A Brief History of Chinese and Japanese Civilizations

A Brief History of Chinese and Japanese Civilizations

Conrad Schirokauer
The City College of The City University of New York

 Harcourt Brace Jovanovich, Inc.
New York   San Diego   Chicago   San Francisco   Atlanta

For Lore and our sons, David and Oliver

Cover photograph by Lore Schirokauer

Calligraphy by Dr. Léon L. Y. Chang, Distinguished Visiting Professor at the Center of Asian Studies, St. John's University; Member, Board of Directors Chinese National Museums.

Maps by J. P. Tremblay

Timelines by Rino Dussi

ISBN: 0-15-505570-4

Library of Congress Catalog Card Number: 78-54115

Printed in the United States of America

Copyrights, acknowledgments and illustration credits on pages 630, 631, and 632.

Preface

The reasons for studying China and Japan can be subsumed under three broad headings: the richness of their long historical records, which form such an important part of the total history of the human race and illuminate the nature of the human condition; the enduring value of their cultural achievements; and the contemporary importance of the world's most populated land and of its most successful non-Western modernized country, the one undergoing a revolution unprecedented in scale, the other now the third largest industrial power in the world. In a day when the roads are filled with Japanese cars and the bookstores with books on Zen, it should no longer be necessary to argue the case for studying East Asia. But setting aside the obvious impact of East Asia on contemporary Western life, surely some acquaintance with the civilizations of China and Japan is required of one who would be an educated person, for to be educated means to be able to see beyond the narrow geographic, temporal, and cultural bounds of one's immediate neighborhood. Indeed, to be educated entails the ability to see oneself in a broader perspective, including the perspective of history. And in this day and age, that means not only the history of one's own tribe or state or even civilization but ideally of all human history—for it is all our history.

That history is woven of many strands, and so we have economic and political history, the study of social structure, of thought, and of art. This text is based on the belief that an introduction to the history of a civilization requires consideration of all these facets of human activity, a general mapping out of the terrain so that the beginner may find his or her bearings and learn enough to consider in which direction to explore further, with some idea of the rewards to be gained for the effort. An introduction then is certainly not a catalog (although it should contain basic data) or a personal synthesis or summation, nor is it the proper vehicle for extending the expanding frontiers of present knowledge. Instead, it should, among other things, introduce the reader to the conventions of a field of study and attempt to convey the state of our present understanding. The basic aim of this text then is to serve as a work of orientation.

v

Thus, for example, where applicable, the standard dynastic framework has been used to provide the basic historical chronology.

History is the study of change and continuity, and both elements are always present, for no generation starts off with a blank slate, nor can even the most fervid traditionalist block changes wrought by the passage of time. In looking at a given segment of history, the scholar does not confront a choice between change and continuity but faces the more difficult task of weighing the change in the continuity, the continuity in the change. Such a determination requires, in the final analysis, as much art as science, and no assessment is ever final. This is so not only because of the continual discovery of new evidence (the dramatic finds of recent Chinese archaeology are a good example) or of new techniques (for example, in the dating of materials) but also because scholars' analytic concepts change, and they learn to ask new questions. Even if that were not the case, history would still have to be rewritten at intervals, inasmuch as the ultimate significance of any individual historical episode depends in the final analysis on the whole story: as long as history itself is unfinished, so is its writing.

If this is true of all history, it is especially the case with the history of East Asia, about which we know a great deal more now than we did just a generation ago, but the areas of our ignorance continue to be enormous. Etienne Balazs (1905–63) once compared students of China to Lilliputians clambering over the Gulliver that is Chinese history, and his words are still apt. Indeed, one of the continuing attractions of the field is that it offers great opportunities to the intellectually adventurous and hardy to work on major problems. Our hope is that the very inadequacies of a text such as this will spur some readers on to these endeavors. Thus for this text to succeed, it must fail: the reader must come away hungry, his appetite whetted but not satiated.

A broad survey such as this is by necessity based on the studies of many scholars (indeed the author's pleasure in wide reading is matched only by his fear of inadvertent plagiarism). No attempt has been made to list all the works consulted. The suggested readings in the appendix have been drawn up in the hope of meeting some of the readers' needs, not of acknowledging the author's indebtedness, although there is considerable overlap. It is also impossible here to list all the individuals who have contributed by offering suggestions, suggesting references, supplying a date or a translation for a term, and so forth, or to acknowledge individually the teachers, students, and colleagues who have influenced my thoughts about the broader problems of history, China and Japan, and the teaching of these subjects. I do, however, want to single out for special mention Professor Arthur F. Wright (1913–76), scholar and humanist, whom I had the privilege of knowing as both teacher and friend.

For reading portions of the book and offering valuable corrections and suggestions, I am indebted to Professors Kwang-Ching Liu, William F. Morton, Robert M. Somers, and H. Paul Varley. In addition Professor Somers read the entire manuscript with unflagging care and sensitivity. I would also like to thank Professor Gary Ledyard, who kept me from straying too far from my area of competence. Further, I wish to acknowledge the research help of Henry Sirotin.

This book would never have been written without the gentle persuasion of William A. Pullin. It owes much to the careful editing of Avery M. Colt, who repeatedly insisted that I spell things out, fill in gaps, and make myself clear, and to Marion Corkett, who saved the book from a flood of errors and embarrassments and combined painstaking care with persistent good humor as she saw the manuscript through its various stages. The author alone, however, is responsible for any errors that slipped through despite everything.

The high cultures of China and Japan are profoundly visual, and the highest art is calligraphy. It therefore gives me particular pleasure to thank Dr. Léon Long Yien Chang (Chang Lung-yen) for gracing this book with the art of his brush. It has also been a pleasure to work with Patricia Smythe, designer, Carla Hirst Wiltenburg, art editor, and Jean Paul Tremblay, cartographer and artist.

My greatest debt is to those who have lived with this book for so long, my forbearing family, for the project ate badly into the time available for me as son, father, and husband. My son Oliver helped in reading final proof—his sharp eyes spotted errors that had eluded everyone else. My wife, Lore, not only helped in innumerable direct and indirect ways but also contributed greatly to the art work, which includes a number of her own photographs.

CONRAD SCHIROKAUER

Note on Calligraphy on the Chapter Title Pages

In drawing the titles, Dr. Léon L. Y. Chang selected calligraphic forms appropriate for the contents of each chapter. Thus Chapters 1 and 2 are written in the Ta Chüan (great seal) form used during the Shang and Chou. The title for Chapter 3 is in the Hsiao Chüan (small seal) form, which was promulgated as standard by the first emperor of the Ch'in. The title for Chapter 4 is written in two styles: the characters in the single column at the right are in the Li (clerical or official) form, which dates from the third century B.C. and was used until the middle of the third century A.D.; the characters at the left are in the Cheng (standard) form, which began during the Three Kingdoms period. Thus the first of these characters designates Wei, one of the Three Kingdoms. The next is Chin, which briefly reunified China. This style of calligraphy was called Chin-li during the T'ang and is now commonly called K'ai-shu. The titles of all subsequent chapters are written in the Cheng, Hsing, or Ts'ao forms (standard, longhand, or cursive), which are illustrated in Figure 4-3.

Note on Names
and Romanization

In Chinese and Japanese, surnames precede given names, and that has been the order followed in this book except for modern Chinese and Japanese scholars who, writing for a Western audience, have adopted the Western name sequence. Furthermore, members of Japanese political and cultural dynasties, as well as certain other individuals, are commonly known by their given names (for example, Tokugawa Ieyasu) or their appellations (for example, Hokusai), and that practice has been followed here.

Chinese geographical names have been rendered in accordance with customary usage. Those for Japan follow the Hepburn system, except that macrons have been omitted for Tokyo. With the exception of Ch'ang-an (modern Sian) and Edo (modern Tokyo), the modern geographical names have been used throughout. This has been done for ease of identification even though it results in some anachronisms. With the exception of geographical names and a few Cantonese names (Sun Yat-sen, Chiang Kai-shek), all Chinese terms have been transliterated according to the Wade-Giles system for Chinese (with a few standard modifications), and all Japanese terms according to the Hepburn system.

The following is intended only as a basic, nontechnical guide to the sounds of Chinese and Japanese as Romanized. It is not an introduction to the phonetics of the languages but does indicate roughly how the various letters should be pronounced.

Vowels

In both Chinese and Japanese, vowels are pronounced as in Italian, German, or Spanish.

> *a* as in c*a*r
> *e* as in sp*e*nd
> *i* as in m*e*
> *o* as in b*o*ld (but in Chinese, sometimes as in s*o*ft, and after
> *k, k', or h* like the *u* in b*u*t)

u as in rude (but hardly pronounced after *tz*, *tz'*, or *ss* in
Chinese or after *s* in Japanese)
ü as the German *ü* or the French *u*

Vowel Combinations

Chinese Diphthongs are always run together. Thus *ai = I* (the personal
pronoun); *ao = ow* as in b*ow*; *ei = a* as in m*ay*; *ou = o* as in l*ow*.

Japanese *Ai* and *ei* are diphthongs pronounced as in Chinese. Other vowels
occurring together are pronounced individually. Long vowels (indicated by a
macron) are pronounced like short vowels but the sound is held longer.

Consonants

In Japanese, consonants approximate their English equivalents. However,
in Chinese, aspirated consonants are distinguished from their unaspirated
counterparts by the use of an apostrophe.

Wade-Giles	Rough English Equivalent	Wade-Giles	Rough English Equivalent
ch	j	ch'	ch
k	g	k'	k
p	b	p'	p
t	d	t'	t
ts, tz	dz	ts', tz'	ts

The consonant *j* is pronounced something like *r*; *ih* is pronounced something
like *ir* as in s*ir*.

In addition to Wade-Giles there are a number of other systems for Romanizing
Chinese. One that is widely used is the Pinyin system adopted by the People's
Republic.

Hanyu Pinyin / Wade-Giles Conversion Table

Pinyin	Wade-Giles	Pinyin	Wade-Giles	Pinyin	Wade-Giles	Pinyin	Wade-Giles
a	a	bao	pao	bo	po	ceng	ts'eng
ai	ai	bei	pei	bu	pu	cha	ch'a
an	an	ben	pen			chai	ch'ai
ang	ang	beng	peng	ca	ts'a	chan	ch'an
ao	ao	bi	pi	cai	ts'ai	chang	ch'ang
		bian	pien	can	ts'an	chao	ch'ao
ba	pa	biao	piao	cang	ts'ang	che	ch'e
bai	pai	bie	pieh	cao	ts'ao	chen	ch'en
ban	pan	bin	pin	ce	ts'e	cheng	ch'eng
bang	pang	bing	ping	cen	ts'en	chi	ch'ih

From Endymion Wilkinson, *The History of Imperial China: A Research Guide*, Harvard East
Asian Monographs, No. 49 (Cambridge, Mass.: Harvard University Press, 1973).

Pinyin	Wade-Giles	Pinyin	Wade-Giles	Pinyin	Wade-Giles	Pinyin	Wade-Giles
chong	ch'ung	fang	fang	ji	chi	lin	lin
chou	ch'ou	fei	fei	jia	chia	ling	ling
chu	ch'u	fen	fen	jian	chien	liu	liu
chuai	ch'uai	feng	feng	jiang	chiang	long	lung
chuan	ch'uan	fo	fo	jiao	chiao	lou	lou
chuang	ch'uang	fou	fou	jie	chieh	lu	lu
chui	ch'ui	fu	fu	jin	chin	luan	luan
chun	ch'un			jing	ching	lun	lun
chuo	ch'o			jiong	chiung	luo	lo
ci	tz'u	ga	ka	jiu	chiu	lü	lü
cong	ts'ung	gai	kai	ju	chü	lüe	lüeh
cou	ts'ou	gan	kan	juan	chüan		
cu	ts'u	gang	kang	jue	chüeh	ma	ma
cuan	ts'uan	gao	kao	jun	chün	mai	mai
cui	ts'ui	ge	ke, ko			man	man
cun	ts'un	gei	kei	ka	k'a	mang	mang
cuo	ts'o	gen	ken	kai	k'ai	mao	mao
		geng	keng	kan	k'an	mei	mei
da	ta	gong	kung	kang	k'ang	men	men
dai	tai	gou	kou	kao	k'ao	meng	meng
dan	tan	gu	ku	ke	k'e, k'o	mi	mi
dang	tang	gua	kua	ken	k'en	mian	mien
dao	tao	guai	kuai	keng	k'eng	miao	miao
de	te	guan	kuan	kong	k'ung	mie	mieh
dei	tei	guang	kuang	kou	k'ou	min	min
deng	teng	gui	kuei	ku	k'u	ming	ming
di	ti	gun	kun	kua	k'ua	miu	miu
dian	tien	guo	kuo	kuai	k'uai	mo	mo
diao	tiao			kuan	k'uan	mou	mou
die	tieh	ha	ha	kuang	k'uang	mu	mu
ding	ting	hai	hai	kui	k'uei		
diu	tiu	han	han	kun	k'un	na	na
dong	tung	hang	hang	kuo	k'uo	nai	nai
dou	tou	hao	hao			nan	nan
du	tu	he	he, ho	la	la	nang	nang
duan	tuan	hei	hei	lai	lai	nao	nao
dui	tui	hen	hen	lan	lan	ne	ne
dun	tun	heng	heng	lang	lang	nei	nei
duo	to	hong	hung	lao	lao	nen	nen
		hou	hou	le	le	neng	neng
e	e, o	hu	hu	lei	lei	ni	ni
ei	ei	hua	hua	leng	leng	nian	nien
en	en	huai	huai	li	li	niang	niang
eng	eng	huan	huan	lia	lia	niao	niao
er	erh	huang	huang	lian	lien	nie	nieh
		hui	hui	liang	liang	nin	nin
fa	fa	hun	hun	liao	liao	ning	ning
fan	fan	huo	huo	lie	lieh	niu	niu

Pinyin	Wade-Giles	*Pinyin*	Wade-Giles	*Pinyin*	Wade-Giles	*Pinyin*	Wade-Giles
nong	nung	ren	jen	tan	t'an	yi	i
nou	nou	reng	jeng	tang	t'ang	yin	yin
nu	nu	ri	jih	tao	t'ao	ying	ying
nuan	nuan	rong	jung	te	t'e	yong	yung
nuo	no	rou	jou	teng	t'eng	you	yu
nü	nü	ru	ju	ti	t'i	yu	yü
në	nüeh	ruan	juan	tian	t'ien	yuan	yüan
		rui	jui	tiao	t'iao	yue	yüeh
o	o	run	jun	tie	t'ieh	yun	yün
ou	ou	ruo	jo	ting	t'ing		
				tong	t'ung	za	tsa
		sa	sa	tou	t'ou	zai	tsai
pa	p'a	sai	sai	tu	t'u	zan	tsan
pai	p'ai	san	san	tuan	t'uan	zang	tsang
pan	p'an	sang	sang	tui	t'ui	zao	tsao
pang	p'ang	sao	sao	tun	t'un	ze	tse
pao	p'ao	se	se	tuo	t'o	zei	tsei
pei	p'ei	sen	sen			zen	tsen
pen	p'en	seng	seng	wa	wa	zeng	tseng
peng	p'eng	sha	sha	wai	wai	zha	cha
pi	p'i	shai	shai	wan	wan	zhai	chai
pian	p'ien	shan	shan	wang	wang	zhan	chan
piao	p'iao	shang	shang	wei	wei	zhang	chang
pie	p'ieh	shao	shao	wen	wen	zhao	chao
pin	p'in	she	she	weng	weng	zhe	che
ping	p'ing	shei	shei	wo	wo	zhei	chei
po	p'o	shen	shen	wu	wu	zhen	chen
pou	p'ou	sheng	sheng			zheng	cheng
pu	p'u	shi	shih	xi	hsi	zhi	chih
		shou	shou	xia	hsia	zhong	chung
qi	ch'i	shu	shu	xian	hsien	zhou	chou
qia	ch'ia	shua	shua	xiang	hsiang	zhu	chu
qian	ch'ien	shuai	shuai	xiao	hsiao	zhua	chua
qiang	ch'iang	shuan	shuan	xie	hsieh	zhuai	chuai
qiao	ch'iao	shuang	shuang	xin	hsin	zhuan	chuan
qie	ch'ieh	shui	shui	xing	hsing	zhuang	chuang
qin	ch'in	shun	shun	xiong	hsiung	zhui	chui
qing	ch'ing	shuo	shuo	xiu	hsiu	zhun	chun
qiong	ch'iung	si	szu	xu	hsü	zhuo	cho
qiu	ch'iu	song	sung	xuan	hsüan	zi	tzu
qu	ch'ü	sou	sou	xue	hsüeh	zong	tsung
quan	ch'üan	su	su	xun	hsün	zou	tsou
que	ch'üeh	suan	suan			zu	tsu
qun	ch'ün	sui	sui	ya	ya	zuan	tsuan
		sun	sun	yan	yen	zui	tsui
ran	jan	suo	so	yang	yang	zun	tsun
rang	jang			yao	yao	zuo	tso
rao	jao	ta	t'a	ye	yeh		
re	je	tai	t'ai				

Contents

11 Japan in the Kamakura Period: 1185–1333   256

12 The Ashikaga Shogunate and the Period of Unification: 1336–1600   280

13 East Asia and Modern Europe: First Encounters   306

PART FOUR   **Traditional China and Japan: The Last Phase**

PART FIVE   **China and Japan in the Modern World**

17 The Intrusion of the West: Japan   402

18 The Emergence of Modern Japan: 1874–1894   424

19 Self-Strengthening in China: 1874–1894   444

20 End of the Old Order and Struggle for the New: China, 1895–1927   464

21 The Limits of Success: Japan, 1895–1931   490

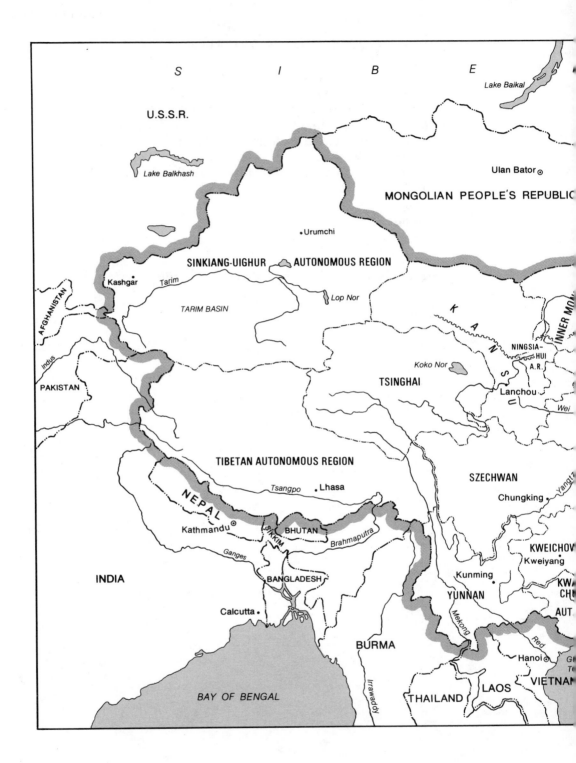

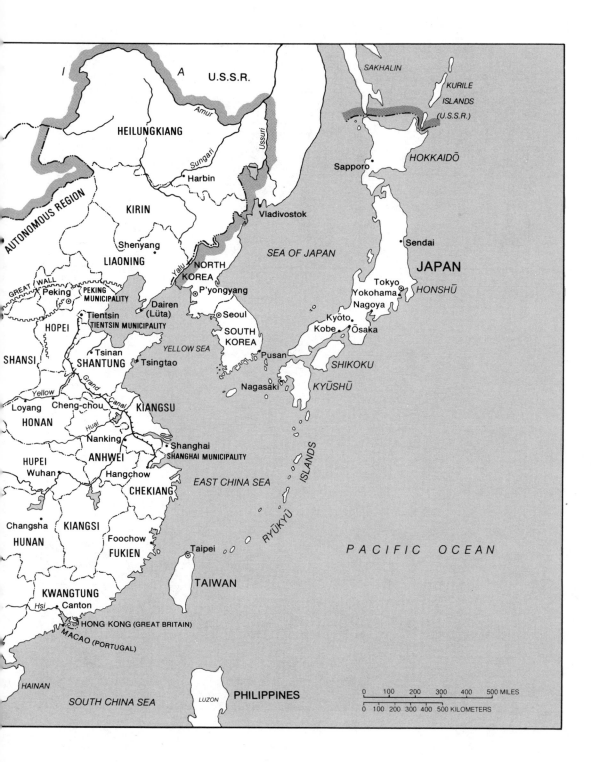

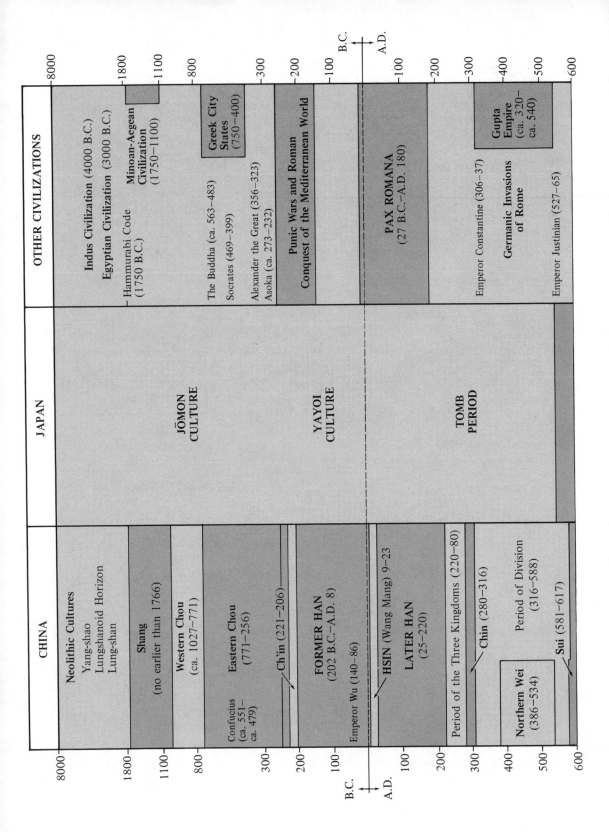

Date	China	Japan	West
600		Late Yamato (552–710)	Muhammad and the Koran
700	T'ANG (617–907) Li Po (701–63) Tu Fu (712–70) Rebellion of An Lu-shan (755–63)	Nara Period (710–84)	Charlemagne (crowned in 800)
800		HEIAN PERIOD (794–1185)	
900	Five Dynasties (907–60)		
1000	Liao (907–1119) SUNG (960–1279) Northern Sung (960–1127)		
1100	Chin (1115–1234) Southern Sung (1127–1279)		The Crusades (1096–1204)
1200		KAMAKURA PERIOD (1185–1333)	Magna Carta Chartres Cathedral
1300	YÜAN (1279–1368)		
1400	MING (1368–1644)	ASHIKAGA PERIOD (1336–1600)	RENAISSANCE Fall of Constantinople
1500			Overseas Exploration
1600		TOKUGAWA PERIOD (1600–1868)	Shakespeare
1700	CH'ING (1644–1911)		Newton THE ENLIGHTENMENT
1800		Meiji (1868–1912) Taishō (1912–26) Shōwa (1926–) } Modern Japan	American and French Revolutions Hegel and Marx
1900	Chinese Republic (1912–49) KMT (1928–49) People's Republic (1949–)		First World War The Great Depression Second World War

Flying Horse. Bronze, Wu-wei, Kansu, second century A.D., 34.5 cm × 45 cm.

PART ONE

The Classical Civilization of China

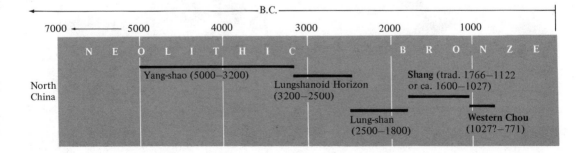

1 *Chinese Antiquity*

The earliest civilization in East Asia originated in China. Although in many ways uniquely Chinese, it established the foundations for the culture that later spread its influence throughout the rest of East Asia and in this respect provides a starting point for the study of the history of the entire region.

Geographic Parameters

In China, as elsewhere, the physical environment provided the opportunities and challenges out of which civilization was wrought, and civilization, in turn, over many centuries shaped and altered the environment. Geography not only provided the setting for history but itself became part of history as new lands were opened to agriculture, marshes were drained, canals were built, moun-

3

tains were terraced, and dikes were constructed to contain rivers. In this sense, Chinese history consists of the interaction of man and nature, each leaving a deep imprint on the other. Yet the basic configurations of the land remained constant. The essential features of climate and landscape did not change.

The outstanding geographical feature of the North is the Yellow River, which flows from the highlands of the west, through the alluvial lowlands of the Great Plain, to empty into the sea near the Shantung Peninsula. It is a region of temperate climate, cold winters and warm summers, but rainfall is scarce. This is particularly true in the arid west, but in the moister areas as well the annual rainfall is extremely variable. Although the area is subject to drought, the soil is fertile. It is a region suitable for growing millet, kaoliang (a kind of sorghum), and, in the moister parts, wheat and beans.

Very different conditions prevail south of a line which runs roughly along the 33rd parallel, following the Tsinling Mountains and the Huai River. Here rain is abundant, the climate subtropical, and the soils are leached. The dominant river is the Yangtze, which is about 3200 miles long, roughly 500 miles longer than the Yellow River. Once the necessary technology was developed and the land laboriously drained, a process that took many centuries, this region proved ideal for rice culture. This grain, destined to be the favorite staple throughout East Asia, appears in the North and the South, in the Chinese Neolithic period. Then, however, it was a rare treat, most likely consumed only by the upper classes on special occasions. Differences in climate and topography (the South is more mountainous) were associated with differences in culture and life style, with the result that within agricultural China the predominant distinction remained that between North and South.

In both North and South the agricultural regions were bordered by areas unsuitable for agriculture; and not until the establishment of the People's Republic in 1949 was there a concerted attempt to integrate the steppelands of Manchuria and Mongolia, the arid regions of far western Sinkiang, or the Tibetan highlands into China proper. The relations between China and the inhabitants of these areas will be explored in due course, but we may note here that these regions, like the jungles and mountains of Kweichow and Yunnan (only 5 to 10 percent level land) in the southwest and the waters of the world's largest ocean on the east, constituted barriers to the spread of the Chinese way of life.

These physical barriers also prevented close contact between China and the other civilizations of Asia. China, however, possessed the natural resources, the size, and the geographical diversity to develop and sustain a civilization varied in place as well as in time. Therefore, the study of the history of China and the exploration of its geography may proceed hand in hand.

Neolithic Cultures

Reports concerning a few fossil teeth discovered in Yunnan Province in 1965 indicate that a humanoid may have lived in southwestern China around a million years ago and had the use of fire. More ample archaeological data exist for the humanoid known as Peking man (*Homo erectus pekinensis*) whose remains, found not far from modern Peking, indicate that he may have lived half a million years ago between two periods of glaciation. Although in terms of cranial capacity and other physiological criteria Peking man was only a proto-human, he used fire and worked with flaked and pebble stone tools. However, any connection between this precursor of Homo sapiens and the historical Chinese people is purely speculative. The origins of China's civilization are best looked for in its Neolithic cultures.

The earliest of these is called Yang-shao after the name of the village where remains of this cultural type were first discovered. The oldest Yang-shao site studied to date goes back to the sixth millennium B.C., but the earliest site of a fully developed Yang-shao settlement originated during the next millennium. This is at Pan-p'o near present Sian in Shensi Province. The archaeological remains reveal a people who lived in small villages, practiced agriculture, raised pigs, made painted pottery, and buried their dead in a special burial ground.

Yang-shao sites are found on terraces near small tributaries of the Wei River and of the great Yellow River. This was the nuclear area of Chinese civilization (see map, Figure 1-1) because, over many centuries, fine-grained sand had been deposited there by the wind to form loess. In the highlands of Shansi, Shensi, and Kansu, the layers of loess reach a thickness of 350 feet. Because loess is fertile, retains moisture, and is easy to work, it favored the development of agriculture and encouraged settlement.

Later North Chinese Neolithic settlements also are usually located on high ground near a stream, close enough to use the water but safe from flooding. This problem was particularly acute in the lower reaches of the Yellow River, which received its name from the heavy load of loess carried in its sluggish waters. Down to the seventh century B.C., people's response to this dangerous river was to evade flooding by moving their settlements upland and to propitiate the river spirits by sacrifice.

The staple grain of the Yang-shao people was millet, and this has remained the foundation of the diet of the ordinary person in North China. Another element of continuity is the Chinese emphasis on raising grain crops together with small animals like the pig (and later the chicken) to supplement the diet. This was the basis of the agricultural technology that, refined over the centuries, provided the economic foundations for Chinese civilization. Indeed it became identified with the Chinese way of life. Chinese civilization never really took hold in areas unsuitable for intensive agriculture.

Yang-shao is often referred to as the painted pottery culture after its characteristic ware, but the very earliest ceramics were cord-marked and unpainted. Both kinds of pottery, the cord-marked and the painted, were built up by coiling, since the potter's wheel did not come into use until the subsequent Lung-shanoid phase of Chinese culture. Pottery with cord markings was apparently once common throughout East Asia—remains have been found on Taiwan and in Japan where the earliest have been dated back to 10,000 B.C. In shape, however, and in appearance, the Chinese and Japanese cord-marked pottery are very far apart. Similarly, Yang-shao painted pottery has not been linked to any

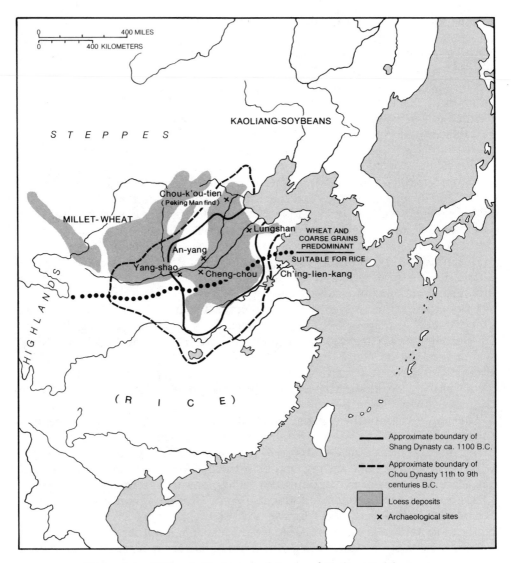

Figure 1-1 **Climatic Regions and Areas of Earliest Settlement**

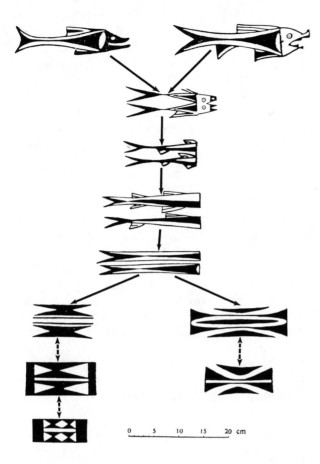

Figure 1-2 Evolution of Yangshao fish designs (from site at Pan-p'o).

0   5   10   15   20 cm

produced outside of China. This ware was usually decorated with symmetrical abstract designs, although fish and human faces also appear. Figure 1-2 exemplifies the decorative process of abstraction and also serves as a reminder that fish was an important supplementary source of food throughout East Asia.

One can speculate about various continuities between Yang-shao and later Chinese culture, such as the care and respect shown for the dead, but what is perhaps more noteworthy is the self-sufficiency of this early self-generated culture. Although some foreign products (for example, wheat, barley, goats) appear during the Stone Age, most of these were introduced in the late Stone Age, and none had a decisive impact. Treacherous seas and the world's largest ocean to the east, semiarid areas to the west, and the Tibetan massif and tropical jungles to the southwest isolated China from centers of civilization elsewhere in Eurasia. The formation of the Silk Road across the dry lands of Central Asia was still far in the future, for it depended on the Bactrian camel, which is not mentioned in Chinese texts until the fourth century B.C.

As the discovery and analysis of archaeological sites continues, a richer and fuller understanding of the Chinese Neolithic is emerging. In addition to the Yang-shao culture, the remains of two other cultures going back to the fifth millennium B.C. have been unearthed. One, located in the southeast and on

Taiwan, produced cord-marked pottery. The other is typified by discoveries at Ch'ing-lien-kang (Kiangsu). It has its own distinct polished and painted pottery and was located in the lower Yangtze River and Huai River valleys. Before radio-carbon dating revealed its antiquity, it had been assigned to the Lungshanoid horizon, along with a number of other cultures more recent than Yang-shao. These cultures were found in the eastern portion of the old Yang-shao nuclear area and also to the east on the North China Plain and along the seaboard north as far as the Bay of Po-hai (north of the Shantung Peninsula) and south as far as the Pearl River in the Canton area. The Lungshanoid horizon included more elaborate and technologically advanced settlements than those of the Yang-shao type. They are called Lungshanoid (literally, "like Lung-shan") because they were transitional between the Yang-shao and the Lung-shan culture of the North China Plain.

The Lung-shan culture is particularly noted for its wheel-made black pottery, very thin and burnished to a high sheen. It is also important for its influence on the later Shang period. For example, it introduced the practice of scapulimancy, divination by applying heat to animal bones (oracle bones) and interpreting the resulting cracks. Lung-shan pottery forms influenced pottery making by the Shang, and even bronze casting, since the technique of pottery making was a direct precursor to bronze casting, which used ceramic molds and high temperature kilns. Although the Bronze Age began with the Shang, regional Neolithic cultures gave way only gradually and had by no means disappeared even in the subsequent Chou period.

Civilization: The Shang

With the Shang, China entered a significant new phase of development, for there now appeared all the characteristics usually associated with the emergence of civilization: the formation of cities, the use of writing, an increase in occupational specialization, and a more complex organization of society. China entered this stage late compared to the ancient civilizations of the Middle East, but all indications are that the process occurred without significant external influence.

Prior to archaeological discoveries made in the 1920s many modern scholars dismissed literary accounts of the Shang as later fabrications, but the historicity of the Shang now has been established without question, although the modern analysis of Shang culture differs widely from the idealized traditional Chinese view. In that view, the Shang was preceded by an earlier dynasty known as the Hsia, but to date no Neolithic culture has been convincingly identified with the Hsia.

The central region of the Shang was northern Honan, where two sites have yielded particularly valuable information. The earliest of these, Cheng-chou, contains Lung-shan remains beneath those of the Shang, providing evidence of the continuity between the two cultures. The later site at Anyang is rich in

Figure 1-3
Inscribed oracle bone.

archaeological materials including oracle bones used for scapulimancy. (See Figure 1-3.) These, along with tortoise shells used for the same purpose, bear a fully developed language. The exact dates of Shang civilization and of the Shang state remain to be determined. Although 1766 B.C.–1122 B.C. are the dates traditionally accepted, there are good arguments in support of the view that the Shang began around 1600 B.C. and came to an end in 1027 B.C.

In addition to the presence of writing and bronze, archaeology reveals other major differences between the Shang and its Neolithic predecessors. One of these is the horse-drawn chariot; another is the size and scale of the Shang's capital cities. The walls surrounding Cheng-chou are estimated as 2385 feet long, 60 feet wide, and 30 feet high. It might have taken 10,000 laborers working 330 days a year no less than 18 years to complete such a wall given the technology of the time. Obviously, this was a society that was capable of mobilizing considerable human resources over a long period.

Written Language

The language that appears on the Shang oracle bones and tortoise shells already included almost all of the grammatical principles of later classical Chinese. The function of words in a sentence is determined basically by placement; for example, the subject precedes the verb, the possessive comes before the pos-

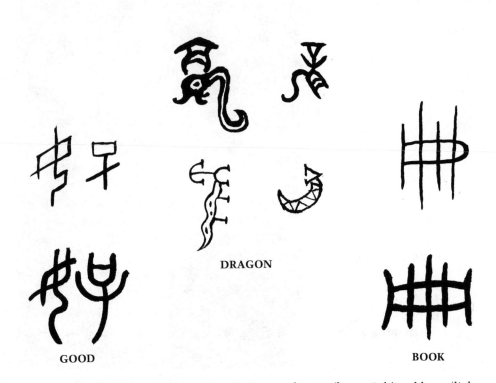

DRAGON

GOOD

BOOK

Figure 1-4   Early Chinese writing: inscriptions on bronze (heavy ink) and bone (lighter ink). Drawn by Dr. Léon L. Y. Chang.

sessed, and so forth. This is a positional grammar not unlike modern English as contrasted with such highly inflected languages as Greek, Latin, or Russian. The Shang further possessed a developed script, which was later stylized and greatly expanded but which nonetheless formed the starting point for writing throughout East Asia.

In its origin and fundamental orientation, this script was strongly visual (see Figure 1-4; Figure 4-3), and writing became the most highly prized of the visual arts, as well as being a means of communication. From early pictograms (stylized pictorial representations of things) and from ideograms (visual representations of a thing or concept through association), the student can learn much about early Chinese culture. The pictogram for "book," for example, suggests that the first books were made of slips of wood or bamboo held together by a thong. The symbol also suggests that the written language, originally developed for communication with the gods in the form of burnt offerings, was now used for human communication as well.

The interpretation of pictograms and ideograms, particularly those for abstract terms like "good" (woman and child), is fascinating but fraught with danger, for many etymologies accepted for centuries have conclusively been shown to be false. Furthermore, many symbols or characters are neither pictograms nor ideograms, but phonograms. The simplest of these are phonetic loans, symbols borrowed for their sound rather than for their meaning. An imaginary English counterpart might be the use of a symbol representing a bee to write the verb "to be," and we could go on and combine "bee" and "leaf" to write "belief," but it would hardly do to conclude from this that people in England conceived of "being" in terms of insect and vegetable life.

Most phonograms are more complex, and the majority of Chinese characters are composed of a combination of pictogramic and phonetic elements, although this was not yet true in the Shang. The development of such compound characters was no doubt a response to the proliferation of phonetic loans, which must have caused great confusion in a language that has an unusually large number of homonyms. In the compound characters, one element (the phonetic) indicates the pronunciation of the word and another (the radical or signific) designates the general category to which the word refers. This principle is illustrated by the word for "black horse." The radical, "horse," is on the left; the phonetic, "li," on the right: together they inform the reader that the "li" under discussion has something to do with horses. The presupposition is, of course, that the reader already knows that there is a word in the language with this sound and meaning. Over the **BLACK HORSE** course of time the significs were standardized and their number reduced, finally resulting in the 214 that still provide the basic organization for most Chinese dictionaries. However, the language has undergone numerous phonetic changes over time, with the result that in modern times the phonetic element is no longer a sure guide to pronunciation.

The inventor of the character used to represent "black horse" had a wide range of emblematic symbols for this very common sound from which to choose. Naturally a symbol with appropriate overtones—in this case "elegant and beautiful"—was selected. In this way, at least at the beginning, the phonetic element was not a completely neutral indicator of sound like the letters of an alphabet or the syllabaries developed much later in Korea and Japan.

The failure of the Chinese to develop a wholly phonetic script shows that the existing system, complex as it is, was adequate to their purposes. The consequences for Chinese thought of this written language are important. The average literate Chinese in later times were no more conscious of the etymology of the words they wrote than are modern English speakers writing about Oxford (where oxen ford the river). Yet the Chinese symbols, unlike their alphabetic counterparts, tended to acquire an identity and life of their own and to function as potent emblems. An example is the rule, effective down to the twentieth century, prohibiting the use of a character that appeared in the name of a ruling emperor or any of his dynastic predecessors. Thus, again in imaginary contemporary terms, Ox*ford* would have to change its name and such words as "af*ford*" would be banned, at least in the United States, because a Gerald Ford had been president.

Like later classical Chinese, the language on the oracle bones is very compact. Because it contains a large number of homophones, classical Chinese is aurally incomprehensible without a visual reference. The spoken language uses many more compounds. Thus the compactness of oracle bone inscriptions suggests that, even at the beginning, there was a gap between the spoken and written languages, a distinction that the visual orientation of the latter helped to perpetuate.

The spoken and the written languages continually influenced each other, but until the twentieth century they remained distinct, and literacy was the highly prized monopoly of a restricted cultural elite who prided themselves on working not with their hands but with their brains. On the other hand, the written language was a unifying element geographically. There was one system of writing (with some local variations prior to 221 B.C.) even though people spoke mutually unintelligible languages. Thus, in modern times, a speaker of Cantonese could not converse with a Mandarin speaker from Peking, but they could communicate in writing and read the same newspapers. And beyond China, scholars in Vietnam, Korea, and Japan were able to participate in Chinese literary culture although they usually did not learn to speak Chinese.

About 100,000 Shang oracle bones have come to light, and some 50,000 inscriptions from these bones have been published. Of the roughly 5000 characters used in the inscriptions, approximately 1500 have been deciphered. The bones were used to address questions to the spirits, usually on behalf of the ruler, and the nature of these questions provides important insights into Shang religion and the activities of the ruler. They ask about the proper timing of military expeditions, hunts, and journeys; inquire about ceremonials and omens; and ask about the weather, the course of an illness, or the sex of an unborn child. The oracle bone inscriptions have also been used to confirm the Shang genealogy contained in the *Records of the Grand Historian* by the great Han historian Ssu-ma Ch'ien (see Chapter 3).

Students of the Shang continue to work on the oracle bones, and new discoveries continue to be made. Of equal or even greater importance, however, are the Shang dynasty bronzes, which furnish dramatic proof of technological advances and provide further information concerning other aspects of Shang civilization.

The Bronzes

Bronze was worked in foundries outside the cities, and the artisans who cast it also had their quarters beyond the city walls. Their houses, provided with floors of stamped earth, testify to a way of life superior to that of the common people who lived in semi-subterranean dwellings.

The peasantry apparently continued to use stone tools, and there was little change in agricultural methods from the Neolithic. At least this seems to be the case, for very few bronze tools have been discovered, and the metal was apparently used mostly for weapons, chariot fittings, and above all for ritual vessels. These were constructed of pieces cast separately in clay models and

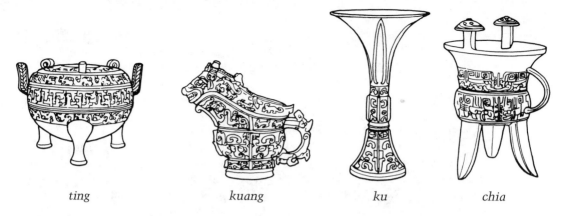

| ting | kuang | ku | chia |

Figure 1-5   Four types of Shang bronze vessels. The *ting* is a cooking vessel; the *kuang*, a wine container; the *ku* and *chia*, drinking vessels.

then joined together. The Shang bronzesmiths are noted for the clarity of detail and perfection of their craftsmanship.

The bronze vessels were cast in many forms (see Figure 1-5), some derived from old pottery traditions, others going back to containers made of more perishable materials such as wood, and still others apparently new with the Shang. They were receptacles for storing or serving various solids and liquids used in the performance of sacred ceremonies. Many of them probably belonged to altar sets such as the one illustrated in Figure 1-6. The pieces in this set date from the late Shang or early Chou, and the set includes vessels in various styles, probably accumulated over a period of time by the family that built

Figure 1-6   Bronze altar set. (Altar table, 19.7 cm × 89.9 cm × 46.4 cm.) Metropolitan Museum of Art, New York.

Crest   C-horn   Tail Quill

Lower jaw Forehead Fang Snout   Upper jaw or trunk   Beak or fang   Eye Leg

Figure 1-7 *T'ao-t'ieh* design.

the tomb from which it was excavated. One type of vessel represented is the tripod, a shape that goes back to the Neolithic and is particularly ingenious in its hollow-leg variety, which is a most effective way of heating liquids rapidly with minimum heat loss. The tripod also appears under a pot with a perforated base to form a steamer.

It is typical of the developed Shang style that all available space is decorated, with the forms of real and imaginary animals figuring prominently. Most clearly visible in the illustration of the altar set are the heads (perhaps of rams) on the handles of the two ritual vessels at the top and the single-legged dragon-like creature that decorates the altar itself. Some of the abstract forms also derive from animals. For example, in the *ku* (the vessel directly in front of the altar at the very center), the vertical decoration, somewhat like the petal of a flower, is a stylized cicada. Since the life cycle of this insect includes a long period of dormancy in the ground, it forms an appropriate symbol for the rebirth of an ancestor in the spirit world, and it was not uncommon, among the wealthy, for a corpse to be buried with a jade cicada in its mouth. The significance of other forms is more difficult to fathom, and this is true of the most common motif of them all, the *t'ao-t'ieh*. (See Figure 1-7.) This mythological being is always presented frontally as though squashed onto a horizontal plane to form a symmetrical design. In the modern language the term "*t'ao-t'ieh*" signifies glutton, and in the late Chou dynasty it was considered a covetous man banished by the Shang to guard a corner of heaven against evil monsters or, more fancifully, as a monster equipped with only a head who tries to devour men but hurts only itself. The trouble with these explanations is that it was only much later (during the Sung dynasty: 960–1279) that the form appearing on the bronzes was identified as a *t'ao-t'ieh* at all.

It was also during the Sung dynasty that Shang bronzes first became objects of study by the student of antiquity and of pride for the collector of art and artifacts. They have ever since been appreciated as works of art, prized not only for their shape and design but also for the various green, blue green, and even reddish patinas created by chemical action as they lay buried in the ground. Unfortunately, the forging of bronzes also has an old history, and a patina is no guarantee of old age; at least one family made forgery a hereditary occupation, burying bronzes in the ground to be disinterred two generations later.

The detailed study of the changing types and styles of bronzes from early Shang through late Chou and into the Han is a fascinating but specialized field of art history. The main stylistic development during the Shang was away from rather controlled decoration kept within the bounds of the vessel toward the more bristling and protruding forms and flanges found in the Late Shang. Some of the Shang forms such as the *ku* are very graceful, but the most powerful pieces have about them an air of ferocious majesty. It is an art that is not easily accessible but that can be most rewarding:

> Our first reaction to the art of the ritual bronze may well be that we are coming into contact with something thoroughly unfamiliar, not to say hostile. The shape of the vessels, and the strangely potent beings they advertise, convey the impression of a spirit that is almost barbaric, and we perhaps have to remind ourselves that they are, after all, highly civilized works of art. But the more prolonged our examination of structure and content, the less acute does this feeling of strangeness and hostility become. We find that we are acquiring a new and first-rate aesthetic experience.[1]

The beauty of these objects lives on even though the religion they served has died.

Shang Religion

Some of the Shang bronzes are decorated with representations of the animals sacrificed in religious ceremonials, and this may also be the significance of a human head that appears on the decoration of a recently excavated vessel as well as of a number of bronze axes found in various tombs. More direct evidence of human immolation is provided by the contents of royal tombs. Some of these are immense. They contain the remains not only of animals but also of people buried alive. In one tomb there are the remains of a chariot complete with horse and driver; in others whole entourages accompany the ruler in death. Human victims were also sacrificed below the foundations of buildings. The people marked out for such grisly deaths were non-Shang "barbarians" captured in war and reduced to slavery. Presumably they were believed to accompany the dead on a journey to the afterworld.

It is not known what kind of sacrifices the ruler made to his ancestors, but it is certain that such sacrifices were an important part of his life. Actually, the names by which the Shang kings are known represent the days assigned for sacrifice to their spirits. Not only was the good will of the ancestral spirits essential for the well-being of the living, the performance of these solemn rituals was also a source of legitimacy for the ruler and helped to sanctify the living hierarchy as an extension of the dead. And just as a ruler presided over mundane society, there was a principle deity, the supreme god or god-on-high, *Shang-ti*, whose powers far exceeded those of the ordinary spirits. *Shang-ti* controlled the basic forces of nature and human destiny and was so elevated that earthly rulers approached him through the intermediation of their ancestral spirits.

Many other deities were worshipped by the king and his people. Jade disks representing a circular heaven have been preserved from the Shang dynasty, as have small square jade pillars that represent the earth. Indeed, jade, respected for its strength and clarity, had its own mystique and was considered to possess protective powers.

To the people of the Shang, the world seemed populated not merely by humans, but also by ghosts, spirits, and mythical monsters. It is probable that various animal gods served as tribal totems. The legend that the progenitor of the Shang was a black bird is very likely of Shang date even though not written down until later. Another later source tells of a god who may be identical with the deity who dispatched the black bird and whose wives gave birth to ten suns and twelve moons. Fortunately, a great archer saved humanity from the overwhelming heat and light by shooting down the excess celestial spheres. Such legends, however garbled in the retelling, are the remnants of what must have been a rich mythology.

Furthermore, there is no reason to suppose that folk religion during the Shang was any less rich in gods of the house and hearth, of the field and well, of mountains and rivers, and so forth, than was the case later on. Unfortunately, there is no access to this material now, and students of folk religion, unlike archaeologists, have no carbon 14 tests for dating the antiquity of their materials.

The elements of Shang religion known to have survived into later times include reverence for ancestors and a concept of the ruler as having important religious functions, expressed in the centrality of his sacred places (already oriented north-south, east-west in the Shang) and in ceremonials that, although in adumbrated form, Chinese rulers continued to perform for three millennia after the end of the Shang.

Government and Society

In the Shang as in other ancient cultures there was no distinction between the secular and the sacred. The capital city was the center of both worlds and so was the king. Kingship was hereditary, but intragenerational succession from older to younger brother was as frequent as intergenerational inheritance, usually from uncle to nephew. Aside from his religious duties, the king was the leader in time of war. In time of peace, he spent much of his time in hunting. Major hunts might go on for months and provided good preparation for warfare, as well as provisions for the table and the altar.

There was not at this early date a distinction between the king as a private and public person: the government can best be thought of as modeled on a patriarchal family in which the king as father had undisputed authority; the running of the state was not considered essentially different from operating a household. To assist the king, there were officials who served in various capacities as needed. They acted as generals in war, served on royal missions, supervised building projects, managed the royal stables and palace, directed the artisans, and took charge of outlying territories assigned to them. The highest officials were no doubt drawn from the nobility that lived in the capital. In war the nobles fought from chariots, using bows and arrows and spears. The less fortunate served as foot soldiers.

Other officials were specialists in divination who may also have been responsible for setting the calendar, a vital function in agrarian society since the correct timing of sowing and reaping and other farm tasks is a matter of life or death. The Shang used a system of counting days in repeating cycles of sixty, which much later, in the second century B.C., was also adopted for keeping track of years.

Less privileged than the nobility but better off than the majority of peasants were the artisans who worked in jade, bronze, bone, and leather; wove hemp and silk; made pottery; built chariots; and otherwise fashioned a material culture richer and more sophisticated than that of previous eras. Most people, however, lived in villages, tilled the land, and lived in houses that were only partly above the ground. Their lives probably did not differ much from those of their descendants in the Western Chou period.

The Western Chou (1027?–771 B.C.)

The Chou dynasty was based to the west of the Shang and seems to have shared in the developed culture of the time even before it conquered the Shang. Consequently there was no sharp break in technological or cultural continuity. Its capital cities, like those of the Shang, were surrounded by stamped-earth walls made of layers of compressed earth hammered down by the workmen. The cities were oriented according to the points of the compass. Important buildings were built on stamped-earth foundations and faced south. During its period of vigor, the court shifted the capital six times, but until the eighth century it remained in the area just west of modern Sian. After the dynasty was forced, in its decline in 771 B.C., to flee from barbarian attack and shifted the capital east, near present Loyang, it officially continued but without real power.

Figure 1-8   Tiger. Chou dynasty, ninth century B.C., 25.2 cm × 75.2 cm. Freer Gallery of Art, Washington, D.C.

During the early Western Chou, bronze was used for the same purposes as under the Shang, and even in style it is difficult to distinguish Late Shang from Early Chou pieces (see Figure 1-6). But change soon set in. Even early Chou bronzes sometimes carry lengthy inscriptions in contrast to the simple indications of ownership that appear on some of the Shang vessels. Certain Shang shapes, the elegant *ku* for instance, disappear as do some Shang motifs including the *t'ao-t'ieh* and the cicada, which are gone by the tenth century. Among animals introduced by the Chou, birds figure prominently. One indication of change is a greater coarseness, a loss of sharpness in detail.

In the late Western Chou (often called Middle Chou by art historians), animal forms tend to dissolve into purely decorative patterns and ribbons. The stripes on the tiger shown in Figure 1-8, however, are not purely decorative since they suggest the skin of the animal and help to create a sense of movement. Such free standing figures first appeared in the Shang and became quite popular during the Chou. The opening on top suggests that such tigers may have been used as structural supports, and this is born out by their sturdiness. Seen from the front, however, the lowered head and bared fangs reveal that this art had not yet lost its bite.

The vessel shown in Figure 1-9, which dates from the middle of the ninth century B.C., clearly illustrates how animal forms were transformed into purely ornamental, repetitive patterns that, like the Yang-shao designs derived from fish, retain only hints of their origin. The effect is decorative rather than awe inspiring, and the inscription on this vessel states that it was commissioned as a bridal gift to a firstborn child. It ends with the words, "may sons and grandsons forever treasure and use it." [2] From their origin as sacred vessels used in solemn (and bloody) religious rites, the vessels have been transformed into treasured family heirlooms. Such changes in the appearance and function of the bronzes are evidence of a slow and gradual process of secularization in the upper reaches of society, a process which was to accelerate in the centuries immediately following the move to the east. It does not imply a questioning or weakening of religious belief but does suggest a more worldly attitude toward life.

Recognition of this trend must not obscure the general continuity of religious belief from Shang to Chou. Here, too, there was no sudden disruption. *Shang-ti* continued to be venerated, although he was increasingly referred to as "*T'ien*," or "Heaven," which gradually replaced the older term. Burial practices also changed. The number of humans and animals buried alive in tombs decreased; greater stress was placed on the observance of proper rites and ritual in dealing with both gods and men. The ruler, styled "Son of Heaven" (a term later applied to emperors), still derived ultimate authority from the divine. One of the key concepts of Chinese political theory, the idea that the sovereign

Figure 1-9 *Hu*, ceremonial wine vessel. Mid-ninth century B.C., 60.6 cm high. Asian Art Museum of San Francisco, Avery Brundage Collection.

ruled by virtue of a Mandate from Heaven, very likely originated from a Chou justification for their overthrow of the Shang. Furthermore, political relationships were more extensive and complex than those of the Shang and required solemn sacrifices to ancestors for the necessary sanctification.

The Chou Political System

After its victory over the Shang, the Chou never attempted to rule the conquered areas directly. Instead, it invested members of the royal family, favored adherents, and allies with the authority to rule over more than a hundred separate territories, which these men were free to administer without interference from the Chou king. These subordinate rulers were given ranks later systematized into a hierarchic order, and they were placed under an obligation to render military service and tribute. Among those granted territory in this manner were the descendants of the Shang royal house, who were thus enabled to continue the performance of their ancestral rites (perhaps relieving the Chou from the threat of supernatural reprisal). In practice these positions were hereditary under a system of primogeniture, but the investiture had to be renewed each generation to legitimize the inheritance, and this was done with solemn rites addressed to ancestors accepted as common to both king and local lord.

The relationship between the Chou kings and the subordinate territorial authorities resembles, to a certain extent, that between lords and vassals in medieval Europe. As a result the Chou political system has often been identified as feudal. Nevertheless, there are major differences, such as the absence in China of subinfeudation (vassals having their own vassals) and the Chinese appeal to bonds of kinship rather than to contractual agreements. Furthermore, the contrasts between the history of postfeudal Europe and post-Chou China make it very difficult to apply to both the term "feudalism" in the sense of a stage of development in a universal historical process. Awareness of the differences between them further serves to restrain the temptation to overinterpret the Chou evidence, which is much more meager than that available for the student of Europe almost two thousand years later. The difficulties are further compounded by disagreements over the definition of "feudalism" itself. This is not the place for a study of comparative feudalism, but, in any case, post-Heian Japan presents a much richer and more fruitful field for such a study than does China's Western Chou because the parallels between Japan and Europe are far more numerous. Nevertheless, the Western Chou will continue to figure in comparative analyses because this was the period when the Chinese political system most resembled the Western feudal order.

About the structure of local village life during the Western Chou and the routine activities of the common people, we are not well informed. This was not the kind of information those who were literate considered important to preserve in writing, and as a result our knowledge of ordinary life in China before relatively recent times remains strictly limited. However, we can learn

something from the folk poetry included in one of China's oldest and most revered classics, *The Book of Songs*, containing poems composed between 1000
and 600 B.C.

The Book of Songs

Folk songs are only one part of the poetry in *The Book of Songs*. There are also
religious hymns and stately songs to accompany royal festive and ceremonial
occasions. There are prayers evoking Lord Millet, reputed ancestor of the
Chou, and songs of courtship and love, ceremonial greeting and warfare, feast-
ing and lamentation. Originally these were sung, but by the Han dynasty the
music, unfortunately, had already been lost. Tradition held that Confucius as
editor determined the selection of poems for inclusion in this book that became part of the classic canon of Confucianism,* a text to be memorized by
anyone aspiring to be considered educated. Even before China had an official
orthodoxy, failure to recognize an allusion to a poem in this anthology marked
out a man as a hopeless boor and ignoramus. For the modern student of Chinese civilization, these poems provide both valuable information and aesthetic
pleasure.

Some songs show ordinary people at work: the men clearing weeds from the
fields, plowing and planting, and harvesting; the girls and women gathering
mulberry leaves for the silkworms, making thread, carrying food hampers out
to the fields for their men to have lunch. There is much about millet—both the
eating variety and that used for brewing wine for use in rites. We hear about
wheat and barley and rice. There are joyful references to granaries full of grain,
and to the men gathering thatch for their roofs in off-season. Mention is made
of lords' fields and private fields and a bailiff is referred to, but the details of the
system are not provided. There are also poems of complaint against the government. One compares tax collectors to big rats. Another tells of the hardships of
military service, men constantly on the march, living in the wilds like rhinoc-
eroses and tigers, day and night without rest. Sometimes a soldier survives
the hardships and dangers of war and returns home only to find that his wife
has given him up for dead and remarried.

The love poems are among the most appealing in the freshness and inno-
cence of their language and in their frankness, for this was a time when girls
were not yet restricted by etiquette from expressing the wish to be married or
their longing for a sweetheart:

> That the mere glimpse of a plain cap
> Could harry me with such longing,
> Cause me pain so dire![3]

---

* *The Book of Songs* is one of the *Five Classics*. The others are *The Classic of Change* (*I Ching*),
The Classic of History, *The Spring and Autumn Annals*, and the *Ritual* (a set of texts including
the *Records of Rites*). Sometimes a now lost classic of *Music* is added to form the *Six Classics*.

Some poems tell of the anguish of the lovelorn or protest against neglect. The following tells of seduction:

> In the wilds there is a dead doe;
> In white rushes it is wrapped.
> There was a girl longing for spring
> A fine gentleman seduced her.
>
> In the woods there are tree stumps;
> In the wilds lies a dead deer,
> Wrapped and bound with white rushes.
> There was a girl fair as jade.
>
> "Ah, not so hasty, not so rough!
> Do not move my girdle-kerchief;
> Do not make the dog bark."[4]

As always, much depends on the vision of the translator. For Liu Wu-chi, whose translation appears above, the poem tells of "the tragedy of love." In the mind of another contemporary scholar, Wai-lim Yip, it is an "animated pastiche of a lovely rural seducement song":

> In the wilds, a dead doe.
> White reeds to wrap it.
> A girl, spring-touched:
> A fine man to seduce her.
> In the woods, bushes.
> In the wilds, a dead deer.
> White reeds in bundles.
> A girl like jade.
> Slowly. Take it easy.
> Don't feel my sash!
> Don't make the dog bark![5]

It is a truism that to translate is to interpret, and much is inevitably lost in the process. But to read is also to interpret, and in reading these poems, later literary and scholarly Chinese "translated" them to conform to their own ideas of what a classic should be, namely a repository of lessons in social and political morality. And commentators worked hard to show how this should be done. For example, the song of longing for the plain-capped youth quoted above was transformed into a lament for the decline in mourning rites, an indication of the decay of filial piety, for white is the color of mourning in China. Thus, in a nineteenth-century English translation following Chinese commentators, the poem begins:

> If I could but see the white cap,
> And the earnest mourner worn to leaness!
> My toiled heart is torn with grief![6]

No matter which translation of the poem about the dead doe we select, it is not the traditional interpretation: *The Book of Songs* we read today is not the same as that read by traditional Chinese scholars, for *all* modern readers bring a different vision to the text. But the study of Chinese civilization cannot even begin without an attempt to understand traditional views and images. This is true of all periods, but it is especially pertinent to a consideration of Chinese antiquity; for the gap between the classical understanding of the poems and the modern is not any wider than that between the account of China's beginnings presented in this chapter and the traditional view once held by educated persons in China and East Asia, people whose own understanding of themselves was intimately linked to their view of history.

The Traditional Chinese View of Antiquity

Virtually all known cultures develop creation myths at an early stage in their growth: myths to explain the origins of the earth and of their peoples. One looks in vain for such myths in the earliest Chinese texts, however, for in the beginning the classical Chinese view was more concerned with great semidivine culture heroes than with a theory of beginnings. P'an-ku, a creator figure, does not appear in literature until quite late, and then he appears in the South rather than the North China Plain. He is first mentioned in a text of the third century A.D., and his story is elaborated still later. Born of a cosmic egg, he continually grew for 18,000 years and separated heaven and earth (he is often shown wielding an axe). When he died, his eyes became the sun and moon; his blood, the rivers and oceans; his hair, the grasses and trees. Humans and animals derived from his body lice.

As exemplified by P'an-ku, it seems, generally, that the earlier a figure is placed in mythological time, the more godlike its attributes; it also seems that the earliest legendary figures were the most recent creations. The result is an inverse ratio between ascribed and actual age: the older, the younger. Thus, the next group of semidivine beings who are placed in the third millennium B.C. were all current during the Han, and perhaps earlier, but do not appear in China's earliest historical record, *The Classic of History*, also known as *The Book of Documents*. To them is attributed the creation of the basic elements of civilization that we now view as the products of a long historical evolution. Fu Hsi was believed to have been the founder of animal husbandry, marriage, the calendar, and musical instruments. The construction of the eight trigrams of *The Classic of Change* (*I Ching*), an ancient divination text (see Chapter 2), is also ascribed to him. Fu Hsi and his sister, or wife, Nü-kua (or Nü-wa) are depicted in the Han with serpent bodies and human heads. Shen-nung, whose name literally means "divine farmer," taught men agriculture and also set up markets and began commerce. Huang Ti (the Yellow Emperor) defeated the "barbarians" in North China. He invented government institutions and was credited with a long list of inventions. His wife taught silk culture and domestic work, and his minister invented the first written signs.

Huang Ti was the first of five emperors, the last two of whom, Yao and Shun, appear in *The Classic of History*, a collection of documents purportedly compiled by Confucius. Such a collection did exist at the time of Confucius and his disciples, but more material was added later. The pre-Chou materials in this book cannot be used as historical sources, but the information it contains about the early Chou is more usable. However, the historicity of Yao and Shun remained unquestioned until modern times. They were accepted as paragons of imperial virtue, as sage-emperors, perfectly just and wise. It was a mark of Yao's impartiality that he passed the throne on not to his son but to Shun, a poor man. Shun earned this distinction because he remained an obedient son even though his wicked stepmother and blind father treated him miserably and even tried several times to kill him. As a final test, Yao married his two daughters to Shun, and when the latter demonstrated his ability to live in harmony with them, Yao was confirmed in the wisdom of his choice. Shun, in turn, passed the throne on to the worthiest official under his reign, Yü, who worked single-heartedly for thirteen years fighting the Great Flood that had long threatened and devastated the land. To channel the waters, he dug great drainage canals.

When Yü died, the people did not accept his designated successor but turned to Yü's son, thereby beginning the practice of hereditary succession and creating the first dynasty, the Hsia. When after many accomplishments the Hsia line produced the brutal and wicked Emperor Chieh, the dynasty was finished, and a new man of virtue appeared to found the Shang. Again, after a long time, the Shang deteriorated and produced Chou Hsin who killed people in abandon, ripped up pregnant women, and otherwise behaved atrociously. The portrait of the wicked last ruler of the Shang is probably a Chou attempt to justify their destruction of the previous dynasty, and very likely, the story of the Hsia decline was also manufactured by the Chou to give their story greater weight. The virtuous founder and the bad last ruler remained stereotypes of Chinese historiography.

Yao, Shun, and Yü may be late reflections of early gods or heroes, but with the Duke of Chou we encounter a genuine historical personage. To him, as a devoted regent for a child emperor, was assigned the credit for fashioning the institutions of the Chou, the last of the Three Dynasties (Hsia, Shang, and Chou), which were considered *the* age of greatness and perfection. Although the Duke of Chou did contribute much to the establishment of the dynasty, his reputation was greatly embellished in later times until he became a figure larger than life. He was turned into a model statesman and philosopher, the hero of Confucius, who was disturbed when the Duke of Chou failed, for an extended period of time, to appear in his dreams. Among the works later attributed to him was *The Rites of Chou*, which presented a schematic and ideal picture of Chou government, a source of inspiration for reformers throughout the history of imperial China. Herrlee G. Creel has well summed up the traditional image of the duke: "Ruler, statesman, cultural innovator, scholar, philosopher: for thousands of years, the Duke of Chou has been regarded as one who succeeded in realizing not one but all the highest Chinese ambitions."[7] In the Confucian view, he was the last of the sages to be emulated by later men, the last man fully to put his lofty ideals into operation.

Decline of the Chou

Traditional Chinese scholars attributed the decline of the Chou to human foibles, but modern historians are more apt to point to institutional trends such as the loosening of the bonds that tied the territorial lords to the king at the center. In any case, by the ninth century, Chou rulers could not prevent fighting among their territories and were even more troubled by the incursions of non-Chinese peoples. It was to evade the latter, that the decision was made to move the capital to the east away from the line of outside attack.

After this move the Chou continued to reign nominally for another five hundred years even though the court no longer had real military, political, or economic power. That it survived so long was partly because no state appeared that was capable of completely supplanting it and founding a new dynasty. But its survival also testifies to a moral authority that faded only slowly over the centuries.

NOTES

1. William Willetts, *Foundations of Chinese Art: From Neolithic Pottery to Modern Architecture* (New York: McGraw-Hill, 1965), p. 95.
2. Michael Sullivan, *The Arts of China* (Berkeley and Los Angeles: University of California Press, 1973), p. 47.
3. Arthur Waley, *The Book of Songs* (New York: Grove Press, 1960), p. 10.
4. Liu Wu-chi, *An Introduction to Chinese Literature* (Bloomington: Indiana University Press, 1966), p. 20.
5. Wai-lim Yip, *Chinese Poetry* (Berkeley and Los Angeles: University of California Press, 1976), p. 53.
6. James Legge, *The Chinese Classics, IV: The She King* (Reprinted Hong Kong: Hong Kong University Press, 1960), p. 216.
7. Herrlee G. Creel, *The Origins of Statecraft in China*, Vol. 1, *The Western Chou Empire* (Chicago: University of Chicago Press, 1970). p. 72.

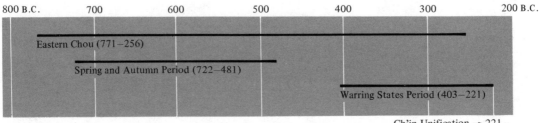

800 B.C.	700	600	500	400	300	200 B.C.

Eastern Chou (771—256)

Spring and Autumn Period (722—481)

Warring States Period (403—221)

Ch'in Unification → 221

2 The Age of Philosophers

The 550 years from 771 to 221 B.C. were a time of social change and political turbulence, during which no one state was able to dominate China. Not only later scholars, but the philosophers of these times, who believed in a harmonious, noncompetitive world order with a single rather than multiple sources of authority, considered this period an age of decline from the heights of the early Chou. The great majority of articulate people who lived through these turbulent centuries did not consider themselves fortunate to have been born into an age when great changes were underway, changes that were to lead to a stronger, more extensive, and more prosperous civilization.

They could not know what the future would bring. For them, it was a bewildering and disturbing time. Old beliefs and assumptions were challenged, prompting questions never before raised and stimulating intellectual exploration in many directions. Some of these new concepts were later abandoned; others became the guidelines for Chinese thought for centuries.

The period from 771 to 256 B.C. is known as the Eastern Chou. Historians also divide the period into the Spring and Autumn Era (722–481 B.C.) and the period of the Warring States (403–221 B.C.). The latter term well describes the history of those years. The former is derived from the *Spring and Autumn Annals,* a chronicle of the years indicated. The *Annals* are alleged to have been edited by Confucius, who is believed to have died in 479 B.C., not long after the *Annals* end. Commentaries were later written to elucidate and give meaning to this dry text. The most interesting of these because of the richness of its historical narrative as well as the nobility of its literary style is the *Tso Chuan* (*Tso Commentary*), which carries Chou history down to 468 B.C.

The Early Eastern Chou (Spring and Autumn Period)

The early Eastern Chou, a time of cultural advance and troubled political relations, introduced several important changes to Chinese life. Soybean cultivation, which had originated northeast of China proper in Manchuria, home of a non-Chinese tribal people, spread to China proper in the second half of the seventh century B.C. A rich source of protein and an important addition to the Chinese diet, this new crop plant also contains nitrogen-fixing bacteria that helped augment the fertility of the soil in which it was grown. During the sixth century B.C., individual states began experimenting with new techniques of governing. The small state of Lu, the home of Confucius, enacted an agricultural reform in 594 B.C. that required peasants to pay land rents directly to the government rather than to their lords. This amounted to an early system of direct taxation. In the second half of the sixth century B.C., another state began to inscribe its laws in bronze, in effect, to develop a written code of law. And in 521 B.C. (during Confucius' lifetime) occurs the first mention of iron in a Chinese text.

Notwithstanding these advances, political relations of the time were troubled. It was a visible sign of the feebleness of the Chou court after its move east that the territorial lords no longer bothered to journey to the court for the ceremony of investiture, and that the king could do nothing about it. China was now divided into a number of independent states which negotiated their differences when they could and fought each other when diplomacy failed. Among the most important states of the seventh century B.C. were Ch'i in Shantung and Chin in Shansi, as well as the semi-Chinese state of Ch'u, which was centered on the Yangtze River and tried unsuccessfully to dominate the North. In the northwest, in Shensi, Ch'in was beginning its process of growth and development. (See map, Figure 2-1.)

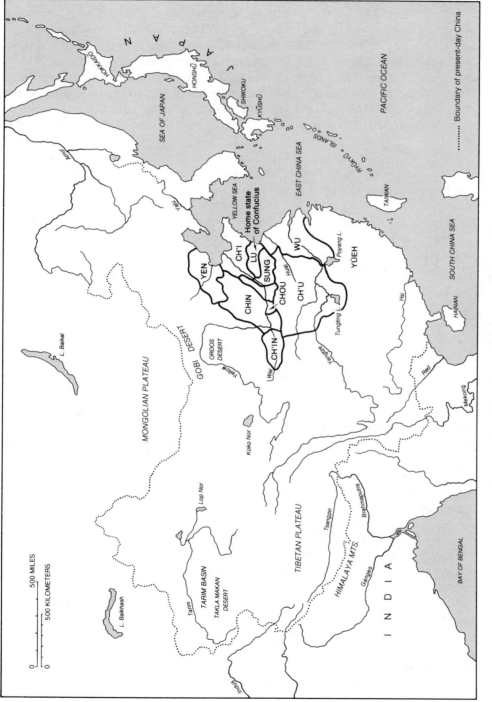

Figure 2-1   China in the Spring and Autumn Era

For a time in the seventh century, the inherent instability of a multistate system was remedied by the formation of a league headed by a strongman (*pa*) and sanctioned by the Chou court, but unlike the Japanese shogunate of much later times (see Chapter 11), this arrangement never developed into an institutionalized system. The failure of multistate alliances led to an increase in international tensions among the Chinese states of the time and created a general aura of suspicion and betrayal in the sixth century. Although treaties were supposedly sanctified by being inscribed on bronze vessels, they were broken at will.

There was as little political stability within states as between states. Here, too, solemn promises and even family connections were not allowed to interfere with political ambition. The old sanctions no longer worked. The secularization already reflected in the late Western Chou bronzes had progressed to skepticism. The old gods were dead; the world in crisis. It was under these conditions that Chinese philosophy developed—conditions very different from those which were stimulating Greeks at about the same time to speculate on the nature of the world.

Confucius

Confucius (ca. 551–ca. 479 B.C.) was apparently of aristocratic lineage and received a traditional education in learning, deportment, and music that would not have been accessible to commoners. His ambition was to play an important role in public affairs, to become a trusted adviser to a ruler, but he never obtained more than minor office. In his middle years he traveled, unsuccessfully, from court to court in search of a ruler who would follow his guidance. In place of a political career he turned to teaching. He was not a wealthy man and supported himself from his pupils' tuition fees. In accepting students he did not consider class distinctions. But he did insist on students making a serious effort: he would not teach those not eager for learning, those not striving themselves for understanding. "If I hold up one corner of a square and a man cannot come back to me with the other three, I won't bother to go over the point again."[1] Not only instruction but much of Chinese literature and art has operated on this principle, conveying a message by suggestion, relying on readers or viewers to work out the full implications by their own efforts.

No known writings of Confucius have been discovered. To study his teachings we must turn to the *Analects* (*Lun Yü*), a collection of his words as passed on by his disciples and assembled after his death. The *Analects* do not consist of systematic philosophical treatises or even students' lecture notes. They are an unorganized collection of statements and conversations, open to varying interpretation. In their totality, however, they give a surprisingly full picture of the man and his ideas.

Confucius believed that his teachings merely transmitted the traditional wisdom and values of Chinese culture, but he was a creative transmitter, a man who understood the old traditions in terms suitable for his own age and thereby revitalized and transformed old values. A good example is his redefinition of nobility as something acquired through virtue and wisdom, not through birth. Confucius' ideal man or true gentleman (*chün-tzu*) is humane, wise, and brave. He is devoted to virtue in contrast to the petty man out for gain. His standard is righteousness. The ultimate virtue is *jen*, which, like most of the central terms of Chinese philosophy, defies translation. It is the ground for all the other virtues, the condition of being fully human in dealing with others— the Chinese character for *jen* consists of "man" and "two."

For Confucius the interaction between men is governed by *li*, a term which encompasses the meaning of sacred ritual, ceremonial, propriety, and good manners. The *li* (like all Chinese words it can be read either as a singular or as a plural) are traditional and, because of their religious associations, had been sanctified and imbued with a quality of magic that they retained even after literal belief in the old religious ideas faded away. For Confucius the *li* themselves, when performed with true sincerity, are what make the individual human. Sacrifices should be performed as though the spirits were present. On the spirits themselves Confucius was noncommittal.

All dealings between people should accord with *li* performed in perfect good faith. Then everyone would perform his role with genuine understanding and devotion. Harmony would result, and there would be no need for physical sanctions, no necessity for laws and punishments. Of crucial importance was the initiative of the ruler, who by following the advice of true gentlemen could initiate benevolent government and win over the people. The people's confidence was essential to the state, more important than arms or even food.

Among the virtues and *li* most important for Confucius were those connected with the family, and he placed special emphasis on filiality, the wholehearted obedience child owes to parent. For Confucius obligations toward a father have priority over those to the state: for example, a son should not turn his father in for stealing a sheep. The relationship between father and son formed one of the classic Five Relationships of Confucianism. The other four were between ruler and minister, husband and wife, elder brother and younger brother, and between friend and friend. They emphasize the importance of reciprocal obligations between people of superior and inferior status and illustrate the existence of these values at the family level, at the community level (friendship), and in state relationships (ruler and minister). The Confucian view of society was essentially hierarchical; while Confucians felt that the values expressed in the Five Relationships applied to all, that did not mean they favored an egalitarian polity. Quite the contrary. Similarly, the Way (*Tao*) to perfection was open to all, but only the morally and intellectually cultivated could understand it. The common people could only be made to follow.

For Confucius and his disciples there was only one, valid and true, eternal and universal Way. The idea that there might be a number of legitimate ways was foreign to people who had no contact with any highly developed, literate civilization radically different from their own. There was one civilized way and that was the Way of antiquity, of the sages, of the Duke of Chou.

Confucius idealized the Duke of Chou and in turn became a model for his own followers. It remained characteristic of Chinese culture that model emulation played a very large part in education and in the search for self-improvement. Confucius himself appears in the *Analects* as a man of moderation: gentle but firm, dignified but not harsh, respectful but at ease. He displays a nice sense of balance, as when he warns both against learning without thinking and against thinking without learning. In one place Confucius gives an account of his own intellectual and spiritual progression, culminating when he reached seventy and was able to follow his heart's desires without transgressing against morality. Like the master of ceremonial who has internalized every movement or the great musician who has become one with his instrument, the Confucian sage perfects his own moral wisdom until he reaches a point at which he no longer needs to worry about a wrong gesture, a missed note, an improper act. In all three cases the efficacy of the performance depends on the authenticity of the state of mind of the performer.

As in the case of all seminal thinkers, there was much Confucius did not say, questions he did not raise, issues he left open; and his language permitted various interpretations. Thus ample opportunity was provided for future elaboration and for disagreements among Confucians. Confucius was only the beginning of Confucianism. His followers honored him but developed in ways he could not have foreseen. There were also those who disagreed with Confucius. In the light of later history, it is important to realize that, during the entire period under discussion here, his teachings never won official acceptance in any state. They remained a minority view. One vigorous challenge to Confucianism originated with a man thought to have been born at the end of the decade in which Confucius died. That man was Mo Tzu.

Mo Tzu

Mo Tzu (ca. 470–ca. 391 B.C.), like Confucius, apparently traveled from court to court to find a patron for his teachings, but little else is known about his life. His ideas are contained in the *Mo Tzu*, a work which also includes writings by later members of his school.

Like Confucius, Mo Tzu emphasized ethics, but the content of his ethics differed radically from those of his predecessor. In place of the Confucian emphasis on filiality and loving one's family first, Mo Tzu advocated universal love. People should love each other impartially regardless of kinship bonds. He argued that the absence of such love accounted for the evils of the age, emphasized that such love is practical, and maintained that it is in accordance with the will of Heaven. For Mo Tzu, Heaven was an intervening deity that punishes the wicked and rewards the good. In Mo Tzu's view all people should pattern themselves on their superiors in a hierarchy leading up to the ruler, who himself should obey Heaven. Universal love did not, for Mo Tzu, mean the abandonment of hierarchy or obedience. Like Confucius, he argued that government posts should go to the capable not to the wellborn. He also resembled Confucius in appealing to the authority of antiquity, although he placed his ideal further back in time, in the era of the mythical Hsia.

Mo Tzu's criteria for judging the validity of a concept or practice were whether it had been employed in antiquity, the evidence of the senses, and its utility. If universal love were not useful, Mo Tzu said, he himself would reject it. On these grounds he passionately denounced offensive warfare. He also bitterly condemned elaborate funerals and rites as wasteful, and attacked the Confucians of his day for waxing fat on the profits they made from managing extravagant funerals. On similar grounds he dismissed music; in his narrow utilitarianism there was no appreciation for the aesthetic side of life. Among the ideas and policies which satisfied his criteria were the use of rewards and punishments and the belief in the retributive power of ghosts and spirits, both helpful in inducing the people to be good. Mo Tzu favored frugality and measures, such as early marriages, that would increase the wealth and human resources of the state.

Mo Tzu's rejection of aesthetic considerations is also evident in his prose style, which lacks variety and adornment but hammers away at his point repetitiously with a kind of relentless logic. Some of his later followers made important contributions to the art of logic, but none took the further step of distinguishing between logic (the principles of reasoning) and rhetoric (the techniques of persuasion). For centuries after the master's death, Mohism lived on as a tightly knit, organized order that provided support for those of its members who attained office and sought to advance the founder's teachings. Some Mohists became experts in defensive warfare ready to come to the assistance of any state threatened by attack. More united than the followers of any other thinker, the Mohists formed a quasi-religious and quasi-military order during the period of the Warring States.

The Warring States: Growth and Conflict

During the Warring States period (403–221 B.C.) and the seventy-eight years that intervened between it and the Spring and Autumn era, the trends already visible earlier accelerated. Competition among the states became ever more intense, more bloody and ruthless. The number of states declined, but those which survived grew bigger until at the end of the period there was only one great state: the Ch'in.

War chariots, which stuck in mud and were clumsy in hilly terrain, were replaced by cavalry. Accompanying the chariot into oblivion were the vestiges of a gentlemanly code of fighting that, in an earlier day, had reportedly reduced the brutality of warfare. Now infantry did most of the fighting: peasant conscripts commanded by professional officers. States fielded giant armies, some said to have numbered a million men, although that may have been hyperbole. Given the proliferation of armed struggle, it is hardly surprising that one of the world's military classics, *The Art of War* (the *Sun Tzu* or *Ping-fa*), should date from the fourth century. It is noteworthy that *The Art of War* stresses the psychology of battle as much as it does the importance of terrain and technical matters. For example, it stresses the need for a general to know his enemy and to rely for victory more on cunning than on brute force. The true art of winning consists in inducing the enemy to destroy himself.

It was a period for professionals in other fields also. It took a skillful diplomat to maneuver a state through the treacherous waters of international relations and an eloquent voice to win a debate. Rhetorical exercises of this sort are preserved in the *Intrigues of the Warring States* (*Chan-kuo ts'e*). Other men developed expertise in agriculture, various fields of science, and in statecraft. Operating in a hazardous international environment and faced with internal threats as well, the rulers of states tended to be interested more in the competence than in the pedigree of those whom they employed.

Society was in flux as aristocratic families fell into decline. Some officials, warriors, and landowners died in the course of war or were replaced when their state was conquered by another. Other aristocrats were simply unable to compete successfully in a world where the old rules no longer prevailed, and men of humble origins could rise provided they were blessed with the proper endowment of ability and luck. Both aristocrats in decline and commoners on the way up became *shih*. This term, originally used for the lower aristocracy of fighting men in the Western Chou, was then expanded to include not only warriors but also men outside the high aristocracy who were conversant with traditional learning and participated in traditional rituals. Some were small landowners; others served noble patrons in various capacities or assumed minor government posts. During the Warring States period the term became further demilitarized. Among the *shih* were various unattached experts, politicians, and thinkers whose disputations brought about a quickening of intellectual life.

Military and social changes were inseparably linked to economic changes, the one reinforcing the other. Economic growth was essential to produce the surplus needed to maintain large armies, and to provide opportunities for men of initiative; conversely, economic growth was itself stimulated by demands for more production to serve new needs. As always, agriculture was the basic enterprise. Reclamation projects opened new lands. Although there are references to irrigation in the seventh century B.C., it did not become important until the Warring States period, and truly ambitious plans had to wait until the third century B.C. A beginning was made in applying iron to agricultural use, for example, to make the cutting edges of spades. Systems of taxation and labor-service were widely adopted and refined as states became increasingly proficient at marshaling the economic resources of the areas under their control. Land became a commodity to be bought and sold.

Among those who did the buying were men who made their fortunes in commerce, for, with the increase in the size of states, merchants could travel freely over wider areas than previously. Roads built for military purposes could also

Figure 2-2   Ancient Chinese coins.

be used for trade. The most notorious merchant of the period was Lü Pu-wei
(d. 235 B.C.), who for many years was the chief counselor of Ch'in and was even
rumored to have been the real father of the ruler who united all of China in 221
B.C. Increased trade spurred the development of metallic currencies, which replaced the cowrie shells used earlier. Figure 2-2 shows an assortment of early
Chinese coins: spade money, knife money, and round coins with a hole in the
center so that they could be strung together. Strings of cash, usually with a
thousand coins to a string, later became standard. As a result of the increase in
trade, cities, growing in commercial importance, expanded physically by con-
structing new outer walls to accommodate more people. As for the items exchanged in trade, they included various kinds of textiles, a wide range of
metals, special timbers, bamboo, jade, and other regional specialties, such as
seafood and pearls from the southeast and even wild animals (bears, foxes, and
so forth) from the Szechwan region. Additional evidence of the richness of the
material culture of the period comes from the arts.

The Arts

In the visual arts the fashion was for the exquisite, the refined, and the expensive. In this last stage of their lengthy development, bronze vessels became objects of aesthetic enjoyment and, most likely, also of ostentation and display.
Some were decorated with scenes of the hunt or war; others, more numerous,

displayed abstract patterns inlaid with gold, silver, or precious and semiprecious stones to add to their sheen and sparkle. Beautifully made bronze belt hooks, inlaid with silver and gold, and fine ivory carvings confirm the era's sophistication of taste, craftsmanship, and design. Figures were often gilded. The little tapir (Figure 2-3), his body covered with intricate designs, exemplifies this stage of artistic development. He is a delightful ornament or toy, but it is difficult to recognize him as a descendant of the majestic and fierce Shang figures that were his progenitors.

The Warring States bronzes and those of the Shang belong to different worlds. Although humans were as brutal to each other as ever, at least the spirits had somewhat relented. Now the noble dead accepted stylized sculptured figures representing humans—images made of clay (in the north) or wood (in the south)—as substitutes for the actual people found in earlier tombs. Tombs, however, continued to hold large quantities of fine objects. This remained the tradition, at least for imperial burials, to the end of the Ming dynasty. By that time, however, lesser folk were content to burn paper money for the departed.

Music was also an important art. Here, too, there was a change between the Spring and Autumn era and the Warring States period, with string and reed instruments becoming more prominent and percussion instruments less so. Mo Tzu was virtually alone in his rejection of music. A number of writers on

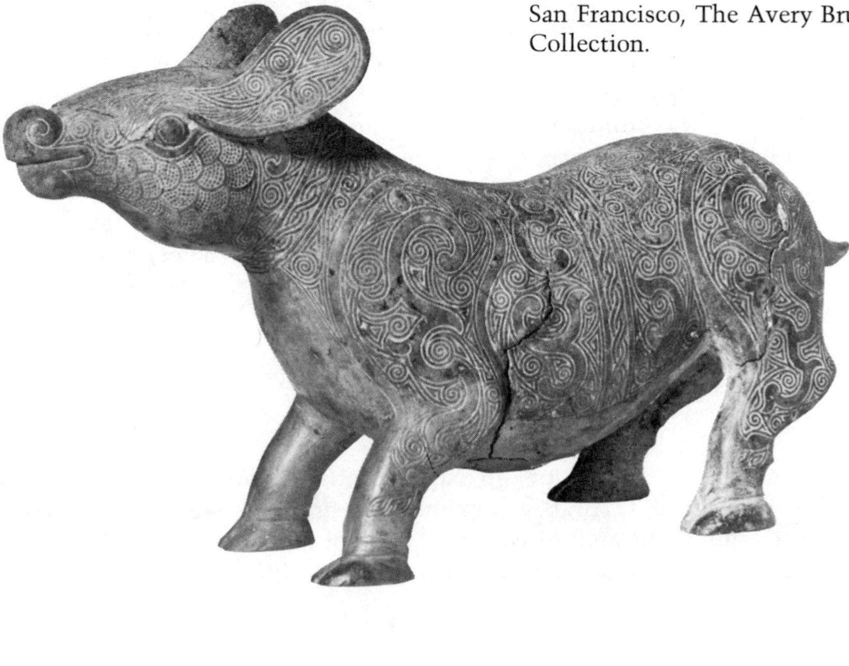

Figure 2-3
Tapir. Late Spring and Autumn
or Early Warring States period, 10.2 cm
× 17.8 cm. Asian Art Musem of
San Francisco, The Avery Brundage
Collection.

Figure 2-4   Bronze bell. Warring States period, 66.4 cm high. Freer Gallery of Art, Washington, D.C.

music made good use of the fact that the character used to write the word for music (*yüeh*) was the same as that for joy (*lo*). For Confucians the importance of music ranked with that of the *li*, for it had the power to transform people. It could make them harmonious, well balanced, well behaved, good subjects or, conversely, cause them to be abandoned, quarrelsome, and depraved. Thus according to Hsün Tzu (whose philosophy is discussed later in this chapter) music is as important as the rites. Another writer, the tough-minded Legalist Han Fei Tzu, paints a vivid picture of what happened when an unworthy duke insisted that a great music master play a piece created by the Yellow Emperor and meant only for the ears of sages:

> As he played the first section of the music, black clouds began to rise from the northwest. With the second section, a fierce wind came forth, followed by violent rain, that tore the curtains and hangings on the terrace, overturned the cups and bowls, and shook down the tiles from the gallery roof. Those who had been sitting in the company fled in all directions, while the duke, overcome with terror, cowered in a corner of the gallery. The state of Chin was visited by a great drought that seared the land for three years, and sores broke out all over Duke P'ing's body.[2]

Our understanding of Chou music has been advanced by the excavation of great bronze bells. Chinese bells were sounded by being struck, not from the inside as are Western bells, but from the outside with a piece of wood. Sets of bells, numbering as many as thirteen, were suspended in wooden racks. Inside the bells there are grooves and marks of scraping and scratching made as the bells were tuned to the right pitch. The bell reproduced in Figure 2-4 has an ornamental dragon handle; the bosses, which improve the quality of the tone, are in the form of coiled snakes; and at the bottom the *t'ao-t'ieh* reappears treated in a playful, ornamental manner. After this age, it disappears entirely.

The division of China into numerous different states encouraged the development of regional cultures and the introduction of foreign elements, such as the animal styles of the steppes. The richest regional culture, however, developed not along China's northern and western frontiers, but in the southern state of Ch'u.

Ch'u and the Culture of the South

The origins of the state of Ch'u are obscure, but already by the eighth century it boasted a ruler who called himself a king. During the Eastern Chou, Ch'u became a major factor in Chinese politics until it was finally destroyed by Ch'in in 223 B.C.

It is not surprising that a major power should develop in the lush region south of the Huai and around the Yangtze River, where warm weather and ample water from rainfall, rivers, and lakes provide ideal conditions for rice cultivation. Rice and fish were staples in the diet of the people of Ch'u. Their technological level was on a par with that of the North: they had iron as well as bronze, made fine ceramics, and employed bronze coins.

Archaeological excavations, especially those from Changsha in Hunan province, reveal a highly sophisticated culture. Ch'u tombs were surrounded by a layer of charcoal and a thicker layer of white clay. Although they became waterlogged, their contents are remarkably well preserved. The finds include not

Figure 2-5
Cover, Laughing Dragon
Box. Wood and cloth covered with painted lacquer,
diam. 26.5 cm, height of
box, 10 cm. Museum of
Fine Arts, Boston.

only a large number of stylized, painted wooden figures of human beings but also jade disks, glass beads, pieces of linen and silk, bows, bamboo mats, slips of bamboo written on with a brush, shields of lacquered leather, musical instruments, and an assortment of lacquerware: bowls, dishes, low tables, and toilet boxes which when opened reveal a set of combs, whisks, hairpins, hairpuffs, and even hairpieces. Many of the lacquer objects are finely painted, red on black or black on red. Changsha is also the site of the oldest painting on silk discovered to date, although that may, of course, be an accident of archaeology. It shows a woman accompanied by a phoenix and a dragon. The dragon became one of the most prominent mythological animals throughout East Asia. Another dragon, called by Max Loehr "partly organism, partly ornament,"[3] appears on the walls and on the lid of the lacquer box known as the Laughing Dragon Box (Figure 2-5). Since the dragon is a majestic and rather awesome animal, however, laughing dragons are exceedingly rare. In East Asia the dragon is always associated with water, not with fire as in the West. It does not belch flames, but is the lord of lakes, rivers, and oceans. It is therefore particularly at home in the watery region of Ch'u.

Other tantalizing glimpses into the world of the supernatural are afforded by drum or gong stands consisting of two birds, standing back to back, either on tigers or on serpents (perhaps the ancestors of dragons), and these may provide a mythological and artistic link with the early culture of North Vietnam. Even more striking are monster heads with antlers, bulging eyes, and long tongues, eating a snake. (See Figure 2-6.) Like the so-called *t'ao-t'ieh* monster of the Shang, these mythological beings offer just a hint about a world of beliefs and observances later disowned and discarded.

Something more about that world can be learned from an anthology of Ch'u poetry translated by David Hawkes as *Ch'u Tz'u: The Songs of the South.* Included in this collection are nine shamanistic songs. Shamanism, widely practiced in Central, North, and Northeast Asia, is based on the belief that a priest, or shaman, when in an inspired trance can summon spirits to appear or, conversely, can release his soul to go on a spiritual journey to the land of the gods.

Figure 2-6
Mythical creature. Excavated in Hsin-yang District, Honan, Late Warring States period, 195 cm high.

Shamans may be of either sex: in Korea and Japan they were women. The songs in the anthology employ erotic imagery, inviting the spirits as to a rendez-vous, but neither the sex nor the number of people calling on the gods is known. Shamanism was later derided, but the songs were preserved because they appealed to antiquarian interests and because they could be reinterpreted as the pleas of a loyal minister to his ruler rather than those of a priest to a god.

The *Ch'u Tz'u* contains China's first nature poetry and was a prime source for the fantastic landscapes beloved by the Han rhapsodists (see Chapter 3). One poem is dedicated to the orange, a reminder of the South's contribution to the diet of China, and to judge by such words as "tangerine" and "mandarin" to the western diet as well. The anthology also contains the longest poem in pre-Han China, the 374-line "Li Sao," or "Encountering Sorrow." A powerful but difficult poem, it is strong in rhythm and in flights of magic and fantasy. This poem, reputed to have been written by Ch'u Yüan, a rejected minister, is interpreted as a political allegory, consistent with the story of his life.

Ch'u Yüan, who served his ruler faithfully and wisely but fell victim to slan-der, personifies the tragedy of the loyal but rejected minister. Banished from court and powerless to change a muddled world, he chose death as the means to preserve his purity and to serve as a model for worthy men. Clasping a large stone, he jumped into the Mi-lo River and thus became China's noblest sui-cide. In time, his story fused with the stories of others who had drowned, and it is remembered in the Dragon Boat Festival, a festival held on the Double Fifth, the fifth day of the fifth month of the lunar calendar. As part of the festival, celebrated from at least the Han dynasty on into the twentieth century, rice cakes were thrown into the water as offerings to Ch'u Yüan's spirit.

Neither the achievements of the South nor its contributions to Chinese cul-ture should be underestimated, but events in the third century B.C. were to demonstrate that power belonged to the North. It was also in the North that intellectual life was at its liveliest.

Mencius and the Development of Confucianism

Like Confucius, Mencius (371–289 B.C.?) traveled in vain from court to court, trying to find a ruler to implement his program, and then turned to teaching as another way to propagate his ideas. He was a great admirer of Confucius and, living at a time of lively debate, was spurred to refine and develop the master's teachings. He shares with Confucius the distinction of being known in the West by the Latinized version of his name, a reflection of the status accorded him by Sung and post-Sung Chinese Confucian scholars. His teachings are contained in the book which bears his name, the *Mencius*.

Mencius contributed importantly to the theory of human nature, a subject of perennial concern to Chinese philosophers. He starts with the position that people are basically good, as shown, for example, by the instantaneous, uncal-culated compassion we feel when we see a child about to fall into a well. We are naturally endowed with a sense (or heart) of compassion that is the beginning, the germ, from which grows our benevolence or humanity (*jen*). Similarly our sense of shame is the germ for dutifulness; our sense of courtesy, for modesty; our sense of right and wrong, for wisdom. These four senses are as much a part of the person as are his four limbs. Challenged with the proposition that human nature is neutral and can, like water, be channeled in any direction, Mencius retorted that the goodness of human nature was like the tendency of water to flow downward.

This view of human nature opened the way for a deepening of the philosophy of individual self-perfection, since "all things are already complete in oneself."[4] Everyone can become a sage by recovering his original nature or finding his lost mind, and thereby know Heaven itself. Mencius thus provided a source of inspiration for the development of Confucian theories of self-cultivation that stimulated later theorists, particularly those of the post-Buddhist age. Additional psychological and metaphysical depth was provided by the "Doctrine of the Mean," a chapter of the *Records of Rites* (*Li Chi*), compiled around 100 B.C. from earlier materials. Still another chapter of the same work, "The Great Learning," stressed the link between self-cultivation and government, viewing the perfection of the individual as the prerequisite for the perfection of society:

> when the personal life is cultivated, the family will be regulated; when the family is regulated, the state will be in order; and when the state is in order, there will be peace throughout the world. From the Son of Heaven down to the common people, all must regard cultivation of the personal life as the root or foundation.[5]

For Confucians of all persuasions, sagehood was by definition expressed in society.

Mencius looked for a perfectly humane prince who would, by his acts and example, transform all with his benevolence. Such a prince was needed, according to Mencius, to bring out and nourish human goodness. Given his belief in human nature, Mencius needed to explain the all too obvious failure of individuals to be good in actual life. His solution was typically Confucian in its insistence that the germs of goodness must be cultivated if they are to grow and flourish. In an eloquent passage he compared the human heart to Ox Mountain. Once, in accordance with its original nature, Ox Mountain was green and covered with vegetation, but it became bald because of the abuse inflicted by man and beast, until anyone looking at it would conclude that its intrinsic nature was to be barren.

To Mencius, it was the function of government to provide the environment for the nurture of human goodness. He vigorously defended familial virtues against Mohist attack and, like Confucius, thought in terms of a political and social hierarchy based on virtue and ability. He made it explicit that those who work with their brains are to be supported by those who work with their hands. But he insisted that the government was responsible for the well-being of all its subjects, that it provide for their material as well as spiritual needs. As the ideal form of land distribution, Mencius advocated the well-field system, thought to have been practiced in antiquity. Under this system, eight families each farmed an outside field and joined together to cultivate the inside field for their lord. The system took its name from the Chinese character for "well," 井 which resembles the arrangement of the nine fields. Once the people's material wants were satisfied, schools should be established to educate them.

Drawing on such sources as *The Classic of History* and *The Book of Songs*, Mencius refined the concept that government is based on divine and moral sanctions by insisting that a dynasty rules by virtue of a Mandate of Heaven, which can be revoked if the ruler does not conduct himself as a ruler should. In one place, Mencius suggests that such a ruler is not a ruler at all, an argument consistent with the principle of the "rectification of names," contained in the *Analects*, which holds that the world could be set in order if only actualities conformed to names, for example, if princes were really princes. In any event, Heaven in making its judgment follows the voice of the people. Mencius quotes a now lost portion of *The Classic of History:* "Heaven sees with the eyes of its people. Heaven hears with the ears of its people."[6] This right of rebellion became a permanent part of Chinese political thought, used by reformers to frighten recalcitrant rulers as well as by those who took up arms against the government. "Removing the mandate" (*ke-ming* in Chinese or *kakumei* in Japanese) became the modern word for revolution.

Taoism

Although Taoism, especially in its first formulation, has a political dimension, its primary emphasis has been on natural harmony more than on the social harmony of the Confucians. For a Taoist, social harmony follows from a return of man to harmony with nature and its underlying reality, the *Tao*, eternal, self-activating, omnipresent, the only and the ultimate reality. The first great Taoist classic, the *Tao Te Ching*, or *Lao Tzu*, dated from the third century although Taoist tradition attributes it to an older contemporary of Confucius called Lao Tzu, or Old Master. There is no reason to doubt the antiquity of its ideas, but a true Taoist philosopher would dismiss such matters as precise dating as inconsequential.

The *Tao Te Ching*, much of which is in verse, is cryptic, paradoxical, highly suggestive, and has been the subject of more Chinese commentaries than any other single text. It is also the most frequently translated Chinese book, for its language invites a multitude of interpretations, notwithstanding that, or perhaps because, one of its messages is the inadequacy of language. The *Tao* cannot be named or defined, for to do so is to make distinctions and thereby miss the totality which is the *Tao*.

Among its themes and images there is a preference for the negative over the positive, nothing over something, the weak over the strong, the soft over the hard, the yielding over the assertive. Non-being is of a higher order of reality than being. Water triumphs by yielding, as does the feminine. Non-action accomplishes more than action. It is the empty center that gives value to the wheel, the pot, the house. Silence is more meaningful than words, ignorance superior to knowledge. The sages admired by Confucians really did society a disservice by introducing moral distinctions, family relationships, learning. Apprehension of the *Tao* is through an incommunicable intuitive identification: "those who know do not speak; those who speak do not know."

The *Lao Tzu* had as its political ideal a return to primal simplicity, when people were content, ignorant, and lived in tune with nature. To attain this idea, the ruler must conduct his government with great delicacy and restraint, like a cook boiling a small fish. He must not interfere with the *Tao* and, by taking no action of his own, must allow everything to happen.

The other great Taoist text, the *Chuang Tzu*, turns its back on politics. The wise man knows that it is better to sit fishing on the banks of a remote mountain stream than to be emperor of the whole world. Chuang Tzu (ca. 369– 286 B.C.), the reputed author of the book which bears his name, had a keen sense of paradox, as when he argued the usefulness of the useless. For him, too, language and debate are not the source of truth. If two men disagree, who is to decide which one is right? The *Tao* is everywhere and in everything, not excluding piss and dung. To understand is to be like Cook Ting, so familiar with every turn and twist in the anatomy of an ox that, over nineteen years, he cut up thousands of oxen without ever having to sharpen his knife. He simply slid his knife through the spaces between the joints.

One of Chuang Tzu's favorite themes is the relativity of ordinary distinctions. He tells a story of waking up from a nap and being unable to tell whether he was Chuang Tzu dreaming he was a butterfly or a butterfly dreaming he was Chuang Tzu. Which is dream and which is "real"? For him, true comprehension leads to ecstatic acceptance of whatever life may bring. Consider Master Yü, who fell ill and became all crooked and contorted, "My back sticks up like a hunchback and my vital organs are on top of me. My chin is hidden in my navel, my shoulders are up above my head and my pigtail points at the sky."[7] True sage, he accepts it all with joy and speculates on what may happen next. Perhaps his left arm will turn into a rooster. If so, he will herald the dawn. Or his right arm may become a crossbow pellet. Then, he will shoot himself a bird. Or his buttocks will turn into cartwheels, "then, with my spirit for a horse, I'll climb up and go for a ride."[8]

There is in Chuang Tzu an ecstatic acceptance of the *Tao* and a celebration of spiritual freedom that expresses itself in soaring flights of imagination. He transcends even the distinction between life and death, and sees both as parts of a single process to be welcomed equally. Only the foolish mourn.

The Taoist sympathy for nature and the natural remained a source of inspiration for Chinese poets and free spirits and provided refreshment for men wearied by the routines of official life. It contributed greatly to the strain in Chinese culture that produced great nature poetry and fine landscape painting.

Apart from the philosophical Taoism of the *Tao Te Ching* and *Chuang Tzu*, there later developed various forms of religious Taoism which built on the lore of the Taoist sages able to ride the winds and live forever. In the Han and after, the search for longevity contributed to the development of Chinese science, and Taoist religious bodies provided havens for displaced peasants. Had Chuang Tzu foreseen the future, he would have indulged in full his fondness for paradox.

In his book, Chuang Tzu's wit and wisdom are often displayed to best advantage against the foil of a logician called Hui Shih (380–305 B.C.?) who inevitably gets the worst of the argument. Hui Shih was one of a number of men who pursued the study of logic as far as it was ever to go in traditional China.

The Logicians

Among those interested in logic were the later members of the Mohist school. Their acuity is revealed in their critique of Chuang Tzu's treatment of all statements as mistaken. This, they point out, is itself a statement. Therefore, if Chuang Tzu's statement is true, it is false; if false, it is true.

Hui Shih delighted in paradoxes, some not unlike those of the Greeks, but the most discussed logical conundrum was the statement by Kung-sun Lung (b. 380 B.C.?) that a white horse is not a horse. The seeming paradox can be explained in terms of the differences between categories of shape (horse) and color (white) or as arising out of a confusion between discussing a term and using it (the term *white horse* is not a horse), but it is perhaps best understood in modern terms as originating out of confusing class membership and identity. A white horse is a member of the class of horses, but this does not imply that it shares all attributes with all members of that class.

During the Warring States period, professional dialecticians won patronage through the brilliance of their debating tactics and their dazzling mental gymnastics, but it was widely felt that their displays had little bearing on practical issues. Since, for other reasons, Mohism also did not survive as a living school after 221 B.C., the logicians had little permanent influence on Chinese thought.

Theories of the Natural Order

In their scientific and philosophic speculations about the world, the Chinese thought of nature in dynamic rather than static terms and considered man a part of the natural process. Animating this process were *yin* and *yang*, paired, complementary opposites whose interaction keeps the world going. *Yin* is associated with the feminine, the passive, the negative, the weak and *yang* with the opposite qualities and forces: the masculine, the active, the positive, the strong. Perhaps reflecting the rhythm of agricultural life, *yin* is cold and winter, *yang* hot and summer. *Yin* is response; *yang* is stimulus. The two terms range widely in application from the popular to the technical, from the concrete to the abstract, and if phenomena are conceived in terms of polarities, the list can go on endlessly.

Similar in some ways to the concept of interaction between *yin* and *yang* is the Chinese conception of the Five Agents, or Five Phases: wood, fire, earth, metal, and water. Since the components of this concept recall the four elements of Greek philosophy, for a long time the Chinese term was translated as the "Five Elements." This translation is misleading, for it implies inertia and passivity rather than the dynamism and self-movement inherent in the Chinese conception. Furthermore, the translation "Five Agents, or Five Phases" more accurately reflects the Chinese view that the processes of nature occur in regular sequence.

Yin and *yang* and the Five Agents, or Phases, have a long history in Chinese thought. Early speculation concerning them is traditionally attributed to Tsou Yen, who supposedly lived in the fourth century B.C. Unfortunately the earliest information concerning him comes from the *Records of the Grand Historian* by Ssu-ma Ch'ien (ca. 145–ca. 90 B.C.). According to Ssu-ma Ch'ien, Tsou Yen held that ever since heaven and earth separated, time has been dominated by each of the Five Phases in turn. A cyclical view of time and history is consistent with the practice of counting time in cycles, confirming the experience of an agricultural people patterning their lives on the annual cycle of seasonal change.

The idea of change is important in Chinese thought. The ancient divination text that was incorporated into the Confucian canon and became the textual reference for much of later metaphysical speculation is called *The Classic of Change* (*I Ching*). Sixty-four hexagrams and the commentaries on them form the heart of the book. Each hexagram was created by combining two trigrams, each of which consists of three lines, either broken or unbroken. Since each trigram has three lines of only two kinds, that is, broken or unbroken, only eight combinations are possible:

Combining the eight trigrams into hexagrams in turn yields sixty-four unique figures. A common method of divination was to select the appropriate hexagram by counting the stalks of the milfoil. The very concept of divination is based on the conviction that nature and man are interrelated.

By identifying the *yin* with the broken line and the *yang* with the unbroken, the *I Ching* illustrates the way this pair of concepts applies to everything. For example, the first hexagram ☰ represents heaven, all *yang*, the second hexagram ☷ represents earth, all *yin*. The rest consist of combinations of the two. In addition to the hexagrams and their explanations, *The Classic of Change* includes influential appendixes that traditionally were ascribed to Confucius. Although this attribution is no longer accepted today, it helped to assure the status of the *I Ching* as a Confucian classic long treasured by those interested in speculations concerning the workings of nature. There were, of course, also Chinese philosophers not given to such speculation. One of the foremost of these was Hsün Tzu.

Hsün Tzu

Hsün Tzu (fl. 298–238 B.C.), along with Confucius and Mencius, counts as one of the three classical Confucian thinkers. If Mencius developed the "tender-hearted" aspects of Confucianism, Hsün Tzu is his "tough-minded" counterpart. Of a critical, analytical turn of mind, he depicts an impersonal world that proceeds according to its own ways oblivious of humankind. It will rain or not rain regardless of people's prayers. The heavenly bodies rotate the same way whether a sage or a villain is on the throne. In a departure from previous Confucian tradition, Hsün Tzu rejects the intrinsic validity of names. He regards the meaning of terms as a matter of conventions instituted by kings. He is also modern in his attitude toward the *li*, which for him provide a necessary and proper outlet for emotions such as joy, grief, reverence, and respect.

Hsün Tzu's emphasis on the psychological aspect of *li*, and of music, is in accord with his theory of human nature. Unlike Mencius, he sees human nature as fundamentally antisocial. But it can be trained. The individual has the potential of consciousness, and Hsün Tzu, like Socrates, assumes that once a person recognizes what is good he will follow it. Moreover, it is precisely because people are bad that they want to become good, just as the ugly yearn for beauty or the poor for wealth. Like his predecessors, he feels that society must be rehabilitated from the top down and emphasizes the importance of rites, music, and education. His ideas were particularly influential during the Han dynasty, although later he was overshadowed by Mencius.

Consistent with his views on human nature, Hsün Tzu accepted the need for coercion and, unlike Confucius or Mencius, counseled that strict laws and punishments be established. Here there is an element of congruity with the last group of thinkers to be discussed in this chapter, the Legalists. It is perhaps not entirely accidental that both the greatest Legalist theorist, Han Fei Tzu, and the greatest practitioner, Li Ssu, began as students of Hsün Tzu.

Han Fei Tzu and Legalism

Han Fei Tzu (d. 233 B.C.) agreed with his teacher that human beings are inherently selfish and antisocial. Even in the family, the parents rejoice when a boy is born, since he will be a support in their old age; but a girl baby may even be put to death since she is a liability. Thus, if calculations of self-interest enter even into the attitudes of parents toward children, how much more is this the case for relationships not bound by ties of natural affection. Unlike the Confucians,

Han Fei Tzu did not believe that the solution to governance lay in a return to an idealized past. He held that conditions had radically changed and that new problems demanded new solutions. He tells of a farmer who while working in the fields one day observed a rabbit dash itself unconscious against a tree stump. That evening the farmer and his family had a feast. The next day and every day thereafter the farmer waited by the stump for the next rabbit. To Han Fei Tzu this farmer was no more foolish than the Confucians waiting for the next sage-ruler. He agreed that benevolent government had worked in antiquity when men were few and their desires did not clash; but, he taught, this was no longer possible in the competitive, struggling world of his time.

Han Fei Tzu was particularly attracted to the concept of practical statecraft that originated in the fourth century B.C., which stressed rationalization of administration, managerial techniques, and the strict enforcement of severe punitive laws. Although Han Fei Tzu referred to the techniques of personnel management associated with such thinkers as the statesman Shen Pu-hai (d. 337 B.C.), he drew more heavily on the doctrines which stressed law, hence the designation "legalist." He emphasized that people should be controlled by the two handles of punishments and rewards. Given the proper legal system, the ruler will not have to do anything and yet will be all powerful. In his advice to the ruler as well as in his general principles, there was an amorality that Confucians always found extremely shocking.

In later times Legalism continued to be associated with institutional innovation but especially with harsh punishments. Its reputation became inseparably identified with that of the regime which implemented a Legalist program. For it was the only doctrine of the Warring States period actually to be put into operation.

The Ch'in: Legalism Applied

The state of Ch'in was located in the west of North China, with its heartland in the Wei River Valley in modern Shensi. This is the same region from which the Chou had conquered North China, and it was to serve as a power base again in the future. The area provided a suitable economic base on which to build a strong political and military apparatus. It was also strategically advantageous, since it was protected from attack by mountains whose passes were easy to defend and yet provided avenues for offensives to the east. In 316 B.C. Ch'in increased its resources without adding to its vulnerability when it expanded into Szechwan, a fertile area well protected by mountains.

When in the eighth century B.C. the Chou retreated to the east, the northwest became a buffer area between the civilization of China and various warlike tribal peoples. The Ch'in made the best of this situation, toughening its armies by fighting the tribesmen and at the same time drawing on the techniques and expertise developed in the centrally located states. Never invaded itself, it welcomed men from war-torn states. Among them were its most famous and most innovative statesmen.

The transformation of Ch'in into a Legalist state is traced back to such a foreigner, a man commonly known as Lord Shang (d. 338 B.C.). Following the example of the most advanced states to the east, he introduced a direct tax on the peasantry, devised a centralized bureaucracy, and divided the state into administrative districts (*hsien*). The hereditary nobility was suppressed, and noble ranks were conferred on those who excelled militarily. Everything was geared to make the state rich and strong.

Lord Shang was also known for the harshness of the legal system he instituted in Ch'in and for establishing a system of mutual responsibility. According to the Han *Records of the Grand Historian*, anyone who failed to report the perpetrator of a crime would be cut in two at the waist, but an informer would receive a reward equal to that given for decapitating an enemy soldier. Lord Shang, like the later Legalists, insisted that the laws apply equally to all regardless of status and followed this dictum when he punished the crown prince for an infraction of the law and had the prince's teacher branded. Later when the prince became king of Ch'in, he had his revenge: Lord Shang reportedly suffered dismemberment, his body torn apart by chariots pulling in opposite directions. By that time, however, he had laid the foundations for Ch'in strength, and perhaps also for the *Book of Lord Shang*. This Legalist text was probably composed not long after Lord Shang's death; quite likely it is based on his words and ideas.

The Warring States period was a ruthless time, and Ch'in was not alone in using bribery and treachery in international relations or in building up a great military machine at home. According to the *Book of Lord Shang*, the people should be made to welcome war. This can best be achieved by making their peacetime lives so harsh that war will seem to them a release. As it was, the Ch'in succeeded not only in mobilizing people for war but also in organizing them in great numbers for projects such as the construction of irrigation networks in the Wei River Valley (Shensi) and the Red Basin (Szechwan), projects which gave the state added economic muscle.

During the third century B.C., Ch'in military might and economic strength were translated into territorial expansion at the expense of rival states. The conquest of China was accelerated and completed under the direction of the man who had become king of Ch'in in 247 B.C. and later became the first emperor of a new China. After 237 B.C., he was assisted by the Legalist minister Li Ssu (d. 208 B.C.), who had once studied under Hsün Tzu but whose policies were more consistent with those of Lord Shang or Han Fei Tzu. Han Fei Tzu himself traveled to Ch'in but ended in prison and was forced to drink poison by Li Ssu, his former fellow student. Whether Li Ssu was motivated by reasons of state or personal jealousy we shall never know.

In 221 B.C. the conquest was completed, and with its completion ended China's longest experiment with a multistate system. The existence of a number of states made for intellectual and artistic diversity and encouraged economic and political experimentation. It enabled a "hundred schools" to flourish. But it was also a period of instability and warfare, sadly lacking in the harmony that all the Chinese philosophers prized.

NOTES

1. Wm. Theodore de Bary, Wing-tsit Chan, and Burton Watson, comps., *Sources of Chinese Tradition* (New York: Columbia University Press, 1960), p. 26.

2. Burton Watson, trans., *Han Fei Tzu—Basic Writings* (New York: Columbia University Press, 1964), pp. 55–56.

3. Quoted in Jan Fontein and Tung Wu, *Unearthing China's Past* (Boston: Museum of Fine Arts, 1973), p. 76.

4. Wing-tsit Chan, *A Source Book in Chinese Philosophy* (Princeton: Princeton University Press, 1963), p. 79.

5. *Ibid.*, pp. 86–87.

6. *Mencius*, V, pt. A, chap. 5, translated by D. C. Lau, *Mencius* (Baltimore: Penguin Books, 1970), p. 144.

7. Burton Watson, trans., *Chuang Tzu—Basic Writings* (New York: Columbia University Press, 1964), p. 80.

8. *Ibid.*, p. 81.

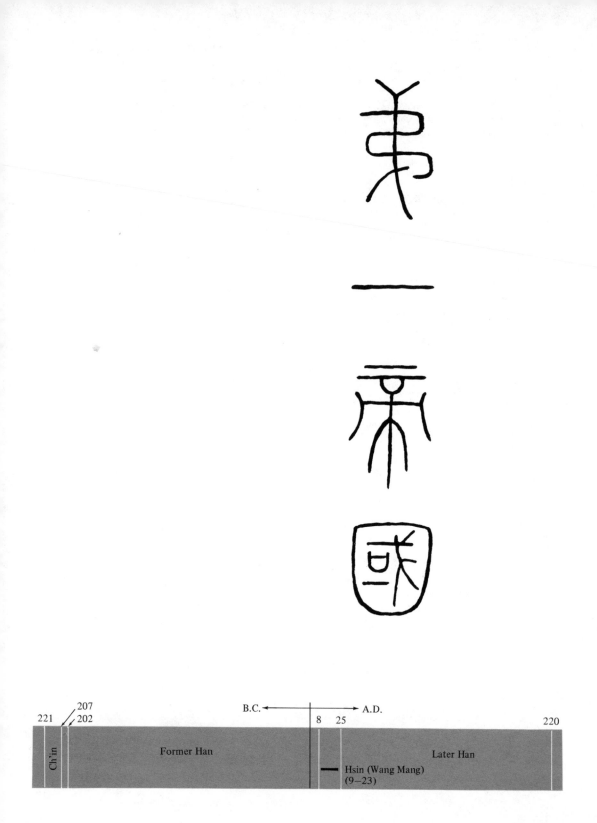

B.C. ←————→ A.D.

| 221 | 207 | | 8 | 25 | | 220 |

Ch'in

Former Han

Later Han

—— Hsin (Wang Mang)
(9–23)

3 The First Empire: 221 B.C. – A.D. 220

      The Ch'in unification of China in 221 B.C. was the beginning of some four hundred years of imperial rule, even though the Ch'in itself barely survived the death of its first emperor. Building on Ch'in foundations, although overtly rejecting many of that regime's policies, the Han erected a more lasting political structure. Under the Han, Chinese civilization was reshaped, and China became a great imperial power comparable in achievements and historical significance to the Roman Empire. (See map, Figure 3-1.) Considering the importance of the period, it is perhaps not inappropriate that our English word "China" is ultimately derived from "Ch'in." On the other hand, the Chinese refer to themselves as the Han people.

The Ch'in Integration

After defeating its rivals and completing its conquests, the Ch'in applied to all its territories the principles first implemented in its own state. Under the direction of the First Emperor and his advisor Li Ssu, China was divided into thirty-six provinces (*chün*), which were in turn subdivided into districts (*hsien*). Administration was entrusted to officials whose assignments, promotions, and demotions depended on their performances. To guard against a revival of feudalism and prevent a resurgence of local opposition, many old and prominent families were forcibly moved to the Ch'in capital where the government could keep a close watch on them.

The physical integration of the realm was fostered by a program of road building. The roads were used by the army but also helped to strengthen economic ties between different regions by encouraging trade. To facilitate travel on the dirt roads, axle lengths were standardized so that the ruts formed by cart wheels in the soft soils of North China would be uniform. The Ch'in further unified its territories by standardizing weights and measures and by issuing a single official coinage to supplant the many different moneys then in circulation. Written communication was facilitated by Li Ssu's standardization of Chinese characters.

The government did not stop at standardization of the script but also sought to control what was written and read, attempting to destroy old ideas as well as institutions. Its opposition to anti-Legalist schools of thought, particularly those which, like the Confucians, "used the past to criticize the present," led to the suppression of scholars and the banning and burning of books. The Ch'in hostility to Confucianism was reciprocated by Confucian hatred of the dynasty. As a result the historical accounts have a strong anti-Ch'in bias and must be used with great care. We cannot really know, for example, whether 460 scholars actually were buried alive by the Ch'in, but this became part of the historical record accepted by Chinese scholars for over two millennia, consistent with the ruthless iconoclasm attributed to the Ch'in.

The founders of the unified empire were highly conscious of their break with the past and set out to establish a regime they hoped would last "ten thousand generations." Since the old title of "king" (*wang*) had lost much of its luster through overuse by the rulers of even small principalities during the long period of Chou breakdown, it seemed hardly adequate for the head of a vast empire who claimed sovereignty over all peoples. Therefore, a new designation was adopted, combining two characters previously used for culture heroes and deities, to convey the full majesty of the ruler. Usually translated "emperor" (*huang-ti*), the title remained in use until 1912.

In theory the emperor's sovereignty had no geographical limit, and he sent military expeditions to establish a Ch'in presence on the coast of South China and in Vietnam, as well as into Inner Mongolia to fight against the Hsiung-nu tribes. Rather than expansion, however, the Ch'in emphasized consolidation of its rule over China, and it tacitly recognized the limits of its powers when it built the Great Wall as the demarcation between China and "barbarism." The wall was constructed partly by linking segments that had previously been erected by individual states for defensive purposes. Although the present wall dates from the fifteenth century, the Ch'in wall is its ancestor, making the dynasty responsible at least in part for China's most spectacular structure.

The Great Wall was only one of a number of large public works projects undertaken by the Ch'in. In addition to the network of roads already mentioned, the dynasty was active in the construction of canals for transportation and for irrigation. All these projects demanded the services of conscript laborers, as did the building of the imperial palace and of a great, lavish tomb for the First Emperor. Known simply as "First Emperor of the Ch'in" (Ch'in Shih Huang-ti), this ruler is depicted in the historical records as a fierce, suspicious, and superstitious man who became increasingly obsessed with the search for an elixir of everlasting life, although that did not diminish his concern for the completion of his tomb. He also reportedly sent a mission of young men and women out to sea in search of the mythical islands of immortality.

To assert his sovereignty, symbolically as well as physically, the First Emperor toured his empire a number of times. On his first eastern tour in 220 B.C., he visited China's most sacred mountain, Mt. T'ai in Shantung, where he performed sacrifices to Heaven. Several other journeys took him to various parts of the empire, and on his fifth tour, he became ill and died. Li Ssu and a eunuch named Chao Kao, however, contrived to keep his death secret until they could return to the capital, forge an order for the heir apparent to commit suicide, and place on the throne the emperor's malleable second son. The alliance between Li Ssu and Chao Kao was short-lived, however, ending in the former's death after imprisonment and torture.

The few remaining years of the dynasty were disruptive. Murder and intrigue ruled at court. The empire was torn by rebellion as the people sought to escape heavy taxes and demands for labor-service. The very harshness of the regime's laws hurt the dynasty in the end by driving into rebellion men who feared severe punishment for only minor lapses. The disintegration of the empire was rapid. The third of the line no longer dared to call himself "emperor," and this "king of Ch'in" surrendered to rebels in 206 B.C.

The Founding of the Han

As the number of rebellions against the Ch'in increased and coalesced, the contest for supremacy among the rebel forces gradually narrowed to two groups: one led by Hsiang Yü (233–202 B.C.), a southern aristocrat of great courage and charisma; the other under Liu Pang (247–195 B.C.), who had a village background and was a shrewd judge of men. The contrasting personalities and backgrounds of the two main protagonists lends color to the drama of their struggles. In the end, Liu Pang's skill in handling men proved more significant than Hsiang Yü's military abilities, and in 202 B.C. Liu Pang emerged victorious, one of only two commoners in all of Chinese history to succeed in founding a major dynasty. The dynasty was the Han, and Liu Pang as emperor is usually referred to by his posthumous imperial title, Han Kao-tsu.

Hsiang Yü had shown signs of wishing to restore the old feudal order. During the struggle Liu Pang also found it expedient to reward his generals and allies generously by granting them vassal states, and he also established "kingdoms" in eastern China for members of his own family. However, once he was in power, he took care to forestall any ambitions his former generals and allies might have entertained. Under one pretext or another, he regained control over the lands assigned to them. These lands were then incorporated into the empire. This left the territories assigned to members of the imperial family. Although these "kingdoms" were managed by court appointed officials, Kao-tsu's successors kept a close watch on them and followed a policy of reducing and eliminating them when possible. The showdown came in 154 B.C. when seven of these states, goaded into revolt, were crushed by the dynasty with unexpected ease.

The Pattern of Former Han History

The fact that it took so long for the Han emperors to eliminate the kingdoms is an indication that the new rulers were only gradually able to consolidate their power, and that the Han system was not created all at once at the beginning of the dynasty. Nor was all change in a single direction. Indeed, for a time, the fate of the imperial Liu family was in doubt; for after the death of Kao-tsu, his strong-willed widow, Empress Lü, took control of the throne and promoted the careers of members of her own family. The Lü family did not, however, gain the throne, and after the empress died in 180 B.C., her clan was massacred. The ambitions and political manipulations of empresses on behalf of their families reemerged during the first century B.C. as a source of dynastic weakness, but under Emperor Wen (180–157 B.C.) the dynasty gained in stability. Then, in Emperor Wu (140–86 B.C.) the Han found its most vigorous ruler, who initiated important changes in domestic and foreign policies. Much of the official symbolism and ritual of his reign indicates that he saw himself as making a new beginning. There was also a notable flowering of culture during this period.

Emperor Wu's reign of over half a century was the longest of the dynasty, more than twice that of Emperor Hsüan (75–48 B.C.), who was noted, among other things, for the favors he showed Confucian scholars. These later years of the Former Han were marked by the rise and fall of a number of families with palace connections, and it was a member of such a family, the controversial minister and usurper Wang Mang, who brought the Former Han to an end when he assumed the throne and established the short-lived Hsin Dynasty (A.D. 9–23). This was followed by a period of confusion and rebellion, and ultimately establishment of the Later Han. This reemergence of the Han dynasty is a testament to the prestige of the Han and its aura of legitimacy.

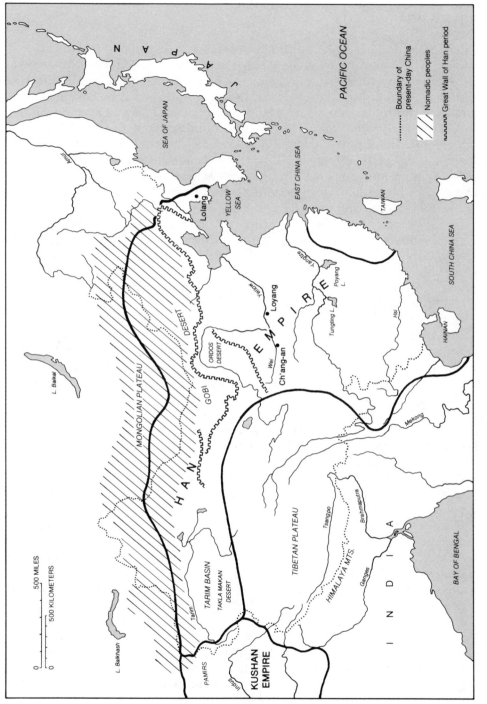

Figure 3-1 **The Han Empire**

Government and Society

In the Han political system ultimate authority was vested in the emperor, although when minor or weak emperors occupied the throne their power might be exercised by empresses or regents. As under the Ch'in, actual administration was entrusted to a bureaucracy. Officials were graded by rank and salary and were controlled from the capital, which under the Former Han was located in Ch'ang-an (modern Sian). At the head of officialdom was the Chancellor, who presided over court conferences attended by other high officials. Such officials, and especially the Chancellors, enjoyed considerable authority, although they had no recourse against a despot such as Emperor Wu, who had five of his last seven Chancellors put to death. Another powerful official was the Director of the Secretariat, who until 68 B.C. was able to determine which documents received the emperor's personal attention. The third great official was the Great Commandant, who was in charge of the military although no strict division was made at this time between the military and civil service. Under these three highest officials were nine ministers, who supervised the business of government and also were charged with palace administration and the conduct of ritual observances.

In theory the formal government of emperor and bureaucracy concerned itself with all aspects of the lives of the people, who, for their part, owed their taxes and labor-services directly to the state. In practice, however, the state usually confined itself to matters vitally affecting the welfare and security of the empire or jeopardizing the dynasty. Local matters were mostly handled by the families of notables, who dominated the local power structure. Some of these owed their eminence to old family lands and connections in a given area; others were founded by wealthy merchants who invested in land; still others acquired their base through holding of high office. In addition to the support of their kin, such families enjoyed the backing of a circle of clients bound by favors and protection rendered over the years, and also maintained permanent "house guests" whose services were particularly useful during the frequent vendettas.

Only exceptional, "harsh" officials tried to combat or ignore this local power structure. Cooperation between officials of the central government and those members of the powerful families who held lower posts in the local administration was the more usual pattern, and local matters were largely left in the hands of the local elite in return for their support. In this way, the central government and the local power holders both supported and restricted each other.

Crucial to the functioning of government was the background of its officials, for government service during the Han was a career largely limited to families of means. Not all such families sought to place members in government, but it was primarily they who could afford the investment in books and instruction required to prepare their sons for a government career. Although the top officials could have one or more sons accepted into the service automatically through "hereditary privilege," most recruiting was done through a system of recommendation by central or, more generally, by high local officials. Initially, calls for capable men went out from the capital sporadically, but under Emperor Wu local authorities were asked every year to send up the names of "filial and honest" men. Already in 165 B.C. Emperor Wen (r. 180–157 B.C.) had personally given written examinations to the men recommended to the government, and such testing later became the rule. Also designed to help prepare men for government service was the imperial university, which was established by Emperor Wu and is said to have reached an enrollment of 30,000 under the Later Han. Entry into that institution was also by recommendation.

Emperor Wu's establishment of the university was one aspect of his patronage of Confucianism. Prior to this, Confucians had already been active in government. Actually the dynastic founder, Kao-tsu, had little patience with pompous and pretentious scholars and once expressed his disdain for the breed by urinating into a pedant's hat. But after he became emperor, Kao-tsu found a need for precedents to guide him and for ceremonies to create a proper air of majesty and decorum at court—and Confucian scholars were experts par excellence in these matters of ritual. More than that, Confucianism offered to the Han emperors a body of classical learning and theory that could legitimize their dynasty and prompt ministers to faithful service. Their patronage of Confucianism did not by any means prevent Emperor Wu or other Han emperors from employing ideas derived from other traditions, and, as we shall see, Confucianism itself was transformed during this period, amalgamated with various cosmologies in theory and combined with Legalist measures in practice.

The dynasty's institutional and ideological policies contributed to the formation of a bureaucracy staffed by men who shared not only a generally similar family background but also an education grounded in classical learning, a common set of historical references, and a fund of basic ideas and widely held values. They were not faceless functionaries simply carrying out directives from above, but men with their own family interests, and heirs to a tradition that, however adulterated, did not teach unthinking compliance to the whims or policies of the ruler. The government's dependence on such officials, armed as they were with economic and moral power, restricted the power of the central government and tended to soften the impact of absolutism, even though it did not save the lives of Emperor Wu's Chancellors. On the other hand, the cohesiveness of officialdom should not be exaggerated. The diversity of geographic and family ties among the officials encouraged the formation of factional political groupings, and the intellectual heritage left ample room for disagreements, including serious policy differences.

A major area of controversy concerned government financial and economic policies. There was general agreement that the prosperity of government and society was based on agriculture, and from the beginnings of the dynasty a land tax and a head tax were the main sources of government revenue. Adult males were also obliged to render a month's labor-service and to serve in the army. Under Emperor Wu the government expanded its economic role and its income. In an attempt to stabilize prices, the government set up a system of official warehouses for the storage of commodities, especially grain. By purchasing grain when it was plentiful and prices were low and selling it in times of scarcity, the government would prevent prices from soaring out of sight. This plan, designed to make a profit for the government, also helped to secure the agrarian tax base by enabling small cultivators to remain solvent. It also served to curb the great merchants whose wealth contrasted with their theoretically low social status. A more direct means of channeling into government coffers some of the wealth gathered by the merchants was the establishment of government monopolies, especially of salt and iron. These affected everyone, for salt was a dietary necessity for peasants living on a largely vegetarian diet and iron too was vital since it was needed for tools.

These measures aroused considerable controversy and in 81 B.C., not long after Emperor Wu's death, gave rise to a famous debate at court. The government's economic policies were defended as fiscally sound and necessary by practical minded men whose realistic arguments had Legalist overtones. Their opponents, suspicious of government interference, warned against official greed and argued for the primacy of moral values. These policies underwent various changes after that, but the tendency during the later years of the Former Han was to abandon the measures. They were later briefly revived, in modified form, by Wang Mang and continued to appear, in one form or another, in subsequent regimes. All the major later dynasties enacted government monopolies.

An important aspect of the debate on the government's economic and fiscal policies concerned the dynasty's foreign policy, since it was Emperor Wu's military spending that created the need to increase government income.

Relations with Foreign Peoples

From early times the Chinese traded, negotiated, and fought with neighboring peoples. During the Warring States period such contacts became quite extensive, including relations with tribal confederations in Manchuria and Korea in the northeast, with the inhabitants of the steppes to the northwest, and with the peoples of the south. Prior to the reign of Emperor Wu, Han foreign policy was generally conciliatory, but that emperor adopted expansionist policies and by force of arms asserted Chinese control over the southeast, including Northern Vietnam, and established Chinese colonies in Korea where they greatly accelerated the diffusion of Chinese culture into that peninsula and beyond to Japan. Emperor Wu's main efforts, however, were reserved for the most troublesome and challenging area of foreign relations, the northern and northwestern frontiers. This was the home of the Hsiung-nu tribes, who had caused trouble to Chinese frontier states as early as the fourth century B.C. and had more recently been the object of a military expedition sent out by the First Emperor of the Ch'in.

Nomad peoples like the Hsiung-nu were often formidable opponents because of their skill in warfare. For them war represented merely a special application of the skills of horsemanship and archery that they practiced every day in guiding and defending their flocks. In contrast, military service for a Chinese peasant required that he interrupt the normal pattern of his life, leave his work, and undergo special training. The mobility of the nomads was an asset not only in attack but also in defense for, traveling lightly with their flocks and tents, they could elude Chinese military expeditions and avoid complete destruction or permanent control, even when the Chinese were able to mobilize their superior resources in manpower and wealth. The interaction between the Chinese and the nomadic peoples they considered barbarian thus became one of the major themes of Chinese history.

One Chinese policy alternative was to apply military force as the Ch'in did, but Kao-tsu, the founder of the Han, decided on a more prudent, conciliatory course. He and his immediate successors wooed the Hsiung-nu leaders through generous gifts, took care to address them as equals, and cemented friendly relations by sending them imperial princesses as brides. Emperor Wu reversed this policy and sent large armies into the Ordos Region, Inner Mongolia, Kansu, and Chinese Turkestan. To maintain surveillance over these areas, he established military colonies in strategic places and pressured local rulers and chiefs to enter into tributary relations with the Han. In addition to accepting Chinese suzerainty, they were required to send princes to the capital, ostensibly to receive a Chinese education, but actually to serve as hostages. There were also exchanges of gifts, in which practice the Chinese emperor more than matched the generosity of the "barbarian" tributaries.

The Hsiung-nu were slow to accede to tributary status but did so in 53 B.C., during the reign of Emperor Hsüan. By that time the tribes had split into northern and southern federations, and it was the latter which gave its allegiance to the Han. The leaders of the steppe had always found it difficult to achieve and maintain political coherence among independent-minded tribesmen thinly spread over vast areas. The Chinese also did what they could to foster division among their neighbors, "using barbarians to control barbarians." Chinese brides continued to figure in the diplomacy of the Han. The most famous was Wang Chao-chün who was married to a Hsiung-nu chief in 33 B.C. and became a much beloved tragic heroine, the central figure in *Autumn in the Palace of Han*, a drama written well over a thousand years later.

More important, at least economically, than the bestowal of brides on "barbarians" were the opportunities for trade that accompanied the tributory system. Much of this trade was conducted in border markets, and Chinese exports included lacquerware, ironware, bronze mirrors, and silk, some of which was woven for the export trade in two imperial workshops in the capital. It was during the Han that Chinese silk first reached Europe over the famous Silk Road; there it became a major luxury article in imperial Rome. The silk was carried to Rome by various middlemen; neither Chinese merchants nor diplomats traveled that far west.

Chinese envoys did cross the Pamirs, however, in search of allies against the Hsiung-nu. Again it was Emperor Wu who took the initiative, sending missions to the Chinese Far West and even a military expedition across the Pamirs to obtain the famous western "blood sweating" horses. (The origin of the term is uncertain.) From even further afield came such exotic luxury items as glass and amber as well as foreign jugglers and slaves. Closer to home, tributary states aided the diplomatic and military expeditions by supplying their needs and also contributed to the upkeep of Chinese garrisons.

Flourishing and Decline

Emperor Wu's vigorous expansionist policy extended Chinese influence further than ever before, but it was an expensive policy that led to tax increases and controversial new fiscal measures. After Emperor Wu's death, taxes were lightened and the new measures modified and softened. This took place under the direction of Ho Kuang, who began his career under Emperor Wu, controlled the government as regent for Emperor Chao (86–74 B.C.), engineered the dethronement of that emperor's heir-apparent after a reign of only twenty-seven days, and replaced him with Emperor Hsüan. Ho Kuang remained in control of the government until his death in 68 B.C. Among the treasures lavished on him in death was a jade suit of the kind shown in Figure 3-2, but his family soon got into political trouble and did not survive him for long. The dynasty continued to enjoy foreign triumphs, including the submission of the Hsiung-nu, and remained culturally productive, but below the surface there were signs that all was not well.

In the traditional Chinese view of the historical process, the end of a dynasty is foreshadowed by a decline in the quality of the rulers, who are depicted as either weak or tyrannical. In the case of the Former Han, the last emperor was a child, not a monster. Other signs of decline included intrigues at court and factionalism in officialdom, a general increase in maladministration, and the spread of corruption. A particularly dangerous development was the narrowing

Figure 3-2   Jade burial suit of the Princess Tou Wan, wife of Liu Sheng (d. 113 B.C.). Man-ch'eng, Hopei, 172 cm long.

of the dynasty's tax base. As powerful and well connected local notables largely succeeded in avoiding taxation, the tax burden on the free peasantry increased to the point where many lacked the resources to cope with poor harvests or unusual family expenses. Frequently an unpaid mortgage resulted in the loss of their land to the large tax-evading proprietors. When this happened the burden on the remaining peasants increased still further. Peasants and government were caught in an accelerating and vicious cycle. When the number of landless peasants exceeded the number of opportunities available for farming as tenants or hired laborers, the unfortunate ones had to survive as best they could, perhaps selling wives and children into slavery—although slaves did not constitute more than 1 percent of the Han population. When all else failed, they took to the hills, living as bandits or rebels while the government floundered.

The Han peace helped to increase agricultural productivity. So did the use of a new plow, fitted with two plowshares and pulled by oxen (or men), and the introduction of a new technique for sowing seed, which used an innovative system of furrows and ridges. Nevertheless, complaints about the inequitable hardships borne by the peasantry were voiced as early as the late second century B.C. The eminent Confucian theorist Tung Chung-shu contrasted the wealth of the rich and the lot of the poor "left without enough land to stick an awl into," burdened by both rents and government exactions, reduced to "eating the food of dogs and swine." He told Emperor Wu:

> Ownership of the land should be limited so that those who do not have enough may be relieved and the road to unlimited encroachment blocked. The rights to salt and iron should revert to the people. Slavery and the right to execute servants on one's own authority should be abolished. Poll taxes and other levies should be reduced and labor services lightened so that the people will be less pressed. Only then can they be well-governed.[1]

Tung Chung-shu's proposal to limit the size of land holdings was turned down. Even a vigorous emperor might hesitate before attacking the economic base of those who staffed his government. It was not until 7 B.C. that an edict was issued limiting the size of estates to around 500 acres, and even then no attempt was made to enforce this measure. The reigning emperor himself exceeded this quota in the amount of land he bestowed on his favorite catamite.

Deterioration in the quality and effectiveness of government, together with an accompanying pattern of agrarian decline, is a recurrent feature of Chinese history. It fits in well with the traditional Chinese concept of dynastic cycles, although the traditional Chinese scholar placed his emphasis more on the moral factors. Since it fosters the notion that history is merely the repetition of things that happened before, the cyclical view of history distracts attention from straight-line change and can even lead to the conclusion that nothing really new ever happened in Chinese history. It is the modern historian's task to remain sensitive both to recurrent patterns of change and to the movement of history in new directions.

Wang Mang and the Hsin Dynasty (A.D. 9–23)

The Wang family first rose to prominence through the influence of the consort of Emperor Yüan (48–33 B.C.), suffered an eclipse under Emperor Ai (7–1 B.C.), and came into its own under Emperor P'ing (1 B.C.–A.D. 6), for whom Wang Mang served as regent. He retained this position for another three years until, with a proper show of reluctance, he consented to follow the advice of ministers and the omens of Heaven and mount the throne himself, establishing the Hsin dynasty. Although *"hsin"* is usually translated "new," renewal rather than innovation was the hallmark of his reign. Wang Mang tried as far as possible to reinstitute the Chou order as represented in idealized form in *The Rites of Chou.* Not only did he change the official nomenclature, reintroducing archaic titles for officials and ancient place names, but he cited ancient precedents in reaffirming imperial ownership of the land and in setting limits to the amount that could be held by any one family, the excess to be assigned to those with inadequate holdings. In this way he tried to prepare the way for a return to the "well-field" system mentioned previously. He also attempted to abolish slavery, initiated an expanded monopoly system, reintroduced price stabilizing storehouses, changed the coinage, and modified the salary system of officials, whose pay was to vary from year to year according to the harvest. It was a complex set of measures, not all pulling in the same direction, and, under the circumstances, hardly enforceable. The land measure, for instance, was revoked after only two years.

Instead of renewing and strengthening the state, Wang Mang's policies disrupted the social and political order, and his policies also disturbed the Hsiung-nu and other non-Chinese peoples whose titular status was now lowered. The dynasty's greatest problems were caused by nature, however. A great crisis was created when the Yellow River spread destruction during one of its periodic shifts in course. Soon Shantung and then the entire Central Plain were in turmoil. Among the most prominent group of displaced peasants pushed into rebellion were the Red Eyebrows, first organized by "Mother Lü." Their choice of red, the color of the Han, reflected their hopes for a restoration of the old dynasty, but they did not have the field to themselves. Other restorationist insurrections arose, often supported by the power and resources of local notables. During the fighting, Wang Mang was killed in the capital. Troops cut his body to pieces and then ate it; his head was placed on display in the marketplace. Civil warfare continued until victory went to a leader belonging to a branch of the imperial Liu family that had settled in Honan.

The Later Han (25–220)

The Later Han is also called the Eastern Han because it moved the capital from Ch'ang-an east to Loyang. This choice of capital suggests the influence of the Honan notables who backed the new government in its formative stage and implies a less vigorous policy toward the non-Chinese peoples to the West. Notables and "barbarians" eventually helped to destroy the dynasty, but during its first three reigns, that is up to the year 88, the new Han enjoyed political stability, a cultural flourishing stimulated by the patronage of education and Confucianism, and all the benefits of economic recovery after the terrible years during which natural disasters and warfare had substantially reduced the population of North China. During the first century A.D., China also reasserted its suzerainty over the Southeast and over Northern Vietnam and reestablished its supremacy over Central Asia, a project facilitated by the split of the Hsiung-nu into a northern and a southern confederation. Pan Ch'ao (31–102), brother of the famous historian Pan Ku, led a Han force over the Pamirs and marched all the way to the Caspian Sea. Since the Later Han took a lenient attitude toward merchants, trade flourished as never before. The international caravan trade continued long after the dynasty ceased to exist.

Despite the initial brilliance of the Later Han, it soon became apparent that the dynasty had no lasting solution for the weaknesses that had undermined its predecessor. The fourth emperor came to the throne as a child, and the first of a succession of consort families monopolized high offices in the capital. In the provinces the estates and clientele of great landed families grew at the expense of the small peasants and the state treasury, occasional warnings by some Confucian officials notwithstanding.

A new element in the complicated politics of the period was the growth of eunuch power. Palace eunuchs, like consorts, enjoyed easy access to the emperor, but, unlike consorts, they did not belong to powerful families well connected in officialdom. Eunuchs were deliberately chosen from insignificant, often aboriginal families to ensure that they would have no outside loyalties but would be solely dependent on imperial favor. This dependency commended them to strong-willed rulers like the founder of the Later Han; his weaker successors, however, sometimes became the instruments rather than the masters of the eunuchs. Earlier, in the Ch'in and during the last half century of the Former Han, individual eunuchs had become powerful, but never before had eunuchs as a group attained the prominence they achieved in the second century. They were even granted the right to perpetuate their power by adopting "sons" to create ersatz families.

Confucian scholars and officials despised eunuchs as less than complete men and strongly disapproved of their access to power through palace politics rather than normal official channels. Since the scholars wrote the histories, the depiction of the eunuch is a stereotype: a man who overcompensates for his physical impotence by giving full vent to his lust for wealth and power. Nevertheless, there are occasional indications that at least some eunuchs, during the Han and later, enjoyed considerable respect and prestige, and some can be credited with genuine accomplishments.

Much of the history of the second century is filled with the ups and downs of the fortunes of consort families, eunuchs, and scholars playing a deadly political game for the highest stakes, a game that, in the end, they all lost. No single consort family managed to establish itself let alone avoid a bloodbath. When scholars denounced eunuchs, the literati suffered persecution, first in 166, again and with more vigor in 169 and after. Punishments ranged from house arrest to death, and among those arrested in 172 were more than a thousand students at the state university. In 189 it was the eunuchs' turn to suffer and die. More than two thousand were killed, including some beardless but otherwise virile men who were mistaken for eunuchs. Five years earlier, in 184, the Yellow Turban Rebellion had demonstrated that dynastic disintegration was well advanced, and the following decades showed that the process could not be reversed simply by slaughtering eunuchs. What was coming to an end was more than a political dynasty—an entire epoch of Chinese civilization was drawing to a close. The end of the Han was one of the great watersheds in the history of Chinese civilization. Much survived, but only in changed form. Before we examine the dynasty's closing years, it is time to explore the texture of that civilization and consider some of its salient features, both those which survived and those which perished. Among the great works that survived to inspire and delight future generations of readers throughout East Asia, none has been more admired than Ssu-ma Ch'ien's great history.

Han Historiography: Ssu-ma Ch'ien and Pan Ku

Ssu-ma Ch'ien (ca. 145–ca. 90 B.C.) devoted his life to the completion of a work begun by his father, a history of his world from the legendary Yellow Emperor to his own day. Even after suffering castration, the price he paid for defending an unsuccessful general against the views of the court and in conflict with Emperor Wu's own opinion, Ssu-ma Ch'ien continued with his great undertaking. Through his writing he sought to fulfill his obligation to his father and to bequeath to posterity a literary and moral legacy of permanent value.

His efforts resulted in the *Shih Chi* (*Records of the Grand Historian*) consisting of five sections: Basic Annals, Chronological Tables, Treatises, Hereditary Houses, and Memoirs. The treatises include essays on rites, music, pitch pipes, the calendar, astronomy, the solemn *feng* and *shan* sacrifices performed at Mt. T'ai, the Yellow River and canals, and economics. The memoirs contain accounts of the lives of famous men, important political and military leaders, philosophers, and such groups as imperial favorites, merchants, and so forth. They also include accounts of non-Chinese people. Ssu-ma Ch'ien's work became the pattern for later histories. It's form, somewhat modified, was followed by later historians including Pan Ku (d. 92), author of *The History of the Former Han*. This history, which is a record of the preceding dynasty written during and sanctioned by the succeeding dynasty, was the first in a series of such dynastic histories. Although the works of Ssu-ma Ch'ien and his successors emphasized political history and subjects of concern to officials, in scope they compare favorably with the works of the historians of classical Western antiquity.

Like all good historians Ssu-ma Ch'ien and Pan Ku strove for objectivity. One device employed by all Chinese historians was copious quotation from original documents. Another was a careful separation between the narrative text and their own editorial comments. However, historians in China could no more transcend their times and origins than could their counterparts elsewhere. The very process of selection reveals their own values and ideals. Ssu-ma Ch'ien freely expressed his enthusiasm for political valor and virtue, his delight in clever stratagems, his fascination with character and personality. His deep feelings give life to his prose. A fine stylist and gifted raconteur, he did not hesitate to invent dialogues or turn to poetry to convey the full force of a historical personage's feelings or personality. His flair for the dramatic is exemplified by the following account of a battle:

> T'ien Tan then rounded up a thousand or more oxen from within the city and had them fitted with coverings of red silk on which dragon shapes had been painted in five colors. He had knives tied to their horns and bundles of grease-soaked reeds to their tails, and then, setting fire to their tails, had them driven out into the night through some twenty or thirty openings which had been tunneled in the city wall. Five thousand of the best soldiers poured out after them. The oxen, maddened by the fires that burned their tails, rushed into the Yen encampment which, it being night, was filled with terror. The oxtail torches burned with a dazzling glare, and wherever the Yen soldiers looked, they saw nothing but dragon shapes. All who stood within the path of the oxen were wounded or killed. The five thousand soldiers, gags in their mouths so they would make no noise, moved forward to attack, while from within the city came an accompaniment of drumming and clamor, the old men and boys all beating on bronze vessels to make a noise until the sound of it shook heaven and earth. The Yen army, taken completely by surprise, fell back in defeat, and the men of Ch'i were able to capture and put to death its commander, Ch'i Chieh.[2]

Pan Ku's style is more sober and restrained, in keeping with his more austere Confucianism.

There is a great deal we would dearly like to know, which the Han historians do not tell. Moreover, portions of their texts, especially some of the annals, are at times dry and dull. Nevertheless, they convey an impressive amount of information and, at their best, they remind us that the study of human beings is what history is all about. For the modern reader it is perhaps especially salutary to read of people who rejected the general pattern of their times, for example, of Yang Wang-shu, a wealthy student of Taoism who, in an age when the highest elite went to their graves dressed in jade, dismayed his family and shocked the world by insisting that he was to be buried naked. Pan Ku reports that he had his way.

The two histories are read for their literary as well as historical qualities. The elegant simplicity of their prose is more in tune with modern tastes than is the elaborateness cultivated in much other Han writing. In their histories Ssu-ma Ch'ien and Pan Ku also helped to preserve many poems that otherwise would have been lost.

Han Poetry

Among the poetic remains of the Han are the verses collected by the Music Bureau established by Emperor Wu. These include hymns and songs for cere-monial occasions and also a group of fresh and simple folk songs. Originally they were sung to the accompaniment of such instruments as the flute, a bam-boo mouth organ known as the *sheng*, the drum, the lute, and/or a stringed in-strument that was the ancestor of the Japanese koto. The music has been lost, and the words alone remain. The dynasty also produced good and important poems in a form limiting lines to five words each. The most characteristic and popular form, however, was the rhapsody, a uniquely Chinese genre.

The rhapsodies (*fu*) often ran to great lengths and combined poetry with prose. There were prose introductions and conclusions, and there might be prose interludes between the streams of verse. They were frequently in the form of a poetic debate and drew on both the rhetorical tradition of the Warring States period and on the rich metaphors and fantastic allegories of the Ch'u tradition. Exotic terminology, verse catalogs, and ornamental embellishments enriched the verse, but in the hands of less than a master, the form was apt to degenerate into mere ostentation and artificiality. Its thematic repertoire in-cluded royal hunts and ceremonies, landscapes, the capital, fauna and flora, fe-male beauty, and musical instruments.

The most highly regarded Han rhapsodist was Ssu-ma Hsiang-ju (179–117 B.C.), a colorful man who as a young and poor scholar eloped with the widowed daughter of a wealthy merchant. Eventually his poetic gifts were recognized by Emperor Wu, and the poet received a post at court. One of his greatest *fu* de-scribes the imperial park. It is too long to quote in full, but the following seg-ment, in Burton Watson's translation, is sufficiently substantial to suggest the scope and flavor of this style of verse.

> Within the park spring the Pa and Ch'an rivers,
> And through it flow the Ching and Wei,
> The Feng, the Hao, the Lao, and the Chüeh,
> Twisting and turning their way
> Through the reaches of the park;
> Eight rivers, coursing onward,
> Spreading in different directions, each with its own form.
> North, south, east, and west
> They race and tumble,
> Pouring through the chasms of Pepper Hill,
> Skirting the banks of the river islets,
> Winding through the cinnamon forests
> And across the broad meadows.
> In wild confusion they swirl
> Along the bases of the tall hills
> And through the mouths of the narrow gorges;
> Dashed upon boulders, maddened by winding escarpments,
> They writhe in anger,

Leaping and curling upward,
Jostling and eddying in great swells
That surge and batter against each other;
Darting and twisting,
Foaming and tossing,
In a thundering chaos;
Arching into hills, billowing like clouds,
They dash to left and right,
Plunging and breaking in waves
That chatter over the shallows;
Crashing against the cliffs, pounding the embankments.
The waters pile up and reel back again,
Skipping across the rises, swooping into the hollows,
Rumbling and murmuring onward;
Deep and powerful,
Fierce and clamorous,
They froth and churn
Like the boiling waters of a caldron,
Casting spray from their crests, until,
After their wild race through the gorges,
Their distant journey from afar,
They subside into silence,
Rolling on in peace to their long destination,
Boundless and without end,
Gliding in soundless and solemn procession,
Shimmering and shining in the sun,
To flow through the giant lakes of the east,
Or spill into the ponds along their banks.[3]

The poet has turned the park into the cosmos fulfilling the intent of the landscape architect who designed it. The poem ends with the emperor virtually giving up his luxuries in order to benefit the people. The *fu* often concluded with a moral message, although only in the case of really serious Confucian poets does that become the main focus. Conversely, one of the most gifted but also most earnestly Confucian of the rhapsodists, Yang Hsiung (53 B.C.–A.D. 18), eventually gave up the form because he felt it was not really suitable for moralizing.

The flair for ornamentation, the cosmological outlook, and the dramatic rendering of movement so striking in Ssu-ma Hsiang-ju's rhapsody are also prominent in the visual arts.

The Visual Arts

Like the imperial park, Han palaces were intended to mirror the universe. Heirs to an ancient tradition of celestial symbolism, the Han built their palaces on a north–south axis (for the emperor always faces south) and recreated on a small scale the symmetry of the cosmos. Especially significant was the

Figure 3-3 Model of a watch tower. Pottery covered with a green iridescent glaze, second century A.D., 88 cm high. Nelson Gallery—Atkins Museum, Kansas City, Missouri.

Ming T'ang (Sacred Hall) where many of the most important ceremonies were performed. Its round roof representing heaven was set on a square structure representing the shape of the earth. Some accounts of the building are replete with numerological symbolism: 8 windows for the 8 winds, and 4 openings for the seasons; 9 apartments for the divisions of the world; 12 halls and 36 doors representing the number of months and of ten-day periods in a year; 72 windows, one for each five-day period. The aesthetic result of such considerations was an architecture of formal symmetry and geometric balance.

But it was not a severe architecture. As in classical Greece, the buildings were decorated in rich colors. Red lacquered wooden supports sustained roofs of sparkling glaze, or sometimes of bronze tiles, contrasting with walls of shining white. Sculpture everywhere contributed to the flamboyance. Columns were carved with human and animal forms, and paintings decorated the interiors. In architecture, as in poetry, people enjoyed intricate patterns, colors galore, and lush variety.

Unfortunately, Han buildings no longer exist, but clay models, preserved in tombs, confirm the impressions created by literary descriptions. Among the most interesting are the models of watchtowers (see Figure 3-3), frequently still showing some paint, roofed in tile, and testifying not only to the style of the period but also to the need for security. Other models show such utilitarian buildings as granaries and storehouses and even a combination privy-pigsty (see Figure 3-4), an example of the Chinese genius for recycling.

Among the favorite subjects of the Han painter was the human figure, especially portraits of exemplars of virtue and other famous men. Most of this art has been lost, but enough remains to document the artists' skill in drawing and placing figures so as to create a sense of interaction even in the absence of a landscape or architectural setting. Examples appear on tiles and also on a famous lacquer basket found in Lolang, the Han colony that Emperor Wu established in Korea. (See Figure 3-5.) Historical and semihistorical scenes are depicted in low relief in Han tombs, giving further indications of formal painting styles. These low reliefs reveal the use of a convention which translates depth into height so that the upper figures are to read as being located behind rather than above the lower. A more naturalistic perspective is found in some tiles discovered in Szechwan. One depicts in detail the process of recovering salt from wells, a process still in use today. The tile shown in Figure 3-6 presents a harvest and threshing scene in the bottom panel, a hunting scene at the top. Except for the oversized fish, the figures are in scale. They move in real space, and the sense of space receding into the distance is remarkable for such an early work. The striking rhapsodies of Ssuma Hsiang-ju, the technique revealed in the tile paintings, and the fineness of its lacquerware, all testify to the advanced state of the culture of Szechwan.

Figure 3-4   Model of a privy-pigsty. Clay, Han dynasty,

Tomb tiles and figures provide much information on Han music, pastimes, and the lives of ordinary people. There are models of wells and stoves, people playing board games, scholars receiving instruction seated on the floor, as is still the custom in Japan. There are models of carts and dogs and tiles depicting everyday activities such as a woman cooking fish.

There are also horses, for in art as in life, horses were cherished. One painter won renown for painting an ideal horse, combining the best features of actual horses owned by several different families, that is, the mouth of one horse, the nostrils of another, and so on. The flying horse shown on page 1 is in bronze.

Figure 3-5   Exemplars of filial piety. Lacquer painting on basketwork box, Lolang, Korea, Later Han dynasty, approx. 5 cm high.

Figure 3-6 Rubbing from
a pottery tile. Kuang-han,
Szechwan, Han dynasty,
42 cm high.

Balanced on a swallow, it gallops through the air. At the opposite pole of Han sculpture are monumental figures: grand, dignified lions, other animals, and mythical beasts.

In the Han, as earlier, the fantastic and mythical were never far from human consciousness, and the dragon (see Figure 3-7) remained a favorite motif throughout Chinese history, giving full play to the artist's talents and imagination. Dragons appear also on the backs of Han mirrors where they represent the

Figure 3-7 Impressed and painted gray tile. Chin-ts'un, Honan, Former Han dynasty. Wadsworth Atheneum, Hartford, Connecticut.

Figure 3-8 Mirror back. Bronze, Later Han dynasty, diam. 17.2 cm. Metropolitan Museum of Art, New York.

east, balancing the tiger on the west. A popular form of mirror design is the "TLV" type, so called because shapes similar to these letters are repeated in the design. (See Figure 3-8.) The square earth (*yin*) at the center is surrounded by circular heaven (*yang*), while the central axis of the world is represented by the mirror's raised boss. The central square also contains the twelve symbols used for computing the lunar calendar, and in the space between heaven and earth move the directional animals and various spirits. The T, L, and V shapes have been variously interpreted as representing the four corners of the world, the seasons, and points of the compass—or alternatively, the mountains and gates of the universe. Similarly the pattern ringing heaven may represent mountains or waves. Such mirrors were valued by the living and (it was believed) by the dead alike, for they were thought always to tell the truth. No demon, no matter what form he assumed, could escape detection by the mirror.

The Intellectual Order

The establishment of empire resulted in the channeling of intellectual as well as political life. Some varieties of thought, that of the Mohists and the dialecticians for instance, disappeared from the scene. On the whole, it was not a time for radical new departures but a period of working out the implications of older ideas and of blending them in new ways. As previously indicated, Confucianism won official endorsement under Emperor Wu, but this did not inhibit the government then or later from employing Legalist policies, including the promulgation of an extensive law code. Confucian ideas shared the political realm with concepts derived from Legalism; similarly, Confucianism shared the intellectual world and interacted with Taoism and various cosmological theories. As a result of its political and intellectual position, Han Confucianism developed in ways which would have startled, perhaps dismayed, its founder.

One corollary to imperial patronage was imperial interference, as when in 51 B.C. scholars were summoned to court to assist the emperor in establishing the "correct" texts of five classics. Textual studies remained a major scholarly preoccupation, generating a dispute between Modern Text scholars, who accepted texts that, early in the dynasty, had been written down in modern characters, and the advocates of Ancient texts, composed in archaic script, that had been "discovered" during the first century B.C. Philosophical and political issues complicated the debate. Of the two groups, the scholars of the Modern Text school were more deeply identified with Han cosmological speculation and the dynasty's claims to cosmic sanctions. Post-Han scholars, however, turned to the more sober antiquarianism of the Ancient Text school. Among the lasting contributions of Han scholarship were China's first real dictionary and the commentaries on the classics, among which those by Cheng Hsüan (127–200) were particularly valuable.

From the beginning, moral teachings have been at the core of Confucianism, and this remained the case during the Han. Of works in this genre, few have been more influential than *The Classic of Filial Piety*, generally thought to be of Han date. Its exemplars of filial piety (see Figure 3-5) have been held up as models for two millennia. Similar in its stress on obedience and selfless service was the *Lessons for Women* by Pan Chao (45–114?), the sister of Pan Ch'ao, who won fame in Central Asia, and of the historian Pan Ku. After the latter's death, Pan Chao completed his history. Her own book emphasizes a woman's obligations to her husband and parents-in-law, and projects an ideal of wifely devotion that extends beyond the grave. In her condemnation of widow remarriage, Pan Chao went beyond the ideas and practices of the time, for such marriages were both frequent and entirely respectable during the Han.

A major Han intellectual enterprise was the construction of a philosophical order to account for all reality, just as Ssu-ma Ch'ien included all of history in his work, and the emperor ruled for all mankind. In their quest for an all encompassing explanation of the political and moral as well as natural order of things, the Han thinkers were necessarily eclectic, joining Confucian moral and political values to cosmological explanations derived from other schools. Basic to their effort was the conviction that the world was an organic whole passing through time in identifiable phases. All phenomena, no matter how diverse, which shared any particular temporal phase were held to be interrelated in a set of extensive correspondences.

There were various versions of such correspondences, employing *yin-yang* theory, Five Agents concepts, the diagrams of *The Book of Changes*, and similar systems. Table 3-1 is based on the order by which the Five Agents were thought to produce each other. Another Han arrangement was fire-water-earth-wood-metal, the sequence in which the Agents overcome each other. Al-

Table 3-1 Correspondences for the Five-Agents System

	THE FIVE AGENTS				
Correspondence	Wood	Fire	Earth	Metal	Water
Seasons	Spring	Summer		Autumn	Winter
Divine Rulers	T'ai Hao	Yen Ti	Yellow Emperor	Shao Hao	Chuan Hsu
Attendant spirits	Kou Mang	Chu Yung	Hou T'u	Ju Shou	Hsuan Ming
Sacrifices	inner door	hearth	inner court	outer court	well
Animals	sheep	fowl	ox	dog	pig
Grains	wheat	beans	panicled millet	hemp	millet
Organs	spleen	lungs	heart	liver	kidneys
Numbers	eight	seven	five	nine	six
Stems	chia/i	ping/ting	mou/chi	keng/hsin	jen/kuei
Colors	green	red	yellow	white	black
Notes	chueh	chih	kung	shang	yu
Tastes	sour	bitter	sweet	acrid	salty
Smells	goatish	burning	fragrant	rank	rotten
Directions	East	South	center	West	North
Creatures	scaly	feathered	naked	hairy	shell-covered
Beasts of the directions	Green Dragon	Scarlet Bird	Yellow Dragon	White Tiger	Black Tortoise
Virtues	benevolence	wisdom	faith	righteousness	decorum
Planets	Jupiter	Mars	Saturn	Venus	Mercury
Officers	Minister of Agriculture	Minister of War	Minister of Works	Minister of Interior	Minister of Justice

From Wm. Theodore de Bary, Wing-tsit Chan, and Burton Watson, *Sources of Chinese Tradition,* vol. I (New York: Columbia University Press, 1960), p. 199.

though not included in the table, this technique could also be used to explain history, past and present. To signify a new beginning, Emperor Wu adopted earth and the corresponding color, yellow, for the dynasty. Another theory, developed near the end of the Former Han, held that the dynasty corresponded to fire and red. This was used by Wang Mang to justify his regime and continued to be accepted even though Wang Mang was discredited.

The acceptance of the idea that all phenomena are interrelated in a set of correspondences gave great satisfaction. Not only did it explain everything, it enabled men to feel at home in the world, part of a temporal as well as spatial continuum. It provided both an impetus to the development of science and the basis for a sophisticated theoretical framework for explaining the world. Since it made Chinese investigators sensitive to phenomena that interact without apparent physical contact, it enabled them to discover and explain such phenomena as the sympathetic vibration of musical instruments and the workings of magnetism, phenomena most perplexing within the context of the Aristotelian physics that Galileo was the first to challenge in the West. Among the most noted Han scientists was Chang Heng (78–139): mathematician (he calculated the value of pi), practical and theoretical astronomer, cartographer (inventor of the grid system for map making), and inventor of a seismograph that registered the direction of earthquakes far from the capital.

The most influential philosopher of the period was Tung Chung-shu, a Modern Text scholar who helped persuade Emperor Wu to sponsor Confucianism. He shared the Han conviction that the architecture of the human body, like that of the Ming T'ang, was the universe in microcosm. Man's head corresponds to heaven, similarly round in shape; his eyes and ears resemble the sun and moon; his body has four limbs, five internal organs, twelve major joints, 366 small joints, corresponding to the four seasons, the Five Agents, the months and days in a year. Man also functions like the universe: his breathing, the opening and closing of his eyes, his mental and emotional processes all have their cosmic counterparts.

This is explained in Tung's book on the *Spring and Autumn Annals*, the scriptural point of reference for his moral and metaphysical ideas. In his view there was correspondence not only between the individual and the universe but between society and nature. This was, of course, an old idea, and it was current in the Han prior to Tung Chung-shu. According to one famous anecdote, one spring a high minister under Emperor Wen passed a group of brawlers who had killed or wounded one another but took no notice of them whatever. Yet when he later saw a man leading an ox panting in the heat, he made it a point to question the man closely. Later he explained that there were lower officials to deal with brawlers, but an unseasonable heat wave causing an ox to pant, that was a matter for the highest officials charged with harmonizing the *yin* and *yang*. Tung emphasized the crucial role of the emperor in educating people who without such guidance could not realize the potential goodness that was in their nature. He also elaborated the doctrine that Heavenly omens such as unseasonable weather, eclipses, earthquakes, and the like were warnings to a ruler. During the later part of the Former Han dynasty and throughout the Later Han, the theory of portents, auspicious as well as ominous, stimulated the development of a whole literature incorporating many folk beliefs, numerological theories, and abstruse teachings.

On the other hand, the more sober tradition associated with Hsün Tzu's scepticism did not die out. On the contrary, in Wang Ch'ung (17–100) it found a great exponent. Wang asserted that Heaven could not possibly be concerned with a creature as insignificant as man, a mere flea or louse in the fold of a garment, a cricket or an ant in a crack. In Wang's writings, Tung's optimism gave way to a fatalistic pessimism. In this he was perhaps ahead of his time, for a century later there was every reason to be pessimistic.

The Fall of the Han

The beginning of the end came for the Han when thousands of desperate people, driven by poverty and plagued by natural calamities, joined a messianic antidynastic movement dedicated to the "Way of Great Peace" (*T'ai-p'ing tao*). This movement offered a potent mixture of folk beliefs and religious Taoism (one of its sacred texts was the *Tao Te Ching*), together with organization and leadership. Located in Shantung, Honan, and six other provinces, the members of this sect were called "Yellow Turbans" after the color of their kerchiefs. The color, in turn, was of religious and political significance. Unlike the similarly Taoist "Five Bushels" sect that flourished in Szechwan, the Yellow Turbans tried to overthrow the dynasty by force, launching their rebellion in 184, the first year of a new sexagenarian cycle.

The dynasty managed to survive this challenge—but only barely, for power now shifted to military leaders supported by the great families who had carved out for themselves solid bases in the provinces. It was a military leader who was responsible for the slaughter of the eunuchs in 189. The official demise of the dynasty was postponed until 220 by the rise of another military strongman, Ts'ao Ts'ao, famous for his brilliance, ruthlessness, and poetry, but his authority was limited to the North. The diplomatic and military maneuvers between Ts'ao Ts'ao and his two rivals in the South and Southwest were embellished by storytellers over the centuries and inspired the much beloved *Romance of the Three Kingdoms*, compiled in its definitive form in the fourteenth century. Among its most famous personalities, in addition to Ts'ao Ts'ao, were two men who served the rival state established in Szechwan: Chu-ko Liang, one of the most brilliant strategists of all time, prototype of the wise, clever, and loyal minister and also admired as a writer, and Kuan Yü so renowned for his strength and valor that he eventually became the god of war in Chinese popular religion.

When Ts'ao Ts'ao died so did the fiction of Han rule. His son deposed the last Han emperor and proclaimed himself founder of a new dynasty, the Wei, but was unable to reunify the country, now divided into three kingdoms.

This time, in contrast to the demise of the Former Han, it was impossible to revive the dynasty. The deterioration of the old order revealed its weaknesses —intellectual as well as political. During the second century there were thinkers who hoped through Confucian and/or Legalist reform to reinvigorate the dynasty, but the end of the Han turned men's minds to more private quests for truth and fulfillment. Han Confucianism had become so strongly identified with the dynasty that it could not long survive without it, and theories that had satisfied intelligent and sensitive men living in an orderly, stable period were perceived as inadequate by those who lived through the turbulent and bloody confusion of the last years of the dynasty and suffered from a sense of civilization in crisis.

NOTES

1. Wm. Theodore de Bary, Wing-tsit Chan, and Burton Watson, comps., *Sources of Chinese Tradition* (New York: Columbia University Press, 1960), pp. 233–34.

2. Burton Watson, trans., *Records of the Historian: Chapters from the Shih-chi of Ssu-ma Ch'ien* (New York: Columbia University Press, 1969), pp. 32–33.

3. Burton Watson, *Chinese Rhyme-Prose* (New York: Columbia University Press, 1971), pp. 38–39.

Maitreya (Miroku). Wood, Asuka period,
123.5 cm high. Kōryūji, Kyōto.

PART TWO

China and Japan in a Buddhist Age

分裂時期之中國

魏晉

南北朝

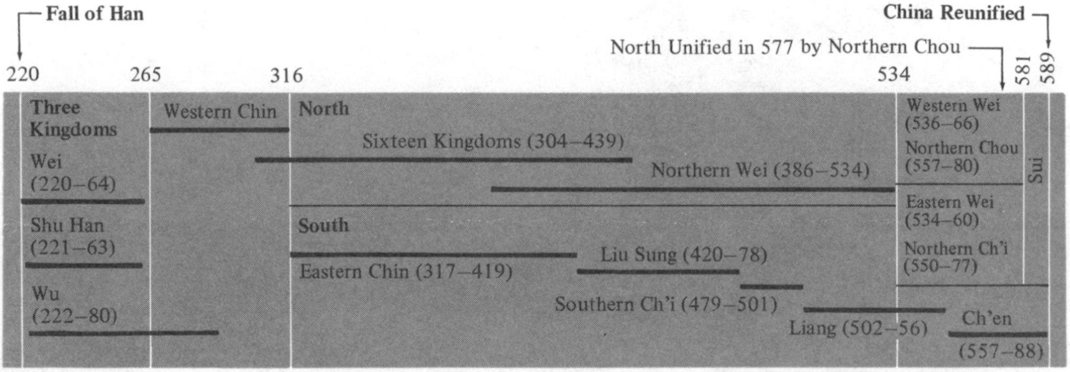

Fall of Han

China Reunified

North Unified in 577 by Northern Chou

| 220 | 265 | 316 | | | 534 | 581 | 589 |

Three Kingdoms

Wei (220–64)

Shu Han (221–63)

Wu (222–80)

Western Chin

North

Sixteen Kingdoms (304–439)

Northern Wei (386–534)

South

Eastern Chin (317–419)

Liu Sung (420–78)

Southern Ch'i (479–501)

Liang (502–56)

Western Wei (536–66)

Northern Chou (557–80)

Eastern Wei (534–60)

Northern Ch'i (550–77)

Ch'en (557–88)

Sui

4 China During the Period of Disunity

Gautama Siddhartha* (ca. 563–483 B.C.), the founder of Buddhism, was roughly contemporary with Confucius, but his teachings did not take hold in China until the collapse of the Han dynasty weakened faith in the imperial Confucian orthodoxy. By that time Buddhism, which had begun as a teaching directed at satisfying the spiritual quest of a small group, had developed into a universal faith. Considerable time passed before this religion from India sank its roots into Chinese soil; but once it had, Buddhism came to pervade the cosmopolitan culture of T'ang China, which in turn left an enduring imprint on the societies of Korea and Japan.

---

* Gautama refers to his clan, and Siddhartha was the name he received at birth. He is also known as Sakyamuni (sage of the Sakya tribe). After he attained enlightenment he was called the Buddha or the Tathagata.

Buddhism in India

Accounts of the Buddha's life were not committed to writing until centuries after his death. These narratives were the work, not of dispassionate scholars, but of faithful believers whose aim was to extol the great founder. Yet, despite the accretions of the mythical and the miraculous in these accounts, the Buddha they reveal is essentially a humane man, not a god. Only later was he deified.

Tradition has it that Gautama Siddhartha was born a prince and brought up in luxury. He was shocked into a search for religious understanding, however, when on three successive outings from the palace he encountered an old man, a sick man, and a dead man—and learned that such is the fate of humankind. He abandoned worldly pleasures to seek religious truth. Initially he became an ascetic and practiced austerities so severe that they almost cost him his life; ultimately he found a middle way between self-deprivation and gratification. His subsequent enlightenment under the bodhi (wisdom) tree (at which time he became the Buddha, or "Enlightened One") was achieved despite the efforts of Mara, the evil one, who first sent demons to assail him, and then sent his daughters (Discontent, Delight, and Desire) to tempt him, all equally in vain. The Buddha's success elicited a suitable cosmic response. The whole earth swayed, and blossoms rained from the heavens. After attaining enlightenment, he spent the remainder of his life teaching his disciples, a following whose growth led to the formation of communities of monks and nuns.

At the core of the Buddha's teachings are the Four Noble Truths. The first of these is that life is suffering. Like many religions throughout the world, Buddhism teaches that pain and unhappiness are unavoidable in life. The traditional response of Indian religions to this perception is to seek for ways to transcend life. Death is not the answer, for in the Indian view, living beings are subject to reincarnation in one painful life after another. According to the law of karma, for every action there is a moral reaction. A life of good deeds leads to reincarnation at a higher and more desirable level in the next cycle; evil deeds lead in the opposite direction. But the ultimate goal is not rebirth as an emperor or millionaire: it is to achieve Nirvana and never be born again. Legend has it that the Buddha himself gained merit in many reincarnations before his final rebirth, and stories of his previous lives have provided rich subject matter for the artist. (See, for example, Figure 6-11.)

The second Truth explains the first, stating that the cause of human suffering is craving, or desire. This in turn leads to the third Truth: that to stop suffering, desire must be stopped. The cause of suffering must be completely understood and halted. This is accomplished by living the ethical life and practicing religious contemplation and the spiritual exercises set out in the last of the Four Truths.

The fourth Truth proclaims the Eightfold Path: right views, right intention, right speed, right action, right livelihood, right effort, right mindfulness, and right concentration. The religious life involves vegetarianism, celibacy, and abstinence from alcoholic beverages, as well as positive religious practices. Carried to perfection it leads to release from reincarnation and to Nirvana: that is, to the absolute, the infinite, the ineffable.

There is much that is subtle in the elaboration of these ideas and in their explication by the Buddha and his followers. The explanation of the doctrine that there is no ego provides an example. That which we think of as the self is merely a temporary assemblage of the five aggregates (material body, sensation, perception, predisposition, and consciousness). At any point in time an individual is a momentary cluster of qualities without any underlying unity. It is a dangerous delusion to think that these qualities pertain to some kind of permanent entity or soul: only by understanding that all is change can Buddhahood be achieved. Transmigration is likened to the passing of a flame from one lamp to another until it is finally extinguished. "Extinguished" is the literal meaning of Nirvana.

Many problems of a doctrinal interpretation were left unanswered by the Buddha, for he was a religious teacher concerned with showing the way to salvation, not a philosopher interested in metaphysics for its own sake. The Buddha's concern for spreading the faith was carried on by later missionaries who undertook hazardous journeys to bring the message to distant lands. As in other religions, such as Christianity, later commentators worked out the philosophical implications of the founder's teachings, producing a mass of writings. These holy scriptures were compiled in the Tripitaka, or "three baskets," which consists of sermons attributed to the Buddha himself (sutras), later treatises (sastras), and monastic rules (vinayas). The enormity of this body of scripture indicates the vast breadth of Buddhism. It had no centralized organization or ecclesiastical hierarchy and developed in a generally tolerant atmosphere conducive to producing a rich variety of schools and sects.

The distinction between the Theravada sects, which still predominate in Sri Lanka and Southeast Asia, and the Mahayana schools, which played the major role in China and continue to do so in Japan, is the result of a major division in Buddhism that occurred early in its history. The word "Mahayana" literally means "greater vehicle," reflecting the claims of its followers to more inclusive and powerful teachings than those of their predecessors in the Hinayana, or "lesser vehicle"—a term generally resented by Theravada Buddhists. A branch of Mahayana Buddhism important for its development of doctrine was the Madhyamika school, which taught that reality is empty or void (*sunya*). Emptiness became an absolute, underlying all phenomena. In innermost essence, everything, including the world of appearances, is Nirvana and empty. If everything is emptiness, then what is it that perceives the emptiness? The Yogacara school held that the ultimate reality is consciousness, that everything is produced by mind.

Mahayana Buddhism developed not only a metaphysical literature whose richness and subtlety are barely hinted at here; it also broadened the appeal of Buddhism to draw in those people who did not have the time, training, or inclination for abstract speculation. A significant development was the growth of devotionalism directed at the Buddha, deifying him and placing him at the head of an expanding pantheon. Other Buddhas also appeared and had their following, especially Maitreya, the Buddha of the future, who exerted a messianic appeal and was often adopted as a symbol by Chinese rebel movements. The three-body doctrine helped to accommodate and justify new forms of Buddhism, for it taught that Buddhahood can be considered under three aspects: the "transformation body," that is, the historical personage of the Buddha, the "enjoyment body," that is, the celestial Buddha as beheld by the devout, and the "truth body" as understood in the abstractions of the metaphysicians.

In addition to the Buddhas, there were numerous lesser gods, but more important than these were the celestial Bodhisattvas, who postponed their own entry into Nirvana in order to help other beings. Somewhat like the Virgin Mary and the saints of Christianity, the Bodhisattvas themselves became objects of veneration and worship, none more than Avalokitesvara (Kuan-yin in Chinese, Kannon in Japanese), famed for the shining quality of his mercy. In China this embodiment of the gentle virtues was gradually transformed into a feminine figure. Sometimes depicted with multiple hands and arms, Avalokitesvara is a favorite subject of Buddhist sculpture. Buddhist art was itself a significant development, dating from the first images of the Buddha that were sculpted in India in the first century A.D. in what was at the time a daring departure from tradition.

Buddhism appealed to people in China, and later to people throughout East Asia, because it addressed itself to human suffering with a directness unmatched in their native traditions. It also provided a well-developed body of doctrine, art, magic and medicine, music and ritual, even heavens and hells for those bewildered by the abstract quality of Nirvana. Buddhism was spread by missionary monks who followed the caravan routes linking the northern part of India with western China. The new religion faced formidable cultural and linguistic barriers among the Chinese and might well have remained simply an exotic foreign faith had not the collapse of the Han dynasty set people to questioning the traditional verities. During the years of dislocation and confusion that followed, China was more open to the message of a foreign religion than ever before. The history of Buddhism in China cannot be understood, therefore, without reference to other aspects of contemporary Chinese history.

China Divided

The three states (Wei, Wu, and Shu Han) into which China was divided after the fall of the Han did not last long. One more effort to reunite the land was made under the Chin (266–316), but when that short-lived dynasty fell, control over the North passed to non-Chinese peoples, some of whom had been settled within China during the Late Han and had increasingly participated in China's military struggles. The capture and devastation of Loyang in 311 by the "barbarians" sent shock waves throughout the Chinese world.

After 316 China was effectively divided. During this period of division (316–589), while the "barbarians" ruled in the North, five dynasties succeeded each other in the South: Eastern Chin, Liu Sung, Southern Ch'i, Liang, and Ch'en. Together with the preceding southern state of Wu, they are generally known as the Six Dynasties.

In the North, meanwhile, there were sixteen regional, overlapping kingdoms between 304 and 439. These short-lived kingdoms, which generally barely managed to survive their founders, provide a contrast to the more substantial achievements of the Northern Wei (386–534). (See map, Figure 4-1.)

The Northern Wei

The nomadic peoples who established states in the North had already been exposed to Chinese civilization in varying degrees prior to their conquests. Typically, they possessed the military skills and resources required to carve out a state but lacked the administrative experience and trained personnel needed to govern a settled agricultural people. They could, to be sure, avoid this problem by turning their new possessions into pasture, but this would be self-defeating since it would destroy the wealth that had drawn them into China in the first place. If they were to enjoy China's wealth on a long term basis, they had to devise a political system more sophisticated than the tribal organization they brought from the steppes. Usually this meant relying on Chinese administrators who knew how to operate a tax system, keep records, and run a government. But the ensuing Sinification had to be kept in check if the conquerors were to retain their power and something of their cultural heritage.

The problem of how to use Chinese personnel and techniques without becoming either Chinese or irrelevant was to face all major dynasties of foreign conquest, including the last of all the dynasties, that of the Manchus (1644–1911). The Northern Wei did not really solve this problem, but it was nevertheless the most successful state in East Asia during the fifth and early sixth centuries. A major shift took place in 493–94 when the regime moved its capital from Shansi, close to its old tribal home, east to the old and venerated city of Loyang, and then went on to gain control of all North China down to the Huai River. In Loyang itself major changes and improvements were made. The Northern Wei organized the capital city into regular wards, an innovation that became the model for the great T'ang capital of Ch'ang-an, as well as for T'ang Loyang. The Northern Wei is also known as the T'o-pa Wei after the Chinese name for the Hsien-pei tribal group who founded it. The Hsien-pei are considered a proto-Mongolian people originally from Manchuria.

Long years of warfare and devastation in the North brought on large scale migrations of Chinese to the South. This influx stimulated social and economic development in the South, but the exodus created a population shortage in the North, so that much arable land remained uncultivated for want of labor. The Northern Wei responded to this problem with massive forced relo-

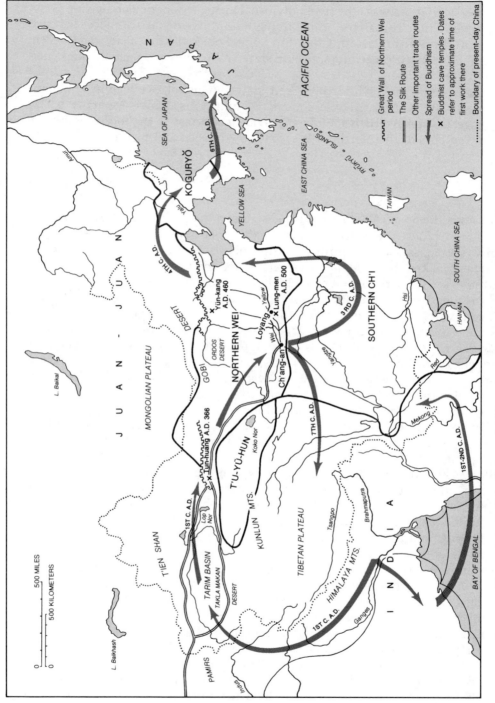

Figure 4-1 Political Map of China Around 500 Showing Also the Spread of Buddhism

cation of populations, so that deserted lands could be reclaimed and government revenues increased. Also, in 486, it established the "equal field" system which not only outlasted the dynasty but also influenced reformers in Japan. Based on the ancient principle that all land belongs to the emperor, this system provided for the allotment of agricultural holdings to each adult peasant for the duration of his or her working life. When a landholder reached old age or died, the land reverted to the state and could be reassigned. Exceptions were made, however, where the nature of cultivation required greater continuity of tenure. Silk culture, for example, involved permanent planting and continuous care of mulberry trees. Although this was not the original intent, such land came to be held in perpetuity by its proprietors. In return for land, cultivators were obliged to make certain tax payments and render labor-services, for example, road building and military service.

The implementation of the "equal field" system in devastated areas did not prevent the Northern Wei from cooperating with landed aristocrats entrenched elsewhere. From the outset, the T'o-pa rulers employed Chinese advisers, and they early on gained support for their rule within the existing Chinese power structure by adopting the nine-rank system. This system, which had originated in 220 as a means for recruiting officials through local recommendation, had by the fourth century become a system for appointing men to office according to their inherited family rank. This emphasis on birth reflected the enduring power and prestige of great Chinese families, some of them descendants of those who had controlled the countryside during the Later Han. Their distinguished ancestry, their embodiment of Confucian traditions, and their aristocratic style and conduct created an aura of distinction that complemented their great landholdings and the strength they derived from a mutually supportive network of marriage relations. Their position was further strengthened by the fact that during the Northern Wei local officials, most of whom were members of great families, enjoyed considerable autonomy. Among other things they had the right to appoint their subordinate officials; thus, by appointing relatives they could perpetuate family power and status. What they lacked, however, was institutionalized military might.

Continuing Chinese influence proved a source of weakness to the Northern Wei. During the last half century of its reign, men from distinguished families were increasingly attracted into the Sinicized central government, in which Chinese was the official language. In Loyang everyone wore Chinese dress, and even T'o-pa nobles had to adopt Chinese names. Many married Chinese wives. This Sinification finally alienated those among the conquering tribes who had not adopted Chinese ways, including the troops stationed in frontier garrisons. They expressed their displeasure in the usual way; by taking up arms. The Northern Wei state was split and came to an end.

Later in the sixth century, the Northwest reemerged as a source of military power, for this was the base from which the Sui eventually reunified China. By that time, an aristocracy of mixed Chinese and Hsien-pei ancestry had developed. This new aristocracy, however, did not enjoy the prestige of the older northeastern families, some of which had moved to Loyang, choosing government service even though it meant severing their local roots. It is of significance for the following Sui and T'ang periods that some of the most distinguished aristocratic families were able to survive despite the turmoil and confusion of the times.

Buddhism in the North

Today the Northern Wei is perhaps best known for its legacy of Buddhist art, particularly the sculpture found in cave temples at Yün-kang in Shansi and Lung-men near Loyang. These works occupy an important place in the history of Chinese art and also influenced the art of Korea and Japan. The Bodhisattva from the caves at Lung-men (see Figure 4-2), for example, shows how by the late Northern Wei Chinese artists had assimilated and transformed an art which, like the concept of creating temples in caves, was Indian in origin. In contrast to the lovingly sensuous modeling of the naked body in three dimensions that is the glory of the Indian sculptor, the essentially linear style of the figure, with its geometric composition and frontal orientation, is characteristically Chinese. At its best, this art reproduced in metal and stone the simple piety and sweet spirituality of a religious age.

Such works of art are but one of the visual signs that mark the beginning of the complex process by which a foreign religion took hold in China and was, in turn, influenced by Chinese styles and viewpoints. When Buddhism first reached China during the first century A.D., it had been introduced as the religion of foreign merchants. Through the period of division the trade routes remained open, since trade was as advantageous to the nomadic peoples who controlled oases and taxed caravans as it was to the buyers and sellers in the more settled regions. As life became more difficult in China, Buddhism both acclimatized itself to Chinese circumstances and became more appealing to those who were disillusioned with the old ways, especially during the century between the collapse of the Han and the fall of Loyang. It spread further during the subsequent period of "barbarian" conquest. Devoted missionaries won patronage from rough tribal leaders by using feats of magic to convince them that Buddhism was a more powerful religion than that of the shamans.

But Buddhism was powerful also in other ways. It enabled tribal chiefs to see themselves in new and grander roles, and it appealed to alien rulers. Through their patronage of this universalistic religion, which like themselves was foreign to China, such rulers could create a broad and venerable base for their claims to legitimacy as they attempted to create multiethnic states.

Political patronage was important, but to survive and prosper Buddhism also had to win a wide following among the Chinese people. In this endeavor its foreign origins were not an asset but a liability. Words and ideas, as well as artistic forms, had to be translated into Chinese terms.

Translating Buddhist texts into Chinese proved a formidable undertaking, since they were the products of a radically different culture and were written in

Figure 4-2   Seated Bodhisattva. Stone,
Lung-men, Late Northern Wei.
Museum of Fine Arts, Boston.

a language totally unlike Chinese. The problems faced by the early Buddhist translators were similar to those which much later plagued Christian missionaries trying to render the Bible into Chinese. Particularly vexing was the need to introduce unfamiliar concepts at the very heart of Buddhism. Just as Christians were later to agonize over ways of translating "God" into Chinese, Buddhists racked their brains over words like "Nirvana." One early solution was to employ Taoist terminology. This had the advantage of sounding familiar. But it could also lead to a great deal of confusion, as when the Taoist term for "non-action" (*wu-wei*) was used to express the quite different concept of Nirvana.

Another possibility was not to translate at all but to transliterate, that is, to employ Chinese characters to approximate the sound rather than the meaning of the original word. Transliteration was most suitable for reproducing foreign proper names in Chinese, and this became the standard practice continued to this day. It was, and still is, also used for technical terms. In both cases the results were apt to be unwieldy and sometimes even misleading, since even in relatively modern times the Chinese reader has found it difficult to divorce the characters from their meanings.

Despite these handicaps scholar-monks made good progress in their work. The greatest of these translators was Kumārajīva, who, like many of his predecessors, was a Central Asian. Early in the fifth century he directed a translation project in Ch'ang-an staffed by some thousand monks. In a vivid comment on the translator's art, he once compared his work to that of a man who chews rice in his mouth and then gives it to another to swallow. He and his staff produced good translations of basic Hinayana and Mahayana texts and were also responsible for the introduction of Madhyamika teachings, but the appeal of these abstract metaphysical theories was limited to a few intellectually inclined monks. Kumārajīva was only one of the many monks from Central Asia whose missionary zeal contributed greatly to the growth of Buddhism in China. But the traffic was not all one way: Chinese also undertook the long pilgrimage to India. The monk Fa Hsien, who made the trip during 399–414, left a detailed account of his travels that serves as a prime source for the history of India during this period.

To overcome cultural barriers, early Buddhist apologists argued that their religion was basically compatible with the Chinese heritage and played down areas of potential conflict. That they enjoyed considerable success is shown by inscriptions at Yün-kang, Lung-men, and elsewhere which reveal that the pious considered the donation of an image not only an expression of their religious faith but also a demonstration of their filial piety, and of reverence for ancestors whose souls were included in their prayers. (The idea of non-self, or non-soul, never had much currency in popular Buddhism nor was it generally taught even by well-educated Chinese monks.) Yet not everyone was convinced by this attempt to fuse Buddhism and filiality. After all, one of the prime dictates of the latter demanded the continuation of the family and thus conflicted with the celibate life of the monk and nun. Withdrawal from the secular world left Buddhists open to charges of antisocial behavior, and the growth of monastic wealth and influence made the Buddhist church vulnerable to political attack. Buddhism had its share of enemies; its progress was not all smooth, nor did it go unchallenged.

Challenges to Buddhist Influence

A strong competitor both for state patronage and popular support was the Taoist church. This had originated in the Later Han and now developed its own organization and priesthood along lines suggested by Buddhism. Frequent disputes arose between Buddhists and Taoists concerning various religious claims. For example, Taoists maintained that Lao Tzu had traveled to India where he became the Buddha, while the Buddhist accounts depicted Lao Tzu and Confucius as disciples of the Buddha, and even portrayed the semidivine founders of Chinese civilization as Bodhisattvas.

Since this rivalry involved power and patronage as well as matters of belief, it also had its fiercer aspects; it was a major factor in the persecution of Buddhism by the Northern Wei during 446–52 and again by another state in the North in 574–78. Instigated by Taoists and Confucians, both persecutions aimed at the destruction of Buddhist monasteries and the elimination of the

Buddhist religious establishment, which had grown wealthy and powerful. (No attempt was made, however, either then or later, to suppress private Buddhist beliefs or ideas.) In both cases the persecution ended as soon as there was a change of ruler, and the new emperor made generous amends. Buddhism had grown too strong to be crushed by government fiat, and the persecutions appear to have done little permanent damage.

Religious persecution revealed considerable tension between church and state, but instead of suppressing the religion, the usual pattern, again exemplified by the Northern Wei, was for the state to place controls on the Buddhist church. This was done in order to prevent the monasteries from becoming havens for tax-dodgers or men escaping their labor obligations, to bar fraudulent transfers of land titles to tax-exempt religious institutions, and to enforce standards for ordination and for clerical conduct. Regulation was achieved by creating a clerical bureaucracy not unlike its secular counterpart. Northern Wei emperors appointed a monk to be Chief of Monks, and he presided over a network of Regional Chiefs of Monks, who in turn supervised the Buddhist orders while also looking after the interests of the religion. Thus the great Northern Wei cave temples were created through a combination of official support by the court and efforts of the Buddhist community itself. In the meantime Buddhism was also making gains under the very different political and social circumstances prevailing in the South.

The South

Spared the nomad incursions and warfare that plagued North China, the South during the period of division enjoyed relative tranquility, despite a series of political intrigues, palace coups, and the like which disturbed life at court. As in the North, here too a hereditary aristocracy of great families stood at the top of the social hierarchy. But in the South the influence of the great families was not merely local—on the contrary, they dominated the courts of a succession of Southern dynasties. Not only did they enjoy exemption from taxation and labor-service, but they had ready access to office and set the whole tone of court life. In the fifth century, they even managed to obtain legislation prohibiting intermarriage between aristocrats and commoners. Their entrenched privileges seriously hampered government efficiency. Yet they were far from invincible. For one thing, their power was constantly being undermined by intense and recurrent conflicts among themselves. Friction between émigré families and those with deeper local roots was endemic. The influence of the aristocratic families was also weakened by their lack of military power and their inability to control military strongmen of nonaristocratic background.

Despite the turbulence of political conflict the South was making significant economic progress. Partly through migration from the disturbed North, partly through development of the land, the fertile area of the lower Yangtze saw a very substantial increase in population and productivity. Further south, Fukien now became truly Chinese for the first time as a result of increased Chinese settlement. As Chinese settlers moved in, the local aborigines were either pushed back into the hills or absorbed into the Chinese population.

Rice culture was the cornerstone of the agricultural economy of the South. Sophisticated wet-field cultivation of rice, much more productive than growing rice on dry land, took time to perfect. Not only did it involve experimentation with various strains of rice, it also entailed the construction of paddy fields and careful irrigation to keep the field wet and to maintain the water at an even temperature. When the fields were laid out on sloping ground or when terraces were constructed on hills, a complicated system of dams and reservoirs was necessary.

In the second century A.D. the Chinese developed a technique for raising seedlings in a nursery and transplanting them later in the paddies when the season was right. Such early planting in nurseries greatly increased the yield, but it also increased the demands for labor. Refugees from the North helped to augment the labor supply, and in that sense made a direct contribution to the growing prosperity of the South. The enlarged labor force was, in turn, sustained by the increased rice yields obtained from wet-field cultivation, which produced more calories per acre than did Northern dry-field agriculture. It is because rice has the ability to support high population density that the development of the South was to be of great consequence for the future history of China.

The South made great strides not only in the economic sphere but also in the development of secular culture. As we have seen, the South had already made important contributions to Chinese literature and the arts. Now its contributions formed the mainstream of Chinese cultural development, largely because the South fell heir to the lively cultural life that had accompanied the collapse of the Han.

Secular Culture and the Arts

When, with the fall of the Han, the old world disintegrated, intellectually as well as physically, thoughtful men were prompted to reexamine old assumptions and find new ways to give meaning to their lives. Whereas the collapse of the old Chou order gave rise to classical Chinese thought, the new civilizational crisis made men receptive to a new religiosity and stimulated a cultural flowering in which the aesthetic dimension of human experience and creativity was accorded full recognition and given free play.

Intellectually there was a turning away from Confucian scholasticism, although some of the most brilliant thinkers of this period, such as Wang Pi (226–249) and Kuo Hsiang (d. 312), continued to accept the validity of Confucian social values. Both these thinkers contributed to the development of what is known as Neo-Taoist philosophy. Wang Pi, writing on the *Tao Te Ching* and the *I Ching*, gave new depth to the concept of non-being (*wu*). For him, original non-being (*pen-wu*) was the ultimate reality, the origin of all being. For Wang it was a source of metaphysical unity in a physical world that was disunited. He was also the first to introduce two complementary concepts that were to have a long history in Chinese philosophy: *t'i* and *yung*, usually translated "substance" and "function," and understood by Wang Pi also in the sense of latent and manifest. A key concept stressed by Kuo Hsiang was the idea of nature or naturalness (*tzu-jan*); the Chinese term has the basic meaning "so of itself."

Many refined and sensitive men turned to mystical nihilism for an explanation of ultimate reality, and sought to attain it through spiritual contemplation, a "sitting in forgetfulness" so complete that forgetting is itself forgotten. Nor were other, less sublime, ways of forgetting neglected. A favorite pastime of the cultured gentleman was "pure talk." In contrast to the "pure criticism" (*ch'ing-i*) directed against the government by Later Han Confucians, "pure talk" (*ch'ing-t'an*) was clever repartee for its own sake. The highest honors went to the man who thought up the most adept and pithy characterization of his acquaintances. This witty, verbal game was far removed from the social and political concerns enjoined by Confucians.

Equally un-Confucian was the veneration of nature as an ultimate, and the search for naturalness in conduct even at the price of the social conventions and ideas of propriety prized by the Confucian tradition. The result was a burst of self-expression in the arts and in the lives of the sophisticated, who let themselves go in music, poetry, and personal attitudes. Most famous are the Seven Sages of the Bamboo Grove (third century), a group of gifted friends noted for their artistic accomplishments and their eccentricity. Wine flowed freely at their gatherings. One man was always followed by a servant carrying a bottle in one hand and a spade in the other—equipped for all eventualities in life or in death. Sometimes he drank stark naked at home. One startled visitor who found him in that state was promptly informed that his house was his pair of trousers; "What are you doing in my trousers?" the "sage" berated him. The men of this age did not invent eccentricity and unorthodox behavior, and they were certainly not the first to enjoy their cups. What was new was that they gave such conduct intellectual respectability.

It is in keeping with the spirit of the age that there was a strong interest in the study as well as in the appreciation of nature. Attempts were made to recreate and accelerate natural processes in alchemical furnaces, in an effort to create gold or the elixir of immortality. Advances in alchemy were matched by those made in medicine, where the object was to find new ways to prolong life, indefinitely if possible. The quest for immortality had long been pursued by followers of religious Taoism. One set of techniques to this end consisted of breathing exercises reminiscent of Indian yoga, but dating well before the appearance of Buddhism in China, and designed to nourish an embryo of immortality within the body in a process of internal alchemy. Refined diets, gymnastics, and sexual practices also formed part of the Taoist repertoire.

When Loyang was captured by the "barbarians," its fall served to confirm the disillusionment and general pessimism felt by residents of the South. The continuing arrival of émigrés from the North reinforced this spirit. The more sophisticated turned to witty conversation, meditation, alchemy, and wine as a diversion from the depressing social and political problems of the day. It was this discontent and yearning for greater stability that made the society of southern China receptive to Buddhism. But it also served to liberate individual impulses to artistic expression, channeling energies that formerly had been devoted to philosophy and government into the secular arts. The result was an outburst of achievements in those arts which are the most highly prized and most closely identified with the Chinese gentleman: poetry, calligraphy, and painting.

Poetry

Many themes characteristic of the time found their finest verbal expression in the poetry of T'ao Chien (365–427), also known as T'ao Yüan-ming, regarded as one of China's greatest poets. After a short career in government, he retired to live the life of a country gentleman, although not without ambivalent feelings toward official life and its obligations. But there is in his verse much about wine, the simple country life, books, and nature. Poems such as this have an enduring appeal:

> I built my cottage among the habitations of men,
> And yet there is no clamor of carriages and horses.
> You ask: "Sir, how can this be done?"
> "A heart that is distant creates its own solitude."
> I pluck chrysanthemums under the eastern hedge,
> Then gaze afar toward the southern hills.
> The mountain air is fresh at the dusk of day;
> The flying birds in flocks return.
> In these things there lies a deep meaning;
> I want to tell it, but have forgotten the words.[1]

T'ao especially loved chrysanthemums and wrote about them often; ever since, this "hermit among the flowers" has been associated with his name. The poem conveys a serene harmony with nature that is a lasting Chinese ideal and a common theme in much later Chinese poetry.

Other fine poets also wrote during this period. But there was at the same time a tendency for poets to indulge in increasingly artificial styles (for example, extreme parallelism in construction, with two lines matching each other word for word) and to exhibit their virtuosity in using an exotic vocabulary, as Han poets had in their rhapsodies. As a result spontaneity, creative freshness, was gradually lost, so that versification was already approaching a dead end when political unification from the North put an end both to the southern courts and their poetry.

More significant than poetic output, per se, was the development of a new attitude toward literature, which grew out of a deep concern with the process of poetic creation. Formerly the poetic art had been viewed as a vehicle for instruction, for example, as an embodiment of Confucian social values. But in an era when the hold of old values was noticeably weakening, the old didacticism gave way to an appreciation of poetic creation in its own right. Hence increased emphasis was placed on stylistic devices, exotic language, and the like. When Hsiao T'ung wrote the preface to his famous literary anthology, *Wen-hsüan* (530), he could frankly explain that his selection was based on purely aesthetic considerations. Two lines of Lu Chi (261–303) give the flavor of the poetry of this period:

> Trying the empty Nothing, and demanding Something
> Banging the silent Zero, in search of Sound.[2]

They are from his famous rhapsody (*fu*) on literature, itself a work of high literary art.

Calligraphy

Of all the visual arts, Chinese scholars traditionally have given first place to calligraphy. (See Figure 4-3.) Behind this high esteem for calligraphy lies the aesthetic appeal and the mystique of the Chinese characters themselves, already noted in our discussion of the first inscriptions on oracle bones. It also reflects the intensively literary nature of Chinese culture. Moreover, the development of cursive script during the Later Han turned writing into an intensely personal art, a vehicle for self-expression and a creative outlet, well suited to educated persons who had been wielding the brush and working with ink since childhood. Calligraphy came to be especially valued as a means for conveying the writer's deepest self, so that according to one T'ang scholar one character was sufficient to reveal the writer. The flow of the lines and the rhythm of the brush creating the abstract beauty of the whole were now far more important than legibility. Thus Chinese appreciation of calligraphy as high art contained much of the pleasure and excitement associated with abstract art, as well as with graphology, in the West.

"In every terrible period of human history there is always a gentleman in a corner cultivating his calligraphy and stringing together a few pearls of expression."[3] Thus wrote Paul Valéry in 1915. If so, it is no wonder that calligraphy flourished during the years following the collapse of the Han, nor that the new emphasis on self-expression was particularly conducive to this art.

The greatest calligrapher of the age was Wang Hsi-chih (321–379), a fourth century master whose art inspired, and served as a model for, generations. He, and two of his sons who also became famous calligraphers, drew inspiration from Taoism with its emphasis on the natural. They sought to express naturalism, itself an abstract quality, through what was in effect "artistic penmanship," except, of course, that they wrote with ink brushes, not pens. It was a magnificent challenge and typifies the artistic strivings of the age. The effort required years of practice. Wang Hsi-chih is said to have destroyed everything

| DRAGON | BOOK | GOOD |

Figure 4-3   Basic forms of calligraphy, from the brush of Dr. Léon L. Y. Chang. The top two characters in the "dragon" column and the top characters in the "book" and "good" columns exemplify the Li form (clerical, or official); the third and fourth characters in the "dragon" column and the second characters in the "book" and "good" columns exemplify the Cheng (also called K'ai) form (regular, or standard); the fifth character in the "dragon" column and the third characters in the "book" and "good" columns exemplify the Hsing form (longhand, or running); the bottom characters in each column exemplify the Ts'ao form (cursive, or shorthand).

he had written before the age of 50 because he was dissatisfied with it. Unfortunately, none of his original work survives. Copies exist, but none is earlier than the Sung. Reproduced here (see Figure 4-4) is a letter by a famous Sung calligrapher and painter who drew inspiration from Wang Hsi-chih and one of his sons. The fourth line (reading right to left) is an example of the musical "continuous stroke" style for which they were famous.

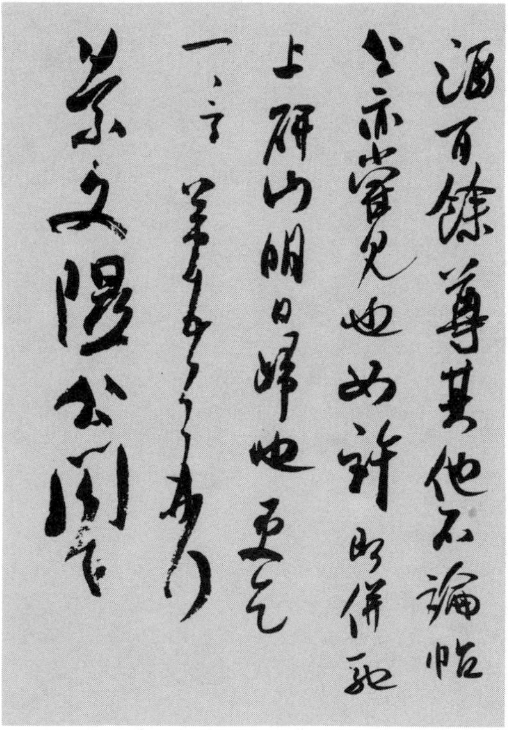

Figure 4-4
Portion of a letter by Mi Fei. (From
Ku Kung Fa Shu No. 11 [Taipei,
Taiwan: National Palace Museum,
1968], p. 11b.) Selected and translated
by Dr. Léon L. Y. Chang.

The text may be translated as follows:

". . . (sent) more than 100 vases of wine (from Yangchow), not to mention
the other (gifts). Concerning the *tieh** which you have seen previously,
with your permission, I shall have it brought to you, too. The *yen-shan*†
will be returned to you by tomorrow.
Awaiting a word from you,
Fei salutes more than once at the Pavilion of
The Honorable Shih Chin-wen."

* *tieh:* a model of calligraphy, either an ink-rubbing or a handwritten original.
† *yen-shan:* a rock of unusual or grotesque shape. Usually placed in front of
an ink-stone on a scholar's desk, *yen-shan* were appreciated as objects of art
and valued as collectors' items.

Painting

In painting, the main subject continued to be the human figure, although the
beginnings of China's great landscape tradition can also be traced back to this
period. Preeminent among the painters was Ku K'ai-chih (ca. 344–ca. 406)
famed for capturing with his brush the essential character of his subjects, as
when by adding three hairs to a chin he succeeded in depicting a man's wisdom. Among the most famous of his paintings still extant, although probably
only a copy, is his hand-scroll illustrating a poem entitled "Admonitions of the
Instructress to the Court Ladies" in which the painted panels alternate with

Figure 4-5   Ku K'ai-chih, Scene 5 from *Admonitions to the Instructress to the Court Ladies.* Ink and color on silk. British Museum, London.

lines of the text. The scene reproduced here (see Figure 4-5) illustrates the lines, "if the words you speak are good, men for a thousand *li* will respond; but if you depart from this principle, even your bedfellow will distrust you." Presumably it is the emperor who is mistrusting the lady, although this scene has sometimes been read the other way around. The other panels also illustrate moral edicts basically Confucian in content, although the artist himself was known for his Taoist eccentricity.

The enhanced interest taken in painting led to the development of art criticism and stimulated the classic formulation of the six rules, or principles, of painting by Hsieh Ho, an early sixth century portrait painter. Most important, but also allowing for the widest latitude of interpretation, is his first principle, which calls on the artist to imbue his painting with a cosmic vitality and sense of life. These terms have been translated by Alexander Soper as "animation through spirit consonance" where "spirit" is a translation of *"ch'i,"* the vital force and stuff of man and the universe.[4] *Ch'i* is also a central concept in Chinese medicine; Manfred Porkert in his pioneering analysis of Chinese medical theory renders it as "configurational energy,"[5] and we will encounter it again as a basic component of Neo-Confucian cosmology and metaphysics. The concept also figures in burial customs. The most eminent dead were fitted with suits of jade to prevent the *ch'i* from leaking out of their bodies; those who could not afford a complete outfit were equipped with stoppers for ears, nose, mouths, and so forth. In the context of aesthetics, it is the quality that causes a painting to reverberate with life.

Hsieh Ho's second law demands structural strength in the brushwork, demonstrating the vital link between painting and calligraphy, which used the same basic tools and techniques. It was largely in the quality of the artists' brushwork that the Chinese looked for an expression of their vital inspiration.

The next three laws require less explanation since they correspond to criteria familiar in the West. They are: fidelity to the object in portraying forms, conformity to kind in applying colors, and proper planning in placing of elements—what we would call composition. The sixth and final principle is very Chinese, for it enjoins the copying of old masters. This is one aspect of the old Chinese veneration for the past. It was a way of preserving old masterpieces and at the same time provided training and discipline for later artists, who by following the brushwork of a great predecessor would gain technical competence and an understanding of the medium, just as apprentice calligraphers today still begin by copying the great masters of their art, internalizing and making it their own. In neither case is there any intent to deceive.

Buddhism in the South

In the South as in the North, Buddhism made great headway, winning substantial support among the aristocracy and the personal patronage of rulers. In contrast to the North where Buddhist missionaries had to deal with "barbarian" rulers, in the South erudite and clever monks won favor by adopting the stance and displaying the skills of the sophisticated gentlemen who dominated society. Thus quick-witted Buddhists became experts in "pure talk" and engaged also in highly abstract metaphysical discussions in which they displayed their command of the Chinese as well as Buddhist intellectual heritage. Given new prominence as a model for the Buddhist as aristocrat was the figure of Vimalakirti, a wealthy layman who enjoyed life to the full and displayed great powers of intellect and a pure and lofty personality. (See Figure 4-6. This depiction of Vimalakirti is from a later period and from Japan, but it illustrates that Buddhism was not only for the poor and ignorant.) Moreover, monasteries erected in beautiful surroundings offered a life of scholarly retreat and contemplation, posing an attractive alternative to the requirements of life in the world.

An outstanding patron of Buddhism in the South was Emperor Wu of Liang (r 502–49), sometimes called the Emperor Bodhisattva. A devout Buddhist, he banished meat and wine from the imperial table; wrote commentaries on holy texts; held great assemblies of monks and laymen, one of which had an attendance of fifty thousand; built temples; and otherwise generously supported

Figure 4-6   Vimalakīrti. Clay,
45.2 cm high.
Pagoda of the Hōryūji.

Buddhism, which he made the official religion. This does not mean that Buddhism enjoyed universal approval in the South any more than it did in the North. Its opponents in the South not only attacked its alleged subversive effects on state and society but also attempted to refute some of its teachings. For example, Fan Chen argued against the concept of the indestructibility of the soul, now a common tenet of Chinese Buddhism, the original teaching of the Buddha notwithstanding. Against Fan Chen's argument that the soul was a passing function of the body, just as keenness is a temporary attribute of a knife, Emperor Wu solicited counterarguments and received fifty-eight refutations and only two replies supporting Fan Chen's anti-Buddhist views. Such arguments provided background for later attacks on Buddhism, but the time was not yet ripe for a major anti-Buddhist reaction. On the contrary, the full flowering of Buddhism in China was still to come, after China was once more united.

In this process of reunification Buddhism too, as we shall see, played its part; for toward the end of the period of division, the contrasts between Buddhism in North and South were fading. Monks traveled between the two areas, and the same texts were studied and recited North and South. Furthermore, Buddhism was better able to contribute to reunification because it had gone far toward adapting itself to Chinese civilization. In architecture, for example, individual

Buddhist halls followed native secular prototypes, and the only major difference between a Buddhist temple and a Han palace compound was the presence in the former of a pagoda. This characteristically East Asian structure, however, owed at least as much to the Han watchtower as it did to the Indian stupa.

China on the Eve of Reunification

The changes that occurred between the fall of the Han and the Sui reunification were far reaching and profound. The division of China had brought with it foreign rulers and a new religion. It had stimulated a new consciousness, which found expression in literature and art. And it had accelerated the development of the South, thus altering China's economic geography. These events are comparable to what took place in the West after the fall of Rome, and in both civilizations, traditional scholarly attitudes toward the post-imperial age have been disparaging. Anti-Buddhist to begin with, traditional Confucians considered the division of the empire a sure indication that something was drastically wrong with the world. But this political division also had its positive side, for, as in the Warring States period, it made for intellectual choice and diversity.

In contrast to the history of the West after the fall of Rome, in China the factors making for political integration were strong enough, under the right leadership, to triumph in the end. Buddhism was one such factor, and Confucianism as a family ethic and as a state rationale persisted even when Confucian philosophy was in eclipse. Nor was the ideal of political unity ever challenged. At the close of the period, the last of the Five Dynasties in the South, the Ch'en (537–89), was attempting to organize a more centralized and therefore more powerful state. Ultimately, however, unification came from the North (specifically the northwest), which was, as always, militarily the strongest area. Unification proved a great and difficult undertaking—and one which in the end succeeded brilliantly.

NOTES

1. Liu Wu-chi, *An Introduction to Chinese Literature* (Bloomington: Indiana University Press, 1966), p. 64.
2. Eric Sackheim, . . . *the silent Zero in search of Sound . . .; An Anthology of Chinese Poems from the Beginning through the Sixth Century* (New York: Grossman Publishers, 1968), p. ii.
3. Quoted in Etienne Balazs, *Chinese Civilization and Bureaucracy* (New Haven: Yale University Press, 1964), p. 226.
4. Alexander Soper, "The First Two Laws of Hsieh Ho," *The Far Eastern Quarterly* 8 (1949): 412–23.
5. Manfred Porkert, *The Theoretical Foundations of Chinese Medicine* (Cambridge: The M.I.T. Press, 1974), p. 62.

隋唐時代

國際交流之文明

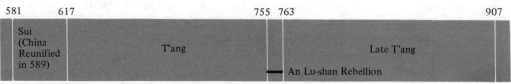

581	617		755	763		907
Sui (China Reunified in 589)		T'ang			Late T'ang	
				An Lu-shan Rebellion		

5 The Cosmopolitan Civilization of the Sui and T'ang: 581-907

China was reunited in 589, and the second imperial period in Chinese history lasted approximately 300 years, until 907. It was during this period that China became the political model and cultural center for all East Asia. Buddhism flourished. Significant changes occurred in government and society. It was the classical period of Chinese poetry. Like the Han (in the first imperial period) the T'ang dynasty followed a powerful but short-lived regime that had accomplished the task of reunification: the Sui. And like the Han, the

101

T'ang dynasty may be thought of as having an earlier and later phase, although there was no formal interruption of T'ang rule. There are other ways, too, in which the two dynasties are comparable, but the differences between them are as instructive as their points of resemblance.

The Sui (581–617)

As we have seen in the previous chapter, the Northern Wei was unable to maintain a unified northern state after 534. In 577 another of the northern states, the Northern Chou (557–81), accomplished military reunification of the North. Four years later a Northern Chou general usurped the throne and founded his own dynasty, the Sui. In 589 the Sui defeated the last of the southern states and, thereafter, incorporated North and South into a single political system. The magnitude of this task has been compared to that facing Charlemagne (742–814) when he attempted to create a new Roman Empire in Europe. Indeed, in terms of land area, diversity of terrain, and variety of local cultures the two situations are quite comparable.

The Sui, unlike the Ch'in, did not attempt to impose a new pattern on China but adopted a policy of fusing various local traditions and amalgamating different elements. The contrast between the two unifying regimes is perhaps most striking in the area of ideology, for the Sui founder, although a convinced Buddhist, also made use of Confucian and Taoist traditions to legitimize his regime and gain acceptance and support. In formulating a legal code the Sui incorporated elements from different legal traditions, North and South. This was done so effectively that it provided the basis for the T'ang and all subsequent legal codes. In other respects also there was a great deal of continuity between the Sui and the early T'ang, which, unlike the Han, did not repudiate the principles and policies of its immediate predecessor.

The Sui emperors, Wen-ti (r. 581–604) and his son Yang-ti (r. 604–18), came from a northwestern aristocratic family of mixed Chinese and foreign ancestry. Politically, they sought through a combination of cultural policies and marriage alliances to reconcile the pretensions of the great aristocratic families of the Northeast and of the South. For example, Yang-ti married a southern princess. The second emperor completed his father's ambitious project of building a canal linking China's two great rivers, the Yellow and the Yangtze, which enabled the political capital in the North to draw on the rich resources of the lower Yangtze. The completed Grand Canal went from Hangchow to Kaifeng and was linked by extensions both to the area of modern Peking and to the Sui-T'ang capital, the new Ch'ang-an, which Wen-ti had built near the site of the old capital of the Former Han. The construction of official granaries further helped to establish a government economic network.

The Sui took equal care to further political consolidation and centralization. The state bureaucracy was reorganized, and a tier of local administration was eliminated to make local government more amenable to central direction. Furthermore, local officials were deprived of the authority to appoint their subordinates, a right they had enjoyed during the period of division. Other measures included the "rule of avoidance," which prohibited an official from serving in his native place, and the stipulation that no official could serve more than one tour of duty in the same locality. After this tour, usually of three years' duration, the official would be reassigned according to merit. Even more important, the Sui instituted a system of recruiting officials by examination. This deprived the hereditary high aristocracy of the monopoly of power they had enjoyed during the period of division, when appointments had been made by recommendation, and opened government service to a somewhat wider class of people, although service was still the prerogative of the wellborn. These measures effectively reduced the ability of officials to establish a personal power base in the areas where they served, reduced the power of the great families to which they belonged, and made officials more responsive to the interests and direction of the central government.

As is to be expected of a unifying dynasty, the Sui was vigorous militarily. Expeditions were sent as far south as Central Vietnam and into Taiwan while, to the west, nomadic peoples were driven out of Kansu and eastern Turkestan. Colonies were established along the western trade routes, and further afield, in Central Asia, such states as Turfan became tributaries. Envoys were exchanged with Japan. The Sui also continued the militia system it had inherited from the northern dynasties and settled many troops in garrisons along the frontiers.

The dynasty's vigorous foreign policy demanded the organization and deployment of considerable military force. Most costly in terms of casualties and materiel were three unsuccessful campaigns against Koguryŏ, the state that controlled northern Korea and much of southern Manchuria. Successive defeats placed an unbearable strain on the dynasty's resources. Insurrection and rebellion became widespread, and the dynasty was doomed. It had overreached itself, trying to accomplish too much too rapidly. In the traditional Chinese view, however, the onus for its demise was assigned to Yang-ti, who was cast as an archetypical bad last emperor, a self-indulgent tyrant—an image that was further embellished in popular literature, which depicts him as living in luxury while the people were starving, and frolicking with the numerous women of his harem, in a room lined with polished bronze screens to serve as mirrors, when he should have been minding the ship of state.

The T'ang: Establishment and Consolidation

The T'ang dynasty emerged from the struggles accompanying the disintegration of the Sui. Its founder was that dynasty's top general, a man related through his mother to the Sui ruling house. Many of his officials had also served the former dynasty. There was consequently no sharp break in the composition or the policy of the ruling group, but the fighting was hard and prolonged. It took up most of the reign of the founding emperor, known posthumously as Kao-tsu (r. 618–26). The emperor's second son won considerable success as a military commander. In 626 he killed the crown prince and an-

Figure 5-1 *Horse and Groom.* Stone relief from tomb of T'ang T'ai-tsung. Design attributed to Yen Li-pen (d. 673). 147.4 cm × 152 cm. University of Pennsylvania Museum, Philadelphia.

other brother, apparently to forestall a plot against himself, and then he forced his father to abdicate. He is known as T'ai-tsung (r. 626–49) and effected the political consolidation of the new dynasty.

T'ai-tsung's physical vigor and military prowess are suggested by the stone panels, over five feet high, showing in relief his favorite mount (see Figure 5-1). It was, however, his political abilities that caused him to become one of China's most admired and idealized rulers. He was particularly skillful in his selection of officials and wise in the knowledge of men. His most famous Confucian minister was Wei Cheng (580–645), on whom he relied for ethical guidance. In a statement after Wei Cheng's death, T'ai-tsung compared his minister to a mirror in which to correct his judgment, just as a bronze mirror is used to correct one's dress and the past serves as a mirror for understanding the rise and fall of states. But although T'ai-tsung sought Wei Cheng's counsel on moral issues, such as the punishment of officials, or the giving and receiving of gifts, he did not allow him to influence major policy decisions such as those concerning peace or war.

The emperor's policies generally followed and furthered those initiated by the Sui. He broadened the geographical composition of the bureaucracy by including men from areas other than his native Northwest, but government remained in the hands of aristocrats. The most pretentious of these were the high aristocrats of the Northeast, who looked down on the "semibarbarian" northwestern families, not excluding the imperial family. T'ai-tsung had a genealogy compiled to define the importance of various families throughout China and rejected the first draft in order to demote one of the great Hopei lineages and to promote the imperial clan to first place.

Additional granaries and schools were built and a new law code promulgated. The code dealt with both criminal and administrative concerns and consisted of primary laws, meant to hold for all time, and secondary laws: regulations open to frequent adjustment to allow for changing conditions and local variations. There was also a refinement of the structure of government. The essential tasks of the central government were performed by Six Ministries (personnel, revenue, rites, war, justice, and public works), which were retained by later dynasties as their central administrative organs.

In foreign affairs T'ai-tsung pursued a strong, aggressive policy. He successfully pushed Chinese power even further west than had the Han, but, like the Sui, failed in Korea. With Chinese power extending all the way to the Pamirs and the land itself at peace, there was a resumption of foreign trade and influence that remained characteristic of the T'ang period. Although many foreigners visited and dwelt in Ch'ang-an during T'ai-tsung's reign, the most famous traveler of the time was a Chinese monk, Hsüan-tsang, who journeyed to India and returned with Buddhist texts and much information about foreign countries. The emperor, characteristically, was more interested in the latter than in the former and even tried to persuade the venerable monk to return to lay life and become a foreign policy adviser. But Hsüan-tsang declined, and the emperor financed the translation projects to which the monk devoted the rest of his life.

T'ai-tsung was favorably disposed to Buddhism, but like his predecessors he was careful to keep the Buddhist establishment under control. Furthermore, since the T'ang ruling house claimed descent from Lao Tzu, Taoism was also shown considerable favor. For example, Hsüan-tsang was ordered to translate the *Tao Te Ching* into Sanskrit for the benefit of the Indian world. This text and also the *Chuang Tzu* even found a place in the T'ang system of civil service examinations, otherwise a major bastion of Confucian influence.

T'ai-tsung's last years were spoiled by disappointments in his sons and heirs. The crown prince became so infatuated with nomad ways, even living in a yurt, that he was finally deposed, and the emperor's favorite son was too deeply involved in intrigues over the succession to be trusted. In the end, the succession went to a weak young prince who, on T'ai-tsung's death, became Emperor Kao-tsung (r. 650–83).

Empress Wu and Emperor Hsüan-tsung

The political history of the century between the death of T'ai-tsung and the outbreak of the devastating rebellion led by General An Lu-shan was dominated by two ruling personalities. The first of these was Wu Chao (625?–706?), one of T'ai-tsung's concubines who won Kao-tsung's affection. She engineered the removal and often the murder of all rivals, and dominated government after Kao-tsung suffered a stroke in 660. After he died, in 683, two of her sons ruled in succession, but in 690, not satisfied to rule through puppets, she proclaimed herself "emperor" of a new dynasty, the Chou, thereby becoming the only woman in Chinese history to rule in her own name. For legitimization Empress Wu turned mainly to Buddhism, proclaiming herself an incarnation of Maitreya and ordering temples set up in every province to expound a sutra, the *Ta-yün-ching*, which prophesied the appearance of a female world ruler seven hundred years after the passing of the Buddha. Her patronage of Buddhism also extended to other temples and sects, and much work was done in the Lung-men caves during her reign. She was especially supportive of Hua-yen Buddhism, which conceived the world as centered on Vairocana Buddha, much as Empress Wu aspired to be the center of the political order.

The legitimacy of Empress Wu's power was also bolstered by a genealogy compiled in 659 that listed families according to the official rank attained by their members, rather than according to their traditional inherited social standing, with the Wu family placed first. Under her rule the bureaucracy was expanded, and many of the new positions were filled through the examination system. Although this opened government careers to a wider group than before, in the final stage of the process, candidates continued to be judged on their appearance and speech, criteria that inevitably favored the wellborn. It was also normal practice for candidates to try to win favor with an examiner prior to the tests. Those who could used their family connections for this purpose; others sent samples of their verse in the hope of impressing the men who held the keys to a government career. Under Empress Wu, men who entered government through the examinations were able for the first time to attain the highest office, even that of Chief Minister, although the Empress herself preferred to bypass this office and work through the "Scholars of the Northern Gate," who formed a kind of personal secretariat. Gradually, however, in the course of the first half of the T'ang, examination graduates acquired great prestige and came to hold the highest offices, even though the majority of officials still entered government service through other means, making use of family connections. At the same time, government service gradually became the most desirable and prestigious career in the empire.

Under Empress Wu, T'ang power reached its furthest geographic extent. (See map, Figure 5-2.) But this expansion was not achieved peacefully; constant fighting occurred, particularly against the Tibetans. In Korea Empress Wu supported the successful efforts of the state of Silla to unify the peninsula. Although China was unable to dominate the newly unified state, relations remained cordial throughout her reign. Until around 700 she remained a vigorous although ruthless ruler, but during her last years the empress, now in her seventies, came under the influence of sycophantic courtiers. She was deposed in 705, and the T'ang was reestablished.

The second major ruler was Hsüan-tsung (r. 713–56), also known as the "Brilliant Emperor" (Ming-huang). His reign is considered the high point of the

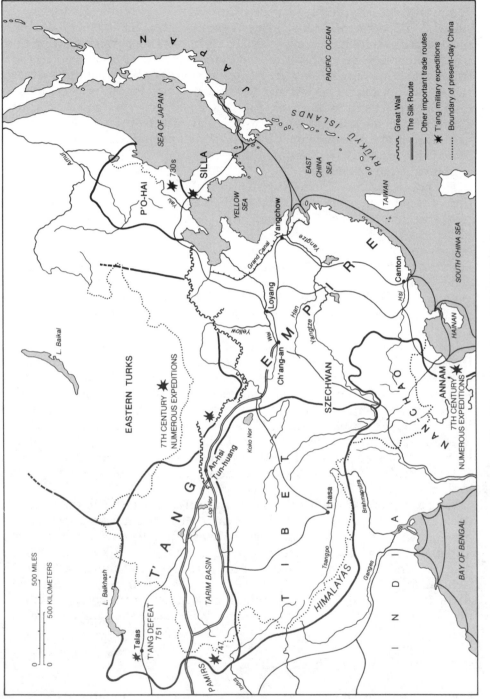

Figure 5-2 The T'ang Empire—Mid-Eighth Century

T'ang: economically, politically, and culturally. His court must have been truly splendid. The emperor, a horse lover, is said to have kept 40,000 horses in the royal stables, including a troupe of dancing horses. Poetry and painting flourished, and horses were a favorite theme for poets, painters, and potters. It is fitting that Han Kan, probably the greatest of the T'ang horse painters, served at Hsüan-tsung's court. This was also the time in which landscape painting came into its own. The most admired of all T'ang painters, Wu Tao-tzu, also lived during this period. It is said of him that one day, after painting a scene on a wall, he walked into it—leaving only the empty wall behind. He must have been a remarkable master to have inspired this story; unfortunately, none of his work is known to have survived.

The political achievements of Hsüan-tsung's government included reformation of the coinage, repair and extension of the Grand Canal, and the implementation of a land registration program. To carry out these measures, he employed special commissions headed by distinguished aristocrats. Men of equally imposing background also staffed the Censorate, the organ of the government charged with the surveillance of the bureaucracy. There was a tendency at this time for officials to polarize into two groups: members of the high aristocracy and those of less exhalted rank. Nevertheless, factors influencing political alignments were too complex to be reduced to simple family or regional patterns.

Important changes in the institution of government also occurred under Hsüan-tsung. The power of the Chief Ministers increased, and a council, or cabinet, of Chief Ministers was established. This development was particularly significant because, near the middle of his reign, the emperor gradually withdrew from active participation in government. In 736 Chief Minister Li Lin-fu became a virtual dictator. He was of aristocratic stock, but he did not have an examination system degree and was often ridiculed by degree holders for his lack of scholarship. Nevertheless, he was an able administrator. When Li Lin-fu died in 752, his place was taken by Yang Kuo-chung, a much less capable man.

Yang Kuo-chung owed his rise to the influence of his cousin, the royal concubine Yang Kuei-fei. A beautiful woman, on the plump side in accord with the T'ang ideal of female beauty, she so captivated the emperor that he neglected all else and was content to entrust the burdens of government to her relatives. The reign that had begun in such brilliance ended in disaster. In 755 General An Lu-shan rebelled, and the court was forced to flee to Szechwan. Along the way, loyal soldiers, blaming Yang Kuei-fei for the country's difficulties, forced the emperor to have her strangled. Hsüan-tsung then abdicated.

City Life in the Capital: Ch'ang-an

Even the most casual glance at a map of the Sui-T'ang capital, Ch'ang-an (see Figure 5-3), is enough to reveal that it was a planned city. Containing about thirty square miles, excluding the palace area, it was the largest planned city

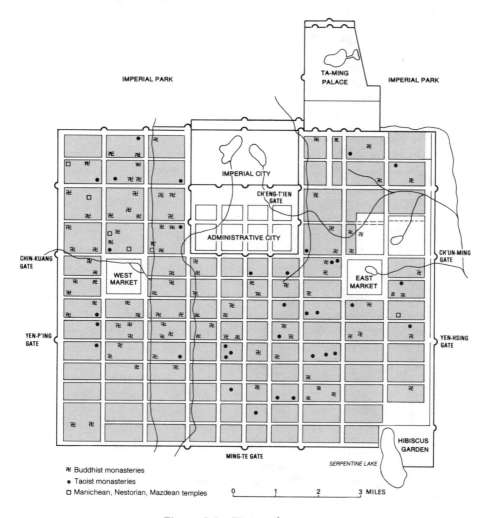

IMPERIAL PARK

TA-MING PALACE

IMPERIAL PARK

IMPERIAL CITY

CH'ENG-T'IEN GATE

ADMINISTRATIVE CITY

CHIN-KUANG GATE

WEST MARKET

EAST MARKET

CH'UN-MING GATE

YEN-P'ING GATE

YEN-HSING GATE

HIBISCUS GARDEN

MING-TE GATE

SERPENTINE LAKE

卍 Buddhist monasteries
● Taoist monasteries
□ Manichean, Nestorian, Mazdean temples

0   1   2   3 MILES

Figure 5-3   T'ang Ch'ang-an.

ever built, and also the largest city encompassed by walls. Its roughly one million inhabitants also made it the most populous city in the world, in its day. Roughly another million people lived in the greater metropolitan area outside the walls.

Many cities grow naturally in response to the social and economic needs of their inhabitants, but planned cities express the values and priorities of their builders. The essential feature of Ch'ang-an is that it was built to be the capital of a great empire. In accord with ancient tradition, it was oriented so that both the city and the imperial palace faced south. The entire city was in a sense the home of the emperor. Its layout resembled that of a typical T'ang house, with a service area in front and a garden in the rear. The imposing presence of the emperor and his government were further emphasized by the grand avenue that led from the main city gate to the palace and the government complex. Five hundred feet wide, it was well calculated to impress envoys from lesser lands with the might and grandeur of the great Chinese Empire.

Figure 5-4 *Armenoid Merchant Holding Wine Skin*. Pottery with three-color glaze, eighth century, 37.2 cm × 25.4 cm. Seattle Art Museum.

The people of the city, including those employed in the government complex, lived in rectangular wards. Each ward was a self-contained unit surrounded by walls, with entry provided through a gate that was closed each night. Two friends in adjacent wards might be able to see each other's houses but find it difficult to visit. Since it was the center of government, Ch'ang-an was hardly the place to escape government surveillance and interference. In contrast to medieval Europe, where the city became a refuge and a center of freedom, in China one sought freedom in remote mountains and hills. Not everyone wished to rusticate in a remote village however; there were many who bitterly bemoaned an enforced absence from the great capital—unless, perhaps, they were posted to the secondary capital of Loyang or to the southern metropolis of Yangchow.

T'ang culture was doubly cosmopolitan: first, in the sense that China was open to cultural influences from India and the distant west; second, in the sense that China, itself, was the cultural model for the other settled societies of East Asia. Both aspects were reflected in the considerable number of foreigners who lived in Ch'ang-an. Some were students. Among these the most numerous were the Koreans, of whom some 8000 were said to be in Ch'ang-an in 640. Other foreigners were engaged in commerce, coming from as far away as India, Iran, Syria, and Arabia. The Armenoid wine-seller shown in Figure 5-4 probably sold his exotic beverage at the West Market, the center for foreign trade, where his customers could also enjoy other exotic foods and beverages and attend performances of foreign acrobats or magicians or see a foreign play.

Stylish T'ang ladies sported foreign coiffures, while painters and potters had a good time rendering the outlandish features of "barbarians" from distant lands. Images of foreigners from all over Central Asia and beyond to Iran were prominent among the clay figurines manufactured in specialty shops to be used for burial with the dead. Among the tomb figures are camel drivers and grooms for the horses, examples of which can be found in almost all museum collections of Chinese art. Information concerning foreign foods, music, and customs can also be found in T'ang writings, particularly poetry. It is characteristic of the robust and cosmopolitan spirit of the period that one of the favorite pastimes of its aristocratic ladies and gentlemen was polo, a game which originated in Persia. The participation of women in such athletic activities and their fondness for riding (see Figure 5-5) are worth emphasizing in the light of the very different ethos that was to prevail in post-T'ang times.

Among the amenities of the capital were the Serpentine Lake and the Hibiscus Garden in the southeast corner of the city, where newly granted degree holders celebrated their good fortune by floating wine cups on the water, and the emperor himself sometimes entered the Purple Cloud Pavilion to observe the festivities. Notably absent, however, were such public buildings as forums, baths, or stadiums found in cities inhabited by citizens rather than subjects. Nor did Ch'ang-an boast great, monumental structures of stone or brick. The men of T'ang were under no illusion concerning the permanence of stone. In their view, it was the written word which endured.

Figure 5-5 *Lady on Horseback.* Painted clay, T'ang, 38.1 cm × 31.1 cm. Collection of Mr. and Mrs. Ezekiel Schloss, New York.

As the map of Ch'ang-an (Figure 5-3) clearly shows, the city was also a religious center. Manichean, Nestorian, and Zoroastrian temples testify to T'ang tolerance and cosmopolitanism, but their congregations, like those of Buddhist temples during the Han, were largely foreign. The opposite was true of the many Taoist and Buddhist establishments. Many of the latter were the chief temples of flourishing sects, and some accommodated pilgrim monks from Korea and Japan. Just as Buddhist pagodas dominated the Ch'ang-an skyline, the Buddhist faith predominated on the intellectual and spiritual horizon. It was the time when Chinese Buddhism came of age.

The Flourishing of Buddhism

Although the state employed Confucian forms and learning, and T'ang emperors often favored Taoism, this was the golden age of Chinese Buddhism. Buddhist monasteries flourished economically; they fulfilled important social roles; and their most outstanding monks had sufficient self-confidence to make their own formulations of doctrine and develop the teaching in new ways. For Buddhist art as well, it was an age of classic fulfillment.

Eight Buddhist sects appeared between 581 and 755, of which four enjoyed only temporary or limited success: the Disciplinary School (Lü), the Fa-hsiang (Dharma Image), the Sect of the Three Stages (San-chieh), the Esoteric School (Mi). The Disciplinary School restricted its concerns to monastic rules, rituals, and regulations. More deeply philosophical (but rejected after it lost imperial patronage) was Fa-hsiang, propounded by the great pilgrim Hsüan-tsang. It was basically a derivation of Yogacara Buddhism as interpreted by Hsüan-tsang's teacher in India. As a school of metaphysical idealism it developed a subtle and complex psychology, but it departed from Mahayana universalism in its insistence on salvation through arduous meditation so that the *manas* (thought center), by attaining perfect wisdom, could restore the purity of *ālaya* (the storehouse) where are found the seeds of karma, some tainted and some pure. Fa-hsiang taught that not all beings possess untainted seeds, and therefore not all were able to achieve salvation, a doctrine of limited appeal in China.

The Sect of the Three Stages (San-chieh) was particularly prone to government suppression. Its devotees divided time into the era of the true teaching, the era of the counterfeit teaching, and the era of the decay of the teaching. Although there was disagreement over exact periodization, the T'ang was generally assigned to the period of decay, a view which T'ang emperors naturally did not appreciate. Empress Wu and Emperor Hsüan-tsung were particularly hostile. The latter, who had an abiding interest in Taoist magic, patronized Esoteric Buddhism (Mi) which was characterized by the use of mantras (mystic syllables), mudras (signs made by the position of the fingers and hands), and mandalas (pictorial representations of the cosmos—"cosmograms"). Although the Esoteric School influenced other sects, it did not flourish as an independent sect in China. It did flourish in Japan in the form of Shingon.

By contrast, the four major sects had considerable influence in China and in Japan. These were: T'ien-t'ai (Tendai, in Japanese), Hua-yen (Kegon, in Japanese), Ch'ing-tu (Jōdo, in Japanese), and Ch'an (familiar to us from the Japanese name, Zen). The school that enjoyed the most official support under the Sui was T'ien-t'ai. Founded by Chih-i (538–97), it took its name from a mountain range in Chekiang. Just as the Sui strove for political and economic integration, T'ien-t'ai developed doctrinal and metaphysical syncretism, that is, it combined elements of the various doctrines and practices. In particular it sought to combine the scholarly tradition of the South with northern pietism and meditation. Thus, a text esteemed in the North was considered Buddha's first sermon, but his last pronouncement, according to T'ien-t'ai, was a sutra popular in the South. The complete Truth for T'ien-t'ai was contained in the Lotus Sutra, believed to have been preached by the Buddha to 12,000 arhats (saints), 6000 nuns, 8000 Bodhisattvas, and 60,000 gods. The great god Brahma attended, accompanied by 12,000 dragons, and there were hundreds of thousands of other supernatural beings. As he talked, a ray of light emanated from the Buddha's forehead revealing 18,000 worlds in each of which a Buddha is preaching. This text was enormously influential in East Asia, and its imagery inspired many artistic representations.

T'ien-t'ai doctrine centered on a tripartite truth: (1) the truth that all phenomena are empty, products of causation without a nature of their own; (2) the truth that they do, however, exist temporarily; (3) the truth that encompasses but transcends emptiness and temporariness. These three truths all involve and require each other—throughout T'ien-t'ai the whole and the parts are one. A rich but unified cosmology is built on this basis: Temporariness consists of ten realms. Since each of these includes the other, a total of one thousand results. Each of these in turn has three aspects—that of living beings, of aggregates, and of space. The result is 3000 worlds interwoven so that all are present in each. Since, therefore, truth is immanent in everything, it follows that all beings contain the Buddha nature and can be saved. One eighth-century T'ien-t'ai patriarch taught that this includes inanimate things, down to the tiniest grain of dust.

Like T'ien-t'ai, Hua-yen taught the doctrine of emptiness and the interpenetration of all phenomena, but its teaching that all phenomena arise simultaneously in reciprocal causation was new. More interested in doctrinal subtleties than T'ien-t'ai, Hua-yen Buddhists distinguished between li, which can be translated as "principle" and is formless, and shih or phenomena. One of its greatest masters was Fa-tsang (643–712), who was generously patronized by Empress Wu. In a famous sermon Fa-tsang once explained Hua-yen doctrine by setting up a Buddha figure surrounded by eight mirrors at the points of the compass. A ninth mirror was placed above the statue and a tenth below. When the Buddha figure was lit by a torch, each mirror reflected not only the Buddha but also all the other mirrors.

The remaining two sects emphasized practice more than doctrine. The Ch'ing-tu, or Pure Land sect, derived its name from the paradise in the West over which presides Amitābha (A-mi-t'o-fo in Chinese, Amida in Japanese), the Buddha of Infinite Light. Another great favorite of Pure Land Buddhists was Kuan-yin, the Bodhisattva of mercy. Drawing on a long Mahayana tradition, this school emphasized faith as the means for gaining rebirth in the land of bliss. The teaching of salvation by faith was often coupled with the idea that this was the appropriate means for a decadent age. A special practice of Pure Land Buddhism was the invocation of Amitābha's name. This, if done with wholehearted sincerity, would gain anyone rebirth in the Pure Land. The popular appeal of this sect was immense, and its spiritual dimensions probably received their furthest development in the teachings of the Japanese master Shinran (1173–1262).

The last school to be discussed was so influential in Japan that in the West it is generally known by its Japanese name, although Ch'an (Zen) was very much Chinese in origin and has affinities with Taoism. It taught meditation as the way for one to pierce through the world of illusion, recognize the Buddha nature within oneself, and obtain enlightenment. Whereas for other schools meditation was only one of many techniques, Ch'an rejected all other practices, such as the performance of meritorious deeds or the study of scriptures. The so-called Northern branch of Ch'an emphasized sitting in silent meditation and attaining enlightenment gradually. Southern Ch'an, founded by the man known as the Sixth Patriarch, Hui-neng (638–713), maintained that illumination comes in a sudden flash, although only after long searching. A Western analogy might be Newton's experience under the apple tree: he discovered the law of gravitation in a sudden flash, but he would never have done so had he not been constantly thinking about the problem, searching for a solution.

Southern Ch'an teachers often employed unorthodox methods to prod their disciples on the road to illumination. Their methods included irreverent or irrelevant answers to questions, contradictory remarks, nonsense syllables—anything to jar the mind out of its ordinary rut. Some masters would strike their disciples in the belief (as with Newton) that enlightenment might come as the result of a sudden physical shock. One widely practiced technique was for the master to assign his pupils a *kung-an* (*kōan*, in Japanese), an enigmatic statement to be pondered until the pupil attained an understanding that transcended everyday reasoning. One famous *kung-an* asks: "what is the sound of one hand clapping?"

If the growth of sects illustrates the inner vigor of Buddhist religion, there were equally impressive outward manifestations of the strength of the Buddhist church. In the countryside, Buddhist temples performed important economic functions: operating mills and oil presses, maintaining vaults for safe-deposit, and performing other banking services including pawnbroking. The temples also held much land that they cultivated with semiservile labor, and they profited from their connections with wealthy patrons who sought to evade taxation by registering land under a temple name. Some temples provided medical care; still others entertainment. Much of their wealth was channeled into building and the arts.

Architecture and Art

Religious persecution and war have taken their toll on the architectural remains of T'ang Buddhism. Remaining temples are limited to a very few pagodas and halls, the largest of which is located on Mt. Wu in Shansi. This is similar in design to the Tōshōdaiji founded by a Chinese monk (see Figures 6-12 and 6-13) in Japan, a worthy expression of T'ang self-confidence. Just as the message of the Buddha was considered universal in its appeal and application, the artistic styles of the T'ang at its height were adopted beyond the seas in Japan. Built facing south, a hall such as this was oriented not to the topographic features of any particular location but to the cosmos that encompasses all.

Large scale T'ang sculpture in wood and bronze has not survived, although the more than life-size bronzes at the Yakushiji in Nara, Japan, are fine representations of the T'ang international style. In China there are a good many stone statues, including a very large Vairocana Buddha (the universal Buddha of Hua-yen and Esoteric Buddhism) just outside the caves at Lung-men. More sculpture is preserved in other caves, with the best examples found at T'ien-lung Shan in Shansi. The Kuanyin shown in Figure 5-6 is a T'ang sculpture in the style seen in eighth-century Ch'ang-an. The sensuous quality of the body, clothed (not hidden) in diaphanous drapery, owes something to Indian influence, particularly that of the Gupta style (Gupta dynasty in India, 320–647). At their very best, T'ang sculptures blend Indian delight in the corporality of mass with a Chinese sense of essentially linear rhythm. It is a combination most suitable for portraying Kuanyin, combining the spiritual qualities of a supernatural being with merciful concern for earthly creatures. The balance between movement and restraint, like that between the worldly and the sacred, was difficult to maintain: in later Buddhist art, corporality degenerates into obesity, and the robes take on a wild, rococo life of their own.

Figure 5-6   Eleven-headed Kuan-yin. Limestone, eighth century, 100.8 cm × 31.7 cm. Freer Gallery, Washington, D.C.

We know that the temples at Ch'ang-an were decorated with great frescoes and that Wu Tao-tzu did some of his best work for Buddhist establishments; a favorite scene was that of Amitābha presiding over his paradise. An important site for T'ang painting is Tun-huang, a major center for the caravan trade, famous not only for the art preserved in its grottoes but also for the many documents discovered there. Kumārajīva's translation of the Lotus Sutra is the most frequently found text, but administrative records, often written on the backs of religious works, make the Tun-huang material a major source for the study of T'ang economic, social, and administrative history. Paintings dating from the Northern Wei and T'ang also provide information on agricultural tools and techniques. Others depict major events in the Buddhist tradition, including scenes from Hsüan-tsang's great journey.

In the ninth century (mid-T'ang) an untrammeled, spontaneous style of painting, largely influenced by Ch'an Buddhism, developed in Szechwan. It is best represented by Wang Mo ("ink Wang") who made pictures by splashing ink on silk, usually while drunk. Ch'an painting flourished in Sung China and Ashikaga Japan, and will be discussed in the chapters on those periods. A popular subject of the Ch'an painter in both lands was a pair of T'ang recluses, wearing expressions of divine lunacy: Han Shan (Cold Mountain), named after the mountain in the T'ien-t'ai range where he made his home, and Shih Te (Foundling), who worked in a monastery kitchen on Cold Mountain and is usually shown holding a broom. Both men wrote poetry. The strong verse of Han Shan has been especially admired and is well represented in English translation.

Poetry

Buddhism influenced the work of other T'ang poets. Foremost among them is Wang Wei (699–759), who is noted also for his landscape painting and his music, both now lost. His best poetry conveys the serenity and calm of the detached, enlightened man:

> I didn't know where the temple was,
> pushing mile on mile among cloudy peaks;
> old trees, peopleless paths,
> deep mountains, somewhere a bell.
> Brook voices choke over craggy boulders,
> sun rays turn cold in the green pines.
> At dusk by the bend of a deserted pond,
> a monk in meditation, taming poison dragons.[1]

The dragons are the passions; the scene is visual yet empty.

Buddhist serenity is but one theme in T'ang poetry. Wang Wei, like other major poets, also wrote verses that reflect secular life. The following, celebrating the military exploits of a young horseman, suggests the period's military vigor:

Alone, he can draw two carved bows at once!
A thousand waves of enemy horsemen cannot daunt him.
Astride his golden saddle, he strings his bow with white-feathered arrows,
And ping! the plumed shower drops five khan dead![2]

Li Po and Tu Fu

During the T'ang the ability to write at least passable poetry was one of the accomplishments expected of a gentleman, and it was usually a prerequisite for passing the civil service examinations. Consequently, the production of poetry was large: over 48,000 T'ang poems by some 2200 writers have been preserved. Their quality, however, is uneven, as would be the case if contemporary American politicians and business executives all were expected to write poetry. Furthermore, during the T'ang, poetry was viewed not as a vocation, but as an avocation—and, sometimes, as a consolation.

Li Po (701–63) and Tu Fu (712–70), China's two most beloved and admired poets, experienced both the brilliance of Hsüan-tsung's reign and the dark times of An Lu-shan's Rebellion. Li Po was actually implicated in a secondary rebellion. Neither man was a political success, although Tu Fu felt this more keenly than did the older poet. Both enjoyed friendship and wine and composed beautiful poetry with multidimensional meanings. They were personal friends, and Tu Fu greatly admired Li Po. Yet, despite all they shared, they differed greatly in personality and in their work. It is the contrasts between them that Chinese scholars and literary men have always stressed.

Like Wang Wei, Li Po's subject matter included nature, but the nature described in poems such as "The Road to Shu Is Steep," which describes Hsüan-tsung's flight to Szechwan during An Lu-shan's Rebellion (see Figure 5-7, in which this subject is treated pictorially) is much more exuberant than that of Wang Wei, more akin to the tradition represented by the Han rhapsodists. Li Po's fondness for nature and for mountains blended well with his freedom of spirit. Although he wrote poems in many forms, he preferred old-style verse (*ku-shih*), which was without the restrictions and limitations placed on verse in the new style (*chin-t'i shih*) and left the poet free to devise his own rhythmic and verbal structure.

Li Po was famous as the poet of wine:

> A pot of wine among the flowers:
> I drink alone, no kith or kin near.
> I raise my cup to invite the moon to join me;
> It and my shadow make a party of three.
> Alas, the moon is unconcerned about drinking,
> And my shadow merely follows me around.
> Briefly I cavort with the moon and my shadow:
> Pleasure must be sought while it is spring.
> I sing and the moon goes back and forth,

> I dance and my shadow falls at random.
> While sober we seek pleasure in fellowship;
> When drunk we go each our own way.
> Then let us pledge a friendship without human ties
> And meet again at the far end of the Milky Way.[3]

It is said that on one nocturnal drinking expedition on a lake, Li Po fell into the water while trying to fish out the moon and died by drowning. This tale may be spurious! But it formed part of the traditional image, part of the legend of Li Po. The Sung painter Liang K'ai captured this image of the slightly inebriated poet floating in space (see Chapter 8, Figure 8-5) with an economy of means that would have pleased Li Po, for his own verse is deceptively simple. He knew that true art does not reveal its skill.

Both poets wrote highly compressed verse, but much of Tu Fu's poetry, unlike that of Li Po, is enriched by a patina of allusions that add weight and majesty to the lines. Also in contrast to Li Po, Tu Fu was particularly effective in new-style poetry, especially the regulated verse (lü-shih) in eight lines with five or seven characters per line, and elaborate rules governing tone and rhyme as well as verbal parallelism. There are occasional poems, poems of friendship and wine, but Tu Fu has perhaps been admired most for his social conscience and compassion. He can be biting in his commentary, as in two frequently quoted lines that form part of a longer poem written shortly before the An Lu-shan Rebellion:

> Inside the red gates wine and meat go bad;
> On the roads are bones of men who died of cold.[4]

Some of his most moving poems describe the suffering and hardships of ordinary people. One concerns the visit at night of a recruiting officer to the village of Shih-hao. An old grandmother informs the officer that only two males are left at home: the old man who has fled and an infant son. She tells him to take her since she can at least cook—and in the morning she is gone.

Tu Fu, like his contemporaries, frequently sent poems to those close to him. The following was written while he was living near the upper reaches of the Yangtze and is addressed to a brother living far away near the mouth of the river. The "wind in the dust" in the third line refers to the warfare that separates the two brothers:

To My Younger Brother

> Rumors that you lodge in a mountain temple
> In Hang-chou, or in Yüeh-chou for sure.
> Wind in the dust prolongs our day of parting,
> Yangtze and Han have wasted my clear autumn.
> My shadow sticks to the trees where gibbons scream,
> But my spirit whirls by the towers sea-serpents breathe.
> Let me go down next year with the spring waters
> And search for you to the end of the white clouds in the East.[5]

In other poems Tu Fu tells of life in the thatched hut he inhabited during exile in Szechwan, and he often voices his dismay at the failure of his political ambitions. His aspirations and disappointments corresponded to the experiences of many of his readers, who admired his artistry and his humanism. Perhaps for all of these reasons, he was venerated as China's foremost poet.

The Rebellion of An Lu-shan (755–763)

The rebellion that drove the emperor in flight to Szechwan and created havoc in the country revealed underlying weakness in the T'ang system. Only a strong emperor or an all-powerful chief minister like Li Lin-fu could prevent the friction between the aristocratic commissions and the regular bureaucracy from getting out of hand. Old institutions were revealed as inadequate under new conditions. The dynasty had adopted the "equal field" (chün-t'ien) system of land allotment developed by the Northern Wei as a way of bringing deserted land back under cultivation or opening up new lands, but this system proved unworkable when there was a shortage rather than a surplus of land. The breakdown of the land system brought in its train the failure of the taxation system, which was based on equal land allotments. Furthermore, most taxes were collected in kind, that is, goods rather than money, and this required a cumbersome system of transport and storage. The old militia system similarly proved inadequate for the dynasty's military requirements, which could only be met by large standing armies composed of professional soldiers.

In 747 a T'ang army crossed the Pamirs, led by a Korean general who had opted for a career under the T'ang rather than returning to his native land. The purpose of this expedition was to prevent Arabs and Tibetans from joining forces. The tactic succeeded, but four years later this same general suffered defeat on the banks of the Talas River near Samarkand. The loss of this battle not only put an end to T'ang ambitions in the area but opened to Islam what had up to then been a Buddhist oriented Central Asia. Earlier, Turkish peoples had caused conflict in the Northwest, but in 736 this area was stabilized when the pro-T'ang Uighurs became the dominant power. In midcentury, however, the dynasty was challenged by an alliance between Tibet and Nan Chao, a southwestern state in the area of modern Yunnan Province. The government's response was to create military provinces along the frontiers. These were placed under the direction of military governors (chieh-tu shih) who were given logistic as well as military authority and gradually assumed other functions of government. Since the central army was in decline, a serious imbalance of power resulted between the home army and the powerful frontier forces. An Lu-shan, a general of Turkish extraction, began his rebellion in control of 160,000 troops in the Northeast.

An Lu-shan's forces seized both Loyang and Ch'ang-an, and he proclaimed himself emperor of a new Yen dynasty. But in 757 he was murdered by his son.

The rebellion then continued, led first by another general of similar background, Shih Ssu-ming, and then by his son. In the meantime, the court had taken refuge in Szechwan, the very large (75,000 square miles) and fertile province famed for its terraced hills, the flooded fields reflecting the light of the moon. (Fertile soil and a favorable climate make Szechwan perfect for rice cultivation, and for other crops as well, for it is said that anything that can be grown anywhere in China can be grown in Szechwan. Ringed by mountains, it is highly defensible. During the Second World War it served as a bastion for the Nationalist Chinese.)

In 763 the court was able to regain the capital, and the T'ang was saved. However, the dynasty was able to accomplish its preservation only with the assistance of foreign, mostly Uighur, troops. Furthermore, it had to be content with purely nominal submission of the virtually independent "governors" in the Northeast, in the region west of the capital, in parts of Honan, and in Szechwan. Regional differences that before the rebellion had been worked out within the system now threatened to pull it apart.

The Late T'ang

One long-term effect of the rebellion of An Lu-shan was the final abandonment of the "equal field" system and with it the practice of assessing taxes according to the number of individuals in a household. Instead, under Emperor Te-tsung (780–805), a new system was instituted that assessed households according to the size of their houses and the amount of land they held. Thus the government officially acknowledged the uneven distribution of land and tried to make the best of it. Since the new taxes were collected twice a year, the system is known as the Two Tax System. Another innovation provided that taxes be calculated in terms of money, although they were still collected in kind. The Two Tax System did not always operate effectively, but this basic approach to taxation persisted for 700 years.

Major economic support for the dynasty came from the South. A main source of revenue was the salt monopoly, for the government controlled all but one of China's major salt producing areas. The government sold monopoly salt to merchants for distribution throughout China, thereby deriving income even from areas not under its political control.

Te-tsung strengthened the dynasty's finances and also built up a large palace army. The history of the T'ang after An Lu-shan was thus not all downhill. Emperor Hsien-tsung (r. 806–20) was especially vigorous in fostering institutional renewal and in reasserting central control over some of the lost provinces. But both of these vigorous emperors relied on men directly dependent on them, the "inner court," rather than using the regular bureaucracy. The result, as in the Later Han, was the emergence of eunuch power. Eunuchs commanded the palace armies and once again formed self-perpetuating "families" through adoption. Hsien-tsung was murdered by eunuchs, whose power grew greatly in the 820s and 830s—an attempted coup against them in 835 failed. Moreover, officialdom at the time was divided into bitterly hostile factions. A dispute that lasted half a century arose out of a disagreement over the results of a special civil service examination held in 808.

Both Te-tsung and Hsien-tsung personally favored Taoism. This was also true of Wu-tsung (840–46) for whom the temptation to meet his great and pressing financial needs by seizing Buddhist riches proved irresistible. He is, consequently, best known for his persecution of the church: monastic lands and wealth were confiscated, monks and nuns were returned to lay life, slaves and dependents were released. In the process irreparable damage was done to many large bronze statues and to buildings. Although the policy of persecution was promptly reversed by Wu-tsung's successor, it was all the more damaging to Buddhism because the religion was already showing signs of a decline in inner vitality. Only two sects continued to flourish: Pure Land, grounded in the hearts of the people, and Ch'an, perhaps the most Chinese form of Buddhism and less dependent than others on patronage.

Late T'ang Poetry and Culture

For about twenty years after Tu Fu's death in 770 no great poetry appeared, but in the 790s Han Yü (768–824) and Po Chü-yi (772–846) began to write in their own distinctive and widely imitated styles. The latter was not only a very prolific poet, author of some 2800 pieces, but was also particularly beloved wherever Chinese influence reached. His "Everlasting Remorse" is the classic poetic rendition of the tragedy of Hsüan-tsung and Yang Kuei-fei. Unlike Tu Fu, he wrote in simple and easy language. Like Tu Fu he had a strong social conscience:

An Old Charcoal Seller

An old charcoal seller
Cuts firewood, burns coal by the southern mountain.
His face, all covered with dust and ash, the color of smoke,
The hair at his temples is gray, his ten fingers black.
The money he makes selling coal, what is it for?
To put clothes on his back and food in his mouth.
The rags on his poor body are thin and threadbare;
Distressed at the low price of coal, he hopes for colder weather.
Night comes, an inch of snow has fallen on the city,
In the morning, he rides his cart along the icy ruts,
His ox weary, he hungry, and the sun already high.
In the mud by the south gate, outside the market, he stops to rest.
All of a sudden, two dashing riders appear;
An imperial envoy, garbed in yellow (his attendant in white),
Holding an official dispatch, he reads a proclamation.
Then turns the cart around, curses the ox, and leads it north.

Figure 5-7 Anonymous, *Ming Huang's* (i.e., Hsüan-tsung's) *Journey to Shu*. Hanging scroll, ink and color on silk, T'ang in style but dates from Sung or later, 55.9 cm × 81 cm. Palace Museum Collection, Taipei.

> One cartload of coal—a thousand or more catties!
> No use appealing to the official spiriting the cart away:
> Half a length of red lace, a slip of damask
> Dropped on the ox—is payment in full![6]

In other poems, he tells of his daily life, his family, and routines. He once described himself as addicted to poetry, bursting forth whenever he sees a fine landscape or meets a beloved friend: "madly singing in the mountains."[7]

Han Yü championed the Old Prose movement (which wanted to return to the style of writing found in the classics) in opposition to the elaborate parallelism and rhetorical flourishes of more recent prose. He is best known for an essay in which he reaffirmed the Confucian Way. Han Yü subsequently became one of the heroes of Sung Confucians who considered him their precursor. In his poetry as in his prose, Han Yü preferred the old styles, writing long poems rich in original and daring similes. A common theme in his work is the classic complaint of the T'ang gentleman–poet: lack of official recognition. A scholar is like a fine horse, in need of proper care if he is to flourish. The trouble with the world lies not in the lack of horses, but in the absence of a ruler who understands horses. Han Yü's works were not always serious; he also showed a lighter side. He wrote an essay admonishing a crocodile and a poem about losing one's teeth.

Other writers of the Late T'ang include the historiographer Liu Chih-chi (661–722), the philosopher Li Ao (d. ca. 844), and the poets Li Ho (791–817) and Li Shang-yin (812?–58). Li Ho, a brilliant man who died young, was long neglected by later Chinese scholars. He had a penchant for quaint and even frankly odd language; as one Chinese critic put it: his verse has a demonic quality. Li Shang-yin, on the other hand, wrote frequently of love—not a common theme in Chinese poetry.

Tu Fu seems to have been the first poet, or at least one of the first, to write on or about paintings. He showed a keen awareness of the perishability of silk and ink. And he was right, for the poems have survived long after the paintings disappeared. The main sources for T'ang landscape painting are literary descriptions and later copies. Long after the T'ang, Wang Wei was credited with having established a gentleman's style of calligraphic painting in monotone, but none of his work has survived. It is said to have contrasted with the precision of line and decorative coloring of the court style, illustrated in Figure 5-7 by a copy made not earlier than the Sung. The coloring, blue and green, is a

Detail Figure 5-7 Anonymous, *Ming Huang's Journey to Shu.*

hallmark of T'ang art, but the pleasure the artist takes in the fantastic mountains is typical of all Chinese landscapists. Here, however, in contrast to later mountainscapes, nature does not overwhelm man. Instead, it provides a setting for his activities. The scene is Emperor Hsüan-tsung's flight to Szechwan during the An Lu-shan Rebellion, although as Michael Sullivan has suggested it really looks more like a pleasure excursion than a precipitous retreat after tragedy and defeat.[8] Be that as it may, this painting is probably as close as we can now get to the style of the T'ang, an important reference point for later Chinese painting as well as a delightful work in its own right.

Collapse of the Dynasty

During its last fifty years, the T'ang dynasty was weakened by conflict and divided loyalties in the capital; mistrust between officials in the capital and their military commanders in the field; and by suspicions, manipulations, and falsifications of all kinds. Even reports concerning natural disasters were falsified, as when an official assured the emperor that a plague of locusts had proven harmless because they had "all impaled themselves on thorns and brambles and died."[9] The story makes a sad litany of mismanagement, corruption, and incompetence. Meanwhile, bandit gangs, a refuge for the desperately poor and dislocated, increased in number, size, and ambition. Forming themselves into confederations, they progressed from raiding to rebellion; what had once been a nuisance now became a threat. Power, whether bandit or "legitimate," went to the strong and ruthless. Ordinary people survived as best they could the depredations of bandits and soldiers alike. Even though the dynasty made occasional gains, each rally amounted to no more than one step forward followed by two steps backward.

The most serious rebellion was led by Wang Hsien-chih, who was succeeded after his death by Huang Ch'ao. The latter destroyed Canton (879), killing many of its foreign as well as Chinese population. He is most notorious, however, for the brutality that he displayed after he captured Ch'ang-an in 880. Huang Ch'ao failed in his ambition to create a new dynasty; after his rebellion, once-unified China was thoroughly fragmented. (See map, Figure 5-8.)

The survival of the court now depended on the tolerance of, and especially the competition among, its neighboring rivals. An important factor in the shifting military and political balance of North China were the policies of the foreign peoples who inhabited the northern borderlands. Among these the Sha-t'o Turks were now the most important. Their intervention on behalf of the dynasty rescued it from destruction several times and enabled the T'ang to survive the Huang Ch'ao Rebellion. In 905 the Sha-t'o Turks concluded an alliance with a people from Mongolia called the Khitan, an alliance that continued through the Five Dynasties period (907–60). Indeed the Sha-t'o Turks themselves formed the second of these dynasties. This was the Later T'ang (923–34), which as its name implies tried to rule in the T'ang tradition. They

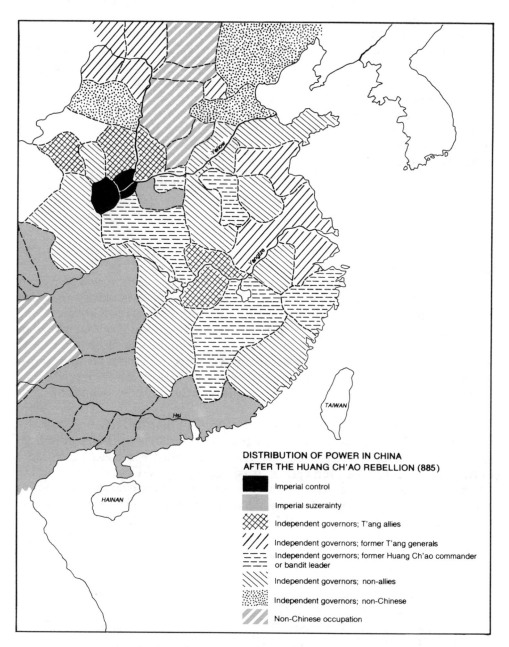

DISTRIBUTION OF POWER IN CHINA
AFTER THE HUANG CH'AO REBELLION (885)

- ■ Imperial control
- ▨ Imperial suzerainty
- ▤ Independent governors; T'ang allies
- ▨ Independent governors; former T'ang generals
- ▤ Independent governors; former Huang Ch'ao commander or bandit leader
- ▨ Independent governors; non-allies
- ▤ Independent governors; non-Chinese
- ▨ Non-Chinese occupation

Figure 5-8   **Distribution of Power in China after the Huang Ch'ao Rebellion**

SOURCE   Adapted from Robert M. Somers, "The Collapse of the T'ang Order," (Ph.D. dissertation, Yale University, 1975), pp. 204–05.

did not succeed in creating a lasting state, but a part of North China remained in foreign hands until the Ming.

The fighting at the end of the T'ang was particularly severe in the Northwest, and it devastated Ch'ang-an. There was panic in the streets, people screaming, scrambling over walls, stampeding while "rebels rage like stamping beasts"; "blood flowing like boiling fountains," severed heads, houses in flames, people eating bark or human flesh; deserted palaces where brambles grow and fox and rabbit run wild. These are some of the images in "The Lament of Lady Ch'i," a long ballad composed by Wei Chung (836–910) after Huang Ch'ao ruined the city. Its most famous lines capture the essence of the tragic contrast between past greatness and present disaster:

> The Inner Treasury is burnt down, its tapestries and
>   embroideries a heap of ashes;
> All along the Street of Heaven one treads to dust
>   the bones of State officials.[10]

Ch'ang-an, which the first Han emperor had made his chief city over a thousand years before, was never again to be China's capital.

The fall of the T'ang brought to an end the story of a great city and a great dynasty. It also marked the end of the hereditary high aristocracy that had dominated the Period of Disunity and had accommodated itself to the T'ang bureaucratic order even after an examination degree carried more weight than a pedigree. In broad terms, the fall of the T'ang brought to a close a period of Chinese martial vigor and self-assertion vis-à-vis its nomadic and seminomadic neighbors. At the same time there was a turning away from the foreign religion that had fascinated and comforted the Chinese people for centuries.

This is not to deny that there were continuities, particularly between the Later T'ang and the Sung, for many of the characteristics of the later period, ranging from the tax system to intellectual developments, are easily traceable to the eighth century or even earlier. It is, therefore, useful to distinguish between the earlier and later parts of the T'ang dynasty. However, it is helpful to keep in mind the accomplishments and historical pattern of the entire T'ang as we turn to consider the history of Japan.

NOTES

1. Burton Watson, *Chinese Lyricism: Shih Poetry from the Second to the Twelfth Century* (New York: Columbia University Press, 1971), p. 175.

2. Chang Yin-nan and Lewis C. Walmsley, *Poems by Wang Wei* (Rutland, Vt.: Charles E. Tuttle, 1959), p. 76.

3. Liu Wu-chi and Irving Yucheng Lo, eds., *Sunflower Splendor* (Garden City, N.Y.: Anchor Press/Doubleday, 1975), p. 109.

4. A. R. Davis, *Tu Fu* (New York: Twayne, 1971), p. 46.

5. A. C. Graham, *Poems of the Late T'ang* (Baltimore: Penguin Books, 1965), p. 47.

6. Liu and Lo, *Sunflower Splendor*, pp. 206–07.

7. Arthur Waley, trans., *One Hundred and Seventy Chinese Poems* (London: Constable & Co., Ltd., 1918; reprinted 1947), p. 144.

8. Michael Sullivan, *The Arts of China* (Berkeley and Los Angeles: University of California Press, 1973), p. 293.

9. Robert M. Somers, *"The Collapse of the T'ang Order,"* (Ph.D. dissertation, Yale University, 1975), p. 102.

10. *Ibid.*, p. 145.

早期之日本

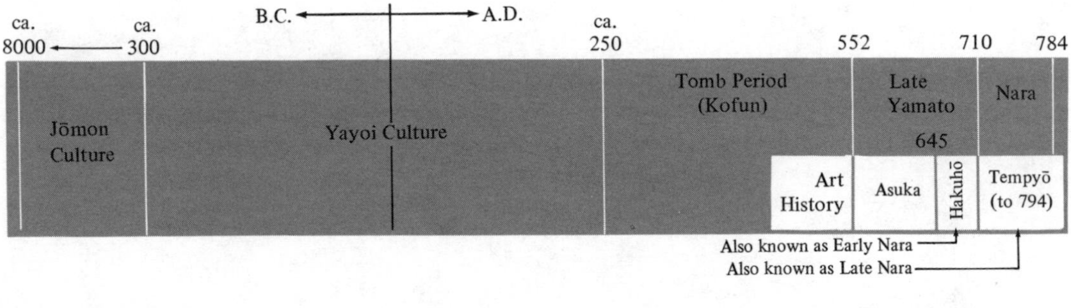

ca. 8000	ca. 300	B.C. ←	→ A.D.	ca. 250		552		710	784

Jōmon Culture

Yayoi Culture

Tomb Period (Kofun)

Late Yamato

645

Nara

Art History

Asuka

Hakuhō

Tempyō (to 794)

Also known as Early Nara —
Also known as Late Nara —

6 Early Japan to 794

A major theme in the history of Japan is the interplay between native and imported elements in culture and government. Although hospitable to T'ang civilization, Japan did not become simply a smaller replica of China, for by the time Buddhist and Chinese influences came to bear, Japanese culture was firmly grounded in its own native traditions.

Geography helps to explain both Japan's receptivity to continental influences and its ability not to be overwhelmed by them. (See map, Figure 6-1.) Although it is considerably smaller than the Chinese giant, Japan is not an unusually small state. For example, Japan's 142,707 square mile area is larger than that of the British Isles (99,909 square miles). Something like four-fifths of this land is too mountainous to permit cultivation. But Japan enjoys a climate warm and wet enough to permit the cultivation of rice, and, through intense cultivation, developed a highly efficient agricultural production that contributed to population growth. The small proportion of arable land thus has been

129

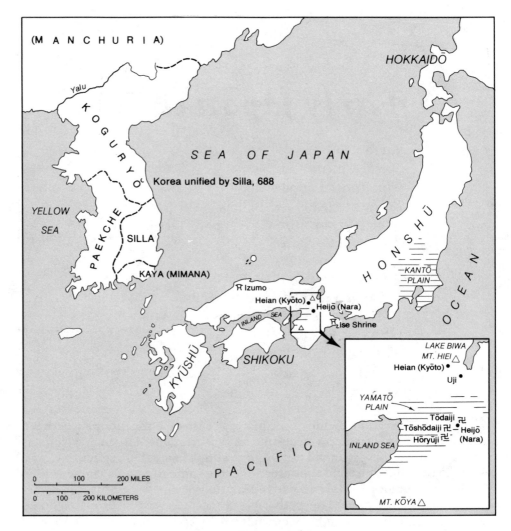

Figure 6-1 **Korea and Japan**

able to support relatively large populations. Japanese mountain ranges were large enough to impede transportation and communication in early times. As a consequence, areas of settlement were originally isolated from each other, encouraging fragmentation of political power and obstructing efforts towards unification of the state and development of a centralized government. However, mountain barriers were not as massive as those in China. Eventually they were overcome.

Endowed with an adequate physical base for the development of its own institutions and traditions, Japan was also profoundly affected by its location on the world map. At its closest point, the island of Kyūshū is about 120 miles from the continent, across the Korean Strait. It was over this route that continental influences entered Japan, for direct contact with China did not become general until late in the seventh century and, even then, remained hazardous. Although conquerors from the mainland may have played an important part in Japan's early history, Japan was too far away to be dominated by mainland powers. Foreign ideas, institutions, and techniques could be adapted to Japanese needs without military or political interference from abroad.

A prime factor preserving the integrity of Japanese culture was linguistic, for Japanese (like Korean) is not related to Chinese. In contrast to the Chinese or Sinitic languages, both Japanese and Korean are agglutinative. That is, they are languages in which words are formed primarily by a process of adding (or "gluing" together) words and word elements. Verbs and adjectives are highly inflected, with differences in tense, mood, level of formality, and so forth expressed by adding to the stem one element after another. The function of nouns in a sentence is indicated through the use of postpositions. These are somewhat similar to English prepositions except that they follow rather than precede nouns, and no noun can appear without one. These postpositions and various particles delineate the structure of sentences, which, in contrast to the compact mode of classical Chinese, tend to be long and rambling. Even when Japanese men of letters immersed themselves in Chinese learning, they continued to speak (and think) in the language they shared with the great majority of their countrymen.

In Japan, as in China and Korea, there is evidence of the presence of man from very early times (for example, tools of chipped stone), but there is not enough data to permit a clear reconstruction of the earliest human society. Similarly, many questions concerning the origins of the Japanese people remain unanswered. There is, for example, no generally accepted theory concerning the place of the Ainu people in early Japanese history. Today some fifteen thousand of these Caucasoid aborigines still live in enclaves in the far north, although they are gradually being assimilated into Japanese society. Another subject of speculation is the role of Southeast Asia in the formation of the Japanese people and their culture, for mixed into the predominantly East Asian pattern of Japanese development are elements suggestive of the south. Most tantalizing is the obscurity which envelops the question of early relations between the inhabitants of Japan and those of the Korean Peninsula.

Jōmon Culture

Shell mounds (heaps of shells, the remains of consumed shellfish) found near the shore provide evidence of the presence, and diet, of a preagricultural culture in Japan. This first distinct neolithic culture, however, takes its name from the Jōmon, or "rope pattern," pottery found at these sites. The Jōmon culture may have originated around 8000 B.C., and it lasted until the third century B.C. Over this vast period of time there were many temporal and regional variations, and it may be that the basic culture is actually an amalgam of cultures originally developed by different peoples.

Figure 6-2 shows an example of the pottery from which the period takes its name. Lacking the potter's wheel, the Jōmon people made their ware by building up coils of clay (or perhaps simply kneading it into shape). They then decorated the vessel by pressing twisted rope into the wet clay to give the pottery its distinctive pattern. Also characteristic of the Jōmon period were clay figurines. The earliest of these frequently had animal subjects, which perhaps were totems. Later, human figures prevailed. (See Figure 6-3.) There are indications that they served as fertility symbols: one even had the bone of an infant baked into it, perhaps expressing hope for safe childbirth, or for a healthy child to take the place of one who had died. J. Edward Kidder has suggested that the figurines' strange eyes were associated with the belief that the "eye is the direct line of communication with the soul."[1] Surviving from prehistoric times, these images evoke a powerful world of primitive magic.

Figure 6-2   Pottery vessel. Aomori, Middle Jōmon period, 44.2 cm high. Osaka University.

Figure 6-3   Jōmon figurine.

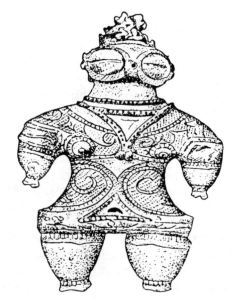

Figure 6-4 Pottery jar. Miyagi, Late Yayoi period 29.2 cm high. Tohoku University, Sendai.

Phallic-shaped stones are another indication of the prevalence of fertility cults. Other discoveries of the Jōmon period include the remains of pit dwellings, various stone implements, and articles of personal ornamentation such as earrings and amulets. Among the latter are late Jōmon stone *magatama*, comma-shaped ornaments also found in early Korean sites. Skulls found at archaeological sites provide evidence of tooth mutilation (certain teeth were removed at the age when boys and girls reached maturity), a practice originating in Southeast Asia. The figurines also suggest that these people tattooed their bodies—a custom reported in early Chinese accounts of Japan.

Yayoi Culture

Beginning in the third century B.C. Jōmon culture was gradually displaced by a new culture, which spread from Kyūshū east to the Kantō Plain. It is called the Yayoi culture after the section of Tokyo where the first archaeological finds were made. At first the new culture and the old had much in common. For example, the earliest Yayoi pottery is close in style to late Jōmon pottery and the custom of tooth mutilation did not disappear in Japan until toward the close of the Yayoi period. By then, however, a society had developed that was dramatically different from its predecessor.

A sense of the difference between the two cultures is suggested by the pottery illustrated in Figure 6-4. Yayoi ware is so even and graceful that for a long while the view prevailed that it was made on the potter's wheel. However, many scholars now believe that, like the Jōmon, it was made by coiling. Small at the base and thin at the neck, the vessel shown here is both functional and aesthetically pleasing. Indeed the shape was so pleasing and served so well that it was later developed into the standard form of the Japanese sake container, the form still in use today.

Other changes that occurred during the Yayoi included the introduction of wet-field rice cultivation, an innovation originating in continental Asia. Such excavations as those of a community near Shizuoka show that Yayoi rice was grown on irrigated paddies; even some of the perforated steamers used for cooking the rice have been recovered. Perhaps some of the crop was stored in the warehouses built on raised posts, a building technique widespread in Southeast Asia. Since there is also ample evidence that fishing was an important source of food, it would seem that not only the sake container but the basic elements of the Japanese diet as well date back to this time.

These changes in fundamental economic activity must have affected most aspects of life. For example, we know that intensive rice cultivation results in an increase in the economic resources of a society, encouraging population growth and geographic expansion. But since we are still dealing with a preliterate period, the impact of these changes on the social, political, and intellectual character of society is largely a matter of speculation. Evidence of links to the continent at this time come from archaeological sites that have yielded: glass beads, bracelets, and disks; iron and bronze weapons; bronze coins and mirrors. These objects reached Japan through the Chinese colony established by the Han in Korea and from native Korean tribes or states.

Various metal objects were also produced in Japan itself. Many locally made weapons have been found. Of particular interest are bronze bells, ranging in size from less than five inches to more than four feet, related in form to some Korean bells but, nevertheless, distinctly Japanese. Some are decorated in low relief, depicting various animals, or scenes that reveal something of daily life. For example, there are scenes of people pounding rice or using dogs to hunt a boar. The bells also portray the boats of the Yayoi and houses covered with thatched roofs.

The Tomb Period

Around the middle of the third century A.D., tomb mounds began to appear. Some of these were quite modest in scale, but others, particularly in the Kansai region, were very large. The most magnificent has been identified as that of "Emperor" Nintoku, the dates of whose reign have been calculated as about 395–427. It occupies eighty acres, is about 2695 feet long, and is of the popular "keyhole" shape (see Figure 6-5). Other tombs were round or square, and all shapes may be found with or without moats. Although such tombs continued to be built into the seventh century, it is convenient for purposes of historical periodization to end the tomb period around the middle of the sixth century when Buddhism became officially acknowledged in Japan. It was under Buddhist influence that the construction of these tumuli was gradually abandoned.

The sheer scale of Nintoku's tomb indicates an ability to put a large number of people to work. Although there is a great deal about the organization of society which remains unknown, there is ample evidence for the presence at this time of warriors who wore armor and rode horses. To account for the appearance of these warriors, scholars have speculated about a possible invasion from Korea. These views gain plausibility in the light of large-scale shifts of peoples on the continent in the fourth century, but the nature of the available historical data makes all historical reconstruction highly speculative.

On the Korean side of the equation, we do know that from the fourth century until the state of Silla unified Korea in 688, three states dominated the area. The oldest of these was Koguryŏ, the state that defeated the armies of the Sui and thereby helped to bring an end to that dynasty. Two other states, Paekche in the Southwest and Silla in the East shared the peninsula. Although each state had its own traditions, all three had been formed out of tribal confederations, which had coalesced into more permanent unions. Even though they were conversant with elements of Chinese civilization, the extent of Chinese influence on these Korean states should not be exaggerated, for this was a time when even at home, in a divided land, Chinese civilization was in retreat.

In the Southeast of the Korean Peninsula was an area identified as Kaya by the Koreans and Mimana by the Japanese. It is extremely difficult to reconstruct the history of this region, but it is clear that there was a close relationship between this area and people living in Southwest Japan, a relationship antedating the appearance of the mounted warriors in Japan.

Figure 6-5   Tomb of Emperor Nintoku, Mozu, Sakai City, Osaka. Middle Tomb period, total length approx. 815.5 m.

Figure 6-6   Folk art
paper showing various
haniwa.

During the next two centuries, numerous Koreans came to Japan, bringing
with them important aspects of mainland culture. One early contribution was
the potter's wheel, and it is hardly surprising that Korean influence is visible in
tomb period pottery. However, the period is best known for a uniquely Japanese kind of clay sculpture called *haniwa*, literally "clay circles," placed on
the outside of the tombs. These *haniwa* included cylindrical representations of
human figures, clay houses, boats, horses, and other animals. (See Figure 6-6.)
Figures of warriors dressed in armor and clay horses, along with bronze and iron
military equipment found inside the tombs, provide evidence for the presence
of mounted fighting men.

There is nothing grim or stern about the figures. The overwhelming impression one gets from groups of *haniwa* is one of warmth and even of joy.
They display no indication of pain, sorrow, or grief, such as one would expect
to find on a tomb. Many of the figures seem to dance and sing. Others depict
scenes of daily life: a poor peasant carrying a hoe, a figure offering a drink of
sake, a mother with a baby on her back. Some were merely elongated cylinders
with holes for eyes and mouth; and the features in others were often out of
proportion.

The Haniwa also provide evidence of the presence of female shamans, who
apparently played a very important role in early Japanese culture. The earliest Chinese accounts of Japan describe an unmarried queen named Pimiko,
who ruled the country of Yamatai with the help of a younger brother, and who
"occupied herself with magic and sorcery, bewitching the people."[2] She lived
in a grand palace and, when she died, was buried in a great mound. This calls to
mind the tumuli of the tomb period. Unfortunately the location of Yamatai
remains unknown, and the identity of Pimiko is also unclear. Yamatai may
refer to Yamato, the old capital district, and Pimiko may mean "sunprincess,"

in which case there would be a link to the origins of the Japanese ruling house, which claimed descent from the Sun Goddess and had its capital in the Yamato district. But, again, this is speculation.

In addition to the findings of archaeology and the accounts in Chinese texts, information concerning this period is found in the *Kojiki* (Record of Ancient Matters) and *Nihon Shoki* (History of Japan), which date from the eighth century but contain earlier materials. Incorporating a melange of legendary and semihistorical accounts, at times contradicting each other, and reflecting the political and intellectual needs of a later age, these books must be used with great care, but they do offer indispensable insights into Japanese antiquity and the Japanese conception of their own history. Here, for example, is found the first statement of the myth that Japanese emperors are of divine descent, a myth later used to sanctify the right to rule of the imperial house.

Shinto Legends and Beliefs

Later emperors claimed as their ancestor the legendary Emperor Jimmu, to whom they attributed the founding of the Japanese state in 660 B.C. The accounts reach back to an unsophisticated creation myth in which a divine brother and sister, Izanagi and Izanami, descend to earth and create the islands of Japan as well as a number of deities. Izanami died after giving birth to the god of fire, and Izanagi, like the Greek Orpheus, followed her to the world of the dead but was driven away by the putrifying condition of her body. When he then purified himself in a stream, a series of deities were born, of which Amataseru, the Sun Goddess, and Susa-no-ō, the storm god, were to be the most important. These two deities in turn produced a third generation of gods. At one point the Sun Goddess was so offended by the conduct of her uncouth husband-brother, who had damaged her rice fields and even defecated in her palace, that she retreated into a cave and refused to reappear, plunging the whole world into darkness. Fortunately the other deities devised an entertainment (which featured a lewd dance) and managed to lure her back out. Susa-no-ō was then banished to Izumo, where he became the progenitor of a line of rulers who were in constant conflict with a line of rulers descended from the Sun Goddess herself. Ninigi, a grandson of the Sun Goddess, settled in northern Kyūshū, bringing with him the three sacred imperial regalia: the mirror (symbol of the sun); the "herb-quelling great sword," which Susa-no-ō had discovered in the body of a giant eight-headed serpent; and a jewel *magatama*. Ninigi's grandson, in turn, fought his way successfully to Yamato, where as Emperor Jimmu he founded the imperial line. His descendants finally defeated the rulers of Izumo and brought other parts of Japan under their rule, but they continued to allow worship at the great shrine at Izumo.

Of the three regions in which these legends are set, Northern Kyūshū and Yamato have yielded abundant evidence for the existence of the tomb culture, but archaeology has not revealed the presence of a major center at Izumo. Nevertheless, the current shrine at Izumo is considered second in holiness only to that of the Sun Goddess herself at Ise. The buildings standing there today are not very old, for both have been rebuilt repeatedly. The shrine at Ise is rebuilt every twenty years. But because they are regarded with great reverence, they preserve certain essential features of very early Japanese architecture: a pleasing simplicity of design; the subtle use of natural materials such as unpainted and undecorated wood and the thatched roof (see Figure 6-7); and the sensitive care shown for the natural setting. But the word "setting" is not quite appropriate: for nature does not play a subordinate role; it is as much a part of the shrine as the building itself. Religious ceremonies were, no doubt, performed outdoors at these sacred places before there were any buildings at all, and it is quite likely that the idea of housing the deities was a foreign import.

Such closeness to nature is a part of early Japanese religious life as expressed in the native animism later termed Shinto, or "the way of the gods" (or spirits, *kami*). In the legendary beginning even rocks and plants could move and speak, and although mythical heroes later put an end to these troublesome powers, the *kami* continued to be identified with nature. They could be found in a special stone, a stream, an old tree, a mountain or any object felt to be imbued with some extraordinary quality. Stories about the *kami* were numerous but they were not systematized, nor were these localized spirits clearly visualized. Just as the *haniwa* are apparently cheerful figures, the religion associated with the *kami* apparently expressed a positive and optimistic attitude toward life. In it the defilements encountered in life could be overcome through ritual purification. These defilements were conceived in physical not ethical terms. Blood was defiling, for example, whether it was spilled on purpose, or by accident, or occurred in menstruation. This concern for ritual cleanliness, noted by the Chinese chroniclers, probably explains the great importance the Japanese have always attached to the bath. This early religion was no match for Buddhism intellectually or in terms of grandeur of vision, but the *kami* were intrinsic to the spiritual life of the communities that looked after them. The very absence of theoretical elaboration or doctrinal demands may have helped to give Shinto its remarkable staying power.

Social Organization

In early Japan, as elsewhere, religion was deeply identified with the prevailing social structure. During the tomb period the elite was organized into lineage groups or clans called *uji*, the members of which traced their descent to an alleged common ancestor, often a deity. The members of an *uji* shared in the worship of their *kami* thereby sanctioning and confirming their sense of solidarity. Each *uji* was headed by a chief who, as a direct descendant of the deity, served both as a head priest and as the patriarchal ruler. Usually the members of an *uji* lived in a specific geographic area, which they dominated by combining political and military power. The horses, weapons, and armor they used have been found by archaeologists.

Figure 6-7   Ise: The Inner Shrine.

Subject to the *uji* elite were the commoners, most of whom lived in villages and tilled the land. Others wove cloth, made pottery, brewed sake, and generally did society's work. They were not completely free, for they were organized into occupational communities called *be* that were governed and protected by the *uji*. The *uji* in turn derived their wealth and manpower from the *be* under their authority. At the bottom of the social scale were a small class of household slaves.

The Yamato State

In the course of time some *uji* became more powerful than others and were able to exert a measure of control over lesser lineages, which accepted a subordinate status. In this way larger political units were formed, and these, in turn, interacted, peacefully or militarily, in a process of political agglomeration. Largely because Japan's mountainous geography worked to the advantage of local power holders, the process of creating a large state was both slow and incomplete. Gradually, however, a single lineage came to occupy a position of authority on the Yamato Plain, the most extensive agricultural region of western Japan. This was the lineage that claimed descent from the Sun Goddess.

The Sun lineage acquired its status in part through the use of arms, but also by exploiting kinship ties and by forming marriage alliances. (The latter was facilitated by the practice of polygamy). The Sun lineage enjoyed the services of other *uji,* some of whom rendered certain military or ritualistic services and others who provided support in outlying areas. This was a highly flexible political system, kept in balance as much by manipulation as by force. The power balance might shift or be disrupted (by a recalcitrant chief or a struggle for the succession) but, on the whole, the system proved resilient.

A powerful inducement for other *uji* to accept the primacy of the Sun lineage was religious, for it was natural for the *uji* to conceive of society in terms of lineage and descent and to give primacy to the descendants of the prime deity. Just as the local *kami* protected their regions, so the Sun Goddess looked after the entire country. By implication, therefore, so should the Yamato line. Government and religion were conceived as one. Even the same word (*matsuri-goto*) was used for both.

During the fifth century the Yamato rulers increased in strength by subordinating the *uji* chiefs to the ruling house. One technique was to assign them places in an official hierarchy and gradually turn them into great ministers of state. However, this process did not proceed unchallenged. For not only the Yamato rulers but also the outlying *uji* were gaining economic and political strength. In the sixth century the power of the outlying *uji* threatened to get out of hand. Nevertheless, the long-term trend favored the center.

Late Yamato (552–710)*

Continental influences, at work since the beginning of the tomb period, became increasingly visible during the Late Yamato age. This tendency was furthered both by the presence of numerous Koreans in Japan and by continued contacts with Korea. Among the skills brought to Japan was the art of writing.

One of the main continental influences was Buddhism. Most likely the Japanese had been introduced to Buddhism before the middle of the sixth century, but in 552 the king of Paekche in Korea is said to have commended the religion to the Japanese and sent them some Buddhist texts and statues. By that time, Buddhism was well established in Paekche, which hoped for Japanese assistance in fighting neighboring Silla.

At the Yamato court the introduction of the new religion set off a bitter controversy. Opposing the acceptance of what they considered a powerful *kami* from abroad were two strong *uji*: the Nakatomi who served as Shinto ritualists and thus had a stake in the religious status quo, and the Mononobe, an *uji* with military responsibilities. Championing the cause of Buddhism were the Soga, who had come to prominence fairly late but enjoyed great influence because they intermarried with the Sun lineage. The Yamato ruler Kinmei (r. 540–71) had many children by his Soga consort to perpetuate the family's influence. The Soga's adoption of Buddhism may have been, in part, an effort to bolster and sanctify their power.

After consulting all sides, Kinmei presented a Buddhist image to the Soga, who established it in their home as their clan *kami*. Shortly afterward, how-

* This designation combines the periods known to art historians as Asuka (552–645) and Hakuhō (645–710).

ever, an epidemic broke out. The Soga's enemies claimed that the epidemic was caused by the local *kami*, angered at the Buddhist intrusion. Buddhism suffered a setback, and the image itself was reportedly thrown into a canal. Both the clan and the religion recovered, however, and in 587 the Soga defeated the Mononobe in war.

The victorious Soga leader, Umako, was now the most powerful man in the land, but he did not seek to displace the Yamato line. Instead, he first had a nephew assume the rulership and then, when this man proved insufficiently pliable, replaced him with a niece, Suiko (r. 592–628). Actual government, however, was conducted by the regent, Prince Shōtoku (Shōtoku Taishi) who became one of Japan's most revered figures. It is impossible now to separate legend from fact in the accounts of his life, but he appears to have been a most remarkable man. Part of his fame came from his generous patronage of Buddhism. He has been credited with sponsoring many temples, including the famous Hōryūji, and staffing them with clergy from Korea. In Korea itself he tried to restore a Japanese client state (Mimana) but without success. He then opened direct relations with China, recently unified by the Sui. Chinese records indicate that the Sui emperor was not amused on receiving a communication addressed, "from the emperor of the sunrise country to the emperor of the sunset country"; nevertheless, during the short Sui period, four Japanese missions were sent to China.

Direct contact with China increased Japanese receptivity to continental imports such as new religious ideas, the Chinese calendar, and concepts of government that the Japanese found useful in their attempt to build a stronger state. The new court ranks introduced in 603 were based on Chinese practice, and Chinese influence is pronounced in the famous seventeen-point "constitution" traditionally ascribed to Prince Shōtoku and dated 607. Its first article is a Confucian discourse on harmony. This is followed by a second commanding reverence for the three treasures of Buddhism (the Buddha, the Law, and the Order). Other articles call on subordinate officials to obey their superiors, and the subordinates are admonished to behave with decorum, avoid greed, be suspicious of flatterers and so on. The "constitution" affirmed the primacy of the sovereign and asserted the monopoly role of government in collecting taxes. Unlike modern constitutions, its purpose was not to organize a form of government, but to promulgate certain moral precepts that *ought* to characterize the conduct of government. Nevertheless, its objectives were clearly political: to strengthen the political power and moral standing of the state.

This was by no means an easy matter. Although the trend in these years was toward adoption of Chinese institutions and an increase in the strength of the central government, the process was neither smooth nor uninterrupted. The death of Prince Shōtoku in 622 led to bloody struggles that culminated in a coup d'etat in 645 led by an imperial prince and by the head of the Nakatomi, which had opposed the Soga from the beginning. This man, Nakatomi no Kamatari, was given the surname Fujiwara and became the founder of a family that was to dominate Japanese government off and on for centuries to come.

The anti-Soga group also included some men who had studied in China, and once in power, they not only continued the practice of sending missions to China but worked to further the adoption of Chinese practices. In 646 the new government proclaimed the Taika (Great Change) reforms. To effect greater control over outlying areas, a new system of provincial administration was announced and provisions were made for an extensive system of roads and post stations. Private ownership of land was abolished as were the *be*. Rice fields were now to be allotted on the model of the Chinese "equal field" system, with the fields reverting to the state for redistribution each generation. A new T'ang-style tax system was also proclaimed and a census ordered, an essential component for the functioning of the new system. The crown prince himself gave up his land to the state, but the implementation of the program was gradual and incomplete. For example, the first census was not taken until 670.

The Nara Period (710–784)

The Late Yamato period came to an end with the establishment, in 710, of a permanent capital at Nara, then called Heijō. Prior to 645 the capital had consisted simply of the ruler's palace, and its location changed with each ruler. (This may have been partly to avoid defilement, for according to Shinto belief a death polluted the place of its occurrence.) Changes in ruler, and hence changes in location, reflected the shifting political realities as rival *uji* maneuvered for power. The adoption of Chinese institutions of government required a more elaborate bureaucratic structure and more formal administrative procedures, however, and these in turn required government buildings: an audience hall, offices, and housing for officials and their staffs. Moving the capital became an increasingly complex business. Fujiwara, the last and largest of the seventh-century capitals, served three emperors before it was abandoned for Heijō.

Heijō was conceived and laid out as a miniature Ch'ang-an. The Japanese ruler was now an emperor in the Chinese sense, a virtuous "son of heaven." He ruled through a divine mandate, but unlike his Chinese counterpart, the Japanese emperor's mandate was irrevocable, entrusted for all time to the ruling house by virtue of divine descent. Chinese concepts were adopted to strengthen the throne, not to weaken it; and the Mencian idea that the mandate could be revoked was disregarded. Individual emperors might exercise a great deal of power, as did Emperor Temmu (r. 672–86) shortly before the Nara period and Emperor Kammu (r. 781–806) at its end, but even weak emperors continued to function as the country's chief priests. The continued importance of this native religious tradition in the Japanese concept of government and throne is also exemplified by the high prominence accorded the peculiarly Japanese Department of Deities, which looked after the imperial Shinto ritual. However, in many other respects Chinese political models were adopted.

Underlying the Nara system of government was the Taihō Code. Promulgated in 702, this body of law further implemented and extended the work of the Taika reforms. The bureaucratic structure of government was more closely modeled on that of the T'ang. The country was divided into three levels of administrative jurisdiction: provinces, districts, and villages. The peasantry was organized into village units whose members, as in China, were mutually responsible for each other's behavior. Rice lands were reorganized into square fields of a standard size. As in China, taxes were to be collected in kind: grain, textiles, and labor-service. In addition, the male population was liable to military conscription. Indeed, a continuing source of military manpower was essential in this period, when the Yamato state was constantly expanding its borders in Honshū and Kyūshū.

Also as in China, the land allotment system was not permitted to interfere with the wealth or status of aristocratic families or with the flourishing religious establishments, which enjoyed special privileges, such as immunity from taxation. Moreover, government office continued to be a prerogative of the wellborn. Government posts were filled by persons of appropriate rank, and rank was hereditary. The Japanese did not seek to broaden the composition of officialdom by adopting a Chinese-style examination system. Thus in Japan, despite much borrowing from the mainland (Buddhism, written language, government organization, law, tax systems, architecture, graded ranks, land reform), the principle of hereditary authority was retained inviolate. The emperor could not lose his right to the throne; aristocratic birth remained a prerequisite for a government post.

Nara Literary Culture

The oldest known literary works of Japan are the *Kojiki* and the *Nihon Shoki*. The former is completely mythological, and only the second half of the latter—that relating to late sixth-century and seventh-century Japan—can be considered historical. The two books helped to preserve and perpetuate the old Shinto legends. However, the authors did more than just compile old traditions. The legends were arranged and presented in ways that would bolster claims of the imperial house to supernatural as well as historical legitimization. Genealogies of the leading aristocratic families were also incorporated in them for the same purpose. In this way, the characteristically Chinese practice of recording the past was adopted to serve Japanese ends.

Both works were written in the Chinese script, the only form of writing available in Japan during the Nara period, but they differ in that the *Nihon Shoki* is written in Chinese while the *Kojiki* is written in a very difficult mixed style that sometimes employs the Chinese characters for their meaning but at other times uses them merely to represent the sounds of eighth-century Japanese.

There are also two famous collections of poetry from this period: the *Man'yōshū* (*Collection of Ten Thousand Leaves*), a collection of roughly 4500 poems, completed around the middle of the eighth century; and the *Kaifūsō*, an anthology completed about the same time. The *Man'yōshū* was written using Chinese symbols to transliterate the spoken Japanese, while the *Kaifūsō* was, in effect, Chinese poetry written by Japanese. It is hardly surprising that the poems written by Japanese in their own language are of superior literary merit.

The *Man'yōshū* poems range widely in form, authorship, and subject. However, the most commonly used poetic form is the *tanka*, a verse in which thirty-one syllables are arranged in five lines in a pattern of 5–7–5–7–7 syllables. Because the Japanese language has a relative absence of stresses while having a superabundance of rhyming possibilities, neither stress nor rhyme have played an important role in Japanese poetry. Hence the relatively greater emphasis on length and balance of lines. As Earl Miner has suggested, the language was so fluid and free that "for centuries only one form, the *tanka*, seemed able to contain it."[3] Already in the *Man'yōshū* the *tanka* prevails, but there are also poems of up to 149 lines. The finest poet included in the *Man'yōshū* is Kakinomoto Hitomaro. Although he also wrote *tanka*, his best poems are longer. Among them is his "On Seeing the Body of a Man Lying among the Stones on the Island of Samine in Sanuki Province." It begins:

> O the precious land of Sanuki,
> Resting where the seaweed glows like gems!
> Perhaps for its precious nature
> I never tire in my gazing on it,
> Perhaps for its holy name
> It is the most divine of sights.
> It will flourish and endure
> Together with the heaven and earth,
> With the shining sun and moon,
> For through successive ages it has come down
> That the landface is the face of a god.[4]

The poem reflects an abiding Japanese love of the land. This quality is an inherent aspect of the Shinto heritage, with its veneration for spirits of the local countryside (*kami*). It is important to bear in mind that the spread of Buddhism in seventh- and eighth-century Japan represented the overlay of one religion on the other, not the replacement of Shinto by Buddhism. The melding of Shinto sensibilities with Buddhist aesthetics was to create a highly refined, beautiful, and evocative artistic tradition.

Early Japanese Buddhism and the Arts

Through the Late Yamato and Nara periods Buddhism continued to exercise a varied appeal. The spiritual content of its religious message was only one, and by no means the dominant, element in this appeal. Many were drawn to Buddhism by the potency of its rituals and the reputed efficacy of its healing power, as is shown by the popularity of the Buddha of Healing (Yakushi). It is hardly surprising that the finest large surviving bronze sculpture of the Nara period is a triad in which the figure of the Healing Buddha occupies the central

Figure 6-8   The Hōryūji, Nara Prefecture.

place. The sculpture is housed in the "Temple of the Buddha of Healing" (Ya-kushiji), which was built by order of an emperor worried by the illness of his consort.

Within the temples, as in Western monasteries, monks and nuns, under the direction of an abbot or abbess, read and copied the scriptures and performed various solemn religious rites, including the chanting of the sutras. Thereby, they hoped to advance not only their own salvation but also to contribute to the welfare of their patrons, who frequently were members of the royal family. Indeed, it was common practice for the emperor to encourage Buddhism and to endow Buddhist temples in an effort to obtain divine protection and acquire religious merit. This is similar to the religious patronage practiced in China, or in Europe where Christian monarchs built cathedrals, endowed religious estab-lishments, and went on crusades. In times of crisis, when the emperor was ill or the state in danger, men and women were even coerced into taking orders and entering a monastery or nunnery, in an act of forced piety.

Japanese Temples

There is no finer expression of the aesthetic impulse of Nara Japan than the emergence of its temple architecture and related arts. The oldest surviving temple, which, incidentally boasts the oldest wooden buildings in the world, is the Hōryūji, near Nara. The original structure, erected by Prince Shōtoku, was rebuilt after being destroyed by fire in 670. Figure 6-8 shows the nucleus of the temple, a quadrangle enclosed by a cloistered walk. Equal emphasis is accorded

Figure 6-9 Kudara Kannon. Painted wood, Asuka period, 204.8 cm high. Hōryūji, Nara Prefecture.

the pagoda and the Golden Hall, balanced against each other at opposite ends of the north–south axis. This layout was characteristic of the temples of the Nara region, but in subsequent temples the Golden Hall was given greater prominence, and there was some experimentation with alternate possible locations for the pagoda. As in China, some temples had double pagodas.

Other buildings commonly found in temples included a lecture hall, usually located to the north or back, a sutra repository to store the scriptures, a belfry, a refectory, and buildings to house monks in their cells. The major buildings stood on a stone base and were roofed in clay tile. Again as in China, these heavy roofs were supported by a system of bracketing that in itself contributed greatly to the aesthetics of the building. Large exterior wooden units were painted red, yellow paint covered the crosscut faces of the brackets, rafters, and so on, and other, intervening spaces were painted white. In their orientation, structure, and ornamentation these were basically continental buildings.

The art housed in these temples was also basically continental; frequently the work of Korean and Chinese artists and craftsmen. Indeed, Nara period temples in Japan are our best source for studying Chinese Buddhist art up through the T'ang in its temporal and regional variations. The Hōryūji itself is a great treasure house. Here we shall mention only two of its most famous sculptures. One is a triad that looks like a bronze version of a Northern Wei stone sculpture. It is signed by an artist whose grandfather came from China and is dedicated to Prince Shōtoku. As Robert Paine has noted, the flatness of this sculpture and its frontal approach are logical consequences of the techniques needed for rock carving but are unrelated to bronze casting, which begins with a model in clay. "An accepted traditionalism, not questions of material, directed these early sculptures in Japan."[5] Another major piece, surely one of the most lovely figures in the Hōryūji, is the Kudara Kannon (which, since "Kudara" is Japanese for "Paekche," is a reminder of the Korean provenance of so much in Japanese Buddhism). The overall effect of this elongated figure is one of great elegance and grace. (See Figure 6-9.)

Figure 6-10 Detail of Maitreya (Miroku). Wood, Asuka period. (The full figure appears on p. 77.)

Also representative of the best temple art of the period is the figure of Maitreya, the Buddha of the future (see Figure 6-10), with its shared Chinese and Korean ancestry, and its remarkable aesthetic fusion of piety and sensuousness. This figure belongs to a temple in Kyōto that traces its origins, although not its current buildings, to Prince Shōtoku. It is a visual reminder of the spiritual, philosophical, and artistic influence of Buddhism in East Asia and of the role of Buddhism in creating linked cultures throughout the region.

The Hōryūji also contains material for the study of painting. The earliest painting is found on the Tamamushi (Jade-Beetle) shrine, so named because it was decorated with iridescent beetle wings set into metal edging, a technique also practiced in Korea. The scene, shown in Figure 6-11, derives from a famous story concerning an earlier incarnation of Sakyamuni. It shows the future Buddha sacrificing himself to feed a starving mother tiger unable to feed her young. The painting, like the story, begins at the top where the future Buddha is shown hanging his clothes on a tree, and it ends at the bottom where the tigress is devouring him. Its linear effects and the elongation of the figure fit in nicely with the general style of the Asuka period. The Hōryūji also contained frescoes that were an important source for the study of T'ang-style painting. They were destroyed by fire in 1949 but can still be studied from photographs.

The Hōryūji was just one of the temples built before the construction of the capital at Nara, where during the eighth century T'ang arts and T'ang styles flourished. The spirit of T'ang architecture is well illustrated by the Golden Hall of the Tōshōdaiji (see Figure 6-12) as seen when one enters the temple

Figure 6-11 *Tamamushi Shrine.* Lacquer on wood, seventh century, 233.7 cm high. Hōryūji, Nara Prefecture.

through the south gate. Although the original roof was more sloping and less steep than the present version, the illustration gives a good idea of the self-assured strength of T'ang building at its best. The careful symmetry of its proportions is exemplified by the bays: the central bay measures sixteen *shaku* (about 25.29 centimeters); the next bay on each side is reduced to fifteen *shaku*; the third set of bays measure thirteen; the end bays (not visible in the illustration) measure eleven *shaku*. The result is a handsome building with the emphasis on the center. Similarly, whereas in the Golden Hall of the Hōryūji the altar was square and therefore ideal for the rite of circumambulation (ritual walking around an "altar"), in the Tōshōdaiji it has been replaced by a rectangular platform affording the central Buddha a position of enhanced prominence.

The Tōshōdaiji was founded by the Chinese monk Chien-chen (pronounced "Ganjin" in Japanese), who finally reached Japan on his sixth attempt, having earlier been frustrated by storms, pirates, shipwrecks, and once by the Chinese authorities. By the time he reached Japan, he had lost his sight. His portrait (see Figure 6-13) is housed at Tōshōdaiji. It is constructed in the dry lacquer technique in which layers of cloth and lacquer are alternately built up, usually on a wooden frame. It is an important starting point for Japanese portrait sculpture,

Figure 6-12   ABOVE, Tōshōdaiji, Nara.
BELOW, Tōshōdaiji: side elevation.

Figure 6-13   *Portrait of Ganjin* (Chien-chen). Dry lacquer, mid-eighth century, 80.7 cm high. Tōshōdaiji, Nara.

as well as being a reminder of the courage and devotion shown by the early Buddhist missionary monks and of the serenity that was their earthly reward.

The main Buddha at Tōshōdaiji is Vairocana, the cosmic Buddha of the Hua-yen sect, called Kegon in Japanese. It was for this Buddha that the most ambitious Nara temple was built, the Tōdaiji. The casting of the Great Buddha, fifty-three feet high and requiring over one million pounds of metal, was a great technical achievement and a truly national undertaking requiring contributions from all quarters. The final act was the painting in of the pupils of the eyes by an Indian monk. This was the highlight of a great celebration, held in 752 amid universal rejoicing, at which ten thousand monks were presented with a vegetarian feast. It was surely one of the most magnificent spectacles in Japanese history. Unfortunately, the present figure in the Tōdaiji has been so much restored that it probably bears little resemblance to the original.

The Tōdaiji was the head temple of the land, for in Japan as in China Hua-yen doctrines appealed to centralizing rulers. The government was also the sponsor of Buddhism in the provinces. In 741 an edict was promulgated requiring that a Buddhist temple and pagoda be established in every province. Each temple was to have twenty monks and ten nuns who were to chant sutras and perform other religious ceremonies on behalf of the emperor and the state. At the same time, however, it was believed that the well-being of the country was impossible without the cooperation of the ancient *kami* as well. Efforts were made to assure the friendly coexistence of the old spirits with the divinities of the new religion. The consent of the Sun Goddess was duly obtained for the construction of the image of the Great Buddha himself as a form of the "Sun Buddha" (Dainichi). Meanwhile, Shinto shrines protected Buddhist temples by ensuring that the local *kami* would welcome them, and Buddhist altars extended their benefits to Shinto gods. Buddhist monks also found room for Shinto deities by treating them as avatars, or manifestations, of their own divinities. One major divinity, Hachiman, was both a Shinto *kami* and a Buddhist bodhisattva. This coexistence between the two religions began at a time when Buddhism itself was only just beginning to filter down to the common people, and probably hastened its acceptance.

Far removed from the eyes of the common people were the treasures housed in a remarkable building that was originally part of the Tōdaiji. Called the Shōsōin, it is a great repository of eighth-century secular art. Like other Japanese storehouses it stands on pillars and is built of logs. These logs expand when it is humid (keeping out moist air) and contract in dry weather (providing ventilation). Inside the Shōsōin are nine or ten thousand objects: books, weapons, mirrors, screens, silks, and objects of gold, lacquer, mother-of-pearl, and glass. Objects used in the dedication ceremonies of the Great Buddha are there. There are even goods from China, India, Persia, Greece, and Rome, testifying to Japanese participation in the cosmopolitan culture of the eighth century. A similar openness to the world is evident elsewhere, in court music for example, which shows Persian influence. Perhaps some of this music was played on the instruments preserved in the Shōsōin.

The Move from Nara

The attempt to turn Japan into a miniature T'ang encountered numerous obstacles in the eighth century, but the problem that finally induced the court to abandon the old capital was similar to one also encountered in China. The Buddhist establishment had attracted such wealth and power that it became a threat to the state. The danger was highlighted by the notorious career of the priest Dōkyō and his relationship to the ex-empress Kōken (r. 749–58), who resumed the throne in 764 to rule as Empress Shōtoku until her death in 770. Seduced by the charms of the priest, this empress housed him in the palace, bestowed on him the highest office of the state, and in 769 even gave him a title used exclusively by abdicated emperors entering the priesthood. Then Dōkyō overreached himself by trying for the throne itself. He encountered strong resistance but was protected as long as the empress remained alive. When she died, however, his political enemies had their revenge and drove him into banishment. There followed a reaction not only against ambitious Buddhist clerics but also against female rulers. After this, there were to be only two more empresses in Japanese history—one in the seventeenth century and one in the eighteenth century.

The Japanese dealt with the problem posed by the power of the Nara sects and the ambitions of their priests by circumvention rather than suppression. The decision to move was made by Emperor Kammu, a strong minded ruler. Nara was abandoned in 784, and after an unsuccessful attempt to establish the capital at another site, it was transferred to Heian, modern Kyōto, in 794. With this move there came to an end the era in which Japan acquired continental ideas, and the process of adaptation and transformation began. The change was not abrupt—the new capital also was modeled on Ch'ang-an—but during the Heian period the divergence between Japan and the continent became increasingly marked.

NOTES

1. J. Edward Kidder, *Japan Before Buddhism* (New York: Frederick A. Praeger, 1966), p. 73.
2. Ryusaku Tsunoda, *Japan in the Chinese Dynastic Histories* (Kyōto: Perkins Oriental Books, 1968), p. 20.
3. Earl Miner, *An Introduction to Japanese Court Poetry* (Stanford: Stanford University Press, 1968), p. 22.
4. *Ibid.*, p. 48.
5. Robert Treat Paine and Alexander Soper, *The Art and Architecture of Japan* (Baltimore: Penguin Books, 1955), p. 12.

平安時代之日本

Military Intervention and Control

	794	858		1068	1156	1185
	Period of Imperial Assertion	Fujiwara Dominance Michinaga in Power (995–1027)		Revival Imperial Family *In* system, 1086–1156		
Art History	Jōgan (Kōnin, Early Heian)		Fujiwara (Late Heian)			

897

7 *Heian Japan*

The Heian period began with a vigorous assertion of imperial power under Emperor Kammu. However, the long-term trend was in the opposite direction. The aristocracy, not the emperor, dominated the age and created a refined culture that left a permanent mark on Japanese life and perceptions of the world.

By keeping the temples out of the new capital of Kyōto and by patronizing the new Tendai and Shingon sects, which had their headquarters in the mountains, Emperor Kammu was able to evade the political influence of the old, city-based orders. Equally energetic and innovative in secular matters, he established new agencies to advise the throne and enforce its decisions, appointed inspectors to examine the books of retiring provincial governors, and replaced the ineffective conscript army with a militia system. In this way he and his immediate successors were able, for almost half a century, to rule in the spirit of the Taika Reforms and the Taihō Code.

This period of imperial assertion was followed by two centuries during which the Fujiwara family enjoyed political and economic ascendance, reducing the throne to an impotence reminiscent of the days of Soga domination. But the Fujiwara remained content to dominate emperors and did not seek to displace the imperial house. During most of subsequent Japanese history as well, emperors continued to function as titular heads of government, symbols of legitimization and objects of veneration, without actual political power. They were manipulated rather than removed, for the religious aura of the imperial person was based on his family's unique divine descent. There is nothing quite comparable to this phenomenon in Western history.

The Fujiwara

The Fujiwara house was founded by Nakatomi no Kamatari, head of the Nakatomi clan who played the leading role in the coup of 645. He was rewarded with the name Fujiwara, literally "wisteria plain," an apparent reference to the wisteria arbor where the anti-Soga plotters met. Kamatari's son Fuhito (659–720) continued the family's influence. He headed the committee that drew up the Taihō Code and became the father-in-law of two emperors and the grandfather of another. After that the family fortunes had their ups and downs, but the Fujiwara continued to be an important factor in Nara politics. For example, the opposition to the priest Dōkyō was led by a Fujiwara. The Fujiwara clan was itself divided into four main branches. It was a subbranch of one of these (the Northern, or "Hokke" branch) that gained power in the Heian period.

Intermarriage with the imperial family was one of the keys to Fujiwara power. The period of Fujiwara dominance is usually dated from 858, the year Fujiwara Yoshifusa (804–72), Grand Minister since 857, placed his own eight-year-old grandson on the throne and assumed the title of Regent for a Minor (sesshō). This was the first time anyone outside the imperial family had filled this position. Yoshifusa was succeeded by his nephew Mototsune (836–91), who was the first to continue as regent even after the emperor was no longer a minor, assuming for that purpose the new title of kampaku, designating a regent for an adult emperor. It was as regents that the Fujiwara institutionalized their power.

The ambitions of this family did not go uncontested. After Mototsune died in 891, there was an interlude without a Fujiwara regent until Tadahira (sesshō, 939–41; kampaku, 941–49) continued the tradition. Most famous of the opponents of the Fujiwara was Sugawara no Michizane (843–903). A noted scholar and calligrapher, he enjoyed great influence for a time but eventually could not withstand the Fujiwara political machinations and ended as a virtual exile in a provincial post. There he died, but his ghost reputedly returned to punish his enemies, leading to a brilliant posthumous career. To put an end to a series of storms, floods, droughts, fires, and other calamities attributed to his angry spirit, he was promoted several times and finally became the patron god of letters and calligraphy, worshipped at the Kitano shrine erected in his honor in the capital.

Other rivals of the Fujiwara were considerably less successful, although the leading Fujiwara statesmen were never without at least some opposition, usually from other branches of the Fujiwara clan. A high point in Fujiwara power was reached under Michinaga (966–1027) who demonstrated great skill in the intrigue and political infighting necessary to succeed at court. He was especially skilled at marriage politics, for he managed to marry four daughters to emperors, two of whom were also his grandsons. Emperors who were the sons of Fujiwara mothers and married to Fujiwara consorts were unlikely to resent the influence of the great family, let alone to resist it. Michinaga himself felt so secure that, although he did become a *sesshō*, he never assumed the title of *kampaku*, preferring the reality to the trappings of power. His successors, however, resumed the title while continuing to derive legitimacy and prestige from their close association with the imperial family. In the meantime, as the emperor's political power waned, his sacerdotal role grew even more important. Indeed the ritual and ceremonial demands on the throne were so great that when the imperial family reasserted its power in the eleventh century, the lead was taken by abdicated emperors who by resigning had freed themselves from the burdensome routine of official observances.

The importance of marriage politics and control of the emperor should not be underestimated, but lasting political power usually is linked to some kind of economic power, and Heian Japan is no exception. In their heyday the Fujiwara were the wealthiest family in the land; their mansions outshone the imperial palace. To understand the source and nature of their wealth, it is necessary to examine changes in Japan's basic economic institutions, changes that had their origins in the Nara period but reached their fruition in Heian times. At the heart of these changes was the development of *shōen*, or estates.

The Shōen

The *shōen* were private landholdings essentially outside of government control. Since there is nothing quite like them in Western history, we are forced to use the Japanese term.

The origins of the *shōen* go back to the Nara period. It will be recalled that Japan had adopted the Chinese "equal field" system for distributing land to peasant cultivators and redistributing the land again upon the proprietor's death. Certain lands were exempt, however: (1) those held by the imperial family and certain aristocratic families, (2) those granted to the great Buddhist temples and Shinto shrines, and (3) agricultural lands "reclaimed" from their original wild state. At first, to encourage opening new lands, lands were assigned for several generations. In the eighth century the law was changed so that they could be retained in perpetuity. Furthermore, there was a natural tendency for all land assignments to become hereditary. This was true of lands assigned to accompany certain ranks and offices and also of lands assigned to cultivators. The complicated and foreign system of land redistribution fell into abeyance, and the last recorded redistribution of land in the central provinces took place in 844.

The development of private landholdings was accompanied by the growth of tax exemptions granted to influential aristocrats and temples. In the course of time, these tax exemptions were broadened to include other privileges such as immunity from inspection or interference by local provincial government officials, who were thus deprived of administrative authority over the shōen. They could not even enter the estates.

Landholdings of this type first appeared in the eighth century and grew thereafter largely by a process of commendation. Small landholders placed their fields under the protection of those powerful enough to enjoy tax exemption and immunities. Thus, a small relatively powerless local landholder might assign his land to a richer and more influential family or religious institution, retaining the right to cultivate the land in exchange for a small rent, less than he would have had to pay to the tax collector. In this way he secured an economic advantage and received protection from the exactions and pressures of the local officials. The new proprietor might in turn commend the land to one of the truly powerful families such as the Fujiwara with their high status at the capital. To obtain their protection, he would in his turn cede certain rights. Furthermore, since the proprietor was usually an absent landlord living in the capital area, he required the services of administrators, and these men too received certain rights to income from the land. These rights, called shiki and entitling the bearer to a certain portion or percentage of the income from the land, could be divided, passed on to one's heirs, or even sold. As a result the system became very complicated—one man might hold different kinds of shiki in one estate and/or hold shiki in several estates. Women too could hold these rights and were able to enjoy an independent source of income not unlike the modern owners of stocks and bonds.

It was a complicated system, but essentially four levels of people were associated with an individual shōen in what Elizabeth Sato characterizes as a "hierarchy of tenures."[1] At the bottom of the scale were the cultivators (shōmin). Above them were the "managers" known variously as "local lords" or "proprietors" (ryōshu), members of influential families resident in the shōen (shōke), and officials (shōkan). Still another step up were the "central proprietors" (ryōke), and at the top of the ladder were the patrons (honke). Frequently the patrons lived, not in the shōen, but at court in the capital.

The appearance and steady growth of large holdings of land outside government jurisdiction continued despite sporadic efforts by the government to halt the process by decree, for those who controlled the government themselves profited from the growth of *shōen*. As a result, it has been estimated that by the twelfth century 90 percent of the land was incorporated into *shōen*. This development naturally had a profound effect on government, and led to an increasing divergence from the Chinese prototypes adopted during the Nara period.

Government and Administration

Since the *shōen* were beyond government jurisdiction, the growth of these lands led to a decline in the power of the government and a decrease in government revenue. Those who operated the government themselves depended on private sources of income. In a gradual but irreversible process, the procedures of the government became increasingly divorced from the exercise of real power. As so often occurs in Japanese history, the old structures were retained even after they ceased to fulfill the purposes for which they had been intended. As their sphere of action shrank, officials became preoccupied with lengthy deliberations on the phrasing of documents and subtle points of ceremonial. In filling official vacancies, birth was the important criterion, and knowledge of precedent the most essential accomplishment. Skill in intrigue, wealth, and good looks were more important assets for the official than intellectual or administrative ability. The emphasis on form was consistent with the Confucian insistence on *li* (propriety, rites, ceremony) and was reinforced by the ethos of the Heian aristocracy, which valued good taste above everything else. It was in keeping with the times that form was stressed at the expense of function, or indeed that form became function.

There were officials who took their duties seriously, and the capital continued to provide the arena where the great families competed for status and its benefits, but the deterioration of the government machinery also took its toll. Not even the basic institutions for maintaining order were exempt. For example, pedigree, not ability, determined who was appointed chief of the Imperial Police. This agency had been established in the early ninth-century reassertion of imperial power and in its heyday exercised wide powers in the capital and even in the provinces. It was the only official source of armed support for the throne. But by the time of Michinaga it lacked the strength even to secure the capital against internal disruptions and disorders. Already in 981 unruly priests from the Tendai monastery on Mt. Hiei marched through the streets of the capital to press their demands without encountering effective resistance, and in 1040 robbers found their way into the imperial palace itself and made off with some of the emperor's clothes.

Clearly government was no longer functioning as it had in Nara or during the period of vigorous imperial rule in early Heian. The period of Fujiwara ascendancy can therefore be considered a time of deterioration in government, a view not inconsistent with the economic growth produced by the opening of new lands, for not only in Japan have old political institutions often been undermined by positive economic developments. However, to focus on the decline of the imperial government may blur the part played by nonofficial but perfectly legal institutions in de facto government, now largely in private lands.

What affected the lives of the people on the *shōen* were not the decisions reached at court but rather those made by the aristocratic families or temples that served as the *shōen*'s patrons. To administer their shōen holdings (and household affairs), these patrons had a *mandokoro*, translated by G. Cameron Hurst as "administrative council." He describes the Fujiwara *mandokoro* as having the following components:

> A documents bureau (*fudono*) "for handling complaints and other types of correspondence"
>
> A secretariat (*kurōdo-dokoro*)
>
> A retainer's office (*samurai-dokoro*) "to coordinate the activities of the warriors in the service of the household"
>
> A stable (*mimaya*)
>
> An attendant's bureau (*zushin-dokoro*) "to control the attendants allotted by the court to high-ranking nobles"
>
> An Office of Court Dress (*gofuku-dokoro*)
>
> A provisions bureau (*shimmotsu-dokoro*), which "handled the receipt and storage of rice and other grains, vegetables, fish, and other foods for the household's meals"
>
> A cook's bureau (*zen-bu*) "in charge of the actual preparation of food"[2]

There was also a Judicial Office (*monchūjo*) for administering justice in those *shōen* where this right belonged to the patron.

Sato describes the administrative process by which the patrons governed the *shōen* as follows:

Matters regarding the transmission, receipt, and distribution of income from the shōen were handled by the shōke's *mandokoro* (administrative office), which communicated directly with the managerial office of the shōen (*honjo*). When the honjo was located on the shōen, the original ryōshu or his descendants as shōke, were responsible for the day-to-day affairs of the shōen. These included assignment of fields to cultivators, distribution of seed and implements, regulation of water supply, collection of revenues, and, if full immunity had been obtained, administration of justice. As one of the chief officials of the honjo of the shōen, the shōke was responsible for forwarding revenues to superior proprietors.

When the honjo of the shōen was in the capital the shōke acted as agent of the absentee proprietor, working primarily as an overseer rather than as an administrator. In some cases, special agents were dispatched from the capital to serve as officials of the shōen.[3]

The Warriors

The Fujiwara were a family of civilian aristocrats who preferred intrigue to war and shared the disdain for the military that was prevalent among the Heian aristocracy. No society seems able to dispense with force entirely, however. Prior to the introduction of conscription and peasant armies, most fighting had been done by *uji* fighting men, that is, trained clan warriors. This class of fighters never disappeared. As less and less land was administered under the "equal field" system, raising conscript armies became less and less practical. In 792, two years before the move to Kyōto, the conscription system was abolished. The central government no longer had the means to raise armies—except as the emperor or his ministers raised fighting men in their own domains—and military power and responsibilities passed to government officials and great families in the provinces.

Since fighting involved costly equipment, such as horse and armor, and training in special techniques, such as archery and swordsmanship, it remained the profession of a rural elite. This elite included former civilian provincial officials to whom the government had delegated military powers, managers who rose within the *shōen* system and were entrusted with defense responsibilities on the estates, and the trained warriors that they formed into bands of fighting men. The development of local warrior organizations varied according to different conditions in different regions of Japan. It was especially prominent in the eastern part of the Kantō region, still a rough frontier area, where formidable warrior leagues grew and clashed.

It was fighting men of this type who kept order in the provinces, performing both police and military functions, as well as fighting for various patrons as they jockeyed for power. For example, such warrior organizations fought on both sides in the Masakado Rebellion (935). Taira no Masakado (d. 940) was a fifth generation descendant of Emperor Kammu. It was the practice in Japan for the descendants of an emperor who were not in the line of succession to be cut off from the imperial line after a certain number of generations, in order to keep the size of the imperial family within manageable limits. At that time they would be given a family name and endowed with rich official posts in the capital or the provinces. Their wealth and distinguished ancestry made them the elite of the provincial elite. Two of the greatest warrior families in Japan had such ex-imperial origins: the Taira (also known as Heike) and the Minamoto (or Genji). The Masakado Rebellion was put down only with great difficulty. At the time of Masakado's Rebellion in the East, there was trouble also in the West. Sent to suppress piracy on the Inland Sea, Fujiwara no Sumitomo (d. 941) instead turned outlaw himself. In the restoration of order, Minamoto no Tsunemoto (d. 961) played a leading role. His son later established an alliance with the Fujiwara house. This branch of the Minamoto, the Seiwa branch or Seiwa Genji, became in effect the Fujiwara's military arm, its "claws and teeth," or, less complimentary, its "running dogs."

In the eleventh century there was more fighting in the Kantō area, with wars from 1028 to 1031, smaller scale fighting between 1051 and 1062, and another war from 1083 to 1087. These wars provided opportunities for building up the strength of the Minamoto in eastern and northern Honshū, so that they became the strongest force in this area, while the Ise branch of the Taira was developing strength in the Inland Sea area and also around the capital. At the same time, in the second half of the eleventh century, the Fujiwara went into decline, their manipulation of marriage politics hampered by a shortage of daughters. Emperor Go-Sanjo (r. 1068–72) came to the throne because his brother's Fujiwara empress was childless. Although he was opposed by the Fujiwara regent, he enjoyed the support of another powerful Fujiwara noble, and this support insured his success.

The revival of the imperial family begun by Go-Sanjo was continued by his son Shirakawa, who became emperor in 1072. He abdicated in 1086 but continued to enjoy great power as retired emperor (In) until his death in 1129. Two more vigorous heads of the imperial line followed, Toba (r. 1107–23; In, 1129–56) and Go-Shirakawa (r. 1155–58; In, to 1192).

The role of the retired emperor (In) was not unlike that of the Fujiwara regent, except that in place of the paramountcy of the family of the emperor's mother, the paternal family now attained supremacy. The resemblance to the Fujiwara went still further, for, despite the ambivalence of Shirakawa, the general policy of the abdicated emperors was to acquire for the imperial family the same type of assets enjoyed by the Fujiwara. As a result the imperial house acquired a vast network of estates and was transformed into the largest land-holder in Japan.

The political situation at this time could and did get very complicated when there was more than one retired emperor on the scene. The ambitions and machinations of the courts, the Fujiwara, and the temples (which had their own armed forces) all contributed to political instability and complicated the politics and the life of the capital. Much of the substance of power continued to shift to the provincial warrior organizations employed by both the imperial and the Fujiwara families to foster their causes, but which soon supplanted them.

The system came to an end under Go-Shirakawa. In 1156 military power was, for the first time, directly involved in capital political disputes; and once the warriors had been called in they could not readily be dismissed. By 1160 the Taira clan were in control of the government. Kyōto remained the political center until 1185, but the last twenty years or so do not really form part of the Heian period. Rather, they constitute an interlude of warrior power that can best be considered as an overture to the Kamakura period. Yet, for another seven hundred years, until 1869, the imperial family and the Fujiwara remained in Kyōto, and the Fujiwara still provided most of the regents. Indeed the Fujiwara family grew so large that men came to be called by the names of the branch families, and even in the twentieth century a member of one of these Fujiwara branches (Konoe) became a prime minister.

The Life of the Heian Aristocracy

Literature is our best source for the study of Heian society, which produced some of Japan's greatest prose and poetry. Its art diaries and other literary works furnish details of the daily life of the upper classes and insights into their values and taste. Most Heian authors were court ladies, and their feminine view of life at the top is unique in the history of East Asia and perhaps the world. Japan's greatest prose work, *The Tale of Genji* was composed by one such woman, Murasaki Shikibu (978–ca. 1016).

The literary eminence of Heian ladies itself suggests something of their social status. Obviously they had ample leisure for reading and writing; *The Tale of Genji* is twice as long as Tolstoy's *War and Peace*. Often they suffered from an excess of leisure. They became bored with long days of inactivity spent in the dimly lit interiors of their homes and welcomed the chance to exchange pleasantries and gossip with an occasional caller. If the caller was a man, he had to conduct the visit seated in front of a screen behind which the lady remained demurely hidden. Fortunately, there were numerous festivals to break up the monotony of the daily routine, and pilgrimages to temples provided further diversion.

Although there were also men who had literary inclinations and the means to pursue them, prose literature was considered the woman's domain; so much so that when Ki no Tsurayuki (869–945) composed the *Tosa Diary*, he pretended that it was written by a woman. Conversely, men continued to be educated in Chinese, which enjoyed undiminished prestige and remained the official language. This Chinese erudition constituted a male preserve from which women were excluded. For them it was not considered a respectable pastime, and those among them who nevertheless indulged in Chinese learning made it a point not to broadcast the fact. Nor was it proper for women to write in Chinese—instead they wrote Japanese using a mixture of Chinese characters and the *kana* syllabary, which now made its appearance. This was a system of phonetic symbols, originally derived from Chinese characters. (See Figure 7-1.) Each symbol represents a syllable. With this system there is no longer any need to employ Chinese characters to represent Japanese sounds, but they were retained nevertheless, since Japanese has numerous homonyms. In the modern language, the Chinese characters, used to write nouns and the stems of verbs and adjectives, float in a sea of *kana*, representing particles, endings, and certain other common words. (Foreign words, however, are today written in an alternate *kana* system) In modern Japan everyone uses this mixed system of writing, but during the Heian period it was used by women. Excluded from writing in Chinese, they were left free to express themselves in their own native language, and in the process they composed the classic works of Japanese prose.

The world described in this literature is a small one for it concerns only a tiny fraction of the Japanese people, those at the pinnacle of society in the capital. Although there are descriptions of travel outside the capital area, the focus

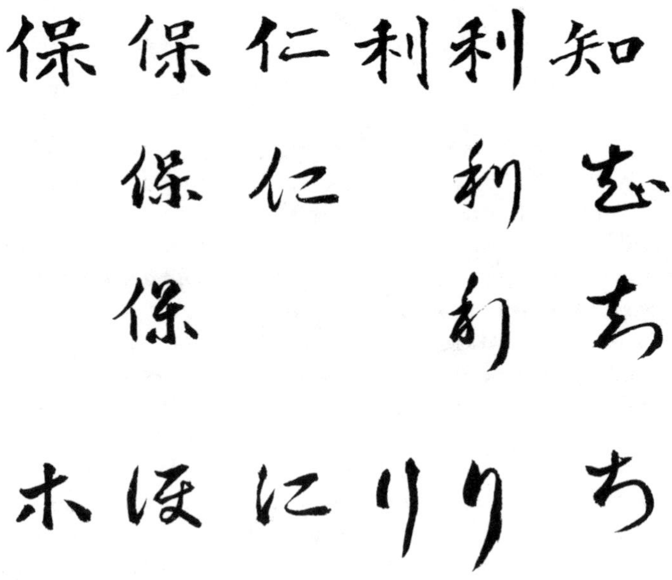

保 保 仁 利 利 知

保 仁 　 利 も

保 　 　 利 ち

木 ほ に り り ち

Figure 7-1 Development of *kana* syllabary. The top row contains Chinese characters and the bottom row shows the *kana* into which they eventually developed. Reading from right to left, the *kana* are pronounced *chi, ri, ri, ni, ho, ho*. All except the third and the last rows are in Hiragana, the most commonly used form; the third and last rows illustrate Katakana, the form used primarily for foreign terms and for emphasis. (Taken from G. B. Sansom, *Japan: A Short Cultural History* (Stanford: Stanford University Press, 1978), p. 238; calligraphy by Dr. Léon L. Y. Chang.

is very much on the capital itself. A provincial appointment, lucrative though it might be, was regarded as tantamount to exile. The provinces were viewed as an uncultured hinterland where even the governing classes were hopelessly vulgar. To these aristocratic ladies, the common people whose labor made society possible were so far removed in manners and appearance as to resemble the inhabitants of another world. At best, they seemed uncouth. At worst, they were regarded as not quite fully human, as when Sei Shōnagon encountered a group of commoners on a pilgrimage and noted in her famous *Pillow Book,* "They looked like so many basket-worms as they crowded together in their hideous clothes, leaving hardly an inch of space between themselves and me. I really felt like pushing them all over sideways."[4]

Geographically limited, constricted in social scope, the world of the Heian aristocracy was also narrow in its intellectual range. The last official Heian government mission to China was sent in 838, and when near the end of the ninth century it was proposed to send another and Sugawara no Michizane was chosen as ambassador, he successfully declined on the grounds that conditions in China were unsettled. Even after order had been restored in China with the establishment of the Sung, relations were not resumed. The Japanese of the Heian period were steeped in the Chinese culture of the T'ang and earlier but, except for some Buddhist monks, displayed a lack of concern for the China of their own time. Perhaps societies, like people, require a period of cultural digestion before they are ready for a new meal. Be that as it may, in the absence of stimuli from abroad, the Heian aristocrats also failed to respond creatively to the changes taking place at home. As we have seen, these changes were momentous, but they were also slow and did not stimulate a reexamination of the old or inspire new intellectual departures. Since the course of historical development went against the fortunes of the court aristocracy, their viewpoint became increasingly pessimistic. This pessimism found an echoing note in Heian Buddhism.

Refinement and Sensibility

What ultimately saved this small world from cultural sterility, and gave meaning to the lives of its inhabitants, was that these people developed the greatest subtlety of refinement within the range of their experience and concerns. At its best, as in the ideal of the perfect gentleman depicted by Murasaki's Genji ("the shining prince"), they sought to fuse life and art through the cultivation of human sensibilities. At its worst, their conduct smacked of effeminacy, and an aesthetic of good taste led to overrefinement.

In this world where aesthetics reigned supreme, great attention was paid to pleasing the eye. Ladies dressed in numerous robes, one over the other (twelve was standard), which they displayed at the wrist in overlapping layers, and the blending of their colors was of the utmost importance in revealing a lady's taste. Often all a man saw of a lady were her sleeves, left hanging outside her carriage or spread beyond a screen behind which she remained invisible. The men were by no means to be outdone in the care they took over their own attire. The following description is from Sei Shōnagon's *Pillow Book:*

> His resplendent, cherry-colored Court cloak was lined with material of the most delightful hue and lustre; he wore dark, grape-colored trousers, boldly splashed with designs of wisteria branches; his crimson under-robe was so glossy that it seemed to sparkle, while underneath one could make out layer upon layer of white and light violet robes.[5]

This concern for appearance also extended to the features of the gentlemen and ladies. Both sexes used cosmetics, applying a white face powder, which in the case of the women was combined with a rosy tint. The ladies took great pride in their long, flowing, glossy hair but plucked their eyebrows and painted in a new set. Such customs are not unfamiliar to the modern world, but far more difficult for us to appreciate are the blackened teeth of the refined Heian beauty. Confined to the aristocracy during the Heian period, this practice, like so many features of Heian taste and sensibility, later spread to the lower classes of society. It became the sign of a married woman, and in the Tokugawa period was also adopted by courtesans.

Specific fashions change, but the concern for visual beauty remained a lasting legacy from the Heian period. Even today, for example, great care is taken over the appearance of food, and its impact on the eye is considered at least as important as its taste.

The emphasis on visual beauty did not mean the neglect of the other senses. Music played an important part in the lives of the Heian aristocracy, and aural and visual pleasure was often combined in courtly dances, at which Genji, of course, excelled. Nor was the sense of smell neglected. The Heian ladies and gentlemen went to great lengths to blend perfumes, and a sensitive nose was a social asset second only to a good eye and ear. Among the aesthetic party contests used to while away the time in polite society, there were even perfume blending competitions such as the one described in *The Tale of Genji*.

Ideals of Courtly Love

The ideal Heian aristocrat was as sensitive in personal relations as in matters of aesthetics: feelings should be as beautiful as dress. Nowhere was this more important than in the love affairs that gave Heian literature its dominant theme, and in this respect, too, literature often mirrored life. Marriages were arranged by and for the family in a game of marriage politics at which the Fujiwara excelled. But for a noble courtier to confine himself to one wife was the rare exception. He was much more likely to have, in addition, one or more secondary wives while conducting still other, more or less clandestine, love affairs. Nor were the ladies expected to remain true to one love for their whole lives either, although few were as amorous as Izumi Shikibu (generally considered the author of the love diary that bears her name). Nevertheless, jealousy posed a recurring problem for a lady of the Heian age who might have to bear long waits between visits from her lover. For the less fortunate and less hardy waiting could become a torture. So unhappy was the author of *The Gossamer Diary* that her writing has been characterized by Ivan Morris as "one long wail of jealousy."[6]

The qualities most valued in a lover were quite similar regardless of sex: beauty and grace, talent and sensibility, and personal thoughtfulness. A gentleman is always considerate. The paragon, Genji, was ever gallant to one lady even though he discovered that she was very unattractive. He found himself in this predicament because Heian men often had no clear idea of the appearance of the women they were wooing, hidden as they were behind screens with only their sleeves showing. (Rare was the thoughtful consideration of a guardian like Genji who provided a lamp of fireflies to shed some illumination for the benefit of his ward's suitor.) Men fell in love with a woman's sense of beauty, her poetic talents, and her calligraphy. As in China, the latter was all-important, since it was thought to reveal a person's character. The Heian version of love at first sight was a gentleman falling hopelessly in love after catching a glimpse of a few beautifully drawn lines.

At every stage of a love affair, and in other social relationships too for that matter, the aesthetics of writing were stressed. At least as important as the literary merits of the poems that were exchanged on all occasions were such matters as the color and texture of the paper, the way it was folded, and the selection of a twig on which to tie the note. Most critical and most eagerly awaited of these poetic missives were the "morning after letters" sent by a lover immediately upon returning home from a night of love, from which he had torn himself away just before dawn with a proper show of reluctance. The first such letter was particularly important as it would provide a good indication of the seriousness and probable duration of the relationship.

In this world of sensitive people, men and women were expected to respond as readily to sadness as to joy. Both sexes cried freely and frequently, and neither felt any hesitation about expressing self-pity. Tears were a sign of depth of feeling and of a genuine awareness of the ephemeral nature of beauty, the transient nature of all that is good and beautiful. Sentiments such as these were expressed in a special vocabulary, using words so rich in their associations as to defy translation, words which became part of the subtle and shifting language of Japanese aesthetics.

Heian Religion: Tendai

When Emperor Kammu turned his back on Nara and moved his capital to Heian-kyō in 794, he crippled the political power of the old sects, but Buddhism continued to grow and flourish. It also continued to enjoy imperial patronage. Kammu himself supported the priest Saichō (767–822) who, dissatisfied with the worldliness of the Nara priesthood, had founded a small temple in 788 on Mt. Hiei northeast of Kyōto. To gain for his temple the kind of prestige enjoyed by the Nara temples, Chinese sanction was a must, so in 804 Saichō traveled to China, the source of Japanese Buddhism. But after his return and throughout his life, his relationship with the Japanese court remained close. His writings show a reverence for the emperor and a love of country not found among the important monks of the Nara period, many of whom were Koreans or, like Saichō's own ancestors, Chinese.

Saichō originally moved to Mt. Hiei because he wanted to escape the corrupt atmosphere of Nara and not because he disagreed with the teachings of Nara Buddhism. However, in China he studied the doctrines of the T'ien-t'ai school, called Tendai in Japanese. On his return he established this sect in Japan, thereby removing himself doctrinally as well as geographically from the Nara temples. The latter resented him bitterly, and when Emperor Kammu died they fought back with some temporary success, as when they disputed the new sect's right to ordain priests, a right not granted to the Tendai temple on Mt. Hiei until 827, by which time Saichō was dead.

The doctrinal content of Saichō's Tendai, like that of its Chinese parent, was grounded in the Lotus Sutra. In contrast to the proponents of some of the older sects, Saichō preached the universal possibility of enlightenment. Everyone could realize his Buddha nature through a life of true religious devotion. On Mt. Hiei, Saichō insisted on strict monastic regimen.

Saichō was more skilled as an organizer than as a theoretician. He built well; and eventually his little temple grew to some three thousand buildings. It flourished on Mt. Hiei until it was destroyed in the sixteenth century for political reasons. In keeping with the syncretic nature of T'ien-t'ai, the Buddhism propagated on Mt. Hiei was broad and accommodating; so much so that it remained the source of new developments in Japanese Buddhism even after the temple community had departed from the earnest religiosity of its founder.

After Saichō's death, a line of abbots succeeded him, among them Ennin, the famous traveler to China, whose diary is a major source of information about the T'ang. Then late in the ninth century there developed a split between the followers of Ennin and those of his successor. This bitter rivalry, fueled as much by jealousy as by doctrinal differences, led to the introduction of force into religious politics and the appearance of bullies (akuso—"vicious monks") who engaged in brawls and combat. The use of violence increased, and by the eleventh century leading Shinto shrines as well as the Tendai temples maintained large standing armies. Particularly troublesome was the monastery of Mt. Hiei, which kept several thousand troops. They repeatedly descended on the capital, terrorizing its inhabitants, to demand ecclesiastical positions, titles, and land rights. Thus the temple on Mt. Hiei, founded and supported as an early Heian solution to problems of temple intervention in politics in Nara, became in the late Heian period itself a major source of widespread distress.

Esoteric Buddhism: Shingon

Contemporary with Saichō was Kūkai (774–835), founder of the other major sect of Heian Buddhism, Shingon. He too studied in China and benefited from imperial patronage, although in his case it came not from Emperor Kammu but from that emperor's successors. Like Saichō he established his main monastery on a mountain, choosing Mt. Kōya on the Kii Peninsula, far removed from the capital. When Kūkai returned from China, Saichō befriended him and showed genuine interest in the doctrines Kūkai brought back with him, but largely through Kūkai's doing, the cordial relations did not last. A year after Saichō's death, Kūkai moved closer to the center of Heian life when he was appointed abbot of Tōji, the great temple at the main (southern) gateway to the capital.

In contrast to Tendai, which flourished in China as it did in Japan, the type of Buddhism introduced by Kūkai was never prominent in China and failed to survive the mid-T'ang persecution of Buddhism. Shingon (mantra, in the original Sanskrit, chen-yen in Chinese) literally means "True Word," thus conveying the importance of mystic verbal formulae in this sect and its insistence on a tradition of oral transmission of secret teachings from master to disciple. Since only the initiate were privy to the full truth, it is known as Esoteric Buddhism. Transmitted in addition to the sacred teachings and verbal utterances were complicated ritual observances involving the mudra (hand positions of the Buddha but also used by Shingon priests) and the use of ritual instruments.

Central to Shingon teachings and observances is Dainichi (Vairocana), the cosmic Buddha whose absolute truth is all encompassing and true everywhere and forever. In his *Ten Stages of Religious Consciousness*, Kūkai ranked the various levels of spiritual life. At the lowest level he ranked animal life, totally lacking in spiritual dimension. Confucianism he ranked as only the second step upwards, with Taoism third. Then came various sects of Hinayana and Mahayana Buddhism, including Tendai (eighth) and Kegon (ninth). At the top he placed Shingon. In this way Shingon incorporated and found a place for other schools of Buddhism, although the Tendai monks were hardly pleased with their place in the Shingon hierarchy. No provision was made in this schema for Shinto, but the name Dainichi (Great Sun) invited identification with the Sun Goddess, and Shingon also proved hospitable to Shinto deities through its concept of duality. This concept held that a single truth manifests itself under two aspects, the nomenal and the phenomenal, so in theory Daini-chi and the Sun Goddess could be considered as two forms of one identical truth.

The teachings of Esoteric Buddhism were complex and difficult to understand; yet it was enormously popular during the Heian period, even over-shadowing Tendai until Ennin introduced esoteric practices into Tendai itself. One reason for the appeal of Shingon was the mystery of its rites. From the beginning, people in Japan had been drawn to Buddhism at least in part by magical elements connected with Buddhist observances, for example, incantations, divination, exorcism, and the medicinal use of herbs. Now they were impressed by the mysterious elements in the secret rituals performed in the interior of Shingon temples, hidden from all but the most deeply initiated of the priests. The people of Heian Japan, with their taste for pageantry, were also attracted by the richness of the colorful Shingon rites.

Much of the prosperity of Shingon can be attributed to the genius of Kūkai (also known by his posthumous name Kōbō Daishi, Great Teacher Kōbō). He was an exceptional man, famed for his brilliance and learning, his artistic talents and, of course, his calligraphy. He is credited with the invention of the *kana* syllabary, and it is just possible that his exposure to a phonetic system of writing (he studied Sanskrit in China) helped influence the development of *kana*. Kūkai is also credited with the introduction of tea to Japan and the building of bridges. A cluster of miraculous stories grew up around his name. To this day, he lies in his grave on Mt. Kōya awaiting the coming of Maitreya. (See Figure 7-2.)

One of Kūkai's most lasting contributions to Shingon, and a major source of its appeal, was his emphasis on the arts. A gifted artist himself, he saw art as the ideal vehicle for transmitting religious truth. He once wrote that the truth cannot be conveyed in writing—only in art—reflecting the Heian tendency to equate truth and beauty. Unlike Tendai, Shingon did not give birth to many new schools of Buddhist thought, but it did leave a rich artistic heritage.

No society is composed entirely of the devout—certainly not that of Heian Japan! The degree of piety felt by those who attended religious observances ranged widely. Sei Shōnagon once remarked that a priest should be handsome, so that the audience will have no inducement to divert their eyes and

Figure 7-2   Mt. Kōya, Wakayama.

thoughts. Frequently, then as now, a visit to a temple was primarily a pleasure trip. On the other hand, in the daily lives of all classes, religion and magic were inextricably interwoven with elements of Buddhism, Shinto, *yin-yang* theory, geomancy, and popular beliefs of all kinds. (Geomancy, *feng-shui* in Chinese, is the Chinese pseudoscience for selecting sites for graves, buildings, or cities according to the topographical configuration of *yin* and *yang*.) The inhabitants of the capital were forever purifying themselves, superstitiously avoided walking in certain directions on certain days, and when ill sought the services of a priest skilled in exorcism. The monastery on Mt. Hiei provides a good example of this fusion of beliefs. It was established northeast of the capital to guard the city against the evils that, according to Chinese beliefs, emanate from that direction. And before he built this Buddhist temple, Saichō was careful to pay his respect to the local Shinto deity. "Thus, by the friendly collaboration of Indian Buddhism, indigenous Shinto, and Chinese geomancy, the protection of the city was assured."[7]

Pietism

In the Later Heian period, revulsion at the worldly (and military) success of the established temples, and hope of rescuing a world falling into increasing disorder, stimulated a pietistic movement. This movement was led by the priests Kūya (903–72) and Genshin (942–1017) and centered around Amida (Amitābha, the Buddha of the Infinite Light, who presides over the Western Paradise). So disrupted was Japanese society in the tenth century that many people were convinced they were about to enter the last of the three Buddhist ages (mappō), the degenerate age of the decline of the Buddha's law. The pietists taught that only faith in Amida could provide salvation in such dire times, and a famous statue of Kūya shows him with little Amidas issuing from his mouth. (See Figure 11-4.) In a spirit of evangelical zeal, he traveled through the countryside and even to the land of the Ainu bringing people his message of Buddhist salvation and leading them in dancing and chanting the name of Amida.

It is characteristic of the Heian period that Genshin propagated his teachings not only in writing but also in art. His work contains terrifying representations of hell. He is best known for a painting not actually his that depicts a raigō, that is, the descent of Amida mercifully coming down to a man's deathbed to gather his soul to paradise. One custom among the devout was for a dying man to hold on to a string attached to the figure of Amida in such a painting. For example, when Michinaga, the strong-minded Fujiwara who was de facto ruler of Japan, lay dying, he repeated the nembutsu (invocation to Amida) while holding on to such a cord, while a chorus of monks chanted the Lotus Sutra. This practice became as widespread as the raigō themselves.

Another deity worthy of mention is Jizō, who began as the bodhisattva who saved souls in hell but became popular as the embodiment of Amida's compassion. Eventually he merged with other gods, until in the course of time he came to be regarded as the protector of children who had died young. He still graces many a roadside shrine in Japan today.

Amidism continued to attract an increasing following and devoted apostles such as Ryōnin (1072–1132), a Tendai monk who placed additional emphasis on the nembutsu. As the Heian period neared its end, the veneration of Amida and the use of the nembutsu spread to all temples, but eventually the new religious force could no longer be contained in the established sects despite their syncretic tendencies. The break came when Hōnen (1133–1212) established Pure Land Buddhism as an independent sect in the Kamakura era.

Literature

The poetry of Japan has its roots in the human heart and flourishes in the countless leaves of words. Because human beings possess interests of so many kinds, it is in poetry that they give expression to the meditations of their hearts in terms of sights appearing before their eyes and the sounds coming to their ears. Hearing the warbler sing among the blossoms and the frog in his fresh waters—is there any living being not given to song? It is poetry which, without exertion, moves heaven and earth, stirs the feelings of gods and spirits invisible to the eye, softens the relations between men and women, calms the hearts of fierce warriors.[8]

These famous lines are from the introduction to the Kokinshū (Collection of Ancient and Modern Times), an imperial anthology of poetry completed around 905, by Ki no Tsurayuki. They express the classic Japanese view of poetry. It is the spontaneous creation of the human heart giving rise to "countless leaves of words." It is a message from the heart to the heart: genuine feelings expressed in the right words. These words were purely Japanese, for although Heian poets also composed Chinese verse, Chinese loan-words were meticulously excluded from poetry written in the Japanese language. The greatest of these short poems are enriched by the resonance of their verbal music, suggestive overtones arising from a richness of shared associations, and by double meanings and plays on words. The result is a poetry which, even more than usual, defies translation.

Among the uses of poetry mentioned by Tsurayuki is that it "softens the relations between men and women." It should come as no surprise then that much of Japanese poetry was love poetry, and that court ladies were among its most outstanding practitioners. Much of this poetry is subtle and delicate, but it can also be strongly passionate. It is full of tears, but does not lack fire:

> On such a night like this
> When no moon lights your way to me,
>   I wake my passion blazing,
> My breast a fire raging, exploding flame
> While within me my heart chars.[9]

The author of this poem was a court lady, Ono no Komachi (fl. ca. 850), but it was characteristic for Japanese poets of both sexes to think that love could best be understood from the woman's point of view.

One of the greatest male poets of the period was the great lover Ariwara no Narihira (823–880). Many of his poems are contained in *The Tales of Ise*, one of Japan's literary classics. This work consists of prose explanations of the occasions which gave rise to each verse, followed by that verse. For example:

> Long ago a young man had an affair with a woman who was well experienced in love. Was he not perhaps a bit uneasy?

> > If it is not me
> > take care not to loosen your sash!
> > Oh, morning glory,
> > even though you are a flower
> > that falls before the evening.

> In reply:

> > By the two of us
> > was this sash tied at parting—
> > One of us alone
> > will not I think unloose it
> > till we two are face to face[10]

Heian literature laid great stress on blending prose and poetry, life and art. Consequently, the art diary—a prose form to which poetry was central—was the favorite literary genre in this period. Some diaries, like Tsurayuki's *Tosa Diary*, were cast into the form of travel accounts while others dealt with life at court, but all contained large numbers of poems. Their attention to feeling and sensibility were shaped, in form and substance, by the requirements of art.

Art as much as life determined their content; and in Heian diaries, as well as in Heian fiction, the distinction between art and life, fact and fiction, was not clearly delineated. Just as the diaries were shaped by art, it was demanded of novels that they remain true to life. The importance of the diary as a literary form and the close relationship between the diary and the novel may be a uniquely Japanese literary phenomenon, but it is not unique to the Heian period: like so many other aspects of Heian culture, it survived even into the twentieth century, helping to account for the popularity of autobiography thinly disguised as fiction, known as the "I novel."

The greatest Japanese novel is, of course, *The Tale of Genji* (ca. 1010) by Murasaki Shikibu. Its influence on Japanese culture was enormous and varied. References to *Genji* echo throughout Japanese literary history down to the present. To make this classic accessible to a modern audience it has been translated into modern Japanese by, among others, Tanizaki Junichirō (1886–1965), one of Japan's outstanding twentieth-century novelists. It has also provided subject matter for the arts (see Figure 7-7) and left its mark on the writing of history. One such history is *The Tale of Glory* (*Eiga monogatari*), an eleventh-century account focusing on the Fujiwara, particularly Michinaga. (The word *"monogatari"* appears alike in novels, histories, and compilations of stories.)

A reason for *The Tale of Genji's* enduring fascination and appeal is its psychological subtlety. Indeed, it is, among other things, the world's first psychological novel, for Lady Murasaki was as interested in the thoughts and feelings of her characters as in their tastes and talents; an interest in surface beauty did not preclude introspection. In structure, the novel shows careful planning and organization, unfolding somewhat like a hand-scroll in which each scene can be enjoyed separately while still forming part of a larger whole held together by the continuity of time and the repetition of motifs.

The Tale of Genji has long been admired for its expression of *mono no aware*. *Aware*, an adjective frequently used by Lady Murasaki, was originally applied to anything genuinely moving. It could refer to joyous as well as sad experiences, but eventually the implication of melancholy predominated. *Mono* means things, and *mono no aware* can be translated as "sensitivity to things." It involves a realization of the ephemeral quality of beauty, of all that is best in life, indeed, of life itself. Clearly in this concept there are resonances of Buddhist teaching, which views life as an illusion, insubstantial as a dream. To the Japanese, it was a beautiful but fleeting dream, and sadness was itself a necessary dimension of beauty.

Of the other terms used in, and applied to, Heian literature, the word *"miyabi"* is particularly appropriate. Translatable as "elegance," "refinement," or "courtliness," it demanded the rejection of anything that was gross or vulgar and the polishing of manners, diction, and feelings to eliminate all roughness and crudity so as to achieve the highest grace. *Aware* and *miyabi* complement each other. In particular they share that sensitivity to beauty that was the hallmark of the Heian era and has been the hallmark of Japanese culture ever since.

Figure 7-3   Pagoda of
Murōji, Nara Prefecture.

The Visual Arts

In art also imported themes and forms were domesticated during the Heian period and were turned into something definitely Japanese. The period is readily divided into two parts for purposes of art history. "Early Heian," also sometimes called the Kōnin or Jōgan period, designates roughly the first century in Kyōto (794–897).

In architecture the reassertion of Japanese taste took a variety of forms. It is particularly notable in the layout of the new temples, for when Saichō and Kūkai turned from the Nara Plain to build their monasteries in the mountains, they abandoned the symmetrical temple plans that had been used around Nara. Down on the plain, architecture could afford to ignore the terrain; but in the mountains, temple styles and layouts had to accommodate themselves to the physical features of the site. On Mount Hiei and elsewhere, the natural setting, rock outcroppings, and trees became integral parts of the temple, as had long been the case with Shinto shrines. But it is interesting to note that even on Mount Kōya, where there was enough space to build a Nara-style temple complex, the traditional plans were abandoned. Changes were also made in building materials and decoration.

During the Nara period the main buildings had been placed on stone platforms; the wood was painted; and the roofs were made of tile. In the Nara tem-

ples, only minor buildings had had their wood left unpainted and had been fitted with roofs of thatch or bark shingles. Now, these techniques were also used
for the main halls. An excellent site at which to observe the resulting aesthetic
is Murōji, set in the mountains some forty miles from Nara, among magnificent straight, cedarlike trees (cryptomeria) such as are also found on Mt. Kōya
and at other locations. Not only in material but also in the size of its buildings,
Murōji is more modest than the Nara temples. Its pagoda (see Figure 7-3) is
only half the size of that at the Hōryūji but makes up in charm and grace what
it lacks in grandeur.

In the Early Heian period, wood replaced clay, bronze, dry lacquer, and stone
as the material of choice for sculpture. Statues, and sometimes their pedestals
as well, were carved out of a single block of wood. Frequently the finished
sculpture was painted or lacquered, but this was never allowed to obscure the
beauty of the wood grain, for that would have offended the artist's sense of respect for his material.

Although some statues of Shinto deities survive from this period, most Early
Heian statuary concerned Buddhist themes. As a result, the art form reflects
the demands of the new forms of that religion, particularly Esoteric Buddhism.
Usually the statues are formal and symmetrical. The flesh is full and firm. The
faces are cast in a serious mien, creating an aura of mystery without the hint of
a smile or any indication of friendliness. A famous example of Early Heian art
is the figure of Sakyamuni (the historic Buddha) at Murōji (see Figure 7-4). It is

Figure 7-4   Sakyamuni. Ninth
   century, 129.6 cm high.
   Murōji, Nara Prefecture.

Figure 7-5 *Womb Mandala.* Painting on silk, ninth century. Tōji, Kyōto.

among other things, a fine example of "wave" drapery, so called because its lines flow like the sea. It has been suggested that the curious swirls at the bottom may be the result of copying in wood an original calligraphic drawing.

The Shingon sect demanded unusual iconographic exactitude in its art, just as it did in its rites. The result was an unwholesome tendency toward sterile formalism, both in reciting the mantras and in religious art. This was especially true of Shingon mandalas, which became very complex as artists tried to represent the cosmos graphically, including all the various deities that were emanations of Dainichi. Some altars, for example, at Tōji in Kyōto, were arranged in mandala fashion, but more usual were painted mandalas, such as that shown in Figure 7-5. This is a depiction of the Womb Mandala, representing the world of phenomena. The red lotus at the center symbolizes the heart of the universe. Dainichi is seated on the seedpod of the lotus. Other Buddhas occupy the petals. Altogether there are 407 deities in the Womb Mandala. Its counterpart, the Diamond Mandala, centers on a white lotus and represents the world containing 1314 gods.

A frequent subject of painting and sculpture is Fudō, the Immovable, a ferocious deity bent on annihilating evil. In the Red Fudō at Mt. Kōya (see Figure 7-6), the red of the figure and the flames behind him dominate the color scheme and help to create a terrifying atmosphere. In his hand he holds a sword the handle of which is a thunderbolt (*vajra*), a symbol originating in India as the weapon of the god Indra, and in Esoteric Buddhism thought to cut through ignorance just as lightning pierces the clouds. A dragon coiled around the blade of the sword adds to the threat. The proportions of the figures and the manner in which the picture fills the space produce a feeling of massiveness character- istic of the art of this age.

Early Heian art at its best achieved a certain majesty, but it has a forbidding quality about it that stands in striking contrast to the sweetness of Late Heian art. Shingon continued to produce art after the ninth century, but the period really belonged to Amida—and to the Fujiwara. Michinaga had a great temple built in the capital reproducing Amida's paradise, containing "columns with bases of ivory, roof ridges of red gold, gilded doors, platforms of crystal."[11] This temple and a similar one built by Emperor Shirakawa are no longer extant. They have to be reconstructed from texts to give us some idea of what Heian Kyōto looked like.

The historical and artistic origins of such temples go back to Chinese images of the Western Paradise and to its closest terrestial approximation, the T'ang palace garden systematically laid out with its lake and bridges. Similarly, a major feature of the Heian mansion (*shinden*) was a garden with one or two artificial hills, carefully placed trees and bamboo, and a pond in which a tiny island was reached by a bridge. A small stream fed the pond and was used to

Figure 7-6   *Red Fudō*. Color on silk, Early Heian, 130.8 cm. Myōin, Mt. Kōya, Wakayama.

float wine cups at banquets in the Chinese manner. To the north of the garden were the living quarters: rectangular buildings joined by roofed corridors. Like all Japanese-style buildings, these structures were raised a few feet off the ground, and usually a little stream ran under a part of the mansion. Inside, the floors were of polished wood. Flexibility was provided by sliding paper screens, and shutters could be moved to combine small rooms into a larger one. Several kinds of screens (see Figure 7-8) provided some privacy. Sparsely furnished, the Heian *shinden* reflected the Japanese appreciation for aesthetic restraint.

Painting

Sliding doors in the Heian *shinden* were frequently decorated with landscapes, such as the picture within a picture shown in Figure 7-7. In painting, as in the other arts, after serving a period of apprenticeship to continental masters, the Japanese went their own way. Japanese-style paintings (*Yamato-e*) depicted native, not Chinese, subjects, including views of the Japanese landscape. The greatest of such paintings still extant illustrate *The Tale of Genji.* In the Genji Scroll, unlike later narrative scrolls, the individual scenes are separated by passages of text. The scene reproduced in Figure 7-7 shows a lady (upper left) looking at pictures while one of her attendants reads aloud the story they illustrate. At the lower left, another lady is having her hair combed. In the foreground is a screen such as was used by a lady when receiving a gentleman caller. In this and similar paintings, the roofs are removed to afford a view from above into the rooms. The treatment of human features is conventionalized

Figure 7-7 *Genji Monogatari*, section of hand-scroll. Color on paper, twelfth century, 21.6 cm high. Tokugawa Museum, Nagoya.

Figure 7-8 *Animal Caricatures* (*Chōjū Giga*), section of hand-scroll. Attributed to Kakuyū (Toba Sōjō). Late twelfth century, 30.5 cm high. Kozanji, Kyōto.

with "straight lines for eyes and hooks for noses." The colors were applied quite thickly to produce a richly decorative effect in keeping with aristocratic taste.

Late in the Heian period there also appeared scrolls (*emaki*) in which no text interrupted the flow of pictorial narrative. Some represent Buddhist hells, but others display a gift for comic caricature. Particularly well known are the animal scrolls attributed to Kakuyū (Sōjō, 1053–1140) but probably completed near the end of the twelfth century. Here frog-priests and rabbit-nobles gambol and disport themselves. In Figure 7-8, a monkey is worshipping not a Buddha but a frog.

The minor arts also illustrate the taste of the Heian aristocrats. See, for example, the garment box shown in Figure 7-9. It is decorated with cart wheels,

Figure 7-9 Garment box. Lacquered wood, Late Heian, 31 cm long. Hōryūji, Nara Prefecture.

Figure 7-10　Byōdōin (Phoenix Pavilion). Uji, Kyōto Prefecture.

made of mother-of-pearl and gold, half immersed in water. The asymmetry of the design and the unifying flow and rhythm, here supplied by the water, are characteristic of the Japanese achievements in decoration.

The Phoenix Pavilion

Sometimes a single site offers a summary of a whole era; for Late Heian art this is true of the Phoenix Pavilion (Byōdōin). (See Figure 7-10.) It is located in Uji, a locale some ten miles from Kyōto that figures prominently in *The Tales of Genji.* The building is associated with the Fujiwaras: it was built by Michinaga's son. And it was built for Amida who occupied the center of a *raigō* in sculpture. Other versions of the *raigō*, painted on the doors and inner walls, show Amida and his entourage descending onto a purely Japanese landscape. Mother-of-pearl insets in the main dais and in some of the columns contribute to the overall richness of effect.

Amida himself is the work of the sculptor Jōchō. He is fashioned in the joined-wood technique, which affords greater freedom of expression than the early Heian process of carving from a single piece of wood. It also allows for a greater and more varied exploitation of the grain. The halo, alive with angels, clouds, and flames, contrasts with the calm of Amida himself. As Robert Paine so eloquently expressed it, "the tranquility of the Absolute is made to harmonize with the Buddha's sympathy for the finite."[12]

The design of the buildings suggests a bird coming in for a landing or ready for flight. Two bronze phoenixes grace its highest roof. It may be considered a mansion for the Buddha himself. And to assure that Amida, too, will enjoy the beauty of the setting and the lovely sight of his hall reflected in the pond, the architect has thoughtfully provided an opening so that he can look out. Here is another example of the unity of building and site that was such a key feature of Heian architecture and which suggests the acceptance of man and nature as one.

NOTES

1. Elizabeth Sato, "The Early Development of the Shōen," in John W. Hall and Jeffrey P. Mass, *Medieval Japan: Essays in Institutional History* (New Haven: Yale University Press, 1974), p. 105.

2. G. Cameron Hurst, Jr., "The Structure of the Heian Court," in Hall and Mass, *Medieval Japan,* p. 52.

3. Sato, "The Early Development of the Shōen," p. 105.

4. Ivan Morris, *The Pillow Book of Sei Shōnagon* (New York: Columbia University Press, 1967), p. 258.

5. *Ibid.,* p. 76.

6. Ivan Morris, *The World of the Shining Prince* (New York: Alfred A. Knopf, 1964), p. 244.

7. Sir George Sansom, *A History of Japan to 1334* (Stanford: Stanford University Press, 1958), p. 118.

8. Earl Miner, *An Introduction to Japanese Court Poetry* (Stanford: Stanford University Press, 1968), p. 18.

9. *Ibid.,* p. 82.

10. H. Jay Harris, trans., *The Tales of Ise* (Rutland, Vt. and Tokyo: Charles E. Tuttle, 1972), p. 76.

11. Robert Treat Paine and Alexander Soper, *The Art and Architecture of Japan* (Baltimore: Penguin Books, 1955), p. 212.

12. *Ibid.,* p. 45.

PART THREE
China and Japan: Gentry and Samurai

ABOVE, Bottle Vase. Kuan porcelain, Sung, 16.8 cm high. Sir Percival David Foundation, London. RIGHT, Chōjirō, *Tea Bowl Named "Shobu."* Raku ware, sixteenth century, 8.9 cm high. Hakone Art Museum.

宋代之中國

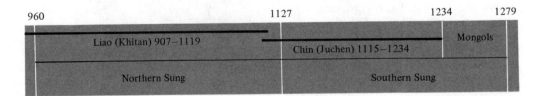

960   1127   1234   1279

Liao (Khitan) 907–1119

Chin (Juchen) 1115–1234

Mongols

Northern Sung   Southern Sung

8 *China During the Sung: 960–1279*

      The Sung period (960–1279) represents a new phase of Chinese history, marked by many features that were to remain characteristic of traditional China. Foremost among these was the full emergence of an elite of scholar-officials who assumed the place once occupied by a hereditary aristocracy. The Sung was also a period of dramatic and far-reaching changes in the economy. In philosophy and in painting especially, the Sung achievement attained classic dimensions, creating a heritage that for centuries to come inspired and challenged thoughtful men throughout East Asia.

The Scholar-Officials

The turbulence which accompanied and followed the decline of the T'ang helped to destroy the old aristocratic families that had been so prominent during the T'ang dynasty. The way was thus cleared for a new and different kind of elite. This elite based its prestige on literary learning, its status and power on office holding, and its wealth on land ownership. Frequently these three attributes reinforced each other. For instance, even though the spread of printing (a Late T'ang invention) made books cheaper and encouraged the diffusion of literacy, a certain economic level had to be achieved before a family could afford to do without the labor of a son in the fields and to pay for his education. Education, in turn, was a prerequisite for an official career, while office holding provided opportunities for the acquisition and protection of wealth.

Sung social structure was more complex than this, however. There were also the overeducated poor and the undereducated rich: the deeply learned scholar who lived a life of frugal obscurity, and the man of wealth who was not fully educated by elite standards and who was ineligible for political appointment and unwelcome in high society. The fact that learning, office, and wealth did not necessarily coincide made for considerable social variety, a variety further enhanced by the contrasts between urban and rural life and by major regional differences. Furthermore, status was a function of the social group. Even a criminal (say, a salt smuggler) might well enjoy high standing within his community although despised by the official elite. It is important to remember that in premodern times the web of government rested only lightly on society and that the world of officialdom was remote from most people's lives. The reminder is necessary, since most of the historical sources stem from that world of the scholar-official, which also supplied traditional China's historians. This scholar-official elite played a crucial role in maintaining Chinese unity, but unity should not be mistaken for uniformity.

To distinguish the new elite from the old aristocracy, scholars commonly use the term "gentry." At the highest level it is used for those who held office in the statewide civil service or were eligible to do so by virtue of success in the civil service examinations. It is also used for families of local prominence. The local gentry were usually educated, although several generations might pass without a family producing a degree holder. Theoretically servants of the emperor, gentry bureaucrats were also susceptible to the pulls of regional and family interests. The local gentry, for their part, generally tried to act as "brokers" between their communities and the state. Actually it appears that this local elite emerged only slowly during the latter part of the Sung and did not become dominant until the Ming dynasty, for in Sung times sheer wealth often determined the pattern of village relations. However, wealth could be invested in education, which in turn conferred social status and opened the way to public office.

In contrast to societies in which status is inherited, the Chinese system neither guaranteed elite families continuity of status nor barred the way for those trying to rise from below. Economically, also, such movement up and down was made possible by the ready transferability of land and other forms of wealth, which was further facilitated by the custom of dividing estates among heirs rather than leaving them intact to a single son. Meanwhile, the examination system provided the institutional means that made it possible for new men to join the scholar-official elite, for the examinations were open to all men, excluding only a small minority such as the sons of criminals and the like.

The Examination System

The system of civil service examinations came into its own in the Sung and (except in the Mongol period) remained the most prestigious means of government recruitment. Although during the Sung many men continued to enter the civil service through other means, such as sponsorship by an official, in later dynasties the examination route represented the norm for entry into government service. The system was only abolished in the twentieth century. During this vast span of time, the system was refined and greatly elaborated, but its basic features were already clearly in evidence in the Sung.

Structurally the system provided for an orderly progression through a series of tests (three during the Sung, more later). These began at the local level, included a metropolitan examination given in the capital to candidates from the entire country, and culminated in a palace examination held under the personal auspices of the emperor. The practices of the T'ang whereby candidates brought personal influence to bear on the examiners were now eliminated, and the government went to great lengths in its attempt to secure impartiality. The papers of candidates, who were identified only by number, were copied by clerks before being submitted for grading in order to prevent a reader from recognizing the author of any paper by its calligraphy. The battle of wits between would-be cheaters and the authorities seeking to enforce honesty lasted as long as the examinations themselves and was pursued with great ingenuity by both sides. Despite occasional scandals the examination system enjoyed a well-deserved reputation for honesty.

Competition was tough, testimony to the great attractions of a government career. It has been estimated that about one out of every five men who took the Sung metropolitan examination was successful, and the average age of those who completed the entire process and received the coveted *chin-shih* (presented scholar) degree was in the midthirties. Since some areas were considerably more advanced culturally and educationally than others, regional quotas were introduced during the Sung to insure representativeness, a practice continued by most later governments. This provided some geographical balance to the bureaucracy but also meant that competition for places was particularly intense in the most advanced areas.

Success in the examinations required first of all a thorough command of the classics, which the candidates had to memorize. Candidates had to be able to identify not only well-known lines but also the most obscure passages, and even sequences of characters that made no sense to anyone who did not know the exact context in which they appeared in a classic text. Tests of memory and exercises demonstrating command over formal literary styles were favored by examiners, since they made grading easier and more objective. Thus formal criteria were stressed in judging the poems that candidates were usually required to compose as part of their examinations. There was a persistent tendency for the examinations to turn into mere technical exercises, testing skills that revealed little about either a man's character or his administrative competence. This remained true even though the candidates were also required to discuss the meaning of designated passages from the classics and to answer questions concerning statecraft that had some theoretical bearing on the policy problems of the day. Despite its shortcomings the examination system did facilitate the careers of China's greatest statesmen during the Sung and later. And it graduated administrators who shared a common intellectual heritage and recognized a common set of values, men who were scholars as well as officials.

The examination system was a pivotal institution profoundly affecting government. It provided a measure of social mobility, largely determined the educational curriculum, and shaped the structure of the lives of those who aspired to a degree. It is no wonder, therefore, that the examinations themselves became a subject of profound concern and intense debate. The tradition of protest against its inadequacies is almost as old as the system itself. There were those who wished to see it abolished altogether, and many others who argued for reforms of various kinds. The examination system, therefore, remained a topic of political debate and scholarly controversy.

The Northern Sung

It is useful and customary to divide the Sung into two periods, each roughly a century and a half in length. "Northern Sung" designates the period from 960 until 1126 when the dynasty had its capital in the North, at Kaifeng. During this period the Sung government ruled over both North and South. However, from the time of the dynasty's founder, Emperor T'ai-tsu (r. 960–76), and his brother T'ai-tsung (r. 976–97), who completed the establishment of the dynasty, the Sung had to tolerate a non-Chinese presence in North China. This was the Liao dynasty (907–1119), which had been created by a tribal people known as the Khitan and included sixteen prefectures on the Chinese side of the Great Wall. Relations between the Sung and the Liao were frequently hostile, but the two states came to terms in 1005 after the Sung emperor, Chentsung (r. 997–1022), had personally taken the field against the Khitan. Negotiations led to a treaty that included provisions for diplomatic exchanges, trade, and a Sung agreement to send the Liao contributions in silk and silver. For the Sung the cost was considerably less than would have been required to finance a military solution, but it was characteristic of the dynasty that it would rather pay than fight.

The Liao, however, were not the Sung's only troublesome neighbors. In 1038 there was a challenge from the West as the leader of the Ordos-based Tangut peoples organized the Hsi Hsia state and invaded Shensi. In 1044, under Emperor Jen-tsung (r. 1022–63), the Sung signed a peace treaty with the Hsi Hsia along the lines of its earlier agreement with the Liao. The Hsi Hsia, however, remained a military problem for the Sung until the Sung lost all of North China to still another power, the Juchen, who established the dynasty known as the Chin (1115–1234).

Initially the Sung had welcomed the emergence of the Chin as an ally, but the dynasty's attempt to "use barbarians against barbarians" ended in disaster. The last two emperors of the Northern Sung, Hui-tsung (r. 1100–26), China's greatest imperial painter and calligrapher (see Figure 8-1) but not equally distinguished as a ruler, and his son, Emperor Ch'in-tsung (r. 1126–27), were taken

Figure 8-1   Sung Hui-tsung, *Five-Colored Parakeet.* Hanging scroll, colors on silk, 53 cm high. Museum of Fine Arts, Boston.

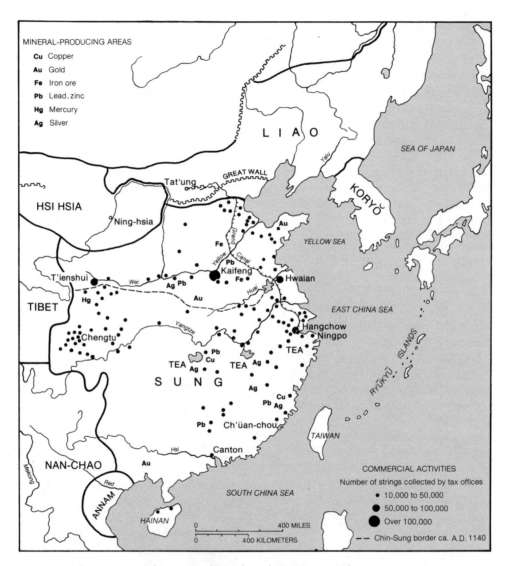

MINERAL-PRODUCING AREAS

Cu Copper
Au Gold
Fe Iron ore
Pb Lead, zinc
Hg Mercury
Ag Silver

LIAO

SEA OF JAPAN

Tat'ung GREAT WALL

KORYŌ

HSI HSIA

Ning-hsia

Au

YELLOW SEA

Fe

T'ienshui

Ag Pb

Pb Kaifeng

Fe

Hwaian

Wei

Au

TIBET

Hg

EAST CHINA SEA

Yangtze

Hangchow
Ningpo

Chengtu

TEA

Pb
Cu

RYŪKYŪ ISLANDS

TEA Ag

TEA Ag

SUNG

Ag

Cu

Pb Ag

Pb

Ch'üan-chou

TAIWAN

Hsi Canton

NAN-CHAO

Au

COMMERCIAL ACTIVITIES

Number of strings collected by tax offices

SOUTH CHINA SEA

• 10,000 to 50,000
● 50,000 to 100,000
⬤ Over 100,000

HAINAN

0 ———— 400 MILES
0 ———— 400 KILOMETERS

--- Chin-Sung border ca. A.D. 1140

Figure 8-2   **Sung China—Political and Commercial**

NOTE To suggest the scope of the Sung economy, this map also indicates tea
and metal production. Economic data taken from the map "Centres
Commerciaux de la Chine des Sung" by Etienne Balazs, published in Françoise
Aubin, ed., *Sung Studies—Etudes Song in Memoriam Etienne Balazs*, Series I,
No. 3 (Paris: Mouton & Co. and Ecole des Hautes Etudes, 1976).

to Manchuria as prisoners of the Juchen and there lived out their lives. The dynasty was able to reestablish itself in the South, but the North, homeland of Chinese civilization, remained lost. Not until the founding of the Ming dynasty in the fourteenth century was the North to come again under Chinese rule. (See map, Figure 8-2.)

Government and Politics

Sung government was basically organized along T'ang lines, but Sung statesmen, careful students of history, were determined to avoid past errors as well as to profit from past achievements. One precedent the dynasty was particularly anxious to avoid was the reemergence of warlords such as had eventually destroyed the T'ang. Emperor T'ai-tsu, the dynastic founder and himself a general, saw to it that power was placed in civilian hands, and his successors pursued the same policy. By such devices as the rotation of troops and frequent changes of command, the court prevented generals from developing personal power and succeeded in keeping commanders in line. Indeed, the military profession suffered a permanent loss of status. From the Sung on, it was a truism that good men are not turned into soldiers any more than good iron is wasted to make nails.

But everything has its price. Despite huge armies and sophisticated weaponry, the dynasty's military record was mediocre. Yet, at the same time, the maintenance and support of the military establishment was expensive, as was the financing of an expanding civilian bureaucracy. Naturally, Sung scholars and officials disagreed over economic and fiscal policies much as they did over the examinations and over the linked issues of foreign and military policy.

The political process during the Sung was complicated by factionalism and infighting. Bureaucratic politics was conducted, not by stable and legitimized political parties united by a common program, but by factions whose members might share some common policy commitments but were more likely to be held together by personal relationships and temporary alliances. Characteristically, factions accused each other of narrow self-interest, and each held its opponents responsible for the development of factionalism itself, a phenomenon condemned by the court and by Confucian theory as inimical to the state.

Each faction sought to obtain the emperor's support for its members and policies. Such imperial support was as crucial in practice as it was in theory, for the disappearance of an aristocratic counterweight served to increase the power of the throne. Nevertheless, Sung emperors were notable in using this power to manipulate rather than to intimidate their officials. Those who fell out of imperial favor usually suffered nothing worse than exile. It is perhaps indicative of the political tone of the dynasty that it had no counterpart to the imperious rulers of the past: no one comparable to Emperor Wu of the Han or T'ai-tsung of the T'ang. Indeed, its most famous emperor was Hui-tsung, already mentioned as an artistic success and political failure. The dynasty also produced China's greatest and most controversial reform minister, Wang An-shih, who was able to initiate new policies so long as he enjoyed the support of Emperor Shen-tsung (r. 1067–85). Wang's policies and career throw much light on state and society in eleventh-century China. They illustrate what government could do and could not do and how the system functioned.

Wang An-shih

Wang An-shih (1021–86) was not the first Sung reformer. That honor went to Fan Chung-yen (989–1052), famed for his definition of a true Confucian as "one who is first in worrying about the world's troubles and last in enjoying its pleasures." Fan and Wang's reforms were part of a Confucian revival that dominated eleventh-century intellectual life. Both men sought to bring government closer to the Confucian ideal, but Wang went far beyond his predecessor in initiating new programs, and in the process, he antagonized his most illustrious contemporaries, among them the dynasty's greatest poet (Su Shih, often known as Su Tung-p'o [1037–1101]), its greatest historian, and its most creative philosophers.

One of Wang's first acts was to establish a finance planning commission (1069). Another act of 1069 rationalized the process of supplying commodities to the capital. This and the establishment in 1072 of a state trade system were designed to save money for the government by breaking the monopoly on government procurement held by large merchants. The latter measure provided that the government should deal directly with small suppliers who now became eligible for government loans. A consistent feature of Wang's economic policies was a preference for dealing in money rather than in commodities. Tax payments in cash were substituted for the customary deliveries of supplies to the palace (1073). Similarly, Wang instituted a tax to finance the hiring of men to perform local government service (1071), a function previously assigned to well-off local families on a rotating basis. He also increased the amount of currency in circulation. Nevertheless, there was a currency shortage brought on by increased demand.

Wang An-shih did not neglect agriculture. To save small farmers from the ruinous short-term interest rates of 60 to 70 percent charged for carry-over loans during the hard months between spring sowing and autumn harvest, he instituted farming loans ("young shoots money") with a maximum interest rate of 20 percent for the season (1069). To deal with the perpetual problem of faulty tax rolls and fraudulent records, Wang also initiated a land survey in 1072.

Another program organized people into groups of 10, 30, and 300 families to ensure collective responsibility for local policing, tax collections, and loan repayments, and to supply men for a local security force that could also function as a military reserve. Another measure designed to cut the dynasty's enormous military expenses provided for placing horses with farmers. In return for maintaining them, the farmers could use the horses in peacetime but were obligated to turn them over to the army in case of military need. This program was not well conceived, however, since farm horses do not make good military steeds.

A number of programs were rendered ineffective because they were sabotaged by officials or were used to oppress the very people they were intended to help. Thus reforms of personnel recruitment and of management were crucial to effective program implementation. Wang An-shih tried to obtain the men he needed by changing the examination system. He included law as a subject to be tested, assigned his own commentaries on the classics as official interpretations to be followed by the candidates in their papers, and stressed the classic known as *The Rites of Chou* (*Chou Li*), since it provided justification for institutional reform. He also tried to circumvent the entire examination system by expanding the state university and ensuring its graduates direct entry into the civil service. Wang further realized that most of the actual work of government, particularly on the local level, was performed, not by the civil service officials who were sent out for a tour of duty to preside over a district or prefecture, but by a subbureaucracy of clerks, petty agents, and various underlings who remained permanently in place. These men shared neither the status nor the learning of the officials, and there was little to restrain them from squeezing maximum profit out of their jobs. Despised as notoriously corrupt, they tended to become still more corrupt to compensate themselves for being despised. Wang's policy was to reduce their number, improve their pay, place them under stricter supervision, and give the most capable among them an opportunity to rise into the regular bureaucracy.

Wang's personality as well as his measures made him many enemies; by 1076 he was out of office. In the middle and late seventies, his program lost momentum, but a full reaction did not set in until the death of his imperial patron, Emperor Shen-tsung. However, there was a partial revival of the reform program under Emperor Hui-tsung. Still later, individual measures similar to those of Wang An-shih were reinstituted from time to time, but no minister again tried to do so much so rapidly.

In China, as elsewhere, political and economic developments were closely intertwined. The economic history of the period is complex, and there is much still to be learned, but clearly the Sung was a period of dramatic economic change.

The Economy

Qualitatively and quantitatively Sung economic changes were so extensive that scholars have termed them revolutionary. Furthermore, they occurred in all three areas of primary economic activity: industry, agriculture, and commerce. (For commerce, metals, and tea see Figure 8-2.) Of this triad, industrial growth peaked during the Northern Sung, whereas agricultural and commercial growth continued even after the loss of the North.

Figure 8-3 The "Rainbow Bridge," Kaifeng. Detail of *Spring Festival on the River* by Chang Tse-tuan. Hand-scroll, ink and light color on silk, early twelfth century, 25.5 cm high. Palace Museum, Peking.

During the Sung, important progress was made in the production of many commodities traditionally associated with China. Thus paper making and all the processes involved in book production advanced; there was progress in salt processing; and notable developments occurred in ceramics. Other kinds of economic activity, such as tea processing and shipbuilding, also gained new eminence, but it is not widely realized that China now also developed a coal and iron industry that was the most advanced in the world. In North China, as later in Europe, deforestation provided the major incentive for coal production. Much of this coal found its way into furnaces used to smelt iron mined in an area stretching in an arc from southern Hopei to northern Kiangsu. Estimates for total annual pig iron production range from 35,000 to as much as 125,000 tons, with the actual figure probably closer to the upper end of this scale. Using coke in blast furnaces fanned by box bellows, the Chinese developed the technology for smelting iron and carbonizing it to produce steel.

Much of the iron and steel went to equip the Sung army of well over one million men, providing them with swords, other weapons, and armor of various kinds. Even their arrows were tipped with steel. Other ferrous metal products included tools for farmers, carpenters, and other workmen; major consumer items such as stoves; and smaller items such as nails and needles. High-grade steel was used to produce bits for drilling wells and to make the chains used to support suspension bridges.

A good deal of the metal, as well as other products, was consumed in the Northern Sung capital, Kaifeng. (See Figure 8-3.) Located near the junction of the Yellow River and the canal system leading to the prosperous southeast, this city had originated as a commercial center and continued to function as such after it also became the political capital. It housed not only government offices, garrisons, warehouses, and arsenals but also private textile concerns, drug and chemical shops, shipyards, building material suppliers, and so forth. There was also a thriving restaurant and hotel industry. In contrast to the symmetrical, planned layout of the T'ang capital, Kaifeng grew organically, and in the process, it outgrew the old system of enclosed wards and spilled beyond its city walls as its inhabitants sought relief from urban congestion.

Some of the mining and manufacturing enterprises were large-scale operations employing hundreds of workers, while other concerns were confined to small workshops. Various kinds of brokers facilitated commercial transactions, and numerous lines of business were organized into guilds or associations that supervised the terms of trade and also served as intermediaries between their members and the government. As in medieval Europe, members of the same profession or guild frequently (but not always) set up shop in the same city street or district.

The growth of manufacturing and the development of Kaifeng and other cities were sustained by an increase in agricultural yields. At the same time, the opening of new markets for rural products stimulated the development of agriculture, now called upon to feed a population that had passed the 100 million mark. The size of harvests was increased by the use of improved farm tools, advances in water control, wider application of fertilizers, and the introduction of new strains of rice, most notably an early ripening variety native to central Vietnam. Different strains of rice (low or high in gluten, drought resistant, early or late ripening) were cultivated to suit local conditions. In the southeast it became common practice for a rice paddy to produce two crops a year, either two harvests of rice or one of rice followed by a crop of wheat or beans grown on the paddy after it was drained.

A major effect of increased agricultural yields was to confirm the South as China's richest and most productive region. In this respect, it left a more permanent influence on subsequent Chinese history than did the development of the coal and iron industries in the North. Economic growth in the North was disrupted by the Juchen invasion in the twelfth century and by that of the Mongols in the thirteenth, by a major shift of the Yellow River in 1194, and by the permanent decline of Kaifeng and its market. In the south, however, advanced agricultural practices continued to spread, enabling commerce and cities to continue to flourish during the Southern Sung.

Before turning to these developments, it is well to recall that economic growth rarely benefits all people equally. It does not prevent corruption, with the price, in the end, being paid by those too poor to afford bribes and presents. Nor does it preclude the wealthy from increasing the size of their holdings and from exploiting those who work the land as tenant sharecroppers or laborers. Sung China could easily support its population, but the poor were as hard pressed as ever. Wang An-shih's reforms notwithstanding, they continued to suffer from inequitable taxation and exorbitant interest rates. Peasant uprisings during the dynasty were rare, but there was unrest and rebellion in the 1120s. Much of the good that Emperor Hui-tsung accomplished by building schools and sponsoring charities was undone by the heavy burden of taxation and the exactions of government. Especially notorious were the emperor's demands for rare plants, stones, and novelties destined to decorate the imperial garden and collected from the people without compensation.

The Southern Sung (1127–1279)

Despite the deployment of catapults, flamethrowers, and incendiary devices made with gunpowder (another Chinese invention), the Sung lost the North. The dynasty carried on under a son of Emperor Hui-tsung, Kao-tsung (r. 1127–62), who at the nadir of his career was forced to flee from the Juchen troops by taking refuge on some islands off the southeast coast. Then, however, the tide of war turned. In 1138 Kao-tsung designated Hangchow as a "temporary capital," and a peace agreement with the Chin was concluded in 1142. The previous year had brought the death in prison of Yüeh Fei (1103–41), one of China's most celebrated generals, subject of a novel and numerous stories and plays, whom later generations extolled as a hero who had paid for his patriotism with his life. Conversely, Ch'in Kuei (1090–1155), the minister who effected the peace, came to be despised as the prototype of the traitor. Later, iron statues representing Ch'in Kuei and his wife in chains were placed on the grounds of Yüeh Fei's tomb beside Hangchow's West Lake. For a long time, visitors used to express their contempt by spitting at the statues, but under the People's Republic a sign was posted prohibiting this practice.

In the treaty of 1142 the Sung accepted the Huai River as its northern boundary, agreed to make annual payments to the Chin, and recognized the Chin as its superior. Nevertheless, relations between the two states remained uneasy. Fighting broke out again between 1161 and 1165. After a period of unfriendly coexistence, cold war once again turned into active warfare, for the last time, from 1206 to 1208. This time the war came to an end only after the Sung handed over to their enemy the severed head of the minister responsible for starting the war. The Juchen state was gradually Sinified during the twelfth century, as indicated by its adoption of such institutions as the examination system, but this did not induce the Sung to look any more kindly on its northern neighbor.

The Southern Sung government was therefore by no means unhappy when the new Mongol power rose in the North to challenge the Chin. When the Mongols destroyed the Chin and occupied North China in 1234, the Sung's situation became precarious. The dynasty continued to hold on for another forty years, however, largely because of its maritime strength. When the end did come, it was hastened by naval treachery.

Among the reasons for the Southern Sung's ability to sustain itself for a century and a half were the geographic defensibility and the prosperity of the South as well as the government's ability to command acceptance as the legitimate regime and to perform the traditional functions of government. However, it also suffered from internal ills: unstable imperial leadership (the first three emperors ended their reigns by abdicating), factional divisiveness in officialdom, monetary policies that eventually produced rampant inflation, and a shrinking tax base resulting from the decline of small landholders and tax evasion by those who held much land. To deal with the latter situation, an ambitious land reform program was launched by Chief Councilor Chia Ssu-tao (1213–75) during the 1260s. Large landowners were required to sell to the government a portion of their holdings, which the government then managed itself. The economic gains thus realized, however, were counterbalanced by the disaffection of the wealthy and powerful at a time when the state required maximum unity against the Mongol threat.

The government had its troubles, but the dynasty continued to inspire loyal devotion to the end—and even beyond. Not only had men sacrificed their lives in its defense even after the cause was hopeless; there were also others who remained loyal even after its demise. This was a new phenomenon in Chinese history, and, as with so many Sung innovations, set a precedent for later ages.

Southern Sung Cities and Commerce

Politically and psychologically the loss of the North was a grave blow to the dynasty, but economically the loss was much less severe, since by this time a good two-thirds of China's population and wealth were in the South. As elsewhere in the world, the development of cities and commerce went hand in hand.

Commercial transactions were facilitated by the use of paper money, a Chinese innovation. This medium of exchange originated in Szechwan with the circulation of private certificates of deposit secured by funds placed in private shops. In the eleventh century, paper money was issued for the first time by the government. As long as these notes were adequately secured by goods or specie (hard money) they worked well. However, the government could not resist the temptation to issue more paper money than it could back with solid reserves. When this became generally known the notes depreciated in value.

A large part of China's internal as well as foreign trade was waterborne, for it was less expensive to transport goods on rivers and canals than to cart them overland. China's oceangoing ships were large, capable of carrying several hundred men. They were navigated with the aid of the compass, a product of China's traditional excellence in the study of magnetism. In other ways, too, the ships were technologically advanced. As enumerated by Mark Elvin, their features included: "watertight bulkheads, buoyancy chambers, bamboo fenders at the waterline, floating anchors to hold them steady during storms, axial rudders in place of steering oars, outrigger and leeboard devices, oars for use in calm weather, scoops for taking samples off the sea floor, sounding lines for determining the depth, compasses for navigation, and small rockets propelled by gunpowder for self-defense."[1] The ships, which carried merchandise, could also be converted to military use, and the superiority of its navy was crucial to the Southern Sung's military security.

The trading cities of the South were known for their prosperity, the fast pace of life, and also for the reputed frivolity and shamelessness of their inhabitants. The greatest city was Hangchow. Situated between the Yangtze (to which it was linked by canal) and the international ports of the southeast coast, it was a government and trade center, home of merchants and officials. Flanked by the Che River and the West Lake, Hangchow, like Venice, was a city of bridges and canals; and it evoked the enthusiasm of that cosmopolitan Venetian Marco Polo, who described it as, "without doubt the finest and most splendid city in the world,"[2] even though by the time he visited it late in the thirteenth century, Hangchow was no longer the capital and the South was generally disdained by China's new Mongol masters.

Hangchow merchants, organized into guilds, offered their customers all kinds of merchandise ranging from the staples of life to exotic perfumes, fine jewelry, and other luxury items. There were bookstores and pet shops. Among the amenities offered by the city were exquisite restaurants, tea houses, cabarets, and baths. Entertainment was also provided by a host of popular performers, chess masters, fortunetellers, acrobats, storytellers, and puppeteers. There were also numerous practitioners of the world's oldest profession, ladies "highly proficient and accomplished in the use of endearments and caresses," who completely captivated Marco Polo and other foreign visitors.[3] Outside the city, the surrounding hills with their Buddhist temples provided opportunities for pleasure excursions, and a favorite pastime was boating and partying on West Lake, still today a favorite resort.

The inhabitants of Sung cities did not escape the grimmer aspects of urban life. The threat of fire was ever present, and the government took various protective measures against this menace. In Kaifeng, the Northern Sung capital, guard stations were placed at fifty-yard intervals, and watchtowers were erected, each manned by 100 firefighting soldiers. In the case of Hangchow, the city was divided into zones. Two thousand soldiers were responsible for the fourteen zones within the city, and another 1200 stood ready to combat fires in eight suburban zones. These firefighters were equipped with buckets, ropes, hatchets, fireproof clothing and other paraphernalia. Despite these precautions, there were frequent and destructive conflagrations. Crime, too, was a fact of urban life, and the cities and towns alike had their share of criminals: confidence men who passed lead off as gold, holdup specialists against whom merchants required special police protection, and other petty criminals who eked out a living as best they could. For those who could not make a decent living, honestly or dishonestly, the city still offered advantages not available in the village. On special occasions, public alms were distributed, and there were state hospitals and dispensaries, and houses for the aged, the decrepit, and the orphaned. If worst came to worst, those dying in poverty at least had the consolation of knowing that they would receive proper burial even if they had no relatives to pay for it.

Since the government derived considerable revenue from foreign trade (for example, through customs duties, licensing fees, sales and transit taxes, and so forth) this was one of the rare times in Chinese history when it actually encouraged overseas commerce. It maintained harbors and canals, built breakwaters, erected beacons, operated warehouses, and even set up hotels. Merchants who attracted foreign shipping to Chinese ports were rewarded. Among the major imports were aromatics and drugs, textiles, minerals, and miscellaneous luxury items, while the primary exports included silks, metals (especially copper coins exported to Japan), and ceramics. The export of the latter was actively encouraged by the government, and the discovery of Sung shards not only throughout South and Southeast Asia but also in the Middle East and along the east coast of Africa attests to the wide popularity of the Sung product. This was the precursor of the later export trade that was to make the word "china" a synonym for "porcelain."

The Confucian Revival

Even during the centuries when Buddhism prevailed as the major spiritual, intellectual, and aesthetic influence, the family ethic and political ideology of Confucianism had never been totally eclipsed. In the Late T'ang, for example, Han Yü had vigorously affirmed the Confucian Way. But during the Sung there was a revitalization of Confucianism, which took many forms. It stimulated a revival of classical scholarship, new achievements in historical studies, and fresh departures in Confucian speculative thought. And it prompted a more earnest devotion to Confucian principles.

Confucianism had always emphasized the study of history, and the Confucian revival brought with it a renewed interest in historiography. Outstanding among the Sung historians was Ssu-ma Kuang (1019–86), a bitter opponent of Wang An-shih. The care and critical intelligence Ssu-ma Kuang employed in examining historical sources, his sophisticated understanding of the historical process, his narrative skill, and the scope of his work have earned the esteem of scholars. In a departure from tradition, he included in the finished work discussions of the discrepancies he had found in the sources and his reasons for choosing one version of events over another. He was a master of detail, who had the confidence and vision to do something no scholar had attempted since the Han: a study of virtually the whole of Chinese history (taking up where the *Tso Chuan* had left off) rather than confining himself to a single dynasty. Animating his work was the conviction that an accurate account of the past could teach moral and practical lessons for the present, and thus he gave his work the title *A Comprehensive Mirror for Aid in Government* (*Tzu-chih t'ung-chien*).

The Confucian emphasis on right understanding of the past (history, philosophy, literature) as a guide to proper life and preparation for service to the state, implied a commitment to education. Confucius himself had become a teacher when he failed in his quest for a ruler to implement his ideas. Thus it is no accident that the Confucian revival under the Sung was accompanied by the burgeoning of schools, both government institutions and private academies. Famed among the latter was the White Deer Grotto Academy, which was run, for a time, by the renowned philosopher Chu Hsi (1130–1200). There, students were exposed to a heavy mixture of moral exhortation and scholarship so that they might emerge both virtuous and erudite. Like dedicated teachers everywhere, the committed Confucian scholars were forever pleading with their students to forget such careerist considerations as passing examinations and to concentrate on the serious business of learning and self-improvement. To become truly educated, the guidance of a teacher was believed extremely important. But for the sake of those who lived in remote places without teachers, Chu Hsi and his friend Lü Tsu-ch'ien (1137–81) compiled an anthology of Sung Confucianism for self-instruction, which became enormously influential in Korea and Japan as well as in China. It draws on the writings of the four Northern Sung thinkers who came to be considered as the founders of the new Confucian philosophy, Chou Tun-i (1017–73), the two brothers Ch'eng Hao (1032–85) and Ch'eng I (1033–1107), and Chang Tsai (1020–77). Its title is *Reflections on Things at Hand (Chin-ssu lu)*.

Reflections deals with many matters of practical concern ranging from guidance on how to manage a family to advice on when to accept political office and when to decline. It includes discussions of political institutions and behavior. Its main emphasis, however, is on self-perfection, which alone makes all the rest possible.

The authors of *Reflections* were careful to distinguish their teachings from the doctrines of Buddhism and Taoism and attacked the teachings of the Buddha and Lao Tzu. Yet, even the staunchest Confucian was not immune to the attractions of Buddhism, although only Ch'an Buddhism appeared to show continuing creative vitality. Meanwhile, a continued interest in Taoism was evidenced when in 1019 the state sponsored the printing of the Taoist Tripitaka (*Tao-tsang*) resembling in length and scope its Buddhist prototype. Given this rich Buddhist and Taoist heritage, it should not come as a surprise to find that Sung Confucian philosophers were influenced by these two traditions even as they sought to undermine them by creating a more sophisticated philosophy of their own.

Neo-Confucian Philosophy

It was the great strength of the new Confucianism that it was at once a creed that gave meaning to the life of the individual, an ideology supporting state and society, and a philosophy that provided a convincing framework for understanding the world. It conceived of the world as an organic whole and itself constituted an organic system in which each aspect reinforced the other in theory as well as in practice.

This new philosophy, known in the West as Neo-Confucianism, received its classic formulation by Chu Hsi, but neither he nor the four Northern Sung philosophers whose work he excerpted in *Reflections* were accepted as orthodox in their own day. It was not until the second quarter of the thirteenth century that Chu Hsi's teachings received official recognition and his commentaries on the *Four Books* were officially accepted. Of these four books, considered repositories of fundamental truth, only the *Analects* had been universally revered by all Confucians throughout history. The other three, *The Mencius*, *The Great Learning*, and *The Doctrine of the Mean* (the last two are chapters from the *Records of Rites*) were subjects of controversy and debate for most of the Sung period.

It was characteristic of East Asian thinkers that they did not present their ideas in systematic philosophical treatises but as commentaries on the classics, in miscellaneous writings (including letters), and in conversations that were recorded by disciples. This made the study of their ideas very demanding but also encouraged successive generations of scholars to reinterpret Confucianism in their own way. Neither in the Sung nor later was Neo-Confucianism a monolithic philosophy.

Sung thinkers, like earlier Chinese philosophers, found it congenial and fruitful to think in terms of complementary opposites, interacting polarities such as inner and outer, substance (*t'i*) and function (*yung*), knowledge and action. Perhaps they were particularly attracted to this mode of thought because it enabled them to make distinctions without doing violence to what they perceived to be an ultimate organic unity. In their metaphysics they naturally employed the ancient *yin* and *yang*, but more central to their thought was the conceptual pair *li* and *ch'i*.

This *li*, not to be confused with the term meaning ritual (which is written with a different character) is usually translated as "principle." Since the Chinese word does not distinguish between singular and plural, *li* can also be understood as a network of principles. Indeed, the accepted Sung etymology of the word was that it originally signified veins running through jade. Thus each individual *li* is part of the entire system, and in the philosophy of Ch'eng I and Chu Hsi, this system constitutes the underlying pattern of reality. In this view nothing can exist if there is no *li* for it. It is characteristic of the Confucian and Neo-Confucian cast of mind that this applies as much to the realm of human conduct as it does to the physical world. The *li* of fatherhood has the same ontological status (order of being or order of reality) as the *li* for mountains. No distinction is made between the former, which is defined in moral terms, and the latter, into which value judgments do not enter, for the world of moral action and that of physical objects is held to be one and the same. Both are comprehensible and both are equally "natural."

Ch'i is a more difficult word to render into English. It can be characterized as the vital force and substance of which man and the universe are made. It can also be conceived of as energy, but energy which occupies space. In its most refined form it occurs as a kind of rarefied ether, but condensed it becomes the most solid metal or rock. Thus in his cosmology Chu Hsi envisioned the world as a sphere in constant rotation, so that the heaviest *ch'i* is held in the center by the centripetal force of the motion. The *ch'i* then becomes progressively lighter and thinner as one moves away from the center. In this way he was able to explain why, for instance, the air at high altitude is thinner than that at sea level.

It was theoretically possible to construct a philosophy based on either concept. Chang Tsai based his theories entirely on *ch'i* whereas Chu Hsi's contemporary Lu Chiu-yüan (1139–93) asserted that *li* alone exists. Ch'eng I and Chu Hsi, however, accepted both as irreducible entities, although *li* had logical and ontological but not temporal priority over *ch'i*. Actually, in Chu Hsi's system *li* was further identified with the Supreme Ultimate (*t'ai-chi*), which had formed the basis of Chou Tun-i's metaphysics. In this way *li* was elevated to a level superior to *ch'i*. Nevertheless, in the actual world *li* never occurs without *ch'i*. This was a very important doctrine, for it enabled the Sung philosophers to accept Mencius' theory of the essential goodness of humankind and to explain man's frequent departures from that goodness: people were composed of good *li* and more or less impure *ch'i*. The ancient sages were born with *ch'i* that was perfectly pure: they were born perfect. But ordinary folk have to cope with more or less turgid *ch'i:* they must work to attain perfection.

For ordinary people, the way to attain perfection is by truly grasping the *li*, but since these are found within everyone as well as out in the world, there was serious disagreement over the proper methodology of self-cultivation. Chu Hsi generally stressed the "investigation of things," by which he meant primarily the study of moral conduct and especially the timeless lessons contained in the classics. Consequently his school was associated with an emphasis on scholarly learning, even though it by no means ruled out more inner-directed endeavors such as silent meditation and reflection. Lu Chiu-yüan, in contrast, foreshadowing the teachings of the major Ming dynasty philosopher Wang Yang-ming, stressed inner illumination. For him, without the reader's innate understanding, even the classics remain without meaning. The truth is within: he once went as far as to say, "the classics are all footnotes to me." The intellectual atmosphere was further enlivened by other Confucians who rejected theoretical speculation and insisted that the true vocation of a scholar lay in concentrating on matters of practical statecraft. But by narrowing their intellectual focus these thinkers also narrowed their appeal, so that they had less influence on the course of Chinese thought than did Chu Hsi or Lu Chiu-yüan.

Associated with Sung Confucianism was a moral seriousness that made heavy demands on men and women. Old strictures like those against widow remarriage, generally disregarded in earlier times, were now taken more seriously. The woman who remained faithful to her betrothed even though he died before their marriage could be consummated took her place among the Confucian paragons. Nor was there anything in Neo-Confucianism to hinder the gradual spread of footbinding,* a practice which caused agonizing pain to many generations of Chinese girls. In a convergence of ethics and aesthetics, tiny feet were thought to enhance a girl's attractiveness and, at the same time, to deter her from straying into mischief. We should note, however, that the practice was apparently rare in Sung times and that it was not part of a Confucian social program.

The Sung philosophers gave the old concept of *jen* (humaneness) a new metaphysical dimension. Chang Tsai proclaimed, "all people are my brothers and sisters, and all things are my companions."[4] It is in keeping with this ideal that the age saw a new growth in secular charities sponsored by eminent Confucians, their lineages, or the state. In Sung poetry, too, there was a continuation of the old tradition of employing verse to protest political and economic conditions and also a new interest in ordinary things and in rendering scenes from everyday life.

Sung Poetry

The Sung was a prolific period for poetry. (One eighteenth-century scholar listed 3812 Sung poets.) There are, for example, a great many poems depicting the hardships of life in the country and the disastrous effects of bad officials and/or bad weather. But it would be wrong to view rural life as just one unrelieved misery. The following is one of four poems in which a Late Northern Sung poet describes life in his native village:

> At cock crow the whole village rouses.
> Gets ready to set off for the middle fields:
> Remind the wife to be sure to fix some millet,
> Shout to the children to shut the gate behind us.
> Spade and hoe catch the morning light;
> Laughter and hubbub mingle on the road.
> Puddles from the night before wet our straw sandals;
> Here's a wild flower to stick in the bun of your hair!
> Clear light breaks through the distant haze;
> Spring skies now are fresh and gay.
> Magnolia covers the wandering hills;
> In the empty field, a brocaded pheasant preens.
> The young people have come like racing clouds;
> Owl-like, an old man squats on his heels alone.

* A procedure used to restrict the growth of the feet. The feet of young female children were wrapped tightly in bandages (about two inches wide and ten feet long). Over a period of time, the four toes of each foot were bent into the sole, and the sole and heel were brought as close together as possible. The great toe was left unbound. This practice probably originated during the Five Dynasties period. It later became more widespread among the upper classes until, in the later dynasties, it not only was prevalent among the high Chinese elite but was also widely practiced in other social strata. It continued well into the twentieth century.

> The yellow earth glistens from the rain that passed;
> Clouds of dust race before the wind.
> Little by little, the whole village gathers,
> Calling greetings from field to field.
> The omens say it will be a good month;
> Let's keep on working, down to sundown![5]

The poetry of this time provides many pictures of daily life and personal routines, glimpses into people's private inner lives, and their responses to misfortunes and joy. And it reflects their broader concerns, as when a Southern Sung patriot, disgusted by his government's peace policy, complains. "Stabled horses die of obesity; strings unstrung break on the bow."[6] At the same time poetry was an art with its own technical demands.

The Northern Sung poem quoted above is in the form of five-character old-style verse, and many fine Sung poems were written in the old forms. These include poems by Su Shih (Su Tung-p'o), who is also famous for expanding the *tz'u* form, which originated during the T'ang but reached its height in the Sung. Written to tunes, of which the titles are all that now remains, the *tz'u* required great skill in fitting the words to the musical pattern. But it allowed the poet unusual freedom in diction, since he was permitted to incorporate colloquial expressions. Actually Su Shih's genius was not bound by any set form. Perhaps his most famous works are two rhapsodies (*fu*) on the Red Cliff, site of a famous battle fought during the Three Kingdoms period. Su Shih also wrote many poems on friendship, drinking, and nature. Like other Sung poets he knew and loved the literature of the past. But he also brought to it a critical spirit. For example, his view of the highly respected and beloved T'ang poet Meng Chiao was by no means representative of his time. The following poem surely will strike a responsive chord in anyone who has ever labored over a poem only to discover that the reward gained was not worth the effort expended.

Reading the Poetry of Meng Chiao—First of Two Poems

> Night: reading Meng Chiao's poems,
> Characters fine as cow's hair.
> By the cold lamp, my eyes blur and swim.
> Good passages I rarely find—
> Lone flowers poking up through the mud—
> But more hard words than the *Odes* and *Li sao*—
> Jumbled rocks clogging the clear stream,
> Making rapids too swift for poling.
> My first impression is of eating little fishes—
> What you get's not worth the trouble;
> Or of boiling tiny mud crabs
> And ending up with empty claws.
> For refinement he might compete with monks
> But he'll never match his master Han Yü.

Man's life is like morning dew,
A flame eating up the oil night by night.
Why should I strain my ears
Listening to the squeaks of this autumn insect?
Better lay aside the book
And drink my cup of jade-white wine.[7]

Su Shih was at the center of a circle of talented friends who not only wrote fine poetry but also excelled in calligraphy and painting, for these were the three arts of the gentleman-scholar. Su and others frequently wrote their poems on a painting, thus combining the three arts in a single work, and Su himself saw a close relationship between poetry, "pictures without form," and paintings, "unspoken poems."[8] For Mei Yao-ch'en (1002–60), poetry itself must go beyond words and "express inexhaustible meaning which exists beyond the words themselves."[9] Su Shih's views on painting were in advance of his time in that he rejected representationalism as childish. For Su, a painting such as the bamboo by his friend Wen T'ung (1018–60), China's first great bamboo painter, was practically a self-portrait, revealing the noble character of the painter. (See Figure 8-4.)

Figure 8-4   *A Broken Branch of Bamboo,* attributed to Wen T'ung. Album leaf, ink on paper, 31 cm × 48.3 cm. Palace Museum Collection, Taipei.

Painting and the Arts

The bamboo branch attributed to Wen T'ung and reproduced here illustrates what the painter can accomplish employing the ink and brush of the calligrapher. Roger Goepper's analysis is worth quoting in full:

> All the elements have been drawn with a single confident brush stroke: the sections of the stem and the branches with a firm and elastic writing brush (*kan-pi*), the counter-pressure of whose springy tip can be felt in the hand; the leaves with a softer and limper brush (*shui-pi*), which submits obediently to the slightest pressure of the hand. The interaction of the graphic forms resulting from these two techniques largely determines the general impression created by the painting, the individual elements becoming fused in a composition filled with tension and vitality. The diagonal upward movement of the stem is answered contrapuntally by the smaller twigs, while the sudden break diverts the thrust from the top left-hand corner and causes it to fade out into the largest blank space in the composition. At the same time this break introduces an element of the unexpected and exciting into the picture; it disturbs the harmonious sequence of its construction and hints at the outside forces that affect the bamboo and determine its fate, as they do with man. The fixed points of the composition lie on the one hand in the knots of the stem, accentuated by small brush dashes, and on the other in the areas of radiation formed by the rhythmic play of the overlapping leaf spears.[10]

Expressiveness and spontaneity were prized by Ch'an painters, some of whom worked in the ink-splash technique of "ink Wang" (see Chapter 5), dashing off their work, destroying what did not come out right, but never laboring over their art, confident that artistic inspiration, like religious enlightenment, comes in a flash. The finest Ch'an painters lived during the Southern Sung and were as unrestricted in subject matter as in style. Thus for Mu-ch'i, one of the greatest masters of the genre, six persimmons could mirror the truth as faithfully as any portrait of the Buddha. Liang K'ai's famous portrait of Li Po (see Figure 8-5) suggests that he and the T'ang poet were kindred spirits. This art was not highly regarded by later Chinese connoisseurs, but it was prized in Japan, where we shall encounter the style again.

There was also less iconoclastic Buddhist art. Particularly notable were gilded wooden figures of Kuan-yin seated in a position of "Royal Ease," with one leg raised supporting an arm. Housed in temples more delicate and refined than their T'ang predecessors and now more generally capped by gracefully curved roofs, such figures were among the best products of the last phase of Buddhist art.

A new age demanded a new means of artistic expression. The towering achievement of Sung art was in landscape painting. Developing styles which first appeared during the Five Dynasties period shortly before the Sung, Sung painters produced classic works of art strikingly different from the paintings of earlier times.

Just as Ssu-ma Kuang sought to encompass all of history in his *Tzu-chih t'ung-chien*, and Neo-Confucian philosophers sought to develop a universal philosophy, the great landscape painters sought to encompass the whole of na-

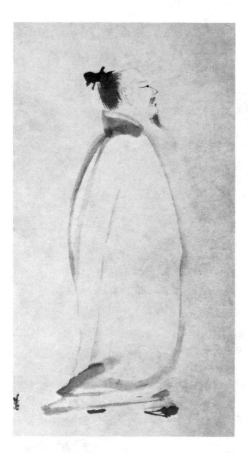

Figure 8-5 Liang K'ai, *Li Po.* Ink on
paper, mid-thirteenth century,
79 cm high. Tokyo National Museum.

ture in their work. Thus they produced works of unparalleled monumentality
such as Fan K'uan's (d. ca. 1023) *Traveling among Streams and Mountains* (see
Figure 8-6). Impressive scope, strength, and dark tones have replaced the rich
colors, the clarity of line, and the decorative charm of earlier landscape paintings (compare Figure 5-7). The principles of composition have also changed.
For the first time we find the classic Chinese perspective in which the picture
surface is divided into three planes, one near and one distant, with the middle
plane occupied by water or mist. Whereas nature in earlier paintings provided a
setting for man, here man is reduced to his proper dimensions, and a road invites the viewer to enter the painting and contemplate the grandeur of nature,
the *li* of the universe.

Fan K'uan was a northerner. In the South, other masters like Tung Yüan
(d. 962) and his disciple Chü-jan (fl. ca. 975) depicted the softer and more at-
mospheric mountainscapes of their region and founded another influential
tradition. The difference between the southern and northern painters was not
only a matter of tone and technique, but as Richard M. Barnhart has suggested
of Tung Yüan, "The southern master appears to have wished to meditate
upon the land, as a poet; the northern masters to dramatize it."[11]

This was also an age which produced fine hand-scrolls through which the
viewer could travel at leisure as the painting was gradually unrolled, an effect

Figure 8-6　Fan K'uan,
*Traveling among Streams
and Mountains*. Hanging
scroll, ink and light
color on silk, 129.6 cm ×
74.9 cm. Palace Museum
Collection, Taipei.

Detail Figure 8-6　Fan K'uan, *Traveling among Streams and Mountains.*

recaptured only with difficulty by the modern museum visitor who sees such a painting completely spread out in a glass case. Frequently in such works the viewer follows a river, and might even, as in the famed Ch'ing-ming Festival Scroll, visit the capital itself. Today this painting provides valuable material for the student of Sung urbanization as well as delight to the lover of art. (See Figure 8-3.)

The world of the Sung painter, northerner and southerner, gentleman-amateur, monk, or professional, was as varied as was the intellectual and literary life of the period. It serves little purpose to list names and styles, but a few more works may illustrate something of the range of Sung art as well as its general direction. The first, by Emperor Hui-tsung, is a classic in its own, much practiced genre. The carefully studied, realistic yet idealized, five-colored parakeet (see Figure 8-1) well meets the standards demanded by the emperor in a famous edict: "Painters are not to imitate their predecessors, but to depict objects as they exist, true to color and form. Simplicity and nobility of line is to be their aim."[12]

Artists who lived after the period of the monumental masters such as Fan K'uan knew that the classical achievement could not be repeated and sought modes of expression more fitting for their own times. Frequently they chose to paint a part of nature rather than the whole, a branch to represent the tree.

One painter who did this was Ma Yüan (ca. 1160–ca. 1225), often known as "One-cornered Ma" because of his tendency to concentrate his compositions in one corner of the surface. One of his themes (see Figure 8-7) is that of the scholar quietly contemplating and enjoying nature. Both the scene and its vision of nature are full of charm. Another favorite Southern Sung painter, along with Ma greatly appreciated in Japan, was Hsia Kuei (fl. ca. 1190–1230). Figure 8-8 reproduces a section of his hand-scroll *A Pure and Remote View of Rivers and Mountains*, a masterpiece in which the artist made the most of the musicality of the medium. Many have imitated his style, but very few were able to achieve the subtlety and strength of his brushwork animating the austerity of his composition.

In one other art form the Sung represents a classic achievement: Sung ceramics have long been admired as combining the vigor of earlier work in this medium with the grace of the ware that was to be produced later. As in painting, there were major differences between northern and southern styles, reflecting in this case not only different tastes and a varied clientele but also differences in the chemical composition of the clays used by potters. Sung wares include stoneware and porcelain, vessels covered with a slip (clay coating) which has been carved away to produce a design, others covered with enamel or decorated with a painting. Colors run from white through grays to black, as well as various hues from lavender to olive. Perhaps most prized are the celadons, blue green ware often decorated with a crackle (network of fine cracks) formed by the glaze cooling more rapidly than the vessel. (See Page 181, left.) Some of this exquisite ware was made especially for the imperial household, and such pieces are fitting representatives of the refinement and elegance which were not least among the Sung's achievements.

Figure 8-7   Ma Yüan, *On a Mountain Path*. Album leaf, ink and light color on silk, 27.4 cm × 43.1 cm. Palace Museum Collection, Taipei.

Figure 8-8   Hsia Kuei, *A Pure and Remote View of Rivers and Mountains.* Section of handscroll, ink on paper, 46.4 cm high. Palace Museum Collection, Taipei.

NOTES

1. Mark Elvin, *The Pattern of the Chinese Past* (Stanford: Stanford University Press, 1973), p. 137.
2. R. E. Latham, trans., *The Travels of Marco Polo* (Baltimore: Penguin Books, 1958), p. 184.
3. *Ibid.*, p. 187.
4. Wing-tsit Chan, *A Source Book in Chinese Philosophy* (Princeton: Princeton University Press, 1963), p. 497.
5. Ch'in Kuan, in Kojiro Yoshikawa, *An Introduction to Sung Poetry*, trans. Burton Watson (Cambridge: Harvard University Press, 1967), pp. 16–17.
6. Liu Wu-chi, *An Introduction to Chinese Literature* (Bloomington: Indiana University Press, 1966), p. 119.
7. Burton Watson, trans., *Su Tung-p'o* (New York: Columbia University Press, 1965), p. 59.
8. Susan Bush, *The Chinese Literati on Painting: Su Shih (1037–1101) to Tung Ch'i-ch'ang (1156–1636)* (Cambridge: Harvard University Press, 1971), p. 25.
9. Jonathan Chaves, *Mei Yao-ch'en and the Development of Early Sung Poetry* (New York: Columbia University Press, 1976), p. 110.
10. Roger Goepper, *The Essence of Chinese Painting* (Boston: Boston Book and Art Shop, 1963), p. 134.
11. Richard M. Barnhart, "Tung Yüan," in Herbert Franke, ed., *Sung Biographies—Painters*, Münchener Ostasiatische Studien, vol. 17 (Wiesbaden: Franz Steiner Verlag, 1976), p. 141.
12. Arthur Waley, quoted in Goepper, *The Essence of Chinese Painting*, p. 106.

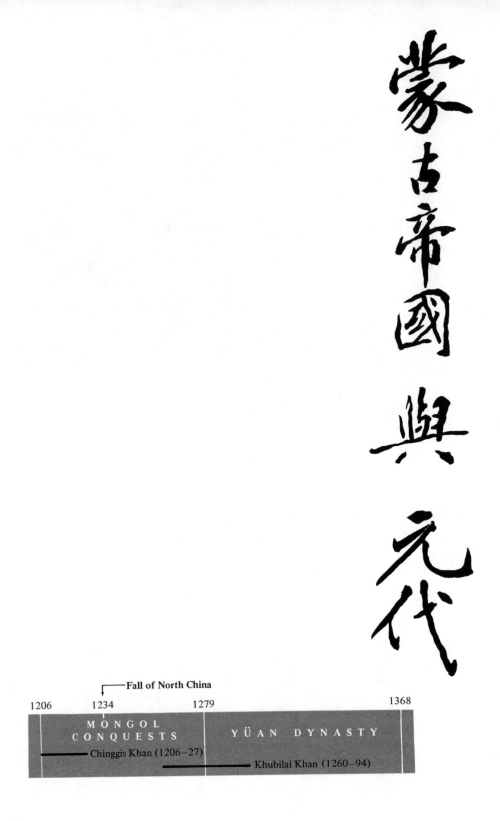

蒙古帝國與元代

Fall of North China

| 1206 | 1234 | 1279 | 1368 |

MONGOL
CONQUESTS

YÜAN DYNASTY

Chinggis Khan (1206–27)

Khubilai Khan (1260–94)

9 The Mongol Empire and the Yüan Dynasty

The Mongols are famed as the world's foremost conquerors, creators of the largest empire in the history of the planet. (See map, Figure 9-1.) They established their supremacy over most of Eurasia, including Russia and Persia, all of Central Asia, China, and Korea. Mongol armies reached as far West as the Adriatic; in the East they took to ships to attack Japan and Java. Even those lands that, like Japan, preserved their independence were affected by the Mongol challenge. For a time, communication between East and West was facilitated by Mongol domination and encouragement of trade. But the Mongol territory was too vast, local cultures too various and deeply rooted, the centrifugal forces too strong for the Mongol Empire to last very long. Ultimately the empire disintegrated.

211

Chinggis Khan: Founding of the Mongol Empire

Temüjin, the man known to the West as Chinggis (Genghis, Jenghis) Khan (ca. 1167–1227), was the son of a Mongolian tribal chieftain. When his father was killed, the boy was forced to flee and spent a number of years wandering. Eventually he returned to his tribe, and began his career as a world conqueror by avenging the murder of his father. Gradually he gained ascendency in the hierarchy of Mongol tribal chiefs. He was almost forty by the time he established his leadership over all the Mongol tribes, which, at a great meeting held in 1206, recognized him as the supreme ruler, the Chinggis Khan. As the supreme ruler he unified the tribes, organized them into a superb fighting force, and started them on the road to conquest and far-flung empire.

Unifying the tribes was a difficult task, not only because they were widely dispersed but also because of the nature of tribal life. The tribesmen were excellent fighters, jealous of their independence. Moreover, there was constant fighting among the tribes, to abduct women for wives and to settle old feuds. It required great determination, political skill, knowledge of men, and a manifest ability to lead, to weld these tribal groups into a people. It also required ruthlessness, drive, military skill, and personal courage. Apparently Chinggis Khan had these qualities. He was able to obtain the support of the hardy tribesmen. Equally significant, both as a testament to his leadership qualities and as an indication of his personal power, was his ability to attract a following of *nökhör*. These were men who renounced all other ties to clan or tribe and gave their patron their sole and complete loyalty. Many of Chinggis Khan's best generals were *nökhör*.

Clans and tribes remained the basic units of Mongol organization, but at a higher level the people were also bound together by loyalty to the Great Khan and by a law code (*jasagh* or *yasa*) first promulgated in 1206 and further expanded thereafter. Also transcending tribal divisions was the army, which was organized on a decimal system in units of tens, hundreds, and thousands. An elite corps, which grew to 10,000 men, formed the core of the Mongol army. At the height of the campaigns, the total army may have numbered nearly 130,000 men. It was joined in those campaigns by almost an equal number of non-Mongol warriors, the forces of other peoples who decided to join the Mongols rather than attempt to resist the whirlwind.

The Mongol army was a superb force in terms of overall direction, organization, and the toughness and ability of its individual fighting men. These fighters lived in the saddle: they could even sleep on horseback while their horses marched. When necessary they withstood great privation and endured all kinds of hardship. They were able to cover enormous distances at great speed, changing mounts several times in the process. The Mongol horses too were very hardy, able to endure extremes of climate, and in winter to find food by digging it out from under the snow or stripping twigs and bark from trees. Moreover, on the command level, the Mongols achieved masterly feats of planning and carrying out their operations. Their enemies were defeated as much by the Mongols' rapid movements and the precise coordination of their far-flung armies as they were by their ferocity and superb tactical discipline.

Whatever the Mongols could not use they destroyed. That was the fate of cities which resisted. As for their inhabitants, the women and children were enslaved, the men either killed or used as living shields in the next battle or assault on a city. Mongol brutality left terror in its wake. Even for Europeans, who lived in a far more military culture than that of China, the encounter with Mongol arms was an overwhelming experience that could only be explained in supernatural terms. According to *The Chronicle of Novgorod*, "God alone knows who they are and whence they came."[1] In Russia, Poland, and Hungary the merciless Mongols appeared as manifestations of God's wrath; their cruelties, acts of divine punishment meted out to sinners.

By the time of his death in 1227, Chinggis Khan had established Mongol supremacy in Central Asia, begun the offensive against Russia, destroyed the Hsi Hsia state, fought the Chin, and captured Peking. His headquarters remained in Mongolia, where Kamakorum served as the capital city, although it did not take on the appearance of a major city with a city wall and permanent buildings until 1235. This was the work of Ögödei (r. 1229–41), who as Great Khan had inherited the richest part of his father's empire. According to Mongol custom, however, other portions had been assigned to Ögödei's brothers, who ruled over three major khanates in Turkestan, Russia, and Persia.

The death of Chinggis Khan and the division of his patrimony did not diminish the momentum of Mongol conquests: in 1231 Mongol troops crossed the Yalu River into Korea and continued their advance in North China, taking Kaifeng in 1233 and Loyang in 1234. Also in 1234 they completed the destruction of the Juchen Chin dynasty. Mongol armies were equally successful in the West, where Kiev fell in 1240, Baghdad in 1258. In 1241 a Mongol army was on the Adriatic. And then they turned back. Western Europe was spared, not because the Mongols were beaten in battle or had been awed by the Western defense, but by a command decision of the Mongol general. The exact reason for the turnabout is not known, but geography most probably played a role. The vast number of horses required by the Mongol army needed great open plains on which to graze.

The Mongols developed a courier system to link their empire; couriers could cover up to 200 miles a day. They also had a written language based on an alphabet borrowed from another tribal people, the Uighurs, and Chinggis Khan created a body of written law, the *yasa*. However, the Mongols lacked an organized political system capable of molding their vast and diverse conquests into a lasting unity. Particularly grave was the absence of a formalized system of succession. Where complex political institutions did exist, as in China and Persia, they were grafted on to a local culture; otherwise, there was simply the old tribal system that had been unified by Temüjin's character and thus could not long survive his death, despite his attempt to create a legal system in the *yasa.* That he created the *yasa,* coming from a tribal culture, is a mark of his genius; that he so greatly underestimated the task of institutionalizing his rule is a mark both of the limits of his genius and of the gulf between the tribal and settled cultures.

Under Chinggis Khan's grandson Khubilai (1215–94), who became Great Khan in 1260, the capital was transferred from Mongolia to Peking (1264). In doing so Khubilai tacitly relinquished the Mongol claim to rule the entire world. Once again the political balance of East Asia was dominated by China, although this time not by Chinese.

China under the Mongols: The Early Years (1211–1260)

Almost half a century passed between Chinggis Khan's first attack on Chinese territory (1211) and the beginning of Khubilai's reign. It was a period that helped to set much of the pattern for later Mongol rule in China. In both the military operations against the Juchen Chin and the subsequent civil administration of North China, the Mongols made use of non-Mongols, particularly Khitan leaders who had a tradition of hostility toward the Chin and Chinese who felt no great loyalty toward the Juchen. The services of such men were essential to the Mongols, operating as they were in unfamiliar terrain and outnumbered by their enemy. Indeed, their ability to use men of non-Mongol background was essential, as the Mongols themselves numbered only around one and a half million people. Thus non-Mongol military leaders were accepted as *nökhör* by the Khan and granted the privileges which went with that status, including the receipt of lands to rule.

Among the non-Mongols in the service of the Khan, Yeh-lü Ch'u-ts'ai (1189–1243) was the most outstanding. As a Sinicized Khitan of royal Liao lineage, and a first place examination graduate under the Chin, Yeh-lü was well equipped to mediate between the Mongols and their Chinese subjects. Summoned to Mongolia by Chinggis Khan in 1218, he became influential as the court astrologer and is said to have played a role in the Mongol decision to stay out of India. But his real prominence came under Ögödei.

At the beginning of Ögödei's reign, Yeh-lü Ch'u-ts'ai was able to persuade the khan to reject the proposal by a group of Mongols that all the territory conquered in North China be turned into pasturage. This was a serious proposal consistent with the Mongol way of life and, especially, with the crucial need for great quantities of horses if the Mongols were to retain their power. Other nomadic peoples, most recently the Juchen, although much less involved than the Mongols in maintaining power outside China, had pondered the same alternatives. But in the end, Yeh-lü Ch'u-ts'ai's position prevailed. He persuaded the khan, not by appealing to Chinese theories of government, but by demonstrating the profits to be gained through an orderly exploitation of a settled and productive population. Yeh-lü was thereupon, in 1229, placed in charge of taxation and created a tax system staffed by civilian officials.

Rising eventually to highest office, he worked hard to fashion a centralized administration along Chinese lines but achieved only partial success. For example, he failed in his attempt to subject privileged non-Chinese in North China to the same taxes imposed on the Chinese population. He did obtain enactment of a census, but he could not disuade Ögödei from granting lands to supporters, which were beyond the government's fiscal control. In this case his proposal would have affected Chinese as well as non-Chinese leaders whose self-interest was at stake. The division of China into large-scale and loosely controlled military commands continued throughout the Mongol period; these commands later evolved into the large provinces into which China was divided during the Ming and Ch'ing.

Yeh-lü rescued Chinese scholars from captivity and found positions for them, including posts as tutors to Mongol nobles, but his revival of the civil service examinations was very short lived. Toward the end of his life he suffered increasing setbacks. Throughout his career he appealed to Mongol greed. In the end he was outbid by Central Asian merchants who argued that they could extract more wealth for the Mongols from China through tax farming than Yeh-lü could through a centralized state tax system. Tax farming was a system by which interested individuals bid against each other for the right to collect the taxes from a certain area for a specified period of time. The bidder who offered to raise the largest amount for the Mongol rulers was awarded the contract. Any amount he could raise over the amount to be given to the government he could keep for himself. Obviously this system appealed to the rapaciousness of both the government and the tax farmer, and the most ruthless measures were used to exact ruinously high taxes. Despite Yeh-lü's protests that this was ultimately a short-sighted policy harmful to the people who produced the wealth, a Muslim businessman was, in 1239, granted the right to collect taxes in North China.

At the time of Yeh-lü Ch'u-ts'ai's death in 1243, it looked as though his work was coming undone. His career demonstrated the difficulties involved in creating a Sino-Mongolian state.

Khubilai Khan and the Early Yüan

Khubilai Khan (r. 1260–94), who in 1264 had transferred the capital to Peking, followed this, in 1271, by the adoption of a Chinese dynastic name, Yüan, as well as Chinese court ceremonials. Chinggis Khan now received a posthumous Chinese title (T'ai-tsu), and Khubilai himself appears in the Chinese histories under the name of Shih-tsu. Previous khans had preferred, as was their tradition, to live among their herds and tents instead of taking up permanent residence in the capital; they spent as much time hunting as they did looking after government operations. Khubilai, in contrast, spent most of his time in Peking or in his summer capital at Shang-tu, in Inner Mongolia. He was careful to give at least an appearance of ruling in a Chinese manner.

His first concern was to make himself truly master of all China, completing the military conquest initiated by his grandfather and continued by Chinggis Khan's successors. The subjugation of the Southern Sung was difficult, for resistance was stiff, and the Mongols had to learn new techniques to operate successfully in the South. They were finally victorious, assisted by the defection of much of the Sung navy. When the Southern Sung fell in 1279, the Mongols became the first nomadic conquerors to rule all of China. (See map, Figure 9-1.)

This did not bring an end to warfare. Although Khubilai's empire was China based, his ambitions were not confined to China. He sent an expedition against Japan in 1274 and, after he was master of all of China, organized a second, more massive attack in 1281. (See Chapter 11.) Both attacks failed. Plans for a third attempt were never carried out. This was largely because in the 1280s Mongol forces were occupied with operations in Southeast Asia where repeated attacks were made on Vietnam and Burma. In 1281 and again in 1292 the khan's fleet attacked Java. These expeditions forced local rulers into ritual submission but did not expand the territory under actual Yüan control. At the same time Khubilai could not afford to neglect China's inner Asian frontier, where he was repeatedly challenged by Ögödei's grandson, Khaidu. There, Khubilai and his successors concentrated on securing Mongolia. This they accomplished but at the cost of giving up their ambition to dominate Central Asia as well.

Within China the long and bitter struggle against the Southern Sung left lasting wounds. Chinese hatred and bitterness were matched by Mongol suspicion and distrust of the southerners. A significant number of Chinese remained loyal to the old dynasty, continued to employ Sung terminology, and dreamed of a Sung restoration while refusing to serve the new power. On the other hand, the Mongols relegated southerners to the lowest category in their fourfold division of society along ethnic lines. Highest status in this system was accorded to the Mongols. Next came persons with special status (*se-mu jen*). These were Mongol allies, largely from Central Asia and the Near East, such as Turks, Persians, and Syrians. They played an important role in government financial administration, often served as managers for Mongol aristocrats, and enjoyed special privileges as financiers. Organized into special guilds, they financed the caravan trade and loaned out money at usurious rates. The third status group, although termed "*han-jen*," which usually means "Chinese," included all inhabitants of North China: those of Khitan, Juchen, or Korean family background as well as native Chinese. Finally, at the bottom, were the 80 percent of the Chinese population which lived in the South, the "*nan-jen*" or "southerners," also referred to by the less neutral term "*man-tzu*," that is, "southern barbarians." This fourfold division of society deeply affected the Yüan's treatment of its subjects. It was expressed in the recruitment and appointment of government officials, in the conduct of legal cases, and in taxation.

Actually, as we have seen, the most cultivated scholars lived in the South. Most resigned themselves to the new order and accepted the Yüan as the recipient of the Heavenly Mandate. But they nevertheless remained alienated from

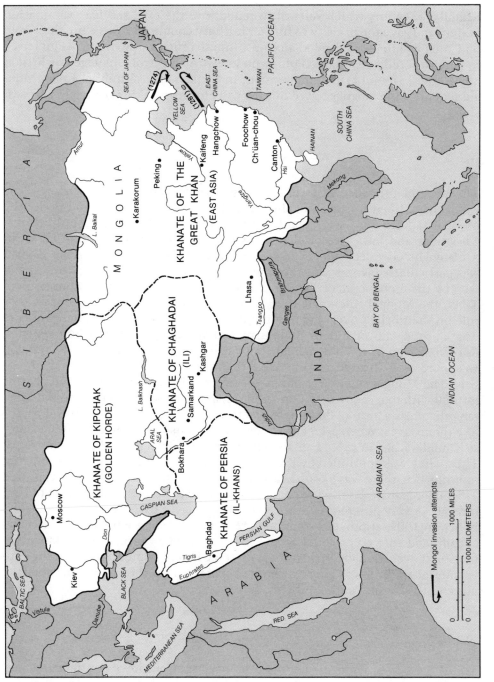

Figure 9-1 The Mongol Empire—Late Thirteenth Century

Khubilai's regime, which refused to reinstitute the civil service examination system and gave top priority to further military conquests. To assure their hold on China and to avoid dependence on Chinese officials, the Mongols preferred to employ foreigners. Marco Polo, who knew the Mongol language but little if any Chinese, found ready employment in the service of Khubilai Khan. Mongol remained the language used by all Yüan emperors in their official court sessions.

Religion

The Mongol tolerance of foreigners also extended to foreign religions. The early khans liked to sponsor religious debates at their courts, and under the Mongols all religions were granted tax exemption. Nestorians and Muslims, Christians and Jews were welcome. After the Taoist master Ch'iu Ch'u-chi (Ch'ang-chu chen-jen [d. 1227]) visited Chinggis Khan in Central Asia, Taoism was particularly favored, but the competition for official patronage was finally won by the proponents of Tibetan Buddhism. After gaining the submission of Tibet, the Mongol rulers left the abbot of a prominent Tibetan monastery to rule on their behalf over this mountainous land, where the dominant religion was an amalgam of Indian Buddhism and the native Tibetan Bon religion. Known as Lamaism, after the Tibetan word designating a monk, this religion was more sophisticated and universal than the native shamanism of the Mongols. The Mongol rulers were impressed by the Lamaist formulae and charms infused with magic power to cure or harm; and they were attracted to the Tibetan religion as a form of Buddhism practiced by a hardy, nonagricultural people like themselves. When a Tibetan lama was established as the official preceptor to Khubilai Khan in 1260, Lamaism became the official faith of the Yüan court. This policy was continued by Khubilai's successors, and as a result of imperial munificence, there was a proliferation of Buddhist art. Much of this art showed Tibetan or Nepalese influence, but it never won the esteem of students of Chinese art. A very different expression of official favor took the form of an edict, issued in 1309, stipulating that anyone striking a lama would have his hand cut off, and that an offender would lose his tongue for insulting a lama. Lamaism, however, made little impact on the Chinese population. Even the conversion of the Mongol people who had remained on the steppe did not take place until the sixteenth century.

The Economy

The Mongol conquerors did not disturb the class structure of South China, nor, to judge by accounts such as that of Marco Polo, did the conquerors inflict permanent damage on the economy of the South. Khubilai even made a start in the reconstruction of the shattered economy of the North, but the South remained the main economic region. There the ceramics and silk industries continued to flourish and a new cotton industry also developed. (Cotton culture may have been borrowed from the aboriginal inhabitants of China's southern provinces; a species of cotton was cultivated in Western Yunnan by the third century A.D. However, cotton did not become important economically until the Yüan.) One of the financial policies that the Mongols adopted from their Chin and Sung predecessors was the use of paper money. Not only did they issue their own paper money, but under Khubilai this became the sole legal currency. During his reign, when the paper currency was well backed, this policy was a success despite the slow inflation that set in after 1280. In other areas too, including the rehabilitation and extension of the Grand Canal, Khubilai's regime accomplished much. He displayed an ability to learn and to adjust to new circumstances in administrative as well as in military matters. What he could not do was to construct a system that would run smoothly of itself, and, unfortunately for the dynasty, there was not to be another Khubilai Khan.

The Yüan after Khubilai Khan

Although the Yüan after Khubilai accomplished more than traditionally hostile Chinese historians would later admit, it never achieved the strength and longevity of a major Chinese dynasty. Lacking a tradition of orderly succession to rulership, the Yüan was troubled by numerous succession disputes. During the forty years after Khubilai's death, seven emperors came to the throne, often to the accompaniment of bloodshed and murder. The last time men from the Mongolian steppe played a major role in these struggles was 1328. Even earlier, in 1307, the Mongolian homeland had been reduced to a province under civil administration. But the elimination of the steppe as a power base did not alleviate internal tensions. Nor was the dynasty able to devise a lasting formula for balancing the diverse elements in government and society.

Court politics were dominated by factionalism, which found expression in fluctuating government policies. Personnel policies were a particularly sensitive area. Not until 1313 was an imperial edict issued reviving the civil service examinations based on the Confucian classics and the commentaries of Chu Hsi. The first tests were given in 1315. Although this was a major concession to the Confucian literati, the system favored the Mongols and their non-Chinese allies, who were given simplified examinations and occupied 30 percent of all government posts. Under these circumstances some Chinese, hungry for office, could not resist the temptation to assume foreign names. In 1335 the Chancellor, Bayan (Chancellor 1335–40), obtained an imperial decree to cancel the examinations and thereby gained the enmity of all Confucians, who viewed the reinstitution of the examinations both as a step toward the normalization of government and as an opportunity for personal advancement. Bayan was overthrown by the Mongol leader, Toghto (d. 1356), who served as Chancellor from 1340 to 1344 and again from 1349 to 1355. Toghto revived the examination in 1342. Although degree holders enjoyed great prestige, the examinations did not regain the prominence they had enjoyed during the Sung, nor did they become the prime method of government recruitment. Still worse from the Chinese scholar's point of view was the persistent Yüan policy of according military officials supremacy over the civilian.

A major cause for concern during the 1340s was the Yellow River, which broke its dikes, flooded, and, most disastrously, began to change its course. One part of the river flowed north of the Shantung Peninsula; another emptied into the Grand Canal, putting it out of commission. Not only did this cause great dislocation and suffering to the inhabitants of the affected areas, it also threatened the economic survival of the dynasty by interrupting shipments of grain from the South. The only alternative to the Grand Canal route was by sea, but the maritime route was in constant danger from an increasingly bold and assertive pirate, Fang Kuo-chen. Clearly a massive effort was required for the government to reestablish control over the river or over the sea route, and it lacked the resources to do both. Given the choice, Toghto decided to concentrate on the more immediately threatening and more manageable inland problem. Furthermore, rather than settle for a superficial and temporary solution, he proposed the digging of a new channel for the Yellow River south of the Shantung Peninsula. Although his plan ran into political opposition, this great feat of hydraulic engineering was successfully carried out during Toghto's second administration. Under the direction of a Chinese engineer it was completed with the labor of 150,000 civilians and 20,000 troops.

Rebellion

The Yellow River problem was solved, but the cost was high, for it strained to the utmost the economic resources of the government and the people. An excessive issue of inadequately backed paper money produced growing inflation, which added its toll to the hardships of the population already suffering from government exactions. The seemingly hopeless situation prompted people to turn to religious salvationism, and the messianic teachings of the White Lotus Society found a responsive audience, as countless people placed their faith in the coming of Maitreya, who would put an end to all suffering and injustice. Under a leader who claimed descent from the Sung imperial line, the society attracted the miserable: dismissed clerks, deserters from the Yellow River project, peddlers, outlaws, the idle, and the displaced. Known as the Red Turbans after their headdresses, these people turned to open rebellion in 1352, and for the next three years much of Central and South China was lost to the Yüan. However, under Toghto's leadership, the dynasty was able for the time being to put down this challenge, ultimately employing forces composed mainly of Chinese soldiers. Yet when Toghto, after the defeat of the Red Turbans, turned his attention to eliminating a rebellious salt smuggler who had seized a town on the Grand Canal and proclaimed a new dynasty, the Mongol Chancellor would not allow a Chinese general to have the glory of applying the *coup de grâce.*

While Toghto was in power, the government maintained control over its military forces by taking great care in the making of appointments, by separating command and supply functions, and by generally exercising central leadership, but after his fall no other political strongman appeared to prevent the formation of regional power centers. These developed when the government made concessions to various commanders combatting a renewed rebellion, which proclaimed itself a revival of the Sung. During the last twelve years of the Yüan, the issue at stake was not so much the survival of the dynasty as the determination of its successor.

It turned out that the future belonged neither to the regional commanders nor to the rebel Sung regime in the North, but to an organization led by Chu Yüan-chang (1328–98) in the South. Chu had been born into a poor family and as a youth served as a novice in a Buddhist monastery. Later he became a beggar and eventually was drawn into the Red Turbans, where he rose to become a military commander. After the defeat of the Red Turbans, he became a leader of his own rebel organization. In contrast to the Red Turbans, who had directed their animosity as much against local landlords as against the dynasty, Chu undertook to reconcile the local elite. By abandoning the messianic radicalism of the earlier rebels and by demonstrating his intention to reconstruct the traditional kind of imperial government, he was able to gain valuable support among the gentry. Although some of the Chinese elite remained faithful to the Yüan and one of the most valiant and loyal defenders of the dynasty was a Chinese general, Chu Yüan-chang could not be stopped. By 1368 it was all over: The Mongol court fled to Mongolia, and a new dynasty, the Ming, was established with its capital at Nanking. Early in his reign Chu Yüan-chang, known posthumously as T'ai-tsu, issued an order proscribing unorthodox religious sects, foremost among them the same White Lotus sect that had inspired his own campaign to power.

Although the Mongols enacted social policies, such as creating hereditary families of artisans, they do not appear to have had a lasting effect on Chinese social structure. The effect of the Mongol period on Chinese political culture is generally considered more important. It is to this period that scholars have looked to explain the contrast between the rather benign government of the Sung and the more authoritarian rule of the Ming. The Mongols had set an example of strong imperial rule and, in their declining years, had provided a lesson of what could happen in the absence of strong central direction. The lesson was not lost on the Ming founder.

Cultural Life

Although fourteenth-century political debates were carried out in Confucian language and Toghto had the support and collaboration of many Chinese scholars, there were others who did not serve the court, which, for its part did not assume the traditional role of cultural patron. Especially at the beginning of the Yüan, highly cultured men found withdrawal from active politics not only appealing but also intellectually and morally respectable. As during the period of division following the collapse of the Han order, a small group of refined, sophisticated men contributed greatly to the development of the artistic heritage. Meanwhile, a good number of talented men, who in more normal times would have taken up a political career, made a living by pursuing occupations that brought them into close daily contact with ordinary, common people. Some became doctors, others took up fortune telling, still others turned to the theater for their livelihood. The result was the creation of great drama and art.

Yüan Drama

The theater arts had a long history in China before drama reached its classic form during the reign of Khubilai Khan. Early shamanistic religious dances, performances of music and acting staged for the amusement of the imperial court, "ballets" such as the T'ang poet Po Chü-yi's favorite, "Rainbow Skirts and Feather Jackets," all form part of the background of the mature Yüan music drama. Equally important was the heritage of popular entertainment, including the various theatricals staged for the benefit of the inhabitants of Sung Kaifeng and Hangchow (both of which had thriving theater districts), featuring not only performances by live actors but also puppet shows and shadow plays. Both these arts have a long pre-Sung history. In the puppet theater some puppets were on strings, others on sticks, still others were controlled by explosive charges, and some productions featured "live puppets," that is, children manipulated by a "puppeteer." In the shadow plays, the audience observed silhouettes of figures manipulated behind a screen and in front of lights. Among the precursors of the Yüan drama, none are more important than the storytellers who had enlivened the urban scene ever since the Sung. Already in Sung Hangchow they were numerous enough to form "guilds." Set up in their stalls, they recited their stories, sometimes to the accompaniment of musical instruments. Each man had his specialty: realistic stories, stories of ghosts and the miraculous, religious tales, stories based on historical episodes. Their art consisted not in simply relating an old story but in making it come vividly alive by dramatic modulations of the voice and other dramatic devices. Cyril Birch tells of a fairly recent practitioner of the art who, " 'in one breath' could produce seven distinct sounds to represent in realistic fashion the screams of a pig in the successive stages of its slaughter."[2] Thus the development of the theater did not inhibit the continuing flourishing of the art of the storyteller, but this art did leave its mark on the formal conventions not only of the theater but also of the novel, and it influenced the content as well as the form of both of these popular genres.

It is therefore not surprising that the plots of many of the 171 Yüan plays still extant are based on earlier materials. Historical episodes such as the marriage of the Han palace beauty Wang Chao-chün to a Hsiung-nu chieftain, the political and military ploys devised by Chu-ko Liang and his contemporaries of the Three Kingdom period, the tragedy brought on by East Asia's most famed *femme fatale*, Yang Kuei-fei, the story of Hsüan-tsang's pilgrimage to India, and other historical and semihistorical events provided the Yüan dramatists with some of their most effective and popular themes. And the plays for their part did much to fix in the popular mind colorful, larger-than-life images of these personages, creations of the poetic imagination at work embellishing the more prosaic historical accounts.

The Yüan theatergoers also enjoyed dramatic renditions of old love stories, such as that of the beautiful Ying-ying and a student named Chang recounted in the highly celebrated thirteenth-century play *The Romance of the Western Chamber* by Wang Shih-fu. In adapting the old tale to the stage, Wang did not hesitate to rework his materials for greater theatrical and literary effect. Thus, in the play, skillful use is made of the refusal of Ying-ying's mother to honor her promise to marry her daughter to whomever will rescue them when they are surrounded by rebels. Ying-ying, already greatly attracted to the young rescuer, now gives him her heart. And the injustice of the mother's act also transforms Nurse Huai-ning from an obstacle into a highly resourceful ally. To please his audience, the playwright departs from the T'ang version of the story and has the drama end with the couple overcoming all obstacles to their happiness, including Ying-ying's mother. After Chang passes his examinations, they are united in marriage. Love triumphs in the end. This happy resolution is characteristic of the genre, for these plays were designed to appeal to an audience not only of connoisseurs but also of ordinary people with little or no formal education, who desired happy endings.

The repertoire of the Yüan theater included many plays expressing a longing for justice. Some featured that model of official rectitude and wisdom Judge Pao (based on a real official, Pao Cheng [999–1062]), a champion of justice who repeatedly uncovers even the most ingenious deceptions of the wicked. Prominent among the villains of such plays are greedy and unscrupulous officials who subvert the moral order they are theoretically committed to uphold. Among the heroes are Robin Hood-like figures, outlaws who have right on their side even as they defy the state and its laws. (Many of these heroes also appear in the Ming novel *The Water Margin*; see Chapter 10). No doubt many members of the audience derived vicarious pleasure from witnessing the punishment of venal and corrupt officials resembling those who in real life went uncorrected. The plays do not deal with contemporary events in any obvious way nor do they directly cast aspersions on the regime. Yet one wonders what a Mongol spectator would have made of the scene in *Autumn in the Palace of Han* where the playwright describes the hardships facing Wang Chao-chün among the "barbarians" when she will have only "tasteless salted flesh" to eat, and for drink "clabbered milk and gruel."[3]

The plays were written for standard actors' roles: leading man, leading lady, villain, and so on. The characters too can be classified into easily recognizable types such as the faithful lovers of *The Romance of the Western Chamber*; the corrupt officials and wise judges of the courtroom dramas; the uncouth but virtuous outlaws; and the beautiful, talented, and strong-minded courtesans. Most plays consisted of four acts between which short interludes, or "wedges," could be inserted. Since stage props were few, characters regularly made speeches of self-identification. The playwrights also used occasional recapitulations, carry-overs from the tradition of the storyteller.

Music played an important part in the theater. The songs or song sequences in each act were in a single mode or key. The lute and zither were the standard instruments of the Yüan northern drama. In contrast to the mellow, refined music of southern drama under the Ming, the Yüan sound was vigorous and spirited. The Yüan drama's roots in the tradition of oral narrative are also revealed in the assignment of all arias to a single performer. Thus in *Autumn in the Palace of Han*, the emperor does all the singing.

The products of the Yüan playwright frequently achieved high literary excellence. Dialogue written in the spoken language of the time lent an earthy freshness to texts, which at times included bawdy vulgarisms such as no respectable Confucian scholar of later times would have allowed to flow from his brush. Such language contributed to the bad repute in which the Yüan drama was held in polite circles under later dynasties, until it was appreciatively rediscovered in the twentieth century. What was valued by the critics were the plays' poetic passages, particularly the lyric songs (*san-ch'ü*) which rank with other major forms of Chinese poetry in their technical intricacy, musical subtlety, and employment of various poetic devices, including the effective use of

Figure 9-2   Kung K'ai, *Emaciated Horse*. Hand-scroll, ink on paper, 30 cm × 57 cm. Abe Collection, Osaka Municipal Museum of Fine Arts.

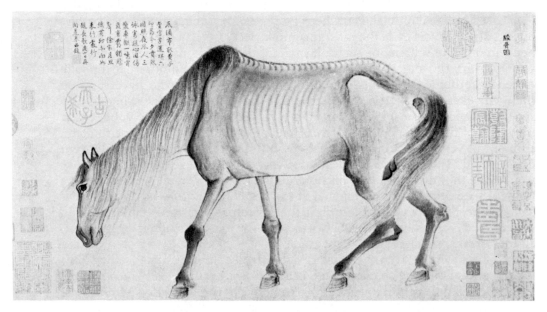

imagery. Just as connoisseurs judged paintings by the quality of their brush-work, critics focused on the merits of the poetry in the plays. Thus a fifteenth-century critic praised the poetry of Ma Chih-yüan, author of *Autumn in the Palace of Han*, as resembling "a phoenix gliding and singing in the highest clouds."[4]

The Romance of the Western Chamber is beloved for its poetry. In it Ying-ying herself is deeply moved when Chang sings to her of love, and "word follows word like the endless dripping of a water-clock."[5] Here Chang's song was accompanied by his zither, but the *san-ch'ü* were sung without accompaniment. In the great plays the poetry is an integral part of the work, contributing to dramatic development. Thus the recurrent image of the moon, which appears more than fifty times in the poetry of *The Romance of the Western Chamber*, helps to give the drama unity and depth. It is present, of course, when after long courtship, the lovers are united. Then, "the bright moon, like water, floods the pavilion and terrace."[6]

The lovers have to suffer through a long period of separation and uncertainty before their union is made permanent at last, but they are fitting representatives of an essentially optimistic and life-affirming theater that combined high art with wide appeal to all classes.

Yüan Painting

In contrast to the theater, in which individuals from all kinds of backgrounds participated and which had something for everyone, Yüan painting was a much more esoteric pursuit. But whereas literary men later disdained the drama as plebeian, the achievements of the great Yüan painters were admired by all later connoisseurs.

The distinction between the professional who sells his wares to the aesthetically naive and the amateur who paints for himself and his friends did not originate in the Yüan, but it was confirmed when the Mongol court ceased to patronize the high arts. Professional artists continued to take pride in the perfection of their techniques and the excellence of their craftsmanship. Gentlemen-amateurs, no less serious about their art, found in brush and ink a vehicle for self-expression and, indeed, for the cultivation of that self. Yüan painting, therefore, often contains an element of self-portraiture, although rarely was this as explicit as in *Emaciated Horse* (Figure 9-2) by the Sung loyalist Kung K'ai (1222–1307), who belonged to the generation that experienced the change of dynasties. His painting expresses the self-image of the Chinese scholars who found themselves condemned to live in a world that did not respect their talents or prize their values; a world in which, as indicated in the poem Kung added to his painting, the stables of the former dynasty remained empty. The horse had long been a symbol of the scholar-official, and was perhaps an especially fitting symbol for the neglected Confucian living under a conqueror who prided himself on his horsemanship. The very gauntness of Kung's haggard

Figure 9-3   Chao Meng-fu. *Autumn Colors on the Ch'iao and Hua Mountains.* Hand-scroll, ink and colors on paper, dated 1296, 28.4 cm × 93.2 cm. National Palace Museum, Taipei.

horse brings out the essential strength of its splendid physique. To those who understood its meaning, the painting was an eloquent, proud, and poignant statement of a bitter shared fate.

The most famous Yüan horse painter was also the outstanding exception to the rule that the gentleman-artist avoided the imperial stable. Chao Meng-fu (1254–1322) held high office under the Mongols and paid the price in lost friendships and inner suffering. Later Chinese scholars, although not approving of his career, were compelled to recognize the force of his genius as a major painter and one of China's truly great calligraphers. Indeed, his paintings of horses were so prized that forgeries abound. Chao's work is illustrated here not by a horse but by *Autumn Colors on the Ch'iao and Hua Mountains* (see Figure 9-3), which exemplifies a deliberate archaism that greatly appealed to the Yüan literati.

As *Autumn Colors* shows, Chao's archaism demanded the complete rejection of the aesthetics of his immediate predecessors. No trace can be found here of the styles of Ma Yüan and Hsia Kuei, and there is a deliberate, consistent avoidance of prettiness. Beyond that, Chao has discarded developments in perspective and ignored size relationships in his attempt to recapture an earlier noble simplicity. Chao and his contemporaries, somewhat like the Pre-Raphaelites of nineteenth-century England, tried to return to the rugged honesty of an earlier age and to unlearn the lessons of the classic period of their art. The Chinese painters, however, were more ready than the Pre-Raphaelites to sacrifice surface beauty for the sake of attaining what Chao called "a sense of antiquity" (ku-i). They also differed in that they conceived of their art in terms of calligraphy: both painting and calligraphy served the purpose of writing down on paper or silk the ideas the gentlemen had in their minds. In the two paintings reproduced in Figures 9-2 and 9-3, the unused space does not serve as a horizon, nor does it contribute to the overall composition. Therefore, the use of this space for calligraphy does not disturb the painting. In a sense the painting, too, is calligraphy just as, in another sense, the calligraphy is painting.

Now, as earlier, calligraphy was prized as a revelation of the lofty character of its cultivated practitioner, an emphasis which made for variety in style, in painting as well as in writing. The master painters of the Yüan did not share a uniform style, nor did individual artists necessarily limit themselves to a single style. There is, for example, a famous anecdote concerning the painter Ni Tsan (1301–74), who one night, while inebriated, painted bamboos that a friend next day criticized for not looking like bamboos. Exemplifying the Yüan painter's disdain for representation, Ni replied that he was delighted: few indeed can paint bamboos so that they do not resemble bamboos in the least! Yet, Ni often painted ordinary bamboos. Bamboos which, like the gentleman-scholar, bend before the wind but do not break were a favorite subject of the literati-painters, who could also find Taoist significance in the fact that the center of this plant is hollow, that is, empty. Reproduced in Figure 9-4 is Ni's

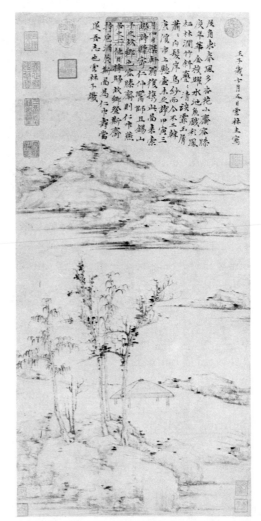

Figure 9-4   Ni Tsan, *The Jung-hsi Studio*. Hanging scroll, ink on paper, dated 1372, 74.7 cm × 35.5 cm. National Palace Museum, Taipei.

Figure 9-5 Wang Meng, *The Forest Grotto at Chü-ch'ü*. Hanging scroll, ink and colors on paper, 68.7 cm × 42.5 cm. National Palace Museum, Taipei.

The Jung-hsi Studio, which exemplifies not only Ni's calligraphic talents but also the cool restraint of his unpeopled landscapes. Like Chao Meng-fu, he has avoided all painterly tricks. He achieved a calm, bland poetry. This aesthetic of the cool and clean is also found in the white and also in the blue-and-white ceramics of the age.

At the opposite stylistic pole from the work of Ni Tsan are the paintings of Wang Meng (ca. 1309–1385), especially his later work in which he employs "unraveled hemp fiber" and S-shaped strokes. (See Figure 9-5). Where Ni Tsan works in monochrome, Wang delights in bright colors. In Ni, nature is stable and empty, but Wang fills his space with natural forces surging around the abodes of his recluses and threatening to burst forth beyond the borders of the painting. Perhaps this was an appropriate statement for a period when social and political forces in China were about to burst through the Yüan dynastic framework.

In considering the cultural achievements of the Yüan, it is worth noting that foreign influence did not enter the world of the literati-painter. Conversely, no appreciation or even an awareness of their art is to be found in the literature of the European visitors, such as Marco Polo and his successors of the fourteenth century. Although there was a Catholic archbishop in Peking and relations across the great Eurasian land mass were often cordial, these relations had a low priority on both sides of the world, for the distances were enormous, and Europe as well as China was faced with far more immediate challenges and opportunities in politics, economics, art, and thought closer to home. In many respects China was ahead of Europe at the time. Literati painting of the type prized in the Yüan was not even considered worthy of note by Europeans prior to the nineteenth century, and it was not until the twentieth century that people in the West learned how to see and value these paintings.

NOTES

1. R. Mitchell and N. Forbes, trans., *The Chronicle of Novgorod 1016–1471* (London: Camden Society, 3rd Series, Vol. 25, 1914), p. 64.

2. Cyril Birch, trans., *Stories from a Ming Collection: The Art of the Chinese Story-Teller* (New York: Grove Press, 1958), pp. 10–11.

3. Cyril Birch, ed., *Anthology of Chinese Literature* (New York: Grove Press, 1965), 1: 483.

4. Chung-wen Shih, *The Golden Age of Chinese Drama: Yüan Tsa-chü* (Princeton: Princeton University Press, 1976), p. 160.

5. *Ibid.*, p. 192.

6. *Ibid.*, p. 159.

10 The Ming Dynasty: 1368–1644

The Ming was the last Chinese dynasty to rule China. The stability of the regime and the general prosperity of the people, as well as notable achievements in literature, philosophy, and the arts, demonstrated the continued vitality of the Chinese tradition and its capacity for growth and transformation. When, toward the end of the Ming period, the first modern Europeans arrived in China, they found much to admire (see Chapter 13). The Ming's Manchu successor, the Ch'ing dynasty, owed much of its success to the solidity of its Ming foundations, social and political.

Chinese Society During the Ming

Traditional accounts of the Ming, as of other dynasties, present Chinese history from the perspective of the capital. This is certainly understandable, for this is where the official records were maintained and the great dynastic histories were commissioned and compiled. Moreover, there is considerable merit in looking at things from this point of view. Not only was the capital the center of government and the residence of the emperor, it was also a primary center of political power, scholarship, and the arts. Decisions and innovations made in the capital shaped the history of China.

But the student of Chinese history must also bear in mind that China is an immense country, highly varied in population, culture, climate, and terrain, and, as observed earlier, one in which the direct impact of government on people living outside the capital was (until very recently) limited. At the local level the central government was represented by the magistrate, who in theory, was responsible for everything that happened in his district. He was supposed to supervise tax collection, provide public security, administer justice, and see to the economic as well as moral needs of the population. Since, however, his staff was small and the average Ming district had a registered population of over 50,000, the magistrate's control and influence were restricted.

Local society operated according to its own rhythms, its patterns influenced and affected by government to be sure, but not determined by it. Indeed, the history of China suggests that occurrences in the provinces had as much influence on the center as acts of the central government had on the provinces. Thus the view from the center needs to be complemented by the study of local history.

Particularly important is the role of the local gentry. They presided over provincial life and gave it much of its tone. The continuity of their prominence in local affairs from the Ming onward contributed greatly to the stability of Chinese society. Hilary J. Beattie's recent study of a district in Anhwei Province provides important insights into the structure of local life.[1] For example, Beattie found that this district's local gentry went back to the early Ming, that the gentry lineages were formally organized in the sixteenth century, and that they were able to survive the rebellions and upheavals of the late years of the dynasty and even the great nineteenth-century Taiping Rebellion. They were able to accomplish this by maintaining solid economic roots in local land ownership and by investing their income in education. Education, in turn, secured their local status, in addition to providing the requisites for competing in the civil service examinations. Members of the gentry who succeeded in becoming officials used their political influence and their economic assets to benefit the lineage, but the gentry were able to sustain themselves even during periods lean in examination success. This suggests that local social and economic status was the primary source of their power and that there was greater continuity in the family background of the local elite than there was among those capable and fortunate enough to gain access to a career in the imperial bureaucracy.

Among the means used to secure lineage cohesion were the periodic compilations of genealogies. These not only fostered a sense of historic continuity among lineage members but also identified the individuals belonging to the lineage. Prominent gentry lineages also maintained ancestral halls and graveyards and conducted ceremonial sacrifices to lineage ancestors. Not infrequently, the income from lineage land was used for these purposes. Lineage solidarity was also maintained by general guides for the conduct of their members and by formal lineage rules. One penalty for severe infractions of these rules was expulsion. The contrast in status between the local elite and the government underlings who served in the subbureaucracy (see Chapter 8) is revealed by the stipulation found in many lineage rules that any member sinking to the occupation of government clerk or runner be promptly expelled. The individual gentry lineages also profited from participation in a complicated network of marriage relationships.

The gentry had considerable influence with government officials assigned to their districts. For one thing, they moved in the same social and cultural circles; they were of the same class and usually had close social ties. Even if uninfluenced by personal associations, however, government officials could hardly disregard the power and influence of the gentry of the district they were sent to administer.

On the other hand, gentry families tended to move to the district capitals. Then, as now, the lure of social, cultural, political, and economic opportunities was a major attraction of urban life. The gentry retained their ties to their local power bases, but as absentee landlords they often succumbed to the temptation to abuse their power, charging high rents, allocating taxes unfairly, charging exorbitant interest on mortgage loans, and so on. A dangerous cleavage developed between the gentry and the peasant tenants who worked their lands. Hostilities were built up, hostilities which found expression during the Late Ming rebellions. Subsequently, however, the Anhwei gentry, sobered by this lesson, appear to have been more ready to observe the frugality enjoined on them by ancestral admonitions and to conform generally to accepted standards of behavior.

There is still a great deal to be learned about urbanization, commercial growth, and economic development in the provinces. Particularly intriguing are regional variations in the pace and direction of these developments and the reasons for variation from one district or province to another. Concerning the general relationship between the center and local communities, the theories of G. William Skinner are especially fruitful. Skinner has suggested that by the middle of the nineteenth century there were in China some 45,000 market towns, each the nucleus of an "autonomous economic system . . . structured spatially according to the principle of centrality and temporally by the periodicity of its market days."[2] He further suggests that in times of dynastic decline and during the insecurity accompanying a change of dynasty, these cells closed themselves off from the larger body politic and that they gradually reopened as peace and stability were reestablished. Although this theory has not been applied to the analysis of the history of specific events in the Ming or any other dynasty, it suggests one way to explain how the local gentry were able to retain their position despite dynastic upheaval.

The Early Ming (1368–1424)

The early Ming was a period of vigorous Chinese military resurgence after the period of Mongol domination. The founder of the dynasty, Chu Yüan-chang (known posthumously as T'ai-tsu), ruled for thirty years (1368–98) and left his imprint on the reigns that followed. His was a martial spirit indeed. For his era name* he chose Hung-wu, which means "grand military achievement," and his military accomplishments were certainly impressive. By the end of his reign, the Ming had won control of all China and dominated the frontier region from Hami, in Sinkiang, north through Inner Mongolia and into northern Manchuria. Beyond that, the Ming had won the subjugation of Korea as well as various Central and Southeast Asian states which sent tribute. (See map, Figure 10-1.) Ch'eng-tsu (r. 1402–24), the third Ming emperor, often referred to by his reign name, Yung-lo, continued his father's expansionist policy, leading five expeditions against the Mongols, intervening in Annam and then incorporating it into the empire, and sending out great maritime expeditions, which established China as a naval power. The early Ming was thus a period of vigorous Chinese military resurgence coming after the period of Mongol domination.

T'ai-tsu was a harsh and autocratic ruler. The position of Chancellor was abolished, and the emperor personally decided all important matters, and even those of secondary significance. A very hard worker, he went through great stacks of memorials: in one period of ten days he is reported to have perused 1660 memorials dealing with 3391 separate matters. In 1382 he appointed four Grand Secretaries to help him with this workload, but it was not until later in the dynasty that the Grand Secretariat developed into an institution. Merciless in exterminating those who stood in his way or were suspected of doing so, he obtained information through a secret service provided with its own prison and torturing apparatus. Officials who displeased the emperor were subjected to beating in open court. Always painful and terribly humiliating, the beating was sometimes so severe that the victim died.

Although harsh and suspicious, T'ai-tsu was also a strong and capable leader. A major objective was to assure control of the countryside. To do this he established the *li-chia* system as a basis for labor-service and local security. Under this system, every ten families in an area constituted a *chia*, and ten *chia*

---

* The Ming founder initiated the practice followed by all subsequent emperors of retaining a single era name throughout his reign. These emperors are therefore often known by their era names rather than by their posthumous epithets. In order to comply with the style of most English language materials, we will refer to Ming emperors by their epithets, indicating the era names in parentheses, but reverse the procedure for the emperors of the Ch'ing (1644–1911). It is easy to tell which is which because the epithets end in *tsu* (progenitor), *tsung* (ancestor), or *ti* (emperor).

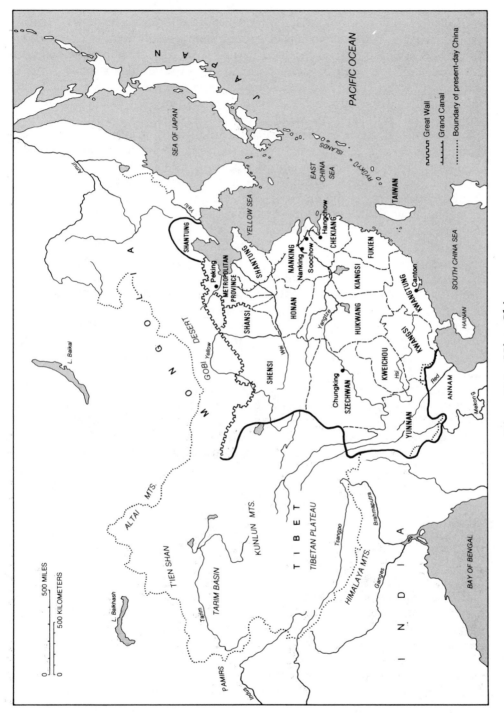

Figure 10-1 **Ming China**

formed a *li*. Each household was required to post a notice on its door indicating the names, ages, and occupations of its members, and all members of a *li* were responsible for each other's conduct. At the same time, the emperor energetically furthered the work of reconstruction and of relief for the poor, some of whom were resettled, and he established an effective tax system. Furthermore, he reestablished the imperial university, founded many schools, and reinstituted the civil service examinations. Confucianism again became the official state doctrine. But the emperor rejected the antiauthoritarian aspects of the thought of Mencius and had eighty-five sections (about one-third of the text) expurgated from *The Mencius* before accepting it as a legitimate book.

Ch'eng-tsu (or Yung-lo) was as politically and militarily vigorous as his father but did not follow the first emperor's example in all respects. After defeating his nephew, the second emperor, in a massive civil war, Ch'eng-tsu moved the capital from Nanking to Peking, which he largely rebuilt. To assure supplies for the capital, he also reconstructed the Grand Canal. Just as severe as his father when it came to purging real or suspected opponents, he was better educated than T'ai-tsu and more generous in his patronage of Confucianism. Not only did he hold more frequent civil service examinations, he also sponsored major scholarly projects. The most grandiose of these was the compilation of a huge literary treasury, which employed more than 2000 scholars and when completed in 1408 resulted in a compendium of 22,877 rolls, or chapters. Under Ch'eng-tsu the complete, unexpurgated *Mencius* was also once more made available.

It is sometimes said that the Ming reaction against the hated Mongols led to an overreaction against all things foreign, but this is not entirely true. For example, Ch'eng-tsu not only sponsored a great compendium of Sung Neo-Confucianism but also patronized the publication of Buddhist works, including a new edition of the Tripitaka. After the death of his wife, he had a Buddhist monastery near Nanking repaired and built there an octagonal porcelain pagoda nine stories tall, more than 276 feet high. It remained standing until destroyed in 1854 during the Taiping Rebellion.

Maritime Expeditions (1405–1433)

The vigor of the early Ming was spectacularly demonstrated by seven great maritime expeditions sent out by imperial command under a Muslim eunuch named Cheng Ho (1371–1433). The first of these voyages included 27,800 men, 62 or 63 large ships, and 255 smaller vessels, and the third was of similar dimensions. Their destinations included not only various areas of Southeast Asia but also the Indian Ocean, Arabia, and the east coast of Africa. The voyages were unique in their scope and official sponsorship, but the technology which made them possible had previously been employed in private ventures not considered worth recording by official historians. Thus it is interesting to observe that on their first voyage the expedition had dealings with Chinese settlers in

Sumatra. Reportedly they also defeated a Chinese "pirate" in those waters, killing 5000 men and bringing the leader back for execution in Peking.

The Chinese sources emphasize that the reason for launching these expeditions was Ch'eng-tsu's desire to locate the nephew from whom he had seized the throne but who had eluded capture. More broadly they may be viewed as an aspect of early Ming military and political assertiveness, for they effectively demonstrated Chinese power and brought tributary envoys to the Ming court, for example, the King of Borneo who died in China in 1408 and was buried outside Nanking, where his grave can still be seen. It is recorded that as a result of the fourth voyage, nineteen countries sent tribute.

Foreign envoys coming to render submission enhanced the court's glory and prestige. Also forthcoming from foreign lands were exotic objects and animals. The emperor was particularly delighted by giraffes, represented in Peking as auspicious "*ch'i-lin*," or "unicorns." Most probably trade was also a motive for the voyages; we know that ships of the first voyage carried silk and embroideries on board. And trade was a major factor in inducing foreign lands to send envoys to China. On the Chinese side, however, the Ming never looked upon trade as something intrinsically worthwhile.

From the official Chinese point of view, these expeditions did not have an economic rationale. Furthermore, their eunuch leadership did not win them friends among Confucian officials. When Ch'eng-tsu died, they lost an enthusiastic supporter, although his successor Hsüan-tsung (Hsüan-te, r. 1426–35) did send out one last expedition. Just as the expeditions can be seen as part of a general early Ming assertiveness toward the rest of the world, their abandonment forms part of a broader pattern as during the reigns of Ch'eng-tsu's successors the dynasty trimmed its ambitions. Furthermore, the crucial land frontier once again demanded military attention: fighting Mongols was a vital enterprise, whereas ocean expeditions were a luxury.

In the absence of a strong naval effort, Chinese waters became the domain of pirates and smugglers, a situation not ameliorated by the dynasty's regulations to control and curb maritime trade. For example, already during the Yung-lo period, the Japanese had been officially limited to one tribute mission every ten years, composed of only two ships with a maximum of 200 men (later raised to 300) to call at Ningpo (Chekiang province). These regulations were not always enforced, for private Chinese interests as well as the Japanese stood to profit by the trade conducted on these occasions. But the regulations illustrate the dynasty's negative attitude toward relations with maritime countries.

The Early Middle Period (1425–1505)

The seventy-five years of the Early Middle Ming were generally a period of peace, stability, and prosperity, under emperors less ambitious for military glory and personal power than T'ai-tsu and Ch'eng-tsu. Hsüan-tsung abandoned the Ming effort to control Annam. However, he did lead one expedition against Mongol raiders in the North. The Mongols were particularly trouble-some under his successor, Ying-tsung, whom they actually captured and held prisoner for a year. As a result Ying-tsung had two reign periods (Cheng-t'ung, 1436–49, and T'ien-shun, 1457–64)—after his release from the Mongols, he spent six and a half years in confinement in a palace in the capital while his brother held the throne. In the 1460s and 1470s there was a revival of Chinese military strength. The Great Wall was strengthened and extended for six hundred miles to protect the northern border of Shensi. Although it goes back to the third century B.C., the wall as it stands today owes much of its imposing mass and extent to the Ming.

Domestically, eunuch influence increased. T'ai-tsu had warned against giving eunuchs positions of responsibility, but under the third emperor, Cheng Ho was but one of a number of capable eunuchs in the emperor's service. Hsüan-tsung went a step further when he established a school for eunuchs, but this did not prevent the continuing hostility of Confucian officials, who seem to have criticized even honest and able eunuchs as a matter of principle. Eunuchs enjoyed unique opportunities for informal, relaxed conversation with emperors who often turned to them for advice or, as in the case of Cheng Ho, entrusted them with important missions.

To preserve himself from drowning in the flood of official business, Hsüan-tsung also selected certain ministers to screen memorials, draft edicts, and the like. This informal group of two to six officials became increasingly influential during the last quarter of the fifteenth century and became known as the Grand Secretariat.

Ming emperors generally believed in doing things on a grand scale. For example, in 1425 the court reportedly had 6300 cooks in its employ, preparing meals not only for the considerable palace population but also for government officials on set occasions. Hsüan-tsung had a special taste for Korean food and sent eunuchs to Korea to bring back, among other things, virgins, eunuchs, and female cooks. He also took an active interest in the arts and was probably the only emperor after Hui-tsung of the Sung to be a gifted painter and poet. Among the noted painters who served for a time at his court was the flower and bird specialist Pien Wen-chih (ca. 1356–1428). Another famous painter was Tai Chin (1388–1462), who worked in the Ma-Hsia tradition of the Southern Sung. His artistic talents did not, however, save him from dismissal when he painted the coat of a fisherman red, a color reserved for the garments of officials. Returning to his native Chekiang, he became a leader in what was known as the Che school of painting.

Hsüan-tsung's reign is also known for its bronzes and especially for its porcelain. Under the Ming, private kilns continued to produce ceramics in traditional styles, but it was the imperial kilns, turning out vast quantities of vessels in many different shapes, which stood at the forefront of technical and artistic development. Whereas the Yung-lo period of Emperor Ch'eng-tsu is noted for its white porcelain, by Hsüan-tsung's reign blue-and-white ware had come into vogue and reached its classic peak. (See Figure 10-2.) During the following reign the imperial kilns enjoyed a monopoly of blue-and-white porcelain, protected by an order prohibiting its private sale. But this could not be maintained for very long. Ming blue-and-white had such appeal that it soon stimulated imitation, and it went on to win admiration not only in East Asia but in such distant lands as Persia and Holland. The porcelain of each reign had its own characteristics. During the fifteenth century, its color range was broadened when white porcelains were decorated by painting them with various enamel colors. The five-colored enamels made during the reign of Emperor Hsien-tsung (Ch'eng-hua, r. 1465–88) are particularly prized.

The Early Middle period came to an end with the death of Hsiao-tsung (Hung-chih, r. 1488–1505), a model of Confucian propriety and a rare monogamist among the Ming emperors. His was generally a calm reign, but after more than 130 years, the dynasty was beginning to show signs of deterioration. The trends which would trouble government during the sixteenth century were already at work beneath the surface.

The Later Middle Period (1506–1590)

This period covers three reigns and the beginnings of a fourth. It was a time when government suffered from inadequate imperial leadership, but the political system still showed a capacity for reform. The first of these emperors, reigning from 1506 to 1521, paid no attention to government but devoted his time and energy to sports, entertainments, sex, and drink. Under the second

Figure 10-2   Plate with bird decoration. Blue-and-white porcelain, Early Ming, probably Hsüan-te, diam. 50.2 cm.

(1522–67), the arts flourished but government did not. The emperor became engrossed in increasingly longer Taoist ceremonies. By the end of his reign, there were ceremonies which continued for twelve or thirteen days and nights. The third emperor, Mu-tsung (Lung-ch'ing, r. 1567–72), reigned for only five years, during which he paid more attention to private pleasures than to public business. The fourth emperor, Shen-tsung (Wan-li, r. 1573–1620), was a minor during the period under consideration here. Throughout the Later Middle period Grand Secretaries and eunuchs wielded great power.

A decline in government honesty and efficiency was apparent both in the capital and in local government. On the district level, the gentry increasingly abused their local power and influence. For example, they frequently bought land from those less powerful and then forced the seller to remain responsible for the taxes. Or conversely, they might sell land and saddle the buyer with a disproportionate share of their own tax burden. Inequities in taxation were harmful both to government finance and to the small peasant proprietor.

But there were also reformers. Most notable was Hai Jui (1513–87), who had a reputation for uprightness, courage, and concern for the common people. As a magistrate he reassessed the land to make taxes more equitable, wiped out corruption so effectively that government clerks were reduced to poverty, and himself led a life of exemplary frugality. His refusal to toady to his superiors earned him powerful enemies, and he came close to losing his life when he submitted a scathing memorial that, among other things, charged the emperor with neglect of government and excessive indulgence in Taoist ceremonies. During the Ming one did not denounce an emperor with impunity: in prison Hai Jui was tortured and condemned to death by strangulation. He was saved only by the death of the emperor. On his release from prison he resumed his career but was forced into retirement when he offended powerful families by forcing them to return lands they had seized illegally. Late in life, in 1585, he was recalled to office, and after he died he was idealized as the perfect official incarnate. About four centuries later, in the 1960s, Hai Jui became the focus of a major controversy. (See Chapter 25.)

A very different kind of reformer was Chang Chü-cheng (1525–82), who dominated government during the reign of Mu-tsung and continued to do so for another ten years during Shen-tsung's minority. He has been described as a Confucian Legalist, for he was convinced that strong and strict government was ultimately for the people's benefit. Efficiency and control were the hallmarks of his policy. Among his achievements were a repair of the Grand Canal, reform of the courier system, new regulations designed to strengthen central control over provincial officials, and a reduction in the total number of officials. He eliminated eunuch influence from the Six Ministries and prevented censors from abusing their authority. He also tried to reform the provincial schools.

Chang was also troubled by what was happening in the civil service examinations. Ever since T'ai-tsu had lent imperial favor to an essay form composed of eight rigidly stipulated sections and known as the "eight-legged essay," the tendency had increasingly been to judge papers on the basis of form rather than content. This eased the task of the examination readers but threatened to turn the examinations into mechanical exercises. Chang, who served as an examiner in 1571, wanted the questions to emphasize current problems and the answers to be graded on content. But in his contempt for "empty" theorizing, he went beyond this and ordered the suppression of private academies. These he also considered undesirable, as potential breeding grounds for political associations and as holders of tax-exempt land. However, the decree banning academies (1579) did little permanent damage to these institutions.

To improve government finances, Chang directed an all-China land survey and also extended to the whole country the "single whip method of taxation," previously tried out in Chekiang and Fukien. This replaced the Two Tax System first instituted during the T'ang. Implementation remained incomplete, but, in principle, the new method provided for the consolidation of tax obligations into a single annual bill. Another important innovation was the use of silver as the value base for tax assessment. The silver tael (ounce) remained the standard monetary unit into the twentieth century.

Chang Chü-cheng made many enemies. They had their revenge after his death, when his family property was confiscated and his sons were tortured. But he left the regime in sound financial condition at a time when it was sustaining heavy military expenditures, fighting Mongol invasions between 1550 and 1570 and maintaining military preparedness thereafter. The government's fiscal health at this time reflected the general economic strength of sixteenth-century China.

The Economy

Peace and stability made for prosperity. During the first century of the Ming, northern agriculture was rehabilitated, but the South remained the most populous and prosperous region. The gradual spread of superior strains of rice, which had begun during the Sung, permitted a steady increase in China's population. By 1600 the population had increased to double the 60 million people who had inhabited China at the start of the Ming. At the same time, the introduction in the sixteenth century of new crops from the Americas laid a foundation for still further population increases which were to follow in the Ch'ing.

Ming economic developments may have been less dramatic than those of the Sung. It is difficult to find major breakthroughs or radically new technologies or types of industries. But the population increase, the flourishing of commerce, and the expanding use of money reveal this to have been a far from stagnant period. Nourished by trade, such great lower Yangtze cities as Nanking, Soochow, and Hangchow prospered. Among the important industries of the period were the porcelain and ceramic kilns centered in Kiangsi, the cotton manufacture of Nanking, and the silk weaving in Soochow. Hopei remained the center of iron manufacture, and Anhwei was known for its dye works. Indigo and sugar cane, along with cotton, were important cash crops grown for the market. A well-known seventeenth-century technical manual, *Creations of Man and Nature,* offers impressive evidence of the inventiveness of Chinese craftsmen within the parameters of their technical and intellectual tradition.

Literacy

Another indication of prosperity was an increase in literacy, not only among the well-educated and ambitious but also among the more humble and less sophisticated. Bookshops did a brisk business. Among their best sellers were collections of model examination papers used by candidates to cram for their tests. But they also sold encyclopedias, colored prints, novels, and collections of short stories. There were also guides which explained the classics in simple language, and books of moral instruction illustrated with tales of wrong-doing and retribution.

The audience for wood block prints was even wider than that for books. Although it was the Japanese who developed the colored wood block print to its highest aesthetic form, the colored print was originated in China and achieved its greatest excellence there in the seventeenth century. The first colored print formed the frontispiece of a Chinese Buddhist sutra and is dated 1346. More colorful and less spiritual were the five-color illustrations of Ming erotica.

There were also, during the Ming, educated men who had failed to advance through the examination system and who, turning to literary careers, helped preserve the popular arts. Two such men were Feng Meng-lung (1574–1646) and Ling Meng-ch'i (1580–1664), authors of widely read anthologies of short stories. Both men were also dramatists and scholars. Feng's interests ranged particularly wide; for instance, he wrote books on gambling as well as on Confucianism. But he is most famous for publishing *Stories, Old and New,* three collections of colloquial short stories based on the promptbooks of the storytellers, who had formed part of the urban entertainment scene at least as far back as Southern Sung Hangchow. Liu Wu-chi's description of the subject matter of Feng's stories reveals their diversity:

> Their range includes: quasi-historical tales of kings and generals, faithful friends and filial sons; romantic yarns of strange lands and peoples; supernatural stories of marvels and prodigies, spirits and ghosts, Buddhist monks and Taoist immortals; realistic stories of scandals in monastic establishments; daring exploits of brigands and thieves; murders, lawsuits, and court trials; domestic tragedies and bloody revenges; social comedies and family reunions.[3]

Ling, son of a noted publisher and scholar, rewrote and retold the stories in the two collections he published, both entitled *Striking the Table in Amazement at the Wonders.*

The Novel

The novel, like the short story, only gradually freed itself from its antecedents in the oral tradition of storytelling, eliminating extraneous material and refining crudities. In composition it remained essentially episodic, and Chinese novels often incorporated passages of verse. Despite their literary excellence, it was not until the twentieth century that novels won respectability in China as a form of high literature. In Japan the novel was an honored part of literary culture, but in China reading a novel was a surreptitious pleasure indulged in by students when their teacher was not looking—or vice versa. Many novels of the Ming period retold old stories or embellished historical episodes; others were adventure stories, serious or comic; and still others were pornographic. The four major novels that have come down to us from the Ming are *The Romance of the Three Kingdoms, The Water Margin* (translated also as *All Men Are Brothers*), *Journey to the West,* and *The Golden Lotus.*

The Romance of the Three Kingdoms (*San kuo chih yen i*) was first published in 1522, although it may have been written in the late Yüan. It is a fictionalized account of the conflict between Wei, Wu, and Shu, the three states which divided China in the third century A.D. In its pages the gifted but badly flawed character of Ts'ao Ts'ao, the martial heroics of Kuan Yü, and the strategic genius and devoted loyalty of Chu-ko Liang come vividly alive. It is no wonder that ordinary people in China formed many of their perceptions of historical figures from this and other novels. This literature was also popular in Korea and Japan where *The Romance of the Three Kingdoms* was widely read and much loved.

A different kind of history supplied the materials for *The Water Margin* (*Shui-hu chuan*), which was based on a Yüan play. It is set in the closing years of the Northern Sung and recounts the deeds of 108 bandit heroes, men driven by the cruel corruption of a decadent government to take justice into their own hands, outlaws who champion the oppressed and avenge the wronged. Numerous episodes, rendered in everyday speech, tell of feats of strength and daring, clever stratagems, and acts of savage but righteous vengeance. The novel's theme did not endear it to the political authorities, and during the Ch'ing dynasty it was officially proscribed. However, it continued to be sold under the counter and enjoyed a broad readership. Among the eminent twentieth-century leaders who read it with profit as well as delight was the young Mao Tse-tung.

The third major Ming novel, *Journey to the West* (*Hsi-yu chi*, translated also as *Monkey*), first published in 1592, describes the trip to India of the T'ang monk Hsüan-tsang. The trip is transformed into a fantastic journey, a heroic pilgrimage, and a tale of delightful satire and high comedy. Monkey is one of three supernatural disciples assigned by Buddha to accompany the priest and protect him from the monsters and demons that threaten him along the way. Many times Monkey saves the day, for he is endowed with penetrating, although mischievous and restless, intelligence and has acquired many magical gifts: he can somersault through the air for leagues with the greatest of ease, has the power to change into all kinds of shapes, and can transform his body hairs into a myriad of monkeys. Over his ear he wears a pin, which becomes an enormous iron cudgel when needed. The novel can be enjoyed as sheer fantasy, or for its satirical accounts of the bureaucratic organization of Heaven and the underworld, or even as a religious (and today Marxist) allegory.

Although the authors of these novels are believed known, the men named are either obscure or the attribution itself is in doubt. The question of authorship of the fourth great Ming novel, *Chin p'ing mei*, translated as *The Golden Lotus*, is even more obscure, and for good reason, since no respectable gentleman would have wanted his name linked to an erotic novel condemned by the Chinese as pornographic. Definitions of pornography change, but when the English translation was first issued in 1939, the more explicit passages had to be rendered into Latin. In its one hundred chapters, *Chin p'ing mei* gives a detailed account of the dissipations of a wealthy lecher. It offers a naturalistic tableau of amorous intrigues within the household and beyond, of drinking parties and sumptuous feasts, and portraits of go-betweens and fortunetellers, doctors and mendicants, singing girls and venal officials, and so on. After a life of sex without love, the hero, reduced to an empty shell, meets a fitting death, and the novel rolls on for another twenty chapters to recount the unraveling of the household.

Ming Drama

In the Ming, drama in the Southern style reached its peak. It differed from the Northern drama (discussed in the preceding chapter) in language, form, and music. Southern plays were much longer, running to forty and more scenes, and the songs, accompanied by the bamboo flute, were assigned to choruses as well as to the leading players. The result has been described as an "undulating cavalcade"[4] composed of scenes varying in length, number of players, and importance. Because of the length of the plays and the familiarity of the audience with their plots, performances of Ming drama, as of Japanese Nō, came to feature selected scenes from a number of plays rather than playing one all the way through. The authors were often sophisticated literary men, writing as much for their peers as for the wider public, at times more concerned to achieve literary excellence than to create effective theater. Ming playwrights were prolific: some 1200 titles are still known. Perhaps some were more frequently read than performed.

Acknowledged as the greatest Ming playwright was T'ang Hsien-tsu (1550–1616), who earned a *chin-shih* degree but had a frustrating official career. In his *The Dream of Han Tan* a young man falls asleep as he is trying to prepare a meal of millet grain. He then sees his whole life in a dream: he comes in first in the *chin-shih* examination, performs great deeds, is slandered and condemned to death, cleared and promoted. As he is about to die, he wakes up to discover that the millet on the stove is nearly ready to eat. This makes him realize that life itself passes as rapidly as a dream. T'ang wrote three other dream plays, and a dream also features importantly in his most admired work, *The Peony Pavilion*. This long play of fifty-five scenes centers on a love so strong that it is able to bring the dead back to life.

Other well known Ming dreams were written on the theme of love. A perennial favorite was the disastrous love of the T'ang emperor Hsüan-tsung for Yang Kuei-fei. The repertoire also contained plays on more contemporary matters. One of the last Southern masterpieces was *The Peach Blossom Fan*, completed in 1699 and depicting the end of the Ming half a century earlier. In it the conflict between traitorous villains and loyal heroes is intertwined with the story of the love shared by a loyal young scholar and a virtuous courtesan. Southern dramas continued to be performed and written, but toward the end of the eighteenth century there arose a new form of theater, based more broadly on popular taste. This was Peking Drama, famed for its actors and singers more than for its writers. Its repertoire consists largely of adaptations of older works.

Painting

The most notable center for painting in the Later Middle Ming was Soochow, where the Wu school flourished ca. 1460–1560. Soochow was a prosperous city, a financial and commercial community located near the juncture of the Grand Canal and the Yangtze River. A great cultural center famed for its poetry and painting, calligraphy and drama, it became a place of refuge for sophisticated people fleeing the uncertainties of political life, a place where the literati could pursue their own interests in peace, the home of the gentleman cultivating his artistic talents without regard for money or career. Soochow was famous, too, for its gardens, conceived and designed as miniature replicas of vast nature.

Designations like "Che school" and "Wu school" are Chinese classifications based on the artist's residence, style, and/or social status. Unfortunately for the modern student, these three categories did not always coincide: not all amateurs resided in Soochow; some professionals adopted "amateur" styles, and so forth. However, in stylistic terms, the Che school declined in the sixteenth century. Its most characteristic contribution to Chinese art was the continuation of Southern Sung academic painting. For fresh departures one must turn to Soochow.

The man who stood at the beginning of the Wu tradition was Shen Chou (1427–1509), who was also a talented poet and calligrapher. He lived in comfort on an estate about ten miles out of town and loved to paint the landscape of Soochow itself. Although deeply influenced by Yüan painting, he gradually developed a style of his own that conveyed a genial warmth and a sense of ease and naturalness.

Figure 10-3 Wen Cheng-ming, *The Seven Junipers of Ch'ang-shu.* Section of hand-scroll, ink on paper, 28.8 cm high; total length, 362 cm.

Wen Cheng-ming (1470–1559) studied painting under Shen Chou and, like his master, was a versatile scholar. He admired and frequently followed the model of Chao Meng-fu, the great Yüan painter, but he was too talented an artist to follow one model only. Nor did he spend a lifetime perfecting a single style or refining a single vision. Instead he worked in many different manners during his long and productive life. Some of his paintings contain references to painting styles going back to the T'ang, styles previously revived during the Southern Sung and the Yüan. Such multiple historical references were among the qualities most admired in his work by Ming and later connoisseurs.

It is not possible to illustrate the work of an artist like Wen Cheng-ming with a single "representative" painting, but *The Seven Junipers of Ch'ang-shu* is one of his most distinctive and powerful (see Figure 10-3). Wen's inscription states that he was copying Chao Meng-fu, but this is "copying" at its most creative, for what it shares with the Yüan painter is the power of its abstraction and the expressiveness of its brushwork. It also shares a love for the old: the trees were originally planted in A.D. 500, and four were replaced in the eleventh century. But here the accent is not on venerable age, but on strength and an explosive vitality that cannot be contained by the edges of the paper. In the artist's own rhapsody (*fu*), which he added to his painting, he invites the viewer on a flight of the imagination:

> Like creaking ropes the junipers dance to the wail of the wind, conjuring up a thousand images: split horns and blunted claws, the wrestling of the dragon with the tiger, great whales rolling in the deep, and giant birds who swoop down on their prey. And now, like ghosts, they vanish, now reappear, vast entangled forms.[5]

Ming Thought: Wang Yang-ming and Others

Like Wen Cheng-ming's junipers, Ming thought could not be confined within the framework intended for it, and it was a contemporary of Wen's by the name of Wang Yang-ming (Wang Shou-jen, 1472–1529) who opened up new intellectual vistas within Neo-Confucianism. Unlike the gentlemen-painters of Soo-

chow, Wang had a very active official career. At its low point he suffered two months in prison and a beating of forty strokes followed by exile in Kweichow, but he subsequently served with great courage and distinction not only as a civil administrator but also as a military commander rendering outstanding service by suppressing rebels.

Ming thinkers had to cope with the problems of living a Confucian life in a world which remained stubbornly un-Confucian. Despite the state's official support for Confucianism, Chinese government and society were as far from resembling the Confucian ideal as ever. How was one to live a proper life in a society that was not right and proper, amid the venality of officials, the social changes induced by economic expansion, and the continuing politicization of government administration?

Ming intellectuals also had to redefine the role of the educated scholar-official-literati in Chinese society. The growth of commerce created a new prosperity, new sources of power, and, de facto, new value systems. At the same time, the spread of literacy undercut the monopoly of classical thought, classical culture, and the status of those with a classical education. Moreover, there was a sense that in a post—classical age perhaps the only way the scholar could make a personal contribution was through specialization—a marked departure from the traditional aim of universal knowledge.

In an effort to define their personal and social roles, the educated were forced to question the nature of their own nature.

> Was it static or dynamic, metaphysical or physical, an abstract ideal or an active force, a moral norm or a trans-moral perfection? . . . How was the individual to understand that nature in relation to his actual self and his society?[6]

The issue at stake was not purely intellectual. It involved a quest not only for knowledge but also for wisdom and a striving for sagehood. For Wang Yang-ming the essential insight came suddenly, at the age of thirty-six after a period of intense thought while he was in exile in Kweichow. His experience has often been likened to the sudden enlightenment sought by Ch'an Buddhists.

Like Lu Chiu-yüan, Wang Yang-ming identified human nature with the mind-heart (hsin), which he in turn identified with principle (li). For Wang, as for Lu, *li* alone exists. Everyone is endowed with goodness and has an innate capacity to know good (*liang-chih*). Self-perfection consists in "extending" this capacity to the utmost. Everyone can attain perfection because all are endowed with the gold of sagehood. People may differ quantitatively in their abilities, but qualitatively they are the same, just as the gold in a small coin is in no way inferior to that in a large one. Thus Wang Yang-ming took it very calmly when a disciple reported that he had gone out for a walk and found the street full of sages. That was only to be expected. However, there is need for strenuous effort to refine the gold by eliminating the dross, that is, "selfish desires." Sagehood does not come easily.

External sources of doctrinal authority, including the classics and the words of the sages, have only a secondary, accessory function. According to Wang Yang-ming, "If words are examined in the mind and found to be wrong, although they have come from the mouth of Confucius, I dare not accept them as correct."[7] Conversely, if the mind finds them correct, it does not matter if the words have been uttered by ordinary folk. The truth is in and of the mind. It remains one whole because the mind and *li* are universal.

As is the case for all Neo-Confucians, the truth that concerns Wang Yang-ming is at once metaphysical and moral. Furthermore, it is not to be grasped by abstract intellectualization but must be lived. What is true of sensory knowledge holds for all knowledge: a person can no more know filial piety without practicing it than he can know the smell of an odor or understand pain without experiencing them. Knowing and acting are not only inseparable, they are two dimensions of a single process: "Knowledge in its genuine and earnest aspect is action, and action in its intelligent and discriminating aspect is knowledge."[8] A man may discourse with great erudition and subtlety on filiality, but it is his conduct which will reveal his depth of understanding. To employ a modern example, a person who "knows" smoking is bad for him but persists in the habit reveals that he does not really "know" this with his whole being. A perfectly integrated personality is, of course, one of the marks of the sage.

Wang Yang-ming had an abiding influence because he spoke to some of the persistent concerns of East Asian thinkers and activists. One may, for example, detect in Mao Tse-tung's discussions of the relationship between theory and practice overtones of the Ming philosopher's insistence on the unity of knowledge and action. Another reason for his influence is that he was the kind of thinker who opens many doors rather than being a rigid systematizer. The thought of the Late Ming can best be understood as developing out of some of the ideas present in his own teachings as well as in reaction to some of his views.

Ming Thought after Wang Yang-ming

Some of Wang Yang-ming's followers and disciples led courageous but quite conventional lives of public service, self-cultivation, and teaching, but others developed the more radical implications of his thought. Thus Wang Yang-ming taught that the mind in itself is above distinctions of good and evil, an idea with a strong Buddhist flavor and compatible with Taoist ideas. The tendency to combine Confucianism, Buddhism, and Taoism was a very old one and attracted a good many Ming intellectuals. It was present in Wang Yang-ming but was carried further by Wang Chi (1498–1585), who freely employed Buddhist and Taoist terms and valued Taoist techniques of breath control. However, he remained a Confucian in his rejection of empty abstract speculation and in his moral values.

Wang Chi and Wang Ken (1483–1541) are considered the founders of the T'ai-chou branch of Wang Yang-ming's teaching, named after Wang Ken's native prefecture where he established a school. Wang Ken was born into a family of salt producers and remained a commoner throughout his life. In 1552 his enthusiasm for the teachings of the sage prompted him to build himself a cart such as he imagined Confucius to have used. He then rode in it to Peking to present a memorial. He attracted much attention in the capital until persuaded by embarrassed fellow disciples of Wang Yang-ming to return south. He remained a vigorous and fervent popular teacher, attracting a good many commoners as students.

In their personal conduct as well as in their teachings, the more radical followers of Wang Yang-ming stretched the parameters of Confucianism to the utmost and went beyond the limits tolerated by the state. Ho Hsin-yin (1517–79) was a courageous defender of free discussion in the academies and so devoted to all humanity that he turned against the family as a restrictive, selfish, exclusive institution. His unorthodox ideas, courageous personal conduct, and reputation as a troublemaker eventually helped land him in prison, where he died after being beaten. Another controversial figure was Li Chih (1527–1602), who carried the individualism implicit in Wang Yang-ming's philosophy to the point of defending selfishness. A thorough nonconformist, he denounced conventional scholars who, he claimed, lacked an authentic commitment to the core values of Confucianism. In 1588 Li Chih shaved his head and became (at least in appearance) a Buddhist monk. But he continued to offend the literati; in 1590 local gentry organized a mob that demolished the temple where Li was staying. Imprisoned in 1602, he committed suicide. Until a modern revival of interest in his ideas, he was best known as an editor of *The Water Margin*, and the novel's opposition to the establishment accords very well with Li's own attitudes. The significance of such men as Ho and Li, however, lies not in their intellectual influence, which was negligible, but in demonstrating the extremes to which Ming thought could be stretched.

Li Chih shocked not only members of the official establishment but also activist Confucians, who were dismayed by the radical subjectivism of this line of thought and appalled by the Buddhistic notion that human nature was beyond good and evil. Such earnest Confucians also saw it as their duty to protest forcefully against political abuses and to object against such un-Confucian conduct as Chang Chü-cheng's refusal to retire from office to observe mourning on the death of his father. Early in the seventeenth century, the Tung-lin Academy, founded in 1604 in Wu-hsi, northwest of Soochow, became a center for such "pure criticism," which cost many Tung-lin men their lives. Conflict between pro-Tung-lin and anti-Tung-lin factions lasted through the final thirty years of the dynasty, but before considering these political events, it is appropriate to turn to another area of activity where Wang Yang-ming's dictum concerning the unity of knowledge and action was applied: the world of art.

Tung Ch'i-ch'ang and Late Ming Painting

Tung Ch'i-ch'ang (1555–1636) was a major painter and calligrapher, the leading connoisseur of his generation, and China's foremost art historian. Many of the ideas of Tung and his circle were not new, but he gave them their final authoritative expression. The key to his analysis was the division of painters into Northern and Southern schools resembling the Northern and Southern branches of Ch'an Buddhism. The assignment of a painter into one group or the other was not based on geography but on the man's social standing and on his style. A "Northern" painter was defined as a professional who stressed technical excellence and fine craftsmanship to produce handsome paintings of maximum visual appeal. In contrast "Southern" painters were literati, men of wide reading and profound learning for whom painting was an experience of self-expression, a chance to allow their genius and sensibility free play, much as in calligraphy. Tung traced these two lines all the way back to the T'ang and cast Wang Wei as the founder of the "Southern" tradition. He also included painters of his own dynasty in his analysis. Furthermore, Tung and his friends affirmed their affiliation with the "Southern" tradition.

Self-identification with a tradition of amateurism did not preclude the study of earlier masters. Tung himself was influenced in calligraphy by Chao Meng-fu and Wen Cheng-ming, and in painting he greatly admired the great masters of the Yüan. But he emphasized the need to "unlearn," and a painting such as his picture of the Ch'ing-pien Mountains (see Figure 10-4) has only a faint resemblance to its purported tenth-century model. Nor is there in this painting any desire to represent mountains as they actually appear to the eye or to define the depth relationships between them by clearly placing them one behind the other. Natural forms are tilted, compressed, and juxtaposed, not to represent nature but to emphasize the painting's formal organization and the interplay of light and dark. The effect of Tung's theories and art on seventeenth-century painting is suggested by Wang Yüan-ch'i (See Chapter 14), who described Tung as having "cleansed the cobwebs from landscape painting in one sweep."[9]

In the final years of the Ming there were artists painting in a number of different styles, many playing on earlier modes. A painter who took as his point of departure the classic Sung landscape but turned it into an expression of his own fantastic imagination was Wu Pin (ca. 1568–1626): Figure 10-5 shows a landscape such as never was nor ever could be. As James Cahill has observed, "Solids evaporate into space, ambiguous definitions of surface unsettle the eye

Figure 10-4 Tung Ch'i-ch'ang,
The Ch'ing-pien Mountain.
Hanging scroll, ink on paper,
dated 1617, 225 cm × 67 cm.

Figure 10-5   Wu Pin,
Landscape. Hanging scroll,
ink and light colors on paper,
306.5 cm × 98.5 cm.

as it moves over them, and the towering construction of spires and cliffs, like the creation of some titanic, demented sculptor, balances on an absurdly narrow base."[10] Paintings such as this suggest both some of the potentialities and some of the dangers inherent in Ming individualism. In the seventeenth century the dynasty, like the painting, found itself balanced on too narrow a base.

Late Ming Government (1590–1644)

A conspicuous feature of the last fifty years of the dynasty was the inadequacy of its emperors. When Chang Chü-cheng died in 1582, Emperor Shen-tsung, then not quite nineteen, saw to it that during his reign no minister would again dominate the government, but soon the emperor himself ceased to bother very much with government. From 1589 to 1615, a period of more than twenty-five years, he did not hold a single general audience, and from 1590 to his death in 1620, he only conducted personal interviews with Grand Secretaries five times. Nor, except on matters of taxation and defense, did he respond to memorials. As a result much of the business of government was left undone. He was particularly remiss in personnel matters. By the end of his reign, not only were the offices in the capital seriously understaffed, but it has been estimated that as many as half of the prefectural and district posts were also unfilled. Whereas at the start he had punished officials who criticized him in their memorials, during the last twenty years he largely ignored even them. Some high officials withdrew from their posts without authorization—they too were ignored.

The emperor did take an interest in military matters. From the 1580s on there was fighting in the southwest against various tribal peoples as well as against the Thais and especially against the Burmese. In the nineties there were campaigns in Inner Mongolia, and large Ming armies fought a Japanese invasion of Korea (see Chapter 12). These military actions were generally successful but enormously expensive. Also costly but not as successful was the Ming military effort in Manchuria, where the Manchu chief Nurhaci founded a state and fought the Ming to a draw (see Chapter 15.)

Emperor Hsi-tsung (T'ien-ch'i, r. 1620–27) was peculiar even by Late Ming standards. He "did not have sufficient leisure to learn to write"[11] but spent all his time on carpentry, creating many pieces of fine furniture, which he lacquered himself. Factionalism, which in the absence of strong imperial leadership had flourished under Shen-tsung, now turned vicious, as a very capable and equally unscrupulous eunuch, Wei Chung-hsien (1568–1627), gained power due to his influence over the emperor. Wei purged all opponents, foremost among them the members of the Tung-lin faction, six of whom died in prison after torture. One of these men, Tso Kuang-tou, in his notes to his sons left vivid descriptions of agonizing pain and suffering, which he interlaced with exclamations of his fervent devotion to the emperor, for example, "my body belongs to my ruler-father."[12] Like Ho Hsin-yin and Li Chih, Tso demonstrated his Confucian selflessness even to the point of death, but his martyr-dom, unlike theirs, testifies to the persuasiveness of a kind of Confucian au-thoritarianism in which even a carpenter-emperor could command the loyalty others might think due, if at all, only to a sage. To the end, the dynasty re-tained the loyalty of most of its officials. A remarkable group of men, compara-ble to the Sung loyalists, remained faithful to the dynasty even after it had come to an end.

Wei Chung-hsien was not content with the realities of power but was also hungry for public recognition. He heaped honors on himself and even had a nephew take the emperor's place in performing sacrifices in the imperial tem-ple. He also encouraged a movement to have temples housing his image built throughout China. But he did not survive Emperor Hsi-tsung for long, and the temples perished shortly after the man. The succeeding emperor, Chuang-lieh-ti (Ch'ung-chen, r. 1627–44), attempted reform during his reign, but the lack of a consistent policy is suggested by the high turnover of the regime's highest officials: from 1621 to 1644 the presidents of the Six Ministries were changed 116 times.

Bureaucratic infighting and corruption was something the dynasty could no longer afford, for during the reign of Shen-tsung the earlier fiscal surplus had been turned into a mounting deficit. But the trouble went deeper.

> The Ming fiscal administration was in essence built on the foundation of a grain economy. With its diversified rates and measurements, self-supporting institutions, regional and departmental self-sufficiency, divided budget, separate channels of cash flow, numerous material and *corvée* labor impositions, and local tax captains, the fiscal machinery was grossly unfit for a new monetary economy. . . . However, [these unsatisfactory features of the Ming fiscal administration] would not have been so appallingly evident had not the wide circulation of silver thoroughly changed the nation's economic outlook. The archaic fiscal structure became more outdated than ever because it was set against the background of a mobile and ex-panding economy.[13]

Furthermore, the delicate balance between the central government and the local elite was upset when the dynasty made too many concessions to the gen-try. Too much was given away, too many fields were removed from the tax rolls. Large landowners were able to find tax-shelters through various manipu-lations, and only peasant freeholders remained to pay taxes. Locally resent-ment against the gentry grew, while the shortage of funds forced the dynasty to neglect vital public works. Grain stored for emergency use was sold off. Even the postal system was shut down. Finally, the regime failed to pay even its most strategically placed troops: when the end came, the capital garrison had not been paid for five months.

Military deserters and dismissed postal employees were among those who took the lead in forming the outlaw gangs that appeared first in Northern Shensi and then spread from there. As they grew in size and strength, they pro-gressed from disorganized raiding to more ambitious objectives. Two groups emerged as most powerful. One established itself in Szechwan and was led by

Chang Hsien-chung (ca. 1605–47), a leader notorious for his brutality. The other was led by Li Tzu-ch'eng (ca. 1605–45), a former postal attendant, whom the official sources depict as a cruel but dedicated leader, and who is celebrated in the People's Republic as a hero.

In 1644 Li Tzu-ch'eng seized Peking, and the Ming emperor committed suicide; but Li proved unable to found a new dynasty, for he had not taken the necessary ideological and administrative steps to win over the members of the scholar-official elite. For them he represented at best an unknown force, but no one could rule China without their cooperation. This was understood by Li's most powerful and capable competitors even though they came from Manchuria. When they came to build their dynasty, they made extensive use of Ming precedents.

NOTES

1. Hilary J. Beattie, "Land and Lineage in China: A Study of T'ung-ch'eng County, Anhwei, in the Ming and Ch'ing Dynasties," (Ph.D. dissertation, Cambridge University), 1973.

2. G. William Skinner, "Chinese Peasants and the Closed Community: An Open and Shut Case," in *Comparative Studies in Society and History* 13 (1971): 272.

3. Liu Wu-chi, *An Introduction to Chinese Literature* (Bloomington: Indiana University Press, 1966), pp. 216–17.

4. K'ung Shang-jen, *The Peach Blossom Fan*, trans. Chen Shih-hsiang and Harold Action (Berkeley and Los Angeles: University of California Press, 1970), p. xiv.

5. Tseng Yu-ho, in Richard Edwards, *The Art of Wen Cheng-ming (1470–1559)* (Ann Arbor: The University of Michigan Museum of Art, 1976), p. 122.

6. Wm. Theodore de Bary and the Conference on Ming Thought, *Self and Society in Ming Thought* (New York: Columbia University Press, 1970), p. 12.

7. Wing-tsit Chan, trans., *Instructions for Practical Living and Other Neo-Confucian Writings* (New York: Columbia University Press, 1963), p. 159.

8. Wing-tsit Chan, *A Source Book in Chinese Philosophy* (Princeton: Princeton University Press, 1963), p. 681.

9. Quoted in James Cahill, *Fantastics and Eccentrics in Chinese Painting* (New York: The Asia Society, 1967), p. 22.

10. James Cahill, *Fantastics and Eccentrics*, p. 36.

11. Quoted in Arthur W. Hummel, ed., *Eminent Chinese of the Ch'ing Period* (Washington, D.C.: U.S. Government Printing Office, 1943), 1: 190.

12. Quoted in Charles O. Hucker, "Confucianism and the Chinese Censorial System," in David S. Nivison and Arthur F. Wright, eds., *Confucianism in Action* (Stanford: Stanford University Press, 1959), p. 208.

13. Ray Huang, "Fiscal Administration During the Ming Dynasty," in Charles O. Hucker, ed., *Chinese Government in Ming Times* (New York: Columbia University Press, 1969), pp. 124–25.

鎌倉時代之日本

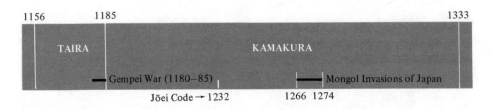

1156　　　1185　　　　　　　　　　　　　　　　　　　1333

TAIRA　　　　　　　　　　　KAMAKURA

—Gempei War (1180–85)　　　　　　—Mongol Invasions of Japan

Jōei Code → 1232　　　　1266 1274

11 Japan in the Kamakura Period: 1185 – 1333

During the Heian period, Japan adapted Chinese institutions, ideas, and styles to suit Japanese needs. A Chinese visitor would have been surprised, puzzled, and even shocked by much of what he might have seen and heard in Heian Japan; but he would also have recognized the similarities, the signs of Chinese influence. But by the thirteenth century the two societies had drawn much further apart: a Sung scholar-official and a Kamakura *bushi* (warrior) or samurai had even less in common than did their aristocratic precursors of the T'ang and Heian eras. China and Japan were moving in divergent directions.

The ascent of the Japanese warrior was a slow process that began well before the Kamakura period, and his dominance of Japanese affairs was incomplete. The sanctity of the throne as the ultimate source of political authority remained unchallenged, and the court in Kyōto retained considerable economic resources and political leverage. Nevertheless, the history of the Kamakura period is largely the history of the *bushi* and the changes he wrought in Japanese institutions, culture, and values. The period gets its very name from the seat of warrior power at Kamakura in Eastern Japan.

The increase in the military strength and economic power of the provincial aristocracy during the late Heian period made it possible for these men to reach out for political power as well and ultimately changed the system of government itself. In the twelfth century the greatest of these families remained the Minamoto (especially the Seiwa Genji branch), relying for their strength on the Kantō region in Eastern Japan, and the Ise Taira based in the West in and around the Inland Sea. Although as provincial warrior aristocrats they shared a certain heritage and values, the rivalry which divided them overshadowed any potential ties of common class interests or feelings of solidarity. The same was true of the civilian court. The political intrigues and fighting that marked this harsh transitional period pitted not only warriors and aristocrats against each other but also warriors against warriors, court nobles against court nobles, and even fathers against sons, in a complicated and treacherous struggle for power.

Triumph and Fall of the Taira (1156–1185)

In 1156 open conflict broke out between the cloistered (retired) emperor and the reigning emperor, and military men were called in on both sides. On one side, supporting the emperor, was a force led by Minamoto no Tameyoshi (1096–1156); on the other side, the cloistered emperor, Go-Shirakawa, had the backing of a coalition led by Taira no Kiyomori (1118–81), which also included among its leaders Tameyoshi's own son, Yoshitomo (1123–60). Military victory in what is known as the Hōgen Conflict went to Kiyomori's coalition, but the real losers were the court and the old civil nobility.

The outcome left Kiyomori in a position of great power, but the victorious coalition was soon dissolved, and further fighting ensued in the Heiji War (1159–60). Once again Kiyomori won, this time defeating his former ally Yoshitomo. These Hōgen and Heiji conflicts were brief and localized, but extremely bitter. They were followed by manhunts and executions, for warriors did not share the civilian aristocrats' qualms about taking life. Gone were the days when the usual penalty for being on the wrong side politically was exile.

These military victories made Kiyomori the de facto ruler. The basis of his power was new, but he used it in the old way, dominating the court and government machinery in the capital and marrying his daughters into the imperial line and also to Fujiwara regents. And in 1180 he placed his grandson on the throne. In his personal deportment, too, he conformed to the standards of taste set by the court. But to the grand Kyōto aristocrats, he remained an arrogant provincial parvenu, worthy only of contempt. An attempt to exert greater control over the court by transferring it to a site near modern Kobe failed. More successful was Kiyomori's handling of the troublesome temple armies. He attacked and burned two of the worst offenders, both in Nara: the great Tōdaiji, and Kōfukuji, the prime temple of the Fujiwara family.

Conditions in the capital were unusually harsh during these years. Storms, earthquakes, and disease afflicted the city, which, as always, was also very susceptible to the ravages of fire. A major conflagration destroyed a third of the city in 1177; in one two-month period after the fire over forty thousand corpses were found in the streets of the capital.

Kiyomori's most serious problem was that in ruling through the old institutions, his regime shared their weaknesses. He could no more exercise real control over the provinces, where the sources of actual power now lay, than could the cloistered emperor. Led by Yoshitomo's son Yoritomo (1147–99), the Minamoto took advantage of this situation to rebuild their power. With the support of many eastern Taira as well as Minamoto families, Yoritomo initiated the Gempei War (1180–85), which culminated in the permanent defeat of the Taira. Contributing to this outcome was the brilliant generalship of Yoshitsune (1159–89), Yoritomo's younger brother, who defeated the Taira at sea as well as on land. Later Yoshitsune himself incurred the suspicion of his powerful brother, who, in the end, turned his armed might against him and forced him into death.

The extent of the fighting, the style of combat which placed a premium on personal valor, the contrast between the Taira (who had adopted many of the ways of Kyōto) and the rougher Eastern warriors, and the impact of the war on subsequent developments have assured the war a lasting place in the Japanese imagination and in literature. It generated one major literary work, *The Tale of the Heike* (*Heike monogatari*), and a host of minor romances, including many which embellished the tale of Yoshitsune and transformed it into a heroic legend.

Establishment of the Bakufu

Yoritomo was not himself a great general, but he was a good judge of men, a consummate politician, and an effective organizer. Carefully he consolidated his position in the East. With his headquarters in the small fishing village of Kamakura, he built a secure base for warrior power. (See map, Figure 11-1.) There he established his *bakufu*, literally "tent government," a term which evokes the military origins of his power.

The power of the Minamoto, like that of the rival Taira, was based on ties of vassalage, aptly defined by Peter Duus as "a personal bond of loyalty and obedience by which a warrior promised service to a lord or chieftain in return for military protection, security, and assistance."[1] The ties of vassalage were more

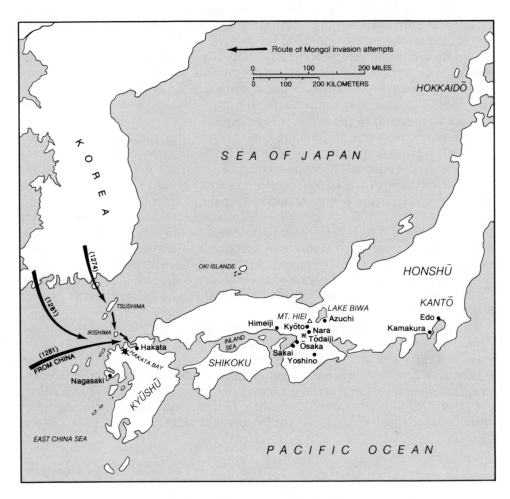

Figure 11-1 **Japan, 1200–1600**

inclusive and expandable than the old kinships bonds; yet the relationship remained personal. It was contractual in the sense that there was at least a tacit
understanding of mutual obligations, but these were never spelled out or incorporated in legal documents. Nor were there legal mechanisms for altering or
dissolving the arrangement. Ideally it called for deep personal devotion of vassal to lord rather than the more abstract loyalty demanded in an impersonal
bureaucratic state; but in practice, especially in turbulent and unsettled times,
much depended on the individuals involved.

From his vassals (*gokenin*, "honorable housemen") Yoritomo demanded and
expected absolute loyalty. Such loyalty was granted him partly as a result of
the confidence he inspired in his men, some of whose families had served the
Minamoto for generations. Others cast their lot with Yoritomo only after they
had been impressed with his visible accomplishments. Calculations of military and political advantage on the part of the lesser lords played a role in aug-
menting Yoritomo's strength, which after the defeat of the Taira, surpassed
that of any possible rival, military or civil. Economic inducements also provided powerful motivation. Those who served him could expect confirmation
of land rights (*shiki*) they already held; and they could hope for further rewards
in the form of rights over land confiscated from the enemies of the Minamoto.
Economic self-interest reinforced the bonds of personal vassalage in Japan just
as in feudal Europe; it was the cement that ensured the cohesiveness of the
system.

There are certain striking resemblances between Kamakura Japan and feudal
Europe. Both featured rule by a military aristocracy that held predominant
local power, a system of vassalage, and the granting of rights to land when
landholding was the main source of wealth. As we shall see, the similarities
did not end there. However, this Kamakura-centered political system functioned in uneasy tandem with the imperial system centered on Kyōto. Rather
than eliminate the old order entirely, Yoritomo tried to use it in his search for
stability. The result was a dual system under which the old aristocracy retained much of its wealth, at least until the early thirteenth century.

The Shogunate

Legitimization for the new order came from the emperor, who in 1192 "appointed" Yoritomo shogun, or to use the full term, Seii Taishōgun ("Barbarian
Suppressing General"). Under the theoretical sovereignty of the emperor, the
shogun's government exercised substantial "delegated" power. This was the
beginning of an institution (the shogunate) that lasted until 1868.

The most important power "delegated" to Yoritomo was legal control over
the staffing of provincial posts, which enabled him to appoint his own men to
administrative positions in the provinces. He was also authorized to appoint
his men to the newly created positions of Military Land Steward (*jitō*) and Military Protector (*shugo*).

Land stewards were appointed to *shōen* and given official responsibility for the collection of rents and the forwarding of dues to the absentee holders of rights in the *shōen*, that is, the court aristocracy, the imperial family, and the great religious establishments. The stewards also received considerable police and judicial authority over the estates, and were rewarded by grants of rights (*shiki*) to a portion of the estate income. For Yoritomo, the right to appoint land stewards provided a way to reward his smaller vassals. These men remained accountable to Kamakura alone, an important point, since tensions between stewards and the Kyōto "proprietors" were frequent.

Military Protectors had much broader jurisdiction than stewards. Placed over one or two provinces, they were charged with the maintenance of security, including the suppression of rebels. They also supervised the shogun's retainers in the area, and thus had considerably more power than the stewards.

The restoration of order benefited everyone, and the new system recognized the economic prerogatives as well as the legitimacy of the Kyōto establishment. However, the advantage lay with Kamakura, since it could exert economic as well as military pressure on Kyōto simply by holding up payments. The arrangement left ample room for discontent in the old capital. This came to a head under the leadership of the ex-emperor Go-Toba (1180–1229), who had abdicated in 1198, at the age of eighteen, after a thirteen-year reign. In 1221 Go-Toba challenged the system and tried to restore imperial power by drawing on the imperial *shōen* and Buddhist monasteries to raise a military force, but he was rapidly and soundly defeated. The end result was to increase the strength of the shogunate, which used the occasion to confiscate three thousand *shōen*, appoint additional stewards in Central and Western Japan, and establish its own deputies in Kyōto, thus further diminishing the power of the imperial establishment.

The Hōjō Regents

Yoritomo established the shogunate on firm foundations, but did not succeed in founding a dynasty of shoguns. During his life he killed off rivals within his own family, and when he died he left only two sons, one aged eleven and the other a wild seventeen-year-old without political judgment. Consequently, Yoritomo's death in 1199 was followed by a struggle for power.

Emerging victorious was the Hōjō, the family of Yoritomo's remarkable, strong-minded widow, Masako (1157–1225). Her father now assumed domination over the shogunal government and became the first in a line of de facto Hōjō rulers, although they never assumed the title of "shogun." That was held by a puppet, who after 1219 was not even a Minamoto, for in that year a Fujiwara infant received the appointment. Meanwhile the Hōjō, by placing family members in key posts, exercised actual control over the *bakufu*. In this way real power was doubly divorced from apparent authority: in theory Japan was ruled by an emperor, but this emperor was actually under the control of his abdicated father (the cloistered emperor); meanwhile, in Kamakura, the power ostensibly "delegated" to the shogun was actually exercised by Hōjō ministers.

Although the overall structure seems complex, organization of the Kamakura *bakufu* remained relatively simple, in keeping with the more modest scope of government itself. An Office of Samurai looked after the affairs of the shogunate's vassals (*gokenin*) and generally supervised military and police matters. A Board of Inquiry (*monchūjo*) dealt with various judicial matters, and under the Hōjō handled cases arising outside of Kamakura itself. General administration was under the jurisdiction of an Office of Administration similar to the household offices used by the great Heian families. Yoritomo, in the end, designated it the *mandokoro*, the usual name for such a household bureau. The heads of these three bureaus participated in a council which advised Yoritomo, who made the final decisions himself. The council was led by the chief of the *mandokoro*, and it was in this capacity that the Hōjō exercised their power. In 1225 an innovative Hōjō statesman created a Council of State to allow for broader warrior participation in government, but the Hōjō soon dominated this body.

The Jōei Code

The Hōjō concept of government is reflected in the Jōei Code of 1232. Adopted a decade after Go-Toba's unsuccessful attempt to reassert imperial authority, it nevertheless insisted on the rights of the court and the Buddhist church, rights which the warriors were not to transgress. The code claimed jurisdiction only over the *bakufu's* warriors, and it was to them that it was addressed. One of its main purposes was to clarify the duties of stewards and constables. Other important articles dealt with land rights, including the property rights of women, who could, in the event of divorce, retain the land they had originally brought into a marriage. The emergence of warrior power did not immediately lead to the suppression of the rights of those who could not bear arms.

Major concerns of the new code were the formulation of warrior ethics, the maintenance of public order, and the pursuit of justice. Severe punishments were stipulated for serious crimes such as treason. The use of abusive language was dealt with very severely, since a warrior would be quick to draw his sword in answer to an insult challenging his honor, thereby starting what might become a drawn-out and disruptive feud. These and other laws were directed at the *bakufu's* warrior constituency—the administration of the concerns of the common people was left largely to local authority.

The code emphasized the impartial administration of justice in settling disputes between warriors, disputes which usually concerned land rights. The adjudication of such matters was one of the shogunate's prime functions, and much of its power and prestige rested on samurai confidence in the equity of its decisions. The Jōei formulary sought to achieve this by setting forth its provisions in a simple and direct manner and by restricting itself to a small number of regulations, for the entire code consisted of only fifty-seven articles. For cases not covered by precedent, it advised recourse to the principles of common sense. This code was not only the first formulation of feudal law in Japan but also remained influential as long as Japan remained feudal.

It is an indication of the effectiveness of Hōjō rule and the solidity of the *bakufu's* basic institutions that this regime was able to withstand a formidable military challenge and survive the strains it placed on the body politic.

The Mongol Invasion and Its Aftermath

The Mongol conquest of East Asia was in full swing at the time the Jōei Code was issued, but it was another third of a century before the momentum of the Mongol conquests was felt in Japan. Before they were faced with the need to defend themselves against the Mongols, the Kamakura statesmen had successfully avoided political or military entanglement in continental affairs, although they did nothing to discourage trade with the Sung, which flourished both before and after the founding of the shogunate. Although this trade consisted mostly of luxury items, it brought on a drain of copper coinage, which posed a problem for Sung finances. Its primary effect in Japan was to stimulate a renewed interest in Chinese culture. The shogunate also maintained cordial relations with Korea: when, in 1227, the depredations of Japanese pirates off the Korean coast prompted Korean complaints, the *bakufu* ordered the offenders arrested and executed.

The Mongols changed all that. In 1266, even before the conquest of the Southern Sung had been completed, Khubilai Khan dispatched his first messenger to Japan demanding submission. This threat produced great consternation at court in Kyōto, but the shogunate remained calm, determined to resist. It took the Mongols until 1274 to organize a military expedition, but in that year a force of about 30,000 Mongols and Koreans was sent to Japan. They landed near Hakata, in North Kyūshū, and fought with a Japanese force assembled by the *bakufu*. Fortunately for the Japanese, a great storm destroyed this expedition. Heavy casualties did not deter Khubilai Khan from trying again. He renewed his demands, only to meet with rebuff; the Japanese showed their determination to resist by executing his envoys. In 1281 Khubilai sent a much larger force, estimated at 140,000 men, to crush the Japanese. But the shogunate, too, had used the intervening years in military preparation: they built a stone wall along Hakata Bay, amassed troops, and trained them in the techniques of group fighting employed by the Mongols, which contrasted with the individual combat customary in Japanese warfare. They fought for seven weeks before nature intervened once more; another great storm, called the *kamikaze* ("divine wind") by the Japanese, settled the issue. About half the men sent by Khubilai perished in this fruitless attempt to add Japan to his empire.

Still the Great Khan did not give up. Preparations for a third attempt were in progress when he died in 1294. Only then was the project abandoned. But the *bakufu* did not know that: it continued the policy of military preparedness until 1312.

In repulsing these attacks, the shogunate achieved a great success and further increased its power vis-à-vis the civilian court. But it had to share the glory of victory with temples and shrines, which claimed credit for securing divine intervention, while it alone bore the burden of paying for the wars. This was especially onerous because fighting the Mongol invaders, unlike internal warfare, brought in no new lands or booty with which to meet the expectations of warriors demanding their just rewards. And the long thirty years of preparation for defense did not even bring military glory. When the shogunate proved unable to satisfy warrior claims, the *bushi* lost confidence in the regime. Their loyalty was weakened, and as they turned for support increasingly to local authorities (Military Protectors and the stronger stewards), centrifugal forces came to the fore. The characteristic Hōjō response was to draw more power into their own hands, a policy not designed to deal with the underlying causes of their deteriorating situation. At the same time, economic pressures and the realities of power also worked against aristocratic civilian interests, as military stewards proved increasingly reluctant to forward payments to Kyōto. Vis-à-vis the cultivators too, the stewards were assuming ever greater powers. If a steward departed too far from custom in his demands, the cultivators could appeal to higher authority (including Kamakura), or they could negotiate with the *jitō* himself. However, the stewards' local authority was so extensive that increasingly they treated the estates as though they were their own property. The policy of excluding the military from interfering with civilian prerogatives was breaking down, and as the shogunate declined, the peculiar Kamakura relationship between court and *bakufu,* aristocrat and warrior, was also coming to an end.

The Warrior and His Ideals

By background and training, the *bushi* was a man very different in kind from the Heian aristocrat. As a fighting man he was called upon to exhibit martial skills and to demonstrate virtues recalling those attributed to the ideal knight of the European Middle Ages: valor, manly pride, vigor, and undying loyalty were among the qualities most highly prized in both societies. For the sake of his lord and the honor of his family name, a samurai should be prepared to face every hardship and make every sacrifice. He was expected to be completely reliable, earnest and sincere, to live a frugal and strenuous life, to care nothing for wealth or luxury, and to treat with contempt considerations of personal gain or calculations of profit or loss. Of course, just as the "refined" Heian period had had its wellborn but uncouth boors utterly incapable of turning out acceptable verse or writing a decent hand, so the "martial" Kamakura period had its full complement of cowards and turncoats: many *bushi* fell far short of the ideal. But in both ages, the widely accepted ideal did serve as a model and as a basis for judging men.

In some ways the demands on the Japanese warrior were harsher than those on his European counterpart, for the Japanese code was not softened by considerations of chivalry toward ladies nor did the rules of warfare provide for the taking of prisoners to be held for ransom. Instead the *bushi* defeated in personal combat expected to lose his head, for it was the practice of the victor to decapitate his enemy and present the head as proof of his triumph.

The complete elaboration of the code of the samurai did not take place until the seventeenth century, but its essential features are evident in the Kamakura period. Virile, selfless, and incorruptible, the ideal samurai gains added mystique through his disdain for death—and not just on the battlefield. To avoid dishonor or demonstrate his sincerity or underline a protest, he should be ready to commit ritual suicide by disembowelment (*seppuku*):

> With that very dagger he stabbed himself below the left nipple, plunging the blade so deep that it almost emerged through his back. Then he stretched the incision in three directions, pulled out his intestines, and wiped the dagger on the sleeve of his cloak. He draped the cloak over his body and leaned heavily on an arm rest; then he summoned his wife . . .[2]

Thus begins the description of Yoshitsune's death recounted in a fourteenth- or fifteenth-century text, and such was the death proper to a noble *bushi*—a death still valued by latter day followers of the samurai ideal, most recently the novelist Mishima (1925–70).

Like the cherry blossom which falls from the tree in its prime, the samurai must have no regrets when his life is cut off. The cherry blossom became the stock symbol of the samurai, suggesting his outlook on life and conveying an aesthetic dimension peculiarly Japanese in flavor. Another important component of the Kamakura view of life was religious, and it is to religion that we now turn.

Kamakura Religion: The Pure Land Sect

The turbulence and uncertainties accompanying the transition from aristocratic to warrior rule tended to confirm the belief that history had indeed entered its final phase of degeneracy (*mappō*) and made people all the more receptive to the solace of religion. One result was the continuing growth and development of the popularizing and pietistic trends exemplified earlier by the activities and teachings of Kūya and Genshin. Hōnen, the founder of the Pure Land sect (Jōdo) in Japan, was very much a part of this tradition. But he carried the invocation of Amida further than his predecessors by teaching that the *nembutsu* was not just one method for attaining salvation but that it was the best and indeed the only method suitable for the age.

When Hōnen expressed his ideas in writing, his book was burned by the monks on Mt. Hiei. He remained a controversial person, suffering in his seventies an exile of four years from which he was allowed to return only a year before he died. Underlying the emphasis on the invocation of Amida was a belief in salvation through faith rather than through works or religious observances— Hōnen himself, on his deathbed, declined to hold the usual cord connected to an Amida to draw him to paradise. His persistent rejection of traditional ritual and scholasticism helps to explain the hostility of the older sects.

Pure Land Amidism was further developed by Hōnen's greatest and most renowned disciple, Shinran (1173–1262), founder of the True Pure Land sect (Jōdō Shinshū). Shinran has been compared to the founders of Christian Protestantism, for, like them, he insisted that humans were so debased that they could not possibly gain salvation through their own efforts or "self-power" but must depend on the "other power" of Amida. Specifically, salvation comes through faith—frequently experienced by the individual in an act of conversion. The boundless compassion of Amida embraces the bad man or woman as well as the good. Indeed the bad individual, conscious of a lack of worth, may be closer to salvation than good individuals who are incapable of resisting self-congratulation on their merits and who rely on their own efforts to attain rebirth in paradise. Once converted and granted faith, each person will naturally bring the message to others, repeating the *nembutsu*, not out of a desire to be saved or for reassurance, but out of gratitude and joy.

Shinran was himself filled with a sense of his own sinfulness. "A bald-headed old fool" is the name he adopted for himself. He also carried rejection of the old monastic observances further than any of his predecessors; he ate meat, and, like Luther, he married a nun. Exiled in consequence, he spent his life proclaiming his religious message among the common people as one of themselves.

Shinran did not intend to found a new sect, nor did he acknowledge having disciples. But he left many followers who developed the True Pure Land sect. One of the best known Kamakura Pure Land evangelists was Ippen (1239–89) who, like Kūya, practiced the dancing *nembutsu* and became the subject of a famous narrative picture scroll. Meanwhile, Shinran's True Pure Land continued to attract followers. In the fifteenth century, during the Ashikaga period, Rennyo (1415–99) organized the community of believers into a disciplined body, ready and able to fight for their beliefs. The True Pure Land sect is still one of the largest religious organizations in Japan, now divided into two branches, each headed by descendants of Shinran. This tradition of hereditary leadership was, of course, made possible by the abandonment of celibacy. It is also consistent with Japanese familism and with Jōdō faith in the benign "other power" of Amida.

Nichiren

Many of the older sects also practiced invocation of the Buddha of the Western Paradise without, however, abandoning their older rituals or beliefs. But not all were tolerant. A vociferous and vehement opponent of Pure Land teachings, as of the doctrines of all the other rival sects new and old, was Nichiren (1222–82), one of Japan's most remarkable religious leaders. Like Hōnen and Shinran, he too was exiled for his advocacy of unacceptable beliefs, but, unlike the others, he was almost put to death; he was saved, according to his followers, only by a miracle, as lightning struck the poised executioner's sword. Nichiren's conviction of the correctness of his teachings was buttressed by his belief that he was a reincarnation of a Bodhisattva specially entrusted with the Lotus Sutra, the one and only text incorporating Buddha's teachings in all their dimensions.

Nichiren, although born into a family of poor fishermen, was a learned man. But like Hōnen and Shinran, his message was simple: faith in the Lotus Sutra, rather than a mastery of its contents, was the requirement for salvation. In place of the invocation of Amida practiced by Pure Land Buddhists, he substituted *"namu myōhō renge-kyō"*—Hail to the Lotus Sutra of the Wonderful Law—usually chanted to the beat of a drum.

In adversity Nichiren demonstrated a depth of conviction and strength of character readily appreciated by warriors who valued similar virtues. Perhaps Nichiren's origins in Eastern Japan also enhanced his standing among the *bushi* who had established the shogunate. Furthermore, he was greatly attached to the land and was Japan-centered to an unusual degree, envisioning Japan as the headquarters for his faith, which from there would spread throughout the world. The very name he chose for himself, Nichiren (*nichi* = sun, *ren* = lotus), indicated his dual devotion to the Land of the Rising Sun and the Lotus Sutra. In his view, the one required the other. Repeatedly he warned that the Lotus was essential for Japan and predicted dire consequences if other sects remained in favor. He prophesied the Mongol invasions, thereby increasing his credibility. Nichiren's concern for state and country, his courage, and his zeal remained an inspiration for his followers in later times. One man is even said to have journeyed to Siberia as a missionary. Nichiren, the man and the faith, have retained their magnetism to the present. Today he is venerated not only in the traditional Lotus sect but also by the Sōka Gakkai (Value Creation Society), a religious body whose membership has burgeoned since the Second World War.

Zen

Pure Land Buddhism and the teachings of Nichiren appealed widely to the warriors, but Zen, with a more limited following, enjoyed official favor and support in Kamakura. Zen practices were not unknown in Japan before the Kamakura period, but it was established only through the efforts of two great monks, Eisai (1141–1215) and Dōgen (1200–1253), who reintroduced Zen (Ch'an) directly from China. Eisai was able to make two trips to the Southern Sung and brought back not only religious ideas but a great enthusiasm for tea, thus initiating the long association between that beverage and Japanese Zen. He was a follower of the Rinzai (Chinese, Lin-chi) school, practicing the use of the *kōan* (*kung-an*) riddles. Eisai found support in Kamakura, but in Kyōto he accommodated himself to the religious life of the old capital by observing Tendai and Shingon practices as well as Zen rules. He even recommended the *nembutsu* and allowed chants and prayers.

Figure 11-2
Zazen.

Dōgen, in contrast, was uncompromising in his attitude toward secular authority. He eventually settled in the mountains remote from Kamakura and Kyōto. He consistently declined wordly honors and built a small temple, which later grew into the great monastery of Eiheiji. Dōgen differed from Eisai also in the type of Zen he preached, for he brought back from China the doctrines of the Sōtō (Chinese, Ts'ao-tao) school, which emphasized sitting in silent meditation (*zazen*) without a specific object or goal in mind, a gradual process of realizing the Buddha nature through the body as well as the mind. In his attitude toward the transmission of the truth, Dōgen was a moderate, accepting scriptural authority as well as the authority of the personal transmission from patriarch to patriarch. The influence enjoyed by the Sōtō school in Japan was much greater than that accorded Ts'ao-tao in China.

The proper practice of Zen made very great demands on its practitioners, demands no less severe than those encountered in military training. Seekers after illumination did not, like the second patriarch, have to sever an arm to demonstrate their seriousness of purpose, but they did have to endure a period of waiting and abuse before they were admitted to the spartan life of the temple. Even now the average day of the Zen Buddhist monk in Japan may run from 3 A.M. to 9 P.M., and is filled with a steady round of religious observances, manual labor, and *zazen*. The latter is itself a rigorous discipline, a period of formal meditation in which no bodily movement is allowed. (See Figure 11-2.) A senior monk makes the rounds with a long flat stick to strike those who show signs of becoming drowsy. Some Zen temples also make provisions for members of the laity who wish to practice meditation without submitting themselves to the full religious life. Ultimately, enlightenment is a personal quest.

The fortunes of Zen were furthered not only by native Japanese monks but also by Chinese masters who traveled to Japan and won considerable influence in Kamakura, where they were favored by the Hōjō regents. For example, the Kenchōji, one of the great Kamakura temples, was built by a Hōjō regent, who invited a Chinese monk to become its abbot. Several of the regents became deeply versed in Zen. Along with Zen these monks brought from China a variety of artistic and cultural influences of which the interest in tea is only one example. The secular influence of Zen became even more marked in the succeeding Ashikaga period. The continuity of Zen influence is reflected in the career of Musō Soseki (1275–1351), also known as Musō Kokushi (Musō the National Master), who successively enjoyed the favor of the Hōjō regent, the emperor Go-Daigo, and the new Ashikaga shogun.

Shinto

No account of the religious scene in the Kamakura period is complete without mentioning the continuing appeal of the native spirits, or *kami* (Shintoism). Old patterns of coexistence between Shinto and Buddhism, and tendencies toward some amalgamation of the two, remained vigorous. Ippen, for example, identified individual Buddhas and bodhisattvas with *kami*; Tendai and Shingon remained hospitable to the old gods, and Shinto in turn borrowed freely from Buddhism. The Inner and Outer shrines at Ise were regarded as Shingon mandalas. It may well be that there was a special affinity between Shingon and Shinto; indeed the major Shinto writer and champion of the imperial house, Kitabatake Chikafusa (1293–1354), ascribed the success of Shingon in Japan, as opposed to China, to its compatibility with Shinto. Another syncretic religion was preached by mountain priests (*yamabushi*), who were themselves combinations of shamans, monks, and Taoist mountain ascetics. They identified mountain *kami* with Buddhist incarnations and emphasized the role of religious retreats in the mountains. In their ceremonials and incantations they blended Shinto and Buddhist elements. This mountain religion (Shugendō) had enjoyed aristocratic patronage during the Heian period but in feudal times turned increasingly toward the common people for support. In the process it furthered the spread of Buddhism to Northern Japan.

Similar recourse to popular support when previous sources of income dried up led to the development of Ise Shinto. The priests at Ise successfully encouraged people to go on pilgrimages to the sacred shrine, which came to rely largely on the offerings of the pious for revenue.

Religious Art

When the Taira destroyed the Tōdaiji and Kōfukuji temples in Nara, they inadvertently prepared the way for a great revival of Buddhist sculpture, stimulated by a happy conjunction of artistic talent and generous patronage. Old works that were damaged or destroyed had to be restored or replaced. Patronage for this effort came both from the *bakufu* and the Court, giving rise to a school of highly talented artists (all of whom chose names ending in "kei"). Artistic inspiration came in part from the sculpture in the old capital area, but the best Kamakura sculptures also convey a new realism and robust vigor, reflecting the martial values of the warrior class in the East. The leading figure of the new school was Unkei (active 1163–1223), whose own career exemplified the blending of the old and the new. He participated in the restoration of some traditional Nara sculptures, but he also traveled and worked in Eastern Japan, where he was exposed to the values and tastes of the warrior class. Both experiences influenced his work.

A good example of the new style is provided by the guardian figures flanking the main entrance of Tōdaiji (see Figure 11-3). This was a joint enterprise in which Unkei, along with others, participated. Almost thirty feet tall, these figures are constructed of many pieces of wood carefully fitted together; Kama-

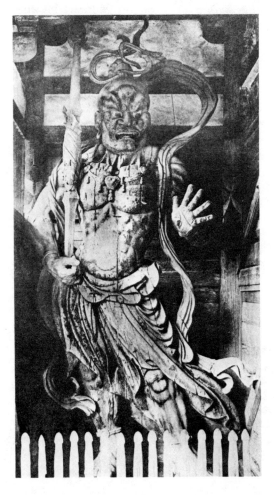

Figure 11-3   Niō (Guardian Figure), Great South Gate. Wood, approx. 808 cm high. Tōdaiji, Nara.

kura sculptors rejected the delicate serenity of late Heian sculpture but not its new technique. In the Tōdaiji figures, the wood is undercut to emphasize tendons and muscle, thereby giving an effect of virility and strength appropriate to martial figures, and to a martial society.

In such guardian figures, ferocity tends to take precedence over realism, but this is not the case in sculpture portraits of milder Buddhist saints and monks. A new device which appears at this time is the use of crystal for the eyes to give them a lifelike sparkle. The figure of Kūya (see Figure 11-4) goes beyond realism: even the words of the priest have to be portrayed.

The figure of Kūya is an example of the influence of Amidism in the arts. A still more impressive symbol of the popularity of Amida in the religious life of this period is the giant, forty-nine foot, figure completed in 1252 and paid for by funds raised from the common people. (See Figure 11-5.) In his compassionate benevolence, the massive Amida leans forward and looks down on pilgrim and sightseer alike. Artistically the figure compares favorably with the badly restored giant Buddha at Nara, but its effectiveness is probably more a function of its dimensions than of any inherent artistic excellence. Originally housed in

Figure 11-4 Kōshō, *Kūya*. Wood, Kamakura, approx. 117 cm high. Rokuharamitsuji, Kyōto.

Figure 11-5 *Amida*. Bronze, Kamakura, approx. 1138 cm high.

its own temple, it now stands outside under the open sky. The figure is partially hollow; inside, steps lead to a little window in Amida's back, through which visitors may look out.

Along with Amida, Kannon continued to enjoy great popularity. Dating from around the middle of the thirteenth century, and thus roughly contemporary with the Kamakura Amida, are the contents of the Sanjūsangendō (Rengeōin) in Kyōto. It features a seated "thousand-armed" Kannon, which is flanked by a thousand standing statues of the same Kannon neatly formed in ranks, a Kamakura reminder of the Buddhist proclivity for repetition. Of greater artistic appeal are some of the realistic Kamakura sculptures also kept in this hall.

The vitality of early Kamakura sculpture gradually waned and the resulting decline in the quality of Buddhist sculpture turned out to be permanent. Craftsmen continued to produce Buddhist figures in imitation of older styles, but there was a dearth of new departures or even creative revivals. The Buddhist religion and the visual arts continued to enrich each other, but after the Kamakura period the relationship between them took a new form.

Chinese influence is visible in some fourteenth-century religious sculpture and can also be studied in Kamakura architecture, which drew on at least two distinctive Chinese traditions. One style of great power was known in Japan as the "Indian Style" (Tenjikuyō), although it was actually imported from Fukien. Its outstanding feature is bracketing constructed along a single, transverse axis and inserted through, rather than mounted on, the supporting columns. The best example of this style is the gate of Tōdaiji (see Figure 11-6), which shelters

Figure 11-6 RIGHT, The Great
South Gate, Tōdaiji, Nara.
ABOVE, The Great South Gate,
Tōdaiji: bracketing.

the two guardian figures discussed above. Like these figures it is an effective expression of some of the qualities associated with the Kamakura period. As Sherman Lee observes, "the gate structure is logical but simple, almost heavy rather than lucid, with a brute strength that overpowers memories of the refined Heian architectural style and which finds no later repetition."[3] This style was short-lived in Japan but survived in Fukien. A later version was reintroduced to Japan from Fukien in the seventeenth century, along with the Huang-po shan (Ōbakusan) sect of Ch'an Buddhism.

Perhaps the Japanese called this style "Indian" because it ran counter to the prevailing fashions of Sung architecture and taste. In any case, they reserved the term "Chinese Style" (Karayō) for buildings modeled on the prevailing continental style. In Kamakura, the Kenchōji (1253) was supposed to be a copy of a famous Ch'an temple in Hangchow and the Engakuji (see Figure 11-7) is said to have been built by an architect who had traveled to Hangchow to study the Chinese model. Unfortunately the Chinese prototypes have not survived, and the Engakuji building is now covered with an incongruous Japanese-style thatched roof. Another important Kamakura period building in the Chinese manner is the Kaisandō of the Eihōji, a Zen temple near Nagoya. (See Figure 11-8.) Along with its general air of elegance, a particularly Chinese feature is its relative verticality when compared to similar buildings in the native Japanese style, which tend to hug the ground. As usual in the Chinese style, the Kaisandō stands on a stone platform, but its roof too has been restored in a Japanese manner, for it should really be of tile. In addition to these two imported architectural styles, the Japanese built many religious as well as secular buildings in the native Japanese style. Also influential was a mixed style combining Japanese and Chinese elements.

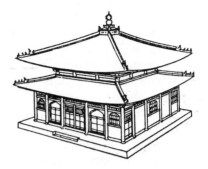

Figure 11-7   LEFT, Engakuji Relic
Hall. Thirteenth century. Kamakura.
ABOVE, Drawing of Engakuji
Relic Hall showing original roof.

Figure 11-8   BELOW, Front View,
Kaisandō of Eihōji, Tajimi,
Nagoya. RIGHT, Kaisandō: side
elevation.

Along with architecture and sculpture, painting also continued to serve religious purposes or to depict religious themes such as gruesome hells watched over by terrifying, grotesque demons, as raging fires threaten the sinners and the blood of the damned gushes and flows in screaming reds. Like their European counterparts, these paintings require no subtle understanding of doctrine or connoisseur's eye. Even the most obtuse will get the message. A secular equivalent may be found in the horrors of war depicted in scenes illustrating battle accounts from such works as the *Tales of the Heiji Period (Heiji monogatari)*, which provided the subject matter for a famous scroll now in the Museum of Fine Arts, Boston. The Kamakura ethos did not allow for pacifism.

Kamakura paintings combine representations of the secular and the sacred. What looks like a landscape may also be an icon. This is true of a famous painting of the Nachi waterfall, which actually represents the *kami* who resides in this, the largest and most revered waterfall in Japan. In an original way this painting combines the Buddhist mandala tradition with the native Japanese religion and the deep love for nature which is intrinsic to it. In the narrative scrolls also, there are scenes showing the beauties of the Japanese landscape rendered in a Japanese manner, although Chinese influence is visible in the Ippen scroll, an influence which was to lead to the development of Chinese-style landscape in the following period.

Both art and craftsmanship are combined in the beautiful and lethal products of the Kamakura sword maker. The attention lavished on swords and richly decorated armor is reminiscent of similar developments in Europe when these were the prized possessions of a warrior class.

Literature

The crosscurrents of Kamakura history and the styles of life prevalent at court, in the military, and in the temple found expression in a rich and variegated literature, much of it of the highest quality. The *Confessions of Lady Nijo*, completed in the first decade of the fourteenth century and thus quite late in the Kamakura period, takes us back to the familiar world of the Heian court lady. In the early chapters we find her conducting her love affairs and paying attention to the fine points of aesthetics against a general background of melancholy awareness that reminds us of *The Tale of Genji*. The last two sections, however, are an account of her life as a Buddhist nun, fulfilling vows to copy the sutras, and traveling to holy sites (including Ise). She also travels to Kamakura, where her advice on dress and decoration is eagerly sought, for in these matters the prestige of the court remained paramount.

Poetry too remained an integral part of court life. Some very fine poetry was produced in the late twelfth and early thirteenth centuries under the auspices of two great poets, father and son: Fujiwara Shunzei (1114–1204) and Fujiwara Teika (1162–1241). The name itself echoes the past; they were descendants of Michinaga, although poetry, not politics, was their world.

In addition to his fame as a poet, Shunzei was recognized by his contemporaries as an arbiter of poetic taste and was influential in developing a new aesthetic, which sought to deepen the expression of melancholy (*aware*) by adding to it a new dimension of profound mystery (*yūgen*). A mood of sadness also colors the word *sabi*, first used as a term of praise by Shunzei, for whom it basically meant "loneliness." These qualities permeated the aesthetic climate of the subsequent Ashikaga period and will be encountered again in our discussion of the characteristic achievements of that era.

Teika presided over the committee which compiled the Shinkokinshū (New Kokinshū, 1205), one of the great collections of Japanese verse and often considered the last of the great imperial anthologies. The following poem by the priest Saigyō (1118–90) is an example of the poetic qualities to be found in the best court poetry:

> While denying his heart,
> Even a priest cannot but know
> The depths of a sad beauty:
> From the marsh a longbill
> Flies off in the autumn dusk.[4]

Buddhism demands that a devout man give up the feelings of his own heart even when they are humbly aesthetic.

> The opening lines of the poem convey the dilemma in subjective, human terms, as the closing lines do in sensuous natural terms. The beginning suggests tragedy, as the priest is drawn back to the lovely but illusory phenomenal world; the end gives something like consolation in the fact that even such a humble sight, which seems almost an aesthetic and human void, affords such beauty and significance. And yet in the balance of the two parts and in the countercurrents within each there is the creative polarity that I have termed celebration and desolation. Beauty is found at the very abyss of human darkness, and yet even the humblest scenes of the illusory world touch the ascetic heart to its depths with mingled suffering and affirmation.[5]

One of Teika's poems included in the anthology is from a series of one hundred poems on the moon. (The composition of such series was one way Japanese poets transcended the limitations of the *tanka*.)

> On her straw-mat bedding
> The Lady of the Bridge of Uji
> Spreads the moonlight out,
> And in the waiting autumn night
> She lies there in the darkening wind.[6]

Even in translation the beauty of the original imagery remains untarnished. In contrast the following is just one example of a poem which dispenses with imagery altogether—a practice not unusual in *tanka*. It was written by Lady Jusami Chikaku who lived around 1300 (after the great age of Saigyō, Shunzei, and Teika). It is included here to remind us that poetry did not end with them and that ladies as well as gentlemen continued to excel in this medium. It deals with one of the recurrent motifs in statements of the woman's side of love, the breaking of love's promises.

> In recent days
> I can no longer say of wretchedness
> That it is wretched,
> For I feel my grief has made me
> No longer truly capable of grief.[7]

The theme is ageless. The private, delicate yet resilient, world of the court poet is far removed from the hurly-burly of politics and warfare; it did not deign to notice the intrigue and the fighting.

A literary man who wrote excellent prose as well as fine poetry was Kamo no Chōmei (1153–1216), who withdrew from the turbulent world to live quietly in a hut on a mountainside near Kyōto. In his *An Account of My Hut*, he wrote about the calamities such as fire, famine, and earthquake suffered by those who remained behind in the world, and about the simplicity and solitude of his own life. Deeply religious, he fell short of the complete detachment taught by Buddhism but found consolation in repeating the *nembutsu*.

Less sophisticated were the stories in *Tales from the Uji Collection*, which in simple and direct language describe the morals and miracles of Buddhism. One story, made famous by a twelfth-century narrative scroll, concerns the holy man of Mt. Shigi who obtained his daily food by sending his begging bowl flying down from his mountain to be filled. When one day the bowl was disdained by a wealthy man, it flew back up the mountain with his entire rice-filled warehouse. The artist had great fun depicting the consternation of the rich man as his storehouse goes flying off. The episode ends happily when the holy man decides to return the rice, and the bowl goes flying back down the mountain carrying one bag, followed by all the other bags flying through the air in single file.

Kamakura literature is also an important source of information about the world of the warrior, as reflected in the military tales and romances. We have already mentioned the tales which grew up around Yoshitsune. Often retold were accounts of his heroic exploits and those of his right-hand man, the stout monk and formidable fighter Benkei, who became his lifelong follower after the young Yoshitsune bested him in a sword fight on a bridge. Stories extolling bravery in battle, engaging accounts of clever stratagems, and celebrations of victory were as appreciated by the Kamakura warrior as by warriors everywhere, but the ultimate tone of the tales is somber. Yoshitsune was, in the end, vanquished (even if one legend has him fleeing to the continent to become Chinggis Khan). Defeat is also the fate of the Taira in *The Tale of the Heike*, the most famous and highly regarded of the military romances, which has as its theme the fall of Taira pride, not the glory of the victorious Minamoto.

Underlying *The Tale of the Heike* is the realization of the transience of victory, the ultimate emptiness of success. Buddhist consciousness of the fleeting nature of all that is best in life saved the Heian age from sinking into mere shallow hedonism and, likewise, rescued the Kamakura from the futile pomposity of the vainglorious. The sweetness of the warrior's triumph is just as ephemeral as the joy of lovers. The opening words of *The Tale of the Heike* sound a note that reveberates throughout the feudal period:

> In the sound of the bell of the Gion Temple echoes the impermanence of all things. The pale hue of the flowers of the teak-tree show the truth that they who prosper must fall. The proud do not last long, but vanish like a spring-night's dream. And the mighty ones too will perish in the end, like dust before the wind.[8]

NOTES

1. Peter Duus, *Feudalism in Japan* (New York: Alfred A. Knopf, 1969), p. 8.

2. Helen Craig McCullough, trans., *Yoshitsune: A Fifteenth Century Japanese Chronicle* (Stanford: Stanford University Press, 1971), p. 290.

3. Sherman Lee, *A History of Far Eastern Art* (New York: Harry N. Abrams, 1964), p. 324.

4. Earl Miner, *An Introduction to Japanese Court Poetry* (Stanford: Stanford University Press, 1968), p. 103.

5. *Ibid.*, pp. 106–107.

6. *Ibid.*, p. 113.

7. *Ibid.*, p. 133.

8. Donald Keene, *Japanese Literature* (New York: Grove Press, 1955), p. 78.

足利及統一之時代

┌─ Fall of Yoshino

1336   1392   1568   1600

A S H I K A G A S H O G U N A T E
(Muromachi: 1336 or 1392–1573)

Kemmu Restoration
(1333–36)

Onin War (1467–77) **SENGOKU** (Warring States)

Period of Unification

Momoyama

1467   (1568–1600 or 1615)

12 The Ashikaga Shogunate and the Period of Unification: 1336–1600

The more than two and a half centuries discussed in this chapter were an unusually rich and complex time in the history of Japan. The period was characterized by extensive interplay between aristocratic and warrior heritages. It was also a period which saw major changes in the organization of Japanese society as old structures declined and new ones gradually and painfully emerged.

For any but the broadest purposes of historical analysis, it may be misleading to think of these centuries as constituting a single period. As indicated by the title of this chapter, it is usual and proper to distinguish between the Ashikaga Shogunate and the period of unification which followed. Furthermore, the Ashikaga* itself may best be divided into three periods, each with its own themes: (1) an initial period (1336–68), when the court failed in a bid for power and the Ashikaga established themselves; (2) a middle period (1368–1467), which saw the shogunate reach its greatest power and then decline; and (3) more than a century of warfare (1467–1573), which changed the political map of Japan.

The Kemmu Restoration (1333–1336)

Between the Kamakura and Ashikaga shogunates, as earlier between the Heian and Kamakura periods, there was a brief interlude. The Kemmu Restoration of Emperor Go-Daigo (1288–1339) was an attempt to reassert the prerogatives of the throne similar to the earlier efforts of Emperor Go-Toba. Since it confronted a much weakened shogunate, the restoration had considerable initial success. Even after Kyōto was lost, there was sufficient momentum to sustain a government in exile in the mountains of Yoshino, south of Nara, which for over half a century provided at least a potential rallying point for those opposed to the Ashikaga. Not until 1392 did it come to an end.

The origins of the restoration go back to the middle of the thirteenth century. Two branches of the imperial family disputed succession to the throne. After the reluctant intervention of the *bakufu*, a compromise was reached whereby the two branches occupied the throne in alternation. It was Go-Daigo's determination to break this agreement and retain the succession in his own line that precipitated the split with the shogunate.

Fighting began in 1331 when the shogunate tried to force Go-Daigo to abdicate. He defied Kamakura and at first suffered setbacks, including capture and exile to the Oki Islands in the Sea of Japan. But the *bakufu* was unable to suppress all those who rose in rebellion. In 1332 the emperor escaped from Oki and was able to return to Kyōto in triumph after Ashikaga Takauji (1305–58), commander of a *bakufu* force sent to destroy him, changed sides. Behind Takauji was the wealth and prestige of the Ashikaga family, which, like Yoritomo, the founder of the shogunate, belonged to the Seiwa Minamoto lineage. Of similarly imposing descent was Nitta Yoshisada (1301–38), who now seized Kamakura in the name of Go-Daigo and put an end to the power of the Hōjō family and to the Kamakura *bakufu*.

The coalition which destroyed the Kamakura shogunate did not last long because the participants had no common program or interests. Moreover, few of

---

* The Ashikaga period is also frequently called the Muromachi period after the section of northeast Kyōto where the shoguns resided, although this term is sometimes applied only to the time after 1392.

the military leaders were attracted by the emperor's vision of a return to rule by the throne, since a genuine imperial restoration would necessarily lead to a reduction of warrior power. Many warriors were alienated and developed a sense of personal grievance when the throne failed to give them what they considered just reward for their services, and imperial justice turned out no better than that dispensed by the Later Hōjō. They were further dismayed by the emperor's adoption of a policy for merging provincial military and civil power and placing it in the hands of civil governors. When Go-Daigo appointed his own son shogun, it disappointed Takauji, and did so without any compensatory increase in the new regime's military strength.

The throne's attempt to turn the clock back cost it the military support required for its survival. But the men who had the military power were themselves divided by conflicting interests and ambitions which could turn brother against brother, as happened in the case of Takauji himself and his brother Tadayoshi (1306–52). A common thread running through the shifting pattern of the political and military history in these years was the rivalry between Takauji and Nitta Yoshisada. The Kemmu Restoration came to an end when Takauji defeated Nitta and then dethroned Go-Daigo. But this did not bring peace, even to the capital. Four times the city was seized by forces of the southern court, the last in 1361, but each time they were forced to relinquish it. The prime motive of the participants in these various campaigns was to strengthen the fortunes of their own families; sometimes a family made certain that it would be on the winning side by having branches fight on both sides of the conflict.

Establishment of the Ashikaga Shogunate (1336–1368)

The power of the Ashikaga, enhanced after the defeat of Nitta Yoshisada, was legitimized in 1338 when Takauji received the coveted title of shogun from the new emperor he had installed in Kyōto. After a period of desultory conflict, the Ashikaga eventually did come to an agreement with the emperor of the southern court (1392). By that time, his position had become hopeless, and he agreed to a resumption of the old arrangement for alternate succession to the throne. Once firmly in control, however, the Ashikaga declined to honor the agreement.

Although the southern court was defeated, later historians did not side with the winner, for the traditional Japanese view accepted the claims of Go-Daigo. The genealogical as well as theoretical basis for these claims was supplied by Kitabatake Chikafusa. In his *The Records of the Legitimate Succession of the Divine Sovereigns*, Chikafusa argued not only for the legitimacy of Go-Daigo but for the sanctity of the correct imperial succession, which ultimately led back to the Sun Goddess. It was this, he claimed, which set Japan apart from other lands and made Japan uniquely divine. The *Taiheiki*, a military romance, supplied stirring accounts of the feats of imperial loyalists, such as Kusonoki

Masahige (d. 1336), an early and faithful adherent to Go-Daigo's cause, and Nitta Yoshisada. It turned these men into popular heroes, shedding luster on the cause they served. One of the legacies of the Kemmu Restoration and the Yoshino court was an embellished and fortified imperial myth.

By contrast, Takauji was cast as the villain of this historical drama. This is an ungenerous view, for the shogun wanted to preserve the status of the throne and protected its dignity, even while denying its occupant any real power. The throne was, after all, the theoretical source of Takauji's own "delegated" authority, and Takauji sought to protect the dignity of the emperor. That the court needed a defender, that it was in disrepute among some of the rough-and-ready warriors newly risen to prominence, is suggested by a number of recorded incidents. One for example, tells of a warrior, probably under the influence of alcohol, who refused to dismount when he encountered the procession of the abdicated emperor. He is quoted as saying, "Did you say 'cloistered emperor' (In) or 'dog' (inu)? If it's a dog, perhaps I'd better shoot it." Adding injury to insult, he then hit the retired emperor's carriage with an arrow, and the upshot was that the carriage overturned and the In tumbled into the street. Takauji promptly had the warrior beheaded.[1]

The disruptions caused by the vicissitudes of political and military fortune should not be exaggerated. The life of Zen Master Musō Soseki indicates that there was a degree of continuity: in the course of his remarkable career, he enjoyed in turn the favor and patronage of the Hōjō, Go-Daigo, and Takauji. Of the latter it is said that he often practiced Zen before going to sleep after a heavy drinking party. Musō's role extended beyond that of a spiritual mentor: it was on his advice that Go-Daigo in 1325 sent an official embassy to China, resuming relations broken off almost five hundred years earlier. Similarly his influence is seen in Takauji's decision to send another mission in 1339. In the latter case, the ship sent was named after the Tenryūji, the great Zen monastery built by Takauji for Musō and dedicated to the memory of Go-Daigo. Its buildings and grounds covered almost one hundred acres west of the capital, and the monastery continued to be involved in voyages to China. Musō also persuaded Takauji to have Zen temples erected throughout the country.

Musō was apparently discreet as well as circumspect and served as an ambassador and negotiator, in addition to being a religious advisor. Through his special relationship with Takauji he was able to obtain valuable patronage for Zen, which even more than before became the officially favored religion. He also left his mark on the physical appearance of the capital, for he was responsible for the fine garden at Tenryūji and deserves much of the credit for the layout of the Saihōji, popularly known as the "moss garden."

Musō was a rather worldly cleric, but monasteries continued to provide a haven for those seeking to retire from the trials and tribulations of an unstable world. Among them was Yoshida Kenkō (1283–1350), poet, court official, and author of The Essays in Idleness (Tsurezuregusa), a prose collection long admired in Japan as a repository of good taste, in social conduct as in art. As in the case of Sei Shōnagon's Pillow Book and Kamo no Chōmei's An Account of

My Hut, and despite the randomness of its organization, Kenkō's work is held together by certain recurrent themes. Particularly significant is his celebration of the aesthetics of the impermanent, for to Kenkō perishability is an essential component and a necessary precondition for beauty. And he voices aesthetic judgments that have become closely associated with Japanese taste, displaying a preference for objects which bear the signs of wear and have acquired the patina of age (*sabi*). He loves the old literature and reiterates the value of *yūgen.* His antiquarianism is pervasive: he admires the old whether it be in poetry, carpentry, or even torture racks for criminals.

Government and Politics under the Ashikaga

Unlike their predecessors, the Ashikaga shoguns did not attempt to establish a new center of power but conducted their affairs from Kyōto and appointed a deputy to look after their interests in the Kantō region. Other deputies were established in Kyūshū, west-central Japan, and in the North. Although the shoguns held the highest civil offices, their actual power depended on their control over their vassals. But the recent disorders had weakened old bonds, and the new shogunate did not command power to the same extent as had the Kamakura *bakufu.* The system of loyalties on which the Ashikaga depended proved to be highly unstable.

The Military Protectors of the Kamakura period now developed into military governors, although their title, *shugo,* remained the same. In the days of its vigor, the Kamakura *bakufu* had tried to limit the power of the *shugo* by assigning men to provinces where they had no family roots or property, and by asserting its right to dismiss and confirm the *shugo,* even though the positions eventually became hereditary. The Ashikaga lacked the strength to reverse the trend toward hereditary appointments. Furthermore, the steady whittling down of the *shiki* of the absentee proprietors, appropriated by local authority, worked to the advantage of the men who controlled the provinces. And in its eagerness to obtain support, the Ashikaga further played into the hands of the military governors by assigning them virtually unlimited rights of taxation and adjudication. Frequently the term *shugo-daimyo* is applied to these provincial power holders who, like the later daimyo, held extensive territory but, unlike the later lords, still participated in central government.

The Ashikaga depended on the *shugo* families for support and appointed some of their leaders to important positions in their own *bakufu* organization. Both *bakufu* and *shugo* were involved in a complicated balance of power, which all parties tried to manipulate to their own advantage. Until the Onin War, the fulcrum of this balance remained in Kyōto. Accordingly, the powerful provincial families established themselves in the capital and assigned deputies to manage the provinces on their behalf.

The situation offered military governors and their deputies opportunities but also posed dangers. They might be able to recruit local warriors as vassals to augment their own military power, but, in the absence of significant moral authority, they could not count on the loyalty of these men, who were concerned about their own family interests and were no more reluctant to switch sides than were their superiors.

To complicate matters still further, the families themselves lost their stability when a practice designed to strengthen families created as many problems as it solved. This happened when families abandoned the old tradition of dividing an estate equitably among a man's heirs. Feasible in times of peace and security, such fragmentation was too dangerous in a period of constant fighting when force alone restrained men in pursuit of wealth and power, and families needed to muster all their economic and human resources to survive. Therefore, to secure the family's future, the property was left intact and passed on to a single heir designated by the family head. This was not necessarily the eldest son, but it was always a son: a daughter would be unable to protect the property militarily. Far from functioning smoothly, however, this system frequently led to bitter rivalries and hard fought succession disputes. These, like all serious conflicts in this period, were settled by force of arms.

John Whitney Hall succinctly defined the ailment of the Ashikaga body politic when he wrote, "The imperial system was now in effect dead, but the system of military allegiances and feudal controls had not fully matured."[2] It was an inherently unstable government, and yet for a while under Yoshimitsu (1358–1408), it worked at least to a degree, and in the period as a whole it neither hampered considerable economic growth nor inhibited fine cultural achievements.

Yoshimitsu and His Age

In 1368 Yoshimitsu, not yet ten, became the third shogun. Initially, however, the shogunate was controlled by the capable Hosokawa Yoriyuki, a member of one of the Ashikaga collateral families powerful in Kyōto and the provinces. Yoriyuki's official appointment was as Chief Administrator (kanrei), the top position in the bakufu, which was always assigned to one of the three most powerful vassal families (Hosokawa, Shiba, or Hatakeyama). His services to the bakufu included administrative reform, settlement of conflicting land claims, and a strengthening of the shogunate's finances. Spending was reduced and new sources of revenue were opened by taxing the wealth of sake breweries and pawnshops. These establishments frequently belonged to the same proprietor, since the original capital of the pawnshops often came from the profits of the sake trade. Indeed, taxes paid by commercial ventures in the capital were crucial to the Ashikaga bakufu, as they provided both a large and a reliable source of income.

When Yoshimitsu took power into his own hands, he continued efforts to strengthen the shogunate. He successfully met several military challenges, and in 1392 he secured the reunification of the two imperial courts. One further campaign (1399) was needed to assure a workable balance of power in the country. Through a series of tours to religious sites, such as Mt. Kōya and Ise, on which he was accompanied by an impressive retinue, Yoshimitsu further displayed his power and was also able to inspect local conditions in person. Lavish patronage of religious establishments no doubt helped to win him support in those quarters as well.

Yoshimitsu, unlike his father and grandfather, the first two Ashikaga shoguns, was born and raised in Kyōto and sought to combine his warrior heritage with the values long cherished in the capital. In gratifying his taste for fine architecture and beautiful gardens, he spared no expense. Unfortunately, his "Palace of Flowers" (Hana no Gosho) has not survived. Politically he demonstrated his dual legacy by assuming the title of Chancellor as well as shogun, and he even managed to have his wife made empress dowager! Yoshimitsu believed in doing things in truly royal style: once he entertained the emperor with twenty days of banqueting, music, and theatrical performances.

This entertainment took place on Yoshimitsu's estate in the northern hills (Kitayama) just beyond Kyōto, graced by the Golden Pavilion (Kinkakuji), a symbol of his good taste as well as of affluence. Although the roof line and parts of the building were covered with gold leaf, the plain surfaces of natural wood, the pavilion's shingled roofs and the grilled shutters and solid doors of the second floor preserved the Japanese tradition of natural simplicity. On the other hand, the paneled doors and arched windows of the top story derive from the standard repertoire of Chinese Zen architecture. With artful casualness, the building is set on an artificial platform in a pond. It combined Chinese and native elements blended harmoniously and in good taste.

Chinese elements in the Golden Pavilion are but one facet of Sung influence on Ashikaga art. Indeed, without the patronage of such men as Yoshimitsu, many valuable Chinese paintings would have been lost. The shogun's fondness for things Chinese extended also to Chinese dress, for he liked to wear Chinese clothes. He reported that the emperor of China visited him in his sleep. When awake, he made an effort to cultivate good relations with the Ming, phrasing his diplomatic communiqués in the properly humble language expected by the Chinese court, which recognized him as the "king" of Japan. As usual, the Chinese responded to foreign tribute by giving even more impressive gifts in return. A lucrative trade ensued in which the Zen monasteries played a major role and from which they derived much wealth. Along with the Tenryūji, a Zen temple founded by Yoshimitsu, the Shōkokuji, played a prominent part in these undertakings. Here communications intended for the Ming were drafted by monks in Chinese. At Chinese request, Yoshimitsu took measures against Japanese pirates who infested East Asian waters.

It is characteristic of the age that Zen monks were welcomed not only for their religious insights but also for their command of Chinese learning and for their poetic talents. For example, the Zen monk Josetsu, of the Shōkokuji temple, was famous as an ink painter, and was patronized both by Yoshimitsu and his successor. Figure 12-1 shows a painting attributed to Josetsu that reflects

Figure 12-1 *Patriarchs of the Three Creeds.* Attributed to Josetsu. Hanging scroll, ink on paper, 98.3 cm × 21.8 cm.

the religious, cultural, and artistic ambiance of the period. In it the three great teachers Sakyamuni, Confucius, and Lao Tzu are shown in harmonious agreement. The "abbreviated" brushwork is in the manner beloved by Zen artists. Each figure is rendered in its own style, and every stroke, every line, counts. The style of this painting is Chinese, and its subject also inspired Sung artists, although none of their paintings survive. It is a theme which reflects the Chinese trend toward religious and philosophical syncretism. Such syncretism was readily accepted in Japan, which had never experienced an institutionalized Taoism competing with a Buddhist establishment and where Buddhism had from the first been mixed with Confucianism. The close relationship between Taoism and Zen has already been discussed. Josetsu's own name is a case in point. It was given to him by a great priest of the Shōkokuji and was derived from the *Tao Te Ching* passage, "the greatest skill is *like clumsiness (josetsu)*."[3] This was his artistic ideal; and his achievement.

The Nō Drama

When Yoshimitsu hosted the emperor for twenty days, among the entertainments offered were performances of Nō, the classic drama of Japan. The roots of Nō go far back into the history of singing and dancing, music and mime, but its developed form was truly the creation of a remarkable father and son. Kan'ami (1333–84), a Shinto priest, and Zeami (or Seami, 1363–1443) developed this highly sophisticated theater out of a tradition of mimetic dance known as "monkey music" (*sarugaku*). Father and son both composed plays

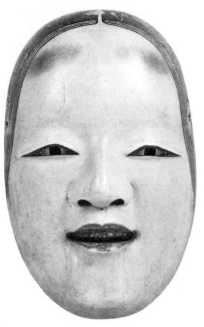

Figure 12-2
Nō mask.

and acted in them, and Zeami also formulated the critical and aesthetic criteria of the art. When Yoshimitsu first saw them perform, he was especially captivated by Zeami, then a good-looking boy of eleven, for the shogun was eclectic in his sexual as well as artistic preferences.

A performance of Nō is presented on a highly polished square wood stage open to the audience on three sides. A raised passageway leads from the actors' dressing room through the audience to the stage. Both stage and passageway are roofed. Three small pine trees placed in front of the passageway and a band of pebbles in front of the stage replicate the drainage area surrounding gutterless buildings, symbolic reminders that Nō performances were originally held out of doors. The stage is bare or almost bare. Occasionally there are symbolic representations of scenery, an outline of a boat, a cube to suggest a well. Likewise, stage properties are few and generally symbolic.

The Nō is often compared to the Greek drama, but the differences are as important as the similarities. For example, both use a chorus, but the chorus in Nō does not participate in the dramatic action. Seated at the side of the stage, the chorus expresses what is in the actor's mind and sings his lines when he dances. The music, produced by a flute and some drums, provides accompaniment and accent.

The actors and the chorus are all male. Some, but not all, of the actors wear highly stylized and exquisitely fashioned masks. The carving of these masks is itself a prized art. The one reproduced in Figure 12-2 represents a young woman. It illustrates the characteristic features of a classic Japanese beauty, found already in the Heian period, with her powdered complexion, artificial eyebrows, and blackened teeth. By subtle body movements and just the right tilt of the head, a great actor can suggest remarkable nuances of mood and emotion, while the frozen faces of the unmasked actors attain a mask-like effect. Attired in elegant costumes, the actors move with deliberate grace, unfolding gestures as full of meaning to the cognoscenti as those employed in the religious observances of esoteric Buddhism.

Nō plays are classified by the Japanese according to subject matter, that is, plays about a god, a warrior, a woman, a mad person, or a demon. It later became customary to include one of each type, in the order listed, in a full program which would take about six hours. The texts are short, and although they contain some fine poetry, they were always meant for the stage. The plots draw heavily on the literary tradition, recreating some of the best loved and most poignant scenes from earlier literature, such as *The Tale of Genji, The Tale of the Heike*, and *The Tales of Ise*. As one might expect, there are plays about Yoshitsune and other notable figures, including the great poetess Komachi, who is portrayed as an old woman suffering because she had caused others to suffer when she was young and beautiful. Others deal with the material of legends; the story of the fishermen who stole the angel's cloak (*Hagomoro*) is a favorite.

The tone is serious; the presentation symbolic. The typical Nō play is not an enactment of a dramatic episode nor a dramatic rendition of a historical or mythological occurrence; it is a retelling after the event. Consider the play based on the death of young Atsumori, reluctantly slain in battle by Kumagai as recounted in *The Tale of the Heike*. The main actors in Zeami's play on this theme are the priest who was once Kumagai and a young reaper who is actually the ghost of Atsumori. Here the purpose of art is not to mirror life but to transform it; setting the action in the play's own past creates the requisite artistic distance. It is an art which eschews realism and aspires to convey a sense of profound meaning beyond the words and scenes on stage. The ultimate criterion, according to Zeami himself, is a play's success in creating *yūgen*, the sense of underlying mystery.

A tone of grave sadness is hard to sustain for hours on end. Even a refined Kyōto aristocrat with his penchant for melancholy must have welcomed the comic relief provided by *kyōgen* (mad or wild words) performed in the interlude between Nō plays. Often in the nature of farce, they show a fondness for broad humor and foolery: servants outwitting their master, a dull country bumpkin sent out to purchase a sculpture of the Buddha and taken in by the trickery of an apprentice posing as a statue, and so on. Livelier than the Nō, the kyōgen are less demanding of the audience, but they lack the aura of poetic mystery which has sustained the Nō tradition in Japan.

Political Decline and Cultural Brilliance

When Yoshimitsu died in 1408 and was succeeded by his son, there was no radical discontinuity in shogunal politics nor even in cultural policies, although his death did bring to an end the favor shown to Zeami. Under the fifth

shogun there were signs of fiscal and political weakness, but the following shogun, the sixth in line, Yoshinori (r. 1428–41), was able to rally the Ashikaga
fortunes. However, Yoshinori's policy of strengthening the *bakufu* necessarily
involved checking the power of strong military governors (*shugo*), and this
turned out to be a dangerous as well as difficult game. It cost Yoshinori his life,
when he was lured to a mansion by a military governor and assassinated.

Yoshinori turned out to be the last strong and vigorous Ashikaga shogun. His
son was eight when he inherited the office and died two years later. He was
followed by another child, Yoshimasa (1436–90). Yoshimasa remained shogun
for thirty years (1443–73) and then retired, having presided over the political
collapse of the regime. From Yoshinori's assassination in 1441 to the outbreak
of the Onin War in 1467, the government went through a process of disintegration. But the Ashikaga shogunate benefited from its historical momentum and
the absence of a viable alternative, since the power of the provincial families,
afflicted by succession disputes, was also declining. It is characteristic of the
age that the Ashikaga downfall came not at the hands of a more powerful family or coalition but as the result of disputes within its own ranks. In 1464 Yoshimasa, still without an heir, designated his brother as next in line, but the
following year his ambitious and strong-minded wife bore him a son. Anxious
to have her son be the next shogun, she found support in a powerful provincial
governor's family, while another family backed the older claimant. Thus the
ground was prepared for the succession struggle that produced the disastrous
Onin War. The outcome of the war did not lead to the triumph of either family,
but it did destroy the authority of the Ashikaga as well as half of the city of
Kyōto, and it wreaked havoc on much of the surrounding country. During
these violent years, Yoshimasa continued to emulate Yoshimitsu in patronizing the arts, for he had the exquisite aesthetic sensibilities long cultivated in
Kyōto. But he completely lacked the qualities of command and decisiveness
required of a shogun, a holder of what was, after all, a military office.

Yoshimasa was as lavish as Yoshimitsu in financing building projects and in
giving entertainments. He too was a great patron of Nō. Like Yoshimitsu his
name is associated with a district in (what were then) the outskirts of Kyōto
and to which he retired (Higashiyama). As a counterpart to Yoshimitsu's
Golden Pavilion, there is Yoshimasa's Silver Pavilion (Ginkakuji), somewhat
smaller, more intimate and more subdued than its predecessor, having two
stories instead of three. (See Figure 12-3.) It too combines, or at least juxta-
poses, Chinese and native elements, featuring a continental second story
placed on a Japanese first story.

A Chinese theme is also echoed in the Ginkakuji's sand garden, identified as
a rendition of the West Lake, outside Hangchow, frequented by Sung painters
and poets like Su Shih (Su Tung-p'o) on their pleasure outings. Near one bank,
however, stands a volcano, also of sand—a miniature Mt. Fuji. Such gardens
were the objects of much care and careful planning. Wealthy patrons like Yoshimasa went to great expense to obtain just the right effect. Transportation
costs were disregarded when a stone was discovered precisely right in shape
and texture and presenting the exact contrast between its rough and smooth

Figure 12-3　The Silver Pavilion (Ginkakuji). Kyōto.

Figure 12-4　Sand and Stone Garden, Ryōanji, Kyōto.

surfaces required for the composition of the garden. As in China, stones themselves were objects of connoisseurship. Similar care went into the selection and pruning of plants and into performing the myriad chores necessary for maintaining a garden at its aesthetic best.

A story is told of a Chinese gentleman who painted the area around a window in his house to resemble the border of a hanging scroll, thus framing the view of his garden, which replaced the usual painted landscape. In Japan, too, the aesthetics of garden design and landscape painting were closely related. The garden artist also could choose rich colorful landscapes, using tree and shrub, rivulet and waterfall, pond and bridge; or he could confine himself to stone and carefully raked sand, much like the ink painter who rejected color. Such sand and stone gardens can be viewed as three-dimensional monochrome landscapes, the sand representing water, the rocks functioning as mountains; or they can be enjoyed as abstract sculptures inviting the viewer to exercise his or her imagination. Like Zen they concentrate on the essentials. The finest are found in the Zen temples of Kyōto. (See Figure 12-4.) Not all of its fifteen stones are visible in this photograph, since the garden is designed so that there is no single point from which they can all be seen at once.

The compound of the Silver Pavilion also contains a small hall, the interior of which is divided between a Buddhist chapel and a new element: a room for the performance of the tea ceremony. Tea grew in popularity after its enthusiastic advocacy by Eisai, the Zen monk who introduced Rinzai to Japan, but it was not until the time of Yoshimasa that the formal consumption of this beverage was developed into a ritual art with its own strict rules and regulations. The accent in the classic tea ceremony is on simplicity and tranquility. Through a small doorway no bigger than a window, the guests crawl into a room about nine feet square, there to enjoy in silent calm the movements of their host as he prepares the tea with motions as deliberate as those of an actor on the Nō stage. After they have drunk the deep green tea, they may exchange a few remarks about the bowl or the flower arrangement prepared for the ceremony. Among the unrefined, the ceremony may be exaggerated into ostentation; in incapable hands it easily degenerates into an empty and pedantic formalism; but when performed with an easy grace by a master, it can convey Japanese good taste at its best. The cult of tea—for such it was—reached perhaps its greatest height during the Momoyama period (1568–1600).

The tea ceremony influenced secular architecture, which during the Ashikaga period adopted many of the features of the tea room. Rush matting (tatami) now covered the whole floor—previously individual mats had been placed on wooden floors as needed to provide a place for people to sit. Sliding doors consisting of paper pasted on a wooden frame (shoji) came into common use, supplementing the earlier sliding partitions (fusuma) with their painted surfaces. Another standard feature is the alcove (tokonoma) with its hanging scroll and flower arrangement. Flower arrangement, like the tea service, became an art, with its own rules and styles passed on through the generations by the masters of distinct schools. It became one of the polite accomplishments expected of those with a claim to refinement.

Poetry and Painting

In Yoshimasa's time poetry continued to be an important part of Kyōto life. In the Heian period it was not uncommon for one poet to supply the first three lines of a *tanka*, leaving it to his companion to complete the poem with a suitable couplet. From such origins grew the linked verse (*renga*) which became a favorite Muromachi pastime, governed by complicated rules:

Of the opening verse (the *hokku*) it was said, "The *hokku* should not be at variance with the topography of the place, whether the mountains or the sea dominate, with the flying flowers or falling leaves of the grasses and trees of the season, with the wind, clouds, mist, fog, rain, dew, frost, snow, heat, cold or quarter of the moon. Objects which excite a ready response possess the greatest interest for inclusion in a *hokku*, such as spring birds or autumn insects. But the *hokku* is not of merit if it looks as though it had been previously prepared." The requirements for the second verse were somewhat less demanding; it had to be closely related to the first and to end in a noun. The third verse was more independent and ended in a particle; the fourth had to be "smooth"; the moon had to occur in a certain verse; cherry-blossoms could not be mentioned before a certain point; autumn and spring had to be repeated in at least three but not more than five successive verses, while summer and winter could be dropped after one mention, etc.[4]

A master like the Zen monk Sōgi (1421–1502), the greatest of the *renga* poets, was able to create fine poetry within this framework. Sōgi also composed *tanka* in the old tradition of court poetry, now coming to an end. The last imperial anthology was compiled in the fifteenth century. The *renga* may not have been a great poetic form itself, but it pointed in new directions.

In painting as in poetry, Zen monks continued to contribute greatly. Josetsu's style of monochrome painting was continued by two Zen monks, Shubun (d. 1450) and Sesshū (1420–1506), both trained at the Shōkokuji. In their work the influence of Sung painting remains clearly visible. The fifteenth-century painter-monks in the great Zen temples could draw on Japanese ink paintings in the Chinese manner going back to the Kamakura period, and the more eminent or fortunate among them might also see the Chinese paintings kept in Japan. The prime source for these was the shogunal collection systematized and cataloged for the first time under Yoshimasa. Most fortunate were those who were able to travel abroad. Thus Shubun drew inspiration from a journey to Korea, and Sesshū was able to travel to and in China. There was no need for him to paint Chinese landscapes from imagination alone.

Sesshū's versatile genius expressed itself in a variety of styles. One of his greatest paintings shows the man who was to become the second Zen patriarch offering his severed arm as a token of his religious commitment, to Bodhidharma, the Indian monk who was the reputed founder of Zen (Ch'an) in China. Another is a long landscape scroll (over fifty-two feet in length) guiding the viewer on a leisurely trip through scenery and seasons. Reproduced here (see Figure 12-5) is his painting of a reknowned beauty spot on the Sea of Japan, Ama-no-Hashidate (the Bridge of Heaven). It was evidently painted on the basis of personal observation in the period shortly before his death. The written identification of the various localities confirms the realism of this solidly constructed painting, while the softness of the painter's brush techniques is appropriate for the gentle Japanese landscape.

Although Zen monks and temples had the greatest influence on the arts in this period, some major contributions were also made by believers in the *nembutsu*, who demonstrated their faith in Amida by incorporating his name in theirs. The aesthetics of Nō may well be compatible with the teachings of Zen, but the greatest names in this theater were, as we have seen, Kan'*ami* and Ze*ami*. And among the main painters in the monochrome style imported from the continent were the three Ami: Nōami (ca. 1394–1471), Geiami (1431–85), and Sōami (d. 1525), father, son, and grandson. These three men were not only fine painters but also served as the shogun's advisers in aesthetic matters, cataloging and evaluating his art collection and passing as masters in the whole gamut of Ashikaga art from flower arranging, tea, and incense to music and the stage.

Also part of the artistic scene were professional painters. Two names that were to remain important as major schools of painting enjoying official favor first appear in the fifteenth century. These schools, like the schools of Nō and other arts, were continued from father to son or, if necessary, to adopted son, perpetuating their traditions much like warrior or merchant families. Their se-

Figure 12-5   Sesshū, *Ama-no-Hashidate*. Hanging scroll, ink and light color on paper, 177.8 cm long.

crets were just as carefully guarded as the formulae of sake brewers or pharmacists. Painting in the old native style (Yamato-e), Tosa Mitsunobu (1434–1525) became official painter to both the imperial court and the *bakufu*. Provided with a generous grant of land, he was able to establish the social and economic position of his family. Meanwhile his contemporary Kano Masanobu (1434–1530) painted in the Chinese manner, although without all of the religious and literary associations found in the work of the nonprofessional artists. Of the two, the Kano line was the more creative. Masanobu's son Montonobu (1476–1559) added color to his paintings. In this he was very likely influenced by the Tosa school.

It is the blending of the imported and the native that produced the characteristic Muromachi taste, a taste common to the aesthetic of the Nō mask, the sand garden, the tea ceremony, and a Sesshū landscape, a taste for the old (*sabi*), the solitary and poor (*wabi*), the astringent (*shibui*), and the profound (*yūgen*). The prestige of Chinese culture was enormous, and Sinophiles versified and painted in Chinese. But, unlike their predecessors of the Nara period, they were selective in their borrowing and rapidly assimilated the new. In later ages Muromachi aesthetic sensibility was challenged, assailed, and even displaced, but it never disappeared completely.

Economic Growth

The economy grew during the Kamakura epoch and even more spectacularly in Ashikaga times. Frequently developments which originated in the earlier period reached fruition in the later. The basis of the economy remained agricultural, and an increasing agricultural yield provided the means for growth. Improvements in farm technology employing better tools and devices such as the water wheel, new crops and new strains of rice, and a greater use of draft animals, were some of the major developments which increased the productivity of the land. This in turn had a positive impact on commerce and manufacturing. Technical progress in such endeavors as mining, sake brewing, and paper production, to mention just a few, further contributed to this process.

An added stimulus came from trade with China and Korea. Initiated by Yoshimitsu, it continued, with minor interruptions, to grow and flourish. To control this commerce and keep the number of ships within agreed upon limits, the Ming issued official tallies valid for trading at a specified port. This system, also helped control piracy by restricting the pirates' ability to trade stolen goods; it lasted until the middle of the sixteenth century. Japanese imports included cotton from Korea, and from China came great quantities of copper coins as well as porcelain, paintings, medicine, and books. A major Japanese export was fine swords. Japan also exported copper, sulphur, folding fans (a Japanese invention), screens, and so forth. The ability to trade products of sophisticated craftsmanship is another index of Japanese accomplishments during this period.

With the growth of commerce, of markets, and of market towns, there appeared guilds (za) formed by merchants and artisans to exercise monopoly rights over the exchange and production of various commodities. To safeguard their rights and privileges, and to obtain protection, these guilds turned to the great religious institutions and powerful families. The pawnbrokers of Kyōto, for example, enjoyed the protection of the Tendai monastery on Mt. Hiei, which on more than one occasion sent armed monks into the capital on behalf of its clients. Temples and shrines, the great families, and the bakufu itself welcomed the guilds as an additional source of revenue and became increasingly dependent on income from this source. As noted earlier, already under Yoshimitsu the Ashikaga shogun relied heavily on income from these quarters, and this trend continued. The prosperity of the pawnbrokers is only one of several signs of the increasing use of money, a development which was both a product of and a stimulus to commercial growth. To facilitate transactions between places distant from each other, bills of exchange came into use.

Around ports and markets, cities grew. The most impressive was Sakai, near modern Ōsaka, which became an autonomous political unit governed by a group of elders who were mostly merchants. Hakata in Kyūshū, the center for trade with Korea, also flourished, as did a number of other well-placed cities.

The growth of cities and similar economic developments suggest parallels with European history, but such parallels hold only to a limited degree. Japanese merchants and cities did not achieve sufficient power to threaten the prevailing order; rather the merchants provided a source of revenue for feudal lords. Social and political institutions were not shattered, but society was enriched by the emergence of a new urban population. One result of political decentralization combined with economic growth was the diffusion of higher culture to the provinces. Conversely, students of Nō and linked verse have pointed out that these arts owe much to popular culture. Sōgi, the great master of linked verse, was himself of obscure parentage. Many more opportunities for men of low birth were created during the warfare which marked the last phase of the Ashikaga period.

War and the Rise of the Daimyo

The Onin War (1467–77) was a major turning point in Japanese history. It not only destroyed the power of the Ashikaga *bakufu* but also put an end to the system on which it was so precariously based. All the military governor families (*shugo*) were drawn into the conflict; they emerged from it with their position seriously, not infrequently fatally, undermined. Not only was the old balance of power demolished; its very constituents were eliminated. The Onin War became merely the first decade of a century of warfare. During this period, the shogun, unable to control even the provinces near Kyōto, was reduced to a symbol preserving the idea and the ideal of a unified state, even as the last vestiges of centralized government were swept away. Meanwhile, beneath the troubled, chaotic surface of events, new developments were at work reshaping the Japanese state and society.

With the collapse of effective central government, what had been a decentralized state gave way to total fragmentation. Japan was divided into countless separate principalities, directed by feudal lords, known as daimyo. These lords competed with each other to preserve their territories and, if possible, to expand them. The sizes of these principalities varied widely; some were no larger than a small castle town while others might be as large as one of the old provinces. Regardless of the size of his holdings, the daimyo's fate depended entirely on his success in the field of battle. What counted was power. Although some of the mid-sixteenth-century daimyo belonged to the old families, many emerged out of the class of local warriors. In these strenuous, difficult times, capable, ambitious, and unscrupulous men struggled to the top using any means at hand; frequently, betrayal was the price of upward mobility. The introduction of formal oaths, unnecessary in an older and simpler age, did not change the situation. Vassals could be counted on for their loyalty only as long as it was in their own best interests to be loyal.

To obtain and hold their vassals, the daimyo granted fiefs and stipends. In place of the old land rights (*shiki*), vassals now received fiefs (that is, the land itself). In return, they were obliged to render military service to their lord and provide the services of a set number of their own fighting men. Without the support of the now defunct system of political centralization, the remnants of the old *shōen* system could not survive.

In the long run, success in this precarious age went to those daimyo who could most effectively mobilize the resources of their domains, turning them into small states. The ultimate consequence of the breakdown of central unity was the creation of smaller but more highly integrated political entities. Daimyo normally asserted their authority over the succession of their vassals and, since political combinations were involved, they also had a say concerning their vassals' marriages. Some daimyo, in their house laws, asserted rights to tax the land in their territory and to regulate economic activities. Frequently, spies were employed to keep the lord informed of the activities and plans of his vassals.

A potent force for integration was the changing nature of warfare. It was found that massed foot soldiers, recruited from the peasantry and armed with spears and the like, were an effective force against the traditional, proud, and expensive mounted warriors. Armies grew larger, and vassals tended to serve as officers commanding troops of commoners.

Sixteenth-century Japan was no exception to the rule that change in offense sooner or later stimulates new developments in defense. The Japanese answer to the new armies was the castle. It was often built on a hill, crowned with a tower, protected by walls, and surrounded by a moat or a natural body of water. In concept and function, they were similar to castles of Europe. On the other hand, nothing like them was known in China.

An added impetus to the use of the new type of armies came after the Portuguese introduced European firearms to Japan in 1543. Within ten years the daimyo of Western Japan were using imported and domestic muskets in their armies. In response, bigger and more elaborate castles became necessary, so that in defense as well as in offense the larger daimyo with ample means had a decisive advantage. For example, Oda Nobunaga was eventually successful in defeating his rivals because he was ready to employ new weapons and techniques, and had the means to do so. In 1575 he won a crucial battle through the superior firepower of his three thousand musketeers; for defense he built a great castle at Azuchi on the shore of Lake Biwa.

The daimyo's castles often served as the center of the daimyo states, and there was a tendency for warriors to gather or to be gathered there. This process naturally removed them from direct supervision of their own land. This resulted in the transformation of villages into peasant communities left to manage their own affairs as long as they provided the payments and services required of them.

This is not to suggest that the peasantry was uniformly docile during this period of fighting and social unrest. On the contrary, the age was marked by peasant uprisings. In one case (Yamashiro Province, near Kyōto) peasants were able to hold power for eight years, but nowhere could they establish permanent peasant power. Their leaders were often low-ranking local warriors whose ambition was to fight their way up the ladder in search of power, status, and wealth. The most notable individual to rise from the peasantry to the very top was Toyotomi Hideyoshi, the strongman who completed unification of the country.

Other uprisings were led by religious sects, particularly the well-organized Ikkō sect, whose members followed a form of Shinran's True Pure Land Buddhism. These sectarians were able to obtain control of the province of Kaga, on the Sea of Japan, and extend their power into neighboring Echizen, as well as holding a strategic stronghold in the Kyōto-Ōsaka area. They could delay but could not finally prevent the process of unification, which destroyed them in the end. The future belonged to the kind of power being developed by the daimyo.

The Process of Unification (1573–1600)

The restoration of central authority in Japan after a century of warfare was accomplished under the direction of three leaders. It was a cumulative process, each man building on the work of his predecessors. Begun by Oda Nobunaga (1534–82), it was completed by Toyotomi Hideyoshi (1536–98), but the final consolidation was left to Tokugawa Ieyasu (1542–1616). Ieyasu established his supremacy in the crucial battle of Sekigahara in 1600 and was then free to organize what was to be Japan's last pre-modern government, the Tokugawa Shogunate (1600–1868).

Nobunaga inherited control of Owari, not one of the great territories but of strategic importance because it was located in central Honshu, between the Kantō and the capital regions. After establishing his military control over this central area, he entered Kyōto in 1568. For another five years the last Ashikaga shogun precariously retained his title; the line came to a formal end in 1573. Nobunaga continued his policy of aggrandizement and became the most powerful man in Japan through a combination of military and political skill applied in a ruthless drive for supremacy. We have already noted his readiness to use firearms; he was also a capable and daring tactician. In 1560 he won one of the decisive battles of his career by defeating an enemy army of some 25,000 with only 2000 men of his own.

After he seized Kyōto, Nobunaga turned his attention to the monks on Mt. Hiei and put an end once and for all to the military proclivities of the great Tendai monastery. He did this by destroying its buildings, slaughtering its monks, and eliminating the unfortunate inhabitants of nearby villages. "The roar of the huge burning monastery, magnified by the cries of countless numbers of the old and young, sounded and resounded to the ends of heaven and earth."[5] An estimated sixteen hundred people lost their lives in this terrible bloodletting. Nobunaga was similarly set in his hostility toward the Ikkō sect. In Echizen province, he was responsible for the death of thirty to forty thousand Ikkō adherents, although he did not eradicate the sect completely. Even Mt. Kōya narrowly escaped Nobunaga's wrath. His hostility to organized Buddhism was one of the factors influencing the friendly reception he accorded the first Jesuit missionaries to enter Japan. (See Chapter 13.)

Nobunaga was politically adroit. He forged valuable alliances through his marriage policies, managed to keep his enemies divided, and retained his followers and allies. A major element in his growing power was his ability to attract new vassals, frequently men who had been the vassals of his rivals. By going over to Nobunaga they could secure their own positions and hope to participate in future gains. Thus success fed on success.

By opening markets, breaking up guild monopolies, destroying toll stations, and encouraging road construction and shipbuilding, Nobunaga fostered trade. He also reorganized the administration of his lands, introducing a new system of tax collection and initiating a land survey. And he began to disarm the peasantry. Both were in full swing when Nobunaga died, betrayed by one of his own generals avenging a wrong. At the time of his death, he had mastered about a third of Japan.

Toyotomi Hideyoshi

Hideyoshi was born into an Owari peasant family but rose to become one of Nobunaga's foremost generals. After Nobunaga's death, he defeated other contenders for the succession and then continued to increase his power much in the manner of Nobunaga, inducing daimyo to acknowledge his supremacy. Unable to subdue the strongest daimyo, Tokugawa Ieyasu, Hideyoshi used diplomacy, marrying his sister to Ieyasu and assigning him very substantial holdings in the Kantō in exchange for domains of less value in central Japan. In this way he saw to it that Ieyasu was both content and at a distance.

Hideyoshi also relocated his own vassals to assure maximum security. Those he trusted most were placed in strategic positions, while those thought to harbor territorial ambitions were provided with hostile neighbors to discourage them. To demonstrate their loyalty, vassals were sometimes required to leave wives and children with Hideyoshi as virtual hostages. Feudal bonds were further strengthened through marriage alliances. Thus, through conquest, diplomacy and manipulation Hideyoshi became, in effect, overlord of all Japan. By 1590 all daimyo swore oaths of loyalty to him. Since he did not belong to the Minamoto lineage, he was ineligible to become shogun. He did have himself adopted into the Fujiwara family, and in 1585 he was appointed regent (*kampaku*). This association with the imperial throne gave added legitimacy to his place at the apex of a system of feudal loyalties.

Hideyoshi's measures of pacification did not stop at the daimyo level. One of his most important acts was the great "sword hunt" of 1588, when all peasants who had not already done so were ordered to surrender their weapons, the metal to be used in building a great statue of the Buddha. By depriving peasants of their weapons he did more than discourage them from rioting or rebelling—although he did that too. A major, and intentional, consequence of the measure was to draw a sharp line between peasant and samurai, to create an unbridgeable gulf between the tiller of the soil and the bearer of arms, where hitherto there had been low-ranking samurai who had also worked the land.

By this time Hideyoshi's land survey was well under way, although it was not completed for all of Japan until 1598. In this great survey, the value of cultivated land was assessed in terms of productivity, not extent; productivity was measured in *koku* of rice, a *koku* being equal to 4.96 bushels. The resulting listings were used to assess the taxes due from each village, and the holdings of the daimyo were also calculated in terms of the assessed value rather than acreage. From this time on, a daimyo, by definition, held land assessed at a minimum of 10,000 *koku*. Large daimyo held much more than that. Some of the greatest had several hundred thousand *koku*, and there were a few with over a million. Hideyoshi personally held two million, not including the lands of his major most trustworthy vassals. Tokugawa Ieyasu held 2,557,000. Like the confiscation of weapons, the land survey, which listed the names of the peasant proprietors, effectively separated farmers and fighters.

An edict of 1591 carried the process still further. The first of its three articles prohibited fighting men from becoming peasants or townsmen, and the second forbade peasants to leave their fields and become merchants or artisans and prohibited the latter from becoming farmers. The third prohibited anyone from employing a samurai who had left his master without permission. If discovered, the offender was to be returned to his master. If this was not done and the culprit was knowingly allowed to go free, then the edict declared that "three persons shall be beheaded in place of the one, and their heads sent to the offender's original master. If this threefold substitution is not affected, then there is no alternative but to punish the new master."[6] In this way, Hideyoshi, who had himself risen from the peasantry to the greatest heights, did his best to make sure that henceforth everyone would remain within his hereditary social status.

Hideyoshi's vision of the world and his own place in it extended well beyond Japan. He took an active interest in overseas trade, suppressed piracy, and undertook other measures to encourage international commerce. One of his two great castles was at Ōsaka, which soon eclipsed Sakai as a trading center and remains today the second largest city in Japan. But Hideyoshi looked abroad for more than trade: he thought in terms of empire. In the 1590s, he demanded the submission of the Philippines by their Spanish governor, although no steps were ever taken to enforce the demand. He also made plans to conquer China, which he then intended to divide among his vassals, much in the same way as he had dealt with his Japanese conquests. Perhaps Hideyoshi's invasion of the continent was partially motivated by a need to satisfy the perpetual land hunger of these vassals or, at least, to find employment for restive samurai. Another factor was his own personality—he was neither the first nor the last world leader whose pride was bloated by success to the point of megalomania.

Whatever Hideyoshi's motivation, he dispatched a force of 150,000 men to Korea in 1592, after Korea had refused him free passage for his troops to march to China. The Japanese force had great initial success and was able to capture Seoul within a month. But they ran into difficulties further north and were bested at sea by the superior ships and seamanship of the Korean fleet under Admiral Yi Sun-sin, famous for his armed "turtle ships." Chinese military intervention and Korean guerrilla fighting also took their toll, and in 1593 peace negotiations were under way. These talks were fruitless, however, and in 1597

Figure 12-6 Himeiji
Castle. Himeiji, Hyōgo.

Hideyoshi sent another force of 140,000 men to Korea. This time they met with stronger resistance, and the whole attempt was suddenly abandoned when Hideyoshi died in 1598, and the Japanese forces immediately returned home. Hideyoshi himself never joined the Korean campaign but left command to his vassals. The fighting helped weaken two of Hideyoshi's most loyal vassals; it also accounts for an infusion of Korean influence in Japanese printing and pottery.

Hideyoshi's grandiose scheme of conquering China failed, and his Korean venture came to naught. Nor was he able to found a dynasty at home. Before he died, he made his most powerful vassals solemnly swear allegiance to his five-year-old son, Hideyori, whom he left in their care as regents. But this proved useless, and in the ensuing struggle for power Ieyasu emerged the winner. His victory at Sekigahara in 1600 was followed by his designation as shogun in 1603, after he had acquired a suitable Minamoto ancestry. Final confirmation of Ieyasu's triumph came with the fall of Ōsaka Castle and the death of Hideyori in 1615. Ieyasu inherited Hideyoshi's power, but unlike Hideyoshi, he concentrated on building a lasting state at home.

Grand Castles and the Arts

The period of unification is usually called the Azuchi-Momoyama epoch (or Momoyama for short) after Nobunaga's Azuchi Castle near Lake Biwa and Hideyoshi's Momoyama Castle in Fushimi, close to Kyōto. In many ways, these castles, along with those of the daimyo, are fitting representatives of the age.

Dominating the surrounding countryside, they featured massive keeps and strong fortifications designed to withstand the new armies and weapons. Their great size was made possible by the wealth obtained by the unifiers and the daimyo as they achieved greater local control. The castles formed nuclei around which grew new cities, as first samurai and then merchants and artisans were attracted to castle towns. The most grandiose of all the castles was built by Hideyoshi in Ōsaka and boasted forty-eight towers. Unfortunately, Hideyoshi's castles and Nobunaga's were all destroyed, although the Ōsaka Castle was later rebuilt.

Most admired among Japan's castles is that at Himeiji, which dates essentially from the early seventeenth century. In recognition of its suggestive white silhouette, it is commonly known as the "Heron Castle." (See Figure 12-6.) Like European castles, it is a stronghold surrounded by moat and wall and protected by massive foundations. But the gracefulness of its higher reaches is reminiscent of a chateau rather than a fortress. Aesthetics were an important consideration in building a castle, and not only to please its owner, for "its purpose was to impress rivals by its elegant interiors as well as to frighten them by its strength."[7] One way to impress people was through richness of decor. The dark interiors of the castle were "lavish to the point of absurdity."[8] Hideyoshi's castle even had locks and bolts of gold and columns and ceilings covered with the precious metal.

Paintings on walls, sliding doors, and screens decorated and brightened the castle interiors. To meet new needs and tastes, the paintings were frequently large. They used striking colors and employed gold-leaf backgrounds. The artist Kano Eitoku (1543–90) epitomized the new style and spirit. Generously patronized by both Nobunaga and Hideyoshi, Eitoku worked at both the Azuchi and Momoyama castles. The Eitoku screen shown in Figure 12-7 was originally one of a pair, but its companion is now lost. It is about twenty feet long

Figure 12-7   Kano Eitoku, *Chinese Lions* (*Kara-shiki*). Section of sixfold screen, 225 cm high. Imperial Household Collection, Tokyo.

and eight feet high and was obviously intended for use in a large room. Two "Chinese lions" are depicted against a gold background:

> Contour lines in ink are dashed on with sure twists and thrusts of the brush, alive and tense in each curve and linear opposition, to form the bodies of the two beasts as an incarnation of controlled ferocity. The flamelike treatment of the manes and tails gives a curvilinear lift, as an upward pull against the bulky weight. Massive and yet with a coiled spring of inner power . . . Eitoku has found the exact pictorial equivalent for the inner threat under a coating of dignity and majesty, such as a Hideyoshi would want to exert over the rebellious feudal barons.[9]

The Kano school was continued by Eitoku's adopted son, Sanraku (1559–1653), in a trend which culminated in the great decorative screens of the early Tokugawa period. In another medium, Momoyama fondness for rich decoration produced elaborate wood carvings such as those on the Kara Gate of the Nishi Honganji in Kyōto, popularly known as the gate which requires a whole day to be properly seen.

Ostentatious and profuse, the Momoyama aesthetic is far removed from Ashikaga restraint. Nothing could be more alien to the aesthetics of the tea ceremony than the monster tea party given by Hideyoshi in 1587, to which literally everyone was invited for ten days of music, theater, and art viewing. This was not the only occasion on which Hideyoshi displayed a penchant for great gatherings and lavish entertainment. Yet the old values also survived, especially in the tea ceremony, although admittedly the fantastic prices paid by wealthy daimyo competing for ownership of a famous bowl or jar were not exactly in keeping with the intended spirit of tea. Sen no Rikyu (1521–91), greatest of the tea masters, stressed harmony, respect, purity, and tranquility in his writings on tea. Patronized by Hideyoshi, he was widely influential until, for reasons unknown, Hideyoshi ordered him to commit suicide. A story told about the great tea master and his son has them visiting another practitioner of the art. When they entered the garden, the son admired the wooden gate, covered with moss, at the end of the path leading to the tea hut, but the father disagreed: "That gate must have been brought from some distant mountain at obvious expense. A rough wicket made by the local farmer would give the place a really quiet and lonely look, and not offend us by bringing up thoughts of difficulty and expense. I doubt if we shall find here any very sensitive or interesting tea ceremony."[10]

Sen no Rikyu is said to have influenced the potter Chōjiro (1576–92), originator of Raku ware, illustrated by the tea bowl on page 181, right. Eschewing the technical virtuosity of Chinese ceramics, the Japanese potter delights in bringing out the qualities of the clay. Another Momoyama tea master, Furuta Oribe (1544–1615), originated a ceramic tradition characterized by thick glazes and rough brushwork, and Korean-influenced Shino Ware exhibited a traditionally Japanese freedom of decoration.

As in China, artists in Japan often worked in more than one style. Both Eitoku and his great contemporary Hasegawa Tōhaku (1539–1610) worked in monochrome as well as in color. In scale, Tōhaku's masterly *Pine Grove* (see Figure 12-8) is typically Momoyama, for it occupies two screens over five feet

Figure 12-8   Hasegawa Tōhaku, *Pine Grove*. Section of sixfold screen, 155.6 cm × 346.9 cm.

(sixty-one inches) high; but it is ink on paper. By his subtle gradations in ink-tone and the fine work of his brush the artist has created the effect of pines seen through the mist. The placing of the trees and the marvelous use of empty space imbue the painting with rhythm and create a poetry which goes beyond decoration.

NOTES

1. H. Paul Varley, *Imperial Restoration in Medieval Japan* (New York: Columbia University Press, 1971), p. 131.
2. John Whitney Hall, *Japan from Prehistory to Modern Times* (New York: Dell Publishing, 1970), p. 110.
3. Jan Fontein and Money L. Hickman, *Zen Painting and Calligraphy* (Boston: Museum of Fine Arts, 1970), p. 93.
4. Donald Keene, *Japanese Literature*, (New York: Grove Press, 1955), pp. 34–35.
5. Ryusaku Tsunoda, Wm. Theodore de Bary, and Donald Keene, comps., *Sources of Japanese Tradition* (New York: Columbia University Press, 1958), p. 316.
6. David John Lu, *Sources of Japanese History* (New York: McGraw-Hill, 1974), 1:189. Trans. from Ōkubo Toshiaki et al, eds., *Shiryō ni yoru Nihon no Ayumi* (Japanese History Through Documents) *Kinseihen* (Early Modern Period) (Tokyo: Yoshikawa Kōbunkan, 1955), pp. 40–41.
7. Sir George Sansom, *A History of Japan, 1334–1615* (Stanford: Stanford University Press, 1961), p. 380.
8. Sir George Sansom, *Japan: A Short Cultural History* (New York: Appleton-Century-Crofts, 1931), p. 437.
9. Elise Grilli, *The Art of the Japanese Screen* (Tokyo and New York: John Weatherhill, 1970), p. 171.
10. Langdon Warner, *The Enduring Art of Japan* (Cambridge: Harvard University Press, 1958), p. 95.

東亞與現代歐洲
初次之接觸

Key Dates

1514—Portuguese Reach China
1543—Portuguese Reach Japan (Shipwreck)
1549—St. Francis Xavier Lands in Kyūshū
1587—Spaniards Arrive in Japan
1601—Matteo Ricci Received by Emperor of China
1614—Persecution of Christians in Japan
1630—Japan Closed to Foreigners
1700—300,000 Christian Converts in China
1742—Pope Decides Against Jesuits in Rites Controversy

13 East Asia and Modern Europe: First Encounters

The early contacts between post-Renaissance Europe and East Asia had nothing like the impact of those which were to follow in the nineteenth century. Even the introduction of European firearms into sixteenth-century Japan merely hastened the unification of the country, accelerating but not changing the course of history. Yet these early relations form more than just an interesting overture to later history. One value of the study of the earlier period is that it affords opportunities for comparison between Chinese and Japanese responses to very similar foreign stimuli. More significant, the ultimate failure of the early missionaries and merchants left East Asia comparatively isolated from developments in Europe just when, for the first time in the history of the globe, what was happening in Europe was inexorably to affect all humanity.

307

The Portuguese in East Asia

The pioneers of European expansion in East Asia, as elsewhere at this time, were the Portuguese, who reached India in 1498, China in 1514, and Japan in 1543. Having wrested control of the seas from their Arab rivals, they established their Asian headquarters at Goa (1510), a small island off the coast of West India. They then went on to capture Malacca (1511), a vital center for the lucrative spice trade, located on the straits which separate the Malay Peninsula from Sumatra. It was the desire to break the Arab spice monopoly that supplied the economic motive for this initial European expansion. Spices were highly valuable relative to their bulk and weight. Easily transported and fetching a high price, they formed an attractive cargo. And there was an assured market for them in Europe, where they added flavor to an otherwise dull diet and made meat palatable in an age when animals were slaughtered in the fall for want of sufficient fodder to sustain them through the winter. They were also used in medicine and in religious ceremonies.

Prospects for trade were hampered, however, by the fact that Europe, needing pepper and other spices from Asia, had no European commodities of equal importance to offer in return. Initially, therefore, Portuguese adventurers in East Asia supported themselves by a mixture of trade and piracy—like their Japanese predecessors in these waters. They were able to do this successfully because they had superior ships and weapons, and were better seamen. Eventually, however, they became the primary carriers of goods in the East Asian trade, taking goods from one Asian country to another—Southeast Asian wares to China, Chinese silk to Japan, and Japanese silver to China. Their profits from this trade were used to purchase spices and other products for European markets. (See map, Figure 13-1.) But before this trade could prosper, they had to secure entry to China and Japan. This posed problems quite different from those they had encountered in seizing a small island off the coast of politically divided India or in driving the Arabs from Malacca.

In China they got off to a very bad start. Not waiting for official permission to trade, they engaged in illegal commerce and even built a fort on Lintin Island, located at the mouth of the river that connects Canton to the sea. Their unruly behavior did not endear them to the Ming authorities, and served to confirm the opinion that these "ocean devils" were a new kind of barbarian. The outrageous behavior of the Portuguese traders was further embellished by the Chinese imagination. When the Portuguese bought kidnapped Chinese children as slaves, the Chinese concluded that their purpose was to eat them. They long continued in the firm belief that they were dealing with barbarous child eaters. Not just a popular rumor held by the ignorant, this belief found its way into the official history of the Ming dynasty.

The first Portuguese envoy to China not only failed to obtain commercial concessions; he ended his life in a Cantonese prison. It was a most inauspicious beginning. But the Portuguese would not leave, and their superiority on the seas made it impossible for the Chinese to drive them out. A *modus vi-*

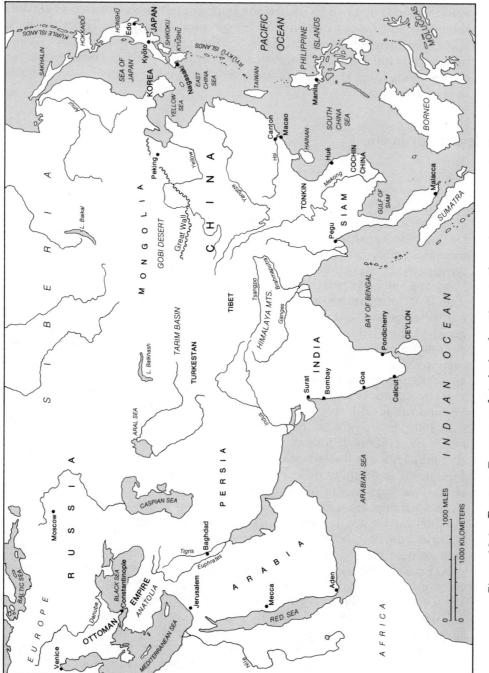

Figure 13-1 Eastern Europe and Asia in the Sixteenth and Seventeenth Centuries

vendi was reached in 1557 when the Portuguese were permitted to establish themselves in Macao in exchange for an annual payment. There the Portuguese administered their own affairs, but the territory remained under Chinese jurisdiction until Macao was ceded to Portugal in 1887. Today Macao and nearby Hong Kong still remain under European control, vestiges of European overseas empire.

The Jesuits in Japan

Trade and booty were not the only objectives of the Europeans who ventured into Asian waters. Missionary work was also important: mid-sixteenth-century Goa boasted some eighty churches and convents. From the beginning, the missionary impulse provided a strong incentive as well as religious sanction for European expansion; and it was the missionary rather than the trader who served as prime intermediary between the civilizations of East Asia and the West from the sixteenth to the twentieth centuries.

Among the early missionaries, the great pioneers and the most impressive leaders were members of the Society of Jesus (Jesuits). Founded in 1540, this tightly organized and rigorously disciplined religious order formed the vanguard of the Catholic Counter-Reformation. They were the "cavalry of the church," prepared to do battle with Protestant heretics in Europe or the heathen in the world beyond. Along with its stress on martial discipline and intensive religious training, the Society was noted for its insistence on intellectual vigor and depth of learning. The latter included secular as well as sacred studies, and the ideal Jesuit was as learned as he was disciplined and devout.

In 1549, less than ten years after the founding of the Jesuit order, St. Francis Xavier (1506–52), one of the original members of the Society, landed in Kyūshū. This was just six years after the Japanese had encountered their first Europeans, some shipwrecked Portuguese who landed on the island of Tanegashima. Xavier was well received and was soon able to establish cordial relations with important men in Kyūshū. First impressions on both sides were favorable. Xavier and his successors liked the Japanese; he himself referred to them as "the best [people] who have yet been discovered."[1] Likewise, the Japanese were impressed by the strong character and dignified bearing of the European priests. The Jesuit combination of martial pride, stern self-discipline, and religious piety fitted well with the ethos of sixteenth-century Japan. Nor did the Christian religion seem altogether strange. On the contrary, initially Christianity, brought to Japan from Goa, seemed just another type of Buddhism. It was similar in some of its ceremonies to those found in Buddhism, and it was difficult for the early priests to convey the subtleties of theology, to explain the difference between God and the cosmic Buddha, for example, or to distinguish Paradise from the Pure Land. At last, the Jesuit fathers concluded that the devil, in all of his malicious cleverness, had deliberately fashioned Buddhism to resemble the true faith so as to confound and confuse the people.

The initial meeting of the Jesuits and the Japanese was facilitated by the similarities in their feudal backgrounds. In Japan, Xavier and other Europeans found a society which resembled their own far more than did any other outside Europe. "The people," wrote Alessandro Valignano (1539–1606), "are all white, courteous and highly civilized, so much so that they surpass all the other known races of the world."[2] Only the Chinese were to receive similar praise—and, indeed, to be regarded as "white." Donald Lach has summarized the qualities the Jesuits found to admire in the Japanese: "their courtesy, propriety, dignity, endurance, frugality, equanimity, industriousness, sagaciousness, cleanliness, simplicity, discipline, and rationality."[3] On the negative side, aside from their paganism, the Jesuits were appalled at the prevalence of sodomy among the military aristocracy and the monks. They criticized the Japanese propensity to suicide and also found fault with the "disloyalty of vassal to master, their dissimulation, ambiguity, and lack of openness in their dealings, their bellicose nature, their inhuman treatment of enemies and unwanted children, their failure to respect the rule of law, and finally their unwillingness to give up the system of concubinage."[4] Nevertheless, the similarities between Japanese culture and their own gave the Jesuits high hopes for the success of their mission.

In their everyday behavior the Jesuits tried to win acceptance by adapting themselves to local manners and customs, as long as these did not run counter to their own creed. "Thus," Valignano observed, "we who come hither from Europe find ourselves as veritable children who have to learn to eat, sit, converse, dress, act politely, and so on."[5] They learned how to squat Japanese style, learned to employ the Japanese language with its various levels of politeness, and mastered the art of tea—the Jesuit dwelling was usually equipped with a tea room so that their guests could be properly entertained. C. R. Boxer has pointed out that the Christian monks came from a land with rather different standards of personal cleanliness: "Physical dirt and religious poverty tended to be closely associated in Catholic Europe where lice were regarded as the inseparable companions of monks and soldiers."[6] But in Japan the devoted monks even learned to wash, a major concession to Japanese sensibilities. Still there were limits: Valignano could not bring himself to endorse the Japanese custom of taking a hot bath every day. That would really be going too far!

Careful attention to the niceties of etiquette was required of the Jesuit fathers in their strategy of working from the top down. It was their hope to transform Japan into a Christian land by first converting the rulers and then allowing the faith to seep down to the populace at large. The purpose of their labors was not to Europeanize Japan or China, but to save souls. They realized that the enthusiastic support of the ruling authority would be an invaluable asset, while without at least the ruler's tacit approval they could do nothing.

This approach met with considerable success in Kyūshū, where they converted important local daimyo, who ordered their people to adopt the foreign faith. Although there were numerous cases of genuine conversion, some daimyo simply saw the light of commerce, adopting a Christian stance in the

Figure 13-2 Namban screen. Section of a sixfold screen, 164 cm × 365.6 cm, Kano Mitsonobu school, ca. 1610. Namban Bunkakan, Ōsaka.

hope of attracting the Portuguese trade to their ports. On at least one occasion it happened that the great Portuguese ship did not appear; they promptly turned their backs on the new faith. The Jesuits themselves became involved in this trade and also in politics. For seven years they even held the overlordship of Nagasaki, granted to them by a Christian daimyo.

Xavier and the monks who came after him realized that real progress for their mission depended on the will not only of local Kyūshū daimyo but of the central government. Xavier's initial trip to Kyōto came at an unpropitious time —the city was in disorder. But Nobunaga soon became a friend of the Jesuits. Attracted by their character and interested in hearing about foreign lands, perhaps he was also happy to talk with someone not part of the hierarchical order which he himself headed. This personal predilection also coincided nicely with reasons of state. It was consistent with his hostility toward the Buddhist orders and with his desire to keep the trading ships coming in. Hideyoshi was similarly well disposed toward the foreign religion. He liked dressing up in Portuguese clothes, complete with rosary, and he once said that the only thing which kept him from converting was the Christian insistence on monogamy.

The political and economic success of the Jesuits helped the spread of Christianity, but power, or the semblance of power, always entails risks. There was the danger that the ruler might perceive the activities of the monks not as assets bolstering his own position but as liabilities, actual or potential threats to his authority. A portent of future disaster came in 1578 when Hideyoshi issued an order expelling the monks. Eager to encourage trade and not really feeling seriously threatened, Hideyoshi did not enforce the decree, but it foreshadowed the persecutions which were to begin in earnest thirty-six years later, in 1614.

There was a surge of popularity for things Western, for instance, "Southern Barbarian Screens," showing the giant black ships of the foreigners. The barbarians themselves were depicted as exceedingly tall and rather ungainly, with sharp, long noses and red hair, wearing the ballooning pantaloons which formed the standard fashion in the Portuguese empire. (See Figure 13-2.) Other scenes, based on paintings from Europe, depicted various barbarian topics: the battle of Lepanto, an Italian court, European cities, maps of the world, not to mention religious subjects. While some artists painted European subjects in Japanese style, others experimented with Western perspective and techniques of shading to produce three-dimensional effects. Nor were Western motifs limited to painting. Western symbols were widely used in decoration, a cross on a bowl, a few words of Latin on a saddle, and so forth. In a letter written in 1594 a missionary described the foreign fad. Writing of non-Christian daimyo he stated:

> They wear rosaries of driftwood on their breasts, hang a crucifix from their shoulder or waist, and sometimes even a handkerchief. Some, who are especially kindly disposed, have memorized the Our Father and the Hail Mary, and recite them as they walk in the streets. This is not done in ridicule of the Christians, but simply to show off their familiarity with the latest fashion, or because they think it good and effective in bringing success in daily life. This has led them to spend no small sums in ordering oval earrings bearing the likeness of Our Lord and the Holy Mother.[7]

This was a passing fashion, but some new products entered Japan to stay, and new words were added to the language, for instance *tabako* (tobacco), *pan* (bread), and *karuta* (playing cards). Another Portuguese contribution was tempura, the popular Japanese dish prepared by deep fat frying vegetables and seafood dipped in batter. The Japanese word is derived from *temporas* (meatless Friday).

The Closing of Japan

Despite the order of 1578, Western influences continued to enter Japan: religious, commercial, cultural. The situation was complicated, however, by the arrival of other Europeans. The first Spaniards arrived from the Philippines, headquarters of the Spanish in Asia, in 1587; and the first Franciscans came from Manila in 1592. By the early 1600s, representatives of the Protestant Dutch and English had also arrived. Although the prospects for trade were attractive, the proliferation of foreigners was disturbing. The various nations competed with each other for Japanese trade. The Dutch and English sought to encourage Japanese suspicions of their Catholic rivals. Moreover, the Japanese were not unaware that the Spanish role in the Philippines was that of colonial master, and that the Spaniards might harbor imperial ambitions with regard to Japan as well. Finally, the Japanese became increasingly concerned that growing Catholic influence might prove subversive of internal stability. The Jesuits had been unable to avoid a degree of involvement in Japanese politics; now the Franciscans, working among the poor, seemed to threaten the traditional social order.

The Jesuits had sought to carry out their missionary activities within the framework of Japanese society and social values. They associated primarily with the upper classes, with a view to working their way down. The Franciscans were suspicious of the Jesuit approach. They were much less well informed concerning conditions in Japan and also much less discreet in their work. Instead of associating with the samurai, the Franciscans worked among the poor and forgotten, the sick and miserable, those at the very bottom of society. The Jesuits did not disguise their contempt for the ignorance and poverty of the Franciscans, the "crazy friars" (frailes idiotas) as they called them, and these sentiments were heartily reciprocated by the friars, who scoffed at Jesuit pretensions.

Rivalry between the Portuguese and the Spanish, between Goa and Manila, compounded the instability of the situation. On one hand, Manila presented the possibility of a new source of profitable trade; on the other, the colonization of the Philippines demonstrated the imperialistic ambitions of the Europeans and the connection between Christian evangelism and colonialism. It was an omen of things to come when Hideyoshi, in 1597, crucified six Franciscan missionaries and eighteen of their Japanese converts after the pilot of a Spanish ship driven ashore in Japan reportedly boasted about the power and ambitions of his king. Ieyasu was at first friendly to the Christians, but he too turned against them. In 1606 Christianity was declared illegal, and in 1614 he undertook a serious campaign to expel the missionaries.

By 1614 there were over 300,000 converts in Japan. The destruction of Christianity was long and painful. Tortures, such as hanging a man upside down with his head in a pit filled with excrement, were used to induce people to renounce their faith. Before it was all over, there were more than 3000 recognized martyrs, of whom less than 70 were Europeans. Others died without achieving martyrdom. In 1637–38 there was a rebellion in Shimabara, near Nagasaki, against a daimyo who combined merciless taxation with cruel suppression of Christianity. Fought under banners on which Christian slogans were written in Portuguese, and led by some masterless samurai, it was a Christian version of the rural uprisings characteristic of the century of warfare before Nobunaga. In its suppression, some 37,000 Christians lost their lives.

Persuasion as well as violence was employed in the campaign against Christianity. Opponents of Christian dogma argued that the idea of a personal creator was absurd and asked why, if God was both omnipotent and good, he should have tempted Adam and Eve and devised eternal punishment in Hell for non-Christians even though they led exemplary lives. According to Christian teaching, even the sage emperors Yao and Shun would end in hell. The First Commandment was attacked as leading to disobedience of parents and lord; a loyal retainer should accompany his lord even into hell.

Such arguments suggest that the Japanese saw Christianity as potentially subversive, not only of the political order, but of the basic social structure, for it challenged accepted values and beliefs and demanded a radical reappraisal of long-revered traditions. Its association with European expansionism posed a threat from abroad, and, as exemplified by the Shimabara Rebellion, it also harbored the seeds of radical disruption at home. Thus the motivation for the government's suppression of Christianity was secular not religious. The shogunate was not worried over the state of its subjects' souls, but it was determined to wipe out a dangerous doctrine. An indication that the government's concerns were secular is provided by the oath of apostasy demanded of all former Christians. In it the recanters had to swear that if they had the slightest thought of renouncing their apostasy, "then let us be punished by God the Father, God the Son, and God the Holy Ghost, St. Mary, and all the Angels and Saints."[8] Thus they had to take a Christian oath that they no longer believed in Christianity! The persecutions succeeded in destroying all but a small underground group of secret Christians, who passed from generation to generation a faith increasingly infused with native elements. Meanwhile every Japanese family was registered with a Buddhist temple, and once a year the family head had to swear that there were no Christians in his household. Incidentally, the resulting demographic data, the most complete for any premodern society, constitutes an invaluable resource for modern scholars.

Not only Christianity but all foreign influences were potentially subversive, including trade which would tend to the advantage of the Kyūshū daimyo rather than the Tokugawa. With this in mind, the Tokugawa *bakufu* gradually closed the country off from the rest of the world. The Spaniards were expelled in 1624, one year after the voluntary withdrawal of the English. In 1630 Japanese were forbidden to go overseas or to return from there or to build ships capable of traveling long distances. The Portuguese were expelled after the Shimabara Rebellion on the grounds of complicity in that uprising. When they sent an embassy in 1640, its members were executed. The only Europeans left were the Dutch (see Figure 13-3), and in 1641 they were moved to the tiny artificial island of Deshima in Nagasaki harbor. There they were isolated and virtually confined, as in a prison. The annual Dutch vessel to Deshima and some limited commerce with China was all that remained to link Japan to the outside world.

The Jesuits in China

The beginnings of the Jesuit missions in China and Japan were closely linked. Xavier himself hoped to begin the work in China. He realized this was not only a great project in itself but also a major step in the Christianization of Japan, providing an answer to the question he was constantly asked there: "If yours is the true faith why have not the Chinese, from whom comes all wisdom, heard of it?"[9] But Xavier died before he could reach his goal. Three further Jesuit attempts to enter China also failed. Then Valignano established a special training center in Macao so that missionaries could study the Chinese language and culture in preparation for work in China. As in Japan, it was Jesuit policy in China to concentrate on gaining the support and, if possible, conversion of the upper classes. To this end, they once more went as far as possible to accommodate themselves to native sensibilities and ways of doing things.

Again, as in Japan, the strong character and attractive personalities of the first missionaries were of great importance in gaining them entree. The outstanding pioneer was Matteo Ricci (1551–1610). A student of law, mathematics, and science, he also knew a good deal about cartography and something of practical mechanics. Once in the East, he was also able to master the Chinese language and the classics. Ricci's ability to make maps and build clocks aroused the interest of the Chinese scholars, while his command of Chinese classical learning impressed them. Slowly Ricci made his way in Chinese officialdom. At last in 1601, after eighteen strenuous years, Ricci was received in an imperial audience and won permission for himself and his colleagues to reside in the capital. (By this time they had discarded the Buddhist robes worn by Jesuits in Japan and had adopted Confucian dress as more acceptable to the Chinese.) In Peking he was able to win over and convert a number of promi-

Figure 13-3 *A Dutch Dinner Party.* Nagasaki color print, 22 cm × 33 cm.

nent men. By the time Ricci died in Peking in 1610, the mission was well established in the capital and accepted by the government. Ricci's body was laid to rest in a plot donated by the emperor.

During the period when the Japanese were persecuting Christians with increasing ferocity, the Jesuits in China labored fruitfully, building on the foundations laid by Ricci. They were particularly successful in demonstrating the superior accuracy of European astronomical predictions. Thereby they succeeded in displacing their Muslim and Chinese competitors and established themselves in the Bureau of Astronomy. This was an important and prestigious office, reflecting the importance of the heavenly bodies in Chinese thought. Jesuit gains in this area were solidified by the work of Adam Schall von Bell (1591–1666), a German Jesuit who was a trained astronomer and served as chief astronomer in Peking. Schall von Bell also assisted in casting cannon for the Ming, although it did not save the dynasty.

The Jesuits made some notable converts among the literati, particularly during the troubled years of the declining Ming. Most notable was Hsü Kuang-ch'i (Paul Hsü, 1562–1633), who translated Euclid's *Elements* and other works on mathematics, hydraulics, astronomy, and geography, thereby becoming the first Chinese translator of European books. With the help of such men, Western science and geography were made available to China, but European influence remained limited. As we shall see in Chapter 14, there was a social and intellectual crisis in China during the early seventeenth century, but this stimulated fresh currents within the Chinese tradition rather than inducing men to explore foreign ideas. Thus, when Li Chih, one of the most forceful and independent Late Ming thinkers, met Ricci, he was impressed with the Jesuit's personality but saw no merit in his proselytizing mission.

The triumph of the Manchus did not seriously disrupt Jesuit activity. Schall von Bell was retained by the new dynasty as their astronomer, and he was followed by the Belgian Jesuit, Ferdinant Verbiest (1633–88), the last of the trio of great and learned missionary fathers. Verbiest, like Schall von Bell, cast cannon and in other ways won the favor of the great Manchu emperor, K'ang-hsi (r. 1662–1722). A good account of Jesuit activities at court comes from the emperor's own brush:

> With Verbiest I had examined each stage of the forging of cannons, and made him build a water fountain that operated in conjunction with an organ, and erect a windmill in the court; with the new group . . . I worked on clocks and mechanics. Pereira taught me to play the tune *"P'u-yen-chou"* on the harpsichord and the structure of the eight-note-scale, Pedrini taught my sons musical theory, and Gheradini painted portraits at the Court. I also learned to calculate the weight and volume of spheres, cubes, and cones . . .[10]

The Emperor accepted the Jesuits' science with alacrity and took their quinine for the sake of his health. He also discussed religion with them, but here they were less successful: "I had asked Verbiest why God had not forgiven his son without making him die, but though he had tried hard to answer I had not understood him."[11] Nevertheless, the middle years of his reign were the high-point of early Christianity in China, after which it declined. By 1700 there were no more than 300,000 Christians in China, roughly the same number as in much smaller Japan a century earlier.

In both cases the missionaries were there on sufferance, dependent on the good will of the authorities. And in China, as earlier in Japan, divisions between the Europeans themselves strongly contributed to their undoing.

The Rites Controversy

The controversy that brought an end to the missionary activity in China centered on the Jesuit policy of accommodation, which was opposed by the rival orders, particularly and vigorously by the Dominicans. It revolved around the question of the proper attitude a Christian should adopt toward Confucianism, its doctrines and practices. This kind of dispute had not arisen in Japan, where Catholic fathers of all orders agreed in their condemnation of Buddhism and Shinto and in their absolute refusal to allow their converts to have anything to do with such heathen religions.

In China, however, the basic strategy used by Ricci and followed by his successors was to accept the teachings of Confucius, "the prince of philosophers." They argued that they had come, not to destroy Confucius, but to make his teachings complete, capping his doctrines with the truths of revealed religion. Like Chinese thinkers intent on using Confucius in new ways, the Jesuits also discarded and condemned previous interpretations and commentaries on the classics. They attacked Neo-Confucianism and developed new theories of their own. In their enthusiasm for the classics, the Jesuits turned Confucius into a religious teacher. Some members of the order went as far as to trace the origin of the Chinese people to the eldest son of Noah. The most extreme even claimed to find Christian prophecies in the *I Ching*. Meanwhile, the Dominicans held that the ancient Chinese were atheists and argued against the Jesuit portrayal of Confucius as a deist. The resulting literature greatly influenced Western understanding of Chinese philosophy. At its best it was a serious effort by Europeans to understand Chinese thought in what they believed to be universally valid terms.

The status of Confucius and the acceptability of the classics were major issues for missionaries operating in a society dominated by the Confucian examination system. Even more troublesome, however, was the related problem posed by Confucian observances. Were the ceremonies in veneration of Confucius, held in the temples of Confucius throughout the land, acts of religious devotion and therefore anathema to a Christian? Or were they social and political in character, secular expressions of respect for China's greatest teacher? Even more important, what about the rites performed by every family in front of the tablets representing its ancestors? Was this a worship of the departed spirits and thus the most iniquitous idolatry? Or did these acts of commemoration to one's forebears merely convey a deep sense of filial piety? Were the two kinds of ceremonials civic and moral in nature, or were they religious, and therefore sacrilegious? Consistent with their stand on Confucianism, the Jesuits claimed the ceremonies were nonreligious and therefore permissible. The Dominicans disagreed.

The issue was fiercely debated, for much was at stake. Theology aside, it is easy to see the practical reasons for the Jesuit standpoint. To exclude Christians from performing the ceremonies for Confucius would be to exclude them from participation in Chinese political life. Worse still, to prohibit the ritual veneration of ancestors would not only deprive Chinese Christians of their sense of family but would make them appear as unfilial, immoral monsters in the eyes of their non-Christian fellows. If Christianity rejected the classics and advocated this kind of nonconformist behavior, it would be turned into a religion subversive of the Chinese state and society. Persecuted and condemned, Christianity would be unable to reach many souls, who would thus be deprived of their chance for salvation.

But the Dominicans could muster strong counterarguments. Why should a church which condemned Protestant Christianity condone Confucian Christianity? The issue was not the acceptability of Christianity to the Chinese but whether the salvation of souls would be fatally jeopardized by tolerating false Confucian doctrines. In their eyes, nothing could be allowed to interfere with the Christian's sacred duty to maintain the purity of the faith.

The Decline of Christianity in China

The question, "when does Christianity cease to be Christianity" was to reappear in the nineteenth century and is not all that different from the question, "when does Marxism cease to be Marxism," which agitates some thinkers today. Such questions are never easy to resolve and perhaps only true believers need grapple with them. Be that as it may, in the papacy, the church had a source of authority that could rule on what was acceptable and what was not. The process of reaching a decision was complicated and involved. What is important here is that the outcome went against the Jesuits. In 1704 the pope favored the Dominicans, and in 1742 a decree was issued which settled all points against the Jesuits. This remained the position of the Catholic Church until 1938. Grand and powerful emperors like K'ang-hsi, however, saw no reason to abide by the judgment of Rome as to what was fitting for their realm. They naturally favored the Jesuit point of view. In the end, the pope would send only those missionaries the emperor of China would not accept.

One major difference between the course of events in China and Japan was that in China neither a desire for trade nor fear of its possible consequences influenced decisions concerning missionary policies, for the trade conducted sporadically by European ships was of only peripheral concern to the Chinese government.

Figure 13-4 Anonymous, *Portrait of Hsiang Fei*. Mid-eighteenth century. Palace Museum, Peking.

Some missionaries remained in China after the break, including the Jesuit Guiseppe Castillione, who served as court painter for half a century, 1715–66. Among other things, he designed a miniature Versailles for the Summer Palace, destroyed in the nineteenth century. Michael Sullivan has described his fusion of artistic traditions as a "synthetic style in which with taste and skill and the utmost discretion, Western perspective and shading, with even an occasional hint of chiaroscuro, were blended to give an added touch of realism to painting otherwise entirely Chinese in manner."[12] Figure 13-4 shows a painting in the European manner done at the Chinese court. It is an anonymous portrait of an imperial concubine playing at being a European peasant girl. Just as Louis XV of France sometimes amused himself by having his courtiers and their ladies assume Chinese dress, the Ch'ing emperor Ch'ien-lung enjoyed exotic Western costume on occasion.

Regardless of the Rites Controversy, the Christians also had opponents in China itself, motivated by the usual combination of self-interest and conviction. There was no Chinese counterpart to Nagasaki: instead, Canton and the surrounding area, the part of China most exposed to the Europeans, already at this time took a negative view of the foreigners. Christianity was proscribed in 1724. Some churches were seized and other acts of persecution occurred, but the suppression of Christianity was not as thorough as that which had taken place in Japan. This was probably because there was no Chinese equivalent to the Shimabara Rebellion—at least not yet. Not until the nineteenth century did the potential of Christianity as an ideology of peasant revolt become evident in China. By the end of the eighteenth century, the number of Chinese converts had been reduced to about half their number at the beginning of the century.

Much research remains to be done on the influence of this period of early Western contact on Chinese thought and civilization. There was certainly some stimulus from the West, but more frequently the Western influence seems not to have progressed much beyond the appreciation of European exotica, such as clocks and other mechanical devices. The influence was much stronger the other way, for the Jesuit reports on China were well received in Europe and helped to create the image of an ideal China dear to the *philosophes* of the European Enlightenment. In the arts there was an enthusiasm for things "Chinesy"—*chinoiserie*. Neither *chinoiserie* in Europe nor *namban* ("Southern Barbarian") art in Japan may have reached great aesthetic heights, but in their relative openness to foreign stimulus, there is a certain resemblance between early modern Europe and Japan (but missing in China) in this period of first encounters.

NOTES

1. C. R. Boxer, *The Christian Century in Japan* (Berkeley and Los Angeles: University of California Press, 1951), Appendix I, p. 401. Also quoted in Donald F. Lach, *Asia in the Making of Europe,* Vol. I, *The Century of Discovery* (Chicago: University of Chicago Press, 1965), p. 284, also pp. 663–64.

2. Boxer, *The Christian Century in Japan,* p. 74.

3. Lach, *Asia in the Making of Europe,* 1:728.

4. *Ibid.*

5. Quoted in Boxer, *The Christian Century in Japan,* p. 75.

6. Boxer, *The Christian Century in Japan,* p. 214.

7. Yoshitomo Okamoto, *The Namban Art of Japan* (Tokyo and New York: John Weatherhill, 1972), p. 77.

8. Boxer, *The Christian Century in Japan,* p. 441.

9. A. H. Rowbotham, *Missionary and Mandarin* (Berkeley and Los Angeles: University of California Press, 1942), p. 46.

10. Quoted in Jonathan Spence, *Emperor of China* (New York: Alfred A. Knopf, 1974), pp. 72–73.

11. *Ibid.,* p. 84.

12. Michael Sullivan, *The Meeting of Eastern and Western Art* (New York: New York Graphic Society, 1973), pp. 66–67.

Hall of Annual Prayers (*Ch'i-nien-tien*). Ch'ing Dynasty (rebuilt late nineteenth century). Peking.

PART FOUR
Traditional China and Japan: The Last Phase

满人治下之中國

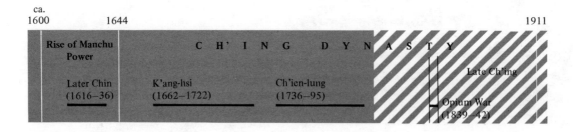

ca.
1600   1644   1911

Rise of Manchu   C H' I N G   D Y N A S T Y
Power
                                                                    Late Ch'ing

Later Chin   K'ang-hsi   Ch'ien-lung
(1616—36)   (1662—1722)   (1736—95)
                                                        Opium War
                                                        (1839—42)

14 *China under the Manchus*

In chapters 14 and 15 we will examine Ch'ing China and Toku-gawa Japan in the period prior to the nineteenth century. This may be considered the last phase of their traditional histories, the period when they did not yet face the full onslaught of the modern world, when challenges from abroad could be contained and even disregarded. The study of this period is crucial not only for an understanding of what was to follow in modern times but also because it affords a last look at the internal dynamics of traditional China and Japan, demonstrating some of the developments implicit in their earlier histories, and enriching our understanding of the relationship between their traditional and modern cultures.

In China, Manchu rulers established the Ch'ing Dynasty (1644–1911), only the second non-Chinese dynasty to rule over all of China and far more successful than the first, the Yüan. Under the Ch'ing, the empire was expanded further than ever before, and for a time China achieved remarkable stability and prosperity. The dynasty's shortcomings in the nineteenth and early twentieth centuries must not be allowed to obscure its accomplishments at its prime.

Formation of the Manchu State

The Ming maintained peace and order in the northern portion of Manchuria partly by diplomacy and partly by establishing "commanderies" under hereditary tribal control. To provide for the security of the Chinese settlers inhabiting the Liao River basin, it also maintained the "Willow Palisades," a line of willows and a deep trench along which checkpoints were maintained. As long as the Ming was strong and the Juchen tribes divided, the frontier area was reasonably stable. However, Ming weakness and the emergence of tribal unity changed all that.

The Manchu state was founded by Nurhachi (1559–1626), who fought, married, and negotiated his way to leadership and power. Originally supported by the Ming, he continued to send tribute to Peking until 1609. But he was powerful enough also to defy the Chinese dynasty when he wished, and in 1616 he declared himself emperor of the Later Chin. In this way Nurhachi identified his regime with the earlier Juchen Chin Dynasty (1115–1234), which had shared China in unfriendly coexistence with the Southern Sung. His ambitions were given more concrete expression by his move that year into the agricultural plain of Manchuria. The Chinese inhabitants were turned into Manchu bond servants (that is, slaves) and were forced to wear their hair in a queue (pigtail) and to shave the rest of their heads in the Manchu fashion. This expansion greatly increased the state's economic and human resources and made Chinese expertise and models available to the new state. But Nurhachi was also concerned to preserve his people's traditions. Thus, when it came to devising a written language, he had his interpreter use the Mongolian script, not Chinese, as his base.

In 1625 Nurhachi established his capital at Mukden, but the following year he suffered his first major military defeat at the hands of a Ming general who made effective use of a new weapon: the cannon. Nurhachi died the same year and was succeeded by his son Abahai (r. 1626–43), who continued to build on his father's foundations. The most important of these was the banner system. This was devised by Nurhachi in 1601 when he formed his troops into companies of 300 men, organized under four large banners, colored yellow, white, blue, and red. In 1615 he added four more banners using the original colors but adding borders to the flags. Each banner was headed by one of Nurhachi's sons who was responsible for the civil as well as military administration of all his troops and their families. In 1621 the first Mongol company was organized, and in 1636 Abahai created the first Chinese company. By the time of the conquest, there were eight Mongol and eight Chinese banners along with the eight Manchu banners. In terms of the number of companies involved, the breakdown was: 278 Manchu, 120 Mongol, and 165 Chinese.

Even before the conquest of China there were more Chinese than Manchus in the Manchu state, and Manchu leaders were strongly motivated to create a political system which would gain the approval and participation of Chinese officials without sacrificing Manchu control. The Manchus created a new institution, the Council of Deliberative Officials, charged with policymaking on the highest level and composed exclusively of Manchus. But Abahai also adopted the Six Ministries, the Censorate, and other Ming institutions. Each of the ministries was headed by a Manchu prince and initially provided with four presidents, two Manchu, one Mongol, and one Chinese. The formula was changed even during Abahai's reign, and it took some time for the details to be worked out, but what was established was the principle that there should be an ethnic balance in the central government under Manchu supervision.

An unequivocal indication that Abahai cherished ambitions beyond Manchuria came in 1636 when he discarded the Later Chin designation and instead called his regime the Ch'ing (pure), at the same time divorcing himself from the Juchen past by changing the name of his people to Manchu. In a series of military campaigns, he reduced Inner Mongolia to vassalage, defeated and gained the submission of Korea, and won control of the Amur River region in the North. But the conquest of North China was achieved after his death by Dorgon (1612–50), acting as regent for Abahai's six-year-old son and heir.

The Conquest

By 1644 the Ming dynasty was in an advanced state of collapse. The last Ming emperor hanged himself just as the rebel forces of Li Tzu-ch'eng entered Peking. (See chapter 10). Li, however, had not formed a stable government, nor had he succeeded in convincing the literati that he was the recipient of the Heavenly Mandate. The immediate key to the military situation was in the hands of the Ming general Wu San-kuei (1612–78), whose army controlled Shanhaikuan, the strategic pass between mountains and sea that formed the eastern terminus of the Great Wall and controlled access from Manchuria into China. When Wu decided to throw in his lot with the Manchus rather than the Chinese rebels, the fate of Li Tzu-ch'eng was sealed. The Ch'ing soldiers entered Peking in June. Dorgon buried the Ming emperor and empress with full honors and announced that he had come to punish the rebels. In October the Ch'ing court was moved from Mukden to Peking.

The subjugation of the South took longer and would have been impossible without the assistance of Wu San-kuei and other Chinese generals, and the acquiescence of many Chinese ready to cooperate with the Ch'ing. The state created in Szechwan by the rebel leader Chang Hsien-chung, who had gained a reputation for terror, soon fell. Chang was killed in 1647. Ming princes tried to keep their cause alive in the South but never really mounted a serious challenge. The last of the princes was put to death by Wu San-kuei in 1662 after being chased into Burma.

The victory of Wu San-kuei and the other Chinese generals did not, however, bring the South under full Ch'ing control, since Wu created a practically autonomous state for himself in Yunnan and Kweichow, with his capital in Kunming. Two other generals long associated with the Manchu cause also carved out states for themselves, one in Kwangtung and the other in Fukien. The destruction of these three states was finally undertaken by Emperor K'ang-hsi, who was only fifteen years old at the time. It took a costly war, known as the War of the Three Feudatories (1673–81), before these states were subdued and incorporated into the Ch'ing state. (See map, Figure 14-1.)

The most prolonged resistance to the new dynasty was along the southeast coast. The main power in this region belonged to Cheng Ch'eng-kung (1624–62), also known as Coxinga, the son of a Chinese pirate and adventurer and a Japanese mother. The father had been baptized by the Portuguese at Macao but became a Ming supporter, and the son too was honored by the beleaguered Ming house—"Coxinga" is actually the Dutch version of the title given him by the Ming. Later, Coxinga and his cause captured the imagination of the Japanese playwright Chikamatsu. From 1646 to 1658 he controlled much of the southeast China coast, and at one point the court ordered the entire coast evacuated to deprive Cheng of the chance for plunder or trade. Originally based in the Amoy region, he later moved to Taiwan (or Formosa, to use the name given to it by the Portuguese). In 1662 Cheng expelled the Dutch from Taiwan where they had maintained posts since 1624. He died the same year, but his son continued to defy the Manchus, who did not suppress him until 1683. The island then was placed under the administration of Fukien Province thus bringing it under mainland control.

Emperor K'ang-hsi, under whom the long process of military consolidation was finally completed, also took measures to win over the Confucian literati. However, some of the most original and provocative thinkers of their generation refused to serve the new dynasty. Among the Ming loyalists, three men stand out as intellectual giants. The youngest of these, Wang Fu-chih (1619–1704), was fifty at the time Emperor K'ang-hsi dismissed the regent who had been governing in his name and began ruling on his own. They thus belong to the generation whose crucial life experience was the collapse of the Ming.

Three Thinkers

Wang Fu-chih, Huang Tsung-hsi (1610–95), and Ku Yen-wu (1613–82) all fought for the Ming while they could and when that was no longer possible refused to serve the new dynasty. Both Huang's teacher, Liu Tsung-chou, and Ku Yen-wu's mother refused to live under the Manchus. Instead they manifested their deep loyalty to the old dynasty by starving themselves to death, a form of suicide consistent with the injunction of filial piety, which prohibits a

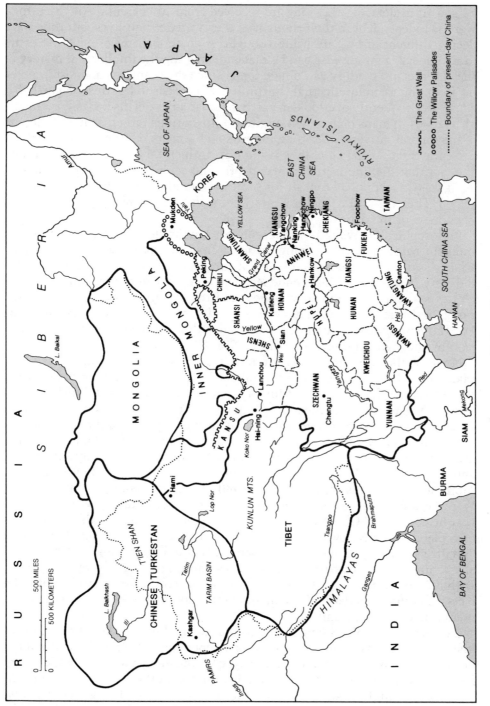

Figure 14-1 Ch'ing China

person from defacing the body he received from his parents. All three men were as independent in their thought as they were in their lives, but they were deeply influenced by Late Ming thought, even though rejecting some of its ideas. Indeed, a strong case can be made for treating the intellectual history of the seventeenth century as a single topic, since the Manchu conquest brought no abrupt break in intellectual continuity. This needs to be stressed, partly because it is frequently overlooked, partly because any brief discussion of a man's ideas tends to focus on his own original contributions rather than on that part of his mental universe which he inherits and accepts relatively unaltered.

Of the three, Wang Fu-chih was the least influential in his own day, despite the fact that his intellectual range, depth, and sophistication were immense. As it was, his work had to wait for some two hundred years before it was published. Then his anti-Manchu views were welcomed by new, modern-minded opponents of the dynasty.

Philosophically, Wang is interesting for having developed a metaphysical monism based on *ch'i*, drawing on ideas first advanced during the Sung by Chang Tsai. The primacy of *ch'i* did not entail a rejection of *li* (principle), but it did deny *li* ontological independence. The view that in the last analysis only *ch'i* exists represents the polar opposite of the elevation of *li* by Wang Yang-ming. In this respect, and in his views on human nature and the desires, Wang Fu-chih represents the intellectual tendency that was given its fullest expression by the eighteenth-century thinker Tai Chen.

None of the three men was interested in abstract theorizing for its own sake. Wang, like the others, was stimulated by the critical problems of his time to undertake a careful study of history, developing analyses and insights still stimulating to modern students. Combining a deep study of *The Classic of Change* with his historical investigations, Wang emphasized the need for people to suit their actions to the exigencies of historical circumstance, recognizing that the policies and institutions of one age are not necessarily suitable for another. This was hardly a new idea, although Wang gave it new emphasis. More radical was his rejection of cultural as well as temporal universalism. Wang regarded culture as molded by a people's environment, with the result that he considered Chinese and "barbarian" cultures equally valid, each in its own place. Wang believed they should be kept apart: Chinese should no more "civilize" foreign peoples than "barbarians" should interfere with China. Ideally Chinese and "barbarians" should resemble fish: passing by each other without taking the least notice. This position contrasted sharply with the facts, of course: "barbarian" Manchu domination over China in the name of universalistic Confucianism.

Like Wang Fu-chih, Huang Tsung-hsi had an abiding interest in the study of history. A great historian, he authored a compendium of Ming thought but did not live to complete a similar undertaking for the Sung and Yüan, which were left to a disciple to finish. Both remain invaluable for the study of Chinese philosophy and intellectual history. Of the three thinkers, Huang was the least hostile to Late Ming thinkers in the tradition of Wang Yang-ming, whose emphasis on the mind was frequently cited by early Ch'ing critics as a cause for the weakness and even collapse of the old dynasty.

Huang's study of history and politics led him to formulate a stringent critique of imperial despotism. This is contained in his *Plan for the Prince (Ming-i tai-fang lu)*, a wide-ranging critical study of government, its measures and institutions. In a scathing attack on the selfishness of imperial despots, he wrote:

> In ancient times the people were considered hosts and the prince was the guest. All of his life the prince spent working for the sake of the people. Now the prince is the host and the people are guests. Because of the prince the people can find peace and happiness nowhere.[1]

Among the policies advocated by Huang were the restoration of a strong chief ministership and tax and land reforms; for a Confucian he was unusually well disposed toward law. But he placed his ultimate faith in education, stressing the importance of schools and reaffirming the Confucian insistence that the emperor and his highest officials attentively listen to the lectures of the wisest in the land. Huang was attracted to the old preimperial system of decentralized government because he felt it provided local officials with maximum authority to exercise their moral and political wisdom.

Ku Yen-wu was in substantial agreement with the ideas Huang expressed in his *Plan for the Prince,* including the need for decentralization, but, unlike Huang, he was bitterly critical of Wang Yang-ming and Late Ming thinkers whose "empty words" he likened to the "pure talk" (*ch'ing-t'an*) of the Chinese scholars during the transition from Late Han to barbarian rule. (See Chapter 4.) Instead, Ku insisted on real and practical learning, solidly based on scholarship. This meant going back to the original sources to reconstruct their meaning rather than relying on Sung and later commentaries. Ku himself wrote important studies in historical geography and inscriptions, but he is especially famous for his work in historical phonetics. His essays, collected under the title *Records of Daily Knowledge (Jih-chih lu)*, show the range and critical spirit also found in the work of his two great contemporaries. But Ku was far more influential than they, for he became the virtual founder of Ch'ing philological scholarship and what was termed "Han Learning," as distinguished from the metaphysical speculation associated with "Sung Learning."

Textual scholarship was a field in which Ch'ing scholars subsequently made great contributions. It was a field encouraged by K'ang-hsi and later emperors. He and his successors were also generous art patrons, but in painting as in thought, some of the most vital achievements were made by men who removed themselves from political life after the fall of the Ming.

Early Ch'ing Painting

Some of the most original painters withdrew to Buddhist monasteries on the fall of the Ming and became monks. One such artist was Hung-jen (1610–63), the greatest of a group of painters from Anhwei. His work has been character-

Figure 14-2 Hung-jen, *The Coming of Autumn*. Hanging scroll, ink on paper, 122.4 cm high.

ized as "sparse, linear, angular, with little vegetation to break up the contours."[2] In his masterpiece, *The Coming of Autumn* (see Figure 14-2), he displays a marvelous sense of structural depth. He was a student of the work of earlier painters, especially Ni Tsan with whom he was already being compared during his lifetime. But the major influence on his work was a profound love for the Yellow Mountains, which he studied and drew constantly. In a sense, therefore, it can be said that nature was his greatest teacher.

Although Hung-jen had his followers, other seventeenth-century painters were too highly individualistic to found schools or perpetuate styles. One of the most eccentric was Chu Ta (ca. 1626–1705), also called Pa-ta Shan-jen, who was distantly related to the Ming imperial house. His personal behavior

Figure 14-3   Chu Ta (Pa-ta Shan-jen), *Fish and Rocks.* Section of hand-scroll, ink on paper, 29.2 cm × 157 cm. The Cleveland Museum of Art.

was distinctly odd: he sang and laughed frequently but refused to speak. His painting was equally unusual: surging landscapes, huge lotuses, and birds and fish with the eyes of a Zen patriarch. His hand-scroll *Fish and Rocks* (see Figure 14-3) begins with a section (not shown here) done with a dry brush, and the brushwork becomes wetter as the painting proceeds—note the water plants and lotuses on the left. Poems and painting remain cryptic in meaning. The strange rock invites speculation, or perhaps it is "simply the outpouring of the artist's passing mood that has condensed into the picture of a rock."[3] Another strong individualist was Kung Hsien (ca. 1618–89). Although his manner of building up his strokes to render light and shade suggests Western influence, his brooding landscapes are the products of his personal vision.

Tao-chi (ca. 1641–1717), or Shih-t'ao, was another descendant of the Ming imperial house who became a Buddhist monk, but in name only. In addition to his paintings he is known for his *Notes on Painting* (*Hua-yü-lu*) in which he writes of the single line from which the whole painting grows. Like all post-Sung painters he is keenly aware of himself as living and working in a post–classical age under the long shadows of the old masters. But he insists on the autonomy of his art, proclaiming that his paintings are as much a part of himself as are his beard and eyebrows, his lungs and bowels. His was a forceful vision, and he had an original technique, particularly in his use of color. Tao-chi eventually became reconciled to the Manchu dynasty and was twice received by Emperor K'ang-hsi. In the more relaxed political atmosphere which followed, he felt free to acknowledge his royal Ming lineage in his seal (the equivalent of a Western artist's signature).

Not all painters of the early Ch'ing were eccentrics or individualists. There were also more orthodox painters. Outstanding were four artists all named Wang. Wang Shih-min (1592–1680) was a student of Tung Ch'i-ch'ang, the great Ming master whose influence on the idea as well as the practice of painting can be seen even in the works of the individualists. Both Wang Shih-min and his friend and second cousin Wang Chien (1598–1677) were influenced by

山川渾厚

草木華滋

甲辰春倣巨然筆為

脩翁老先生壽 王翬

Figure 14-4   Wang Hui,
*Landscape in the Style of
Chü-jan.* Hanging scroll,
ink on paper, dated 1664,
131 cm × 65.5 cm.
Collection of Mr. and
Mrs. Earl Morse.

Yüan painting. Their most gifted student was Wang Hui (1632–1717). His landscape, done in the style of the Sung master Chü-jan, shown in Figure 14-4 is typical in that he uses a past master as his point of departure to create a painting very much his own. The overall composition may not be new, but as Wen Fong has pointed out, his originality lies in the vitality of his brushwork, which infuses his painting with kinetic energy.[4]

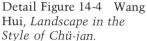

Detail Figure 14-4   Wang Hui, *Landscape in the Style of Chü-jan.*

In 1691 Wang Hui received an imperial commission to supervise the painting of a series of scrolls commemorating K'ang-hsi's southern tour. Shown even more favor by the emperor was Wang Yüan-ch'i (1642–1715), who became K'ang-hsi's chief artistic adviser in 1700. His fascination with form and structure and his concentration on surface space have been compared with Cézanne. Both "seem to have occupied a comparable position in their respective painting traditions; each in his way representing the rejection of a traditional, rationalized spatial organization in favor of a formal construction in abstract space."[5] They differ in that the art of Wang Yüan-ch'i, like that of Wang Hui, was at heart calligraphic. Another difference was that the Chinese artist had the good fortune to be understood and appreciated by the political and artistic establishment of his day.

The Reign of K'ang-hsi

Emperor K'ang-hsi was on the throne from 1662 to 1722 and actually ruled from 1668 on. As already noted, he was able to complete the Manchu conquest of China in campaigns fought largely by Chinese troops under Chinese generals. After the incorporation of Taiwan, K'ang-hsi turned his attention to China's borders in the North and West. In the Amur River region his army destroyed a Russian Cossack base. This success was followed by the Treaty of Nerchinsk signed with Russia in 1689, which settled frontier problems between the two great empires and regularized relations between them. It also removed the threat of a possible alliance between the Russians and a confederation of Western Mongols. Against the latter, K'ang-hsi personally led his troops in 1696–97 and won a great victory. Around the middle of the seventeenth century, Western Mongols had intervened in the politico-religious struggles taking place in Tibet and had remained as conquerors. Under K'ang-hsi, the Ch'ing too became deeply involved. In 1720 Ch'ing armies entered Tibet and installed a pro-Chinese Dalai Lama (the spiritual and secular ruler of Tibet). This was to be the first but not the last Ch'ing intervention in Tibet.

K'ang-hsi's martial exploits were, in part, a reflection of a conscious sense of identification with his Manchu forebears and his desire to preserve the traditional Manchu way of life, which he saw as essential to maintaining Manchu supremacy. Another expression of this feeling was the organization of great hunting expeditions, in which he took considerable delight. To help preserve Manchu distinctiveness, one of the first acts of K'ang-hsi's reign was the closing of Manchuria to Chinese immigration. During the Ch'ing, Manchus were not allowed to marry Chinese, and Manchu women were not allowed to bind their feet. K'ang-hsi was very much the Manchu, but he was not anti-Chinese. Like previous non-Chinese invaders, however, he felt impelled to take steps to avoid being submerged in the larger Chinese population and more sophisticated Chinese culture.

Under K'ang-hsi a strict balance was maintained between Manchus and Chinese in the top metropolitan administrative posts, and in the provinces, generally, a Chinese governor was counterbalanced by a governor-general, usually placed over two provinces, who was a Manchu, a Mongol, or a Chinese bannerman. Military security was provided first of all by hereditary banner forces garrisoned in strategic locations throughout China. They lived apart from the general population in their own communities and were commanded by a general responsible directly to Peking. Another group used by the emperor were his Chinese bondservants, who managed the imperial household and could be used for confidential tasks. Like eunuchs, they were dependent on imperial favor, but unlike eunuchs, they did not offend Chinese feelings. Bondservants were used by K'ang-hsi to submit secret memorials on conditions in the provinces and also managed the emperor's personal treasury and the monopolies, including the maritime customs.

K'ang-hsi was a very vigorous man. He rose well before dawn each day to go through a great stack of memorials before receiving officials, beginning at 5 A.M. (later changed to 7 A.M. to accommodate officials not living near the palace). His tours of personal inspection in the South are famous. To show his benevolence, he reduced taxes and forced Manchu aristocrats to desist from seizing Chinese lands. He was also a man of wide intellectual interests, including, as we have seen, Western learning. He won the affection of many of the Chinese literati by holding a special examination in 1679, and not only patronized artists but sponsored the compilation of the official Ming history, a great phrase dictionary, a giant encyclopedia, and an exhaustive dictionary of Chinese characters. The philosophy of Chu Hsi received his special support.

Yung-cheng

K'ang-hsi's reign was of a length unprecedented in China's history, and he was altogether one of the most successful Chinese emperors, but he was unable to provide for a smooth succession. After his death, the throne was seized in a military coup by a prince who became Emperor Yung-cheng (r. 1723–35). After he became emperor, Yung-cheng censored the record of his accession to the throne and also suppressed other writings he deemed inimical to his regime, particularly those with an anti-Manchu bias. He was a tough and hard-working ruler bent on effective government at minimum expense. His main institutional innovation was the formation of a five-man Grand Council, which became the chief body concerned with high policy, superseding the Grand Secretariat, which was now reduced to handling routine administration. Like his father, Yung-cheng used military force to preserve the dynasty's position in Outer Mongolia, and when Tibet was torn by civil war during 1717–28, he intervened militarily, leaving a Ch'ing resident backed by a military garrison to pursue the dynasty's interests. His reign was despotic, efficient, vigorous, and brief. By the simple device of sealing the name of the heir-apparent in a box kept in the throne room, Yung-cheng was able to assure that on his death there would be no struggle over the succession. Thus he prepared the way for what was to be the Ch'ing's most splendid reign.

Ch'ien-lung

During Ch'ien-lung's reign (1736–95), the Ch'ing achieved its greatest prosperity, and geographic expansion into Central Asia reached its greatest extent. (See map, p. 329.) This was made possible not only by Chinese strength but also by the disunity and declining strength of the Inner Asian peoples. The declining vitality of these peoples has been subject to various interpretations. As summarized by Morris Rossabi, the most plausible explanations include the diminishing importance of the international caravan trade in an age of developing maritime commerce, a trend toward the development of sedentary societies marked by urbanization, and Russian expansion that reduced the area to which tribes could flee in retreat, thereby reducing their mobility.[6]

Under Ch'ien-lung, Chinese Turkestan was incorporated into the Ch'ing dynasty's rule and renamed Sinkiang, while to the West, Ili was conquered and garrisoned. The Ch'ing also dominated Outer Mongolia after inflicting a final defeat on the Western Mongols. Its policy there was to preserve Mongol institutions, but it allowed Chinese merchants to enter and exploit the people, thus reinforcing the anti-Chinese animosities of the animal-herding Mongols. It is no accident that when the Ch'ing fell in the twentieth century, the Mongols promptly declared their independence. Throughout this period there were continued Mongol interventions in Tibet and a reciprocal spread of Tibetan Lamaism in Mongolia. Ch'ien-lung again sent armies into Tibet and firmly established the Dalai Lama as ruler, with a Ch'ing resident and garrison to preserve Chinese suzereinty. Other than that, no attempt was made to integrate Tibet into the empire after the manner of Sinkiang. Further afield, military campaigns against the Annamese, Burmese, Nepalese, and Gurkhas forced these peoples to submit and send tribute.

This expansion involved millions of square miles and brought into the empire non-Chinese peoples (such as Uighurs, Kazakhs, Kirghiz, and Mongols) who were at least potentially hostile. It was also a very expensive enterprise. The dynasty enjoyed unprecedented prosperity and managed in the mid-1780s to accumulate a healthy financial reserve, but its resources were not inexhaustible. Yet the emperor delighted in the glory and wealth. He built a sumptuous summer residence, partly of Western design, and undertook grand tours of the empire, including six tours of the South. In his policy toward the literati, he combined K'ang-hsi's generous patronage of scholarship with Yung-cheng's suspiciousness of anti-Manchu writings. The greatest project sponsored by him was the *Complete Library of the Four Treasuries* (*Ssu-k'u ch'üan-shu*) of 36,000 volumes. It preserved many books, but it was also intended as a means of ferreting out and suppressing those deemed offensive.

Decorative Arts

The splendor and opulence of the age was reflected in its ceramics and decorative arts. In this respect also the Ch'ien-lung period built on the achievements of the two preceding reigns. Under K'ang-hsi, the royal kilns produced great numbers of bowls, vases, plates, and vessels, many of them manufactured especially for the growing foreign market. Among the most admired are oxblood vases, although more common were pieces whose basic color was green (*famille verte*). The plate shown in Figure 14-5 is painted to show a scene with six ladies sitting on a terrace. Along with their artistic qualities, such decorated ceramics provide much information about dress, architecture, and upper-class life and leisure.

In the Yung-cheng period a pinkish rose color (*famille rose*) became the favorite. Fine copies of Sung ware were produced during the Ch'ien-lung period, but there was no return to Sung tastes. Among the most exquisite and finely crafted products of the Ch'ien-lung kilns were porcelains produced at the imperial kilns. Fine examples of the colorful ceramics in many shapes abound in museum collections.

Bright colors were an important feature of interior decoration. The use of colored tiles as well as paint helped to produce a vibrant effect. Enamelware (especially cloisonné—that is, ware on which the enameled areas are separated by thin strips of metal), intricately carved lacquers and ivories, ornate embroideries, highly decorated furniture all testify to the era's taste for fine craftsmanship and rich detail. The entire style of this era evoked the enthusiasm of European visitors and helped to encourage the eighteenth-century European craze for "chinoiserie" and the manufacture, both in China and in Europe, of

Figure 14-5 Dish painting in *famille verte* enamels. K'ang-hsi period, diam. 61 cm.

highly commercial Sino-European products for the Western market. At their best, Chinese art objects of the eighteenth century are impressive in their high craftsmanship. Yet, to borrow a term used by early eighteenth-century Chinese scholars in their discussions of painting, the art was rather "overripe."

During the last years of the Ch'ien-lung era there were definite indications that the dynasty had passed its peak and that there was trouble ahead. Before discussing these, however, it is well to consider some of the other aspects of the century when the Ch'ing was strong and seemed well.

Culture of the Literati in the Eighteenth Century

Scholarship continued to flourish in eighteenth-century China. At the beginning of the dynasty, Ku Yen-wu, as already noted, wrote extensively on both statescraft and philology. Modern readers know him best for the former, but his immediate successors were more interested in his contributions to the latter. As a result, Ch'ing scholars made important, even iconoclastic, discoveries concerning the questionable historicity of parts of such venerated classics as *The Classic of Change, The Classic of History,* and the *Records of Rites.* However, the concentration on philology easily led to the view that textual studies alone were truly "solid" (in the sense that they avoided abstract speculation) and "practical" (in the sense that this seemed the best way to uncover the meaning of the classics). The resulting narrowing of intellectual interest is exemplified by the contrast between Yen Yüan (1635–1704) and his chief disciple, Li Kung (1659–1733). Although Yen Yüan was born too late to be a Ming loyalist, he shared the concerns of the generation that lived through the Ming-

Ch'ing transition. Accordingly, Yen condemned quiet sitting and book learning as standing in the way of true self-cultivation capable of "changing the world"; and he studied military science and medicine. But Li Kung expounded his teachings in the form of commentaries on the classics.

A major scholar and theorist was Tai Chen (1723–77), who made important contributions to linguistics, astronomy, mathematics, and geography as well as philosophy. Like most of the creative seventeenth-century thinkers, he rejected the metaphysical existence of *li*, which he considered simply the pattern of things. Similarly he disputed Chu Hsi's dualistic theory of human nature, insisting that this went against the teachings of Mencius, that human nature is one whole and all good, and that moral perfection consists in the fulfillment of one's natural inclinations.

Tai Chen shared his age's faith in philology, but this was not true of his contemporary Chang Hsüeh-ch'eng (1738–1801), who strongly disliked philologi-

Figure 14-6 Kao Ch'i-p'ei, *Young Crane under a Wu-t'ung Tree.* Hanging scroll, ink on paper, 95 cm × 44 cm.

cal studies and sought for meaning in the study and writing of history. Chang is perhaps most famous for his thesis that "the six classics are all history," by which he meant that they were not "empty" theoretical discussions but that they document antiquity and illustrate the Tao. A scholar must not stop at the facts but get at the meaning. Chang once compared a work of history to a living organism: Its facts are like bones, the writing is like the skin, and its meaning corresponds to the organism's vital spirit.

Along with history and philosophy, another subject of perennial concern to Chinese scholars was the function and evaluation of literature. The poet Yüan Mei (1716–97) held that the purpose of poetry is to express emotion, that it must give pleasure, and rejected the didactic view, held, among others, by Chang Hsüeh-ch'eng, that it must convey moral instruction. Yüan's poetry and prose reflect the life of a talented, refined eighteenth-century hedonist, unconventional within the bounds of good taste, and marginally aware of the exotic West. One of his prize possessions was a large Western mirror much admired by his lady pupils. Among Yüan's less conventional works are a cookbook and a collection of ghost stories. His interest in the latter was shared by his friend, the painter Lo P'ing (1735–99), the youngest, and last, of the so-called "Eight Eccentrics of Yangchow," a man who claimed actually to have seen the apparitions he painted.

In the eighteenth century, painters of various schools were at work: professionals working in the meticulous and mannered "northern" style, eclectics drawing on diverse traditions and models, and individualists striving, sometimes excessively, for originality. An interesting and prolific artist was the Manchu painter Kao Ch'i-p'ei (1672–1734). Even in the Sung and earlier, artists had experimented with unconventional materials instead of using a brush, but none had gone as far as Kao who painted with the balls of his fingers, the side of his hand, and a long fingernail split like a pen for drawing lines. Some six hundred years separate Kao's *Young Crane under a Wu-t'ung Tree* (see Figure 14-6) and Emperor Hui-tsung's parakeet (see Figure 8-1). In that time not only the means but the purpose of art, and the artist's self-conception, had changed.

Ch'ing painters and scholars generally perceived themselves as latecomers in a long and revered tradition. As such they faced a dilemma similar to that of painters, poets, and composers of our own time who no longer feel they can contribute to the traditional lines of development in their arts, that is, be another Rembrandt, Beethoven, and so forth. The classical masters had said what needed to be said, and the creative opportunities available to those who would imitate or compete with them were limited. Moreover, what had been valid for one age could not serve another. But if the time for classical achievements was past, future directions were by no means clear.

It was characteristic of the age—and here the analogy to our own times is also instructive—that old canons of art were rejected. Thus some artists cultivated the notion that the epitome of art was non-art, that is, the deliberate cultivation of innocent awkwardness. Similarly, it was now quite acceptable for an eccentric to display his eccentricity by selling his paintings. Both Kao and Lo did so without jeopardizing their "amateur" status. The favorite place for such men was Yangchow, where wealthy salt merchants derived prestige as well as pleasure from supporting a world of painting, poetry, and calligraphy. Including, but extending beyond, the circle of such sophisticates was the audience for popular drama and vernacular literature. The latter in particular reached new heights.

Ch'ing Fiction

Many of the dynasty's best writers and thinkers were men who had failed in the examination route to success, an experience which perhaps helped them to view society with a measure of critical and even satiric detachment. The examinations themselves were a favorite target. P'u Sung-ling (1640–1715), a short story writer, wrote this account of the seven transformations of a candidate in the provincial examination:

> When he first enters the examination compound and walks along, panting under his heavy load of luggage, he is just like a beggar. Next, while undergoing the personal body search and being scolded by the clerks and shouted at by the soldiers, he is just like a prisoner. When he finally enters his cell and, along with the other candidates, stretches his neck to peer out, he is just like the larva of a bee. When the examination is finished at last and he leaves, his mind in a haze and his legs tottering, he is just like a sick bird that has been released from a cage. While he is wondering when the results will be announced and waiting to learn whether he passed or failed, so nervous that he is startled even by the rustling of the trees and the grass and is unable to sit or stand still, his restlessness is like that of a monkey on a leash. When at last the results are announced and he has definitely failed, he loses his vitality like one dead, rolls over on his side, and lies without moving, like a poisoned fly. Then, when he pulls himself together and stands up, he is provoked by every sight and sound, gradually flings away everything within his reach, and complains of the illiteracy of the examiners. When he calms down at last, he finds everything in the room broken. At this time he is like a pigeon smashing its own precious eggs. These are the seven transformations of a candidate.[7]

This examination was held in a labyrinthine compound, with the candidates housed in individual cells where they had to spend the night. It was an eerie place sealed off from the rest of the world, for during an examination session the great gates could not be opened for any reason whatsoever. (If a man died during the examination, his body was wrapped in straw matting and thrown over the wall.) Thus it was a perfect setting for numerous tales of ghosts, usually the spirits of jilted maidens come to wreak their vengeance on the men who had done them wrong.

One of the two outstanding novels of the Ch'ing was *The Scholars* (*Ju-lin wai-shih*), by Wu Ching-tzu (1701–54). It is primarily a satire on the examination system but also catches in its net an assortment of other human follies, and presents vignettes of the pompous and the ignorant, the unworldly scholar and those who cheat him, the intricacies of social and political life, and so on. Although it is episodic in organization and somewhat uneven in quality, it incorporates certain technical advances in the art of storytelling, notably in the way it allows its characters to reveal their personalities gradually rather than labeling them at the very start. It is a fine work of literature as well as a treasure house for the social historian.

China's most beloved and greatest novel is *The Dream of the Red Chamber* (*Hung-lou meng*), also translated as *The Story of the Stone*. Like *The Scholars* it offers priceless insights into Ch'ing society, this time from the vantage point of a large, eminent family in decline. With rich detail embedded in its narrative fabric, it reveals much about how such a family was organized and functioned, the relationship between the generations and the sexes, the life of women, the status of servants, and so on, and it does this with fine psychological characterization based on the personal experience of its author, Ts'ao Hsüeh-ch'in (?1715–63). Ts'ao's Buddhist-Taoist view of life gives the novel philosophical depth; C. T. Hsia has written that "it embodies the supreme tragic expression in Chinese literature,"[8] and that for its main protagonist, "the ultimate tragic conflict lies in a tug of war between the opposing claims of compassion and detachment."[9]

Despite its excellence *The Dream of the Red Chamber* did not gain respectability in scholarly circles; it was not until modern times that the novel was appreciated as a serious literary genre on a level with poetry, essays, and history. As a literary genre, the novel was considered frivolous and low class by the elite, who nevertheless read novels when no one was looking. Today, the novel is regarded as the period's greatest literary achievement and remains one of its most valuable mirrors, reflecting a society which was prosperous but whose continued well-being was far from assured.

Economic Prosperity

The eighteenth century was a period of great prosperity in China. Economic development had been retarded by the destruction and dislocation that accompanied the collapse of the Ming, but once peace and order were restored by the Ch'ing, the economy more than recovered.

The central economic fact of this period was an increase in agricultural production. This was partly the result of the maximum geographical spread of known products and techniques: superior strains of rice, improved irrigation methods, and better fertilizers, such as soybean cakes. However, production was also increased through the introduction of new crops originally native to America: corn, the sweet potato, and the peanut. The sweet potato and the peanut were of special importance because they did not require the same quality soil or climatic conditions as other products of Chinese agriculture and thus could be grown on land not previously cultivated. One beneficial result of increased output was tax reduction: with agricultural production up, tax rates could be lowered without reducing revenues. Emperor Yung-cheng's reform of the tax system particularly benefited poor peasant farmers. The century saw an increase in Chinese life expectancy and an all-around improvement in the standard of living. These, in turn, undoubtedly made further contributions to agricultural production and to economic development generally.

Agriculture provided a foundation for the development of trade and manufacturing. Of the latter, the pottery kilns have already been mentioned. Another industry which now flourished was the cotton trade. Silk and hemp, brewing and paper, mining and metal working deserve mention as areas of strong activity, as do the spread of tea and sugar production. Stimulated by an increase in internal trade there was a growth of market towns and the flourishing of merchant guilds, which operated on an interprovincial and interregional basis. The salt merchants of Yangchow, dealing in a government monopoly, were especially prosperous. Although the total value of internal trade far outweighed that of foreign commerce, the latter, too, contributed to Chinese well-being. Throughout the century the balance of overseas trade was in China's favor, and there was a strong inflow of gold and silver.

A major result of agricultural growth, peace, and prosperity was an increase in the size of China's population. By the end of the eighteenth century more people lived in China than in Europe; the Chinese population was in the neighborhood of 300 million, about double what it had been two centuries earlier. An increased population made increased demands on the economy. Growth in production could not keep up with expanding population. Thus, by the end of the eighteenth century, population growth was putting new strains on the economy, the state, and society. It may be worth noting that this phenomenon was not unique to China. The improvement in the living standards of Chinese peasants in this period was mirrored in other parts of the world (for example, France and Japan), and the stresses resulting from population growth helped to undermine the traditional order in China as elsewhere. The challenge of population growth did not go unnoticed. The Chinese scholar Hung Liang-chi (1746 −1809) first wrote about the dangers inherent in this process in 1793.

The new population pressures resulted in population shifts: the "filling up" of previously marginal areas in China, and the emigration of Chinese people into Southeast Asia, where they subsequently became important minorities in a number of states. Population pressures also helped contribute to the increasing difficulty even superbly educated men had in winning an official appointment, for there was no increase in the number of positions in the civil service to keep pace with the growing numbers of candidates. Even in the Sung there were cases of men who spent a lifetime taking examinations—when the emperor asked his age, one such man replied, "fifty years ago twenty-three." Now the aged *chin-shih* became a stock figure in literature. The government even relaxed standards for men over seventy so that, past retirement age, they could at least enjoy the psychological satisfaction of receiving a degree. In an effort to weed out candidates, new examinations were introduced. Thus in 1788 the re-

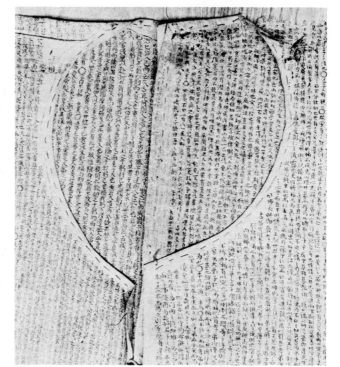

Figure 14-7 Cheating
shirt. Fujii Museum (Fujii
Saiseikai Yurinkan),
Kyōto.

examination of provincial and metropolitan graduates was introduced. That brought the total minimum number of examinations required for the *chin-shih* to eight, not counting a final placement examination. By this time the criteria for judging papers had become exceedingly formalistic. Candidates spent years practicing eight-legged essays, and bookshops did a thriving business selling model answers. In the meantime, the old battle of wits between examiners and cheaters remained a draw. (See the "cheating shirt," Figure 14-7.)

The unsatisfactory state of the examination system, and the tendency of the government to tinker and elaborate rather than reform and innovate, suggests a dangerous hardening of the institutional arteries, and during the last twenty years of Ch'ien-lung's reign there were other signs of trouble. One institution Ch'ing statesmen were not worried about because it seemed to be working well was the system for dealing with European trade. Yet the mission of Lord Macartney to Peking in 1793 (the same year Hung Liang-chi set down his thoughts concerning the population problem) indicated that the British did not share the Ch'ing satisfaction with the status quo.

The Canton System

During the period of dynastic consolidation there was very little Sino-European trade. Then from 1685 to 1759 there was multiport trade, while the British East India Company and others tried out the Chinese market and the Chinese gradually developed the components of what became the Canton System (1760–1842). It is called the Canton System because trade was now confined to the single port of Canton where a special area was set aside for the warehouses (called "factories") of the foreign traders. The traders were allowed to reside there but were not allowed to bring their wives and settle down.

In all their transactions foreign traders were required to deal with a group of Chinese merchants who had been granted a monopoly of foreign trade. These merchants belonged to the Cohong, an association of firms (or hong) established for that purpose. In theory the Cohong was composed of a maximum of thirteen hong, but in practice there were only seven or eight such establishments, supervised by an imperial official who usually squeezed a good deal of personal profit out of his position. Each foreign ship was placed under the responsibility of a particular hong, which handled not only commercial matters but also saw to it that duties were paid and that the foreigners conducted themselves properly. Under this system, the foreigners were not granted direct access to Chinese officials, nor was allowance made for government-to-government relations. On the British side the prime agent was the East India Company, which enjoyed a monopoly of trade between England and China.

These arrangements suited the Chinese more than they did the English; the purpose of Macartney's mission was to expand trade and open European-style diplomatic relations. He failed, and for the time being the system continued to operate as before. Not until the nineteenth century did China face a Europe which could no longer be contained.

Internal Decay

As the expense of military campaigns far beyond the bounds of China proper mounted, the resources of even the prosperous Ch'ien-lung regime were strained to the utmost, while administrative laxity and corruption were rendering the government less efficient and more expensive. The worst offender was a Manchu favorite of Emperor Ch'ien-lung, a man named Ho-shen (1750–99), who rode high for twenty-three years. Assured of imperial support, he built up a network of corruption and amassed a huge fortune, leaving the enormous sum of 20 million taels when he died. Although bitterly detested he could not be removed, for he never lost Ch'ien-lung's confidence and affection. An attack on Ho-shen implied an attack on the aging emperor's own judgment and, furthermore, suggested the presence of the disease of factionalism. Perhaps Ch'ien-lung was especially sensitive to any signs of factionalism since his father, Emperor Yung-cheng, had written a very strong critique on this subject. Like his political authority, the moral and intellectual authority of the emperor were now beyond question. Emperor Ch'ien-lung abdicated after his sixtieth year of rule in order not to rule longer than his illustrious grandfather, but he continued to dominate the government until his death in 1799. Only then was Ho-shen removed and, in lieu of execution, allowed to take his own life.

As always, the burden of extravagance and corruption was borne by the common people. As a result many of them joined in the White Lotus Rebellion, which broke out in 1796 and was not completely suppressed until 1804. At its height it affected Szechwan, Hupeh, Honan, Kansu, and Shensi. The rebellion drew its following by promising the coming of Maitreya, a restoration of the Ming, and the rescue of the people from all suffering. It gained momentum as it attracted the destitute and displaced and proved the power of its cause. It was also assisted by the ineffectiveness of the dynasty's response: government generals used the occasion to line their own pockets and bannermen proved their total incompetence. Not until after Ho-shen's fall did the government make real headway. A new, very capable commander was appointed, disaffected areas were slowly taken from the rebels, and militia bands organized by the local elite, whose members had the most to lose from radical social change, proved effective in putting down insurgency.

Ho-shen and the rebellion were both destroyed in the end, but corruption in government and misery in the countryside remained to plague the dynasty in the nineteenth century. Yet on the local level Chinese society remained resilient. The problems faced by the government and the people were not without precedent and seemed capable of solution within the boundaries of existing values and institutions. On the international level, the perennial problem of invasion from Inner Asia had been laid to rest, but a new, very different and threatening foreign problem was about to emerge. Entering the new century, China was stable but not particularly vigorous; and perhaps this very stability was a liability when China was drawn into the unstable world of modern global history.

NOTES

1. Wm. Theodore de Bary, Wing-tsit Chan, and Burton Watson, comps., *Sources of Chinese Tradition* (New York: Columbia University Press, 1960), pp. 387–88.

2. James Cahill, *Fantastics and Eccentrics in Chinese Painting* (New York: The Asia Society, 1967), p. 44.

3. Roger Goepper, *The Essence of Chinese Painting* (Boston: Boston Book and Art Shop, 1963), p.138.

4. Wen Fong, quoted in Roderick Whitfield, *In Pursuit of Antiquity: Chinese Paintings of the Ming and Ch'ing Dynasties from the Collection of Mr. and Mrs. Earl Morse* (Princeton: The Art Museum, Princeton University, 1969), p. 41.

5. *Ibid.*, p. 183.

6. Morris Rossabi, *China and Inner Asia—From 1368 to the Present Day* (New York: Pica Press, 1975), pp. 139–40. Rossabi does not think Buddhism was a major factor, although it may have contributed to the decline. *Ibid.*, pp. 140–41.

7. Quoted in Ichisada Miyazaki, *China's Examination Hell,* trans. Conrad Schirokauer (Tokyo and New York: John Weatherhill, 1976), pp. 57–58.

8. C. T. Hsia, *The Classic Chinese Novel* (New York: Columbia University Press, 1968), p. 246.

9. *Ibid.*, p. 264.

徳川時代之日本

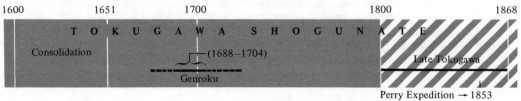

| 1600 | | 1651 | | 1700 | | | 1800 | | 1868 |

TOKUGAWA SHOGUNATE

Consolidation

(1688–1704)

Genroku

Late Tokugawa

Perry Expedition → 1853

15 *Tokugawa Japan*

Although Tokugawa Ieyasu did not assume the title of shogun until 1603, it is customary and convenient to date the beginning of the Tokugawa period from the battle of Sekigahara, in 1600. The Tokugawa thus antedates the Ch'ing by forty-four years; interestingly, its end also antedates the end of the Ch'ing by forty-four years.

During the seventeenth and eighteenth centuries, Japan enjoyed peace, considerable economic growth, and a flourishing urban culture. To guard against dangers from abroad, the shogun adopted a policy of seclusion from the rest of the world, and at home the regime sought social stability by freezing class lines. Consequently, the Tokugawa has been seen as a conservative, even reactionary, period charged with suppressing change and retarding Japan's modern-

349

ization. Tokugawa rigidity has also been cited in explanation of the persistence of traditional elements even in contemporary Japan. But the remarkable ease of the transition after Japan was reopened in the mid-nineteenth century, and the rapidity of Japan's modernization thereafter, would have been impossible without the foundations laid in the Tokugawa period.

The Political System

The essential structure of the Tokugawa political system was devised by Ieyasu and completed by his two immediate successors, Hidetada (1616–23) and Iemitsu (1623–51). By the middle of the seventeenth century, the system was in full operation. For example, it was Iemitsu who persecuted the Christians and closed the country to all but the Dutch and Chinese at Nagasaki, but the basic policy of seclusion had been set by the founder. The main problem facing the Tokugawa, however, came at home, not from abroad.

Ieyasu rose to supremacy as the leader of a group of daimyo, each of whom was backed by his own vassals and supported by his independent power base. The daimyo were by no means all deeply committed to the Tokugawa. Hideyoshi's recent failure to establish a dynasty demonstrated, if any demonstration was needed, the folly of relying solely on the loyalty of such men, especially when passing on the succession to a minor. Ieyasu himself assured the smooth transfer of power to his son by resigning from the office of shogun, in 1605, after holding it for only two years. But he continued in actual control until his death, working to ensure the continuity of Tokugawa rule.

All the daimyo were the shogun's vassals, bound to him by solemn oath, and when a daimyo's heir succeeded to his domain, the new daimyo had to sign his pledge of vassalage to the shogun in blood. Still, some vassals were more reliable than others, and the Tokugawa classified them into three groups. Least trusted and potentially the most dangerous were the "outside," or allied, daimyo (*tozama*), who were too powerful to be considered Tokugawa subordinates. Virtually all of these, like Ieyasu, had been vassals of Hideyoshi. Some had supported Ieyasu at the battle of Sekigahara, but others came over to the Tokugawa only after the outcome of that battle left them no other choice. More trustworthy were the "house daimyo" (*fudai*), most of whom had been Tokugawa family vassals raised to daimyo status by the Tokugawa and thus, unlike the outside daimyo, they were indebted to the *bakufu* for their status and domains. The third group, the "collateral daimyo" (*shimpan*), were daimyo belonging to Tokugawa branch families. The Tokugawa also held its own lands, which supported its direct retainers. Some of these held fiefs of less than the 10,000 *koku* required for daimyo status, but many of them received stipends directly from the *bakufu*.

When Ieyasu was transferred to the Kantō region by Hideyoshi, he chose as his headquarters the centrally located village of Edo (modern Tokyo), then consisting of about one hundred houses but destined to become one of the world's great cities. The shogunate also maintained castles at Ōsaka and Shizuoka (then called Sumpu) as well as the Nijo Castle in Kyōto, residence of a *bakufu* deputy responsible for the government of the capital city and serving concurrently as the shogun's representative at the Imperial court.

To secure itself militarily, the Tokugawa placed its house daimyo in strategic areas. It dominated the Kantō, central Japan, and Kyōto-Ōsaka regions, while the outside daimyo had their territories in the outer areas. A number of policies were initiated to keep the daimyo from acquiring too much strength. They were restricted to one castle each and had to secure *bakufu* permission before they could repair this castle. They were allowed to maintain only a fixed number of men at arms, and, in line with the seclusion policy, were forbidden to build large ships. To keep the daimyo from forming political alliances which might threaten the *bakufu*, they were required to obtain *bakufu* assent for their marriage plans.

During the first half of the seventeenth century the shogunate enacted a vigorous policy of increasing its own strength at the expense of the daimyo. In this period there were 281 cases in which daimyo were transferred from one fief to another, shuffles which strengthened some and weakened others. Another 213 domains were confiscated outright. This happened sometimes as a disciplinary measure, as when a lord proved incompetent or the domain was torn by a succession dispute. More often confiscation resulted from failure to produce an heir. Deathbed adoptions of an heir were not recognized. By such means the Tokugawa more than tripled the size of its holdings, until its own domain was calculated as worth 6.8 million *koku* of rice. The distribution of their holdings also favored the Tokugawa economically, as it did militarily, since they were in possession of many of Japan's mines and most of the important cities such as Ōsaka, Kyōto, and Nagasaki. In the mid-Tokugawa period collateral daimyo held land worth 2.6 million *koku*; house daimyo, 6.7 million; and outside daimyo, 9.8 million. It is indicative of the decline of their economic and political power that religious institutions held only around 600,000 *koku*, and the emperor and the court nobility could draw on land worth only 187,000 *koku*.

To see to it that the daimyo obeyed *bakufu* orders, the shogunate sent out its own inspectors. It also devised a highly effective system of strengthening itself politically (while at the same time draining the daimyo financially) by requiring them to spend alternate years in residence in Edo, where the *bakufu* could keep them under surveillance. When they did go back home to their domains, they had to leave their wives and children behind as hostages. This system of alternate attendance (*sankin kōtai*) forced the daimyo to spend large sums traveling back and forth with their retinues. The maintenance of suitably elaborate residences in Edo was a further strain on daimyo resources. The daimyo were also called upon to support public projects such as waterworks or the repair of the shogun's castle at Edo, but such exactions were not as burdensome as the constant expense of alternate attendance. The residence requirement had the additional effect of turning Edo into a capital not only of the *bakufu* but of all Japan.

In theory the shogun was the emperor's deputy as well as the feudal overlord of all the daimyo. Thus he had political legitimacy as well as standing at the apex of the military hierarchy. This dual role made him, in effect, responsible for the conduct of foreign affairs. The early *bakufu* also asserted its financial predominance when it reserved for itself the right to issue paper currency. Its regulations extended even to the dress of the daimyo. The final provision of a code issued in 1635 declared, "all matters are to be carried out in accordance with the laws of Edo."[1] The *bakufu's* own domain comprised about a fourth of Japan.

Bakufu-Han Relations

Despite this tendency of the shogunate to establish its preeminence as the central power, the daimyo remained largely free to manage affairs in their own domains or *han*. The *bakufu* usually interfered only when the daimyo proved themselves incapable of managing their *han*, or when problems involving more than one *han* arose. The daimyo themselves were naturally concerned to develop the strength of their own domains while keeping *bakufu* interference to a minimum. Even while tightening the administration of their *han*, their self-interest lay in preserving the decentralized aspect of the larger political system, thereby retaining their own feudal autonomy. Tokugawa government is sometimes described as a "centralized feudalism." Using this terminology, we may say that it was to the daimyo's advantage to keep the system feudal. Their ability to accomplish this is suggested by another expression used by scholars, *"baku-han,"* signifying a system composed of the *bakufu* and the *han.* Both formulations allude to the mixed composition of the Tokugawa system.

Under the fourth shogun, Ietsuna (1651–80), the daimyo regained much of the ground they had lost under his three predecessors. *Bakufu* policy was reversed. There was a drastic decline in the number of daimyo transferred and *han* confiscated. Deathbed adoptions were recognized as legitimate. The shogunate even began permitting *han* to issue their own paper money, a policy which led to the proliferation of local currencies. Anxious to protect their own money, some *han* in the eighteenth century prohibited the use of outside currencies—including the *bakufu's* money!

The vigorous but eccentric fifth shogun, Tsunayoshi (1680–1709) presided over a reassertion of *bakufu* power, which earned him the enmity of the daimyo and lasting ignominy. A scant five years after his death, Tsunayoshi was satirized in a puppet play by Chikamatsu. He was an easy target, for he carried to an extreme his Buddhist devotion to the preservation of animal life and especially his solicitude for dogs. His exaggerated concern for these animals was often expressed at the expense of human well-being and sometimes at the cost of human life; this earned him the epithet "dog shogun." Despite the shogun's personality quirks, his period saw a great flowering of culture as well as a significant return to the policies of the early Tokugawa. However, this resurgence of centralizing activity did not lead to a permanent shift in the power balance nor did it initiate a long-term trend toward greater *bakufu* control. If it had, the shogun's historical image would have been rather different.

Until the end of the Tokugawa, the pendulum continued to swing between the *bakufu* and the *han*. The history and dynamics of this process have been analyzed by Harold Bolitho, who has shown that periods of *bakufu* assertiveness tended to occur under vigorous shoguns working in conjuction with trusted advisors drawn from among the shogunate's low-ranking retainers. Unencumbered by fief or vassals, totally dependent on the shogun, they became his men, free from potential conflicts of interest. Under such regimes, the high-ranking Senior Councilors, always selected from among the house daimyo (*fudai*), were treated with an outward show of respect, but in actual practice they were bypassed and disregarded. Little love was lost between the *fudai* and the new men.

When the shogun was a minor or an incompetent, control over the *bakufu* reverted back to the Senior Councilors, descendants of the Tokugawa's most favored and highly trusted vassals. The service of these vassals had formed the core of Ieyasu's strength, and accordingly he relied on their descendants for continued loyal service to his house. While these men were conscious of their heritage of special obligations toward the shogunate, they also had to consider their particular responsibilities and opportunities as daimyo. The tensions between shogunate and *han*, characteristic of the system, were mirrored in their own persons as they faced the demands of *bakufu* and *han*, demands often in conflict with each other. The usual pattern was for them to act more as daimyo than as *bakufu* officials. It was they who were responsible for the relaxation of *bakufu* policies. Such Senior Councilors did not work to strengthen the shogunate at the expense of the *han* nor were they prepared to sacrifice *han* privileges for the sake of the larger body politic. There were even cases of *han* held by incumbent Senior Councilors prohibiting the export of grain badly needed to combat famine elsewhere in Japan. Thus there were periodic shifts in the balance of power between the *bakufu* and the *han*, but the issue was never resolved completely in favor of one or the other.

The more than 250 *han* varied widely in size, local conditions, and prosperity, nor were all the lands held by a daimyo necessarily contiguous. Some domains were more easily organized than others. In general, the daimyo tended to centralize the administration of their *han* even while guarding their independence vis-à-vis Edo. Operating on a smaller scale than the *bakufu*, the *han* governments were generally more successful in controlling their lord's retainers. Accordingly, the trend for samurai to be divorced from the land and concentrated in the *han* capitals, already visible in the sixteenth century, continued strong under the Tokugawa. By the last decade of the seventeenth century over 80 percent of the daimyo were paying stipends to their samurai. Looking at the system in terms of the samurai rather than their lords, it is significant that by the end of the eighteenth century 90 percent of the samurai were entirely dependent on their stipends. Only 10 percent still retained local roots in the country districts.

Assigned to various administrative, financial, and military duties, the samurai staffed the increasingly bureaucratized administrative machinery of the domains and the *bakufu*. Many of them were now occupied more with government than with military affairs, and numerous samurai followed the urgings of the Tokugawa that in times of peace samurai should devote themselves to study. In this respect as in others, Ieyasu had shown the way when he showed special favor to the Confucian scholar Hayashi Razan (1583–1657), whose family continued to supply the heads of the *bakufu's* Confucian Academy. Sung Confucianism meshed with Ieyasu's anti-Buddhist proclivities. Furthermore, in Japan as in China it proved entirely compatible with bureaucratic government. Intellectually as well as professionally, the samurai of 1800 was quite different from his ancestor of two centuries earlier. In other ways also, Japan experienced great changes during this period.

Economic and Social Change

Economic growth was made possible by peace. Moreover, it was stimulated by a rise in demand created by the need to support the roughly 7 percent of the population which enjoyed samurai status and to meet the growing expenses of the daimyo.

Agricultural productivity increased very substantially. During the Tokugawa, cultivated acreage doubled. Other factors contributing to the increase in output were improvements in technology, the practice of multiple cropping, better seed strains, and improved fertilizers. Useful knowledge was disseminated through agricultural handbooks and manuals. The development of a market network was accompanied by regional specialization in cash crops such as cotton, mulberry trees for the rearing of silk worms, indigo, tobacco, sugar cane, and so forth, but grain continued to be grown in all parts of Japan. Population rose from about 18 million at the beginning of the Tokugawa to around 30 million by the middle of the period. From then until the end of the Tokugawa there were fluctuations in population but no additional long-term increase, as hunger and disease took their toll. Historians report three major Tokugawa famines, 1732–33, 1783–87, and 1833–36, and many lesser ones. As an agricultural land, Japan remained at the mercy of the elements; too much rain or too little, a cold wave, typhoons, or locusts brought widespread starvation. In desperate times people resorted to infanticide.

With the samurai now largely removed from the land, the villages were left virtually autonomous units. They were responsible for the payment of taxes to the *han* government or, in the case of those held directly by the Tokugawa, to the *bakufu.* Within the village, neither the benefits of agricultural growth nor the burdens of taxation were shared equally: there were wide gradations in wealth and power in the countryside. Since tax reassessments were infrequent, wealthy peasants who were able to open new lands and otherwise increase their yields found their incomes rising and were able to accumulate funds with which to acquire still more land.

An increased use of money brought with it a decline in the traditional village social-economic order, under which the economic functions and relations of a household were determined by its standing within the extended family to which it belonged. The main house of the extended family had claims on the services of the lesser households as well as some obligations to look after the poorer members. Furthermore, the heads of the main houses formed the traditional village leadership. During the Tokugawa, wealthy villagers turned more and more to hired labor or tenant farmers to work their land. They also put their money to work in rural commerce and industry, and engaged in money-lending, the processing of vegetable oils, the production of soya sauce, and sake brewing. Since these wealthy villagers did not necessarily belong to the old main-house families, there were considerable tensions in the village.

These tensions were accentuated by economic disparities. In contrast to those who profited from the commercialization of agriculture were the poorer villagers and the landless, who shared little, if at all, in the prosperity of the countryside. They, in particular, suffered the dislocations caused by economic and social change as contractural relationships replaced those based on family. Most often they endured in silence, but there were also times when they gave vent to their resentment in uprisings. Peasant unrest was on the increase in the late Tokugawa. An indication of this change is the contrast between early Tokugawa rural uprisings, which were often led by village headmen, and those of the late period, which were frequently directed in the first place against those wealthy and powerful village leaders. However, neither the uprisings nor the changes in agricultural technology seriously threatened the basic stability of the village. Violence was a form of protest, not a means toward revolution. Changes in agriculture increased yield but did not alter the basic pattern of rice farming with its need for intensive labor and community cooperation.

The official Confucian theory recognized only four social classes and thus failed to reflect the more complex social stratification of the countryside. Nor did moral admonitions and sumptuary laws directed at wealthy peasants (laws defining who could own what) change matters. Still less acceptable in Confucian eyes was the growing wealth of the merchant class, theoretically considered economic parasites and relegated to the bottom of society. The authorities found that they could control the merchants politically and keep them in their place socially, but they were too dependent on their services to do them permanent harm, as a class, economically. In addition to Edo, where a little over half of the population consisted of townspeople (*chōnin*), Ōsaka developed as a prosperous commercial and shipping center while Kyōto also continued as a major city. *Han* capitals, like Edo, originally founded as political and military centers, also became foci for marketing systems and centers of trade. Privileged merchants, usually operating under license, supplied the link between the cities and the rural hinterlands, and between the local centers and the capital.

Merchants also handled the warehousing of rice and other commodities and were licensed to operate the *han* monopolies. Brokers converted rice into cash or credit for the sellers. Important merchants acted as financial and forwarding agents for the daimyo, handling shipments to Ōsaka for exchange or to Edo for the daimyo's consumption. They supplied banking services, dealing in the manifold *han* currencies, transferring funds, and repeatedly issuing loans to the political authorities and to hard-pressed samurai. The position of individual commercial establishments could be precarious, and in extreme cases a wealthy merchant with heavy loans out to the powerful might suffer confiscation so that the loans could go unpaid, as happened to a great Ōsaka merchant in 1705. However, these were exceptions, and government measures to force creditors to settle for less than full repayment or for the cancellation of loans simply had the effect of raising the cost of new loans, since the authorities never found a way to eliminate the need for such borrowing. The *bakufu*, daimyo, and samurai depended on the merchants as fiscal agents, and the merchants prospered; so much so, indeed, that in the second half of the eighteenth century there were over two hundred mercantile establishments valued at over 200,000 gold *ryo*, a monetary unit worth roughly a *koku* of rice. Such merchants were fully the economic equals of daimyo. Some of the great modern commercial and financial empires go back to the early Tokugawa, most notably the largest of them all, the house of Mitsui founded in 1620.

As in the villages, there were also great differences in status and wealth among the town dwellers, and for every great merchant there were many more humble shopkeepers and artisans producing and repairing the various utensils required for everyday life. At the very bottom of society were people who did not belong even theoretically in the four Confucian classes. Bearing the designation *"hinin"* (non-people) were beggars, traveling performers, prostitutes, scavengers, and so forth. These were outcasts by occupation. Still worse off were pariahs* whose position beyond the pale of ordinary society was hereditary. Their origins are unknown but go back into much earlier Japanese history. Some were people engaged in butchering and tanning, tasks considered unclean. Others were simple artisans working in straw and reed (for example, making baskets, straw sandals, mats, and the like) or rural families who farmed. Considered defiling, they were discriminated against in law and kept in enforced segregation. The number of people falling into these categories is estimated at around 380,000 for the closing years of the Tokugawa.

Classes and Values

As part of his efforts to create an enduring order Ieyasu followed Hideyoshi's example in drawing a clear line between samurai and commoner, using all the weight of the law and official ideology. On the surface at least, there was no conflict with the four classes of Confucian theory, for the character read *shih* in Chinese and designating the scholar (at the top of the social hierarchy) was in Japanese pronounced *samurai*. There were, to be sure, exceptions here and there to the rigid maintenance of hereditary class identity. It did happen that destitute *rōnin*, masterless samurai, dropped out of their own class, and that through marriage or adoption an alliance was sometimes formed between the family of an affluent commoner and that of an impoverished samurai, but such

---

* Formerly they were known as the *eta*, but this term has become pejorative, and at present the term *burakumin* is commonly used.

cases of social mobility remained uncommon. Members of the warrior class proudly cherished their status while most urbanites contented themselves with the pursuit of wealth and its attendant pleasures.

The most visible sign of the samurai's privilege was his sole right to wear swords, symbols of the samurai even after they had ceased to be his major tools. In an era of peace, when his duties were largely civil, the samurai was sent to school to attain a certain minimal mastery of Chinese learning and, more importantly, to absorb the Confucian ethic of dutiful obedience to superiors and conscientious concern for those below him on the social scale. He was also expected to acquire a degree of proficiency in at least one of the martial arts, although during the long years of peace these became "a matter of formal gymnastics and disciplined choreography"[2] rather than practical military techniques. Ideally the samurai was supposed to combine the virtues of the Confucian scholar and those of the old time *bushi*, to serve as both the moral leader and the defender of society, totally devoted to his moral duty (*giri*) even at the expense of his life.

This combination of Confucian and warrior values is apparent in the writings of Yamaga Soko (1622–95). A student of Hayashi Razan and a devotee of the martial arts, he is considered a founding father of modern *bushido*, a more systematized and Confucianized version of the old code of the warrior. One of his followers became the leader of the famed forty-seven *ronin* who persevered in seeking vengeance for the wrong done their dead lord. In 1703 their carefully nurtured plans were rewarded with success as they stormed into the Kyōto mansion of the offending daimyo and killed him. They immediately achieved the status of heroes and have remained popular exemplars of the ideal of loyalty. Theirs was an act of warrior courage and devotion, but it was also illegal. For a time the shogunate debated what should be done. Then the shogun (Tsunayoshi) decided to uphold the substance of the civil law while preserving the warrior's honor: they were ordered to commit ritual suicide. Playwrights lost no time in adapting their story for the puppet theater and kabuki stage. It has remained a Japanese favorite; in the twentieth century both the cinema and the television versions were enormously popular.

The puppet theater and kabuki belonged to the world of the town dweller and not to that of the samurai proper, for whom the aristocratic Nō drama was considered more suitable. Nevertheless, the popularity of *Chūshingura* (Treasury of Royal Retainers), to give the drama of the forty-seven *ronin* its proper title, shows that commoners could appreciate this aspect of samurai culture. And there was a good deal more on which samurai and commoners, urban and rural, could agree. The official morality was presented through periodic lectures, and was spread by the many schools which came into existence during the Tokugawa period. (By 1800, 40 to 50 percent of all Japanese males were literate to some degree.) As in China, the official Confucian values gave support to the hierarchical order within the family as well as in society at large, although the overriding emphasis on filial piety was somewhat relaxed among urban commoners.

Hierarchical principles of organization operated throughout the society as did a tendency to rank people in grades. Like samurai, even the inhabitants of the demimonde of the pleasure quarters in the great cities were carefully ranked. The great merchant establishments resembled feudal fiefs not only in their wealth but also in their expectation of lifelong loyal service from their employees, who in turn, were entitled to be treated with due paternalistic solicitude. This relationship survives in Japanese industry to this day.

Merchant and samurai held many values in common, but there were also major differences in their mores and norms. It was a mark of samurai pride to regard considerations of financial benefit as beneath contempt. Fukuzawa Yukichi (1853–1901) in his famous autobiography tells how his father took his children out of school when, much to his horror, their teacher began to instruct them in arithmetic; a subject fit only for merchants and their offspring. Merchants perceived the distinction in much the same way:

> A samurai's child is reared by samurai parents and becomes a samurai himself because they teach him the warrior's code. A merchant's child is reared by merchant parents and becomes a merchant because they teach him the way of commerce. A samurai seeks a fair name in disregard for profit, but a merchant, with no thought to his reputation, gathers profit and amasses a fortune. This is the way of life proper to each.[3]

The speaker is a rich merchant in a puppet play whose son has married the daughter of a samurai. They are addressed to his son's father-in-law, who now regrets having married his daughter outside her class.

The merchant's occupation was legitimized by the strain in Buddhism that considered all occupations as legitimate forms of devotion and, especially, by "Heart Learning" (Shingaku), a religion founded by a Kyōto merchant and philosopher, Ishida Baigan (1685–1744). Heart Learning combined elements of Shinto, Confucianism, and Buddhism to create an ethic for the artisan and merchant, reinforcing a traditional morality that stressed honesty, frugality, and devotion to one's trade. Long years of training and supervision in the system of craft and business apprenticeships helped to perpetuate values as well as skills. Meanwhile, a different ethos developed in the urban pleasure quarters officially designated by the *bakufu* as the sole areas where courtesans were permitted to ply their trade. Here a new theater and new arts flourished. However, the older aristocratic traditions also remained very much alive. Thus the distinctive character of the classes of Tokugawa Japan as well as their influence on each other is evidenced by developments in the arts.

The Aesthetic Culture of the Aristocracy

The upper classes of the Tokugawa period inherited and perpetuated much of the Ashikaga cultural tradition. Such arts as the tea ceremony and flower arranging were continued without major change. Government officials still patronized schools of Sino-Japanese painting in the Kano line and the native style of painting produced by Tosa artists. The Nō theater continued to receive enthusiastic support; indeed, the shogun Tsunayoshi was so enamored of the art that he himself performed in Nō plays. Although new plays were written for the Nō stage, there were few fresh departures or new themes.

The variety of Tokugawa architectural style reminds us, however, that aristocratic taste was by no means uniform, that the simple aesthetics of the tea ceremony could coexist with a love for the ornate that would have delighted the men and women of Hideyoshi's time. The detached imperial villa at Katsura, outside Kyōto, is an exquisite example of studied simplicity in the use of natural materials. It is famed, not only for its architectural excellence, but equally for the subtle composition of its garden and tea houses. In striking contrast to the calculated restraint shown at Katsura is the profuse display at Nikkō, the mausoleum where Ieyasu's remains are interred. In chaotic flamboyance, its brightly painted and gilded decorations luxuriate in endless variety, free of any restraining notions of functional or aesthetic logic. A similar indulgence in decoration at the expense of form marks the final phase of the Gothic style in Europe, but the structures at Nikkō are ultimately saved from empty vulgarity by their setting in a magnificent forest, creating as Alexander Soper says, "a serene depth of shadow into which their tumult sinks without an echo."[4]

In Kyōto the aristocratic aesthetic tradition, going back to court circles in the Heian period, was given new life in a final surge of vitality. The movement was led by Hon'ami Koetsu (1558–1637), descendant of a family of professional sword repairers and sword connoisseurs, and was tinged with elements of artistic defiance, for Koetsu and his group rejected the values of the new military class, especially their continued patronage of Chinese styles in art and philosophy.

Koetsu's movement was practical, not merely intellectual. On a site north of Kyōto, granted him by Ieyasu in recognition of his prominence as a member of that city's Nichiren Buddhist community, Koetsu established an artistic and religious colony of fifty-five houses. Here a new group of artists and craftsmen sought to carry on the artistic traditions of Heian Japan. Their success is indicated by the fact that Koetsu became the arbiter of taste for his generation in the old imperial capital.

Koetsu had, of course, been trained in his family's traditional art: sword repair and connoisseurship, but his talents were far-ranging. His tea bowls are considered among the very finest achievements in Raku Ware; he made new departures in lacquer inlay work and was equally accomplished in the medium of cast metal vessels. He excelled in painting and, above all, in calligraphy. Frequently he worked in collaboration with other artists. An example is the handscroll *Thousand Cranes* painted by Tawaraya Sōtatsu (d. 1643?) with Koetsu contributing the bold and free calligraphy. The result is a decorative elegance that does honor to the old tradition. (See Figure 15-1.)

Sōtatsu was a younger contemporary of Koetsu and apparently related to him by marriage. Tawaraya was the name of Sōtatsu's fan and painting atelier (that

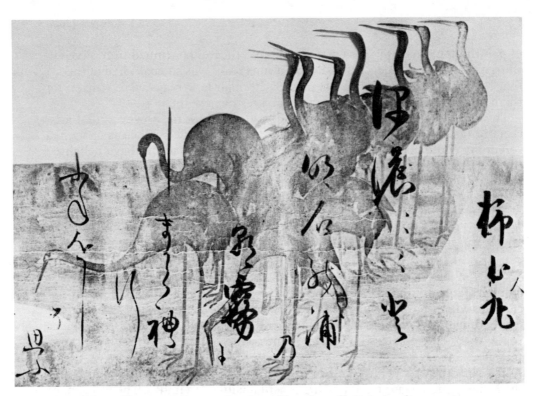

Figure 15-1 *Thousand Cranes.* Section of hand-scroll. Painting by
Tawaraya Sōtatsu, calligraphy by Hon'ami Koetsu. Gold and silver underpainting
on paper, 341 cm × 1460 cm.

is, workshop) in Kyōto. Although influenced by Koetsu, Sōtatsu did not actually move out of town to the former's arts village. Both men were con-
sciously influenced by the Heian tradition, which, among other things, originated the art of painting on fans. Also characteristically native in inspiration is
the softness of Sōtatsu's "boneless" technique, which avoids the strong ink
lines found in the work of the Kano painters. This style, as well as a gift for
composition, he carried over to his work on large screens. Hiroshi Mizuo[5] has
pointed out the influence of fan-painting techniques on such masterpieces as
Sōtatsu's pair of screens *The God of Wind and the God of Thunder.* (See Figure 15-2.) The two screens form a single composition, with the pivot in the
empty center pulling the swirling gods in and preventing them from spinning
right off the painted surface. In this and in his *bugaku* (court dance) screen pair,
Sōtatsu reveals his greatness as a master of dynamic movement.

A third great pair of screens, *Waves at Matsushima*, shows Sōtatsu as a
daring stylist. It is this quality of decorative stylization that is most characteristic of the third great artist in this tradition, Ogata Kōrin (1658–1716), who
studied and copied Sōtatsu's works. It is from the last syllable of his name,
Kō*rin*, that there was derived the term "Rimpa" ("Rin school") designating
the entire school of artists. A perennial favorite is Korin's pair of iris screens.

Figure 15-2 Tawaraya Sōtatsu, *God of Wind.* One of a pair of twofold screens. Color on foil, 153.7 cm × 171 cm.

Elise Grilli compares this pair to Mozart's variations on a musical theme; the painter, like the composer, "first stating his motif, then adding variations, shifts, repetitions, pauses, leaps, intervals, changes of tempo, accents, chords, rise and fall, with changes of mood from major to minor."[6] The iris theme derives from a poem by Narihira in *The Tales of Ise,* but it is not the literary reference but Kōrin's color orchestration and his superb eye for the decorative that link him most clearly to the native Japanese tradition. (See Figure 15-3.)

Figure 15-3 Ogata Kōrin, *Irises.* One of a pair of sixfold screens. Color on gold foil over paper, 151.2 cm × 360.7 cm.

Genroku Urban Culture

Equally Japanese but drawing its nourishment from different roots was the urban culture of Edo, which reached a high point during the Genroku Era. Technically this era name applies to a period of only sixteen years, 1688–1704, but more broadly it designates the cultural life of the last quarter of the seventeenth century and the first quarter of the eighteenth. It was a remarkable period during which some of Japan's most creative artists were at work. These include the foremost playwright, Chikamatsu (1653–1724); the most gifted traditional short story writer, Saikaku (1642–93); Moronobu (1618–94), generally credited with developing the Japanese print; and Bashō (1644–94), the Tokugawa period's finest poet, master of the haiku.

Most large cities of the world have "pleasure districts," which are more or less tolerated by the political authorities, that is, sections of town devoted to bohemian life, erotic activities, entertainment, and gambling. The cities of Tokugawa Japan were no exception. But rarely, if ever, have such quarters produced a first-rate aesthetic as they did in seventeenth-century Yoshiwara, the home of Edo's "floating world." Here, and in similar quarters in the other large towns, the Japanese tradition of aesthetic discrimination once more led to keen appreciation of stylistic excellence in dress and coiffure, in gesture and perfume, and in life itself. The worldly flair of the man-about-town was greatly admired; the spirit and elegant chic of the great courtesans who presided over this world were particularly appreciated. There was nothing but disdain for the country boor, for the gaudy or gauche.

The Japanese Print

The life and values of this "floating world" left their imprint on Japanese culture: on fiction, and the stage, and particularly on the visual arts. A unique achievement is the *ukiyo-e*, "pictures of the floating world," perhaps the last major accomplishment of the native tradition of Japanese art.

Among the precursors of the *ukiyo-e* were genre paintings such as early seventeenth-century screens depicting kabuki performances in the dry river bed in Kyōto or spring excursions to picnic under blossoming cherry trees, and *ukiyo-e* painting remained an important art even after the full development of the color woodcut. The immediate antecedents of the prints were illustrations for books such as the *Yoshiwara Pillow* (1660), a combination sex manual and "courtesan critique," combining two of the perpetually popular themes of the prints. The production of erotica, much of it unpublishable even today, and of portraits of courtesans remained two of the mainstays of the *ukiyo-e* artist.

The fullest expression of *ukiyo-e* was the Japanese print. Portraits of courtesans, theater scenes, nature subjects, or scenes from urban life were carved in wood blocks. These were then inked and printed on paper. First efforts were

Figure 15-4 Okumura Masanobu,
*Girl in Transparent Dress Tying Her
Obi.* Woodcut print.

highly experimental. Hishikawa Moronobu, sometimes considered the founder of the Japanese print, consolidated these early efforts. His work represents
the establishment of the genre.

   At the beginning the prints were in black and white, but then color was
added, first by hand, then by developing techniques of multicolor printing. The
early prints were limited first to basic red and green, but by the middle of the
eighteenth century three- or four-color prints were produced. A versatile master who contributed importantly to the development of the print was Okumura Masanobu (1686–1764). Figure 15-4 shows an eighteenth-century beauty
dressed in a characteristically sumptuous kimono. In the center of the stamp at
the bottom is a gourd, colored red. The text to the right of the gourd reads,
"The genuine brush of the Japanese painter Okumura Masanobu. Tori-shio
Street Picture Wholesale Shop." To the left, the text resumes, "Sale of red pic-

tures and illustrated books. The red gourd seal is enclosed. Okumura."[7] The lower part of the kimono is in bright red (*beni*) while the upper part is yellowish, with the obi (sash) decorated with a brown design painted in lacquer.

Masanobu was a many-sided master whose virtuosity extended to a variety of styles and who himself influenced other artists such as the creator of the hand-colored print illustrated in Figure 15-5. This print depicts the interior of a house in Yoshiwara and features a game of backgammon. The composition experiments with the receding perspective of European painting. The print also shows such standard features of Japanese interior architecture as rooms separated by sliding partitions, the *tatami* floor, and that sense of spaciousness created by the virtual absence of furniture.

Masanobu was a publisher as well as an artist, but usually these functions were separate, carried out by different people. Indeed, numerous people had a hand in the creation of a print. The publisher was very important. He not only distributed and sold the block prints but also commissioned them from the artist with more or less explicit instructions on subject and style, with an eye on what would sell. The artist drew the picture and designed the print, but then turned it over to the engraver and the printer. The craftsmanship of these men did much to determine the quality of the finished product. However, the artist's contribution remained central. The essential vision was his.

Figure 15-5   *Game of Backgammon in the Yoshiwara.* Attributed to Torii Kiyotada (fl. ca. 1720–50). Hand-colored woodcut print.

The Popular Theater: Kabuki and Bunraku

A favorite pastime of the Genroku man-about-town, and an unceasing source of inspiration for the print-artist, was the popular kabuki theater, whose celebrated actors enjoyed as much acclaim and attracted as avid a group of admirers as did the most elegant of Yoshiwara courtesans. A similarly enthusiastic audience was drawn to *bunraku*, the puppet theater.

Important in the evolution of kabuki were the dances and skits presented in Kyōto during the early years of the seventeenth century by a troupe of female performers led by a priestess named Okuni. But this women's kabuki lasted only until 1629, when it was banned by the authorities. This action was not prompted by the *bakufu's* disapproval of the offstage behavior of the actress-courtesans, but by its desire to put an end to the periodic outbursts of violence that erupted as rivals competed for the favors of these ladies. Then, for two decades, young men's kabuki flourished, until it too ran into similar difficulties and was prohibited in 1652, after which date all actors were mature men. Even then kabuki continued to be under government restrictions, tolerated as a form of plebeian amusement, licensed and controlled, since, like other indecorous pleasures, it could not be suppressed.

Kabuki theater was wildly popular during the Tokugawa period, pleasing its audience with its spectacular scenery, gorgeous costumes, and expressions of violent passion. It was very much an actor's art, dominated by dynasties of actors who felt quite free to take liberties with the texts of the plays. The virtuoso performances of the great actors were greeted by shouts of approval from the audience. The raised walkway on which the actors made their way to the stage through the audience also provided a link between performers and spectators. Particularly esteemed was the artistry of the men who played the female roles. These masters devoted their lives to achieving stylizations of posture, gesture, and voice, conveying the quintessence of femininity, always operating in that "slender margin between the real and unreal,"[8] which Chikamatsu defined as the true province of art. In this sense, the *bakufu's* prohibition against female performers enriched kabuki artistically.

Chikamatsu wrote for the kabuki stage but actually preferred the puppet theater (*bunraku*), in which large wooden puppets manipulated by three-man teams acted out a story told by a group of chanters, accompanied by the three-stringed *samisen*. This theater achieved such popularity that live actors even imitated the movements of the puppets. Even after kabuki carried the day in Edo, *bunraku* continued to flourish in Ōsaka. The puppets, like the masks employed in Nō, assured that the action on stage would not be a mere mirror of ordinary life but would have a more stylized and symbolic aspect. For the playwright, *bunraku* held an added attraction in that the puppets, unlike their flesh and blood counterparts, did not meddle with his text. There are also scenes of violence and fantastic stage business which, impossible for live actors, pose no problems for figures that do not bleed and are not bound by the usual limits of human physiology. Spectacular elements helped to attract a wide audience to this theater and are used frequently by Chikamatsu in his plays on historical subjects, such as *The Battle of Coxinga*, his most famous work in this genre.

Chikamatsu also wrote more subtle domestic plays set in his own contemporary world. These center on conflicts between moral obligations (*giri*) and human emotions (*ninjō*), the irreconcilable tensions between duty and feeling. One, for example, tells of the tragic love of a small shopkeeper and a lovely courtesan whom he cannot ransom from her house for lack of funds. A frequent solution is the lovers' flight to death, a trip which provides the poetic high point of the play. Often the ladies exhibit greater strength of character than the men, but both are turned into romantic heroes through the purity and intensity of their emotions. Art imitates life, but life also imitates art: the plays produced such a rash of love suicides that the government finally banned all plays with the words "love suicide" in the title.

Popular Prose Literature

In prose the life and mentality of the townspeople were best expressed in the writing of Saikaku, Chikamatsu's senior by eleven years. Both writers chronicled as well as molded the urban culture of the Genroku period.

The life of Saikaku's typical urbanite was centered on love and money. Although he also wrote about samurai, his best work deals with recognizable city types: the miser and money grubber, the playboy who squanders his patrimony, the young beauty mismatched to an elderly husband, the fan maker, and men and women in love with love. His erotic works, exuberant and witty, mixing humor and sex, were in keeping with the times and are of a robust directness far removed from the subtle delicacy of Heian sensibility even when, as in his later works, he recounted the darker aspects of his subject matter. In his writing, too, can be seen the conflict between duty and feeling which animated the plays of Chikamatsu. Saikaku was not only the finest of prose writers but also a prolific composer of *haikai* (light verse), a poetic genre widely popular among the townspeople.

Tokugawa Poetry: The Haiku

A haiku is a poem with seventeen syllables arranged in three lines 5/7/5. Its antecedents are very old, for this is the form of the opening lines of the old thirty-one syllable *tanka*. It was also the usual form for the opening lines of the *renga* (linked verse). From the Ashikaga on, linked verse remained highly popular, and in the sixteenth and seventeenth centuries this was especially true of *haikai*, or light verse, enlivened by infusions of everyday speech and of humor.

That some of the resulting verse departed considerably from the refined taste of the aristocracy is shown by a famous pair of links in a sixteenth-century anthology:

> Bitter, bitter it was
> And yet somehow funny.

> Even when
> My father lay dying
> I went on farting.[9]

Vulgar as it is, the second verse does contrast sharply with the first, as required in this poetic form. The popularity of *haikai* is attested by the appearance of several seventeenth-century anthologies, one of which contained verses by over 650 contributors.

The haiku came into its own thanks to the work of Matsuo Bashō, an almost exact contemporary of Saikaku. Bashō was born a samurai but gave up his rank to live the life of a commoner, earning his living as a master poet. His own pupils came from all strata of society from wealthy samurai to beggars. His finest poetry was written in the last decade of his life and shows the influence of Zen, which he began studying in 1681, but few of his haiku are overtly religious.

Not every seventeen-syllable poem is a true haiku, for the real measure of a haiku lies not in its formal structure or surface meaning but in its resonance, not in what it says but in what is left unsaid. It invites, indeed demands, that the reader himself become an artist, entering into its spirit and exploring (even creating) its manifold shades of meaning. As Harold G. Henderson observes, "really great haiku suggest so much that more words would lessen their meaning."[10] This may be true of great poetry generally, but it is especially true of what must be the shortest poetic form in any major poetic tradition.

The essence of haiku is that rather than describe a scene or feeling, it presents the reader with a series of images, which when connected in the imagination, yield a wealth of associations, visions, and emotions. Consider, for example, Bashō's best known haiku:

> An old pond
> Frog jumps in
> Sound of water.

Characteristically it presents a scene from nature composed of two elements. The first ("an old pond") supplies the setting. But more than that, it implies a condition—the stillness of water, shaded perhaps by overhanging boughs—that contrasts with the subsequent action ("frog jumps in"), and results in a delightful visual image, which also has aural resonance, that is, splashing water. The inner spring of the poem is the juxtaposition of two contrasting elements, a juxtaposition that sets off waves in the reader's mind.

Some of Bashō's finest poems were composed on his travels and are contained in his *The Narrow Road of Oku*. One such haiku reads:

At Yoshino
I'll show you cherry blossoms—
Cypress umbrella.[11]

He wrote the poem on his umbrella, and there is a gentle whimsy in Bashō's idea of sharing the beauty of the cherry blossoms with his umbrella. The word translated "umbrella" can also mean "hat." Figure 15-6 shows Bashō, with his traveling hat, ready to begin his trip.

The painting itself is an example of the genre known as *haiga* in which a *haiku* and a painting (*ga*) were integrated. It is by Yokoi Kinkoku (1761–1832) and exemplifies "literati painting" (*bunjinga*; Chinese, *wen-jen-hua*) in the general manner of Yosa Buson (1716–83), the most eminent artist in this mode. These artists looked to China for basic inspiration, although they did not limit themselves to Chinese subjects in their art. Like their Chinese models, Buson and other *bunjin* wrote poetry as well as painting pictures, but they represent only one of several trends during the post-Genroku period.

Art and Literature after the Genroku Period

After the Genroku period artists continued to work in the Genroku genres, but the classic age of the popular theater, the print, and haiku was past. Notable among the *ukiyo-e* artists of this time was the strikingly original Tōshūsai

Figure 15-6
Yokoi Kinkoku,
Portrait of Bashō.
Ink and color on paper.

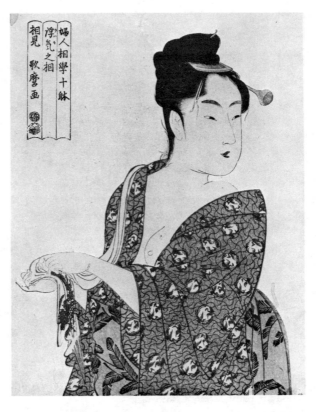

Figure 15-7
Kitagawa Utamaro,
Beauty Wringing Out a Towel.
Woodcut print,
37.8 cm × 25.1 cm.

Sharaku (dates unknown), famous for the prints of actors that he turned out during a ten-month outburst of creativity in 1794–95. His prints, theatrical, psychologically penetrating, and bitterly satirical, ran counter to the tastes of his time. More appreciated in his own day was Suzuki Harunobu (1724–70), who excelled in the subtle use of color and in the freshness of his young beauties. Controversial and uneven was the prolific Kitagawa Utamaro (1754–1806), who achieved great popularity with his prints of the ladies of the "floating world." Reproduced in Figure 15-7 is one of a series on the physiognomies of women, this one illustrating the "wanton" type.

With the end of the eighteenth century, there was a falling off in the artistic quality of the figure prints, but the *ukiyo-e* tradition retained enough vigor to achieve excellence in another form—the landscape print. A master of this art was the "old man mad with painting," Katsushika Hokusai (1760–1849), an eclectic genius. He is represented here by one of his depictions of the scenery along the Tōkaidō, the great road leading to Edo traveled by the daimyo and their retinues. (See Figure 15-8.) Less versatile but at his best producing works imbued with a delicate lyricism was Andō Hiroshige (1797–1858), who was still alive when Commodore Perry arrived in Japan (1853).

In the course of two centuries the Japanese artists and craftsmen achieved a level of artistic and technical excellence unrivaled anywhere in the world. They developed styles appropriate to their medium, creating an art of colors

Figure 15-8 Katsushika Hokusai, *The Station Hodogaya on the Tōkaidō*. Woodcut print, 25.9 × 38.8 cm.

and planes and of crisp lines, with only a hint of the old calligraphic tradition. It was an art of great immediate appeal, not only to the Tokugawa townspeople and country folk looking for a souvenir of their trip to the great city, but also to European artists who, later in the nineteenth century, found they had much to learn from this art.

Prose and poetry continued to be produced and enjoyed by a wide audience, although they did not again reach the quality attained by Saikaku or Bashō. Perhaps the best loved of the later haiku poets was Kobayashi Issa (1763–1827). He achieved a wide identification with nature and showed sympathy for even the humblest of animals and insects.

> Lean frog,
> don't give up the fight!
> Issa is here![12]

Intellectual Currents

During the Tokugawa period, Buddhism, out of favor politically, showed little intellectual or religious creativity. But secular theorizing flourished as never before, as Japanese scholars assimilated and developed the various strands of what in the West is known as Neo-Confucianism, and explored alternate ways of thought. As a result, the Tokugawa achievement in philosophy and the originality and complexity of the period's intellectual history are unmatched by any previous period of Japanese history.

In Japan, as in China, the appeal of Neo-Confucianism was varied and profound. In it, many found religious fulfillment, intellectual stimulation, and moral inspiration. Sung Neo-Confucianism enjoyed the support of the *bakufu* from the time of Hayashi Razan and Ieyasu down to the end of the Tokugawa era. Important as this was, the effectiveness of official patronage was limited, since in Japan, unlike China, there was no civil service examination system to enforce orthodoxy, and Japan's political divisions provided diverse sources of patronage for scholars. When the shogunate, in its most restrictive period, officially prohibited heterodox doctrines in 1790, it had little permanent effect on Japanese intellectual life.

Among the outstanding exponents of Sung Confucianism after Razan was Yamazaki Ansai (1618–82), a stern and forceful teacher who stressed "devotion within, righteousness without" and was so dedicated to Chu Hsi that he said he would follow the master even into error. Some Tokugawa Confucians were extreme Sinophiles, but Ansai did not let his veneration for the Chinese philosophers interfere with his love for Japan. When asked the supremely hypothetical question: what should be done were Confucius and Mencius to lead a Chinese invasion of Japan, he answered that he would capture the two sages and put them at the service of his own land. Deeply interested in Shinto, Ansai attempted to fuse Confucian ethics with Shinto religion. Other major orthodox thinkers include the moralist Kaibara Ekken (1630–1714) and Muro Kyūsō (1658–1734). Most Confucians justified the shogunate by incorporating it into the hierarchy of loyalty, but Kyūsō argued that the Tokugawa ruled by virtue of a heavenly mandate. He found it necessary to defend Sung philosophy against increasingly vigorous challenges from other schools, the Japanese counterparts of the varieties of Confucianism that developed on the continent after the Sung.

The man considered the founder of the Wang Yang-ming school in Japan was Nakae Tōju (1608–48). Like the Chinese philosopher, he stressed the inner light of man and insisted on the importance of action. It was his lofty and unselfish character especially that attracted the admiration of contemporaries and of later activist intellectuals. His best known disciple, Kumazawa Banzan (1619–91) ran into political difficulties, not because of his unorthodox philosophic ideas, but for unconventional policy recommendations, including a relaxation of the daimyo's attendance requirements in Edo to save expenses. He was traditionally Confucian in his concern for the well-being of the peasantry and in his lack of sympathy for the merchant class, as reflected in his advocacy of a return to a barter economy using rice in place of money.

In Japan, as in China, Chu Hsi's philosophy was repudiated by those who denied the authority of the Sung scholars and insisted on going back to the classical sources. This was the stance of Yamaga Sokō, whose connection with *bushidō* was noted earlier in this chapter. Others who argued that the Sung thinkers had distorted the authentic Confucian message differed on the contents of that message. A great teacher and moralist known for his humanism and his emphasis on *jen* (loving benevolence) was Itō Jinsai (1627–1705), who drew inspiration from the *Analects:*

> The *Analects* is like the boundless universe which men live in without comprehending its full magnitude. Enduring and immutable throughout the ages; in every part of the world it serves as an infallible guide. Is it not, indeed, great![13]

Philosophically Itō rejected the Neo-Confucian distinction between *li* and *ch'i*, two concepts by then as much at home in Japan as in China.

Another attack on the Sung philosophy of principle (*li*) was made by Ogyū Sorai (1666–1728), who insisted on going back not just to the *Analects* but to the earlier Six Classics, according to him the genuine repositories of true doctrine. A complex, many-sided thinker, in his political thought he represented the tough-minded pole of Confucianism with its emphasis on rites and institutions. Like some of the seventeenth-century Chinese critics of Sung philosophy, Ogyū Sorai was interested in practical as well as theoretical subjects. A prolific writer, he dealt with many topics: philosophy and politics; literature, linguistics, and music; military science; and economics.

Historiography and "National Learning"

A perennial field of Confucian scholarship was the study of history, but in the Tokugawa period it was not only Confucian scholars who were interested in the Japanese past.

Hayashi Razan, himself, began work on a history of Japan which was completed by his son and accepted as the official history of the shogunate. Among those who made major contributions to scholarship was the statesman and scholar Arai Hakuseki (1657–1725), noted for his careful attention to the evidence and a willingness to reexamine traditional beliefs.

A different emphasis appeared in *The Great History of Japan (Dainihonshi)*, which was begun in the seventeenth century under the sponsorship of the Lord of Mito, Tokugawa Mitsukuni (1628–1700), but not completed until the twentieth century. Mitsukuni, a grandson of Ieyasu, enlisted the services of a Chinese emigree Ming loyalist, Chu Shun-shui (1600–1682). The resulting history was highly moralistic and loyalist in tone, exalting the Japanese imperial house. Since, in theory, the shogun himself derived his authority from this source, there was nothing inherently anti*bakufu* in Mito historiography. That its focus on the emperor rather than on the shogun was potentially subversive, however, was shown later when it provided an emperor-centered source for nationalistic sentiments, and eventually it supplied ammunition for the anti*bakufu* arguments of the movement to "restore the emperor," which culminated in the Meiji Restoration of 1868.

Interest in Japan's past often went hand in hand with a new appreciation of the Shinto tradition, attracting Confucians such as Yamazaki Ansai and stimulating non-Confucian scholars of the "National Learning" variety. This school began with the study of old Japanese literature, such as the *Man'yōshū*, and its greatest exponent made the study of the *Kojiki* his life's work. This was Motoori Norinaga (1730–1801) who believed that the *Kojiki* mirrored the age of the *kami,* whom he accepted as both real and irrational. According to Motoori, it is arrogant not to recognize the limitations of the human intellect and wrong to attempt to understand the *kami* rationally. Indeed the irrationality of the old legends was a sign of their truth, for "who would fabricate such shallow sounding, incredible things?"[14] For Motoori, the *kami* are the starting point: "People try to explain matters in the age of *kami* by referring to human affairs whereas I have understood human affairs by referring to the matters in the age of *kami.*"[15] Supreme among the *kami* was the Sun Goddess. In Motoori, absolute faith in the *kami* did not conflict with fine empirical scholarship, and his belief in nonrational understanding enabled him to appreciate the old Heian aesthetic, and to value especially the feminine sensibility of that age. Motoori left a dual heritage, academic philology and ideological nativism. Among those who drew on the latter aspect of Motoori's thought the most influential was Hirata Atsutane (1776–1843), an ultranationalist whose narrow Japanism proved attractive to many in the nineteenth and twentieth centuries.

Dutch Learning

In Tokugawa Japan European learning equaled "Dutch Learning," for the Dutch remained the only Westerners allowed even limited access to Japan. Their annual audience with the shogun provided an occasion for the Japanese to satisfy their curiosity about the exotic:

> He [the shogun, mistaken for the emperor by the Dutch chronicler] order'd us to take off our Cappa, or Cloak, being our Garment of Ceremony, then to stand upright, that he might have a full view of us; again to walk, to stand still, to compliment each other, to dance, to jump, to play the drunkard, to speak broken Japanese, to read Dutch, to paint, to sing, to put our cloaks on and off. Meanwhile we obey'd the Emperor's commands in the best manner we could. I join'd to my dance a lovesong in High German. In this manner, and with innumerable such other apish tricks, we must suffer ourselves to contribute to the Emperor's and Court's diversion.[16]

This is from a report of the embassy of 1691 or 1692. The "Red-haired Barbarians," as the Dutch were commonly known, continued to be objects of wild rumor. But they also drew the attention of serious scholars after the *bakufu,* in 1720, permitted the importation of books on all subjects except Christianity. One result was the influence of Western art which we have already noted in the discussion of the *ukiyo-e,* and in the eighteenth century, there were also Japanese painters who produced reputable Western-style works in oil.

Most remarkable were the achievements of a small group of truly dedicated scholars who wrestled with the difficulties of the Dutch language and laboriously made the first translations, compiled the early dictionaries, and wrote the first treatises on Western subjects, initially concerning geography, astronomy, medicine, and other sciences. Thus Shiba Kōkan (1738–1818), the first in Japan to produce copper engravings, was fascinated by the realistic aspect of Western art, by its ability to portray objects as they appear to the eye. The practical, scientific value of Western studies had already been recognized by Arai Hakuseki, and to Shiba, too, this is what was of value in the Western tradition. For spiritual nourishment the Japanese continued to turn to their own heritage, thus foreshadowing the nineteenth-century formula "Eastern ethics—Western science." Thanks to *bakufu* policy, they knew little about Western political, philosophical, or religious thought.

By the end of the eighteenth century, there were also scholars of Dutch Learning who turned to matters political, military, and economic at considerable personal risk. Hayashi Shihei (1738–93) was arrested for defying a *bakufu* prohibition by publishing a book dealing with political issues: he advocated defense preparations against the threat he saw impending from abroad. Takano Chōei (1804–50) and Watanabe Kanzan (1795–1841) were persecuted for disagreeing with the *bakufu's* seclusion policy and ended as suicides. Honda Toshiaki (1744–1821), who wanted to turn Japan into the England of the East, complete with mercantile empire, escaped persecution by not publishing his ideas.

Implicit in the views of the scholars of Dutch Learning was dissatisfaction with the Tokugawa seclusion policy, which stood in the way of their learning more about Western civilization and prevented them from traveling overseas. Meanwhile, by stressing the royal line, Mito Confucians and National Learning scholars also helped to weaken the *bakufu* ideologically. And even orthodox Confucianism did not really require a shogun or a *bakufu*.

Thus, by 1800 there were fissures in the Tokugawa's intellectual as well as political and economic foundations, but it was a new challenge from abroad that eventually destroyed them.

NOTES

1. Harold Bolitho, *Treasures among Men: The Fudai Daimyo in Tokugawa Japan* (New Haven: Yale University Press, 1974), p. 17.

2. Ronald P. Dore, *Education in Tokugawa Japan* (Berkeley and Los Angeles: University of California Press, 1965), p. 151.

3. Donald Keene, *Four Major Plays of Chikamatsu* (New York: Columbia University Press, 1961), p. 151.

4. Robert Treat Paine and Alexander Soper, *The Art and Architecture of Japan* (Baltimore: Penguin Books, 1955), p. 274.

5. See Hiroshi Mizuo, *Edo Painting: Sotatsu and Korin*, trans. John M. Shields (New York and Tokyo: Weatherhill/Heibonsha, 1974), pp. 40–41.

6. Elise Grilli, *The Art of the Japanese Screen* (Tokyo and New York: John Weatherhill, 1970), pp. 111–12.

7. Willy Boller, *Masterpieces of the Japanese Color Woodcut; Collection W. Boller,* Photo. by R. Spreng (Boston: Boston Book and Art Shop, [1950?]), p. 20.

8. Attributed to Chikamatsu by his friend Hozumi Ikan. Hozumi's account of Chikamatsu's views has been translated by Donald Keene as "Chikamatsu on the Art of the Puppet Stage," in Donald Keene, ed., *Anthology of Japanese Literature* (New York: Grove Press, 1955), p. 389.

9. Ryusaku Tsunoda, Wm. Theodore de Bary, and Donald Keene, comps., *Sources of Japanese Tradition* (New York: Columbia University Press, 1958), p. 454.

10. Harold G. Henderson, *An Introduction to Haiku* (New York: Doubleday, 1958), p. 8.

11. Calvin French, *The Poet-Painters: Buson and His Followers,* exhibition catalog (Ann Arbor: University of Michigan Museum of Art, 1974), p. 132.

12. Henderson, *An Introduction to Haiku,* p. 133.

13. Tsunoda et al., *Sources of Japanese Tradition,* p. 419.

14. *Ibid.,* p. 524.

15. Shigeru Matsumoto, *Motoori Norinaga, 1730–1801* (Cambridge: Harvard University Press, 1970), p. 81.

16. E. Kaempfer, quoted in Donald Keene, *The Japanese Discovery of Europe,* revised edition (Stanford: Stanford University Press, 1969), p. 4.

PART FIVE
China and Japan in the Modern World

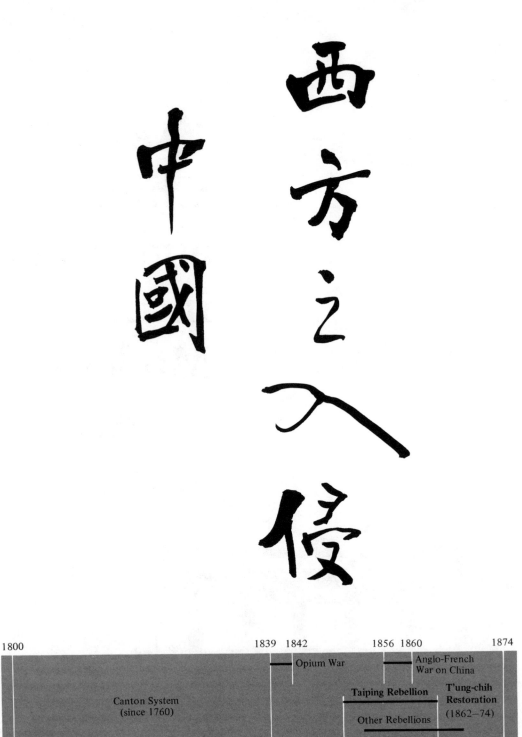

西方之入侵

中國

1800		1839 1842	1856 1860	1874
		Opium War	Anglo-French War on China	
Canton System (since 1760)			Taiping Rebellion	T'ung-chih Restoration (1862–74)
			Other Rebellions	
		1850	1864	

16 The Intrusion of the West: China

In the nineteenth century China and Japan had to deal with a world in which Europe was supreme. Intellectual, political, and economic forces at work since the Renaissance had steadily transformed European civilization and produced unprecedented wealth and power. The process was accelerated in the late eighteenth century by industrialization and the French Revolution, explosions that set off tremors reaching eventually all around the globe. During the century, the economic revolution created new wealth, new tech-

379

nology, new appetites, and new problems, first in England and then in other countries of Western Europe. The nation-state offered its citizens more, but it also made greater demands on them than had the old empires in Europe or elsewhere. It was also a tumultuous period of intense economic competition, stringent national rivalries, bitter class conflicts, and sharp clashes between old values and ideas and new. Yet few Europeans questioned the superiority—moral, intellectual, economic, and political—of their civilization.

The new Europe, powerful and aggressive, challenged all other civilizations. Ultimately it left its mark everywhere. Those areas which, like East Asia, did not become outright colonies still had to face the challenge of European intrusion. In the process, they initiated changes that ultimately were to be just as profound as those which took place in colonized lands. On the other hand, terms such as "the intrusion of the West" or "westernization" should not be allowed to obscure the fact that the "West" itself was changing, and that it was a pluralistic civilization differing in its various national manifestations.

To understand developments in China and Japan, it is necessary to bear in mind what was happening in Europe at the same time. Militarily the nineteenth century was the age of sea power, and Great Britain was the major sea power of the age. Thus Britain was able to create the largest of the European overseas empires, and it was Britain which took the lead in dealings with nineteenth-century China, and initiated a new era in Chinese history by forcing China to abandon the Canton System and to open her doors to the West. (See map, Figure 16-1). The pivotal event was the Opium War (1839–42).

Breakdown of the Canton System: Sino-British Tensions

As noted earlier, Chinese contact with the West in the eighteenth century was limited to commerce; there were no diplomatic relations. Even commerce was strictly limited by the Canton System, that is, all Western commerce with China was carried out through the port of Canton (see Figure 16-2), Western residence in Canton was strictly regulated, and the terms of trade allowed Western merchants to deal with only a small group of Chinese firms (the Cohong), which had a monopoly on foreign trade. Western traders, used to more open commercial dealing in other parts of the globe, and chafing under the lack of respect shown to Westerners in China, became increasingly resentful. Thus, well before the actual outbreak of war, the limitations imposed by the Canton System seemed likely to lead to a clash between the increasingly aggressive Europeans and a Manchu-Chinese Empire past its prime.

Exacerbating political and economic tensions was the incompatibility of the Chinese and English views of themselves and their respective places in the world. Both were supremely self-confident and proud of their own civilizations. Both were narrowly culture-bound. Thus when the Macartney mission arrived in Peking in 1793 in the hope of broadening the terms of trade and initiating treaty relations with China, the presents sent to Emperor Ch'ien-lung

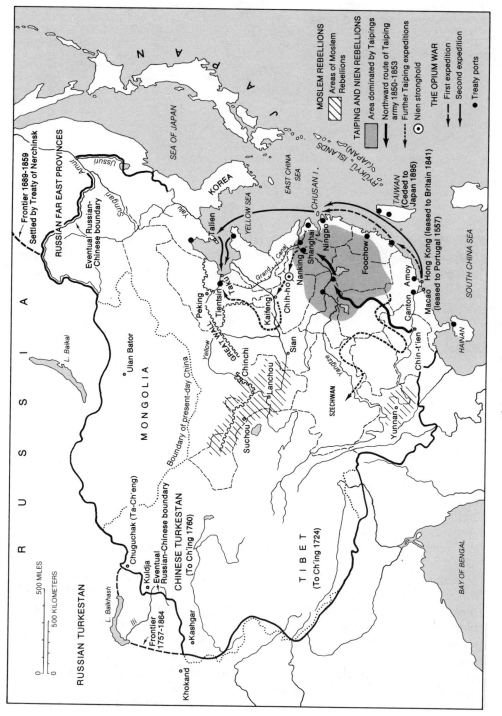

Figure 16-1 **China in the Nineteenth Century**

Figure 16-2 *Canton, ca. 1760.* Artist unknown. Gouache on silk, 47.7 cm × 73.7 cm. One of four creating a panorama of the waterfront. Peabody Museum, Salem.

by England's George III were promptly labeled as "tribute" by the Chinese. Ch'ien-lung responded to the English monarch by praising his "respectful spirit of submission"[1] and, in the gracious but condescending language appropriate for addressing a barbarian king residing in the outer reaches of the world, turned down all his requests, political and economic. He saw no merit in the English request for representation in Peking nor did he favor increased trade, "As your Ambassador can see for himself, we possess all things. I set no value on objects strange or ingenious, and have no use for your country's manufactures."[2]

On the English side, Lord Macartney refused to perform the ceremonial kowtow expected of barbarian envoys and performed by the Chinese themselves toward their superiors and by the emperor toward Heaven. Macartney was confident that the Chinese would perceive "that superiority which Englishmen, wherever they go, cannot conceal."[3] In the end, the Chinese allowed an informal audience that did not require the full kowtow (three kneelings and nine prostrations), but in their self-assessments the Chinese and the English remained as far apart as two peoples have ever been. The English sent another mission to China in 1816 headed by Lord Amherst, but he did not even get an audience at court.

The British motive for coming to China was and continued to be primarily economic. In contrast to China's self-sufficiency and Emperor Ch'ien-lung's disdain for foreign products, there was a Chinese product in great demand in Britain. This was tea. First imported in tiny quantities in the late seventeenth century, tea was initially taken up as an exotic beverage with medicinal properties, then popularized as a benign alternative to gin, and finally was considered a necessity of English life, with the East India Company required by Act of Parliament to keep a year's supply in stock at all times. Tea imports reached fifteen million pounds in 1785 and double that amount in the decade preceding the Opium War. Not only did the East India Company depend on the income from the tea trade, the British government also had a direct stake in tea, since about one-tenth of its entire revenue came from a tax on Chinese tea. Not until the 1820s did the Company begin experimenting with tea growing in India, and it was many years before Indian tea provided an alternative to the tea of China. The importance of Chinese tea extended even to American history: it was Chinese tea that was dumped from East India Company ships in the famous Boston Tea Party (1773).

The British problem was how to pay for this tea. There was no market for British woolens in China, and the "sing-song" trade in clocks, music boxes, and curios was insufficient to strike a balance of trade. Until the last third of the century, the sale of British imports covered 10 percent or less of the cost of exports, with the rest paid for in cash and precious metals. Unable to find anything European that the Chinese wanted in sufficient quantity, the English turned toward India and the "country trade." This was the term for trade between India and various places from the Indian Ocean to the China seas conducted under East India Company license by the private firms of British subjects. Money obtained in Canton by the "country traders" was put on deposit there for the Company against bills of exchange on London. In this way, England, India, and China were connected by a trade and payments triangle.

The Opium Trade

Until 1823 the largest commodity imported to China from India was cotton, but this never reached the volume necessary to balance the trade. That was accomplished by opium. Opium had long been used for medicinal purposes, but the smoking, or more accurately, the inhaling of opium fumes through a pipe, began in the seventeenth century. The spread of the practice was sufficient to provoke an imperial edict of prohibition in 1729, but this and subsequent efforts to suppress the drug were unsuccessful and opium consumption continued to increase. Distributed by a network of illegal wholesalers and retailers with the connivance of dishonest officials, it spread among people of diverse occupations but proved particularly attractive to Chinese soldiers and government underlings. The drug was debilitating and habit forming. (See Figure 16-3.) Withdrawal was excruciatingly painful. Over time the addict developed a tolerance for opium and needed more and more of the drug to achieve a "high." The addict became a slave to opium. Thus, to pay for tea the Chinese were sold a poison. Since the opium was brought to China by country traders, the East India Company disclaimed responsibility for the illegal traffic in China. At the same time, however, it profited from the sale of opium in India where it monopolized the Bengal crop (Patna) and did what it could to control West Indian production (Malwa). In India itself, where the British as the paramount power felt a certain sense of responsibility, consumption of opium for nonmedicinal purposes was strictly prohibited.

The Chinese market for opium developed at such a pace that the balance of trade was reversed. During the 1820s and 1830s silver to pay for opium imports seems to have left China in large quantities. This, in turn, helped cause a decline in the exchange rate between copper coinage and silver, which upset the basis of the Chinese monetary system. Thus, what began as a public health problem now became a fiscal problem as well. In 1834, the Company's monopoly of the China trade was abolished by the British government. This opened the gates of trade still wider on the British side, resulting in an increased flow of opium to China, and an increased flow of silver out of China. Thus abolition of the Company's monopoly made the problem worse.

Abolition of the Company's trade monopoly was a victory for English advocates of free trade, who were as antagonistic to restraints on trade abroad as they were at home. The immediate effect in China was to put an end to the system of Cohong-Company relations in Canton. Now in place of the Select Committee of the East India Company, the British side was represented by an official of the crown. To initiate the new relations, Britain sent out Lord Napier as First Superintendent of Trade with instructions to establish direct contact with the Ch'ing viceroy, to protect British rights, and to assert jurisdiction

Figure 16-3   Opium Smokers.

over Englishmen in Canton. To accomplish these aims, he was ordered to use a moderate and conciliatory approach. Napier, however, more ambitious than diplomatic, immediately took an adamant stand on the issue of direct communication with the viceroy. He violated Chinese regulations by not waiting in Macao for permission to proceed to Canton and by sending a letter rather than petitioning through the hong merchants. With neither side willing to back down, the impasse developed into a showdown. All Chinese employees were withdrawn from the British community, food was cut off, and trade was stopped. Napier finally withdrew to Macao, where he died. This all took place in 1834. Unfortunately, in the ensuing lull no progress was made toward finding a new *modus vivendi* between the two sides.

For a brief moment the Chinese considered legalizing opium, but in 1836 the government decided on suppression instead. Dealers and addicts were prosecuted with great vigor, and imprisonments and executions were widespread, with the result that the price of opium dropped precipitously. This program was well under way when Lin Tse-hsü (1785–1850), a man of excellent reputation and demonstrated intellect and ability, arrived in Canton in March 1839. As imperial commissioner, he was charged with stamping out the drug trade once and for all.

In Canton, Lin Tse-hsü conducted a highly successful campaign against Chinese dealers and consumers. He also severely punished the corrupt officials who had connived at the trade. To deal with the foreign source of the opium, he appealed to Queen Victoria: "Suppose there were people from another country who carried opium for sale to England and seduced your people into buying and smoking it; certainly your honorable ruler would deeply hate it and be bitterly aroused."[4] He also admonished the foreign merchants, and he backed moral suasion with force.

What Lin demanded was that the foreigners surrender all their opium and sign a pledge to refrain from importing the drug in the future at the risk of confiscation and death. To effect compliance, he used the same weapons of isolating the foreign traders employed successfully in 1834 against Napier. Elliot, the British Superintendent of Trade, took a fateful step in response when he ordered the British merchants to turn their opium over to him for delivery to the Chinese authorities. By this act Elliot relieved the merchants of large amounts of opium they had been unable to sell because of the efficacy of the Chinese prohibitions, and he further made the British government responsible for eventual compensation. No wonder that the merchants enthusiastically dumped their opium: 21,306 chests were delivered to Lin Tse-hsü. It took the Chinese twenty-three days to destroy it all.

In England great pressures were exerted on the government by firms interested in the China trade demanding prompt and vigorous military action. Lin meanwhile, pleased with his victory, continued to press Elliot on the issue of the bonds or pledges, but here he did not succeed. The Superintendent of Trade argued that it was against British law to compel the merchants to sign the bonds and that the imposition of the death penalty without the benefits of

English judicial procedure was also contrary to British law. What was at stake here was the issue of British jurisdiction over British subjects, a source of Anglo-Chinese friction since 1784, when the British had refused to submit to Chinese justice. The issue came to the fore again in the summer of 1839 when a group of English sailors killed a Chinese villager in the Canton hinterland. Refusing to turn the men over to Lin Tse-hsü, Elliot tried them himself, but when they were returned to England the men were freed, since the home court ruled that Elliot had exceeded his authority.

The first clash of the war took place in November 1839, when the Chinese tried to protect one of the only two ships whose captains had signed the bond despite Elliot's stand and now wanted to trade. When a British ship fired a shot across the bow of the offending vessel, the Chinese intervened with twenty-one war junks, which, however, were no match for the foreign ships. In December trade with the British was stopped, and on January 31, 1840, a formal declaration of war was announced by the governor-general of India acting in the name of the home government.

The Opium War (1839–1842)

In June 1840, the British force, consisting of sixteen warships, four armed steamers, twenty-seven transports, a troop ship, and 4000 Irish, Scottish, and Indian soldiers, arrived in China. First the British blockaded Canton and then they moved north. They were fired on at Amoy while trying to deliver a letter from Prime Minister Palmerston under a white flag of truce, a symbol the Chinese did not understand. They then seized Chusan Island, south of the Yangtze estuary, and Ting-hai, the chief city there. The main body of the fleet sailed another 800 miles north to Pei-ho, near Tientsin, where Palmerston's letter was accepted. By this time the emperor had lost confidence in Lin Tse-hsü whose tough policy had led to military retaliation. Lin was dismissed, disgraced, and exiled to Ili in Central Asia. His place was taken by the Manchu prince Ch'i-shan (d.1854), who pursued a policy of flattery and accommodation to get the British to return to Canton for further negotiations. This they did in September 1840.

When the negotiations with Ch'i-shan in Canton turned out unsatisfactorily from the British point of view, they resumed military operations, with the result that in January 1841 Ch'i-shan was forced to sign the Convention of Ch'uan-pi, which provided for the cession of Hong Kong, an indemnity payable to Britain, equality of diplomatic relations, and the reopening of Canton. Both Ch'i-shan for the Ch'ing and Elliot for the British thought they had done very well, but neither government accepted their work. The Chinese emperor was indignant at how much had been conceded while Palmerston fumed that Elliot had demanded too little. The reactions of the Chinese and British governments showed all too clearly how far apart they still were in their appraisal of the situation. Caught in the middle were the negotiators. Like Lin Tse-hsü earlier,

Figure 16-4 *Foreign Devil.*
A Chinese sketch, ca. 1839.

now Ch'i-shan came to feel the imperial displeasure: his property was confiscated and he was sent to exile on the Amur. Elliot too was dismissed; his next position was as consul-general in Texas.

In the renewed fighting Canton was besieged in February 1841, but the siege was lifted on payment of a ransom of 6 million Spanish silver dollars. However, before their departure the British experienced the growing hostility of the local population. They were attacked by a body of troops organized by the local gentry. Although militarily ineffective, the attack was an indication of popular sentiment. (See Figure 16-4.)

In August Elliot was relieved by Pottinger, and the last phase of the war began when the British moved north, occupying Amoy in August and Ting-hai in October. Reinforcements were sent from India, increasing the naval force and bringing troop strength up to 10,000. With this force Pottinger continued the campaign, advancing up the Yangtze until his guns threatened Nanking. In Nanking on August 29, 1842, the treaty was signed that brought the war to a close. It was a dictated peace imposed by the Western victor on the vanquished Chinese.

The Treaty System

The Treaty of Nanking (together with the supplementary Treaty of the Bogue, October 1843) set the pattern for treaties China later signed with the United States and France in 1844, established the basic pattern for China's relations with the West for the next century, and supplied the model for similar treaties imposed on Japan. The Treaty of Nanking marked the end of the Canton System. The Cohong monopoly was abolished. Five ports—Canton, Amoy, Foochow, Ningpo, and Shanghai—were opened to Western trade. Britain received the right to appoint consuls to these cities, where British merchants were now allowed to trade and to reside together with their families. The treaty also stipulated that henceforth official communications were to be made on a basis of equality. This implied adoption, even if reluctant, of the European instead of the Chinese practice of international relations.

The Chinese were forced to pay an indemnity of 21 million Spanish silver dollars. Of this amount 12 million was for war expenses, in keeping with the normal European practice of forcing the loser to pay for the cost of a war. Another 6 million was paid as reparations for the opium handed over to Commissioner Lin, while the remaining 3 million went to settle the debts owed by the hong merchants to British merchants, thus liquidating another aspect of the old Canton System.

An important provision of the treaty established a moderate Chinese tariff of from 4 to 13 percent on imports, with an average rate of 5 percent. The Chinese, whose statutory customs levies had been even lower, did not realize that by agreeing to this provision they were relinquishing the freedom to set their own tariffs. On the British side there was the conviction that, as Adam Smith had taught, the removal of constraints on trade would benefit all by allowing everyone to concentrate on what he did best.

The British, having acquired an empire in India, with all the burdens of government that it entailed, did not seek to create another in China. Trade not territory was their aim. But they did demand and obtain a Chinese base. Hong Kong Island, at that time the site of a tiny fishing village, was ceded to them in perpetuity. Well-located and with an excellent harbor, it developed into a major international port.

The issue of legal jurisdiction over British subjects was settled by the Treaty of the Bogue, which provided for extraterritoriality, that is, the right of British subjects to be tried according to British law in British consular courts. The British, having only recently reformed their own legal system, were convinced of its superiority. There were precedents in Chinese history for allowing "barbarians" to manage their own affairs, but in modern terms extraterritoriality amounted to a limitation on Chinese sovereignty.

The Treaty of the Bogue also provided for most-favored-nation treatment. This obliged China to grant to Britain any rights China conceded in the future to any other power. Its effect was to prevent China from playing the powers off against each other. It meant that once a nation had obtained a concession it automatically was enjoyed by all the other states enjoying most-favored-nation status.

In the 1844 treaties the United States and France also received this status. In the American treaty China agreed to allow for the maintenance of churches and hospitals in the treaty ports, and to treaty revision in twelve years, while the French won the right to propagate Catholicism.

The status of the opium trade was left unsettled in the original treaties, and American agreement to outlaw smuggling did not slow down the growth of opium traffic, which was legalized under the next round of treaty settlements, 1858–60. From the annual 30,000 chests a year prior to the Opium War, this trade reached 87,000 chests in 1879 and then declined as native Chinese production of opium increased. British opium imports were down to about 50,000 chests when in 1906 the Ch'ing took strong measures against the drug. British imports finally came to a stop in 1917, but opium smoking remained a serious social problem until the early 1950s.

For China the treaties solved nothing. A particularly ominous development was the permission granted foreign gunboats to anchor at the treaty ports, for when additional ports were opened it gave foreign powers the right to navigate China's inland waterways. The cumulative effect of the treaties was to reduce China to a status of inequality, forcing her to relinquish powers that no European state would have surrendered.

China and the West (1842–1860)

The Chinese were slow to realize the full implications of the Treaty of Nanking, and only a very few men at court had any inkling of the dimensions of the "barbarian" challenge. The best "barbarian" experts could suggest was for China to acquire "barbarian" arms and to employ the old diplomacy of playing off one "barbarian" against another. Less well informed officials suggested that future military operations take advantage of the supposed physical peculiarities of the "barbarians," for example, their stiff waists and straight legs, which made them dependent on horses and ships, or their poor night vision.

Negotiations with the foreign powers were handled by the viceroy of Kwangtung and Kwangsi. The first viceroy managed the English by charm and conciliation, "sharing their cup and spoon to hold their hearts,"[5] but he was later replaced by a more hard-line, intransigent official. Frustrated in attempts at local negotiation, the British demanded direct representation in Peking. They also pressed for treaty revision because the opening of the new ports had not led to the anticipated increase in trade. Behind the demands for freer trade was the persistent belief that only artificial restrictions prevented the development of a giant market in China for British textiles and other products.

One cause for friction between the English and the Chinese was the repeated postponement of the opening of Canton in view of the strong antiforeign feeling of its people. The continuation of the opium trade did not help matters, and Chinese antagonism toward Europeans was reinforced by the development of a new commerce in Chinese laborers. These men were often procured against their will, crowded into dismal "coolie" vessels, and transported as contract laborers to work the plantations of Cuba and Peru. The boom set off by the discovery of gold in California in 1848 also brought Chinese immigrants to the United States, but they came as free laborers, their passage organized by Chinese merchants. By 1852 there were 25,000 Chinese in the American West, and by 1887 there were twice that number in California.

There were some efforts at cooperation during these years. With Chinese consent, the British set about suppressing piracy. More important was the establishment of the Foreign Inspectorate of Customs in Shanghai in 1854, after the Ch'ing officials had been ejected by rebels. The Inspectorate became responsible for the collection of tariffs and the prevention of smuggling. By the new treaties of 1858, its authority was extended to all treaty ports, and it became an important source of support for the dynasty.

Despite such collaboration, however, there remained more discord than harmony, and in 1856 war broke out once more. The immediate cause of the war was the Arrow Affair. The Arrow was a Chinese-owned but Hong Kong-registered lorcha, a vessel with a Western hull but Chinese rigging, which although flying the British flag was boarded by Chinese officials, who seized twelve Chinese men whom they charged with piracy. When the viceroy returned the men but refused to apologize and guarantee there would be no repetition of the event, the British responded by seizing Canton. Then they withdrew, and there was a lull in the fighting while the British were occupied fighting a war in India set off by the Sepoy Mutiny of 1857 (sepoys were Indian soldiers). When the war in China was resumed in December 1857, however, the English were joined by the French.

As in the first war, the Europeans again moved north, and again the first attempt at peace failed, since the Ch'ing emperor refused to ratify the British and French Treaties of Tientsin negotiated in 1858. Hostilities then recommenced. This time the allies entered Peking itself in 1860, and Elgin, the British commander, vented his anger by burning down the imperial summer palace. In October the Conventions of Peking were signed to supplement the Treaties of Tientsin, which now also took effect. In addition to the usual indemnity, China was forced to open eleven new ports, to grant rights to travel in the interior, and to allow foreign envoys to reside in Peking. In 1860 the French also surreptitiously inserted into the Chinese text a provision granting missionaries the right to buy land and erect buildings in all parts of China.

Russian Gains

The peace agreements were secured through the mediation of the Russian ambassador to Peking, who used the opportunity to consolidate the gains Russia had made to date and to obtain new concessions for his country. Under Peter the Great and Catherine the Great, Russia's land empire had expanded into the area west of the Pamirs known as Russian Turkestan, and in 1851 Russia obtained trading privileges and the right to station consuls at Kuldja and Chuguchak (Ta-ch'eng) in the Ili region of Chinese Turkestan east of the Pamirs. Now Kashgar, southwest of Kuldja, and Urga (Ulan Bator) in Outer Mongolia were also opened to them.

The most massive Russian gains, however, were in the Northeast. In the Amur region Nikolai Muraviev, governor-general of Siberia, had been putting pressure on the Ch'ing since 1847. Now, in 1860, the entire area north of the Amur was ceded to the Russians, who also received the lands east of the Ussuri River, which were incorporated into the Russian Empire as the Amur and Maritime Provinces. In the latter Muraviev founded Vladivostok ("Ruler of the East," in Russian). Russia also now received most-favored-nation status. The gains Russia made at this time remain a source of conflict between the Russians and Chinese today.

Internal Crisis

The encroachments of the foreign powers, serious as they were, constituted only one of the threats facing the dynasty. An even greater danger to the regime developed internally as the government proved unable to deal with long-term problems that would have taxed the ingenuity and energy even of an honest and effective government. Foremost were the problems created by population pressures, for the population continued to increase in the nineteenth century as it had in the eighteenth. By 1850 the number of inhabitants in China had risen to about 430 million, without any comparable increase in productivity or resources. As ever, the poor suffered most, and they were legion, for the uneven distribution of land left many people landless, destitute, and in despair. The situation was made worse by government neglect of public works. The opium trade also contributed to the economic crisis, for silver continued to leave China, further disrupting the silver-copper ratio and thereby increasing the farmer's tax burden, which was calculated in scarce silver but paid in copper cash.

Government leadership was totally inadequate. Emperor Chia-ch'ing (1796–1820) tried to remedy the government's financial problems by cutting expenses but was unable to solve the underlying fiscal and economic problems. Sale of official posts and titles helped the treasury but did not raise the quality of the bureaucracy nor help the people who ultimately supplied the funds.

Emperor Tao-kuang (1821–50) continued his father's policy of frugality. It is said that he himself wore old and patched clothes. His partial success in reforming the official salt monopoly system did not compensate for his failure to reinvigorate the Grand Canal or Yellow River managements, however. The former was impassible by 1849, after which tax grain had to be shipped by sea. The abandonment of the canal cost thousands their jobs. Emperor Tao-kuang did not live to see the Yellow River disaster of 1852. Since 1194 the great river had flown into the sea south of Shantung Peninsula but now, silted up, it shifted to the north, spreading flood and devastation over a wide area.

The next emperor, Hsien-feng (1851–61), was nineteen when he inherited the throne and proved equally incapable of dealing with an increasingly menacing situation. Even while rebellion threatened the dynasty, a major scandal involving bribery and cheating shook the examination system.

Famine, poverty, and corruption gave rise to banditry and armed uprisings, as had so often happened in the past. The most formidable threat to the dynasty came from the Taiping revolutionaries. To aggravate the crisis even further, the dynasty also had to contend with rebellions elsewhere. In the border regions of Anhwei, Kiangsu, Honan, and Shantung, there was the Nien Rebellion (1853–68) led by secret societies, probably related to the White Lotus Society. There was also a Muslim rebellion in Yunnan (1855–73) and the Tungan Rebellion in the Northwest (1862–75). Yet it was the Taipings who came closest to destroying the Ch'ing in a civil war that in terms of bloodshed and devastation was the costliest in human history. It is estimated that more than 20 million people lost their lives.

The Taiping Rebellion (1850–1864)

The founder of the Taiping movement was a village school teacher named Hung Hsiu-ch'üan (1814–64) who belonged to the Hakka minority, which many centuries earlier had migrated from the North to the Southeast, where they remained a distinct ethnic group. Originally Hung hoped for a conventional civil service career and four times went to Canton to participate in the examination for the licentiate, only to fail each time. Shocked by his third failure he became seriously ill and for forty days was subject to fits of delirium during which he experienced visions. These visions he later interpreted with the aid of a Christian tract he picked up in Canton, where Protestant missionaries had made a beginning in their effort to bring their faith to China. He also received some instruction from an American Southern Baptist missionary. On the basis of his limited knowledge of the Bible and Christianity, he proceeded to work out his own form of Sinicized Christianity.

Central to Hung's faith was his conviction that in his visions he had seen God, who had bestowed on Hung the divine mission to save mankind and exterminate demons. He had also met Jesus and was given to understand that Christ was his own elder brother. This recasting of Christianity into a familiar familistic mode had its appeal for Hung's Chinese audience but dismayed Western Christian missionaries, who were further appalled by Hung's claims that he himself was a source of new revelation.

The emphasis in Taiping Christianity was on the Old Testament rather than the New Testament, on the Ten Commandments not on the Sermon on the Mount. Hung's militant zeal in obeying the first commandment by destroying Buddhist and Taoist "idols" and even Confucian tablets soon cost him his position as a village teacher. He became an itinerant preacher among the Hakka communities in Kwangsi, gaining converts and disciples as he went about spreading the word among the downtrodden and dispossessed, whom he recruited into the Association of God Worshippers. To the poor and miserable, he held out a vision of the "Heavenly Kingdom of Great Peace" (T'ai-p'ing t'ien-kuo), an egalitarian, God-ordained utopia.

In keeping with both Christianity and native traditions, Hung and his disciples laid great stress on a strict, even puritanical, morality. Opium, tobacco, gambling, alcohol, prostitution, sexual misconduct, and foot binding were all strictly prohibited. Women were put on an equal basis with men in theory and, to a remarkable extent, also in practice. Also, consonant with both the Christian belief in the brotherhood of man and native Chinese utopian ideas was a strong strain of economic egalitarianism, a kind of simple communism. Property was to be shared in common, and in 1850 the members of the Association were asked to turn over their funds to a public treasury that would provide for everyone's future needs.

What stood in the way of realizing this utopia were the demons, mostly Manchus. By July 1850 the Association had attracted 10,000 adherents, primarily in Kwangsi province. In defiance of the Ch'ing they now cut off their queues, the long braids of hair hanging down from the back of the head, which had been introduced by the Manchus as a sign of Chinese subjugation. Since they also refused to shave the forepart of their heads, the government called them the "long-haired rebels."

Millenarian religious beliefs, utopian egalitarianism, moral righteousness, and hatred of the Manchus proved a potent combination when fused into a program of organized armed resistance. At this stage the Taipings also enjoyed good leadership. One of the outstanding secondary leaders was Yang Hsiuch'ing, originally a charcoal burner, who was a talented organizer and strategist. Starting from their base in Kwangsi, the Taiping forces made rapid military progress. One of their favorite tactics in attacking cities was to use their contingent of coal miners to dig tunnels to undermine the defending walls. The incompetence of the government forces was also a help. As the Taiping armies advanced, they picked up strength. It has been estimated that their number reached over one million by the time they took Nanking in 1853.

After such a quick advance, with their ranks swollen by new adherents only partially versed in Taiping tenets, the leadership decided it was time to call a halt and consolidate. The "Heavenly Kingdom of Great Peace" had formally been proclaimed in 1851. Now, with its capital at Nanking, the attempt was made to turn it into a solid regime. To continue military operations, two expeditions were sent out. A small force was dispatched north and reached within twenty miles of Tientsin before suffering reverses and defeat. Large forces were sent west and enjoyed considerable success until 1856, but also were eventually defeated. The future of the rebellion depended in large part on the success of its planned consolidation.

Taiping Programs and Policies

The Taipings proclaimed a revolutionary program of political and economic reorganization. They did not want simply to establish a new regime on the old pattern but to change the pattern itself. The source for their official terminology and many of their ideas was *The Rites of Chou*, long a source of radical thought in China.

The Taiping land program was based on a system of land classification according to nine grades found in *The Rites of Chou*. The idea was that everyone would receive an equal amount of land, measured in terms of productivity of the soil, so that all their personal needs would be met. Any production over and above what was needed by the assignees was to be contributed to common granaries and treasuries. The system did not recognize private property.

The basic political structure was a unit of twenty-five families consisting of five groups of five families each. The leadership of these and larger units was to combine civil and military duties and also to see after the spiritual welfare of the people. Taiping Christianity was propagated by Sunday services conducted by these leaders. It developed its own hymns and literature including *The Three Character Classic* written in the vernacular. Taiping writings also served as the subject matter for a new examination system open to women as well as to men. In other respects, too, women were made equal to men, and there were female military units. Marriages took place in church and were monogamous.

Taiping treatment of Westerners was cordial but clumsy. They lost much good will by employing condescending language and expressions of superiority not unlike those used by Peking. After the British failed to obtain Taiping recognition of their treaty rights, they decided on a policy of neutrality, and the other powers soon followed suit. This remained the policy of the foreign powers through the 1850s.

Dissension and Weakness

A turning point for the Taiping regime came in 1856 in the form of a leadership crisis they could ill afford. Yang Hsiu-ch'ing, more ambitious than devout, had increased his power to the point of reducing Hung to a mere figurehead. To legitimize his position, Yang went into trances and claimed to be acting on God's orders, but he was unable to convince the other leaders. When he overreached himself, they turned on him. Yang, along with his family and thousands of followers, was killed, but no strong successor appeared to take his place. Meanwhile Hung Hsiu-ch'üan was preoccupied with his religious visions. By the time Hung's cousin Hung Jen-kan (1822–64) came into prominence in 1859, it was too late to restructure the regime. Hung Jen-kan was the most Westernized of the Taiping leaders but had neither the time nor the power to build the centralized and modern state he had in mind. His leadership lasted only until 1861.

Failure of the leadership was one source of Taiping weakness. Inadequate implementation of stated policies was another. Practice did not conform to theory. For example, Hung Hsiu-ch'üan and the other leaders kept numerous concubines despite the Taiping call for monogamy. Moreover, there were many missed opportunities: the failure to strike before the dynasty could re-group; the failure to cooperate with secret societies and other opponents of the regime who did not share the Taiping faith; the failure to cultivate good relations with the foreign powers.

To make matters worse, Taiping revolutionary ideas repelled all those Chinese who identified with the basic Confucian way of life and understood that the Taiping program was not merely anti-Manchu but anti-Confucian, and thus subversive to the traditional social order. Consequently the Taipings not only failed to recruit gentry support, but they antagonized this key element in Chinese society. To the literati, rule by "civilized" Manchus was preferable to rule by "barbarized" Chinese.

Tseng Kuo-fan and the Defeat of the Taipings

What ultimately saved the dynasty was a new kind of military force organized by Tseng Kuo-fan (1811–72), a dedicated Confucian and a product of the examination system. Unlike the old armies organized under the banner system (see pages 326–27), Tseng's army was a strictly regional force from Hunan, staffed by officers of similar regional and ideological background personally selected by him. They, in turn, recruited soldiers from their own home areas or from members of their own clans. A paternalistic attitude of officers toward their men, a generous pay scale honestly administered, careful moral indoctrination, and common regional ties all helped to produce a well-disciplined force high in morale.

Ch'ing statesmen were aware that strong regional armies such as Tseng's threatened the balance of power between the central government and the regions, and were ultimately dangerous to the authority of the dynasty. But the traditional armies of the regime had proved hopelessly inadequate, and the Manchu rulers had no choice but to trust their defense to Tseng. Although organized in Hunan, where it began its operations, the army also fought the Taipings in other provinces. It was not always victorious: twice Tseng suffered such serious reverses that he attempted suicide. But in the long run a well-led and highly motivated army, honestly administered and true to its purpose, proved superior to the Taiping forces.

The dynasty also benefited from the services of two other remarkable leaders, Tso Tsung-t'ang (1812–85) and Li Hung-chang (1823–1901). Tso and Li led armies similarly organized on the new model. After the treaties of 1860 the Western powers also sided with the regime that had made such extensive concessions to them. A Western commander and Western officers led a force of four or five thousand Chinese troops in the Shanghai area. An American adventurer, Frederick T. Ward, was its first commander, and he was succeeded by the English officer Charles George Gordon ("Chinese" Gordon) as leader of the "Ever Victorious Army." Customs revenues helped loyalists purchase foreign arms and establish arsenals.

After a series of victories the loyalist armies laid siege to Nanking, and when the situation became hopeless in the Taiping capital Hung Hsiu-ch'üan committed suicide. Shortly thereafter, on July 19, 1864, the city fell to an army commanded by Tseng Kuo-fan's brother. As had happened often in this bitter war on both sides, the fall of Nanking was followed by a bloodbath. Hung's son managed to flee but was discovered in Kiangsi and executed. The Taipings, once so close to victory, were completely eradicated, leaving only the force of their example to inspire future revolutionaries. For many years Tseng Kuo-fan was widely admired as a great Confucian statesman, steadfast in his loyalty to the dynasty when he could have used his provincial power base for his own personal ends. But a hundred years later the tables of historical evaluation were reversed, and in the new China led by another Hunanese, Mao Tse-tung, the Taipings were cast as heroes.

Although the other uprisings against the dynasty did not threaten the Ch'ing as severely as had the Taipings, it still took considerable fighting to suppress them. In the campaigns against the highly mobile mounted Nien bands and the Muslim rebellions, Tseng Kuo-fan, Li Hung-chang, and Tso Tsung-t'ang again played a prominent part.

According to Chinese political theory, force was merely an adjunct of government. The suppression of the Taipings, the Niens, and other rebels was only one aspect of the general effort to revitalize the dynasty.

The T'ung-chih Restoration

The leading statesmen and scholars of the T'ung-chih period (1862–74) thought of themselves as engaged in a restoration (chung-hsing*), that is, a dynastic revival similar to the revival of the Han dynasty by the founder of the Later Han, or to the resurgence of the T'ang after the rebellion of An Lu-shan. From this sense of historical precedent they derived the confidence to initiate a broad program, which they hoped would revitalize the dynasty. Although their accomplishments fell far short of their goals, they achieved enough to induce modern scholars also to employ the term "restoration."

To cope with the dislocations wrought by warfare, the T'ung-chih leaders applied old remedies: relief projects were instituted, public works projects initiated, land reclaimed and water controlled, granaries set up, expenses cut, taxes reduced in the ravaged lower Yangtze Valley. As always, priority was placed on agriculture.

An aspect of the revival dear to the hearts of its Confucian sponsors was a strengthening of scholarship by reprinting old texts, founding new academies, opening libraries, and the like. Examination system reform was similarly high

---

* A different term (wei-hsin in Chinese, ishin in Japanese) was used by the Japanese to designate their Meiji Restoration. Although the Japanese term comes from the Chinese Book of Songs and has the meaning of "making new," or "renovation," it lacks the historical referents and programmatic content of the Chinese term.

on the list of priorities, as was the elimination of corruption from the bureaucracy. In the examinations, questions dealing with practical problems of statecraft were introduced, and attempts were made to limit the sale of degrees and offices. By such measures, the reformers sought to raise the level of honesty and elevate the moral tone of officialdom so as to reestablish the moral authority of the officials and the government they served. However, nothing effective was done about the solidly entrenched and notoriously corrupt sub-bureaucracy of clerks and other underlings.

Furthermore, the dynasty was powerless to reverse the trend toward regionalism, which ultimately had grave consequences for the center and the provinces alike. In the latter, the disruption of old bonds with the central government removed many of the political constraints on local wealth and power. It thus set in motion a restructuring of local society that ultimately was to prove dangerous both to the state and to the social order.

T'ung-chih was only six when he came to the throne, and the real leadership was in the hands of his uncle Prince Kung (1833–98) and his young mother, the Empress Dowager Tz'u Hsi (1835–1908). Foreign policy was largely under the direction of Prince Kung, who expressed the regime's order of priorities thus:

> The situation today may be compared (to the diseases of a human body). Both the Taiping and the Nien bandits are gaining victories and constitute an organic disease. Russia, with her territory adjoining ours, aiming to nibble away our territory like a silk worm, may be considered a threat at our bosom. As to England, her purpose is to trade, but she acts violently, without any regard for human decency. If she is not kept within limits, we shall not be able to stand on our feet. Hence she may be compared to an affliction of our limbs. Therefore we should suppress the Taipings and the Nien bandits first, get the Russians under control next, and attend to the British last.[6]

It was apparent to Prince Kung that new approaches to foreign policy would be required if these objectives were to be met. In 1861 he sponsored the establishment of a new agency to deal with the foreign powers and related matters. This was the Tsungli Yamen (Office of General Management), not an independent ministry but a subcommittee of the Grand Council supervising a number of offices. (See Figure 16-5.) As such its influence depended on that of its presiding officer and his associates. It was, accordingly, most influential during the 1860s, when Prince Kung was at the height of his authority. An important innovation introduced by the Tsungli Yamen was its appeal to international law, using Henry Wheaton's *Elements of International Law*, a standard text translated by the American missionary W. A. P. Martin.

Prince Kung, recognizing that Chinese officials would be at a disadvantage in dealing with foreigners unless they had a better understanding of foreign languages and learning, was instrumental in having the Tsungli Yamen establish a school (the T'ung-wen kuan) for foreign languages and other nontraditional subjects in 1862. The foreign language staff was foreign and included Martin, who became the school's president in 1869. By that time astronomy and math-

Figure 16-5 Three members of the Tsungli Yamen and statesmen of the T'ung-chih period. LEFT TO RIGHT, Shen Kuei-fen, President of the Ministry of War; Tung Hsün, President of the Ministry of Finance; Mao Ch'ang-hsi, President of the Ministry of Works.

ematics had also been introduced, despite the objections of the distinguished Mongol scholar, General Secretary Wo-jen who said: "From ancient down to modern times your slave has never heard of anyone who could use mathematics to raise the nation from a state of decline or to strengthen it in time of weakness."[7] Wo-jen (d. 1871) was not alone in his objections to this extension of "barbarian" influence.

Nevertheless, similar schools were established at Shanghai, Canton, and Foochow in association with arsenals and shipyards sponsored by Tseng Kuo-fan, Tso Tsung-t'ang, and Li Hung-chang. (See Figure 16-6.) Foreigners were relied on to run both the military and the educational establishments. In this way the foundations of "self-strengthening" and of modernization were laid, but the emphasis remained heavily military. This was true even of Feng Kuei-fen (1809–74), an advocate of learning from the barbarians, who had the audacity to propose that examination degrees, including the *chin-shih*, be presented to men demonstrating accomplishment in Western mechanical skills.

During the 1860s, following the close of hostilities, Chinese cooperation with the foreign powers brought certain advantages to the Ch'ing, although there were some on both sides who were opposed to cooperation. (For example,

Wo-jen and men of similar views felt that China should resist all foreign influence and seek the expulsion of all foreigners; while the British mercantile community frowned on the efforts of Rutherford Alcock, English minister in Peking, to work amicably with the government.)

An important area of cooperation was the Maritime Customs Service. The first director of the service, Horatio Nelson Lay, had acquired a fleet of eight gunboats for the Chinese in England. But although these were paid for by the Chinese, he arranged that the captain of the fleet should receive all his orders through and at the discretion of Lay himself! This was unacceptable to the Ch'ing. There were protests. China's first effort to acquire a modern navy ended with disbandment of the little fleet (known as the Lay-Osborn flotilla), and Lay was pensioned off.

Matters improved, however, when Robert Hart succeeded Lay in 1863. Hart's attitude was the opposite of Lay's. He insisted that the customs was a Chinese service, that Chinese officials were to be treated as "brother officers," and he gave the Ch'ing government well intentioned and frequently helpful advice on modernization while building the service into an important source of support for the dynasty.

Cooperation between the Ch'ing and the powers was further exemplified by the first Chinese diplomatic mission to the West, which was headed by the retiring American minister to Peking, Anson Burlingame. Accompanied by a

Figure 16-6   Scene at the Nanking Arsenal.

Manchu and a Chinese official, Burlingame left China in 1867 for a trip to Washington, several European capitals, and St. Petersburg, where he died. Somewhat carried away by his own eloquence he told Americans that China was ready to extend "her arms toward the shining banners of Western civilization."[8] In Washington he concluded a treaty rather favorable to China.

The most important negotiations for treaty revision, however, were conducted in Peking by the British. These culminated in the Alcock Convention of 1869 which included some concessions to the Chinese, among them the provision that British subjects under the most-favored-nation clause would enjoy privileges extended to other nationals only if they accepted the conditions under which those privileges were granted. It also allowed China to open a consulate in Hong Kong and contained provisions concerning duties and taxes. These concessions may not appear very far reaching, but the English merchant community felt threatened by them, and their opposition proved strong enough to prevent the ratification of the convention.

A fatal blow to the policy of cooperation came in 1870 in Tientsin. A Catholic nunnery there had made the mistake of offering small payments for orphans brought to the mission, and rumors spread that the children had been kidnapped and that the sisters removed the children's hearts and eyes to make medicine. The tense situation erupted into violence, and a mob took the lives of the French consul and twenty other foreigners, including ten nuns, in what came to be known as the Tientsin Massacre. The powers mobilized their gunboats. Diplomacy finally settled the issue, largely because France's defeat in the Franco-Prussian War the same year deprived France of military power and forced the French to concentrate on domestic problems. But the decade ended with demonstrations of the gap between the two civilizations and with feelings of mutual bitterness and disdain. Tseng Kuo-fan was given the difficult task of negotiating with the Westerners after the tragic Tientsin Massacre. Tseng died in 1872. As the T'ung-chih period came to an end, the internal reform also lost momentum.

Thirty years after the Opium War the dynasty had survived despite the maladies attacking it from within and without. The progress of the disease had been halted. But time was to show that there had been no genuine cure and that, in the long run, the medicine itself had potentially lethal side effects. In Japan, in contrast, the old regime had fallen, and work had begun on the creation of a new state and society.

NOTES

1. John K. Fairbank, Edwin O. Reischauer, and Albert Craig, *East Asia: Tradition and Transformation* (Boston: Houghton Mifflin, 1973), p. 257.
2. Franz Schurmann and Orville Schell, *The China Reader: Imperial China* (New York: Vintage Books, 1967), pp. 105–13, which reproduce Harley F. MacNair, *Modern Chinese History, Selected Readings* (Shanghai: Commercial Press Ltd., 1923), pp. 2–9.

3. John K. Fairbank, *Trade and Diplomacy on the China Coast: The Opening of the Treaty Ports, 1842–1854* (Cambridge: Harvard University Press, 1953), p. 59, which quotes H. B. Morse, *The Chronicles of the East India Company Trading to China, 1635–1834*, 5 vols. (Oxford, 1926, 1929), 2: 247–52.

4. Ssu-yü Teng and John K. Fairbank, *China's Response to the West: A Documentary Survey, 1839–1923* (Cambridge: Harvard University Press, 1954), p. 26.

5. *Ibid.*, p. 38.

6. *Ibid.*, p. 48.

7. *Ibid.*, p. 76.

8. Quoted in Immanuel C. Y. Hsü, *China's Entrance into the Family of Nations: The Diplomatic Phase, 1858–1880* (Cambridge: Harvard University Press, 1960), p. 168.

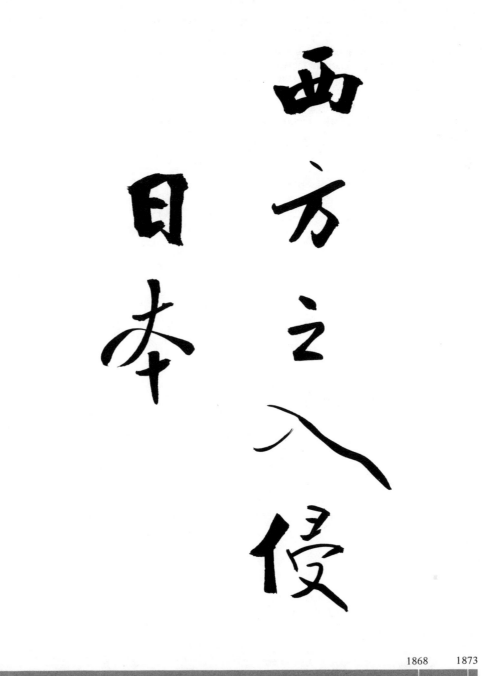

西方之入侵

日本

17 The Intrusion of the West: Japan

Like China, Japan in the middle of the nineteenth century had to come to terms with vigorous and expanding Western powers that could no longer be contained by the old system of "barbarian" management. Also for Japan as for China, the threat from abroad came in a period of political weakness at home. However, despite these similarities, Japanese and Chinese history in the nineteenth century, as in the twelfth or twentieth, offers a study in contrasts. The similarities are just sufficient to make these contrasts meaningful.

Problems at Midcentury

Japan differed from China not only in the rapidity of Japanese response to the West but also in the depth of the changes which this set off in Japanese society; a milder foreign challenge provoked a stronger domestic response. This happened not only because Japan was smaller than China and historically more open to foreign influence but because the internal dynamics of Tokugawa history had already produced the essential ingredients of change even though it took the threat from abroad to set them in motion.

A major source of trouble and distress during the late Tokugawa was the inability of the ruling class to cope with a money economy. The samurai who had to convert a substantial portion of his rice stipend into cash was constantly at the mercy of a fluctuating market which he could not understand and would not study. Even the daimyo, burdened with the heavy expenses of periodic attendance in Edo, and required to maintain separate establishments in the *bakufu* and *han* capitals, found themselves in financial difficulty. One way for a daimyo to improve his finances was to cut stipends, further aggravating the situation of the samurai. This hurt even the small minority of high-ranking men, but the effects were most serious, even devastating, on the bulk of samurai who ranked low in status and stipend.

Some samurai married daughters of wealthy merchants, but many lived in desperate circumstances. They pawned their swords, worked at humble crafts, such as umbrella making and sandal weaving, and tried to hide their misery from the world. A samurai was taught that he should use a toothpick even when he had not eaten.

The samurai were not dissatisfied with the basic social system in which, after all, they formed the ruling class. But they were unhappy at the discrepancy between the theoretical elevation of their status and the reality of their poverty. Not only was their poverty demeaning, but the spectacle of contrasting merchant wealth hurt their pride. It seemed the height of injustice that society should reward the selfish money-making trader and condemn to indigence the warrior whose life was one of service. This helps explain the rapidity with which men of samurai background eventually dismantled the system.

The immediate focus of samurai discontent was not with the Tokugawa order, however, but with the character and abilities of the men in power. There was deep resentment against incompetence and corruption in high places, and it was felt that government could be reformed by putting into office more capable men, including able men from the lower ranks of the samurai class. In staffing the *bakufu* and *han* bureaucracies, ability and competence should take precedence over family.

City merchants and rural entrepreneurs flourished economically and were acquiescent politically, but below them the rural and urban poor included many who earned barely enough to keep themselves alive. Crop failures in the 1820s and 1830s and a national famine in 1836 caused great misery and brought masses of displaced peasants into the cities. The government did supply relief but not enough to forestall violence. Four hundred incidents of violent protest were recorded between 1813 and 1868. One which made a great impression occurred in Ōsaka in 1837. It was led by Ōshio Heihachiro (1793–1837), a low-ranking *bakufu* official and follower of Wang Yang-ming's philosophy of action, but it was poorly planned and quickly suppressed. Peasant discontent during these years also found expression in the rise of messianic religious movements. But neither religious sects nor uprisings ever reached anything like the dimensions of the Taiping Rebellion in China. Tokugawa samurai, unlike Ch'ing gentry, were never called upon as a class to defend their regime against the masses nor did they experience a serious threat from below.

Reform Programs

The *bakufu* itself faced financial problems. By 1800 its annual budget showed a small deficit, the beginning of a trend. For more than a century it had coped with fiscal crises by resorting to two devices: forced loans and currency devaluation. Now it did so again. Between 1819 and 1837 there were nineteen instances of currency devaluation. These brought temporary relief, but they did not effect long range improvements in the shogunate's finances. Nor did they free it from dependence on the market and on the merchants who understood and manipulated the market. There was in Tokugawa Japan no system or theory for regular deficit financing.

The reforms undertaken by Mizuno Tadakuni (1793–1851) during 1841–43 were reminiscent of earlier *bakufu* efforts and in spirit went back to Ieyasu himself. They included recoinage and forced loans, dismissal of officials to reduce costs, and sumptuary laws intended to preserve morals and save money. Censorship became stricter. An effort (by no means the *bakufu's* first) was made to force peasants to return to their lands. This was in keeping with the Confucian view of the primacy of agriculture as well as with the Tokugawa's policy of strict class separation but hardly solved any problems. A program to create solid areas of *bakufu* control around Edo and Ōsaka proved too ambitious. It called for the creation of a *bakufu*-controlled zone of twenty-five square miles around Edo and twelve square miles around Ōsaka by moving certain daimyo and housemen out of these areas, but the plan was never carried out. In the hope of fighting inflation, merchant monopolies were broken up, but the result was economic chaos and still further inflation. Despite the retrenchment policy, an expensive and ostentatious formal procession to the Tokugawa mausoleum at Nikkō was organized in an effort to shore up the *bakufu's* prestige. In the end Mizuno's program produced more resentment than improvement.

The various domains (*han*), faced with similar problems, attempted local reform programs of their own. Here and there *han* government machinery was reformed, stipends and other costs were cut, agriculture was encouraged, and commercial policies were changed. The results were often as disappointing as

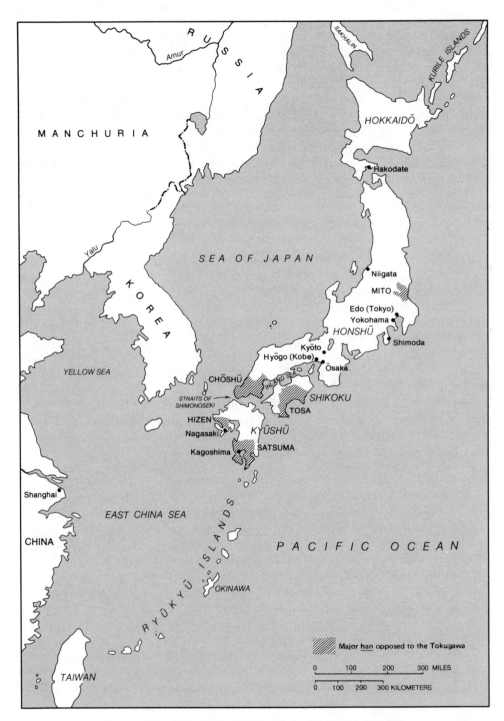

Figure 17-1 **Japan on the Eve of the Meiji Restoration**

they were for the shogunate—often but not always. The political division of Japan allowed for local variations and experimentation so that some domains were more successful than others.

Two of the most successful *han* were Satsuma in Kyūshū and Chōshū in Southwest Honshū. (See map, Figure 17-1.) In interesting and important ways these were untypical domains. For one thing, they were both large, outside *han* (*tozama*), that is, *han* that had arisen independently of the Tokugawa, which prior to 1600 they sometimes opposed and sometimes supported, but as equals not subordinates. In the seventeenth century they accepted Tokugawa supremacy since they had no other alternative, but their commitment to the Tokugawa order was not beyond question. In line with Tokugawa policy, Satsuma and Chōshū had their domains transferred and reduced in size in the seventeenth century. One consequence was that they kept alive an anti-Tokugawa feudal tradition. Another result was that the reduction in the size of their domains left them with a much higher than average ratio of samurai to the land. In Satsuma this led to the formation of a class of samurai who worked the land (*goshi*) and a tight control of the countryside, which experienced not a single peasant uprising throughout the Tokugawa period. Satsuma backwardness was also an asset to the domain in the sense that it worked against the erosion of samurai values found in economically more advanced and urbane regions. Both Chōshū and Satsuma also had special family ties with the court in Kyōto, the most likely focus for any anti*bakufu* movement.

In both *han*, finances were put in order and a budget surplus was built up, although by different methods. In Chōshū a rigorous cost-cutting program was initiated, major improvements were made in *han* financial administration, and there was a reform of the land tax. Most *han* monopolies were abolished, since they were unprofitable for the government and unpopular among the people. Only the profitable shipping and warehouse monopolies at Shimonoseki were continued. Otherwise, commodity transactions were turned over to merchants for a fee. Satsuma, in contrast, derived much of its income from its monopolies, especially the monopoly on sugar from the Ryūkyū Islands (Liu-ch'iu, in Chinese), which were a Satsuma dependency. At the same time Satsuma directed the Ryūkyūs to continue sending tribute to China in order to foster trade between China and the islands, which thus became a source of Chinese goods for Satsuma. The sugar monopoly was strictly enforced: private sale of sugar was a crime punishable by death. The sugar was brought to market in Ōsaka in the *han*'s own ships, and at every stage from production to sale everything was done to insure maximum profit for the Satsuma treasury.

These programs required vigorous leadership, since they naturally ran up against the opposition of merchants and others who benefited from doing things the old way. Both Chōshū and Satsuma were fortunate in having reform-minded daimyo who raised to power young samurai of middle or low rank, men who tended to be much more innovative and energetic than conservative samurai of high rank. Particularly in Chōshū such differences in back-

ground and outlook within the samurai class led to bitter political antago-
nisms and produced a period of turbulence in *han* politics.

The fact that reform was more successful in Chōshū and Satsuma than in
the *bakufu* suggests that it was easier to implement reform in a well-organized, remote domain than in the central region where the economic changes
were most advanced and political pressures and responsibilities were far
greater. Reform attempts in the other *han* varied in success, but the Chōshū
and Satsuma cases are particularly important, since these two large and
wealthy domains were to play a crucial role in the eventual overthrow of the
Tokugawa.

Intellectual Currents

Economic, social, and political changes were accompanied by intellectual res-
tiveness and the continued development of potentially anti*bakufu* strains of
thought. These, it will be recalled (see Chapter 15), included the Shinto revival-
ists of the School of National Learning, members of the Mito school who
stressed the centrality of the emperor, and the proponents of "Dutch Learning."

Frequently, ideas from one or more of these currents were combined. For example, Aizawa Seishisai (1782–1863), of Mito, combined the values of Confucianism and of *bushidō* with Shinto mythology in his discussion of Japan's
unique polity (*kokutai*). To reconcile the Japanese theory of imperial divine descent going back to the Sun Goddess with the Confucian doctrine of the Mandate of Heaven, Mito scholars developed the idea that the emperor ruled by
virtue of his unique descent, but that the shogun's legitimacy was derived from
a mandate he received from the emperor. The implication was that what the
emperor granted he could also revoke if the *bakufu* failed in its duties and obligations.

An example of an influential writer who combined advocacy of an irrational
and frequently naive nativism with a good understanding of, and appreciation
for, Western medicine was Hirata Atsutane, whose long life straddled the eighteenth and nineteenth centuries. Hirata was himself a physician and had studied Dutch medical texts in translation. To reconcile his adulation of Japan
with his appreciation for the foreign science, Hirata maintained that Japan had
originally been pure and free of disease: the need for a powerful medical science arose only after Japan was infected by foreign contacts.

During the first half of the nineteenth century interest in such practical
Western sciences as astronomy, medicine, and mathematics continued to
grow. The *bakufu* itself, in 1811, set up a bureau that translated Dutch books
into Japanese even while it maintained its seclusionist policies. Outstanding
among the students of Western science was the Confucian scholar Sakuma
Shōzan (1811–64), who conducted experiments in chemistry and glassmaking
and later became an expert in the casting of guns; he was a serious thinker
about the principles as well as the products of Western technology. Seeking to

Figure 17-2
Commodore Perry.
Artist unknown.
Woodcut print,
nineteenth century,
26 cm × 24.5 cm.

preserve Confucian values and at the same time to adopt Western technology, Sakuma sought a rationale with room for both. His solution was incorporated in the formula "Eastern ethics and Western science." This became a very influential slogan after the Meiji Restoration, but Sakuma did not live to see the day, for he was murdered by an antiforeign extremist from Chōshū in 1864.

Sakuma's intellectual strategy was essentially one of compartmentalization: the native and foreign traditions were assigned different functions. Each had its distinct role. Most students of Dutch painting would have agreed, for they valued Western techniques more for their practical results than for any aesthetic merit. Yet, like all generalizations, this demands qualification. Hokusai, who lived until 1849, once contrasted the use of shading for decorative purposes in Chinese and Japanese art with its employment to create an effect of three dimensionality in the West. He concluded, "One must understand both methods: there must be life and death in everything one paints."[1]

The "Opening" of Japan

The "opening" of China to the West was a result of the Opium War and subsequent treaties with the European powers. In Japan, the "opening" resulted from an armed mission by Commodore Matthew C. Perry of the United States Navy (1853). (See Figure 17-2.) The treaties which followed that momentous event ended the Tokugawa policy of seclusion. They thus contributed to the growing instability of the Tokugawa system and helped to pave the way for a very different future.

Before 1853 there were a number of Western attempts to induce the Japanese to broaden their foreign policy, but these efforts were sporadic since they were not supported by substantial economic and political interests of the kind at work in China. Regarded as poor and remote, Japan was considered an area of relatively low priority by the great powers. The first approaches came from Japan's nearest Eurasian neighbor, the Russian Empire, and took place in the North, in the Kurile Islands, Sakhalin, and Hokkaidō. In 1778 and again in 1792 the Russians requested trade relations in Hokkaidō, and in 1804 a similar request was made in Nagasaki. All were refused. British ships seeking trade or ship's stores were also turned away. British whaling ships sometimes requested supplies, but in 1825 the *bakufu* ordered that all foreign ships should be driven from Japanese waters. In 1837 a private American-British attempt to open relations with Japan fared no better. But in 1842 the shogunate relaxed the edicts of 1825 and ordered that foreign ships accidentally arriving in Japan were to be provided with water, food, and fuel. China's defeat in the Opium War and the opening of new ports increased the number of Western vessels in East Asia and hence the pressure on Japan.

This changing situation could not be ignored. To begin with, the lessons of Chinese weakness and Western strength were not lost on Japanese observers. Information concerning Western science, industry, and military capabilities continued to be provided by scholars of "Dutch Learning." Information also came from China: Wei Yüan's *An Illustrated Gazeteer of the Maritime Countries (Hai-kuo t'u-chih)* was widely read after it appeared in a Japanese edition in 1847. Furthermore, the Japanese were making progress in mastering Western technology. By the 1840s the domains of Mito, Hizen, and Satsuma were casting guns using Western methods. In 1850 Hizen possessed the first reverberatory furnace needed to produce iron suitable for making modern cannons. As we have already noted, a few courageous students of the West had suggested abandoning the policy of seclusion well before the arrival of Perry. The Dutch, too, had warned the *bakufu* of the designs of the stronger Western nations.

In 1846 an American mission to Japan ended in failure, but with the acquisition of California in 1848 the interest of the United States in Japan increased, since Nagasaki, five hundred miles from Shanghai, was a convenient fueling stop for ships bound from San Fransisco to that port. Putting real pressure on Japan for the first time, the United States government sent out Commodore Perry with eleven ships, three of them steam frigates. Perry and his fleet reached Japan in July 1853, forced the Japanese to accept a letter from the American president to the emperor, and announced that he would return for an answer the following spring.

No match militarily for the American fleet, the *bakufu* realized that it would have to accede at least in part to American demands. In preparation for that unpopular move, it took the unprecedented step of soliciting daimyo opinion only to receive divided and unhelpful advice. The *bakufu* did not gain the backing it had hoped for but did reveal its own weakness.

When Perry returned in February 1854, an initial treaty was signed that provided for the opening of Shimoda and Hakodate to ships seeking provisions, assured that the shipwrecked would receive good treatment, and permitted the United States later to send a consul to Japan. Similar treaties with Britain and France followed in 1855, and the Dutch and Russians negotiated broader agreements in 1857. Still, there was no commercial treaty satisfactory to Western mercantile interests. The task of negotiating such an agreement was left to the first American consul, Townsend Harris, who arrived in Japan in 1856 and gradually succeeded in persuading the shogunate to make concessions. (See Figure 17-3.) The resulting treaty was signed in 1858, and another round of treaties with the Dutch, Russians, British, and French followed.

At the end of this process, Japan's international situation was similar to that of China. First there was the matter of opening ports. This began with Shimoda on the Izu Peninsula and Hakodate in Hokkaidō; it was extended to Nagasaki and Kanagawa (for which Yokohama was substituted); and dates were set for the opening of Niigata, Hyōgo (modern Kobe), and the admission of foreign res-

Figure 17-3 *Harris's Procession on the Way to Edo.* Artist unknown. Watercolor, 53.5 cm × 38.8 cm. Peabody Museum, Salem.

idents but not trade into Ōsaka and Edo. As in the case of China, the treaties provided for most-favored-nation treatment and extraterritoriality. Japan also lost her tariff autonomy and was limited to relatively low import duties.

Domestic Politics

For the *bakufu* these were very difficult years, for it was forced to accede to the foreign powers without enjoying support at home. Each failure in foreign affairs provided additional ammunition to its domestic enemies. The *bakufu* was itself divided by factionalism and policy differences. An attempt was made after Perry's arrival to broaden the shogunate's political base by drawing on the advice of nonhouse daiymo. The Lord of Mito, Tokugawa Nariaki (1800–1860), a persistent advocate of resistance to the West, was placed in charge of national defense. These measures, however, failed to strengthen the *bakufu*—too many men were pulling in opposite directions.

When the shogun died without an heir in 1858, a bitter dispute took place over the rival claims of two candidates for the succession. One of these was still a boy, but he had the strongest claim by descent. He also had the backing of most of the house daimyo (*fudai*) including that of Ii Naosuke, the greatest of the *fudai*. The other candidate was Hitotsubashi (later Tokugawa) Keiki, the capable son of the Lord of Mito. It will be recalled that Mito was a collateral house of the Tokugawa, eligible to supply shoguns if the main line failed to produce an heir.

The immediate issue in the succession dispute concerned control over the *bakufu*, for Keiki's accession was seen as a threat to the continued control over the shogunate by the *fudai*. At the same time, foreign policy was also involved, for the *bakufu* officials, as men on the spot, were more inclined to make concessions to the foreigners. The great lords, on the other hand, demanded a vigorous defense policy against the intruders from the West. Furthermore, the Lord of Mito and some of his peers envisioned their own *han* as playing important roles in building up military strength against the West. Thus his advocacy of a strong foreign policy was consistent with his desire to strengthen his own *han* at the expense of the center.

The split in the *bakufu* increased the political importance of the imperial court. Nariaki even appealed to Kyōto for support for his son's candidacy. And when the shogun tried to obtain imperial approval for the treaty negotiated with Harris, it failed.

The crisis of 1858 was temporarily resolved when Ii Naosuke took charge of the *bakufu*. He did so as Grand Councilor (*tairō*), a high post more often than not left vacant, and which had previously been held by several members of the Ii family. The effective power of this position depended on the authority of the incumbent, and the strong-minded Ii Naosuke used it to dominate the shogunate. He proceeded to sign the treaty with the United States without prior imperial approval, vigorously reasserted *bakufu* power, purged his enemies, forced into retirement or house arrest the daimyo who had opposed him and were on the losing side in the succession dispute, including the Lord of Mito, and punished some of the court nobles and Mito loyalists. For a moment the *bakufu* was revitalized. But it was only for a moment: In March 1860 Ii was assassinated by a group of samurai, mostly from Mito.

Before committing suicide Ii's assassins drew up a document expressing their devotion to the cause for which they had killed and for which they were about to die. It can be summed up in the two phrases that became the slogans for the movement against the Tokugawa: *Sonnō*—"Revere the Emperor"—and *Jōi*—"Expel the Barbarians."

Sonnō Jōi

As we observed earlier, Mito was the home of an emperor-centered school of historiography and political thought, and its lord was one of the most fervent advocates of a strong military policy to "expel the barbarians." It is therefore not surprising that Mito thought influenced the passionate and brilliant young man who became the main spokesman and hero of the *Sonnō Jōi* movement. This was Yoshida Shōin (1830–59), the son of a low ranking Chōshū samurai. Yoshida was influenced by *bushidō* in the tradition of Yamaga Sokō, by books on military science, and by Confucianism. From Sakuma Shōzan he learned about the West. Then he became acquainted with Mito ideas on a study trip to northern Japan, which, since it was unauthorized, cost him his samurai rank. Apprehensive of the West and convinced of the importance of knowing one's enemy, he tried to stow away on one of Commodore Perry's ships but was caught and placed under house arrest in Chōshū. After his release he started a school there and attracted disciples, including Kido Kōin, one of the three leading statesmen of the Meiji Restoration, and the future Meiji leaders Itō Hirobumi and Yamagata Aritomo.

Yoshida condemned the *bakufu* for its handling of the foreign problem. Its failure to expel the barbarians, he felt, reflected incompetence, dereliction of duty, and a lack of proper reverence for the throne. Like many men of lower samurai origins, he was impatient with a system that rewarded birth more than ability or talent, and he saw the *bakufu*'s inability to eject the foreigner as a consequence of this system. What was needed to redress the situation, he believed, were pure and selfless officials who would act out of true loyalty rather than mindless obedience. Thus Yoshida's teaching combined elements of moral revival at home, opposition to the foreigner, and championship of the throne.

Initially Yoshida favored the appointment of new men to the *bakufu*, but after the signing of the treaty with the United States in 1858, he concluded that the *bakufu* must be overthrown. Both personal fulfillment and national salvation required an act of unselfish self-sacrifice by a national hero. Yoshida sought to achieve both aims himself. In 1858 he plotted the assassination of the emissary sent by the shogun to the imperial court to persuade the emperor to agree to the commercial treaty with the United States. Word leaked out. Yoshida was arrested and sent to Edo where he was beheaded the following year.

Mixed Reactions to the West

In this turbulent era Japanese reactions to the West varied widely. Some Japanese, like the Confucian Shinoya Tōin (1810–67), had an absolute hatred of everything Western. He even belittled the script in which the foreigners wrote, describing it as:

> confused and irregular, wriggling like snakes or larvae of mosquitoes. The straight ones are like dog's teeth, the round ones are like worms. The crooked ones are like the forelegs of a mantis, the stretched ones are like slime lines left by snails. They resemble dried bones or decaying skulls, rotten bellies of dead snakes or parched vipers.[2]

It is not surprising that a culture which prized calligraphy on the Chinese model should find the strictly utilitarian Western script aesthetically unappetizing, but Shinoya's invective goes beyond mere distaste. Every word betrays, indeed is meant to express, horror and disgust at the beast that had now come among them.

But there were others who were determined to learn from the West, even if only to use that knowledge to defeat the foreigner. Their slogan was *kaikoku jōi:* "open the country to drive out the barbarians." The learning process continued. In 1857 the *bakufu* opened an "Institute for the Investigation of Barbarian Books" near Edo Castle. Not only the *bakufu* but also some of the domains sent men on study trips abroad; in the case of the *han* this was often done illegally. The process of adopting Western technology, begun as we have seen even before Perry's arrival, was accelerated. An indication of the people's receptivity to the new knowledge is provided by the popularity of the writings of Fukuzawa Yukichi (1835–1901), who went abroad twice in the early sixties and published seven books prior to the Restoration, beginning with *Conditions in the West (Seiyō jijō),* the first volume of which appeared in 1866 and promptly sold 150,000 copies. Another 100,000 copies were sold in pirated editions. These works, written in a simple style (easy enough for Fukuzawa's housemaid to read), were filled with detailed descriptions of Western institutions and life: hospitals and schools, tax systems and museums, climate and clothes, cutlery, and beds and chamberpots. Fukuzawa went on to become a leading Meiji intellectual, but the turbulent years just prior to the Restoration were dangerous for men of his outlook.

In contrast to men like Yoshida Shōin, others hoped for a reconciliation of the court and *bakufu,* and there were some who still hoped the *bakufu* could take the lead in creating a more modern state. These issues, at work during the sixties, were finally buried in the Restoration.

Last Years of the Shogunate: 1860–1867

After the assassination of Ii Naosuke in 1860 the *bakufu* leadership turned to a policy of compromise. An effort was made to effect a "union of the court and military" that was confirmed by the shogun's marriage to the emperor's sister. In return for affirming the emperor's primacy, the *bakufu* obtained assent for its foreign policy. It also sought to win daimyo support by relaxing the old requirements for attendance at Edo. However, this policy ran into the opposition of Kyōto loyalists, activists of the *sonnō jōi* persuasion, samurai, and voluntary *rōnin* who had escaped the bonds of feudal discipline by requesting to leave their lords' service. Psychologically this was not difficult, since their loyalty to their lords had become bureaucratized and since they now felt the claims of a higher loyalty to the throne. Men of extremist dedication, ready to sacrifice their lives for the cause, terrorized the streets of Kyōto in the early sixties and made the capital unsafe for moderates.

Foreigners, too, were subject to attack. The opening of the ports had been followed by a marked rise in the price of rice, causing great economic distress. Xenophobia, that is, intense patriotism coupled with hatred of foreigners, was reinforced by economic hardship caused by the Westerners. Several foreigners were assassinated by fervent samurai in 1859, and in 1861 Townsend Harris' Dutch interpreter was cut down, and the British legation in Edo was attacked. In 1862 a British merchant lost his life at the hands of Satsuma samurai. When the British were unable to obtain satisfaction from the *bakufu*, they took matters into their own hands. In August 1863 they bombarded Kagoshima, the Satsuma capital, in order to force punishment of the guilty and payment of an indemnity.

A similar incident involving Chōshū took place in the summer of 1863. By that time extremists had won control of the court and with Chōshū backing had forced the shogun to accept June 25, 1863 as the date for the expulsion of the barbarians. The *bakufu*, caught between intransigent foreigners and the insistent court, interpreted the agreement to mean that negotiations for the closing of the ports would begin on that day, but Chōshū and the loyalists interpreted it more literally. When Chōshū guns began firing on foreign ships in the Straits of Shimonoseki, the foreign ships fired back. First American warships came to shell the fortifications; then French ships landed parties which destroyed the fort and ammunition. Still Chōshū persisted in firing on foreign vessels, until in September 1864 a combined British, French, Dutch, and American fleet demolished the forts and forced Chōshū to come to terms. These losses, plus a defeat inflicted on Chōshū adherents by a Satsuma-Aizu force in Kyōto in August 1864, stimulated Chōshū to overhaul its military forces. It had already undertaken to purchase Western arms and ships. Now peasant militia were organized, and mixed rifle units were formed—staffed by commoners and samurai, a radical departure from Tokugawa practice and from the basic principles of Tokugawa society. One of these units was commanded by Itō Hirobumi, recently returned from study in England.

Satsuma's reponse to defeat, although not as radical as Chōshū's, was similar in its appreciation of the superiority of Western weapons. With British help the domain began acquiring Western ships, forming the nucleus of what was to become the Imperial Japanese Navy. The British supported Satsuma partly because they were disillusioned with the *bakufu* and partly because the French were supporting the shogunate with arms in the hope of building a strong French role in a reconstituted shogunate. In both Chōshū and Satsuma there was less talk about "expelling the barbarians" and more about "enriching the country and strengthening the army," at least among the leaders.

The politics of these years were even more than usually full of complications and intrigues, and as long as Chōshū and Satsuma remained on opposite sides the situation remained fluid. Traditionally unfriendly to each other, competing for power in Kyōto, and differing in their policy recommendations, they were nevertheless unified in their opposition to a restoration of Tokugawa power. There were two wars against Chōshū. In the first, 1864–65, a large *bakufu* force with men from many domains defeated Chōshū. This in turn set off a civil war in Chōshū from which the revolutionaries with their mixed rifle regiments emerged victors. This led to a second *bakufu* war against Chōshū, but before this second war began, in 1866, Satsuma and Chōshū made a secret alliance. When war did come, Satsuma and some other powerful *han* remained on the sidelines. Chōshū, although outnumbered, defeated the *bakufu.*

After this defeat by a single *han,* the *bakufu* (under the direction of Hitotsu-bashi Keiki, who inherited the position of shogun in 1866) tried to save what it could. There were attempts to work out a daimyo coalition and calls for imperial restoration. In November the shogun accepted a proposal that he resign in favor of a council of daimyo under the emperor. According to this arrangement he was to retain his lands and as the most powerful lord in Japan serve as prime minister. However, this was unacceptable to the *sonnō* advocates in Satsuma and Chōshū and to the restorationists at court, including the court noble Iwakura Tonomi (1825–83), a master politician. On January 3, 1868, forces from Satsuma and other *han* seized the palace and proclaimed the restoration. The shogunate was destroyed. Tokugawa lands were confiscated, and the shogun himself was reduced to the status of an ordinary daimyo. A short civil war ensued. There was fighting in Edo and in northern Honshū but no real contest. Last to surrender was the *bakufu* navy in May 1869.

Formation of a New Government (Meiji Restoration)

The men who overthrew the Tokugawa in January 1868 did not subscribe to any clear and well-defined program. There was general agreement on the abolition of the shogunate and "restoration" of the emperor, but this meant no more than that the emperor should once again be at the center of the political system, functioning as the source of legitimacy and providing a sense of continuity. It definitely did not mean that actual power should be given to the sixteen-year-old Meiji Emperor (1852–1912; r. 1867–1912),* nor did it necessarily imply the destruction of feudalism, for there were those who envisioned the restoration in terms of a new feudal system headed by the emperor. On the other hand, Japanese scholars had long been aware that the Chinese system provided a bureaucratic alternative to feudalism. This, very likely, eased the shift to bureacratic centralization.

The new leaders did not always see eye to eye, but they did share certain qualities: they were all of similar age (35–43) and rank, and came from the victorious *han* or the court aristocracy, although the *han* coalition was soon broadened to include men from Tosa and Hizen. The three most eminent leaders in the early years of the restoration were Ōkubo Toshimichi (1830–78), Kido Kōin (1833–77), and Saigō Takamori (1827–77). Both Ōkubo and Kido had risen to leadership in their own domains (Satsuma and Chōshū), through their influence in the domain's bureaucratic establishment and among the loyalist activists. Of the two, Ōkubo was the stronger personality, disciplined, formal, and somewhat intimidating; completely dedicated to the nation; cautious and practical. Kido was more lively but also more volatile, less self-confident but more concerned than Ōkubo with strengthening the popular base of the government. But he was just as devoted to building a strong state.

Ōkubo's was the single strongest voice in government during 1873–78. One of his initial tasks was to retain the cooperation of Saigō, the military leader of the Satsuma forces which had joined with Chōshū to overthrow the Tokugawa. Saigō was a man of imposing physique and great physical strength. He was known for his outstanding courage, and possessed many of the traditional warrior virtues, such as generosity and contempt for money. More conservative than the others, he was devoted to Satsuma and its samurai but worked with the others at least until 1873. They were united in their conviction that the country must be strengthened to resist the West.

For the sake of national self-preservation the leaders were prepared to enact vast changes, but it took time to plan and carry these out, and indeed, to consolidate their own power in a land where, as Kido complained, "we are surrounded on four sides by little *bakufu*."[3] To insure that the emperor would not become a focus of opposition to reform, Ōkubo argued that he should be moved to Edo, renamed Tōkyō (Eastern Capital) in September 1868. This took place the following year when the emperor moved into the shogun's former castle, which was finally, after much debate, renamed the "imperial palace" in 1871.

The Charter

Even before the move, in April 1868 while the emperor was still in Kyōto, a Charter Oath was issued in his name to provide a general if vague statement of purpose for the new regime. It consisted of five articles:

---

* His name was Mutsuhito, but, as in the case of the emperors of Ch'ing China, it is customary to refer to him and to his successors by the names of their reign periods.

1. An assembly widely convoked shall be established and all matters of state shall be decided by public discussion.
2. All classes high and low shall unite in vigorously promoting the economy and welfare of the nation.
3. All civil and military officials and the common people as well shall be allowed to fulfill their aspirations, so that there may be no discontent among them.
4. Base customs of former times shall be abandoned and all actions shall conform to the principles of international justice.
5. Knowledge shall be sought throughout the world and thus shall be strengthened the foundation of the Imperial polity.[4]

Although the government was reorganized to provide for an assembly in keeping with the first article, power remained with the original leadership, and the attempt to implement this provision was soon abandoned. In contrast, the end of seclusion, the acceptance of international law, and the openness to foreign ideas conveyed by the last two articles did take place. Symbolic of this shift was the audience granted representatives of the foreign powers by the emperor in Kyōto just a month before the Charter Oath was issued. The document itself was drafted by two men familiar with Western thought; it was then revised by Kido. The ramifications of the Charter Oath were far from clear, but the last article, to seek for knowledge "throughout the world" was taken very seriously. Furthermore, the entire document illustrates the gulf between Japanese and Chinese leaders at this time. No Chinese government would have issued such a document in an attempt to gain political strength.

Dismantling Feudalism

While the machinery of the central government underwent various reorganizations, the prime need was for the government to extend and consolidate its authority. Since the continued existence of the feudal domains was a major obstacle to this, the government leaders undertook the delicate but essential task of abolishing the *han*. In March 1869, Kido and Ōkubo were able to use their influence to induce the daimyo of Chōshū and Satsuma to return their domains to the emperor. They were joined in this act by the lords of Tosa and Hizen, and many others followed suit, anxious to be in the good graces of the new government and expecting to be appointed governors of their former domains, which they were. The real blow came in 1871 when, in the name of national unity, the domains were completely abolished and the whole country was reorganized into prefectures. This was made palatable to the daimyo by generous financial arrangements. The daimyo were allowed to retain a tenth of the former domain revenue as personal income while the government assumed responsibility for *han* debts and financial obligations. The daimyo were also assured continued high social standing and prestige. Finally, in 1884, they were elevated to the peerage.

By background and experience the new leadership was keenly sensitive to the importance of military power. Initially the new government was entirely dependent on forces from the supporting domains, but this would hardly do for a government truly national in scope. Accordingly the leaders set about forming a new army freed from local loyalties. Rejecting the views of Saigō, who envisioned a samurai army that would insure the warrior class a brilliant and useful role in Japan's future, the leaders decided in 1872 to build their army on the basis of conscription. In January 1873, the new measure, largely the work of Yamagata Aritomo (1838–1922), "father of the Japanese Army," became law.

The restoration had a profound effect on the samurai. The new army, by eliminating distinctions between commoners and samurai, cut right to the heart of the status system. Anyone could become a warrior now. Other marks of samurai distinctiveness were eliminated or eroded. In 1870 commoners were allowed to acquire surnames and were released from previous occupational and residential restrictions. In 1871 the wearing of swords by samurai was made optional—five years later it was to be prohibited entirely.

The samurai's position was further undermined by the dismantling of feudalism. The abolition of the *han* threatened their economic position because the *han* had traditionally been the source of samurai stipends, and the burden of continuing stipend payments at the usual rate was more than the central government could afford. In addition, without the old domains, the samurai no longer had any social or political functions to perform. Accordingly, they were pensioned off. But in view of their number, 5 or 6 percent of the total population, the government could not afford to treat them as generously as it did the daimyo. At first samurai stipends were reduced on a sliding scale from half to a tenth of what they had been, then they were given the right to commute these into twenty year bonds (1873), and finally they were forced to accept the bonds (1876).

Reduction and commutation of samurai stipends was only one of the measures taken to establish the new government on a sound financial basis. In addition to monetary and banking reforms, a tax system was created (1873). These fiscal measures were largely the work of Ōkuma Shigenobu (1838–1922), a man from Hizen who was to remain prominent in Meiji politics, and Itō Hirobumi (1841–1909), of Chōshū. The main source of government revenue was, as before, agriculture, but in place of the old percentage of the crop payable by the village to the daimyo, the tax was now collected by the government in money in accordance with the assessed value of the land. It was payable by the owner, and for this purpose ownership rights had to be clearly established. This was not done in favor of the absentee feudal interest long divorced from the land, nor did ownership pass equitably to all peasants. Instead, certificates were issued to the cultivators and wealthy villagers who had paid the tax during Tokugawa times. In this way tenancy was perpetuated, and since poor peasants were often unable to meet their taxes and thus were forced to mortgage their land, the rate of tenancy increased, rising from about 25 percent before the new system to about 40 percent twenty years later.

Disaffection and Opposition

The creation of a modern political, military, and fiscal system benefited the state but hurt some of the people. The peasantry was unhappy, not only about the land system but also about forced military service, and showed its displeasure by staging uprisings with increasing frequency from 1866 to 1873. Many of the large merchant houses that had developed symbiotic relationships with the *bakufu* or daimyo also suffered during these years and some went bankrupt.

More serious for the regime was samurai discontent. The new government was itself led by former samurai, and for many men the new order meant a release from old restrictions and the opening of new opportunities. Since the samurai were the educated class with administrative experience, it was they who supplied the personnel for local and national government, provided officers for the army, teachers for the schools, and much of society's leadership. Yet there were many who did not make a successful transition, who were unable to respond positively to the new vocations now opened to them or to use their payments to establish themselves in new lines of endeavor. And among the leaders as well as the supporters of the Meiji government were men who firmly believed that its purpose was the restoration of the old, not the creation of the new. A split between conservatives and modernizers developed early in the Restoration and came to a head in 1873.

The Crisis of 1873

The crisis centered on the issue of going to war with Korea in order to force that country to open her doors to Japan. Those who advocated war, such as Saigō and the Tosa samurai Itagaki Taisuke (1836–1919), did so not only out of nationalist motives but also because they saw war as an occasion to provide employment for the samurai, an opportunity to give them a greater role in the new society, a means to preserve their military heritage. Saigō, a military leader with great charisma and devotion to the way of the warrior, asked to be sent to Korea as ambassador so that the Koreans, by killing him, would provide a cause for going to war.

A decision for war was made in the summer of 1873, in the absence of Ōkubo, Kido, and other important leaders who were abroad, in America and Europe. They were on a diplomatic and study mission headed by Iwakura Tomomi, the noble who had played a leading role at court in bringing about the Meiji Restoration. The purposes of the Iwakura mission were to convey the Meiji Emperor's respects to the heads of state of the treaty powers and build good will, to discuss subjects for later treaty revision, and to provide its distinguished members with an opportunity to observe and study the West at first hand. Its major accomplishment was in fulfilling the last mentioned objective, for the trip made a deep impression on the Japanese leaders who were exposed for the first time to the West and saw at first hand the evidence of Western strength. They returned home with a new realization of the magnitude of the task facing Japan in her quest for equality, and a new appreciation of the importance and complexity of modernization. They were convinced of the urgent priority of domestic change.

When the mission returned Ōkubo led the opposition to the Korean venture on the grounds that Japan could not yet afford such an undertaking. Ōkubo, Kido, and Iwakura prevailed, with the support of many officials and the court. It was decided to abandon the Korean expedition and to concentrate on internal development. The decision split the government. Bitterly disappointed, the war advocates, including Saigō and Itagaki, resigned. In opposition they provided leadership for those who were disaffected by the new government and its policies, an opposition which would prove troublesome to those in power. But their departure left the government in the hands of a group of men unified by a commitment to modernization. Most prominent among them were Ōkubo, Itō, Ōkuma, and Iwakura.

By 1873 the Meiji government had survived the difficult period of initial consolidation. It had established the institutional foundations for the new state, had found a means of defense and national security, and with the resolution of the 1873 crisis, had charted the basic course of development at home and peace abroad that was to dominate Japanese policies during the next twenty years.

The Meaning of the Restoration

A major aspect of the Restoration was increased openness to the West. Signs of at least superficial Westernization were already in evidence in the early 1870s, when the gentleman of fashion sported a foreign umbrella and watch and indulged in beef stew. Faddish Westernism was satirized in one of the bestsellers of the day, *Auguranabe* (*Idle Talks in the Sukiyaki House*) (1871–72) by Kanagaki Robun (1829–1904). Ōkubo ate bread and drank dark tea for breakfast and wore Western clothes even at home. In 1872 Western dress was made mandatory at court and other official functions. The Gregorian calendar was adopted the same year. After the Tokyo fire of 1872, Tokyo's main avenue, the Ginza, was rebuilt with brick buildings, colonnades, and gas lamps to provide lighting. (See Figure 17-4.) Supervising the work was an English architect, one of 214 Westerners employed by the government in 1872, over half of them English.

By contrast there was an effort to turn Japan into a Shinto state. In 1868 Shinto was proclaimed the basis for the government and a Department of Shinto was established with precedence over the other government departments. There was a drive to purify Shinto, to eliminate Buddhist influences that had steadily seeped into Shinto, and to make Shinto the only religion of

Figure 17-4   The Ginza, 1873.

Japan. This drive, however, ran into opposition from Buddhists and also conflicted with Western pressures for the legalization of Christianity. In 1872 the
Department of Shinto was abolished, and in 1873 the old ban on Christianity
was lifted.

The Restoration leaders opted for the new, and they were able to initiate far-
reaching changes partly because they inherited from Tokugawa times a political system that reached much deeper and more effectively into society than did
that of China. Furthermore, they introduced the new in the name of the emperor, a symbol of continuity with the old. This made it easier for them to innovate but also assured the survival of old values and ideas. In the light of
hindsight they appear in the dual role of preservers of tradition and initiators of
East Asia's first cultural revolution.

The Meiji Restoration bears very little resemblance to the contemporary
T'ung-chih Restoration in China,* for it laid stress on innovation rather than
renovation or renewal. In many essential ways the restoration was revolutionary: it destroyed the feudal system and created a centralized state; it eliminated the old class lines and legally opened all careers to all men; in all areas of
human activity it prepared the way for the profound changes that during the
next century were to transform the very countryside of Japan. But if it was a
revolution, it was a revolution from above, an aristocratic revolution, to borrow
a term from Thomas C. Smith.[5] If it was not a restoration in the nineteenth-
century Chinese sense, neither was it a revolution as the term is applied to

* On the meaning of the Chinese and Japanese terms, see note, page 396.

twentieth-century China. Relatively peaceful, it was not the product of a mass movement nor of a radical social ideology, and it did not radically change the structure of village life or the mode of agricultural production. It eliminated the samurai as a legally defined, privileged class, but, led by men who were themselves samurai, did so gently and in terms samurai could understand.

NOTES

1. Michiaki Kawakita, *Modern Currents in Japanese Art*, Heibonsha Survey of Japanese Art, Vol. 24, trans. Charles S. Terry (New York and Tokyo: Weatherhill/Heibonsha, 1974), p. 29.

2. Marius B. Jansen, ed., *Changing Japanese Attitudes Toward Modernization* (Princeton: Princeton University Press, 1969), pp. 57–58; quoting van Gulik, "Kakkaron: A Japanese Echo of the Opium War," *Monumenta Serica* 4 (1939): 542–43.

3. Albert Craig and Donald Shively, eds., *Personality in Japanese History* (Berkeley and Los Angeles: University of California Press, 1970), p. 297.

4. Ishii Ryosuke, *Japanese Legislation in the Meiji Era*, trans. William J. Chambliss (Tokyo: Pan-Pacific Press, 1958), p. 145. Frequently quoted, as in William G. Beasley, *The Meiji Restoration* (Stanford: Stanford University Press, 1972), p. 325.

5. See Thomas C. Smith, "Japan's Aristocratic Revolution," *Yale Review* 50 (Spring 1961): 370–83. Also see Marius B. Jansen, "The Meiji State: 1868–1912," in James B. Crowley, ed., *Modern East Asia: Essays in Interpretation* (New York: Harcourt Brace Jovanovich, 1970), pp. 95–121, which cites Smith on p. 103.

現代日本之形成

1868   1877   1889   1890   1894   1912

The Restoration

Satsuma
Rebellion

Promulgation of
the Constitution

Rescript on
Education

Start of the
Sino-Japanese War

M E I J I   J A P A N

18 The Emergence of Modern Japan: 1874–1894

During the last thirty years of the nineteenth century the Western challenge to the rest of the globe became more intense, more formidable, and more complex. With continued progress in science and technology, the power of the economically advanced countries continued to grow while capitalism and nationalism fueled competition over the acquisition of colonies. As the area left for possible expansion diminished, the race gained momentum. In these thirty years Europeans expanded their colonial empires by over 10 million square miles, about a fifth of the world's land area, inhabited by nearly 150 million people, about 10 percent of the world's population. Much of this expansion took place in Africa, but new colonies were formed also in Southeast Asia. Northeast Asia came under imperialist pressure leading to the Sino-Japanese War of 1894–95 fought over Korea. Japan's victory in that war demonstrated that she had by that time become a participant in, rather than a victim of, the new imperialism.

The leading maritime power in the world continued to be Great Britain, which, as before, had the largest foreign commercial stake in China and Japan. Russia persisted in its overland expansion into and beyond Central Asia. Two other powers, France and the United States, maintained an interest in East Asian developments. In Europe, the emergence of Germany after the Franco-Prussian War (1870) provided a conservative alternative to England's liberal model for modernization. After the war the German Chancellor, Otto von Bismarck (1815–98), adopted a policy of encouraging France to compensate for her losses in Europe by building an overseas empire. This gave an impetus to France's ambitions in Southeast Asia that led to war between France and China in 1883–85. The world was becoming smaller, and, for the weak or weakened, more dangerous.

Relations between China and Japan during the twenty years discussed in this chapter began with a minor clash and ended with a war that had profound internal effects in both countries and changed the balance of power between them for the next half century. The minor clash occurred in 1874 when Japan sent an expedition to Taiwan ostensibly to punish aborigines who had killed some Okinawans shipwrecked on their shores. Its real purpose was to mollify those who resented the abandonment of the Korean expedition so earnestly advocated by Saigō and his friends. An expedition to Taiwan was a smaller and less dangerous undertaking. It was successful, and the result was that China was forced to pay an indemnity and to recognize Japanese sovereignty over the Ryūkū Islands, of which Okinawa is the largest. This ended the ties that the Ryūkyūs had maintained with China even while they were Satsuma vassals. Thus for China the war brought the first of a series of alienations of tributaries, but in Japan it did little to reconcile the samurai.

Statesmen in both China and Japan saw their primary task as that of strengthening their states against the predatory foreign powers, of stemming and if possible reversing the tide of humiliating concessions incorporated in the unequal treaties. But they differed not only in their methods and achievements, but also in their views of what had to be done and for what ultimate ends. In the process, Japan during these years changed more rapidly than China.

For Japan the years between the Restoration and the Sino-Japanese War were a period of conscious learning from the West in an effort to become a modern nation accepted as an equal by the powers of the world. It was a time of great changes: in government and politics, in the economy, in people's ideas, in education—a time of building national strength. These changes were neither smooth nor simple. In the intricate interplay of old and new, foreign and traditional, some old ways went the way of the samurai's sword and topknot, but others were retained and put to new uses. This is a process that still continues in the second half of the twentieth century, but the Sino-Japanese War marked the end of a crucial stage, for by then Japan had achieved many of her initial objectives: a centralized government, a modernizing economy, and sufficient military strength to warrant international respect.

Political Developments

Acting in the name of the emperor, a small oligarchy (group of leaders) dominated the government during the 1870s and 1880s, but not without opposition. Embittered samurai resorted to arms, first in an uprising in Hizen in 1874 and then, more seriously, in 1877 in Satsuma. The Satsuma Rebellion was led by Saigō Takamori, who had withdrawn from the government after the 1873 decision against the Korean expedition. The number of those who threw in their lot with the rebellion rose as high as 42,000. Its suppression strained the military resources of the Restoration government, but after half a year the rebellion was crushed. The Satsuma Rebellion was the last stand of the samurai. When the military situation became hopeless, Saigō killed himself in the approved warrior manner. His was a martyr's death for a lost cause. Saigō died under official condemnation as a traitor, but the Meiji government soon rehabilitated him, and government leaders joined in expressions of admiration and acclaim for the man who came to be regarded as *the* hero of the Restoration. Not only conservatives but representatives of the most diverse political persuasions praised the magnanimity of his spirit and transformed Saigō into a legendary hero, celebrated in poems and songs (including an army marching song), portrayed on stage and in an extensive literature, depicted in portraits and prints, even identified with the planet Mars.

Protest against the government continued, on occasion, to take a violent turn. Less than half a year after Saigō's death, some of his sympathizers assassinated Ōkubo Toshimichi, also from Satsuma, who had worked so hard and successfully to create the new Japanese state. There were other assassination attempts as well, both successful and unsuccessful. More important in the long run, however, was the formation of nonviolent political opposition, animated not only by objections to one or another aspect of the government's policies, but also in protest against the political domination exercised by a few oligarchs from Chōshū and Satsuma, men who had exclusive control over the centers of power. Basing their position on the first article of the 1868 Charter Oath, opposition leaders early in 1874 demanded the creation of an elected legislature. Prominent among them was Itagaki Taisuke, the Tosa leader who, like Saigō, had left the government in 1873 over the Korean issue. In Tosa and then elsewhere antigovernment organizations voiced the discontent of local interests, demanding political rights, local self-government, and formation of a national assembly. The advocates of a constitution, and the leaders of what became known as the movement for popular rights, drew upon Western political theories for support. They argued also that the adoption of representative institutions would create greater unity between the people and the emperor. In their view a constitution was needed not in order to limit the emperor's powers but in order to control his advisers.

The men in power were not adverse to some kind of constitution as a necessary and even desirable component of modernization. By the end of 1878, Kido, Ōkubo, and Saigō were all dead. Of the older men only Iwakura remained important, and three younger men who had already contributed significantly to the Meiji state now gained major prominence: Itō Hirobumi and Yamagata Aritomo, both from Chōshū, and Ōkuma Shigenobu from Hizen. Yamagata was the creator of the new army while Itō took the lead in political modernization and Ōkuma served as Finance Minister. But there were tensions between Itō and Ōkuma. In 1881 the latter precipitated a break when he wrote a memorandum advocating the adoption of an English-style political system. His proposals that the majority party in parliament form the government, that the cabinet be responsible to parliament, and that the first elections be held in 1883 clashed with the conservative and gradualist views of his colleagues. First his proposals were rejected; then when he joined in public criticism of the government over its sale of a certain government project in Hokkaidō, Ōkuma was dismissed. At the same time the government announced that a constitution would be granted to take effect in 1890.

Formation of Parties

In response Itagaki and his associates formed the Jiyūtō (Liberal party), and Ōkuma followed by organizing the Kaishintō (Progressive party). Both parties advocated constitutional government with meaningful powers exercised by a parliament, but they differed considerably in ideology and composition. The Jiyūtō, linked to Tosa, was influenced by the ideas of Rousseau and the French Revolution. It drew much of its support from the rural areas, where peasants and landlords were unhappy that their taxes remained as high as they had been under the Tokugawa and resented bearing a heavier tax burden than that required of commerce and industry. Ōkuma's party (linked to Hizen) was, in contrast, more urban and more moderate, advocating English-style liberalism. It had the backing of merchants and industrialists. Although they both opposed the government, the two parties fought each other energetically. At the same time the parties were troubled by internal factionalism; party splits were based on master-follower and patron-client relations rather than on differences in programs.

The organized opposition was further hampered by the need to operate under restrictive laws, including some promulgated to control political criticism before the parties were formed. Restrictive press laws enacted in 1875 and revised in 1877 gave the Home Minister power to suppress publications and provided fines or imprisonment for offenders. The 1880 Public Meeting Law placed all political meetings under police supervision. Included among those prohibited from attending such meetings were teachers and students. Nor were political associations allowed to recruit members or to combine or correspond with similar bodies. Finally the 1887 Peace Preservation Law increased the Home Minister's powers of censorship and gave the police authority to expel people from a given area: 570 were shortly removed from Tokyo in this fashion.

The Liberal party was hurt not only by differences among its leaders but even more by antagonism within its membership, including conflicts between tenants and landlords. It proved impossible to contain within one party both radicals who supported and even led peasant riots and the substantial land-owners who were the objects of these attacks. In 1884 the party was dissolved. At the end of the same year Ōkuma and his followers left the Progressive party, although others stayed to keep it in existence. Criticism of the government continued, but this initial attempt to organize political parties turned out to have been premature.

The Meiji Constitution

While suppressing its critics the government was also taking steps to increase its effectiveness. A system of centralized local administration was established that put an end to the Tokugawa tradition of local self-government. Villages and towns were now headed by officials appointed by the Home Ministry in Tokyo, which also controlled the police. In the late seventies (1878–80), local assemblies were created as sounding boards of public opinion, but their rights were limited to debate and their membership restricted to men of means. The details of bureaucratic procedure were worked out and a civil service system fashioned. A new code of criminal law was enacted, and work was begun on civil and commercial codes.

To prepare for the promised constitution-making, Itō spent a year and a half in Europe during 1882–83, mostly studying German theories and practices, for he and his fellow oligarchs already had a general idea of the kind of conservative constitution they wanted. After his return, a number of steps were taken in preparation for the constitution: a new peerage was created in 1884 composed of the old court nobility, ex-daimyo, and some members of the oligarchy; in 1885 a European-style cabinet was created with Itō as premier; and in 1888 the Privy Council was organized as the highest government advisory board.

In 1889 work on the constitution was completed, and it was promulgated as a "gift" from the Emperor to the people. It continued in force until 1945. To the Emperor was reserved the power to declare war, conclude treaties, and command the army. He also had the right to open, recess, and dissolve the legislature; the power to veto the latter's decisions; and the right to issue his own ordinances. The cabinet was responsible not to the legislature but to the emperor. The Diet, as the legislature was called, consisted of two houses, the House of Peers and the House of Representatives. The latter was elected by a constituency limited to about half a million voters out of a total population of around forty million. The most consequential power of the Diet was the power of the purse, but, borrowing from the Prussian example, the constitution provided for automatic renewal of the previous year's budget whenever the Diet failed to pass a new budget. Only the emperor could take the initiative to revise the constitution.

The constitution favored the men who had been governing in the emperor's name and who viewed government, like the emperor in whose name it functioned, as operating on a level above the divisive and unedifying world of party politics. But the parties turned out to be stronger than the oligarchs had expected. In the first election of 1890 the reconstituted Liberal party (Jiyūtō) won 130 seats, the Progressives (Kaishintō) led once again by Ōkuma won 47, and only 79 members favoring the government were elected. As a result of this growing party strength there was a stiff parliamentary battle over the budget in the first session of the Diet, which was resolved only after the premier, Yamagata, resorted to bribery and force. When the budget failed to pass the following year, the Diet was dissolved. During the subsequent elections (1892) the government used the police to discourage the opposition but failed to obtain a more tractable Diet. Another election was held in 1894, but the constitution worked no better. It was the war with China over Korea that broke the political deadlock of that year and provided temporary unity in the body politic. During the war the government enjoyed enthusiastic support at home. By that time Japan was quite different from what it had been twenty years earlier when the oligarchs rejected intervention in Korea. The political developments were just one dimension of the transformation of Japan.

Western Influences on Values and Ideas

Enthusiasm for aspects of Western science and technology went back, as we have seen, to Tokugawa proponents of "Dutch Learning," and from the very start of Meiji, there was a fashion for Western styles, including styles of dress. Representative of Japanese attitudes, the Meiji Emperor himself wore Western clothes and dressed his hair in the Western manner. See, for example, the emperor's portrait by Takahashi Yūichi (1828–94) shown in Figure 18-1.

Not only the subject, but also the artist, was influenced by Western styles. Takahashi was very conscious of his precursors: he revered Shiba Kōkan. Like Shiba and his own teacher, the prominent Western-style painter Kawakami Togai (1827–81), Takahashi placed great value on realism in his works. Most of these, unlike the emperor's portrait, were still-life studies of familiar objects, and his most famous work is a realistic painting of a salmon. A major difference between Kawakami and Takahashi is that whereas the former saw Western art as no more than a necessary component of Western learning to be mastered for technical reasons, Takahashi also valued it as art.

Figure 18-1
Takahashi Yūichi,
*Portrait of the Meiji
Emperor.* Oil, 1880.

Similarly men turned to the West in other fields, not only for practical reasons but because they were attracted by the intrinsic nature of Western achievements. Prominent among such men were the intellectuals who, in 1873, formed the Meirokusha, a prestigious society devoted to the study of all aspects of Western knowledge. These same men led what was known as the movement for "civilization and enlightenment" (*bummei kaika*). A leading theorist of this movement was Fukuzawa Yukichi, whose books on the West were mentioned earlier.

"Civilization and Enlightenment"

In eighteenth-century Europe the intellectual movement known as the Enlightenment sought to put all traditional ideas and institutions to the test of reason. Impressed by the achievements of science as exemplified in the work of Sir Isaac Newton (1642–1727), such philosophers as Voltaire (1694–1778) and Diderot (1713–84) believed that reason could produce similar progress in solving human problems and that the main obstacles to truth and happiness were irrationality and superstition. Their greatest monument was the encyclopedia compiled by Diderot and his associates, a summation of the accomplishments of reason in all fields of human knowledge.

Japanese intellectuals like Fukuzawa Yukichi were strongly influenced by the heritage of the European Enlightenment, particularly the emphasis on reason as an instrument for achieving progress. Their faith in progress was also confirmed by such influential nineteenth-century Western historians as H. T. Buckle (1821–62) and François Guizot (1787–1874). Indeed, the belief in progress remained a major nineteenth-century conviction even after the faith in reason had faded.

A corollary to this new concept of historical progress, in Japan as in the West, was a negative reevaluation of Chinese civilization, now seen as unchanging and therefore decadent. No longer did the Japanese look up to China as the land of classical civilization; on the contrary, China was now a negative model, and as her troubles continued Japanese intellectuals tended to regard her with condescension as well as concern. Now the source of "enlightenment" was in the West.

One of Fukuzawa's prime goals in advancing the cause of "civilization and enlightenment" was to stimulate in Japan the development of an independent and responsible citizenry. "It would not be far from wrong," he once complained, "to say that Japan has a government but no people."[1] Tracing the lack of individual independence back to the traditional family, Fukuzawa advocated fundamental changes in that basic social institution. Ridiculing the ancient paragons of filial piety, he urged limitations on parental demands and authority. He also recommended greater equality between the sexes, championed monogamy, argued that women should be educated and allowed to hold property, and compared the Japanese woman to a dwarfed ornamental tree, artificially stunted.

According to Fukuzawa, history was made by the people not by a few great leaders, and he thought it wrong to place too much faith in government or to give the political authorities too much power. His view of the role of government resembled the concept of the minimal state held by early European liberals. Consistent with these ideas he did not enter government himself but disseminated his views in books and through a newspaper he founded. He also established what became Keiō University, a distinguished private university in Tokyo whose graduates played an important part in the world of business and industry.

In Fukuzawa's mind the independence of the people and the independence of the country were linked; indeed, the former was a prerequisite for the latter. This view was widely held among the proponents of "enlightenment." For instance, the translator of the best seller *Self-Help* by Samuel Smiles, whose Japanese version was published in Tokyo in 1871, explained that Western nations were strong because they possessed the spirit of liberty. John Stuart Mill's *On Liberty* appeared in Japanese translation the same year; Rousseau's *The Social Contract* was published in installments during 1882–84. Fukuzawa, with his faith in progress, believed that the ultimate universal movement of history is in the direction of democracy and that individual liberty makes for national strength.

Natural Law

Fukuzawa's liberalism of the early seventies was based on the eighteenth-century Western concept of natural law, that is, that human affairs are governed by inherent concepts of right just as the physical world is governed by the laws of nature. This belief resembled the Neo-Confucian concept of *li* ("principle") in linking the natural and human orders, but the European doctrine, unlike the Chinese, included the affirmation of innate human rights. It postulated an affirmative body of law stating the inherent rights of man in society, in whose name societies could overthrow unjust governments and establish new ones. It was to natural law that the American colonists appealed when they declared their independence in 1776, and that the French revolutionaries appealed to when they promulgated their Declaration of the Rights of Man in 1789.

Social Darwinism

The concept of natural law, however, was soon displaced by another more recent Western import: Social Darwinism. There were various versions of this doctrine, most notably those developed by the enormously influential Herbert Spencer (1820–1903), but all were based on the theory of evolution by natural selection presented in Darwin's famous *Origin of the Species* (1859). Darwin held that over time the various forms of life adapt to changing natural conditions and to competition with each other, and that those which adapt best are most likely to survive. This theory was summarized by the catch phrase "survival of the fittest." Social Darwinism was the application of these doctrines to human history, explaining the rise and fall of nations, for example, in terms of competition, adaptation, and "survival of the fittest."

Social Darwinism seemed entirely apropos to the Japanese experience. It explained why China and Japan had been unable to resist the Western powers, but held out the promise that a nation did not have to accept permanent inferiority. Instead it justified Japanese efforts to develop national strength by mastering the learning and techniques of the West. It purported to have a "scientific" basis. And, unlike natural law with its moralistic overtones, it turned strength itself into a moral criterion, and it provided a justification for imperialism to support the expansionism of any ambitious state. Relations among nations could thus be viewed as one vast struggle for existence in which the fittest survived.

In the mid-seventies Fukuzawa first became skeptical of natural law, and then abandoned it. One effect was a loss of confidence in international law and a new view of international relations as an arena in which nations struggle for survival. Already in 1876 Fukuzawa remarked, "a few cannons are worth more than a hundred volumes of international law."[2] By 1882 he was willing to accept even autocracy if it meant strengthening the nation. Furthermore, he favored imperialist expansion both to assure Japan's safety and to bring the benefits of "civilization" to neighboring countries such as Korea. Thus he welcomed the war when it came in 1894.

Fukuzawa found words of praise for some aspects of the Japanese tradition, including the samurai value of loyal service, but continued to look primarily to the West for his models and ideas. However, he avoided the extremes of Westernization. In early Meiji some thinkers allowed their enthusiasm to get the better of their judgment, and there were all kinds of extreme proposals for radical Westernization, including one to make English the national language. However, not all supporters of Western ways were genuine enthusiasts. Many desired to impress Westerners in order to be accepted as equals and to speed treaty revision. This was the motive behind a variety of movements, ranging from a drive to reform public morals to the revision of the legal code. It also accounts for one of the symbols of the era, the Rokumeikan, a hall completed in 1883 to accommodate mixed foreign and Japanese social gatherings. Designed by an English architect in the elaborate manner of the European Renaissance, it provided the setting for dinners, card parties, and fancy dress balls.

The Arts

In the arts, Western influence was both audible and visible. It affected the music taught in the schools and that performed in military bands. In painting, we have already noted the work of Takahashi, but the impact of the West was

Figure 18-2   Kobayashi Kiyochika, *Train at Night*. Woodcut print.

Figure 18-3
Kuroda Seiki,
Morning Toilet.
Oil, 1893,
178.5 cm × 98 cm.

visible also in more traditional genres. Sometimes called the last of the major *ukiyo-e* artists was Kobayashi Kiyochika (1847–1915). He introduced Western light and shading into *ukiyo-e,* using the principles of Western perspective but retaining a traditional Japanese sense of color. (See Figure 18-2.)

Western styles of painting were advanced not only by foreign artists who taught in Japan but also by Japanese who studied abroad, particularly in France, and brought back new styles and ways of looking at the world. Kuroda Seiki (1866–1924) studied in France from 1884 to 1893, and it was there that he painted *Morning Toilet* (Figure 18-3), which caused a stir when exhibited in Tokyo in 1894 and created a storm of controversy when shown in more conservative Kyōto the following year. Japan had never had a tradition of painting the nude, and there were protests that Kuroda's painting was pornography, not art. But Kuroda won the battle and went on to become one of Japan's most influential Western-style painters.

The initial enthusiasm for Western art led to the neglect and even disdain of traditional art, which shocked the American Ernest Fenollosa (1853–1908) when he came to Japan in 1878 to teach at Tokyo University. Fenollosa did what he could to make the new generation of Westernized Japanese aware of the greatness of their artistic heritage. He, himself, was an admirer of the last of the masters of the Kano school, Kano Hōgai (1828–88), and together with the younger Okakura Tenshin (1862–1913) sparked a revived interest in traditional styles. The two men were assisted by a reaction, which set in during the late eighties, against excessive Westernization. Many were attracted to the formula, "Eastern ethics; Western technology," a concept earlier advanced by Sakuma Shōzan, and there was now more talk about a national "essence" but little agreement on how it should be defined. Some feared that acceptance of a foreign culture was a step toward national decline and sought for ways to be both modern and Japanese, to adopt the universalist aspects of Western culture while retaining what was of value in their own particularist past.

The educated and sensitive were especially troubled by the tensions inherent in a program of modernization under traditionalist auspices. Western scientific rationalism could, by questioning the founding myth, undermine the throne itself. In 1892 a Tokyo University professor was forced to resign after he wrote that Shinto was a "survival of a primitive form of worship."[3] That was sacrilege. Similarly, Western individualism, fostered by the policy of modernization, clashed with the old family values that, Fukuzawa notwithstanding, continued strong and remained in official favor. In Japan, as in other modernizing countries, individuals experienced the need to make difficult choices. For many the resolution of conflicts was eased by the national triumph in war, but the problems, as we shall see, were to remain.

Education

Japanese intellectual and political leaders were quick to realize the importance of education in fashioning a new Japan capable of competing with the West. In this, as in other areas, they showed great interest in the practices and institutions of European countries and of the United States. For example, one of the members of the Iwakura Mission paid special attention to education and wrote fifteen volumes on the subject after his return home.

At the beginning of the Meiji period, Japan sent many students overseas to obtain the advanced training it could not provide at home. One-eighth of the Ministry of Education's first budget (1873) was designated for this purpose, and 250 students were sent abroad on government scholarships that year. Furthermore, many foreign instructors were brought to Japan to teach in various specialized schools. These, however, were temporary expedients to be used until Japan's own modern educational system was in operation. By the late 1880s the number of foreign instructors was down, and only some 50 to 80 students annually were being sent abroad by the government. A landmark in the history of higher education was the establishment of Tokyo University in 1877 with four faculties: physical science, law, literature, and medicine.

Considerable progress was made in building a complete educational system, yet actual accomplishments fell short of the ambitious plan drawn up in 1872. This called for 8 universities, 256 middle schools, and 53,760 elementary schools, but thirty years later, in 1902, there were only 2 universities, 222 middle schools, and 27,076 elementary schools. Similarly, the government had to retreat from its 1872 ordinance making four years of education compulsory for all children. Among the difficulties this program encountered were money problems (elementary education was locally financed), teacher shortages, and the reluctance of rural parents to send their children to school. However, by the time four years of compulsory education were reintroduced in 1900, the great majority of children who were supposed to be in school were in actual attendance, and in 1907 the government was able to increase the period to six years. By that time the teachers were predominantly graduates of Japanese Normal Schools (teacher training institutes, the first of which was established in Tokyo in 1872).

When the Ministry of Education was first established in 1871, the French system of highly centralized administration was adopted. Although local schools were locally financed, the ministry not only determined the general direction of education but prescribed textbooks, supervised teacher training, and generally controlled the curriculum of schools throughout the country. Government educational policy therefore was decisive in determining what was taught.

There was wide agreement among political leaders that an essential function of the educational system was to provide the people with the skills necessary for modernization. They realized that not only factories and businesses but also armies and navies require a certain level of literacy and a command of simple arithmetic among the rank and file, as well as higher education for managers and officers. Beyond that, the leaders recognized that schools foster values and looked to them to mold the Japanese people into a nation. On the question of specific moral content, however, there were intense disagreements reflecting different visions of Japan's future. In the seventies when enthusiasm for the West ran high, even elementary readers and moral texts were frequently translated from English and French for use in Japanese schools. But there were also critics who insisted that the schools should preserve traditional Confucian and Japanese values. Another influential position was opposed to both Western liberal values and to traditional ideals but looked to the schools to indoctrinate the populace with modern, nationalist values. An influential proponent of this last position was Mori Arinori (1847–89), Minister of Education from 1885 until he was assassinated by a nationalist fanatic in 1889.

Although Mori had a strong hand in shaping the educational system, the most important Meiji pronouncement on the subject was drafted under the influence of the emperor's Confucian Lecturer. This was the Rescript on Education, which was issued in 1890. For half a century it remained the basic statement of the purpose of education, memorized by generations of Japanese school children. It begins by attributing "the glory of the fundamental character of Our Empire" to the Imperial Ancestors who "deeply and firmly implanted virtue" and calls upon His Majesty's subjects to observe the usual Confucian virtues beginning with filiality toward their parents, enjoins them to "pursue learning and cultivate arts" for the sake of intellectual and moral development, and "to advance public good and promote common interests." Furthermore, "should emergency arise, offer yourselves courageously to the State, and thus guard and maintain the prosperity of Our Imperial Throne coeval with heaven and earth."[4] In this document, Confucianism is identified with the throne (no mention is made of its foreign origins), and a premium is placed on patriotic service to the state and the throne. These values were further drummed into school children in compulsory ethics classes. Education was to serve both to prepare Japan for the future and to preserve elements of the past, or rather, to prepare Japan for the future in the name of the past.

Meanwhile the religious orientation of the state had also been settled. In 1882 Shinto was divided into Shrine Shinto and Sect Shinto. Most Shinto shrines, including the most prominent such as Ise and Izumo, came under Shrine Shinto and were now transformed into state institutions supposedly patriotic rather than religious in character, operating on a higher plane than the merely "religious" bodies such as the various forms of Buddhism, Christianity (legalized in 1873), and Sect Shinto. This formula permitted the government to identify itself with the Shinto tradition from which was derived the mystique of the emperor, source of its own authority, while at the same time meeting the demands for religious tolerance voiced by Japanese reformers and Western nations.

Modernizing the Economy

In the twenty years that followed consolidation of the Meiji regime, Japan laid the foundations for a modern industrial economy. The nation was still primarily agrarian, but Western experience had shown that capital accumulated through the sale of surplus agricultural production, and labor obtained through the migration of surplus rural population to the cities, were necessary conditions for industrial development. Both conditions existed in Meiji Japan.

Japanese agriculture had become more efficient due to the introduction of new seed strains, new fertilizers, and new methods of cultivation. New land for farming was being opened, especially in Hokkaidō. New applications of science to agriculture were being tried at experimental stations and agricultural colleges. In consequence, during the fourteen years preceding the Sino-Japanese War rice yields increased by 30 percent and other crops showed comparable gains; per capita rice consumption increased. Agriculture was further stimulated by the development of a substantial export market for silk and tea, and a growing domestic demand for cotton. Thus trade also helped generate capital needed for investment in manufacturing.

Increased agricultural production did not result in major changes for the cultivator, however. Village government and the organization of village labor remained largely the same. Rents remained high: it was not unusual for a peasant's rent to equal half his rice crop. Profits resulting from the commercialization of agriculture went to the landlord, who handled the sale, rather than to the tenant. Even the creation of factory jobs did little to relieve population pressure on the land. Much of the factory labor was performed by peasant girls sent to the city to supplement their families' farm incomes for a number of years before they were married. Housed in company dormitories and strictly supervised, they were an untrained but inexpensive work force. When times were bad and factory operations slowed down, they could be laid off and returned to their villages. It was a system advantageous to both the landlord and the industrialist.

In Western countries the industrial revolution had been largely carried out by private enterprise. In Japan, however, where it was government policy to modernize so as to catch up with the West, the government itself took the initiative. The Meiji regime invested heavily in the economic infrastructure, that is, those basic public services that must be in place before an industrial economy can grow: education, transportation, communications, and so forth. As previously mentioned, students were sent abroad at public expense, for example, to study Western technologies, and foreigners were brought to Japan to teach in their areas of expertise. A major investment was made in railroads. The first line was completed in 1872, running between Tokyo and Yokohama. By the mid-nineties there were two thousand miles of track, much of it privately owned, for government initiative was followed by private investment once the feasibility, and especially the profitability, of railroads had been established.

This sequence of state initiative followed by private development can also be observed in manufacturing. The government took the lead, for example, in establishing and operating cement works, plants manufacturing glass and tiles, textile mills (silk and cotton), shipyards, mines, and munition works. The government felt these industries were essential, but private interests were unwilling to risk their capital in untried ventures, with little prospect of profits in the near term. Thus, if such ventures were to be started, the government would have to start them and finance the initial period of operations. It did so.

The Zaibatsu

The expenditure of capital required for this effort, the payments due to samurai on their bonds, the costs of the Satsuma Rebellion, and an adverse balance of trade combined to create a government financial crisis. Rising inflation damaged the government's purchasing power and also hurt the samurai, whose income depended on the interest paid on their bonds. These problems came to a head in 1880. The government's response was mainly to cut back on expenditures, and, thereby, it gradually brought the situation under control. As part of this economy move the government decided, late in 1880, to sell at public auction all its enterprises with the exception of the munitions plants. The

buyers were usually men who were friendly with government leaders and recognized the long-term advantages of buying the factories, which were selling at
bargain prices. These enterprises did not become profitable immediately, but
when they did the result was that a small group of well-connected firms enjoyed a controlling position in the modern sector of the economy. These were
the *zaibatsu*, huge financial and industrial combines.

The *zaibatsu* were usually organized by new entrepreneurs, for most of the
old Tokugawa merchant houses were too set in their ways to make a successful transition into the new world of Meiji. The outstanding exception to
this generalization was the house of Mitsui, originally established in Edo as a
textile house and also enriched by its banking activities. When it became apparent that government initiatives were creating new economic opportunities
in commerce and industry, Mitsui brought new men into the firm to take advantage of them. The new leadership was vigorous and capable, establishing
first a bank and then a trading company. These institutions became important factors in Japan's foreign commerce; they also engaged in domestic transactions, profiting handsomely from handling army supply contracts during the
Satsuma Rebellion. In 1881 Mitsui bought government coal mines, which ultimately contributed greatly to its wealth and power. By that time the traditional drapery business had been relegated to a sideline and delegated to a subordinate house.

A contrast to Mitsui is offered by the Mitsubishi *zaibatsu*, founded by Iwasaki Yatarō (1834–85), a former Tosa samurai bold and ruthless in the wars of
commerce. Iwasaki developed a strong shipping business by obtaining government contracts, government subsidies, and for a time even government guarantee of its dividend payments. At one point the government lent the company
ships, a loan that eventually became a gift. Mitsubishi also benefited greatly
during the Formosan expedition of 1874 and again during the Satsuma Rebellion from doing government business. The firm grew strong enough to displace
some of its foreign competitors, and around its shipping business it developed
banking and insurance facilities and entered foreign trade. It also went into
mining, and its acquisition of the government-established Nagasaki shipyard
assured its future as the leader in shipbuilding and heavy industry, although
Iwasaki did not live long enough to see the shipyard turn a profit. Iwasaki ruled
the combine like a personal domain, but he also recruited an able managerial
staff composed largely of graduates of Fukuzawa's Keiō University.

For Iwasaki personal ambition and patriotism were fused. As he conceived it,
his mission was to compete with the great foreign shipping companies, and he
was convinced that whatever benefited his company was also good for the nation. Not everyone, however, agreed with this assessment. For a time Iwasaki
had to face the competition of a rival company, one of whose organizers was
Shibusawa Eiichi (1840–1931), one of the great Meiji entrepreneurs and
bankers, founder of the Tokyo Chamber of Commerce and Bankers' Association, a believer in joint-stock companies, in competition, and in business independence from government. Iwasaki won this battle, but Shibusawa remained

enormously influential, not only because of his economic power but also because of his energetic advocacy of higher business standards and of the view that business could contribute most to the public good by remaining independent of government.

The success of such men as Iwasaki and Shibusawa should not obscure the fact that new ventures continued to entail risk. Not all new ventures were successful. For example, the attempt to introduce sheep raising into Japan was a failure. Initial attempts at organizing insurance companies were similarly ill-conceived, since they used rates and tables appropriate for European rather than Japanese conditions. But insurance companies were finally established, and altogether successes outnumbered failures.

One reason for the success of the *zaibatsu* and other new companies was their ability to attract capable and dedicated executives. Formerly, many capable members of the samurai class had refused to enter the business world because concern with money making was considered abhorrent. But this obstacle was largely overcome after the Restoration, not merely because the status of the samurai was changing, but because commercial and industrial development were required for the good of the state, and the member of a samurai family who helped build a strong bank, trading company, manufacturing industry, and so forth was rendering a service to the emperor and to Japan. Indeed, the government's initial sponsorship of many enterprises lent them some of the prestige of government service. The fact that many of the companies were created by men of samurai origins also helped make business socially acceptable.

The association of business with government also influenced business ideology in Japan. From the beginning, the ethos of modern Japanese business focused on its contributions to the Japanese nation, not on the laissez-faire notions of economic liberalism that prevailed in the West. The company did not exist only, or even primarily, to make a profit for its shareholders. Similarly, the internal organization of the business firm followed different lines in Japan; old values of group solidarity and mutual responsibility between the samurai and his lord were incorporated into the business structure to give all participants in the venture a strong sense of company loyalty.

In discussing the *zaibatsu* and other modern firms it should not be supposed that large-scale trading, mining, and manufacturing represented the whole of Japanese business. On the contrary, many small-scale traditional establishments continued to function well past the early Meiji era. But the new firms did represent a major growth and change in economic activity, and signaled a change in Japanese perceptions of their role in international affairs as well. This was reflected in economic terms by the government's efforts to preserve economic independence, for example, by protecting home markets, conserving foreign exchange, and avoiding dependence on foreign capital so as to assure Japanese ownership of railways and other large-scale enterprises. It was reflected, also, in Japanese foreign policy, and especially in the modernization and deployment of the Japanese military.

The Military

Japanese military forces engaged in three major military operations in the twenty years following the Restoration: the Formosa expedition of 1874, the Satsuma Rebellion of 1877, and the Sino-Japanese War of 1894–95. The first two operations were fought primarily for domestic purposes, as the new Meiji government sought to consolidate its power. The Sino-Japanese War, on the other hand, was an outward looking venture from the start, a test of strength with China on the Korean Peninsula. An even more striking difference, however, was the difference in the quality of Japanese military organization, armament, and tactical skill in 1874–77 and 1894.

The Formosa expedition of 1874 was far from brilliant. The landing was poorly executed, hygiene was so defective that disease took a great toll, and equipment had to be abandoned because it was unsuitable for use in a tropical climate. Similarly, the force which suppressed the Satsuma Rebellion did so because of its superiority in numbers and equipment rather than because of its military excellence.

To improve the quality of the army, a major reorganization was carried out in 1878 under the direction of Yamagata. A general staff was established along German lines, and Germany became the overall model for the army, which had previously been influenced by France. By strengthening the reserves, the military potential was greatly increased. During the ten or fifteen years before the Sino-Japanese War, generous military appropriations had enabled the army to acquire modern equipment, mostly manufactured in Japanese arsenals and plants, while the creation of a Staff College and improved training methods further strengthened the army and made it more modern. Like Yamagata, most of the leading generals were from Chōshū.

Naval modernization was similar to that of the army except that England was the model and continued to be a source from which some of the larger vessels were purchased. In 1894 the navy possessed twenty-eight modern ships with a total displacement of 57,000 tons and also twenty-four torpedo boats. Most important, Japan had the facilities to maintain, repair, and arm her fleet. From the start most of the naval leadership came from Satsuma.

The military is a good example of the way in which the various facets of modernization were intertwined and supported each other, for the armed forces both benefited and contributed to the process. Not only did they stimulate new industries, ranging from armaments to tin cans, but it was also in the army that the rural conscript was for the first time exposed to a wider and more modern world. Indeed, when conscription was first introduced, many men from backward districts were quite bewildered by the accouterments of modern life. There are reports that some bowed in reverence to the stove in their barracks, taking it for some kind of god. For many men, the army provided the first introduction to shoes. Before the spread of education, some men learned to read and write in the army. All were exposed to the new values of nationalism and loyalty to the emperor. Most also learned to smoke (cigarettes were first reported in 1877) and to drink (native beverages and also excellent Japanese beer, first brewed in the 1870s), and they had their first experience with the modern city. Soldiers also enjoyed a better diet, receiving more meat than the average Japanese. But discipline was very harsh, and draft dodging was prevalent: in 1889 almost one-tenth of those eligible avoided conscription. Nevertheless, the vast majority did serve.

The Test of War

For the country as a whole this was a period of crucial and remarkable change and of highly visible accomplishments. These accomplishments did not come cheap, but that they were genuine was demonstrated by Japan's impressive victory in the Sino-Japanese War. The triumph of Japan's army, which rapidly made its way north through Korea, crossed the Yalu River into Manchuria, and captured Port Arthur on the Liaotung Peninsula, was matched by the victory Japan's naval forces won over the Chinese at sea.

The events leading up to this conflict are discussed in the next chapter, but essentially Japan went to war to counter Chinese dominance in Korea. The motivations of Japan's leaders included alarm over the prospect of a weak Korea open to Western (particularly Russian) aggression as well as more positive empire-building sentiments. Many believed that bringing the peninsula under Japanese influence would foster needed reforms in a reactionary country, and there were Koreans who shared this view. As it turned out, the war did not assure Japanese security let alone Korean progress. But it did signal the beginning of the Japanese Empire. It did not resolve the tensions created during the preceding years, but it did usher in a new phase of Japan's modern history.

NOTES

1. Quoted in Carmen Blacker, *The Japanese Enlightenment: A Study of the Writings of Fukuzawa Yukichi* (London: Cambridge University Press, 1964), p. 111.
2. *Ibid.*, p. 128.
3. Quoted in Kenneth Pyle, *The New Generation in Meiji Japan: Problems in Cultural Identity, 1885–95* (Stanford: Stanford University Press, 1969), p. 124.
4. "Rescript on Education," in John Lu, *Sources of Japanese History* (New York: McGraw-Hill, 1974), 2: 70–71.

中國之發奮自彊

19 Self-Strengthening in China: 1874–1894

In China, the defeat of the Taiping Rebellion gave the Ch'ing dynasty a new lease on life. Other military victories over Muslim rebels in the West further bolstered the regime. On the other hand, as the impetus of the T'ung-chih Restoration slowed, the reform movement faded, and old abuses reappeared. For example, the purchase of examination degrees and government posts continued to be widespread.

In the twenty years preceding the Sino-Japanese War (1894–95) pressures from the Western powers—Russia in Central Asia, France and Britain in Southeast Asia—increasingly restricted the scope of Chinese influence among peoples traditionally considered tributaries of the imperial throne. These pressures, along with the intrusion into China's internal affairs represented by

445

the treaty system, led Ch'ing statesmen to attempt selective modernization as a way to strengthen and preserve their state and society. This effort is known as the Self-Strengthening movement.

In Japan an ambitious modernization program succeeded, at least partly, because it was sponsored by a vigorous new government and accompanied by significant social and political change. For a number of reasons, "self-strengthening" accomplished less in China: contrasts in geographic scale, in historical traditions, and in social structure spring readily to mind. The political situation, too, was very different.

The Empress Dowager and the Government

The dominant figure at court during the last phase of the Ch'ing dynasty (which outlasted her by only three years) was the Dowager Empress Tz'u Hsi (1835–1908). (See Figure 20-1.) The intelligent and educated daughter of a minor Manchu official, she entered the palace as a low-ranking concubine but had the good fortune to bear the Hsien-feng emperor his only son. After the Hsien-feng emperor died, she became co-regent for her son, the T'ung-chih emperor. Skillfully using her position to increase her power, she dominated her son and, it is rumored, encouraged him in the debaucheries that weakened his constitution and brought him to the grave at the youthful age of nineteen (1875). She then manipulated the succession in order to place on the throne her four-year-old nephew, the Kuang-hsü emperor (r. 1875–1908), and continued to make the decisions even when he ostensibly assumed the imperial duties in 1889. At first Prince Kung had provided a counterforce at court, but his power declined in the seventies, and in 1884 he was removed from government altogether.

The Empress Dowager was a strong-willed woman, an expert at the arts of political infighting and manipulation. One of her most reliable supporters was the Manchu bannerman Jung-lu (1836–1903), to whom she gave important military commands. Yet, it was an anomaly to have a woman in control of the court, and her prestige was not enhanced by rumors that she was responsible for the murder of her rivals. Corruption in very high places also took its toll. The very powerful eunuch Li Lien-ying (d. 1911) was totally loyal to his mistress but also totally corrupt, using his influence to amass a fortune. Tz'u Hsi herself accepted payments from officials and misspent government funds. The most notorious case of financial abuse was her use of money intended for the navy to rebuild the summer palace destroyed in 1860 by Elgin and his troops during the second war between Britain and China. Eventually the navy department, established in 1885, became a branch of the imperial household, and China's most famous and magnificent "ship" was made of marble. (See Figure 19-1.)

Tz'u Hsi's prime political aim was to continue in power. She had no profound aversion, but neither did she have any commitment, to the policy of se-

Figure 19-1 Marble Pavilion in the shape of a ship. Summer Palace, Peking.

lective modernization advocated by the champions of self-strengthening, and her understanding of the West was very limited. It was to her immediate political advantage to avoid dependence on any single group of officials and to manipulate a number of strong governors-general who had gained in power as a result of the Taiping Rebellion. These indispensable provincial administrators could no longer be controlled by the court at will, but fortunately for Peking, they remained absolutely loyal to the dynasty. The governors-general operated their own political and financial machines and commanded substantial military forces, but they were still dependent on Peking's power of appointment. Major policy decisions continued to be made in Peking. During this period, the central government was also strengthened financially by the receipts from the Maritime Customs. Thus the West helped to preserve the dynasty even as it was undermining its foundations.

Most powerful of the governors-general was Li Hung-chang, who from 1870 was firmly established in Tientsin, where he commanded an army, sponsored self-strengthening efforts, and successfully avoided transfer. A protégé of Tseng Kuo-fan, he shared his master's devotion to the dynasty but not his Confucian probity. From his headquarters, not far from Peking, Li was able to dominate China's policy toward Korea, but he could not control its foreign policy elsewhere. Arguing for the priority of maritime defense, he had unsuccessfully opposed the emphasis on inner Asia, which produced Tso Tsung-t'ang's campaigns of the 1870s, and in the eighties he failed again when he tried to prevent war with France (1884–85). His opposition earned him the denunciations of his enemies, who castigated him as an arch traitor comparable to Ch'in Kuei, always blamed for the Sung's failure to regain the North from the Juchen. The war, along with other developments in foreign relations, is discussed below; but first, consideration of the Self-Strengthening movement is in order. It was a movement in which Li played a major part.

Self-Strengthening

The Self-Strengthening movement is readily divisible into three stages. Initially, during the period of the T'ung-chih Restoration (1862–74), it was strongly military in orientation and produced arsenals, the Foochow dockyard, and schools offering instruction principally in subjects of military application. In its middle phase, 1872–85, interest in the military continued, but efforts were expanded to include projects in transportation (shipping and railways), communication (telegraph), and mining. The final period (from China's defeat by France in 1885 until the outbreak of the Sino-Japanese War in 1894) was one of continued concern for military modernization, but there was also a further broadening of industrial capacity, including the development of light industry. Since there was a good deal of continuity among the protagonists and in their projects, we will discuss their ideas and programs topically rather than chronologically.

The Theory

A willingness to adopt new means to strengthen and reform the state animated the works of a long line of Confucian scholars, from the Sung through the Ch'ing. As it became apparent during the early years of the nineteenth century that the dynasty was in serious trouble, more scholars turned against the philological emphasis of the school of Han learning and focused on what today would be called policy studies. *Huang-ch'ao ching-shih wen-pien* (*A Compilation of Essays on Statecraft*), published in 1827, is a case in point. It is a collection of essays on social, political, and economic matters written by various Ch'ing officials and compiled by Ho Ch'ang-lin (1785–1841). Concern for reform and willingness to take a hard, critical look at financial and political institutions characterized the writings of leading intellectuals and, in the work of Wei Yüan, began to merge with an interest in the West, although Wei still proposed to apply the old formula of using barbarians against barbarians. Feng

Kuei-fen went further, seeing the West as a threat, to be sure, but also as a source for solving the dangerous problems it had created. He was the first in China to urge the use of "barbarian techniques" against the "barbarians", the hallmark of the Self-Strengthening movement.

Although the ideas of self-strengthening were well established by the 1870s, the classic theoretical formulation came in 1898 from the brush of Chang Chih-tung (1837–1909), a leading scholar-official and governor-general of the Late Ch'ing. Like Sakuma Shōzan earlier in Japan, Chang wanted to preserve traditional values while adopting Western science and technology. The idea was that Chinese learning would remain the heart of Chinese civilization, while Western learning would have a subordinate supporting and technical role. This was expressed in terms of the traditional Neo-Confucian dichotomy of *t'i* (substance) and *yung* (function): Western means for Chinese ends. The basic pattern of Chinese civilization was to remain sacrosanct, but it was to be protected by Western techniques. The techniques to be adopted were initially military but gradually, as already indicated, came to include a great deal more. In the process the details of the prescription were altered without changing the basic plan.

Conservative opponents of self-strengthening, on the other hand, feared that Chinese civilization would be contaminated by borrowing from the West, since, as they well knew, ends are affected by means. In the Confucian formulation, *t'i* and *yung* are aspects of a single whole. The Confucian tradition had always been concerned with means as well as ends, and generations of scholars had insisted that the Way did not consist merely of "empty" abstractions but was concerned with practical realities. There was no essence apart from application. And there was a great deal more to the West than mere techniques. It was fallacious to believe that China could merely borrow the techniques of the West without becoming entangled in manifestations of Western culture.

If China went ahead with efforts to adopt Western techniques while preserving traditional culture, the best that could be hoped for would be an uneasy compartmentalization. Individuals who came in contact with the West would have to separate the modern from the traditional elements in their lives. Those parts of the country that had the most direct experience with the West, such as the treaty ports, would have to be isolated from the traditional Chinese hinterlands. In others words, to preserve tradition in a period of modernization, the country would have to be protected from the kind of radical social reappraisal hailed in Japan by champions of "reason" like Fukuzawa Yukichi. The contrast with Japan is instructive, for there social change was sanctioned by an appeal to nationalism as symbolized by the throne, whereas in China Confucianism was much too closely associated with the social structure to allow for a similar development. Meiji Japan demonstrated that elements of Confucianism were compatible with modernization but also that modernization involved changes reaching into the very heart of a civilization.

An indication of the inadequacy of self-strengthening theory was China's failure to educate a new leadership, both fully Confucian and modern.

Education

The Self-Strengthening movement was led by impressive and capable men, such as Li Hung-chang, but there was a lack of competent middle-echelon officers and managers, as well as technical personnel such as scientists and engineers. The fastest way to make up this deficit was to send students overseas for training, which the Chinese did. However, this approach had only mixed success. The most extensive effort of this sort was made between 1872 and 1881, when 120 students were sent to the United States under the supervision of Yung Wing (1828–1912), Yale class of 1854, and the first Chinese to graduate from an American university. The boys were between fifteen and seventeen years old, young enough to master new subjects, but also immature and easily swayed by their foreign environment. To assure continued Confucian training, they were accompanied by a traditional Confucian mentor. Nevertheless, they soon adopted American ways: participating in American sports, dating and in some cases eventually marrying American girls, and in a few instances even converting to Christianity. Yung Wing himself married an American and ended up making his home in Hartford, Connecticut.

The mission had been launched with the backing of Tseng Kuo-fan and Li Hung-chang, but Li withdrew his support when the students were denied admission to West Point and when they were fiercely attacked by Peking officials for neglecting their Confucian studies. The mission, poorly managed from the beginning, was abandoned. Among its participants were some of the first, but by no means the last, Chinese students who in the course of their overseas stay became alienated from their culture.

The obvious alternative to study abroad was to supply instruction in modern subjects at home. As we have seen, the advocates of self-strengthening were active from the start in doing just that, establishing the T'ung-wen Kuan in the capital and other schools in conjunction with several arsenals and the Foochow dockyard. By 1894 the government also operated a telegraph school, a naval and military medical school, and a mining school. These schools typically offered a curriculum encompassing both the classical studies required for success in the examination system and the new subjects for which they were established. Since command of traditional learning remained the key to entry into the civil service, students naturally tended to concentrate on that, for without an examination degree career opportunities were limited. The most famous graduate of the Foochow dockyard school was Yen Fu (1853–1921), who was sent to England to continue his studies at the naval college in Greenwich but after returning home to China was unable to pass the provincial examination. He became famous not as an admiral but as a writer and translator.

It did occur to some reformers to broaden the content of the examinations to allow candidates credit for mastering modern subjects, but suggestions along these lines encountered formidable opposition, since they were likely to affect the Confucian core of the civilization. A minor concession was finally made in 1887, which provided that 3 out of some 1500 provincial examination graduates might be granted that degree after being examined in Western along with (not in place of) traditional subjects. They would then be eligible for the *chin-shih* examination on the same terms as the other candidates. Creation of a leadership versed in modern subjects would have required major changes in the content and function of the examination system or its elimination altogether.

Economic Self-Strengthening

In China, as in Japan, there were those who wished to adopt Western technology so as to build up their country's economic strength. In Japan a strong central government took the lead in modernizing crucial sectors of the economy and successfully involved members of the upper classes in this undertaking. In China, on the other hand, there was no major sustained national effort. Leadership came from political sponsors (usually regional strong men, typically, governors-general); central government involvement was half-hearted; and the upper classes were divided over whether or not the effort was worthwhile. These differences were reflected in the results achieved.

In the first phase of the Self-Strengthening movement, the focus was military. Early projects included gun factories in Shanghai and Soochow, the Kiangnan Arsenal in Shanghai and another arsenal in Nanking, the Foochow dockyard, and a machine factory in Tientsin. These enterprises, partly due, perhaps, to their political sponsorship and operation under official control, suffered from bureaucratic corruption and poor management. Furthermore, they depended on foreigners for expertise and supervision of operations, but the individuals hired to perform these crucial tasks were frequently unqualified for the job.

During the second phase of the Self-Strengthening movement, "government operated merchant enterprises" (*kuan-tu shang-pan*) became the rule. These were mixed companies established under the patronage of a political sponsor, with capital from both the public and private sectors. Private financing was very much desired, but capital was scarce in China and other forms of investment were more prestigious or more lucrative than modern business enterprises. Private investment came primarily from Chinese businessmen resident in the treaty ports. They had participated in the growth of these centers of international trade and were familiar with modern-style business ventures and techniques. However, their capital was limited; hence the need for public funds, usually provided by the political sponsor.

The new companies applied modern technology to a somewhat broader range of activities than had been true in the initial phase. The new Western-style establishments included a shipping company, textile mills, the beginnings of a telegraph service, and the K'ai-p'ing Coal Mines.

The shipping firm known as the China Merchants Steam Navigation Company is a good example of the *kuan-tu shang-pan*. Albert Feuerwerker's study of this concern is particularly interesting for the light it sheds on the role of the political sponsor in economic development at this time.[1] When private capital proved insufficient to finance the company, the sponsor Li Hung-chang put up the rest from public funds. To help the company make a go of it, Li secured the shipping line a monopoly on the transportation of tax grain and official freight bound for Tientsin. He obtained tariff concessions for the company and protected it from its domestic critics and enemies. In exchange, Li exercised a large measure of control, appointing and dismissing its managers, employing its ships to transport his troops, and using its payroll to provide sinecures for political followers. He also used its earnings to buy warships. To advance his policy in Korea, Li had the company lend money to the Korean government.

The overall record of this and similar companies was mixed. The investors made money and their political sponsors benefited. But after an initial spurt, the companies failed to establish a pattern of sustained growth. Instead, they stagnated. Moreover, they failed to train Chinese technical personnel. They were plagued by incompetent managers, by nepotism and corruption. Even their political sponsors, high officials in the areas where the enterprises operated, exploited the companies, regarding them as sources of patronage and revenue along the lines of the traditional salt administration, rather than as key investments for the modernization of the country.

During the last phase of the Self-Strengthening movement, attempts were made to decrease government participation by organizing joint government-merchant companies and to eliminate government influence entirely by founding private enterprises, but these had very limited success. Absent in China was the close relationship between business and government found in Japan. By the mid-nineties, there was a modern sector in the Chinese economy, but it was largely limited to the periphery of the empire (for example, the treaty ports and Hong Kong), where Chinese merchants were able to hold their own quite successfully against foreign competition.

The total economic impact of imperialism on China during this period is a subject of debate. Obviously tariff restrictions and other concessions forced on the Chinese were designed to benefit Western interests vis-à-vis the Chinese economy. Yet the balance of evidence to date suggests that the traditional Chinese economy, beyond the treaty ports and their immediate hinterlands, remained little affected during this period. Some of the traditional handicraft industries (for example, spinning) were damaged by foreign competition, while others (for example, weaving) held their own or even expanded slightly. Since labor was cheap but capital scarce (and therefore expensive), it did not pay to build factories to produce everything the people needed. Furthermore, the prospective owners of modern factories had to consider not only the cost of their products but also the cost of marketing, including high transportation charges.

To say that traditional economic patterns continued to prevail in China's interior is not to say that all was well. On the contrary. All that continuity implied was that China's economic and social problems had a familiar ring. As Kwang-Ching Liu has put it:

> The chief cause of rural tension continued to be excessive and unequal taxation, the tyranny of yamen underlings, landlordism and usury—social injustice reinforced by administrative abuse.[2]

Missionary Efforts and Christian Influence

The Western presence in nineteenth-century China was no more confined to trade and politics than it had been during the Late Ming encounter. Once again missionaries were drawn to China as a promising area for their endeavors, but now there were Protestant as well as Catholic missionaries. An early Protestant arrival was Robert Morrison of the London Missionary Society. He reached Canton in 1807, learned the language, brought out a Chinese-English dictionary and a Chinese version of the Bible (later used by the Taipings), founded the school where Yung Wing received his early education, and set up a printing press. Other missionaries, many of them Americans, brought Western medicine and other aspects of Western secular knowledge to China.

The missionaries made a notable effort in education: by 1877 there were 347 missionary schools in China with almost six thousand pupils. Such schools helped spread knowledge about the West as well as helping to propagate the religion. A notable missionary-educator was W. A. P. Martin, who contributed to the Self-Strengthening movement. When Martin became head of the T'ung-wen Kuan, he greatly raised its standards and later was appointed first president of Peking University. Missionaries were also important as a major source of information about China for their home countries. The first foreign language newspaper published in China was a missionary publication, and missionaries also contributed to scholarship. Outstanding among the missionaries who became Sinologists was James Legge, a master translator who rendered the Chinese classics into sonorous Victorian prose. In this and other ways, missionaries with varying degrees of sophistication and self-awareness served as cultural intermediaries.

As indicated by the growth of their schools, the missionaries met with some success, but their strength was largely in the treaty ports, and the results were hardly commensurate with their efforts. By the end of the century, the number of Catholic missionaries in China had climbed to about 750, and there were approximately half a million Catholics in China, up from around 160,000 at the beginning of the century. (See Figure 19-2.) The Protestants had less success: in 1890 there appear to have been only slightly over 37,000 converts served by roughly 1300 missionaries, representing forty-one different religious societies. The Tientsin Massacre of 1870 had demonstrated the potential fervor of antimissionary sentiment, and nothing happened to reduce hostilities during the next quarter of a century.

The reasons for the poor showing of Christianity are many and various. They include difficulties in translation and communication analogous to those that plagued Buddhist missionaries a millennium and a half earlier. The most important concepts of Christianity such as sin or the trinity were the most difficult to translate, none more so than the most sacred idea of all, the idea of God. Agreement on how to translate "God" into Chinese was never reached; three versions, one Catholic and two Protestant, remained current. As before, differences in culture compounded the difficulties in communication.

Figure 19-2   The French Cathedral at Canton, built on the former site of the governor's yamen.

The nineteenth-century missionary, however, also encountered problems which he did not share with his predecessors, for the Chinese associated Christianity with both the Taiping Rebellion and the unequal treaties. The former showed Christianity as subversive to the social and political order, while the latter brought the missionaries special privileges. Both were resented. Furthermore, the aura of power also drew to Christian establishments false converts; individuals attracted by the possibilities of a treaty port career, and opportunists out to obtain missionary protection for their own ends. Popular resentment of the missions was fired by scurrilous stories and bitter attacks, such as those which employed a homonym for the transliteration of "Jesus" to depict Christ as a pig. (See Figure 19-3.) This hostility was encouraged by the elite who saw in Christianity a superstitious religion that threatened their own status and values. It was no accident that anti-Christian riots often occurred when the examinations were being held in the provincial capitals.

Here there is an interesting contrast with the situation in Japan, where 30 percent of Christian converts during the Meiji period were from samurai backgrounds. Christianity served the spiritual needs and provided a vehicle for social protest for samurai who found themselves on the losing side of the Restoration struggle. As a result in the 1880s and 1890s a prestigious native clergy was developing in Japan, and Christianity remained more influential than the slow growth of the churches would indicate. In post-Taiping China too, Christianity continued to appeal to people dissatisfied with the status quo, and it counted among its converts some notable protesters, including Sun Yat-sen (see below). But the elite remained hostile, and the real cutting edge of protest was to be elsewhere: too radical for the nineteenth century, Christianity turned out to be insufficiently radical for the twentieth.

In the meantime, missionaries contributed to the Western perception of China. Working in the treaty ports, dealing not with Confucian gentlemen but with men on the margin of respectable society, the missionaries frequently developed a very negative view of China and its inhabitants, an image the reverse of the idealistic picture painted earlier by the Jesuits:

> The universal practice of lying and dishonest dealings; the unblushing lewdness of old and young; harsh cruelty toward prisoners by officers, and tyranny over slaves by masters—all form a full unchecked torrent of human depravity, and prove the existence of a kind and degree of moral degeneration of which an excessive statement can scarcely be made, or an adequate conception hardly be formed.[3]

These words, dated 1848, were written by S. Wells Williams who, after his service in China, became an influential American expert on China. Similar sentiments were expressed throughout the century.

Figure 19-3 *The [Foreign] Devils Worshipping the Incarnation of the Pig [Jesus].*

Endings and Beginnings

Perhaps the most interesting themes in the intellectual and artistic life of an era are those which reflect the end of a tradition and look toward a new future. Such a time had arrived in China. For some time sensitive men had been conscious that they were living in the last stages of a great tradition. The sense of ending was intensified by awareness of dynastic decay. For some, the sense of impending national change represented an exciting challenge. For the majority, however, the mood was one of uncertainty, apprehension, and regret. This mood is caught particularly well in a poem by Wang P'eng-yü (1818–97), an official who served as a Ch'ing censor:

Tune: "The Fish Poacher"

In Reply to a Poem from Tz'u-shan, Thanking Me for the Gift of Sung and Yüan Lyrics I Had Had Printed

Now that the lyric voice wavers in wind-blown dust
Who is to speak the sorrows of his heart?
Ten years of carving, seeking from each new block
The truest music of the string unswept,
Only to sigh now
Finding my griefs in tune
With every beat that leaves the ivory fret!
I sigh for the men of old
Pour wine in honor of the noble dead:
Does any spirit rhymester
Understand my heartbreak?

The craft of letters
Furnishes kindling, covers jars:
True bell or tinkling cymbal, who can tell?
Tu Fu, who lifelong courted the perfect phrase
—Did his verse help him, though it made men marvel?
Take what you find here,
See if an odd page, a forgotten tune
Still has the power to engage your mind.
My toiling over
I'll drink myself merry, climb the Golden Terrace,
Thrash out a wild song from my lute
And let the storms rage at will.[4]

Among those who welcomed the winds from the West were a small group of remarkable men, some with experience abroad in an official or unofficial capacity. An example of the former is Kuo Sung-tao (1818–91), China's first minister to England and the first Chinese representative to be stationed in any Western country. Another was Wang T'ao (1828–97), who spent two years in Scotland assisting James Legge in his translations and who also visited Japan. One of the founders of modern journalism in China, he favored the adoption of Western political institutions, not just their science and technology. There were other men like Kuo and Wang, for instance Cheng Kuan-ying (fl. 1884), a famous scholar-comprador, modernizer, and writer. Such men were interested in Western "substance" (not just "function"), while retaining their prime commitment to the Confucian tradition.

Still more important for the future were a number of younger men whose formative years fell into this period, although they did not become influential until the late nineties. There are three names in particular to which we will return: Yen Fu, born in 1853; K'ang Yu-wei, 1858; and Sun Yat-sen, 1866. The discussion of their ideas must wait, however, for it was not until China was jolted by her defeat in the Sino-Japanese War that they came to the fore.

Foreign Relations

Western pressures continued to affect China's foreign relations in the twenty years prior to the Sino-Japanese War, but the nature of these pressures began to alter. The initial conflicts had been over Western efforts to open trade and diplomatic relations with China proper; in the 1870s and 1880s foreign intervention in lands constituting peripheral areas of the empire or traditionally tributary states were the major causes of friction. (See map, Figure 19-4.)

Even as Japan was engaged in the Taiwan expedition, the Ch'ing government was troubled by a dangerous situation in Central Asia. In 1871 the Russians used a Muslim rebellion in Sinkiang as a pretext for occupying the Ili region, where a lucrative trade had developed. In Sinkiang itself, Yakub Beg (1830–77), a Muslim leader from Kokand in Central Asia, obtained Russian and British recognition for his breakaway state. In response to these alarming developments, the Ch'ing court assigned the task of suppressing the rebellion to Tso Tsung-t'ang, who had just finished crushing Muslim rebellions in Shensi and Kansu. He carried out the task with great success. By 1877, the government's control over Sinkiang was being reestablished and Yakub Beg was driven to his death. After difficult and protracted negotiations, the Russians returned nearly all of Ili (1881).

This strong showing in Central Asia, an area to which the Chinese were traditionally sensitive, bolstered morale, and Chinese successes in the diplomatic negotiations which followed encouraged those who were opposed to accommodation with the West. Indeed, the success of China's Central Asian policy encouraged them to demand an equally strong policy in dealing with the maritime powers. Pressure from this source was too strong to be ignored and constituted a major factor leading to confrontation and then to war with France in 1884–85. At issue was French expansion into Vietnam.

Vietnam and the Sino-French War of 1884–1885

North Vietnam had been annexed by the Han in 111 B.C., but after A.D. 939 native Vietnamese regimes prevailed, the major exception being the short period of Ming domination, 1406–26. The leader of the resistance against the

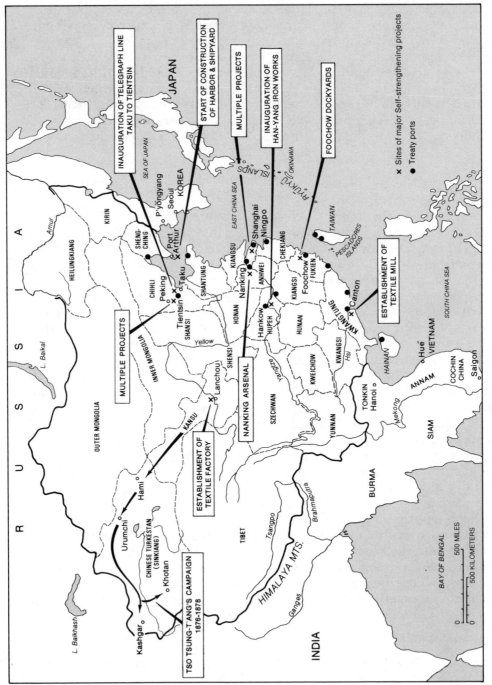

Figure 19-4　China During the Self-Strengthening Period

Ming, Le Loi, established the Later Li dynasty (1428–1789), with its capital at Hanoi and its government organized along Chinese lines. As in Korea, the determination to maintain political independence from China went hand in hand with admiration for Chinese culture and institutions. It is the Chinese influence on Vietnam which sets it apart from the other, more Indian oriented states of Southeast Asia.

China also served as the model for the Nguyen dynasty (1802–1945), which from its capital at Húe in Central Vietnam ruled the country through a bureaucracy modeled as closely as possible on that of China. The Chinese model was powerful, yet differences in size and culture between China and Vietnam required adjustments and compromises. To give just one example, Chinese influence was much stronger on civil government than on the military, for military theory and practice in Vietnam (as in the rest of continental Southeast Asia) centered on the elephant.

Vietnam's location in a cultural frontier area made for a rich and complex culture but was also a source of political weakness. One result was that the social and cultural gap between village and bureaucracy was greater in Vietnam than in China. Another result was the difficulty the Vietnamese state experienced in its efforts to incorporate the south, which had been gradually taken over from the Cambodians (regarded by the Vietnamese as "barbarians") during the century from roughly 1650 to 1750. Under the Nguyen dynasty this continued to be an area of large landlords and impoverished peasants, a region where the central bureaucracy operated inadequately. The area also suffered from educational backwardness, with the result that very few southerners were able to succeed in Vietnam's Chinese-style civil service examination system.

Vietnam's long coastline and elongated shape, as well as the presence of minority peoples within its boundaries, further hampered government efforts to fashion a strong unified state capable of withstanding Western encroachments. French missionaries and military men had early shown an interest in the area and had assisted in the founding of the Nguyen dynasty itself. Nearly 400 Frenchmen served the dynasty's founder and first emperor, Gia-long (r. 1801–20). Catholicism also made headway: it has been estimated that there were more Catholics in Vietnam than in all of China. For much the same reasons as had earlier animated anti-Christian policies in China and Japan, the Vietnamese authorities turned against the foreign religion, but their suppression of Catholicism gave the French an excuse for intervention.

French interest in Vietnam increased during the reign of Louis Napoleon. In 1859 France seized Saigon. Under a treaty signed three years later, the French gained control over three southern provinces, and five years later they seized the remaining three provinces in the South. These southern provinces became the French colony called Cochin China. During 1862–63 the French also established a protectorate over Cambodia. French interests were not limited to the South but included Central and North Vietnam (Annam and Tonkin). Treaties concluded in 1862 and 1874 contained various provisions eroding

Vietnamese sovereignty, and when disorders occurred in North Vietnam in 1882, France used the occasion to seize Hanoi.

Throughout this period of increasing French penetration, the Vietnamese court had continued its traditional tributary relations with Peking. When the French took Hanoi, the Vietnamese court responded by seeking both help from the Ch'ing and support from the Black Flags, an armed remnant of the Taipings which had been forced out of China and was fighting the French in Vietnam.

The Ch'ing responded by sending troops. Considerable wavering and diplomatic maneuvering followed in both Peking and Paris, but in the end no means were found to reconcile the Chinese wish to preserve their historic tributary relations with Southeast Asia and the French determination to create an empire in this region. The resulting war was fought in Vietnam, on Taiwan and the Pescadores, and along the nearby coast of China proper, where the Foochow dockyards and the fleet built there were among the war's casualties.

In the peace agreement that followed, China was forced to abandon her claim to suzerainty over Vietnam. The French colony of Cochin China, and the French protectorates of Annam and Tonkin, were joined by protectorates over Cambodia and (in the 1890s) Laos, to constitute French Indo-China.

Chinese influence in Southeast Asia was further diminished in 1886 when Britain completed the conquest of Burma, and China formally recognized this situation as well. Then in 1887, China ceded Macao to Portugal, officially recognizing the de facto situation there. Thus in the last third of the nineteenth century the foreign powers tried to gain further concessions and proceeded to establish themselves in tributary areas which had been part of the traditional Chinese imperial order, although not of China proper. In the face of this challenge, the Chinese made concessions where necessary and resisted where feasible. When areas of major importance were at stake, their policy was quite forceful. The struggle over Korea is an example.

Korea and the Sino-Japanese War of 1894–1895

Like Vietnam, Korea had adopted Chinese political institutions and ideology and maintained a tributary relationship with China while guarding her political independence. Again, as in Vietnam, differences in size, social organization, and cultural tradition insured the development of a distinct Sino-Korean culture. In the nineteenth century, however, Korea was sorely troubled by internal problems and external pressures. The Yi dynasty (1392–1910), then in its fifth century, was in serious decline. Korea's peasantry suffered from "a skewered or concentrated pattern of landholding; small average per capita holdings; high rates of tenancy; a regressive tax structure; false registration of taxable land; extortion and illegal charges and gratuities at tax collection time; and usury, especially official usury in the management of the grain loan system."[5] There was a serious uprising in the North in 1811. In 1833 there were rice riots in Seoul. And in 1862 there were rebellions in the South.

During the years 1864 to 1873, there was a last attempt to save the situation by means of a traditional program of reform initiated by the regent, or Taewŏngun (Grand Prince, 1821–98), who was the father of the king. The reform program proved strong enough to provoke a reaction but was not sufficiently drastic, even in conception, to transform Korea into a strong and viable state capable of dealing with the dangers of the modern world.

That world was gradually closing in on Korea. During the first two-thirds of the century a number of incidents occurred involving Western ships and foreign demands. Korea's initial policy was to resist all attempts to "open" the country by referring those seeking to establish diplomatic relations back to Peking. This policy was successful as long as it was directed at countries for whom Korea was of peripheral concern, but this had never been the case for Japan. Japan, therefore, was the most insistent of the powers trying to pry Korea loose from the Chinese orbit. In 1876 Japan forced Korea to sign a treaty establishing diplomatic relations and providing for the opening of three ports to trade. The treaty also stipulated that Korea was now "independent," but this did not settle matters since China still considered Korea a tributary. Insurrections in Seoul in 1882 and 1884 led to increased Chinese and Japanese involvement in Korea, including military involvement, always on opposing sides. But outright war was averted by talks between Itō Hirobumi and Li Hung-chang, which led to a formal agreement between China and Japan to withdraw their forces and inform each other if either decided in the future that it was necessary to send in troops.

During the next years the Chinese Resident in Korea was Yüan Shih-k'ai (1859–1916), a protégé of Li Hung-chang, originally sent to Korea to train Korean troops. Yüan successfully executed Li's policy of vigorous assertion of Chinese control, dominating the court, effecting a partial union of Korean and Chinese commercial customs, and setting up a telegraph service and a merchant route between Korea and China.

Conflicting ambitions in Korea made war between China and Japan highly probable; the catalyst was the Tonghak Rebellion. Tonghak, literally "Eastern Learning," was a religion founded by Ch'oe Si-hyong (1824–64). In content it consisted of an amalgam of Chinese, Buddhist, and native Korean religious ideas and practices. As so often before in East Asian history, the religious organization took on a political dimension, serving as a vehicle for expressions of discontent with a regime in decay, and for agitation against government corruption and foreign encroachments. Finally outlawed, it was involved in considerable rioting in 1893, which turned to rebellion the following year when Korea was struck by famine. When the Korean government requested Chinese assistance, Li Hung-chang responded by sending 1500 men and informing the Japanese, whose troops were already on the way. The rebellion was quickly suppressed, but it proved easier to send than to remove the troops.

When Japanese soldiers entered Seoul, broke into the palace, and kidnapped the king and queen, Li responded by sending more troops and war was inevitable. It was a war which everyone, except the Japanese, expected China to win, but all parties were stunned when Japan defeated China on sea and on land. Begun in July 1894, the war was all over by March of 1895. In retrospect the reasons for the outcome are easy to see: Japan was better equipped, better led, and more united than China, a country which was hampered by internal division, corruption, and inadequate leadership in the field. Powerful governors-general considered it Li Hung-chang's war and were slow in participating; the southern navy remained aloof.

The Treaty of Shimonoseki (April 1895)

The war was terminated by the Treaty of Shimonoseki. China relinquished all claims to a special role in Korea and recognized that country as an independent state (although its troubles were far from over). In addition, China paid Japan an indemnity and ceded it Taiwan and the Pescadores, thus starting the formation of the Japanese empire. A further indication that the Japanese had now joined the ranks of the imperialist nations was the extension to Japan of most-favored-nation status, along with the opening of seven additional Chinese ports. Japan was also to receive the Liaotung Peninsula but, after diplomatic intervention by Russia, Germany, and France, had to settle for an additional indemnity instead. The effects of the treaty on Korea, on domestic Chinese and Japanese politics, and on international relations in the area are discussed in the following chapters. Here it should be noted that the treaty marked an unprecedented shift in the East Asian balance of power, a shift from China to Japan that was to continue until Japan's defeat in the Second World War.

China in Perspective

Japan's victory over China toward the end of the nineteenth century has helped to produce a stark and misleading image of contrasting Japanese success and Chinese failure. History is more complicated than that. For Japan the acquisition of empire brought at least as many problems as it did solutions: the history of Japan in modern times has hardly been smooth and easy. Furthermore, compared to any non-Western political entity other than Japan, nineteenth-century China comes off rather well, both in terms of the preservation of sovereignty and in fashioning a response to the onslaught from abroad. Since this book focuses on China and Japan, it naturally tends to view one in terms of the other and emphasize the contrasts between them, but it is necessary to bear in mind the limits of this perspective even while making the most of its advantages. A study devoted, for example, to China and India during the same period might show modern Chinese history in quite a different and more positive light.

NOTES

1. Albert Feuerwerker, *China's Early Industrialization: Sheng Hsuan-huai (1844–1916) and Mandarin Enterprise* (Cambridge: Harvard University Press, 1958).

2. Kwang-Ching Liu, in Ping-ti Ho and Tang Tsou, *China in Crisis* (Chicago: University of Chicago Press, 1968), 1: 117.

3. Harold Isaacs, *Images of Asia: American Views of China and India* (New York: Capricorn, 1962), p. 136, quoting S. Wells Williams, *The Middle Kingdom* (New York: 1883), 1: xiv–xv.

4. Cyril Birch, ed., *Anthology of Chinese Literature* (New York: Grove Press, 1972), 2: 294.

5. James B. Palais, *Politics and Policy in Traditional Korea* (Cambridge: Harvard University Press, 1975), p. 63.

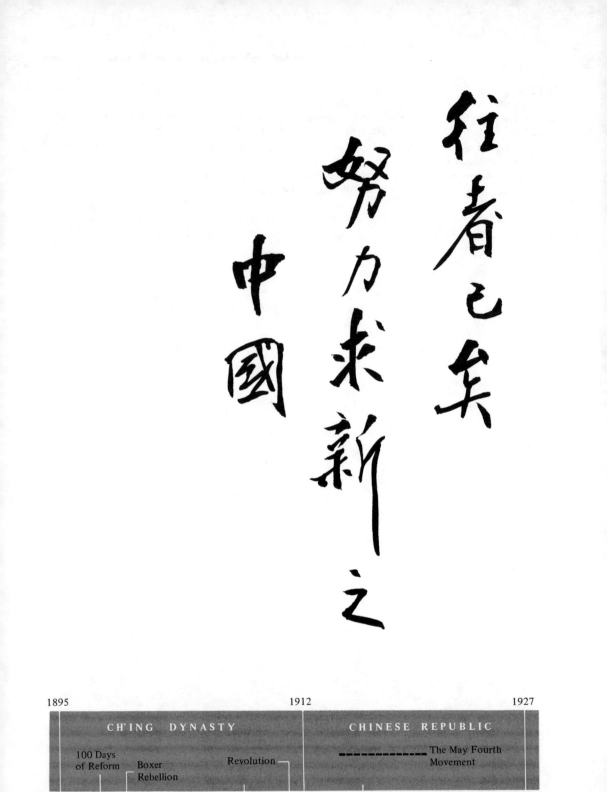

往者已矣
努力求新之
中國

1895   1912   1927

CH'ING DYNASTY   **CHINESE REPUBLIC**

100 Days of Reform   Revolution   — — — — — — The May Fourth Movement

Boxer Rebellion

1898   1900   Death of Tz'u Hsi → 1908   1911   1916 ← Death of Yuan Shih-k'ai

20 End of the Old Order and Struggle for the New: China, 1895–1927

China's defeat by Japan ushered in a period of profound change, accelerating at a pace that often bewildered the participants. As a result, the radical of one decade frequently found himself left behind by events in the next. Politically, intellectually, and in many other respects, the forces of reform, reaction, and revolution competed, interacted, and interlocked in complex patterns. The disintegration of the old was more apparent than the shape of the new. Bisecting the period chronologically and politically was the revolution of 1911, more an end than a beginning.

In foreign affairs the period began with a round of concessions forced on China by the imperialist powers, in a process that reached its greatest intensity during the first six months of 1898. Internally it began with a movement for reform, which also climaxed in 1898 when it culminated in a "hundred days" of intense reform (at least on paper) from June 11 to September 20 of that year. New foreign demands helped to spur the reformers in their efforts, but the defeat of 1895 was the major event that brought them to the fore and gave them an audience.

K'ang Yu-wei and the "Hundred Days of Reform"

In 1895, a small group of reformers began an energetic campaign to urge major changes in China. Working primarily through study groups and journalism, they sought to spread their ideas in an intellectual climate newly receptive to radical ideas. A willingness to reexamine basic assumptions about the very nature of reality distinguished the men who emerged in the nineties from their modernizing predecessors. At the same time, the radicals of this generation, unlike those of the generation to follow, had received a thorough Confucian education and had a command of traditional learning. Steeped in the old culture, they felt the pull of the past even as they charted a bold course for a new future.

A major influence on a whole generation of reformers was Yen Fu, the one-time naval student at Greenwich. Now in his forties, he was emboldened by events to publicize his ideas, which he did first in a series of essays, and then in a number of very influential translations of Western works: Thomas Huxley's *Ethics and Evolution* (1898), Adam Smith's *Wealth of Nations* (1900), John Stuart Mill's *On Liberty* (1903), and others. Yen argued that Western learning was needed to release Chinese energies. He rejected much of the Chinese tradition while praising the West, particularly Social-Darwinism, with its dynamic view of history as evolutionary and progressive, and the high value it placed on struggle.

The leader of the reform movement was K'ang Yu-wei (1858–1927). Unlike Yen Fu, who was no political activist, theorists like K'ang Yu-wei and his younger followers, T'an Ssu-t'ung (1865–98) and Liang Ch'i-ch'ao (1873–1929), tried to implement programs as well as publish critiques. K'ang himself was a thinker who, deeply grounded in Buddhism as well as Confucianism, elaborated a highly original theory to provide a seemingly Confucian basis for ideas which went well beyond the Confucian tradition. Drawing on the Modern Text school of classical interpretation which, founded in the Han, enjoyed something of a revival in the late Ch'ing, K'ang argued that Confucius was not merely a transmitter of ancient teachings but a prophet who, ahead of his time, cast his message in subtle language full of hidden meanings. Confucius, according to K'ang, saw history as a universal progress through three stages, each with its appropriate form of government: the Age of Disorder (rule by an absolute monarch), the Age of Approaching Peace (rule by a constitutional monarch), and the Age of Great Peace (rule by the people). K'ang's Confucius was thus a seer and prophet not only for China but for the entire world. This was K'ang's solution to the problem of how to be modern without rejecting everything that was native and old, when modernization implied wholesale borrowing from abroad, not only of technology but of institutions and ideas. After the failure of his reform attempts, when K'ang was in exile, he elaborated on his vision of utopia. He portrayed a future when the whole world would be united in love and harmony under a single popularly elected government, which would operate hospitals, schools, and nurseries; administering a society in which all divisive institutions would have disappeared, including even the family.

Another radical reinterpretation of tradition came from T'an Ssu-t'ung, a brilliant man destined to become a martyr. T'an did not confine his radical vision to a distant utopia but argued that the monarchy should be replaced by a republic, and attacked the traditional Confucian family distinctions in the name of *jen*, the central Confucian virtue frequently translated "benevolence" or "humanity." Neo-Confucian thinkers had earlier given *jen* a cosmic dimension, but T'an drew on modern scientific concepts to develop his metaphysics of *jen* in which *jen* is identified with ether (*yi-t'ai*, a transliteration of the Western word). K'ang Yu-wei, too, equated *jen* with ether and electricity.

K'ang Yu-wei and his followers sought in their practical program to transform China into a modern and modernizing constitutional monarchy along the lines of Meiji Japan. Thanks to the patronage of a reformist governor, K'ang's disciples were able to carry out some of their program in Hunan, but their greatest moment came in 1898 when K'ang received the support of Emperor Kuang-hsü, who aided the reform movement in an attempt to assert himself and shake off the control of the Empress Dowager. (See Figure 20-1.) For a "hundred days" (actually 103 days), there was a flood of decrees reforming the examination system, remodeling the political apparatus, promoting industry, and otherwise modernizing state and society. It was an ambitious program, but the edicts are more significant as expressions of intent than indicators of accomplishment, for many of them were never implemented. Opposition was strong, not only among high-placed Manchu and Chinese officials but also from the Empress Dowager. She was not necessarily opposed to reform but was alarmed over the reformers' extremism. Furthermore, she was aware of the threat to her own position implied in the reform movement and was unwilling to be shunted into political oblivion. A showdown was inevitable. Realizing this, the emperor and the reformers turned to Yüan Shih-k'ai, formerly Li Hung-chang's representative in Korea, since Yüan was a reform-minded military man then training a modern military force. But at the crucial point, Yüan failed to execute the emperor's orders, which included putting to death Jung-lu, the Manchu general known for his loyalty to the Empress Dowager. Instead, Yüan confided in

Figure 20-1   The Empress Dowager seated on the Imperial Throne.

Jung-lu, and the outcome was a coup that placed the Empress Dowager again in command of the throne. Emperor Kuang-hsü continued as a figurehead.

K'ang Yu-wei and Liang Ch'i-ch'ao managed to flee to Japan, but T'an Ssu-t'ung remained behind to give his life for the cause. Although many of the reform edicts were rescinded, the Empress Dowager did give her approval to moderate reforms, including military modernization and reforms in education and the monetary and fiscal systems. That little was accomplished even then was due to the weakness of the central government and the enormity of the problems facing the dynasty. By no means the least of these was China's perilous international situation.

The Scramble for Concessions

China's display of weakness in the war against Japan brought in its wake an imperialist scramble for special rights and privileges in which Russia, France, Britain, Germany, and Japan pursued their immediate national interests and jockeyed for position in case China collapsed completely. (See map, Figure 20-2.)

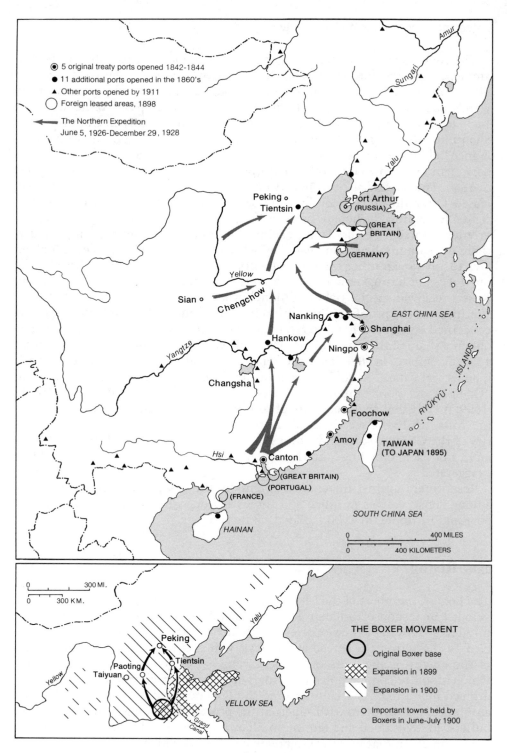

Figure 20-2 **China, 1895–1927**

The concessions extracted from China were economic and political. For example, the powers forced loans on the Ch'ing, which were secured by Chinese tax revenues, such as maritime customs. Long-term leases of Chinese territory were granted to the powers, including the right to develop economic resources such as mines and railroads. Thus Germany leased territory in Kiaochow and Shantung; Russia leased Port Arthur in the southern Liaotung Peninsula; France held leases on land around Kwang-chow Bay; and Britain obtained Weihaiwei and the Kowloon New Territories, adjacent to the Kowloon area ceded in 1860. The powers also frequently obtained the right to police the areas they leased. Often the powers combined leaseholds, railroad rights, and commercial rights, to create a "sphere of interest," that is, an area in which they were the privileged foreign power, as, for example, Germany was in Shantung. Finally, there were "non-alienation" pacts by which China agreed not to cede a given area to any power other than the signatory: the Yangtze Valley to Britain, the provinces bordering French Indo-China to France, Fukien to Japan. In addition, Russia received special rights in Manchuria.

Britain, as the prime trading nation in China, pursued an ambiguous policy, concerned on the one hand to retain access to all of China and on the other to obtain a share of the concessions. The United States at this time was acquiring a Pacific empire. In 1898 it annexed Hawaii and, after war with Spain, the Philippines and Guam. At the urging of Britain, the United States then adopted an "Open Door" policy enunciated in two diplomatic notes. The first of these (1899) merely demanded equality of commercial opportunity for all the powers in China, while the second (1900) also affirmed a desire to preserve the integrity of the Chinese state and Chinese territory. This was a declaration of principle, not backed by force; neither its altruism nor its effectiveness should be exaggerated.

Resentment against the encroachments of the powers was strong, not only among conservatives in office and the exiled opposition, but also among the poor and illiterate. In 1900 it flared up in violence.

The Boxer Rising

The Boxers, members of the *I-ho ch'üan* (Righteous and Harmonious Fists), developed in response to harsh economic conditions and resentment over the privileges enjoyed by missionaries and their converts. Passions were further fueled by alarm over the spread of railways, which cut across the land regardless of the graves of ancestors or the requirements of geomancy, railways along which stood telephone poles carrying wires from which rust-filled rainwater dripped blood red. As a counterforce the Boxers relied on rituals, spells, and amulets to endow them with supernatural powers, including invulnerability to bullets. In 1898 flood and famine in Shantung combined with the advance of the Germans in that province to create conditions which led to the first Boxer rising there in May of that year.

Originally antidynastic, the Boxers changed direction when they received the support of Ch'ing officials prepared to use the movement against the powers. Thus encouraged, the Boxers spread, venting their rage on Chinese and foreign Christians, especially Catholics. On June 13, 1900 they entered Peking. Eight days later the court issued a declaration of war on all the treaty powers. Officially the Boxers were placed under the command of imperial princes, and there followed a dramatic two-month siege of the legation quarter in Peking, where 451 guards defended 473 foreign civilians and some 3000 Chinese Christians who had fled there for protection. The ordeal of the besieged was grim, but they were spared the worst, for the Boxers and the Chinese troops were undisciplined, ill-organized, and uncoordinated. The city was full of looting and violence, but the legation quarter was still intact when an international relief expedition reached Peking on August 15 and forced the court to flee the capital.

During these dangerous and dramatic events, southern governors-general chose to ignore the court's declaration of war, claiming it was made under duress (forced by the Boxers); hence the term "Boxer Rebellion." The powers, nevertheless, demanded from the Ch'ing court a very harsh settlement. It included a huge indemnity (450 million taels, 67.5 million pounds sterling) to be paid from customs and salt revenues. Other provisions required the punishment of pro-Boxer officials and of certain cities, where the civil service examinations were suspended. The powers received the right to station permanent legation guards in the capital and to place troops between Peking and the sea. The Boxer rising also provided Russia with an excuse to occupy Manchuria, where some Russians remained until Russia's defeat by Japan in the war of 1904–05.

The failure of the Boxers meant a further decline in China's international position and struck a blow at the dynasty whose policies had led to ignominious flight. A convincing demonstration of the futility of the old ways, it propelled the Ch'ing government into a serious attempt at reform.

Economic Developments

During the period 1895–1911, the modern sector of the Chinese economy continued to develop at a steady pace, but it was dominated by foreign capital. Not only were extensive railway concessions granted to the treaty powers, but Chinese railroads, like that linking Peking and Hankow, were financed by foreign capital. Foreign capital also controlled much of China's mining and shipping, and it was a major factor in manufacturing, both for the export trade (tea, silk, soybeans, and so forth) and for the domestic market (textiles, tobacco, and so forth). Modern banking was another area of foreign domination, prompting the Ch'ing government in 1898 to approve the creation of the Commercial Bank of China, a modern bank functioning as a "government operated merchant enterprise" (kuan-tu shang-pan). Two more banks were formed in 1905 and 1907.

Except for railways and mines, foreign investments were concentrated in the treaty ports, and it was there also that Chinese factories gradually developed, taking advantage of modern services and the security to be found in foreign concession areas. Chinese enterprises were particularly important in textile manufacturing. Most remained small (by 1912 only 750 employed more than one hundred workers), but they were an important part of China's economic modernization. It was also during this period that Shanghai became China's largest city, a status it retains today.

The development of a modern economic sector in Shanghai and, to a lesser extent, in other treaty ports, was accompanied by changes in social structure. A Chinese business class developed, as did a class of urban laborers who at times expressed their resentment over terrible working conditions by going on strike. In the city, too, the old family system lost its economic underpinnings, and there was an audience receptive to new values and ideas. Some of these were revolutionary, but government leaders too were now convinced of the need for extensive change.

Eleventh-Hour Reform

Even while continuing to denounce K'ang Yu-wei, the Ch'ing regime after 1900 pursued a reform program similar to that of 1898. By making extensive changes, the Empress Dowager hoped to save the dynasty and transform the Ch'ing into a state capable of surviving in the modern world. The reforms were in earnest, and some, like the drive against opium, accomplished much, but frequently the measures taken to save the Ch'ing had a way of working against the dynasty instead.

The educational reforms, which received high priority, are an example. In 1905 the government took the radical step of abolishing the examination system, and by the end of the decade even remote provinces boasted new schools, teaching new subjects and ideas. Chinese students also studied abroad in record numbers, especially in Japan where by 1906 there were at least 8000 of them, many supported by their provincial governments. There, away from their families, they enjoyed a new personal and intellectual liberty. Even those who did not manage to complete their education drank in the heady wine of new ideas. The most influential intellectual of the decade was Liang Ch'i-ch'ao, from whose writings many learned about the major events of world history for the first time, and were introduced to Western social and political thought from Rousseau to the twentieth century. The example of Japan was itself a powerful influence, as were books translated from Japanese. More books were translated into Chinese from Japanese than from any other language, and many Japanese loan words entered the Chinese language, thus reversing the flow which had taken place over a millenium before.

In this way Chinese students learned about Western history and law, science and logic, and above all became convinced of the truths of evolutionism, with its positive evaluation of struggle, and of nationalism, with its shift of loyalty from culture to nation. The Japanese example showed that nationalism was compatible with the preservation of elements of traditional culture, but a commitment to nationalism did imply a willingness to jettison those elements of tradition which failed to contribute to national development. Toward the end of the decade students became increasingly restive and revolutionary. The new education was intended to mold the men who would save the dynasty, but it fashioned those who helped to bury it.

Manchu political reform included restructuring the government along modern lines and the development of a constitution. After a study mission abroad (1905–06) and subsequent deliberations, the government in 1908 announced a nine-year plan of constitutional reform beginning with provincial assemblies in 1909. Although elected on a limited franchise, these assemblies, as well as the central legislative council convened in 1910, became not sources of popular support but centers of opposition.

Nothing was more urgent than the creation of a modern military force, but here too the reform program backfired. The new forces proved unreliable because they were either influenced by new, subversive ideas or were loyal to their commanders rather than the throne. The main beneficiary of military modernization turned out to be Yüan Shih-k'ai, who as governor-general of Chihli from 1901 to 1907 built up an army with which he retained ties even after he was dismissed from the government in 1908.

The government had some foreign policy success, especially in reasserting Chinese sovereignty over Tibet, but failed to emerge as a plausible focus for nationalism. Not only was it handicapped by its non-Han ethnic origins, but during this very difficult and dangerous period of rapid change, there was a deterioration in the quality of dynastic leadership after the Empress Dowager and Emperor Kuang-hsü both died in 1908. The new emperor was an infant, and the regent was inept.

The Revolution of 1911 and Sun Yat-sen

In its program of modernization the dynasty was seriously handicapped by its financial weakness. This became painfully apparent in its handling of the railway issue. In order to regain foreign railway concessions, a railway recovery movement was organized by provincial gentry and merchants who created their own railway companies. The Ch'ing government, however, wanted to centralize power, and in 1911 decided to nationalize the major railway lines. Lacking the necessary financial resources, it was able to do so only by contracting foreign loans, inevitably with strings attached. The loans and the subsequent disbanding of provincial railway companies caused a furor, nowhere more so than in Szechwan, where local gentry who had invested in the provincial railway company felt cheated by the price the government was willing to pay for their shares. Provincial interests resented the threat to provincial autonomy. Nationalists were indignant over the foreign loans that financed the transaction. This was the prelude to revolt. The insurrection which actually set off the revolution took place in Wuchang on October 10 and was conducted by men only very loosely connected with the Revolutionary Alliance, the main revolutionary organization in the land.

The Revolutionary Alliance (T'ung-meng hui, also translated "United League") was formed in Tokyo in 1905 when a number of revolutionary groups joined together under the leadership of Sun Yat-sen (1866–1925). Sun was born into a Kwangtung peasant family, received a Christian education in Hawaii, and studied medicine in Hong Kong. He founded his first revolutionary organization in Hawaii in 1894, and overseas Chinese communities remained an important source of moral and financial support. Over the years he elaborated his "Three Principles of the People"—nationalism, democracy, and the people's livelihood. His political program called for the toppling of the Ch'ing dynasty and the establishment of a republic. Sun was influenced by Henry George's "single tax" theory, which held that unearned increases in land values (as when farm land rises in value because it is sought for commercial development) should go to the community rather than to the individual landholder. Sun, however, did not work out a full-fledged economic program. This may have been just as well, since the Three Principles were broad enough to attract the varied and loosely organized membership of the Revolutionary Alliance; details might only have raised questions and disagreements.

Yüan Shih-k'ai and the Warlord Era

After the October 10 incident, province after province broke with the dynasty, which turned for help to Yüan Shih-k'ai. Yüan's former army commanders stood to gain by supporting him and did so, but neither Yüan nor the revolutionaries were strong enough to impose their will on all of China. At the same time, all the contenders for power were anxious to achieve sufficient political stability to prevent foreign intervention and were thus ready for a compromise. The result was that the Manchu child-emperor formally abdicated on February 12, 1912, and after Sun stepped aside, Yüan accepted the presidency of a republic with a two-chambered legislature. Yüan agreed to move the capital to Nanking, but once in office he evaded this provision.

In the absence of well-organized political parties or deep-rooted republican sentiments among the public, there was little to restrain Yüan, who rapidly developed into a dictator. Elections were duly held in February 1913, but Yüan bullied the parliament. The leader of its largest party, the Nationalist party (KMT, Kuomintang), was assassinated in March 1913. That summer Yüan forced a showdown by ordering the dismissal of pro-Nationalist southern military governors. When they revolted in what is sometimes known as the Second Revolution, Yüan crushed them easily. For the next two years, China's military governors remained loyal.

During the First World War, Japan presented Yüan Shih-k'ai with the notorious twenty-one demands, divided into five groups: (1) recognition of Japanese rights in Shantung; (2) extension of Japanese rights in Mongolia and Manchuria; (3) Sino-Japanese joint operation of China's largest iron and steel company; (4) China not to cede or lease any coastal area to any power other than Japan; and (5) provisions which would have obliged the Chinese government to employ Japanese political, financial, and military advisers, given the Japanese partial control over the police, and obliged China to purchase Japanese arms. Yüan managed to avoid the last and most onorous group of demands, which would have reduced China to a virtual Japanese satellite. However, with the other powers preoccupied in Europe, Yüan was forced to accept Japan's seizure of Germany's holdings in Shantung, grant Japan new rights in Southern Manchuria and Inner Mongolia, and acknowledge her special interest in China's largest iron and steel works, which had previously served as security for Japanese loans. The domestic result was a wave of anti-Japanese nationalist outrage, which expressed itself in protests and boycotts. Yüan himself made no attempt to mobilize nationalist feelings for his own cause but occupied himself in preparing the way for a restoration of dynastic rule, with himself as emperor. The new regime was proclaimed in December 1915 to begin on New Year's Day. It could be argued, and was by an American advisor to Yüan, that China was not ready for a republic, but the new dynasty encountered overwhelming hostility. In March 1916 Yüan gave way and officially abandoned his imperial ambitions. But he never regained his old prestige, and died a failure in June of that year.

The collapse of Yüan Shih-k'ai's plans demonstrated that it was impossible to return to the old order and revealed just how far the central government had disintegrated since it first lost the initiative to the provinces during the Taiping Rebellion. Now all that remained in the way of a national government was an empty shell, which served to provide a facade of legitimacy under presidents who were puppets of the warlord forces that controlled the capital region.

After the fall of Yüan Shih-k'ai, the pattern of Chinese politics became exceedingly complex. Although a national government ruled in Peking, actual power lay in the hands of regional strongmen (warlords) who dominated the areas under their control largely through force of arms, and who struggled with each other to enlarge or protect their holdings. They constantly entered into and betrayed alliances with each other, and the foreign powers (especially Japan and the Soviet Union), fishing in these troubled waters, sought to play the warlords off against each other, and against the central government, for their own benefit.

Some of the warlords had been generals under Yüan Shih-k'ai; others had begun their careers as bandits. In ideology they varied widely, ranging from advocates of Confucianism to one prominent general who adopted Christianity. In personality they ran the gamut from ruthless butchers to benevolent commanders, selfish despots to rulers interested in social welfare and education;

but those who oppressed and squeezed the people were the more numerous. Conditions varied in different regions, but "the terror, oppression, tax demands, bloodshed, intrigue, and pillaging of the warlord era made those dozen years a nightmare."[1] It was a period of bitter suffering, when the disintegration of the old values and institutions was more apparent than the growth of the new. It was also a period of great intellectual ferment and artistic creativity.

Intellectual Ferment

Revolutionary ideas were current among Chinese students in Tokyo during the first decade of the century and were welcomed by the magazines and schools of China proper. Pedants were mocked and corruption was castigated. There were demands for improved social conditions, the education of women, and an end to footbinding. The defeat of 1895 elicited demands for more effective resistance to imperialism, but more than that, it gave rise to a wave of social commentary: critiques of the old and advocacy of the new. This tendency increased after 1900, and again after the government abolished the examination system. Abolition of the examination system was particularly significant because, without weakening the traditional respect accorded scholars and intellectuals, it removed the institutional prop for Confucianism and opened the way for new patterns of thought and new approaches to social and political problems. Moreover, by lifting the requirement of a Confucian education, it further encouraged the modernization of education for prospective scholars and office holders.

It was a sign of the times that the conservative Lin Shu (1852–1924), the most famous and prolific translator of Western fiction into classical Chinese, now translated *Uncle Tom's Cabin*. Furthermore, new ideas also led to new actions. A modern-style student protest took place as early as 1903 when the Russians delayed a promised evacuation of troops from Manchuria. The first antiimperialist boycott came in 1905 in protest against United States legislation excluding Chinese laborers from entering that country.

It did not take the fall of the Ch'ing to produce iconoclasm and protest, but these tendencies became deeper and more widespread after the dynasty collapsed. An important landmark was the founding of *New Youth* (1915) by Ch'en Tu-hsiu (1879–1942), just returned from Japan. In the first issue of this influential journal, Ch'en issued an eloquent call for the rejuvenation of China accompanied by an equally strong denunciation of the old tradition. A prime target for the new intellectuals was Confucianism, still advocated by, among others, K'ang Yu-wei, who tried to cast it in a new role as an official religion for the Chinese state. It was K'ang's great misfortune that in the late Ch'ing he could not construct a Confucian justification for modernization which was persuasive to scholars grounded in the classics, and that afterward he was equally unsuccessful in devising a modern justification for Confucianism acceptable to those whose primary loyalty was to the nation. Confucianism was not destroyed, but it was put very much on the defensive.

New Youth not only opposed the traditional teachings, it also opposed the language in which they were written. The journal opened its pages to Hu Shih (1891–1962), a former student of the American philosopher John Dewey, and China's leading champion of the vernacular language (*pai-hua*). Hu Shih argued that people should write the spoken language not the language of the classics, and that the vernacular should be taught in the schools. He praised the literary merits of the old novels written in the vernacular, which had long been widely read but never before enjoyed respectability. The campaign for the vernacular was a success. The transition did not come all at once: classical expressions had a way of creeping into the vernacular, and newly borrowed terms stood in the way of easy comprehension. Nevertheless, the new language was both more accessible and more modern than the old. Introduced into the elementary schools in 1920, it was universally used in the schools by the end of the decade.

New Youth was also the first magazine to publish Lu Hsün (Chou Shu-jen, 1881–1936) who became China's most acclaimed writer of the twentieth century. Lu Hsün had gone to Japan to study medicine but decided to devote himself to combating not physical ailments but China's spiritual ills. His bitter satire cut like a sharp scalpel, but a scalpel wielded by a humanist who hoped to cure, not kill. His protagonist in "A Madman's Diary" (*New Youth*, 1918) discovers the reality underneath the gloss of "virtue and morality" in the old histories: a history of man eating man. He ends with the plea, "Perhaps there are still children who have not eaten men? Save the children . . ."[2]

Many of the leaders of the new thought were on the faculty of Peking University, now directed by a tolerant European-educated intellectual, and their ideas found a ready following among the students at this and other Chinese universities. On May 4, 1919, some 3000 of these students staged a dramatic demonstration to protest further interference in Chinese affairs by the imperialist powers. China had entered the World War on the allied side, and sent labor battalions to France, in order to gain a voice in the peace settlement. But when the powers met at Versailles, they ignored China, and assigned Germany's former possessions in Shantung to Japan. The students were outraged. The demonstration became violent. There were arrests. These were followed by more protest: a wave of strikes and a show of merchant and labor support for the students. This was particularly significant because the growth of the modern-minded merchant and labor classes in China's large cities had been stimulated by the wartime withdrawal of European firms from East Asia. Imports fell, exports grew, and Chinese commercial and industrial concerns made the most of their opportunities.

In the end the government had to retreat. Those who had been arrested were released, and those who had ordered the arrests were forced to resign. China never signed the ill-fated Treaty of Versailles.

The May Fourth incident came to symbolize the currents of intellectual and cultural change first articulated in *New Youth* and gave rise to the term "May Fourth movement," usually used to designate the whole period from 1915 to the early 1920s. The incident gave intellectuals a heightened sense of urgency and turned what had been a trickle of protest into a tide. A flood of publications followed, introducing new and radical ideas. There was action as well as talk. In private life young men and women rejected arranged marriages and began to question the whole family system. There was also increased social action, particularly in the area of organizing labor unions.

The May Fourth movement had long-term revolutionary consequences. In the short term, however, the eddies of Chinese intellectual and cultural life were as confused as ever. There were intense disagreements concerning the future direction of Chinese culture and, in the absence of an official orthodoxy, a tremendous variety of competing ideas, theories, and styles.

Intellectual Alternatives

In the wake of the May Fourth movement there was vigorous disagreement about basic values and directions. Among those who turned back to the Chinese tradition after witnessing the spectacle of Europe's self-destruction in the First World War was the former champion of the West, Liang Ch'i-ch'ao. Liang now hoped to combine the best of both worlds and achieve a synthesis in which the Chinese elements would predominate (just as Sung Neo-Confucianism had synthesized Buddhism into an essentially Confucian framework), but in the twentieth century this turned out to be an extraordinarily difficult task.

An important debate began in 1923 between the proponents of science and metaphysics, a debate which also involved differences over the interpretation and evaluation of Chinese and Western cultures. Among the advocates of the former were the proponents of scientism, that is, the belief that science holds the answers for all intellectual problems (including problems of value) and that the scientific method is the only method for arriving at truth. These tenets were challenged by those who argued that science is applicable only to a limited field of study, such as the study of nature, and that moral values have to be based on deeper metaphysical truths that by their very nature are beyond the reach of scientific methodology. Since similar problems agitated the West at this time, Chinese thinkers drew not only on the ideas of such classic European philosophers as Immanuel Kant but also on the thought of contemporaries as varied as John Dewey and Henri Bergson, the French exponent of vitalism. Those who identified with the Chinese tradition further drew on the insights of Neo-Confucianism and Buddhism, particularly the former.

Noteworthy among the defenders of tradition were Liang Shu-ming (Liang Sou-ming, 1893–), also well known for his work in rural reconstruction, and Chang Chün-mai (Carson Chang, 1887–1969) later the leader of a small political party opposed to both the Chinese Communist party (CCP) and the KMT. The most influential traditionalist philosophers whose most important works were written in the 1930s were Fung Yu-lan (1895–), a proponent of Chu Hsi's Neo-Confucianism, and Hsiung Shih-li (1885–1969), who developed the opposite, mind-centered stream of Neo-Confucian philosophy drawing on the thought of Wang Yang-ming.

Among the champions of science and Western values were the scientist Ting Wen-chiang (T.V. Ting, 1887–1936) and Hu Shih, the father of the vernacular language movement. Hu Shih was a leading liberal who advocated a gradualist, piecemeal problem-solving approach to China's ills in the face of attacks not only from the traditionalists on the right but also from the left. His message increasingly fell on deaf ears, for his approach required time, and time was precisely what China lacked. More often than not, this included time to digest the heady dose of new intellectual imports. Similarly, liberal individualism was another luxury which many felt a nation and a civilization in crisis could ill afford.

Cultural Alternatives

It is a truism as applicable to modern China as elsewhere that painting reflects the times, yet the most beloved twentieth-century painter was singularly unaffected by either the impact of the West or the heady excitement of the May Fourth movement. This was Ch'i Pai-shih (1863–1957), already in his fifties at the time of the May Fourth incident. Ch'i began as a humble carpenter and did not turn to painting until his mid-twenties, but his industry and longevity more than made up for his late start. It is estimated that he produced more than 10,000 paintings. Ch'i was a great admirer of the seventeenth-century individualist Chu Ta but essentially followed his own inner vision. He was not given to theorizing but did express his attitude toward representation: "The excellence of a painting lies in its being like, yet unlike. Too much likeness flatters the vulgar taste; too much unlikeness deceives the world."[3] Although his work includes landscapes and portraits, he is at his best in depicting the humble forms of life, including rodents and insects, with a loving and gentle humor reminiscent of the haiku of Kobayashi Issa. (See Figure 20-3.) His pictures are statements of his own benevolent vision. They show, to quote a Chinese critic, "a loving sympathy for the little insects and crabs and flowers he draws," and have "an enlivening gaiety of manner and spirit," so that, "his pictures are really all pictures of his own gentle humanism."[4]

There were other painters and calligraphers in the twenties and thirties who remained uninfluenced by the West, but many felt that the new age required a new style. Among those who tried to combine elements of the Chinese and Western traditions were the followers of a school of painters established in Canton by Kao Lun (Kao Chien-fu, 1879–1951). Kao sought to combine Western shading and perspective with Chinese brushwork and was also influenced by

Figure 20-3 Ch'i Pai-shih,
The Night Marauders.
Hanging scroll, Chinese ink
on paper.

Japanese decorativeness. He also sought to bring Chinese painting up to date by including in his works new subject matter, such as the airplanes in Figure 20-4.

In Shanghai, meanwhile, a small group of artists tried to transplant French-style bohemianism into that international city. Hsü Pei-hung (Péon Ju) (1895–1953), for example, affected the long hair and general appearance popular in the artists' quarter of Paris when he returned from that city in 1927. Hsü also brought back a thorough mastery of the French academic style. The subject of the painting shown in Figure 20-5 comes from the Warring States period, but in style it is a typical product of a European art school of the time, although it is

Figure 20-4   Kao Lun (Kao Chien-fu),
Landscape with Airplanes.
Hanging scroll. Art Gallery, Chinese
University of Hong Kong.

Figure 20-5   Hsü Pei-hung, *T'ien-heng Wu-pai Shih*. Oil.

executed with great technical skill. Somewhat more contemporary in his Western tastes was Liu Hai-su (1895–), founder of the Shanghai Art School (1920), where he introduced the use of a nude model for the first time in China. This was also one of the first schools to offer a full course of instruction in Western music. Liu drew his inspiration from French postimpressionists like Matisse and Cézanne. Later, however, Liu returned to painting in a traditional manner, and Hsü too abandoned his Western dress for a Chinese gown. Today Hsü is perhaps most appreciated for his later paintings of horses, which are modern, yet essentially Chinese.

The literature of the period is an excellent source for the student of social and psychological history, but more than that it mirrored the temper of the age. As Leo Ou-fan Lee has noted, "the May Fourth Movement had unleashed not only a literary and an intellectual revolution: it also propelled an emotional one."[5] While there were also experiments with form such as Hsü Chih-mo's (1896–1931) effort to recast Chinese verse in an English mold, complete with rhyme, the dominant quality of the period was an unabashedly romantic outpouring of feelings released by the removal of Confucian restraints and encouraged by the example of European romanticism.

One strain, as analyzed by Lee, was the passive-sentimental, presided over by the hero of Goethe's *The Sorrows of Young Werther* read in China (as in Japan) as "a sentimental sob story." The subjectivism of these writers was not unlike that of the writers of "I" novels in Japan. Another strain was dynamic and heroic. Its ideal was Prometheus, who braved Zeus's wrath and stole fire for mankind. Holding a promise of release from alienation, it was compatible with a revolutionary political stance. For Kuo Mo-jo (1892–), once an admirer of Goethe, Lenin became beyond all else a Promethean hero. Perhaps the strongest expression of Promethean martyrdom came from Lu Hsün, "I have stolen fire from other countries, intending to cook my own flesh. I think that if the taste is good, the other chewers on their part may get something out of it, and I shall not sacrifice my body in vain."[6]

Controversies and rivalries stimulated the formation of literary and intellectual societies as like-minded men joined together to publish journals for their causes and denounce those of the opposition. Revolutionaries were not alone in arguing that literature should have a social purpose, but as the years passed without any improvement in Chinese conditions, the attractions of revolutionary creeds increased. Writers of revolutionary persuasion such as Mao Tun (Shen Yen-ping, 1896–) employed their talents in depicting and analyzing the defects in the old society and portraying the idealism of those out to change things. Such themes appeared not only in the work of Communist writers like Mao Tun but are found also in the work of the anarchist Pa Chin (Li Fei-kang, 1904–), best known for his depiction of the disintegration of a large, eminent family in the novel appropriately entitled *Family* (1931), a part of his *Turbulent Stream* trilogy (1931–40). Such works provide important material for the student of social as well as literary history.

Marxism in China: The Early Years

Marxism was not unknown in China, but it held little appeal prior to the Russian Revolution. The most radical Chinese, like their Japanese counterparts, were most impressed by the teachings of anarchism, which opposed the state as an authoritarian institution and sought to rely on man's natural social tendencies to create a just society. Those few who were drawn to socialism were attracted more by its egalitarianism than by concepts of class warfare. The writings of Marx and Engels offered the vision of a perfect society, but their thesis that socialism could only be achieved after capitalism had run its course suggested that Marxism was inappropriate for a society only just entering "the capitalist stage of development."

The success of the Russian Revolution (1917) altered the picture considerably. Faced with a similar problem in applying Marxism to Russia, Lenin amended Marxist theory to fit the needs of his own country, and thereby also made it more relevant to the Chinese. His theory that imperialism was the last stage of capitalism gave new historical importance to countries such as China, which were the objects of imperialist expansion. It also suggested that the imperialist nations were themselves on the verge of the transition to socialist states. Most significant for the Chinese situation, perhaps, was Lenin's concept of the Communist party as the vanguard of revolution, which showed a way in which party intellectuals could help make history even in a precapitalist state, and thus justified their efforts.

Furthermore, Marxism was modern and claimed "scientific" validity for its doctrines. It shared the prestige accorded by Chinese intellectuals to what was Western and "advanced," even as it opposed the dominant forms of social, economic, and political organization in the West. A Western heresy which could be used against the West, it promised to undo China's humiliation and to place China once again in the forefront of world history. Most important of all, it worked. The Russian Revolution demonstrated its effectiveness. To many, and not only in China, it seemed the wave of the future.

The appeal of Marxism in China was varied. Li Ta-chao (1888–1927), professor and librarian at Peking University and an ardent revolutionary, was attracted to it initially as a vehicle for national revolution. Ch'en Tu-hsiu (1879–1942), the editor of *New Youth* and, for a time, a champion of science and democracy, was attracted to Marxism as a more effective means of achieving modernization. Others were drawn to it for still other reasons. Whatever their reasons, a core of Marxist intellectuals was available as potential leaders by the time the Comintern* agent Grigorii Voitinsky arrived in China, in the spring of 1920, to prepare for the organization of the Chinese Communist party (CCP). Organization of the CCP took place in the following year.

---

* The Third International (*Com*munist *Intern*ational) founded in Moscow in 1919 to coordinate Communist movements around the world.

At its first gathering in July 1921, the CCP elected Ch'en Tu-hsiu its Secretary General. Despite very considerable misgivings, the leadership of the fledgling party submitted to a Comintern policy of maximum cooperation with the Kuomintang, with which a formal agreement was reached in 1923. Under this arrangement, at the insistence of Sun Yat-sen, the two parties were not allied as equals with the CCP as a "block without," but CCP members were admitted into the KMT as individuals, forming a "block within," and subjecting themselves to KMT party discipline. The CCP leadership was suspicious of the KMT and found it difficult to accept the Comintern's theoretical analysis of the KMT as a multiclass party. But it submitted to Comintern discipline and the logic of the situation in China, where the few hundred Communists were outnumbered by the thousands of KMT members and had little contact with the masses they sought to lead. This initial period of CCP-KMT cooperation lasted until 1927. Although the CCP greatly expanded during these years, the KMT remained definitely the senior partner.

The Nationalists (KMT) and Sun Yat-sen (1913–1923)

After the failure of the "second revolution" of 1913, Sun Yat-sen was once again forced into exile in Japan, where he tried to win Japanese support for his revolution. After the death of Yüan Shih-k'ai, he was able to return to China and establish a revolutionary base in Canton, where he retained a precarious foothold dependent on the good will of the local warlord.

Denied foreign backing despite his efforts to obtain support in Japan and elsewhere, Sun was also handicapped by the weakness of the KMT party organization, which was held together only loosely, and largely through loyalty to Sun himself. Meanwhile, the success of the Russian Revolution provided a striking contrast to the failure of the revolution Sun tried to lead in China. Further, Sun was favorably disposed to the U.S.S.R. by the Soviet Union's initial renunciation of Czarist rights in China. This corresponded to a new antiimperialist emphasis in his own thought and rhetoric. The end of Manchu rule had not led to marked improvement in China's lot vis-à-vis the foreign powers, and a stronger antiimperialist line seemed called for.

Sun was therefore ready to work with the Communists, and in 1923 he concluded an agreement with the Comintern agent Adolf Joffe, who concurred with Sun's view that China was not ready for socialism and that the immediate task ahead was the achievement of national unity and independence. Through this pact with Joffe, Sun received valuable assistance and aid. Under the guidance of the Comintern agent Mikhail Borodin (Grusenberg), the KMT was reorganized into a more structured and disciplined organization than ever before, while General Galen (Blücher) performed the same service for the KMT army. Sun Yat-sen made some minor ideological compromises but did not basically depart from his previous views. Of his Three Principles of the People, that of nationalism was now redirected so as to be antiimperialist rather than anti-Manchu. The principle of the people's livelihood now gave greater emphasis to farmers.

KMT and CCP Cooperation (1923–1927)

For both sides, the agreement of 1923 was a marriage of convenience, and at first it worked to the advantage of both parties. The KMT gained guidance and support while CCP members rose to important positions in the KMT organization, and the party reached out to organize urban workers and made a beginning in rural organization. A good example of a CCP leader occupying an important KMT office is provided by Chou En-lai (1898–1976), who became head of the political department of the Whampoa Military Academy, headed by Chiang Kai-shek (1887–1975). At Whampoa the cream of the KMT officer corps was trained and prepared to lead an army to reunify China and establish a national regime.

In accord with Marxist principles, the CCP devoted its main efforts to organizing the urban labor movement, which had already won its first victory in the Hong Kong Seamen's Strike of 1922. Shanghai and Canton were particularly fertile grounds for the labor organizer, since in these cities the textile and other light industries continued their pre–First World War growth, assisted in part by the wartime lull in foreign competition. Of some 2.7 million cotton spindles in China around 1920, 1.3 million were in Chinese controlled factories, and 500 thousand were owned by Japanese. In Chinese and foreign plants alike, working conditions remained very harsh.

Under these circumstances, the CCP's work met with substantial success. It gained greatly by its leadership during and following the incident of May 30, 1925, when Chinese demonstrators were fired on by the police of the International Settlement in Shanghai, killing ten and wounding more than fifty. A general strike and boycott followed; in Hong Kong and Canton the labor movement held out for sixteen months. The strike did not achieve its goals, but CCP party membership increased from around 1000 in early 1925 to an estimated 20,000 by the summer of 1926.

Sun Yat-sen did not live to witness the May 30 incident, for he died of liver cancer in March 1925. In death he was glorified even more than he had been while alive, but his image as the father of the revolution did not suffice, in the absence of a clearly designated heir apparent, to keep the only-recently reorganized KMT united. Furthermore, his ideological legacy was open to a variety of interpretations. His last major statement of the Three Principles of the People, issued in 1924, stressed the first principle, nationalism, which included opposition to foreign imperialism and also provided for self-determination for China's minorities.

The second principle, democracy, contained proposals for popular elections, initiative, recall, and referendum, but full democracy was to come about only after a preparatory period of political tutelage. In terms of political structure, Sun envisioned a republic with five branches of government: the standard Western trilogy (legislative, executive, judicial), plus two contributions from traditional Chinese government: an examination branch to test applicants for government posts, and a censorial branch to monitor the performance of government officials and to control corruption.

Finally, the principle of the people's livelihood aimed at both economic egalitarianism and economic development. It incorporated a Henry Georgian plan to tax the unearned increment on land values in order to equalize land holdings. An additional refinement was a land tax based on each landholder's assessment of the value of his land. To prevent underassessment, the state was to have the right to purchase the land at the declared value. Sun also had a grandiose vision of Chinese industrialization, but this was unrealistic since it called for enormous investments from a Europe which could ill afford them. More realistic was a proposal for state ownership of major industries. He remained critical of Marxist ideas of class struggle, preferring an emphasis on the unification of the Chinese people.

Prominent among the leaders competing for KMT leadership after Sun Yat-sen's death was Wang Ching-wei (1883–1944), who had been associated with Sun in Japan and gained a reputation for revolutionary heroism when he attempted to assassinate the Manchu Prince Regent in 1910. Wang, however, could not dominate the party and had to work with various factions and other leaders. In 1926 it became apparent that the most formidable challenger for the leadership was Chiang Kai-shek. After the pact with Joffe in 1923, Sun had sent Chiang to Moscow to study the Soviet military. On his return to China, Chiang was appointed to head the newly formed Whampoa Military Academy, where he was highly successful, esteemed alike by the Soviet advisors and by the officer candidates, whom he exhorted to do their utmost for the KMT and the Three Principles of the People.

While Wang Ching-wei loosely presided over the KMT, the CCP steadily gained influence in the party, much to the alarm of the KMT right and of Chiang Kai-shek. In March, 1926, Chiang decided to act: he declared martial law, arrested Soviet advisors, and took steps to restrain the CCP influence in the KMT, while managing to retain the cooperation of both the CCP and of its Soviet supporters, since he required their assistance for the military unification of the country. This he began in the summer of 1926, when he embarked on the Northern Expedition (see map, Figure 20-2), setting out with his army from Canton. Although there was some heavy fighting against warlord armies, the force made rapid headway on its march to the Yangtze, and some warlords decided to bring their forces over to the Nationalist side. In the fall of 1926, the Nationalist victories enabled them to shift the capital from Canton to more centrally located Wuhan.* There Wang Ching-wei headed a civilian KMT government but lacked the power to control Chiang and his army.

* Wuhan refers to the three cities (Wuchang, Hanyang, and Hankow) where the Han River flows into the Yangtze.

The Break Between the KMT and the CCP

On its march north to the Yangtze, the KMT army was assisted by popular support for the revolutionary cause, and nowhere was this support more enthusiastic than among the Communist-led workers of Shanghai, where the General Labor Union seized control of the city even before the arrival of the Nationalist troops. Elsewhere too there was an increase in labor activity. This alarmed Chinese bankers and industrialists who, ready to support a national but not a social revolution, financed the increasingly anti-Communist Chiang Kai-shek. In April, 1927, Chiang finally broke with the CCP completely by initiating a bloody campaign of suppression in Shanghai, which then spread to other cities. Union and party headquarters were raided; those who resisted were killed; suspected Communists were shot on sight. CCP cells were destroyed and unions disbanded in a devastating sweep that left the urban CCP shattered.

The CCP's work in organizing city factory workers was entirely consistent with Marxist theory, but the majority of the Chinese people continued to be peasants. Marx, as a student of the French Revolution, despised the peasantry. He referred to them as "the class which represents barbarism within civilization."[7] But Lenin, operating in a primarily agrarian land, assigned the peasantry a supporting role in the Russian Revolution. The CCP, although it concentrated on the cities, had not neglected the peasants. In 1921, China's first modern peasant movement was organized by P'eng Pai (1896–1929), and by 1927 the CCP was at work in a number of provinces, most notably Hunan, where the young Mao Tse-tung (1893–1976) wrote a famous report urging the party to concentrate on rural revolution and predicting, "In a very short time . . . several hundred million peasants will rise like a mighty storm, like a hurricane, a force so swift and violent that no power, however great, will be able to hold it back."[8] In another famous passage in the same report, he defended the need for peasant violence:

> A revolution is not a dinner party, or writing an essay, or painting a picture, or doing embroidery; it cannot be so refined, so leisurely and gentle, so temperate, kind, courteous, restrained, and magnanimous. A revolution is an insurrection, an act of violence by which one class overthrows another.[9]

In Hunan, as in other parts of China's rice producing region, tenancy rates were high, and the poorer peasants were sorely burdened by heavy rental payments and crushing debts. Tenants had few rights, and they faced the recurring specter of losing their leases. Furthermore, the demise of the old order helped to undermine the social functions and destroy the ideological moorings of the old rural gentry, now increasingly transformed from local elites into simple landlords. It was, as Mao saw, a volatile situation, fraught with revolutionary potential. But the Chinese party and its Soviet advisers remained urban minded.

After Chiang's April coup, the CCP broke with him but continued to work with the government at Wuhan, which also broke with Chiang. But here again the needs of the social revolution clashed with those of the national revolution, since the Wuhan regime depended for military support on armies officered largely by men of the landlord class, which was the prime object of peasant wrath. In this situation Comintern directives were wavering and contradictory, reflecting not Chinese realities but rather the exigencies of Stalin's intraparty maneuvers back in Moscow. The end result was that in June the CCP was expelled from Wuhan. Borodin and other Soviet advisers had to return to the U.S.S.R. For the CCP there began a difficult period of regrouping and reorganization.

Establishment of the Nationalist Government

After Chiang Kai-shek's coup in Shanghai, he established a government in Nanking, which remained the capital after the completion of the Northern Expedition. The expedition was resumed in 1928, by which time the Wuhan leaders had bowed to the inevitable and made their peace with Chiang, as had a number of warlords whose forces now assisted the Nationalist army in its drive north and actually outnumbered the KMT's own troops. In June 1928, after a scant two months of fighting, Peking fell. China again had a national government, but the often nominal incorporation of warlord armies into the government forces meant that national unification was far from complete. Warlordism remained an essential feature of Chinese politics until the very end of the republican period in 1949.

During 1927 antiimperialist mobs attacked British concessions in two cities, and violence in Nanking in March left six foreigners dead, a number wounded, and foreign businesses and homes raided. Such incidents were officially attributed to Chiang Kai-shek's leftist rivals, and the foreign powers concluded that he was the most acceptable leader for China, that is, that his government would negotiate rather than expropriate their holdings. Thus Chiang's victory reassured the powers; except for the Japanese, who had plans of their own for Manchuria and Inner Mongolia. Japan had restored its holdings in Shantung to Chinese sovereignty after the American-sponsored Washington Conference of 1921–22 attended by nine powers with an interest in East Asia (Britain, the United States, France, Italy, Japan, China, Belgium, the Netherlands, and Portugal) to settle issues left over from the First World War. But now Japan sent troops to Shantung claiming that they were needed to protect Japanese lives and property, and there was fighting with Chinese soldiers in 1928. Still more ominous was the assassination that same year of the warlord of Manchuria, Chang Tso-lin, by a group of Japanese army officers who hoped this would pave the way for seizure of Manchuria. Acting on their own, without the knowledge or approval of their government, the Japanese officers did not get their way in 1928, but their act did serve as a prelude to the Japanese militarism and expansionism that threatened China during the thirties, even as the Nanking government tried to cope with warlords and revolutionaries at home, in its attempt to achieve a stable government.

NOTES

1. James E. Sheridan, *China in Disintegration: The Republican Era in Chinese History, 1912– 1949* (New York: The Free Press, 1975), p. 90.

2. Lu Hsün, "A Madman's Diary," in *Selected Works of Lu Hsün* (Peking: Foreign Language Press, 1956), pp. 8–21; reprinted in Ranbir Vohra, *The Chinese Revolution: 1900–1950* (Boston: Houghton Mifflin, 1974), pp. 62–71; quote p. 71.

3. See the biographical entry for Ch'i Pai-shih in Howard L. Boorman, ed., *Biographical Dictionary of Republican China* (New York: Columbia University Press, 1967–71) 1: 302–04. Ch'i's statement is quoted on p. 302.

4. Michael Sullivan, *Chinese Art in the Twentieth Century* (Berkeley and Los Angeles: University of California Press, 1959), p. 42.

5. Leo Ou-fan Lee, *The Romantic Generation of Modern Chinese Writers* (Cambridge: Harvard University Press, 1973), p. 265.

6. Quoted in Lee, *The Romantic Generation*, p. 291.

7. Karl Marx, quoted in Lucien Bianco, *Origins of the Chinese Revolution: 1915–1949*, trans. Murial Bell (Stanford: Stanford University Press, 1971), p. 74.

8. Mao Tse-tung, "Report on an Investigation of the Peasant Movement in Hunan," in *Selected Works of Mao Tse-tung* (Peking: Foreign Languages Press, 1967), Vol. 1; reprinted in Vohra, *The Chinese Revolution: 1900–1950*, p. 115.

9. *Ibid.*, p. 117.

日本

成功と限度

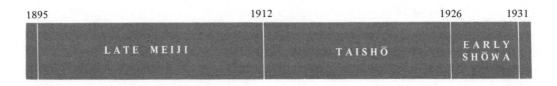

1895   1912   1926   1931

LATE MEIJI   TAISHŌ   EARLY SHŌWA

21 The Limits of Success: Japan, 1895–1931

Japan could take great pride in her victory over China in 1894–95, a tangible measure of the success of Meiji modernization, and the years that followed brought further national achievements. But they did not bring stability in Japan's foreign relations or in her domestic life. The achievement of full status as a world power proved no easy task in a world dominated by Western superpowers: even Japan's triumph over China was laced with bitterness when France, Germany, and Russia interceded to force her to relinquish the

Liaotung Peninsula. Meanwhile, internally, political, economic, and cultural developments created problems as well as opportunities.

For Japan, as for China, the year 1912 provides an appropriate date for historical periodization, although in Japan it marked the demise not of a dynasty but of an individual, the Meiji emperor. However, since this was the emperor who had presided over Japan's transformation since 1867, his passing was felt at the time to signify the end of an era, a judgment in which modern scholars have generally concurred. We will therefore begin this chapter by considering developments from 1895 to 1912.

Late Meiji Foreign Policy and Expansion

From the very beginning, the foreign policy goals of the Meiji leaders had been to achieve national security and equality of national status. But how were security and equality to be defined, and how were they to be attained?

A highly influential view of what constituted Japanese security was that of Yamagata Aritomo, architect of Japan's modern army, and an important political figure in or out of office. Yamagata was not a fanatical imperialist, but he was a hard-headed, realistic nationalist. The army's German advisor argued that Korea was the key to Japan's security, and Yamagata concurred in this analysis. In 1890 Yamagata propounded the thesis that Japan must not only defend its "line of sovereignty" but secure its "line of interest," which ran through Korea.

At the same time the Japanese navy was heavily influenced by the ideas of Admiral Mahan, an American advocate of the importance of sea power. From the navy's point of view, Japanese security demanded Japanese naval domination of the surrounding seas. The acquisition of Taiwan as a result of the Sino-Japanese War gratified the navy as a major step in this direction, but the army was very unhappy at having had to relinquish the strategic Liaotung Peninsula.

Equality was an equally elusive concept, but everyone agreed that at the very least it required the elimination of extraterritoriality and the restoration of tariff autonomy. Already in the 1870s work began on revision of the law codes to bring them into line with Western practices, so that the powers would no longer have reason to insist on maintaining jurisdiction over their own subjects. Even before the lengthy process of revising the codes had been completed, there was strong and vociferous public demand for an end to extraterritoriality. One result was that in 1886 the government was forced to back down from a compromise it had negotiated providing for mixed courts under Japanese and foreign judges. Appreciation of the intensity of public pressure was one of the factors that induced the British, in 1894 shortly before the start of the Sino-Japanese War, to relinquish extraterritoriality when the new legal codes came into effect (1889). Other countries followed suit. In return, foreign merchants were no longer limited to the treaty ports. These treaties also secured tariff autonomy, and in 1911 Japan regained full control over her customs duties.

By that time, Japan, under the most-favored-nation clause of the Treaty of Shimonoseki, was enjoying extraterritorial rights in China and benefiting from China's lack of tariff autonomy. As a result Japan's exports to China increased not only numerically but also in terms of the proportion of her total exports which went to China. This rose from less than 10 percent prior to 1894 to 25 percent by the First World War. A commercial treaty negotiated with China in 1896 gave Japan the right to establish factories in the treaty ports, spurring her investments in China.

During the Late Meiji period imperialism was a cause for national pride in the colonizing countries of the West, and in Japan, too, the acquisition of overseas colonies and interests was hailed as a sign of national fulfillment. Conversely, there was a sense of great public disappointment and outrage when French, German, and Russian intervention forced Japan to give up the Liaotung Peninsula. The government's reaction to this setback was to follow a prudent foreign policy while increasing military spending.

Accordingly, Japan exercised careful restraint during the Boxer Rebellion (1900). However, this stance was not emulated by Japan's chief rival in Northeast Asia, Czarist Russia, which had demonstrated its intent to become a major power in the area by undertaking the construction of the great Trans-Siberian Railway (1891–1903). In 1896 Russia had obtained permission to run tracks across northern Manchuria direct to Vladivostok, and the Boxer Rebellion was used to entrench Russian interests in Manchuria. Russia's lease of Port Arthur on the Liaotung Peninsula gave it a much needed warm water port, but it also grated on the Japanese, who had so recently been denied the peninsula. Nor did Russia refrain from interfering in Korea, where it allied itself to conservative opponents of Japanese-backed reformers. Agreements reached in 1896, 1897, and 1898 kept this rivalry from exploding into war, but the Russian moves in Manchuria furthered Japanese apprehension about Russian ambitions in Northeast Asia.

Japan was not the only nation concerned over Russian expansion in East Asia. Great Britain, which had not joined in the Triple Intervention following the Sino-Japanese War, had long been alarmed over Russian expansion in Central Asia and was also apprehensive over Russia's plans for China. In 1902 Britain cast aside its policy of "splendid isolation" to enter into an alliance with Japan. Great Britain now recognized Japan's special interests in Korea, and each nation recognized the other's interests in China. Furthermore, Great Britain and Japan agreed that each would remain neutral in the event the other fought a war against a single enemy in East Asia and would come to the other's assistance if either were attacked by two powers at once. This meant that in the event of a war between Japan and Russia, Britain would enter on the Japanese side if France or Germany supported Russia. Japan would not have to face a European coalition alone. Aside from strengthening Japan's hand vis-à-vis Russia, this alliance with the foremost world power gave Japan new prestige and confidence. At the same time, Russia showed every intention of wishing to maintain and expand its position in East Asia.

The conflicting imperialist ambitions of Russia and Japan led to the Russo-Japanese War of 1904–05, fought both on land (mostly in Manchuria) and at sea. For both belligerents the cost was heavy, but the victories went to Japan. Despite some hard fighting, Russian troops were driven back on land; while in two separate naval actions the Japanese destroyed virtually the entire Russian navy. The naval war was spectacular. Japan attacked the Russian Pacific fleet at Port Arthur, just before the declaration of war. Russia's Baltic fleet then sailed all the way around Africa because Britain would not allow it passage through the Suez Canal, only to be met and destroyed by the Japanese navy in the Tsushima Straits, which run between Japan and Korea.

In Russia these defeats had fateful consequences. The discredited government of the Czar, long the object of terrorist attacks, now faced full-scale rebellion. The Revolution of 1905 was a precursor of the Revolution of 1917, which overthrew the regime. For their part the Japanese, although victorious, were thoroughly exhausted. It was essential that the war be brought to a close. Thus both sides were happy to respond affirmatively to an offer from the United States to mediate their disputes, and a peace conference was subsequently held in Portsmouth, New Hampshire.

In the resulting treaty, Japan gained recognition of its supremacy in Korea, the transfer of Russian interests in Manchuria (the railway and the leasehold on the Liaotung Peninsula), and cession of the southern half of Sakhalin Island (north of Hokkaidō). Going into the negotiations Japan had demanded all of Sakhalin and also a war indemnity, but Russia successfully resisted these demands, much to the anger of the Japanese public, which, not informed of their country's inability to continue the war, expected more of the settlement. At home the treaty was greeted by riots. Elsewhere in Asia people were impressed by this first victory of a non-Western nation over a European power.

One immediate result of Japan's victory over Russia was economic expansion in Manchuria where the semiofficial South Manchurian Railway Company was soon engaged in shipping, public utilities, and mining as well as railroading. From the start the Japanese government held half of the company's shares and appointed its officers. Although private Japanese firms also entered Manchuria, it has been calculated that in 1914, 79 percent of all Japanese investments in Manchuria were in the South Manchurian Railway. Furthermore, 69 percent of all Japanese investments in China prior to the First World War were in Manchuria. The remainder was largely concentrated in Shanghai.

Colonialism in Korea and Taiwan

In 1906 Itō Hirobumi was sent to Korea as Resident General with wide powers over the Korean government, but in 1909 he was assassinated by a Korean nationalist, and in the following year Japan annexed Korea outright. Korea was then placed under the control of a governor-general, always a military man, although after 1919 a civilian could legally have been appointed to this post.

Like other imperialist powers, Japan governed its colonies for the benefit of the homeland. In both Taiwan and Korea, Japan's policies were designed to control the local population and to exploit the local resources through selective modernization. Japanese rule over Taiwan and Korea, accordingly, shared certain characteristics: in both cases the police were prominent, and dissent was repressed; transportation and communications networks were developed; the landholding system was remodeled and agricultural production encouraged; public health was improved, leading to an increase in the population; schools were fostered, emphasizing Japanese studies and spreading the use of the Japanese language. In both cases too many of the benefits of modernization went to the Japanese who dominated the colonial administrative machinery and operated the larger colonial enterprises.

There were, however, also enormous differences between the two colonies—differences extending beyond such obvious factors as climate (Taiwan is suitable for sugar plantations, Korea not) or Korea's more strategic geographic location. From the beginning, Japanese rule over Taiwan, while vigorous and firm, was not as harsh as that over Korea. There were, no doubt, numerous reasons for this, but important among them was the difference in historical background between Taiwan and Korea. When Japan assumed control over Taiwan after the Treaty of Shimonoseki, it encountered only sporadic resistance, for the island had only recently been fully incorporated into the political and cultural life of the mainland; even though its residents were almost all Chinese (ca. 3 million Chinese as compared to ca. 120,000 aborigines), they were as yet uninfluenced by modern nationalism and lacked a deep-rooted tradition of local cultural and political independence.

Korea, by contrast, boasted a culture older than that of Japan and a tradition of fierce independence. It also contained an old hereditary elite resentful of Japanese intrusion, and after 1895, a small but dedicated group of nationalists. Although the leadership against the Japanese takeover was traditional in composition and organization, violence was widespread. Japanese retaliation (by burning villages and committing other acts of terror) enflamed it even more. Between August 1907 and June 1911, the Japanese recorded 2852 clashes involving 141,815 insurgents. Until 1919 Japanese rule remained totally uncompromising. On March 1 of that year, there was a massive nationalist protest which the Japanese repressed ferociously. Then, in the twenties, the colonial administration was partially relaxed, but this was followed by further severity in the thirties.

Under Japanese rule the average Korean suffered economically. The land survey conducted between 1911 and 1918 favored large landholders. Tenancy increased. The largest landholder in Korea came to be the Oriental Development Company, a semigovernment corporation originally chartered in 1908 with the intent of opening new lands for Japanese immigrant farmers. When that plan proved unrealistic, the company bought up Korean-worked paddy fields instead. This was a development consistent with Korea's role as a supplier of inexpensive rice for Japan. After the First World War, the Japanese greatly expanded rice production in Korea, but there was still not enough for both Japanese and Koreans, and Korean rice consumption declined. In the twenties and thirties a beginning was made in industrial development, especially in the north, which was suitable for hydroelectric plants.

As demonstrated by the 1919 protest, the Japanese built up a vast reservoir of ill will in Korea, and there were nationalists in exile yearning for an end to Japanese rule. Others, however, acquiesced and/or cooperated, and both Taiwan and Korea continued to contribute to the Japanese sense of national accomplishment as well as to the Japanese economy.

Late Meiji Economic Developments

War against China in the 1890s, and against Russia during the following decade, stimulated the Japanese domestic economy. Both wars were followed by an outburst of nationalist sentiment that gave a strong boost to heavy industry (for example, the Yawata Steel Works, established in 1897) and to armaments, including shipbuilding. After 1906, Japan produced ships comparable in size and quality to any in the world. Japanese technology continued to progress and advances were made in new fields such as electrical engineering. Light industry, particularly textiles, continued to flourish and remained predominant in the modern sector. The single most important item of export, accounting for nearly half the total, was in partly finished goods, especially silk. (Because of superior quality control, Japanese silk was more in demand abroad than was the silk of China.) An index of the changing nature of the economy were trade figures which reveal an increasing emphasis on the import of raw materials and the export of manufactured goods. Other statistics indicate increases in productivity, in the labor force, and in urbanization, opening up a widening gulf between the city and the country.

Not everyone in the cities benefited from these developments. Those working in the numerous small traditional establishments experienced little change in their living conditions. Especially harsh were the working and living conditions of those who labored in the factories and shops. These were comparable to those in Western countries at a comparably early stage of industrialization. During the first decade of the twentieth century, 60 percent of the work force was still female, and efforts to improve the lot of women and children working in the factories made headway only slowly. Not until 1916 did a law take effect giving them some protection, such as limiting their working day to eleven hours. An act promulgated in 1900 outlawed strikes, but when conditions became too bad, male workers, for whom a factory job was not an interlude prior to marriage but a lifelong occupation, rebelled, sometimes violently. Thus in 1909, three infantry companies were required to quell violence in the Ashio Copper Mines. Another labor action which made a deep impression was the streetcar strike in Tokyo in 1911.

The distress of the workers was also of great concern to radical intellectuals. Beginning in the early nineties, there was a small radical movement composed

of Christian socialists and anarchists. They exhibited great courage in opposing the war with Russia. Even after the war had begun, they held antiwar ral-
lies in the Tokyo Y.M.C.A. However, barred by the government from forming a
political party and facing government repression, they were unable to expand
their influence beyond the world of intellectuals and college students. In 1911,
twelve of their leaders were convicted, on very flimsy evidence, of plotting the
death of the emperor, and were executed.

Among the main beneficiaries of economic growth were the huge industrial-
financial combines (*zaibatsu*), which retained their close ties with government. The dominant political party during this period, the Seiyūkai (Association of Friends of Constitutional Government), also had a stake in economic
development, since projects for railway and harbor development were a major
means by which it won regional support and built up its political power.

Late Meiji Politics

During the Sino-Japanese War the oligarchs and the party-controlled Diet were
united in pursuit of common national aims, but after the war the political
struggles resumed. The oligarchs, enjoying the prerogatives of *genrō* ("elder
statesmen"), advised the emperor on all important matters. As participants in
the fashioning of the new state and architects of its major institutions, they
enjoyed great prestige as well as the support of their protégés and associates in
that process. The party politicians, on the other hand, resented the *genrō*'s tendency to perpetuate their power and to limit political decision making to a
small group of hand-picked insiders. Their main weapon against a prime minister who defied them was that under the constitution only the Diet could au-
thorize increases in the budget.

Complicating the political situation but also making for compromise rather
than confrontation were divisions within both the oligarchy and the party
leadership. Among the former, Yamagata, a disciplined rather austere military
man, was committed to "transcendental government," dedicated to emperor
and nation and above political partisanship. His main *genrō* rival was Itō, a
more flexible conservative, the man who had supervised the writing of the constitution. Itō was more willing than Yamagata to compromise with the party
forces.

Similarly not all Diet members were adamantly opposed to collaborating
with the *genrō*. Some lost their enthusiasm for opposing a government which
could dissolve the Diet and thereby subject them to costly campaigns for re-
election. Furthermore, the oligarchs could—and did—trade office for support.
Accommodation had its appeal to both sides, but initially it was an uneasy accommodation; there were four dissolutions of the Diet between 1895 and
1900.

Another political factor was the influence of the military. As stipulated in
the constitution, the chief of the general staff reported directly to the emperor
concerning command matters, thus bypassing the Minister of War and the cab-

inet. In 1900 the military's power was further strengthened when Yamagata obtained imperial ordinances specifying that only officers on active duty could serve as Minister of the Army or Minister of the Navy. This in effect gave the military veto power over any cabinet, for it could break a cabinet simply by ordering the army or navy minister to resign. However, control over funds for army expansion remained in the hands of the party politicians of the lower house.

Up to 1901 the oligarchs themselves served as prime minister, but after that date Yamagata's protégé Katsura Tarō (1847–1913) and Itō's protégé, Saionji Kimmochi (1849–1940) alternated as prime minister for the remainder of the Meiji period. Katsura, like Yamagata, was a general from Chōshū; Saionji was a court noble with liberal views but possessing little inclination to political leadership.

Katsura and Saionji were able to govern because they had the cooperation of the Seiyūkai, a party founded in 1900 by Itō who saw this as the way to obtain assured support in the Diet. In 1903 Itō turned the presidency of the party over to Saionji, but the real organizing force within the party was Hara Kei (1856–1921), an ex-bureaucrat who became the leading party politician of his generation. Hara greatly strengthened the party by building support within the bureaucracy during his first term as Home Minister (1906–08) and also used his power to appoint energetic partymen as prefectural governors. He further provided the party with sturdy local roots by freely resorting to the pork barrel, building up a constituency among the local men of means who constituted the limited electorate.

The financial and business community, including the *zaibatsu*, was interested in maintaining a political atmosphere favorable to itself, and political leaders for their part welcomed business support. Thus Itō, when he organized the Seiyūkai, obtained the support of Shibusawa Eiichi and other prominent business leaders, although many remained aloof. The head of Mitsui was so intent on establishing his firm's independence from government that he even discontinued the practice of extending loans to Itō without collateral. However, the trend was toward closer association between the *zaibatsu* and politics, as exemplified by the close relationship between Mitsubishi and Katsura after 1908. During Katsura's second ministry (1908–11), his chief economic advisor was the head of the Mitsubishi Bank.

The relative strength of the participants in the political process did not remain unchanged. The *genrō* enjoyed great influence as long as they remained active, but theirs was a personal not an institutional power, and it tended to diminish with time. As the participants in the original Restoration diminished in number, the power of the oligarchs to orchestrate politics decreased. Katsura as prime minister did not always follow Yamagata's advice. Furthermore, the *genrō* lost an important source of support when a new generation of bureaucrats came to the fore. These new officials did not owe their positions to *genrō* patronage, for after 1885 entrance to and promotion in the bureaucracy were determined by examinations. As servants of the emperor, the bureaucracy enjoyed high prestige and considerable influence.

Political compromise eroded much of the idealism found in the early move-ment for people's rights, but the Seiyūkai prospered. Indeed the increase of its strength in the Diet alarmed the party's opponents in that body, but this oppo-sition was divided and diverse. It included not only those who opposed the Seiyūkai's compromise on principle, but also small and shifting groups of in-dependents, and a series of "loyalist" parties that habitually supported the cabinet.

Decision making was complicated, and government policies were deter-mined by the interaction of various power centers, none of which could rule alone. The system functioned as long as there were sufficient funds to finance the military's and the Seiyūkai's highest priority projects, and as long as none of the participants felt their essential interests threatened. When that ceased to be the case, it brought on the Taishō political crisis.

Literature and Art

Early Meiji literature had largely continued Tokugawa traditions, but during the Late Meiji a modern literature developed under the influence of Western literature and literary theories. The beginning of the modern Japanese novel can be traced to Tsubouchi Shōyō (1859–1935), a translator of Shakespeare and an advocate of realism, that is, the view that literature should portray actual life. In his *The Essence of the Novel* (1885) Tsubouchi argued for the adoption of realism in place of the earlier didacticism or literature written solely for en-tertainment. Futabatei Shimei (1864–1909) then wrote the realistic novel, *Drifting Cloud* (1887–89), a psychological study of a rather ordinary man, told not in the customary literary style but in more colloquial form.

Following the introduction of realism, two other Western literary theories became particularly influential: romanticism, with its emphasis on the expres-sion of feelings, and naturalism, which aimed at treating man with scientific detachment as advocated by the French writer Émile Zola. Although in Europe naturalism was hostile to romanticism, this was not necessarily the case in Japan, where Shimazaki Tōson (1873–1943) won fame both for his romantic poetry and for a naturalistic novel, *The Broken Commandment* (1906). This novel was an account of a member of the pariah class (*burakumin*, see Chapter 15) who tries to keep the pledge he made to his father never to reveal that he was born into this group (which was still the object of social discrimination and contempt even though not subject to any legal restrictions).

Two writers of the Late Meiji era stand out in particular, producing works of lasting literary merit that transcended their age, even as they reflected its con-cerns: Mori Ōgai (1862–1922) and Natsume Sōseki (1867–1916). Both men had a period of study abroad and were deeply influenced by the West, but both achieved greatness by drawing on their own Japanese heritage.

Ōgai's time abroad was spent mainly in Germany, where he studied medi-cine, and on his return to Japan he embarked on a distinguished career as an army surgeon, rising in 1907 to the rank of surgeon-general. His literary work was diverse, for he was a prolific and excellent translator as well as a writer of original works. Among his finest translations are his renderings of Goethe, including the full *Faust,* and of Shakespeare, which he translated from the German. He also translated modern German poetry, with the result that more modern German verse was available in Japanese translation than in English. Furthermore, he introduced German aesthetic philosophy to Japan and also had an influence on the development of modern Japanese theater: the performance of his translation of an Ibsen play in 1908 was one of the major cultural events of the Late Meiji.

Ōgai's first story, *Maihime* ("The Dancing Girl," 1890) recounts the doomed romance between a Japanese student sent by his government to Germany and a German girl named Alice. It became a precursor of the many "I novels," thinly disguised autobiographical works, which became one of the standard genres of modern Japanese fiction, although it also owes something to the old tradition of literary diaries.

After his initial romantic period, Ōgai went on to write works of increasing psychological insight and philosophical depth. He also turned increasingly to Japanese themes, as in his novel *The Wild Goose.* Ōgai was greatly moved when his friend General Nogi (1849–1912), hero of the Russo-Japanese War, followed the Meiji Emperor into death by committing ritual suicide along with his wife. After this event Ōgai published painstakingly researched accounts of samurai. One late work particularly acclaimed in Japan is his *Chibu Chūsai,* an account of a late Tokugawa physician with whom Ōgai identified.

Natsume Sōseki studied in England, where he was thoroughly miserable. A meager government stipend forced him to live in poverty, and he had virtually no friends. Later he described himself as having been "as lonely as a stray dog in a pack of wolves."[1] Both this experience of loneliness, and the extensive reading he did while in England, were reflected in his subsequent work. Sōseki returned from Europe to teach English literature at Tokyo Imperial University, before resigning this position to devote himself wholly to writing. He was acclaimed not only for his fiction but also for poetry in Chinese, haiku, and literary criticism. He once described his mind as half Japanese and half Western, and his early novels reflect English influence, particularly that of Meredith, but in his mature work the Japanese element predominates. Fortunately, much of his work is available in good English translations.

In his early novels *I Am a Cat* (1905) and *Botchan* (1906), Sōseki presents slices of Meiji life portrayed with affectionate good humor. Also in 1906, in a mere week, he wrote a remarkable painterly and diarylike book, *The Grass Pillow,* also translated as *The Three Cornered World,* for "An artist is a person who lives in the triangle which remains after the angle which we may call common sense has been removed from this four-cornered world."[2] The main theme of Sōseki's mature works is human isolation, studied in characters given to deep introspection. Like Ōgai, Sōseki was deeply moved by the death of the Meiji Emperor and General Nogi's suicide, which entered into *Kokoro* (1914), a novel concerning the relationship between a young man and his mentor, called "Sensei" ("master" or "teacher"). In the novel Sōseki links Sensei's personal tragedy and his suicide in 1912 to the death of the emperor and the general, and the larger tragedy of the passing of a generation and with it of the old ethical values, for Sensei perceives that he has become an anachronism.

Painters, like writers, were grouped in several schools. The disciples of Okakura Tenshin, for example, continued to avoid the extremes of formalistic traditionalism and imitative modernism, while seeking a middle ground that would be both modern and Japanese. One member of this school was Yokoyama Taikan (1868–1958). His screen, shown in Figure 21-1, depicts a perennial favorite of Chinese and Japanese scholars, the poet T'ao Ch'ien, whose blend of regret and relief at withdrawal from public life continued to strike a responsive chord in the complicated world of the twentieth century.

Among the artists working in purely European styles was Kuroda Seiki, whose nude had so shocked Kyōto in the nineties. He continued to paint in an impressionistic manner and had many followers and imitators. Some attempts at rendering Japanese themes in Western style produced paintings which are little more than historical curiosities, but in other cases there was a happier result. The painting by Sakaki Teitoku (1858–1939) shown in Figure 21-2 was executed in oil around 1910. While the young men blow traditional bamboo flutes, two young ladies play violins.

Figure 21-1 Yokoyama Taikan, *T'ao Ch'ien*. Detail from one of a pair of sixfold screens, *Master Five Willows*. Color on paper, 1912, 169.4 cm × 361.2 cm. Tokyo National Museum.

Western influence on the visual arts was often direct and immediate. For instance, the noted Japanese artist Umehara Ryūzaburō (1888–) studied in France during the Late Meiji, met Renoir in 1909, and became his favorite pupil. The strongest influence on Japanese sculpture during this period was Rodin, who enjoyed a great vogue in Japan, especially after a major exhibition of his work in Tokyo in 1912. The Japanese continued to be informed, enthusiastic, and sensitive patrons of the visual arts.

There was also an interest in modernizing music. The Meiji government early on sponsored Western military music, and in 1879 the Ministry of Education agreed to a proposal made by Izawa Shūnji (1851–1917) to combine Japanese and Western music in the schools. Izawa had studied vocal physiology in the United States and persuaded the Ministry of Education to bring Luther Whiting Mason (1828–96) from Boston to Japan to help develop songs for use

Figure 21-2   Sakaki Teitoku, *Concert Using Japanese and Western Instruments*. Oil, 1910. Takakiyo Mitsui Collection.

in the elementary schools. The first of the song books to be completed (1881) consisted half of Western songs supplied with Japanese words ("Auld Lang Syne," for example, was turned into a song about fireflies) and half of Japanese pieces harmonized in the Western manner.

Meiji popular music was more freely eclectic than that taught in the schools. During the last decade of the nineteenth century and the beginning of the twentieth, Japanese composers began working with the forms of classical Western music (sonatas, cantatas, and so forth), and thanks to the efforts of the Tokyo School of Music good performers were available on the piano and violin, as well as on the koto and other traditional instruments also taught at the school. Actually, performers made greater progress than composers. The important compositions were still to come. Furthermore, as William P. Malm has suggested, "the training of generations of Japanese youth to harmonically oriented music has created a series of mental blocks which shut out the special musical potentialities of traditional styles."[3] The rediscovery of the latter, and their creative employment in original compositions, did not take place until after the Second World War.

The Taishō Political Crisis (1912–1913)

The Meiji Emperor was succeeded, in 1912, by the Taishō Emperor (r. 1912–26). The transition was marked by a grave sense of unease in the country, not only due to the change in emperors, but also to social and economic conditions in the nation generally. Nevertheless, the crisis of 1912–13 was undoubtedly aggravated by the loss of the old emperor, who had given his people a sense of continuity even as he presided over the profound changes of the Restoration.

The crisis arose when it became apparent that Japan's financial condition required a cutback in government spending. The cutback brought two major interest groups into conflict. The dominant political party, the Seiyūkai, was determined to save its domestic spending program—in part because its political support depended on it, while the army, anxious to build two new divisions, pressed for increased military spending.

Although the Seiyūkai won support at the polls, Prime Minister Saionji was forced out of office in December 1912, when the army ordered the Minister of the Army to resign his post. While the *genrō* deliberated and sought for a successor to Saionji, a number of politicians, journalists, and businessmen organized a movement "to protect constitutional government," which led to mass demonstrations reminiscent of those greeting news of the Portsmouth Treaty in 1905. Called on to form a government once more, Katsura was no longer willing to compromise with the Seiyūkai, but he failed in an attempt to weld his bureaucratic followers and opposition politicians into a party strong enough to defeat the Seiyūkai. When the Seiyūkai threatened a vote of no confidence in the Diet, Katsura tried to save the situation by obtaining an imperial order forcing the Seiyūkai to give up its planned no-confidence motion. This was a stratagem employed previously by embattled prime ministers, but it did not work this time, for the Seiyūkai turned down the order. One consequence of Katsura's failure was to discredit such use of an imperial order, with the result that it was never attempted again.

Katsura died in 1913, but the coalition he had created held together under the leadership of Katō Komei (1859–1926), whose background included graduation from Tokyo Imperial University, service in Mitsubishi, and a career in the Foreign Office capped by an appointment as Foreign Minister at the age of forty. He enjoyed a financial advantage from his marriage into the family which controlled Mitsubishi. A capable and determined man, he was personally reserved. But this was no handicap, for there was no need for party leaders like Katō or Hara to cultivate mass support. The power of a party leader depended on his strength *within* his party, although this was influenced by the party's success at the polls.

The emergence of a strong second party meant that from now on the Seiyūkai faced a rival for control of the lower house. The parties represented a cross section of skills and resources needed to make participation in government viable. As Arthur E. Tiedemann observes, "Each party had associated with it the three essential ingredients for achieving political power: professional politicians to do the nitty-gritty of day-to-day party management; former bureaucrats who had the administrative talents required to form a viable alternative government acceptable to the genrō; and businessmen who could supply the funds and influence essential to successful election campaigns."[4] Thus Japan came to be governed by a two-party system that lasted until 1932.

The Taishō political crisis confirmed the importance of the Diet and of the parties, but it was not until 1918 (when Hara became Prime Minister) that the prime ministership went to a man who had made his career as a party politician. Meanwhile, there were three intervening prime ministers: Admiral Ya-mamoto Gombei, 1913–14, the first head of government from Satsuma since 1897; the septuagenarian Ōkuma Shigenobu, 1914–16, who was committed to destroying the Seiyūkai but failed; and Terauchi Masatake, 1916–18, a Chōshū general who had been governor-general of Korea. It was the Ōkuma and Tera-uchi governments which guided Japan during the First World War.

Japan During the First World War

When the Western powers became immersed in the struggle which was to bring an end to Europe's predominance in the world, new opportunities were opened for the expansion of the Japanese empire and industry.

In August 1914 Japan declared war on Germany and within three months proceeded to seize German holdings in Shantung and the German islands in the Pacific. In January 1915 the Ōkuma government presented the Twenty-One Demands to China. Japan obtained additional rights on the continent but at the cost of stirring up strong Chinese resentment. A prominent critic of this policy was the pro-German Yamagata, who wanted an understanding with China in order to prepare for the war he anticipated against the West.

Much larger and more costly than Japan's military effort against Germany during the First World War was the country's effort against the Russians (1918–22). The Russian Revolution of 1917 had taken Russia out of the war and created disorder in Russia's East Asian territories. In Japan there was considerable disagreement over how to take advantage of a situation further complicated by the presence of Czech troops who were fighting their way out of Russia and were determined to continue the war against Germany. By mid-summer 1918 Japan controlled the eastern portion of the Trans-Siberian Railway and had seized Vladivostok. The United States then changed its earlier opposition to intervention, although President Wilson envisioned only a limited military operation. The Japanese, however, sent 75,000 troops, three times more than those sent by the Allies (United States, Britain, France, and Canada). In the light of Soviet victories and the absence of a viable alternative, the United States withdrew its forces in January 1919 and the other Allies soon did the same. This left only the Japanese, who continued their efforts in the vain hope of at least keeping the U.S.S.R. from controlling eastern Siberia.

Japan was able to pay for such a costly undertaking largely because of the great economic boom she experienced during the First World War, when there was an unprecedented demand for her industrial products and a withdrawal of the European competition. Old industries expanded and new ones grew up as exports surged. Japan earned enough foreign exchange to change her status from a debtor to a creditor nation. But while some prospered, others suffered. The sudden economic expansion produced inflation and workers' wages, as well as the income of men in traditional occupations such as fishing, failed to keep pace. Especially serious was the increase in the price of rice, which rose until people could no longer afford this most basic food. In August 1918, rice riots erupted in cities, towns, and villages all over Japan. Even as Japanese troops were setting off for Siberia other soldiers were firing on hungry people rioting at home. The bitter irony was not lost on Japanese radicals. The immediate effect of the turbulence was to bring down the Terauchi government. When the *genrō* met to choose a new prime minister, they settled on the Seiyūkai leader Hara Kei.

Politics and Policies (1918–1924)

Hara Kei had spent his career building up the Seiyūkai in preparation for the day of party rule, but when he finally attained the prime ministership he was too set in his ways to embark on significant new policies or to devise meaningful changes in the structure of government. The changes he initiated from 1918 until he was assassinated by a demented fanatic in November 1921 were minor, and his concerns tended to remain partisan. Democratic intellectuals, the leaders of labor and farmer unions, and students were disillusioned when the government turned a deaf ear to their demands for universal suffrage, and instead passed an election law which retained a tax qualification for voting and reconstructed local electoral districts to favor the Seiyūkai. Abuse of office, financial scandals, and actions prompted by narrow partisanship had damaged the public image of the parties for years, and the record of the first party prime minister did nothing to alter this. Liberals who had placed their hopes in parliamentary reform either became cynical or looked elsewhere, while the public at large was apathetic.

In foreign affairs Hara's prime ministership began with the peace conference at Versailles, where Japan failed to obtain a declaration of racial equality but did have its rights in China and the Pacific confirmed. His government then adopted a policy of cooperation with the United States, the only possible source for capital badly needed by Japanese industry facing difficult adjustments after peace brought an end to wartime prosperity. The first product of the new policy was the Washington Conference of 1921–22, in which Japan's alliance with Britain was replaced by a Four Power Pact signed by France, Great Britain, Japan, and the United States. The conference also produced an agreement to limit construction of capital ships (that is, large warships) by the signatories, so as to maintain the existing balance of naval power. Under this agreement Japan promised to build no more than three capital ships for every five built by the United States and five built by Great Britain. In addition, Japan agreed to a Nine Power Treaty in February 1922, in which she acceded to the American Open Door policy. Also in the same month Japan reached an agreement with China that provided for the restoration of Chinese sovereignty over Shantung but retention by Japan of economic rights there. Finally, in October 1922, Japan agreed to withdraw from Siberia.

These actions were taken as part of a general policy of getting along with the United States and conciliating China, a policy followed by Shidehara Kijūrō when he served as foreign minister from 1924 to 1927 and again from 1929 to

December 1931. Its purpose was to avert another anti-Japanese outburst and costly boycotts of Japanese goods, in order to permit continuing Japanese economic expansion. After 1914 Japanese investments in China accelerated. By 1931 over 80 percent of Japan's total foreign investments were in China, where they accounted for 35.1 percent of all foreign investments in that country.* In 1930, 63 percent of Japanese investments in China were in Manchuria and another 25 percent in Shanghai, where Japanese engaged in trade, banking, and textile manufacturing. They were especially prominent in the latter: in 1930 Japanese owned 39.6 percent of the Chinese textile industry (calculated in spindles). They were also a very major factor in China's iron industry, with interests in Hankow and Manchuria.

Hara was initially succeeded by his finance minister, but this man lacked Hara's political skills and stayed in office only until June 1922. Three nonparty prime ministers followed, two were admirals (Katō Tomasaburō and Yamamoto Gombei) and one a bureaucrat (Kiyoura Keigo) who organized his cabinet entirely from the House of Peers but resigned when faced with a three-party coalition in control of the Diet. The leader of the strongest of these parties, the Kenseikai (Constitutional Government Association, established 1916) was Katō Kōmei, who had last served as foreign minister under Ōkuma during the war. He was now called upon to form a new government.

The most momentous event of the years between Hara and Katō was geological, not political: in September 1923 the Tokyo-Yokohama area was devastated by a severe earthquake followed by a conflagration, which came close to leveling the area. The red sky was visible all night from a hundred miles away. Around 150,000 people lost their lives. As so often in a disaster, the earthquake and fires brought out the best and the worst in the population. While some courageously and selflessly helped their fellows, others joined in hysterical mobs rampaging through the city killing Koreans. The police reacted to the emergency by rounding up socialists, anarchists, and Communists as a "security measure," and there were cases of police torture and killing.

Party Government (1924–1931)

The main accomplishments of party government came during the two years Katō was prime minister (1924–26). Foremost among them was the passage of a "universal" suffrage act, which gave the vote to all males twenty-five and over. To still the fears of conservatives apprehensive over the possible spread of radical ideas, a Peace Preservation Law was also passed. This made it a crime to advocate change in the national political structure or to urge the abolition of private property. The Katō government never invoked the law, but it was available to later, less liberal regimes.

* Great Britain accounted for 36.7 percent of foreign investments in China, but this represented only 5 to 6 percent of all British overseas investments. Other countries accounting for over 5 percent of foreign investments in China were: U.S.S.R., 8.4; United States, 6.1; France, 5.9.

Katō also tried to reform the House of Peers (changing its composition and reducing its powers) but succeeded in making only minor changes. His government was more successful in introducing moderate social reforms, including the legalization of labor unions, the establishment of standards for factory conditions, the setting up of procedures for mediating labor disputes, and the provision of health insurance for workers. There was, however, no similar program to alleviate the problems of the rural poor.

Katō soon became embroiled in difficult political negotiations with other parties and the House of Peers among others. When Katō died in 1926, he had not transformed Japanese politics, but he did leave a record of accomplishment which might, under different circumstances, have served as a basis for building a strong system of party rule. That this did not happen is partly the result of the kinds of problems Japan had to face during the five years following Katō's death, but it also reflects the weaknesses of the parties themselves. Even the increased suffrage was a mixed blessing, for the larger electorate made election campaigns more expensive, so that politicians were more open to corruption.

From 1927 to 1929 the government was in the hands of Tanaka Giichi, a general from Chōshū who had entered politics and had been elected president of the Seiyūkai in 1925. During his term of office, Japan held its first election conducted under universal manhood suffrage. This took place in February 1928, but was followed by the large-scale arrest of radicals, many of whom were forced to spend long years in prison. Tanaka's administration was also marred by political irregularities and by his inept handling of the nation's economic problems. In his policy toward China, Tanaka departed from Shidehara's conciliatory approach. Under political pressure at home, Tanaka was also concerned over the safety of Japanese residents in Shantung during the Kuomintang's northern advance, yet unwilling to evacuate them. He therefore sent to Shantung the troops already mentioned in the preceding chapter. It was also during his tenure in office that Chang Tso-lin, the warlord of Manchuria, was assassinated. The collapse of the Tanaka government came when he incurred the displeasure of the Shōwa Emperor (r. 1926–) and court by failing to obtain from the army suitable punishment for Chang Tso-lin's murderers. This was one of the rare instances in which the emperor personally intervened in a political decision. The episode was also a harbinger of future unilateral army action, but first, party government had one more chance.

In 1929, Hamaguchi Ōsachi became prime minister, and in 1930 his party, the Minseitō, product of a merger of the Kenseitō and another party, won the election. Shidehara once again became foreign minister and resumed his policy of reconciliation with China and cooperation with Britain and the United States, as signified in the London Naval Treaty of 1930, which included provisions extending the 5:5:3 ratio to other than capital ships. Ratification of the treaty was obtained only after heated debate and the forced resignation of the naval chief of staff. It generated much anger and bitterness among the military and members of patriotic societies, such as the young man who shot the prime minister in November 1930. Hamaguchi never recovered from his wounds, but he did not resign until April 1931. From April until December 1931, the Minseitō cabinet continued under Wakatsuki Reijirō (1866–1949), who earlier had served as Katō's home minister and as prime minister from January 1926 to April 1927. Wakatsuki was an experienced politician, but during 1931 the government lost control over the army.

The restlessness of the military was not Hamaguchi's only problem. During most of the twenties Japan was beset by persistent economic difficulties, including an unfavorable balance of payments, failure of employment opportunities to increase fast enough to keep up with population growth, and a sharp decline in the price of rice, which helped consumers but hurt farmers. The giant *zaibatsu* profited from new technology, the economics of large-scale management, and the failure of weaker firms, but the period was very hard on small operators and especially difficult for tenant farmers. To solve the balance of payments problem, there were at various times during the decade calls for the government to cut expenses and follow a policy of retrenchment in order to reduce the cost of Japanese goods and improve their competitive position in international trade. This was the policy followed by Hamaguchi, who also strengthened the yen by returning to the gold standard. Unfortunately, he initiated this program just as the world depression was getting under way and persisted in it despite great economic dislocations and suffering. From 1925 to 1930 the real income of farmers declined by about a third. The poorest were, as always, the hardest hit. As in earlier periods of famine, there were cases of peasants eating bark and digging for roots or maintaining life by selling their daughters into brothels.

The government's economic failure undermined the prestige of the political parties, which even in normal times had not enjoyed much public esteem. No mass movement arose directed against them, but there was also little in their record to inspire people to man the barricades in their defense. Their enemies included those dissatisfied not only with their policies and politics but with just about every facet of twenties liberalism and internationalism.

The Arts

Internationalism was represented not only in politics but also in the arts. Tokyo was not far behind Paris or London in experimenting with the latest styles and techniques. Indeed it sometimes led the other capitals, as when in 1922 Frank Lloyd Wright built the Imperial Hotel in Tokyo, a break with Japan's own version of the European Art Nouveau. The American architect, himself influenced by the Japanese tradition, was not the only stimulating visitor from abroad during the Taishō and early Shōwa years. Japanese scientists, for example, could converse with Einstein on his visit to their country in 1919, and music lovers enjoyed concerts by eminent foreign performers: both Kreisler and Heifetz gave concerts in Tokyo in 1923. Bach, Mozart, and Beethoven were becoming as much a part of the musical life of Japan as of any other country, foreshadowing the time when, after the Second World War, the Japanese were acknowledged as the pioneers in teaching young children to play the violin and also became the world's foremost manufacturers of pianos.

A grand piano dominates the four panel screen (see Figure 21-3) painted in 1926 by Nakamura Daizaburō (1898–1947), which is representative of the followers of the Okakura school. Not only the traditional dress of the young lady playing by the light of an electric lamp but the technique and aesthetics of the painting recall the earliest Japanese art rather than contemporary Western styles. Conversely there were Japanese artists who, like Hsü Pei-hung in China, depicted traditional subjects in Western style, but the most successful modernists were modern in both subject and technique.

A major influence for modernism was the *White Birch* (*Shirakaba*) journal, which was published from 1910 to 1923, and was edited by a group of humanistic writers, including most notably Shiga Naoya (1883–1971). In contrast to the school of naturalism, the *White Birch* group was dedicated to the exploration of the inner self, the pursuit of deeper personal understanding and self-expression, as in the "I novel" or in individualistic art. International in their orientation, seeking to become "children of the world" (their expression), they introduced a host of European writers and published articles on the work and theories of such artists as Van Gogh, Cézanne, and Rodin, and sponsored art exhibits.

Much of the art produced during this period was merely imitative, but one artist who was able to go beyond imitation to develop his own style was Umehara Ryūzaburō, whom we have already encountered as a disciple of Renoir. However, his work also owes something to the Japanese tradition he absorbed while still a child in Kyōto, where he became thoroughly familiar with the

Figure 21-3   Nakamura Daizaburō, *At the Piano*. Fourfold screen, color on silk, 1926, 164.5 cm × 302 cm. Kyōto Municipal Museum of Art.

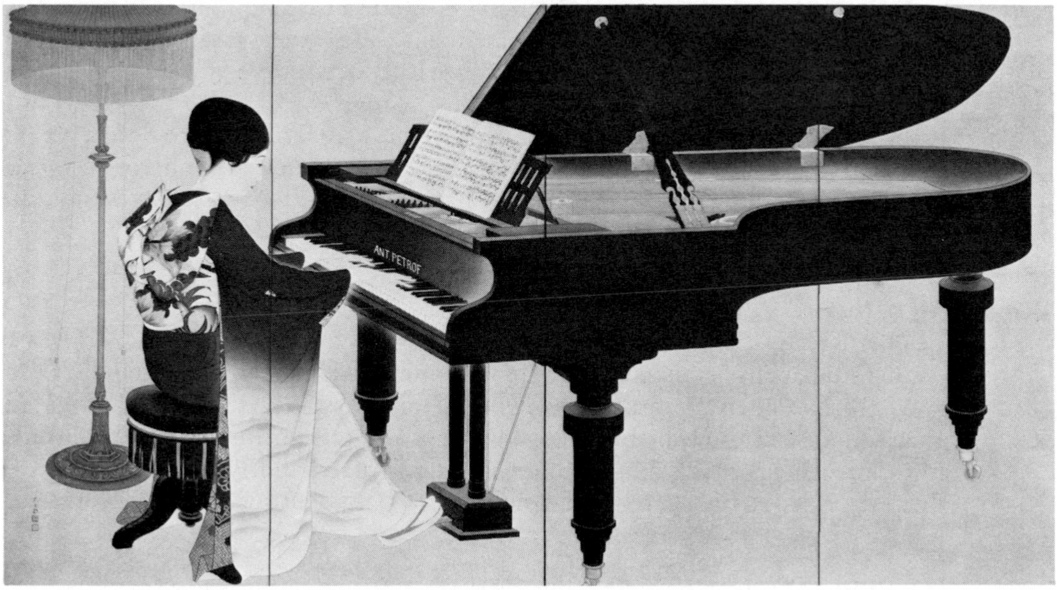

Figure 21-4   Umehara Ryūzaburō, *Cannes*. Oil, 1956, 32.5 cm × 49.5 cm.

styles of Sōtatsu and Korin as still practiced in his family's silk kimono business. The secret of his lively coloring lay in his use of semitransparent gold paint which allowed the color beneath to shine through. A prolific and long-lived artist, he is illustrated here by a work of his old age, painted when he was on his third visit to the French Riviera. (See Figure 21-4.)

European pointillism, cubism, futurism, dadaism, surrealism, and so on, all had their impact on the Japanese avant-garde, here represented by a painting dated 1926. (See Figure 21-5.) The artist, Tōgō Seiji (1897–), was in Europe at the time and was influenced by French and Italian futurism and dadaism, but here exhibits an inclination toward cubism. The title, *Saltimbanques*, is French for "traveling showmen." It is a cheerfully decorative picture, modern in style and subject matter. And it is just one of many works in which it would take a very keen eye, not to speak of considerable imagination, to detect a particularly Japanese element. The painter works in a medium which, for better or worse, is not bound to any particular national tradition, in contrast to the writer whose very language is linked to his historical culture.

Popular Culture

Avant-garde art in Japan as elsewhere was produced by and for the few, but the flow of influence from abroad was by no means restricted to the sophisticated or wealthy. After the war there was a wave of Western influence on the pattern of life, affecting people's diet, housing, and dress, particularly in the great cities, where there was a boom in bread consumption, the wearing of Western dress in public became prevalent, and it became the fashion to include at least one Western-style room in a house.

On the Ginza the "modern boy" (*mobo*) and "modern girl" (*moga*) appeared, dressed and coiffured in the very latest styles imported from overseas. They might be on their way to the movies, for film was now coming into its own, throwing off the shackles of the theatrical heritage that had dominated the early years of Japanese film making, when the narrator was as important as the pictures and female roles were played by men. Although there was always an audience for films filled with melodrama and sword action, others dealt with the problems and joys of daily life. It was in the twenties that the foundations were laid for the great achievements to come in Japanese films.

There was also a great increase in sports activity, not least of which was baseball, although the formation of professional teams had to wait until the thirties. Another new sport was golf, including, in that crowded land, "baby" or miniature golf. After golf or tennis, one could relax in a café or a fellow could practice the latest steps with a taxi dancer at the Florida or another dance hall. The old demi-monde dominated by the geisha, a world so fondly chronicled by Nagai Kafū (1879–1959), was on the decline, and modern mass culture was in the ascendancy.

Figure 21-5 Tōgō Seiji, *Saltimbanques.* Oil, 1926, 114 cm × 71 cm. Tokyo National Museum of Modern Art.

Although centered on the cities, the new popular culture was rapidly diffused now that even the remotest village was accessible by train and car, not to speak of the radio, which was introduced in 1925. Furthermore, mass circulation magazines, some directed at a general audience, others written especially for women or young people, turned out huge printings catering to the unquenchable thirst of the Japanese public for reading matter.

Literature

Among the still active older writers whose reputations were established during the Late Meiji was Shimazaki Tōson, who after *The Broken Commandment* had turned to autobiographical writings published, as was so often the case, serially in magazines. Another master of the autobiographical form was Shiga Naoya, already mentioned as a member of the *White Birch* group, which rejected the pessimism of the naturalists. In the hands of the many lesser writers who indulged in the genre, the detailed examination of everyday life was apt to produce tedium rather than insight, but there was always a public for such works.

A highly gifted writer who rejected the autobiographical mode was Akutagawa Ryūnosuke (1892–1927), author of some 150 short stories between 1917 and 1927. Many of these are modern psychological reinterpretations of old tales such as can be found in the *Tales from the Uji Collection.* In the West he is probably best known for "Rashomon," a tale in which the story of a murder and rape is told from the viewpoint of three protagonists and a witness. This story inspired one of the finest films of Kurosawa Akira, released in 1950. Akutagawa's carefully crafted stories are frequently eerie, but they are saved from being merely macabre by the keenness of his psychological portrayals. Pessimistic, given to self-doubt, and distressed at the changing world about him, he committed suicide in 1927 citing "a vague unease."

In poetry as in art some dedicated themselves to new experiments while others continued working with the old forms. In the nineteenth century, Shiki Masaoka (1867–1902), known primarily as a haiku poet, made notable contributions toward revitalizing traditional poetry, and many *tanka* and haiku continued to be written and published in every decade of the twentieth century. Others, however, looked to the West for models of poetry for a modern age. Some even employed the Roman alphabet (*rōmaji*). Foreign influence did not necessarily produce timeless verse; one poet proclaimed, "my sorrow wears the thin garb of one-sided love."[5]

The most admired master of free verse was Hagiwara Sakutarō (1886–1942), who employed the colloquial language to compose poems intensely personal both in their music and in their symbolism. The following is from a collection entitled *Howling at the Moon* (*Tsuki no hoeru,* 1917):

Bamboos

Out of the shimmering earth
The bamboos grow, the green
Bamboos; and there, below,
Their growing roots grow lean
As thinlier they grow
Until their tiny tails,
A glitter of hairlets make
Veined meshes, flimsy veils
Incredible a-quake

Out of the frozen earth
The bamboos grow, the tough
Intent bamboos that flow
Sky-tall with an almost rough
Interior rage to grow.
To grow. In hardening frost
Their knots swell hard with ooze.
To grow. The blue sky crosses
With growth, with green bamboos.[6]

A major prose writer was Tanizaki Junichirō (1886–1965), who began with a fascination with the West but gradually returned to the Japanese heritage. His artistic journey was paralleled by his physical move from Tokyo to Kyōto after the great earthquake of 1923. In 1919 he published *Some Prefer Nettles,* a title taken from a line in a poem by Yüan Mei, "some insects eat sugar, some prefer nettles."[7] The protagonist in this novel is unhappily married to a "stridently" modern wife. He finds comfort in the arms of a Eurasian prostitute, symbolic of the West, but, as the novel unfolds, he is increasingly attracted to a traditional Kyōto beauty representing the old culture of Japan. Some of Tanizaki's best work still lay in the future, including his masterpiece, *The Makioka Sisters,* which was written during the Second World War. One theme in this long, panoramic novel is the contrast between two of the sisters, one traditional in appearance and mentality, the other modern. Tanizaki's devotion to tradition also led him to translate *The Tale of Genji* into modern Japanese. An identification with tradition was also to characterize the work of Kawabata Yasunari (1899–1972), but during the twenties this famous writer was just at the beginning of his brilliant literary career.

Intellectual Trends

Japanese students of philosophy were for many years under strong German influence, predominantly that of Kant and Hegel and their later elaborators. After the war, along with German idealism, the phenomenalism of Husserl and Heidegger and the vitalism of Bergson and Eucken also attracted a Japanese audience. Outstanding among the philosphers who digested Western philosophy and assimilated it into their own original work was Nishida Kitarō (1870–1945), strongly steeped in Buddhism and best known for his philosophy of transcendent nothingness. Other theorists exploring subjects as seemingly far apart as aesthetics and politics grappled with the relationship between the universal principles valid everywhere and accessible to the intellect, and the particularist values imbedded in the unique culture of Japan, which must be apprehended by direct experience. In theoretical as in literary writings, the emphasis tended to be on the latter.

Nishida is said never to have discussed politics in his many years as a professor of philosophy at Kyōto University, but some of the most influential thinkers of the time were also important political theorists. Most widely read were Minobe Tatsukichi (1873–1948) and Yoshino Sakuzō (1878–1933), both deeply versed in German thought. Minobe was a legal scholar who followed his teacher at Heidelberg, Georg Jellinek, in making a distinction between sovereignty, which belongs to the whole state, and the power to rule, which is supervised by the emperor. In this sense, the emperor becomes the "highest organ" of the state, limited by the other components of the state and by the constitution. The constitution, furthermore, in Japan as elsewhere (according to Minobe) allows, and indeed requires, continuing change in the direction of increasing rationality, responsible government, and popular participation.

Minobe's work gained wide currency, and his book was the most frequently assigned text in courses on constitutional law. In 1932 he was appointed to the House of Peers.

Yoshino did not obtain such Establishment approval, but his many articles were widely read. A Christian populist and a democrat, he was a philosophical idealist who argued for democracy as an absolute rather than on utilitarian or pragmatic grounds. He also held an idealistic view of the nation and rejected any suggestion that democracy was incompatible with the Japanese tradition: "Those who argue that democracy is not compatible with the national spirit believe in the anachronistic and erroneous notion that the Emperor and people are mutually exclusive of each other."[8] Democracy would fulfill, not diminish, the emperor's role.

The postwar world also witnessed a revival of interest in anarchism and socialism, suppressed in 1911, and Japanese intellectuals were drawn to Marxist ideals even as they were impressed by the Russian Revolution. After a brief period of political activity, Yoshino returned to academic life, but more radical intellectuals continued to seek political involvement. This they could find in the labor movement, which conducted a dramatic dockyard strike in Kobe in 1921. By 1929, there were 300,000 workers in labor unions, but the labor parties formed after passage of the universal suffrage act suffered from an excess of factionalism and a lack of mass participation. This was also true of the Japanese Communist party, which was dominated by intellectuals. Some of these Marxists were people of great personal stature, but none was able to create a Marxism suitable to the particular conditions of Japan, nor did any have theoretical influence on international Marxism. Also more important for its program than for its literary accomplishment was a proletarian literary movement exemplified by such novels as *The Cannery Boat* (1929) by Kobayashi Takiji (1903–33), in which the workers revolt against a brutal captain. Even though much of this literature was propagandistic, it did serve to make the reader and writer more sensitive to social conditions, thereby opening up new terrain for Japanese literature.

These years also saw the beginning of a feminist movement, which campaigned for women's rights at a time when they were minors under the law and were completely excluded from the political process. Despite the efforts of several organizations and some dedicated leaders, change in this area was very slow.

While leftists were dissatisfied with what they considered the slow pace of progress in Japan, there were also ideologues who rejected much of the modern world and envisioned a very different future for their country. Among them were men who, conscious of the hardships suffered by the countryside, condemned the life and values of the cities and called for a return to virtuous agrarianism. Among the most severe critics of the parties and *zaibatsu* was Kita Ikki (1883–1937), who combined advocacy of imperialistic assertiveness abroad with a call for egalitarianism at home to bring emperor and people together. Unhappy with Japan's political organization as well as her stance in the world, he looked not to the electorate or mass popular movements for salvation, but placed his faith in change from above enacted by a few dedicated men. Accordingly, his ideas found a friendly reception in small societies of superpatriots and among young army officers who saw themselves as continuing in the tradition of the *rōnin* who had selflessly terrorized Kyōto during the closing days of the Tokugawa; he also found more recent exemplars among post-Edo "patriots," including the ex-samurai who after Saigō's death had founded the Genyōsha (Black Ocean Society, 1881) in Fukuoka (Northern Kyūshū) and the related Kokuryūkai (Amur River Society, also translated Black Dragon Society, 1901), one dedicated to expansion in Korea, the other concentrating on Manchuria, both employing intimidation and assassination among their techniques.

The story of the attempts made by these men to effect a "Shōwa Restoration" belongs in the thirties, but Kita Ikki's most influential book was written in 1919. The seeds planted in one decade bore fruit in the next. The rejection in the thirties of party government and the general internationalism that had prevailed in the twenties revealed that these had as yet shallow roots. Whether they would have flourished in a gentler international climate, we do not know, but their later reemergence after the Second World War suggests, at the very least, that the possiblity existed.

NOTES

1. Quoted in Sōseki Natsume, *Ten Nights of Dream—Hearing Things—The Heredity of Taste*, trans. Aiko Itō and Graeme Wilson (Rutland, Vt. and Tokyo: Charles E. Tuttle, 1974), p. 12.

2. Natsume Soseki, *The Three Cornered World*, trans. Alan Turney (Chicago: Henry Regnery, 1965), p. iii.

3. William P. Malm, "The Modern Music of Meiji Japan," in Donald H. Shively, ed., *Tradition and Modernization in Japanese Culture* (Princeton: Princeton University Press, 1971), p. 300.

4. Arthur E. Tiedemann, "Big Business and Politics in Prewar Japan," in James W. Morley, ed., *Dilemmas of Growth in Prewar Japan* (Princeton: Princeton University Press, 1971), pp. 278–79.

5. Quoted in Donald Keene, ed., *Modern Japanese Literature: An Anthology* (New York: Grove Press, 1956), p. 20.

6. Hagiwara Sakutarō, *Face at the Bottom of the World and Other Poems*, trans. Graeme Wilson (Rutland, Vt. and Tokyo: Charles E. Tuttle, 1969), p. 51.

7. Arthur Waley, *Yüan Mei, Eighteenth Century Chinese Poet* (New York: Grove Press, 1956), p. 150.

8. Tetsuo Najita, "Some Reflections on Idealism in the Political Thought of Yoshino Sakuzō," in Bernard Silberman and H. D. Harootunian, eds., *Japan in Crisis: Essays on Taishō Democracy* (Princeton: Princeton University Press, 1974), p. 40.

國民黨之中國

軍閥主義之日本與

第二次世界大戰

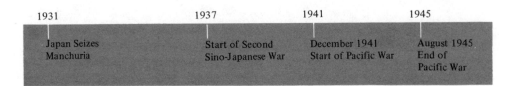

1931	1937	1941	1945
Japan Seizes Manchuria	Start of Second Sino-Japanese War	December 1941 Start of Pacific War	August 1945 End of Pacific War

22

Nationalist China, Militarist Japan, and the Second World War

For much of the world the 1930s were bleak and somber years. In the capitalist nations of the West, the Great Depression ushered in an economic crisis that deepened the rifts in society and threatened existing institutions. In the Soviet Union, struggling to catch up with the West economically, the decade was marred by the brutalities of forced collectivization and Stalin's purge trials. To many people desperate for vigorous action, dictatorship of one kind or another seemed the most effective way of pulling a nation together, and it was not in Italy and Germany alone that fascism was viewed as a non-Communist means to achieve national unity and greatness. The crisis of Western democracy was not lost on observers in East Asia, where traditions of liberal constitutionalism were shallow at best.

During most of the decade those nations which preserved democratic government were preoccupied with domestic problems and the strongest, the United States, was committed to a policy of isolationism. International statesmanship was at a low ebb; national leaders gave only lip service to the principles of collective security embodied in the League of Nations. The weakness of the League was first revealed by its failure to mount an adequate response to Japan's seizure of Manchuria in 1931; the League's condemnation of Japan for aggression was not followed by sanctions. Those who had relied on the community of nations to provide collective security had been proved wrong. Japan withdrew from the League (1933), and China realized that it could not expect aid from that quarter. The League itself emerged from the episode seriously damaged; the lesson was not lost on Hitler or Mussolini.

The Manchurian Incident and Its Aftermath

Party government as it developed in the 1920s derived its legitimacy from the emperor, but there were those in Japan who believed that it was failing its sacred trust. In the name of the emperor, the enemies of constitutional government criticized the political manipulations of the Diet leaders, their ties with business, and the lackluster conduct of foreign affairs—especially the policy of accommodation with the West and conciliation of China, exemplified by the Washington Conference of 1921–22. These sentiments animated the members of various patriotic organizations in Japan. They also prevailed in the army, which considered itself an independent agent of the imperial will and resented cuts made in its budget during the twenties. In the army, dissatisfaction with the political ethos and government policies was thus combined with resentment against restrictions imposed by a civilian government and a sense of a separate mission for which the army was responsible to the emperor alone.

Among the most vehement critics of party government were radical egalitarians like Kita Ikki, who favored nationalizing industry, and radical agrarians like Gondo Saikyo (1866–1937), who would have abolished industry altogether and returned Japan to rural simplicity. Although their visions of the future might differ, such men agreed on two things: that the existing government obtruded on the imperial will and must be swept away, and that Japan had a divine mission overseas.

Such ideas formed the rallying point for small societies of extremists given to direct action. Some, like the Cherry Society, which planned an unsuccessful military coup in Tokyo in March 1931, were composed entirely of army officers, none higher in rank than lieutenant colonel. Indeed, the army was a major source of extreme right-wing patriotic discontent. When the government lost control of the army, the gates to imperialist adventurism were flung open.

The assassination of the Manchurian warlord Chang Tso-lin in 1928 was the work of men such as these. They hoped that Chang's murder would lead to a war in which this vast, strategically important and potentially wealthy area would be conquered for Japan. The attempt failed, but the extremists were not discouraged. Indeed, another attempt in this direction appealed to the superpatriots, not only because it might gain Manchuria, but also because it would strengthen their support in the army, increase the army's power and popularity at home, and undermine the government by political parties they so detested. For these champions of a "Shōwa Restoration" felt that party government was a betrayal of the divine emperor, whom they regarded as the very embodiment of Japan's "national polity" (*kokutai*), a term which became an "incantatory symbol,"[1] all the more powerful for being rather vague.

The shift of attention to Manchuria was consistent with the aggressive Pan-Asianism popular in "patriotic" circles. Others, in the army and also in the Seiyūkai, were well disposed toward overseas expansion under army auspices. In the fall of 1931 the time seemed ripe, for China was hampered by floods in the Yangtze Valley, and the Western powers were neutralized by the depression.

The seizure of Manchuria was masterminded by officers below general rank serving with the Kwantung Army on the Liaotung Peninsula. It was these officers, none with a rank higher than colonel, who fabricated an excuse for hostilities: a supposed Chinese attempt to sabotage the South Manchuria Railway Company. And they saw to it that the fighting continued until the army controlled the entire area. Although certain high army officials in Tokyo very likely knew of the plot, it was carried out without the knowledge, let alone the authorization, of the civilian government in Tokyo, which, once informed, tried to halt the operations but found itself powerless to do so. An attempted military coup in Tokyo in October did not immediately topple the government but did succeed in intimidating civilian political leaders. The Wakatsuki government, divided and helpless, resigned in December. It was followed by a Seiyūkai government under Inukai Ki (1855–1932), which for another half year tried to maintain a semblance of party control.

Events moved swiftly on the continent and at home. In Manchuria the army consolidated its hold and established a puppet state, which early in 1932 declared its independence from China. Manchukuo, as it was known, was placed under the titular rule of P'u-yi who, as an infant, had been the last emperor of China, but it was actually the army's domain. Meanwhile the fighting had spread to China proper; for six strenuous weeks, Japanese and Chinese fought around Shanghai until a truce was finally arranged. Japanese efforts to make a general settlement with China and obtain recognition of Manchukuo were rebuffed, and, condemned by the League of Nations, Japan found herself isolated in world diplomacy. In May 1933 Japan and China concluded a truce that left Japanese troops in control of the area they had seized in China north of the Great Wall, but this did not prevent Japanese soldiers from interfering in the adjacent Chinese demilitarized area nor from exerting continuous pressure in that area. The arrangement lasted for an uneasy four years, but a truce is not a peace, nor necessarily even a prelude to peace, as became clear when full-scale war broke out in the summer of 1937. In the meantime in Manchuria, and now also in Korea, the Japanese concentrated on the development of heavy industry, building up an industrial base on the continent under army control.

At home, 1932 was also an eventful year as members of the patriotic societies continued to implement their schemes by assassinating prominent men, including the head of the house of Mitsui. On May 15 they raided the Tokyo power station, a bank, Seiyūkai headquarters, and the official residence of the prime minister. They failed to provoke a military takeover but did succeed in killing Inukai and bringing an end to party cabinets. The next two cabinets, in office from May 1932 to March 1936, did include party men but were headed by admirals, who were considered more moderate than certain potential prime ministers from the army.

Japanese Domestic Politics and the Road to War

When the fanatic and inexperienced men who staged the May 15 incident were brought to trial, they were treated with great respect. They were allowed to expound their doctrines for days at a time and given a national podium from which to proclaim the selflessness of their patriotic motives. In this way they largely succeeded in creating for themselves an image of martyrdom that won considerable public support. The light sentences that were meted out after the trials were at last completed further discouraged those who hoped for a return to civilian rule. The political parties continued to function, and in 1936 the leftist Social Mass Party managed to win half a million votes. The following year that party's total climbed to 900,000 votes, and it captured 37 seats in the lower house of the Diet. In that same election the Seiyūkai and Minseitō together polled some 7 million votes, giving them 354 out of a total of 466 seats. But their showing in the polls was to little avail. The parties were too weak to serve as a counterweight to the military. Those who wished to preserve constitutional government chose to compromise with the military establishment in the hope of averting a complete overthrow of the existing order, as envisioned by the military extremists. Those who compromised included Saionji, last of the *genrō,* who also hoped to protect the throne from involvement in divisive politics.

In this situation the most important immediate issue concerned not the balance between military and civilian power so much as the control of the military itself, for the actions in Manchuria and the violence at home demonstrated not only the decline of civilian control but highlighted a breakdown in military discipline made possible by the lack of unity within the army. The lines of army factionalism were very complex; for example, there was a division between those officers who studied at the Central War College and those who attended officers' training school. However, two main groups stood out. The more extreme faction, led by Generals Araki Sadao (1877–1966) and Mazaki Jinzaburō (1876–1956), was known as the *kōdōha* or "Imperial Way faction," since it emphasized the imperial mystique and advocated an ill-defined doctrine of direct imperial rule. Like the radical civilian theorists of the right, it opposed existing political and economic institutions, but it placed its faith not in institutional change but in a moral and spiritual transformation which would assure a glorious future for both army and country. In contrast the *tōseiha*, or "Control faction," led by General Nagata Tetsuzan (1884–1935), was much more ready to work with the *zaibatsu* and bureaucracy in order to turn Japan into a modern militarist state prepared for total war. Both factions envisioned a forceful foreign policy, but the *kōdōha* put greater stress on fighting communism and therefore was more adamantly opposed to the U.S.S.R. than were the more pragmatic *tōseiha* leaders.

For a few years after late 1931, the advantage lay with the Imperial Way faction, but it suffered a setback in 1935 when General Mazaki was dismissed from his post as director-general of military education. A lieutenant colonel retaliated by assassinating General Nagata, and the Control faction reacted to this by arresting the officer and laying plans for the transfer of other firebrands to Manchuria. The lieutenant colonel's trial was still in progress when, on February 26, 1936, a group of junior *kōdōha* officers, commanding over _ ... nd men, seized the center of the capital and killed a number of prominent ac ; although some of their intended victims managed to elude them, including Admiral Okada Keisuke (1868–1952), the prime minister, who escaped by a fluke (his brother-in-law, who looked like Okada, was killed instead). The young officers hoped that their action would bring down the old system and that generals Araki and Mazaki would take the lead in restructuring the state, but these senior generals remained aloof. As in 1928, the emperor intervened, and the navy responded to the crisis with vigor. On the third day of the insurrection, the rebels surrendered. This time the leaders were tried rapidly and in secret. One of those who perished at the hands of a firing squad was Kita Ikki, who had not participated in the mutiny but was too closely associated with the young officers and their movement to escape punishment.

The elimination of the Imperial Way faction left the Control faction in command of the army and increased the army's power in government, since it could now threaten a second mutiny if it did not get its way. One consequence of these events was a substantial increase in the military budget for the army and navy. Japan now withdrew from the naval limitation agreement. This opened the possibility that she might have to compete with the combined might of the Western powers and the U.S.S.R. To cope with the latter, Japan signed, in December 1936, an anti-Comintern pact with Germany.

Domestically there ensued an intensification of propaganda and indoctrination, coupled with a continuation of repression directed at the radical left and also victimizing those whose ardor for emperor and national polity (*kokutai*) was deemed insufficient. The most notorious case took place in 1935 when Minobe, the distinguished legal theorist, was charged with demeaning the emperor by considering him merely "the highest organ of the state." Minobe defended himself with spirit but was forced to resign from the House of Peers. Even then, in 1936 while living in seclusion, the old man suffered an attempt on his life which left him wounded. By that time his books had been banned. Censorship increased in severity, and expressions of intense national chauvinism filled the media.

The abandonment of the gold standard and the military buildup largely paid for by deficit financing enabled Japan to recover from the depth of the depression, but agriculture remained depressed and small firms benefited much less than did the *zaibatsu*. The international situation was also very problematic. The great powers refused to recognize Manchukuo or agree that Japan was entitled to an Asian version of the Monroe doctrine. Nor was anyone able to devise a formula regarding China acceptable to both the Japanese army and the Chinese government.

During 1936, the Chiang Kai-shek government, as noted below, showed a new firmness in its attitude toward Japan, whose army, after the conquest of Manchuria, was steadily moving into "autonomous zones" in North China. Until the summer of 1937, Japanese pressure was primarily economic and political, but there was the danger than an unplanned military incident might escalate into a major war. This is, in effect, what happened after a clash between Chinese and Japanese soldiers in July on the Marco Polo Bridge outside Peking, when the Chinese drew the line and refused further concessions. The ensuing hostilities signified the beginnings of a war that in 1941 became part of an even more extensive and destructive war (the Second World War), although this is not what the Japanese intended in 1937.

China under the Nationalists

For a decade, from 1927 to 1937, the Nationalist government in Nanking maintained peace with Japan, but it was, as we have seen, a tenuous peace made possible by concessions and requiring military preparedness to resist further demands. Underlying the initial policy of appeasing Japan was the conviction on the part of Chiang Kai-shek and the Kuomintang leadership that China's most pressing need was for internal unification, for even after the completion of the northern expedition in 1928, the government actually controlled only the lower Yangtze Valley. Elsewhere it was dependent on the questionable, self-serving allegiance of local power holders.

In 1930, in a costly campaign with heavy casualties on both sides, the government defeated the combined warlord armies of Feng Yü-hsiang and Yen Hsi-shan and thereby secured its authority in the North. Nanking was strengthened by this victory but lacked the power to subdue the remaining warlords once and for all. Instead it temporized with them, tried to prevent the formation of antigovernment warlord coalitions, and settled for expressions of warlord allegiance until such time as it could establish central control. The power and prestige of the Nanking regime were increased when it defeated a rebellion in Fukien in 1933–34, and especially after it obtained control over Kwangtung and the submission of Kwangsi in 1936. Its campaigns against the

Communists (see below) provided occasions for the dispatch of central government troops into warlord provinces, especially after the Communists began their Long March in 1934, and similarly the Japanese threat proved useful in eventually bringing certain warlords into line. Thus the trend was in favor of Nanking, but the actual balance between central and local power varied widely in different parts of China. The tenacity of the warlord phenomenon in certain regions is illustrated by Szechwan, in parts of which warlords remained powerful even after the Nationalists moved their wartime capital to that province. Similarly, remote western provinces such as Sinkiang remained virtually autonomous.

The need to unify the country and to withstand the menace of Japan, as well as his own background, were among the factors influencing Chiang Kai-shek to make the military his first priority. This was reflected in the government's expenditures, for its budgets consistently favored the army. Military considerations were paramount also in such projects as road and railway construction. Taking the place of the ousted Russian military advisors were a series of German military men, who tried to introduce German military doctrines (including concepts of military organization not necessarily suitable to the Chinese situation) and also helped to arrange for the import of German arms and munitions. In 1935, at the height of their influence, there were seventy German advisors in China. After the anti-Comintern pact between Germany and Japan, their number decreased until the last men were recalled in 1938. Noteworthy within the army were the graduates of the Whampoa Military Academy, particularly those who completed the course during Chiang Kai-shek's tenure as director, for they enjoyed an especially close relationship with their supreme commander.

It was also Whampoa graduates who during 1931 formed the Blue Shirts, a secret police group pledged to complete obedience to Chiang Kai-shek. They and the so-called CC clique (led by two Ch'en brothers trusted by Chiang) were influenced in ideology and organization by European fascism. The Blue Shirts were greatly feared because of their spying and terrorist activities, including assassinations. The CC clique, too, had considerable power but it failed in its prime aim, which was to revitalize the Kuomintang. After the split with the Communists, the KMT purged many of its own most dedicated revolutionaries. This discouraged those who remained from entertaining potentially dangerous ideas and created an atmosphere attractive to men who, concentrating on their own personal careers, would not rock the boat.

The deterioration of the party was a particularly serious matter because the Nanking government suffered from factional politics and favoritism as well as from bureaucratic overorganization, which spawned departments with overlapping functions and countless committees grinding out lengthy reports and recommendations, detailing programs that consumed vast quantities of paper but were rarely implemented. Coordination was poor. It sometimes happened, for example, that government censors suppressed news items deliberately issued by the government itself. The conduct of official business lumbered along unless quickened by the personal intervention of Chiang Kai-shek, whose power was steadily on the increase. It was power based on the loyalty of the military and the Blue Shirts, core partisans such as the CC clique, the financial backing of bankers and businessmen (including the relatives of Chiang's wife), and on a semblance of balance of various political cliques and factions manipulated by Chiang himself. It was a power that made Chiang indispensable to government, but he lacked the charisma to inspire his officials, who feared rather than loved him. Nor did he have the gift of eloquence with which to rouse the people had he so desired. Negative sanctions, such as the executions sporadically ordered by Chiang when an exceptionally flagrant case of corruption was brought to his attention, were not enough: the regime lacked drive and direction.

One problem was that the regime was ideologically weak. Sun Yat-sen became the object of an official cult, but his ideas were not further refined or developed. Instead emphasis was shifted toward a revival of Confucianism. In contrast to Sun's admiration for the Taipings, Chiang sought to emulate Tseng Kuo-fan, who in his day had successfully stemmed a revolution by revitalizing Confucian values. Chiang's regard for Confucius and Tseng was already apparent during his days at Whampoa but became even more obvious in 1934 when he launched an extensive program to foster traditional values known as the New Life movement. This movement exhorted the populace to observe four vaguely defined Confucian virtues and spelled out the criteria for proper behavior in detailed instructions. The people were to sit and stand straight, eat quietly, refrain from indiscriminate spitting, and so forth, in the hope that they would thus acquire discipline. It did not work. Officials and commoners continued to act much as before. The government never did devise an ideology able to arouse the enthusiasm of its own personnel, command the respect of the people, or convince intellectuals. Censorship clearly was not the answer, although even foreign correspondents were subjected to it, some complaining that it was worse in China than in Japan.

Ineffectiveness also characterized Nationalist economic policies, as when exports were subjected to the same tariffs as imports, and the imports of raw material were taxed as heavily as those of finished goods. Thus China's industry failed to draw much profit from the government's success when, during 1928 and 1929, it at last regained the tariff autonomy China had lost in the Opium War. It was the modern sector of the economy that supplied the great bulk of Nanking's revenue in a period when military expenses and debt service added up to between 60 and 80 percent of the government's annual expenditures. But despite its early links with the business community, the Kuomintang regime retained the traditional government attitude toward private business as a source to be exploited for revenue rather than as an asset to be fostered as a component of national strength. In 1933, embroiled in heavy borrowing from the banks, the government took control of the banking system in a move which benefited the treasury but not the modern private sector. Overall, the modern sector did grow during the decade but only at roughly the same pace as during the years between the fall of the Ch'ing and the establishment of the regime in Nanking.

During the early thirties the traditional agrarian sector of the economy, which accounted for most of China's production and employed the vast majority of its people, was sorely hurt by the fall of prices produced by the depression. The agrarian sector was further afflicted by severe weather conditions, including the Yangtze flood of 1931, and by the exactions of the tax collector who piled surtax on surtax (later changed to special assessments), with the result that the taxes on agriculture continued to increase despite the decline in farm prices. Taxation, like the climate, varied widely, making generalization very risky. Even in the same province, the tax burden paid by one district was often much more than that paid by another, and this was true even in provinces like Kiangsu and Chekiang, which were firmly controlled by the government. The same difficulty applies to attempts to generalize about the prevalence or burdens of tenancy, which was much more frequent in the south than in the north. Nevertheless, since the government did nothing to change the status quo in the village and on the land, the poorest and the weakest suffered most. Like so much legislation promulgated during those years, the law passed in 1930 limiting rents to $37^1/_2$ percent of the harvest was not enforced. Payments of 50 percent were common and 60 percent was not unusual. Programs for developing cooperatives and fostering rural reconstruction were organized, but their benefits rarely filtered down to the rural poor. In 1937 there was a price recovery, and harvests were good, but by that time millions had suffered bitter poverty and despair.

Chiang Kai-shek and his supporters wanted to unify the country and to stabilize society. They wished to consolidate the revolution that had brought them into power, not to expand it. Therefore they put a premium on suppressing those forces which would lead to further and continued revolution. The regime was intent on destroying communism and the Communists, who maintained that the revolution was unfinished and proclaimed their readiness to lead it to completion. To Chiang Kai-shek nothing was more urgent than the elimination, once and for all, of his old enemies, the Chinese Communist Party. For the CCP too these were crucial years.

The Chinese Communists (1927–1934)

The Shanghai massacre and the subsequent suppression of the CCP and its associated labor movement had effectively eliminated the party as an urban force and thereby altered its geographical distribution and profoundly affected its strategy and leadership. For some years it remained unclear just what direction the movement would take. Neither the Comintern nor its Chinese followers was willing simply to write off the cities. After urban insurrection failed, as in the Canton Commune established for four days in December 1927 and greeted by the populace with profound apathy, an attempt was made to capture cities by armed force, as in the case of Changsha in Hunan in 1930. But this also failed. Although no one was ready to say so, at least in public, Moscow clearly did not have the formula for success. Meanwhile in China various groups and factions contended for power and the adoption of their policies.

One of these groups was the CCP military force, which underwent a crucial reorganization in the Chingkang Mountains on the Hunan-Kiangsi border, where, in the spring of 1928, Chu Teh (1886–1976) joined Mao Tse-tung, who had arrived the previous fall. In command of some 2000 troops, the two leaders laid the groundwork for the Red Army, with Chu Teh taking military command and Mao in charge of political organization and indoctrination. As Mao was to say in 1938: "Political power grows out of the barrel of a gun. Our principle is that the Party commands the gun; the gun shall never be allowed to command the Party."[2] Through indoctrination, the recruitment of soldiers into the party, and the formation of soldiers' committees, Mao secured the control of the party over the army, while on the military side Chu and Mao emphasized guerrilla warfare, which put a premium on mobility and surprise, rapid retreats to avoid battle with superior enemy forces, lightning strikes to pick off small contingents of the enemy, and constant harassment to keep the enemy off balance. Essential to this type of warfare is popular support to provide intelligence, supplies, and recruits, as well as cover for guerrillas under enemy pursuit. Peasant participation and support were secured by redistributing land and furthering the revolution in the countryside.

This strategy focused on the development and expansion of rural CCP controlled bases, and in the early thirties there were a number of such areas. The largest were in Kiangsi, where in December 1931 the founding of the Chinese Soviet Republic was proclaimed. The basic agrarian policy was "land to the tiller," involving the confiscation of large holdings and their reassignment to the poor, with "middle peasants" left largely unaffected, but there was a good deal of disagreement over definitions as well as wide variations in the degree of local implementation of the program. During the Kiangsi period, Mao and Chu were influential leaders, but they had by no means won complete acceptance of either their programs or their leadership, even after party headquarters were moved to Kiangsi from Shanghai, a shift which signified recognition of the new power center in the CCP and a defeat for those oriented toward the Comintern in Moscow. Factionalism continued to undermine party unity, but the most severe challenge was external.

Chiang Kai-shek's first three "annihilation campaigns" came in 1930–31 and helped strengthen rather than weaken the CCP as the Red Army employed its tactics to good effect and captured weapons, men, and land. The fourth campaign, 1932–33, again ended in defeat for the Nationalists. In the fifth campaign, begun late in 1933, Chiang, on German advice, changed his strategy. Deploying some 750,000 men supported by 150 airplanes, he surrounded the Kiangsi Soviet and gradually tightened the circle of his blockade. When in the fall of 1934 their situation became untenable, the Communist forces abandoned their Kiangsi base, broke through a point in the KMT blockade manned by former warlord armies, and began their Long March. (See map, Figure 22-1.)

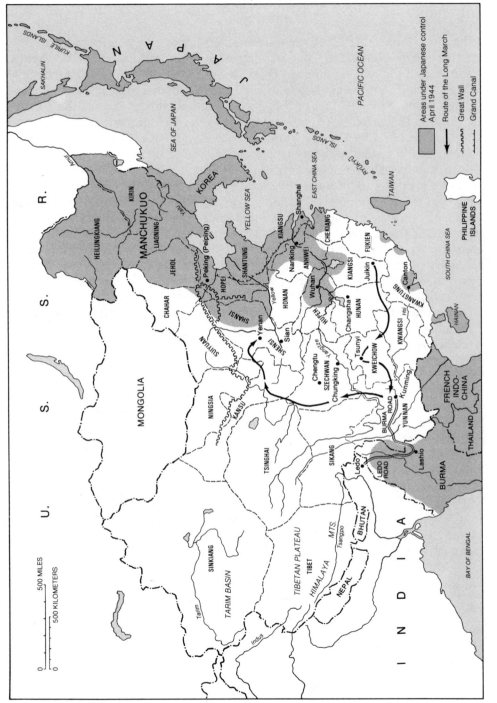

Figure 22-1 **China, 1930–Spring 1944**

(For Japan's maximum occupation of China, see Figure 22-4.)

The Long March

When the Communists left Kiangsi, their first priority was survival, and their destination was not clear. That was settled at an important conference held at Tsunyi in Kweichow in January 1935, when it was decided to proceed to Shensi, where a small soviet was already in existence. In Shensi the CCP would be out of easy reach of the KMT armies. They would be able to act on their earlier declaration of war against Japan and might even hope for some assistance from the U.S.S.R. At the Tsunyi conference Mao gained a new prominence, although he did not actually control the party until the forties.

The march itself, was a heroic accomplishment, a vindication of Mao's belief in the power of the human will and determination. In just over a year, the marchers covered some 6000 miles, traversing snow-covered mountain passes where they froze in their thin clothes and crossing treacherous bogs and marshes. To the hardships provided by nature was added the hostility of man, for there was rarely a day without some fighting. At one point they had no alternative but to cross a mountain torrent spanned by a thirteen-chain suspension bridge from which the enemy, armed and waiting on the other side, had removed the planks.

A terrible ordeal was the six- or seven-day crossing of the grasslands of Chunghai in the Chinese-Tibetan border region. Here heavy rainfall and poor drainage had created a waterlogged plain in which green grass grew on multiple layers of rotting grass beneath. First a vanguard was sent to chart the way, and in the central grasslands they could find no place dry enough to sleep so the men had to remain standing all night long, leaning against each other. The rest of the army followed through the slippery, treacherous terrain, trudging on despite hunger and fatigue, trying to ward off rain and hail and survive the unbearable cold of the nights. Since the men carried only a very small amount of grain, they subsisted mostly on wild grasses and vegetables eaten raw because there was no firewood for cooking. Sometimes the vegetables turned out to be poisonous, and the stagnant water reportedly smelled of horse's urine.

The marchers succeeded in overcoming this and other obstacles but at great cost. Of about 100,000 who set out from Kiangsi, less than 10 percent completed the march. Some were left behind to work in various areas, but many more perished. The loss was only partially offset by new recruits who joined along the way. After completion of the march, including the men already in Shensi, the Communists were about 20,000 strong.

The survivors of the march emerged toughened and filled with a sense of solidarity forged by shared hardships and common suffering. There was also a heightened self-confidence, a conviction that the movement would surmount all obstacles. Something of this spirit is conveyed in a poem Mao wrote shortly before reaching Shensi:

> Lofty the sky
>   and pale the clouds—
> We watch the wild geese
>   fly south till they vanish.

> We count the thousand
>   leagues already travelled.
> If we do not reach
>   the Great Wall we are not true men.
>
> High on the crest
>   of Liup'an Mountain
> Our banners billow
>   in the west wind.
> Today we hold
>   the long rope in our hands.
> When shall we put bonds
>   upon the grey dragon?[3]

The saga of the Long March continued to be celebrated in poetry and prose. It remains today a source of heroic inspiration.

United Front and War

With the Communists in Shensi, Chiang remained as determined as ever to crush them, but their call for a united front against Japan had special appeal for the troops of Marshal Chang Hsüeh-liang, son of Chang Tso-lin, the former warlord of Manchuria. Although assigned to the task, Chang's forces were less than enthusiastic in fighting the CCP. To breathe some life into the anti-Communist campaign, Chiang Kai-shek flew to Sian in December. But he had misjudged the situation. Instead of pledging themselves to renewed anti-Communist efforts, Marshal Chang and some of his men seized Chiang Kai-shek and held him prisoner for two weeks while his fate was being negotiated. Exactly what transpired is not clear, but, after Communist intercession, Chiang was finally released, having agreed to terminate his campaign against the Communists and lead a united front against Japan. He was at the time China's most distinguished military man, the leader of the government recognized as legitimate at home and abroad, the heir to the mantle of Sun Yat-sen. Even his enemies saw him as the only man possessing the political, military, and ideological authority to lead China in an effort to stop the Japanese.

The Sian incident led to the formation of a united front in 1937. Following the KMT's 1936 success against Kwangtung and Kwangsi, formation of the united front was viewed with dismay by Japanese army officers intent on dominating North China. As already noted, matters came to a head after the Marco Polo Bridge clash in early July 1937. This rapidly expanded into large-scale fighting. By the end of July the Japanese were in possession of Peking and Tientsin, and in August Japanese forces attacked Shanghai, where Chiang used some of his best German trained troops in three months of bloody fighting, with heavy casualties. After Shanghai came Nanking, which fell in December, followed by the notorious "Rape of Nanking," during which Japanese soldiers terrorized the inhabitants, killing and raping, burning and looting, leaving an estimated 100,000 dead. The Japanese acquired a reputation for terrible cruelty, which stiffened the determination of the Chinese people to resist.

Japan's prime minister at this time was Prince Konoe Fumimaro (1891–1945), a descendant of the Fujiwaras and protégé of Saionji. He was to hold office from June 1937 to January 1939 and from July 1940 to July 1941. Japanese policy making continued to be a very complicated process, since there was no centralized, coordinated, long-range planning. The general staff, for example, did not share the optimism of the armies in the field, yet the government continued to expand the war, encouraged by a string of victories. As the war escalated so did the Japanese government's aims and rhetoric. What had begun as a search for a pro-Japanese North China turned into a holy crusade against the West and Communism. Unable to obtain Chinese recognition of Manchukuo, the Konoe government in 1938 declared Chiang's regime illegitimate and vowed to destroy it. Japanese troops continued their advance, taking Canton in October, Wuhan in December. Chiang still showed no inclination to submit. In November Konoe proclaimed Japan's determination to establish a "New Order in East Asia" to include Japan, Manchukuo, and China in a political, economic, and cultural union, a bastion against (Western) imperialism and against Soviet Communism. Those who did not see the light were to be brought to their senses by force. The military fracas of July 1937 had been transformed into a holy war suffused with a mystic belief in Japan's mission to create a new East Asia.

By this time the Nationalist government, following a strategy of "trading space for time," had moved its capital to Chungking in Szechwan, where it was joined by many refugees from occupied China. Not only universities but hundreds of factories were transported piecemeal to the wartime capital to help produce for the war effort. In Chungking, Chiang held on gamely, on the defensive. Before the Japanese attack on Pearl Harbor, the Chinese did obtain some financial assistance from outside, and beginning in August 1941, they were also aided by the Flying Tigers, volunteer American pilots later incorporated into the Fourteenth U.S. Air Force, commanded by General Claire L. Chennault. However, the West's support remained primarily moral, and the U.S.S.R. alone sent some official assistance. Although Chungking suffered repeated bombings during 1939–41, at the battlefront these two years were marked by skirmishes rather than massive campaigns, as both sides worked to consolidate their positions. In 1940 the Japanese established a puppet regime in Nanking headed by Wang Ching-wei, the erstwhile follower of Sun Yat-sen and leader of the left wing of the KMT.

Expansion of the War into a Pacific War

A major Japanese foreign policy concern during the thirties was Japanese relations with the U.S.S.R. During 1938–39 there were several military clashes in the border area along Russia's frontier with Korea and Manchukuo. In these operations, quite large in scale and involving the deployment of armor, Japan was not successful. Furthermore, the Japanese were caught off guard diplomatically when Germany, without any warning, came to terms with the Soviet Union in August 1939. Japan was therefore neutral when the Second World War began in Europe shortly afterward. However, the dramatic success of the German blitzkrieg strengthened the hands of those in Tokyo who favored a pro-German policy, and in September 1940, Konoe signed the Tripartite Pact forming an alliance with Germany and Italy.

The Germans again surprised the Japanese in June 1941 when Hitler invaded Russia. While some in Japan maintained that Japan should join the attack on the U.S.S.R., others argued that, with the Soviet Union preoccupied in Europe, the time was ripe for Japan to move into oil- and mineral-rich Southeast Asia and thereby advance its mission, now expanded into the creation of a "Greater East Asia Co-Prosperity Sphere." Without the resources of Southeast Asia, it was argued, Japan would never achieve naval supremacy in the Pacific.

Konoe hoped that, armed with the Tripartite Pact, he would be able to reach his aims without going to war with the United States, but the American government was becoming increasingly alarmed over Japanese expansion. When in the summer of 1941 Japan moved troops into southern Indo-China, the United States, Britain, and Holland (then in control of the East Indies, modern Indonesia) retaliated by applying the economic sanctions they had withheld in 1931. The principal and crucial product cut off from Japan by this action was oil.

The United States was now determined that Japan should withdraw from China as well as Indo-China. For Japan this would have meant a reversal of the policy pursued in China since 1931 and the relinquishment of the vision of Japanese primacy in East Asia. Dependent on oil and rubber from Southeast Asia, the Japanese were in no position to carry on protracted negotiations. Their choice was to fight or retreat. When it became clear to Konoe that the situation had reached an impasse, he resigned, to be followed by General Tōjō Hideki (1884–1948), prime minister from October 1941 to July 1944. (See Figure 22-2.) When last minute negotiations proved fruitless, the Japanese decided on war as the least unpalatable alternative. It began on December 7, 1941, with a surprise attack on Pearl Harbor, in Hawaii, which destroyed 7 American battleships and 120 aircraft, and left 2400 dead.

China During the War

The conviction that eventually the United States would enter the war against Japan sustained Chiang Kai-shek during the long years when China faced Japan virtually alone. When as a result of Pearl Harbor this did happen, it naturally buoyed the spirit of the Chinese, now allied to the one country powerful enough to crush Japan. More material forms of support were also soon forthcoming, although there was never enough because in 1942 Japan cut off the government's last land route to its allies by seizing Burma and closing the Burma Road. Thereafter, supplies had to be flown in from India to Yunnan over

Figure 22-2 General Tōjō.

the Himalaya Mountains (the "hump"). In addition, China ranked low in the American war effort. The Allies decided first to concentrate on the defeat of Germany, and the island-hopping strategy adopted against Japan largely by-passed China, although the Allies appreciated the fact that China tied down vast numbers of Japanese troops that otherwise might have been used elsewhere.

The top American military man in China was General Joseph Stilwell, who in 1942 became Chiang's chief-of-staff as well as commander of American forces in the China-Burma-India theater. Stilwell was a fine soldier but no diplomat. He had high regard for the ordinary Chinese fighting man but scarcely concealed his irritation and impatience with the inefficiencies and corruption he encountered in Chungking, and his disgust at Chiang's policy of preparing for a postwar showdown with the CCP rather than joining in a single-minded effort against the Japanese enemy. The relationship between the two men deteriorated until Chiang requested and received Stilwell's recall in 1944.

Stilwell was replaced by General Albert Wedemeyer, who was more friendly to Chiang, but also was critical of conditions in the Chinese army, which were, by all accounts, horrendous. Induction was tantamount to a death sentence. Those who could possibly afford to do so bribed the conscription officer. The remainder were marched off, bound together with ropes, to join their units, often many miles and days away. Underfed and exhausted, many recruits never completed the trip. Those who did found that food was equally scarce at the front and medical services almost completely lacking.

Misery and corruption were not unique to the military. Even in times of famine (as in Honan during 1942–43) peasants were sorely oppressed by the demands of the landlord and the tax collector, while the urban middle class suffered from mounting inflation. This had already reached an annual rate of 40 to 50 percent between 1937 and 1939, climbed to 160 percent for 1939–42, and mounted to an average of 300 percent for 1942–45. By 1943 the real value in terms of purchasing power of the salaries paid to bureaucrats was only one-tenth what they had received in 1937, while teachers were down to 5 percent of their former earnings. The result was widespread demoralization of the Chinese military and civilian populations under Nationalist control. The secret police were unable to root out corruption. Government exhortations and the publication of Chiang Kai-shek's book *China's Destiny* (1943) did not suffice to reinvigorate ideological commitment to the government and the KMT.

A major reason for the wartime deterioration of the KMT was that Japan's seizure of the eastern seaboard and China's major cities had deprived the Nationalists of their usual sources of support, the great business centers of east China. In Szechwan they became critically dependent on the local landlords, precisely the elements in society that were most resistant to change and reform. Moreover, Chiang was unwilling to commit his troops to battle with the Japanese more than was absolutely necessary, or to do anything which might strengthen the armies of the CCP, because he was convinced that after the war with Japan there would be an all-out confrontation with the Communists that would determine China's future. As a consequence, he missed whatever opportunity might have existed for building a modern Chinese force with American assistance, and for translating anti-Japanese nationalism into support for his own regime.

The shortcomings of the Chungking government were highlighted by the accomplishments of the Communists, headquartered in Yenan. (See Figure 22-3.) During the war years, from 1937 to 1945, the party expanded its membership from roughly forty thousand to over one million, and its troop strength increased tenfold to an estimated 900 thousand, not counting guerrillas and militiamen. Furthermore, the Communists enjoyed widespread peasant support in North China, where they established themselves as the effective government in the countryside behind the Japanese lines. The Japanese, concentrated in the cities and guarding their lines of supply, did not have the manpower to patrol the rural areas constantly and effectively.

In the areas nominally under Japanese control, the Communists were often able to fuse social revolution and national resistance, for example, redistributing to the peasants land owned by landlords collaborating with the Japanese. Similarly, the lands of men who had fled to KMT areas were available for reassignment. In accordance with arrangements under the united front, the CCP did not follow a radical program of land confiscation and redistribution, but by enforcing limits on rents and interest payments and by restructuring the tax system, they favored the poor. In addition, they reorganized village government so as to give the people a larger voice in decision making and formed mass organizations for such groups as women and young people. All of these steps had the effect of liberating important segments of the population from oppressive conditions of life. Poor peasant farmers were released from the exactions of landlord and tax collector; village government was freed from the tyranny of local landlords and elites; women and youth were liberated from the Confucian familial tradition. The result was a tremendous unleashing of new enthusiasms and, of course, support for the CCP. Thus, the Communists were succeeding precisely where Chiang and the KMT had failed.

The Communist role in providing effective resistance against the Japanese was particularly important in those areas which felt the full force of Japanese attempts to terrorize the countryside into submission, as in the notorious "kill all, burn all, destroy all" policy implemented in parts of North China in 1941 and 1942. Areas were selected where this policy was literally implemented, with the effect that previously apolitical peasants, equally distrustful of all government, were turned into determined fighters. The twin lessons of nationalism and revolution were further brought home to the people through indoctrination programs and, particularly, through a campaign to combat illiteracy, conveying new ideas to the peasantry even as it gave them access to the written word, shattering the old elite monopoly on learning.

The social and national policies attracted many; not only peasants but also intellectuals from the cities joined the Communists. To insure discipline and preserve the cohesion of the movement, swollen by new adherents, the party under Mao (now firmly established as leader) organized a rectification cam-

Figure 22-3   Yenan in 1960. After the Long March and during the war, the CCP leaders lived and worked in the Yenan caves.

paign to assure "correct" understanding of party ideology and to bring art and literature into line. Art for its own sake or for the purpose of self-expression was condemned, and those guilty of being insufficiently mass oriented were induced to confess their faults. Many were sent down to work in villages, factories, or battle zones to "learn from the masses."

From the war, the CCP emerged stronger than it had ever been before, although the outcome of the civil war that followed was by no means obvious to observers at the time (see below). It is one of the ironies of the war that the Japanese, who proclaimed that they were combating communism in China, instead contributed to its ultimate success.

Japan at War

Well before Pearl Harbor the effects of the continued war in China were felt by the Japanese people as militarization and authoritarianism increased at home. The National General Mobilization Law of 1938 strengthened the prime minister at the expense of the Diet, and the government began to place the economy on a war basis, with rationing, economic controls, and resource allocations. In October 1940, the political parties were merged into the Imperial Rule Assistance Association, which, however, did not become a mass popular party along the lines of European facism but served primarily as a vehicle for the dissemination of propaganda throughout Japan. Similarly labor unions were combined into a single patriotic organization. Great pressures were exerted to bring educational institutions and the public communications media into line so that the whole of Japan would speak with one collective voice. To effect the "spiritual mobilization" of the country, the government tried to purge Western influence from Japanese life. Not only were foreign liberal ideas banned, but such elements of popular culture as permanent waves and jazz, so popular during the twenties, were now suppressed. Efforts were made to remove Western loan words from the language, and the people were bombarded with exhortations to observe traditional values and revere the divine emperor. To mobilize the public down to the ward level, the people were formed into small neighborhood organizations.

Before the war was over the people were to suffer a great deal, but at first the war went spectacularly well for Japan. By the middle of 1942 Japan controlled the Philippines, Malaya, Burma, and the East Indies, and was assured of the cooperation of friendly regimes in Indo-China (controlled by Vichy France) and in Thailand. However, Japan's attempt to win over the population of the conquered areas by encouraging their native religious traditions, exploiting their resentment against Western imperialism, and teaching them the Japanese language was more than offset by Japan's own imperialistic exploitation, by the harshness of its rule, and by the cruelty of its soldiers, brutalized by the treatment meted out to them in the Japanese army. The slogan "Asia for the Asians" did not disguise the realities of Japanese rule.

In June 1942 Japan was checked at the battle of Midway. (See map, Figure 22-4.) The American use of aircraft based on carriers and the extensive employment of submarines, which took a tremendous toll of vital Japanese shipping, were two of the factors contributing to Japan's ultimate defeat. Another was the island-hopping strategy whereby the American forces seized islands selectively for use as bases for further advances, bypassing others with their Japanese forces intact but out of action. The closer the American forces came to the Japanese homeland, the easier it was for them to bomb Japan itself. Such raids were aimed not only at military and industrial installations, but also at economic targets and population centers. Incendiary bombs were dropped in order to sap the morale of the people, who by the last years of the war, were suffering from scarcities of all kinds, including food and other daily necessities, many of which were available only on the black market. The last year of the war was especially terrible; on one night in March 1945, some 100,000 people died as the result of a firebomb raid on Tokyo, and a similar raid in May devastated another large part of Japan's capital city. Short of resources, and with its cities in ruins, Japan during the last months of the war was reduced to desperate measures, such as the use of flying bombs directed by suicide pilots, called kamikaze after the "divine wind" that once had saved the land from the Mongols.

While internal propaganda persisted until the end in urging the people to ever greater efforts, it was clear to some political leaders that Japan could not win. After the fall of Saipan, largest of the Mariana Islands, General Tōjō was forced out of office in July 1944, but there was no change either in the fortunes of war or in policy under his successor General Koiso Kuniaki (1880–1950). Koiso remained in office until April 1945, when he was succeeded by Admiral Suzuki Kantaro (1867–1948). Some civilian leaders sent out peace feelers to the Allies, but their efforts were hampered by the noncooperation of the Soviet Union, anxious to have the war continue long enough to allow it to participate, and by the demand issued at Potsdam in July 1945, insisting on Japan's unconditional surrender. The demand for unconditional surrender reflected the Allied belief that it had been a mistake to allow the First World War to end in an armistice rather than in a full capitulation. The Allies felt that the armistice had permitted Hitler to claim that Germany had been "betrayed" into defeat, not beaten on the field of battle, and that he had been able to use this emotionally charged argument to generate the popular support that brought the Nazi party to power. Determined not to commit a similar mistake in the Second World War, the Allies demanded an unconditional surrender. But the insistence on an unconditional surrender actually stiffened Japanese resistance because it left the fate of the emperor in doubt, and this was impossible for the Japanese to accept.

The end came in August 1945. On August 6 the United States dropped an atomic bomb on Hiroshima (see Figure 22-5) in southwestern Honshū, razing over 80 percent of the buildings and leaving some 200,000 people dead or injured and countless others to continue their lives under the specter of radiation sickness. This holocaust added a new chapter to the horrors of war.

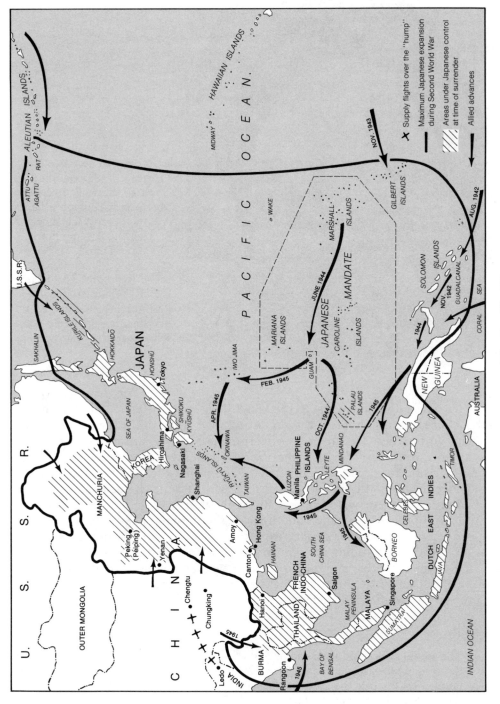

Figure 22-4 **The Pacific War**

Figure 22-5 Hiroshima. Through the vault over the Memorial Cenotaph for the Atomic Bomb Victims can be seen the Atomic Bomb Memorial Dome. The steel skeleton of the dome and the gutted building (formerly the city's Industrial Promotion Hall) have been left standing unaltered, in witness to the tragedy.

Two days later, on August 8, the U.S.S.R. entered the war, and on the ninth the United States dropped a second atomic bomb, this time on Nagasaki. Twice during these fateful days a government deadlock was broken by the personal intervention of the emperor, each time in favor of peace. Even after the final decision for peace, diehards tried to continue the war by a last resort to violence in the tradition of the terrorists who had first helped steer Japan toward militarism and war. They set fire to the homes of the prime minister and president of the privy council and invaded the imperial palace in search of the recording of the emperor's peace message, but they failed. When all was lost, several leaders, including the war minister, committed ritual suicide.

On August 15 the imperial recording was broadcast over the radio, and throughout Japan the people, for the first time, heard the voice of their emperor. In the formal language appropriate to his elevated status, he informed them that the war was lost. This is how Ōe Kenzaburō, ten years old at the time, recollects the impact of the broadcast:

> The adults sat around their radios and cried. The children gathered outside in the dusty road and whispered their bewilderment. We were most confused and disappointed by the fact that the Emperor had spoken in a *human* voice, no different from any adult's. None of us understood what he was saying, but we had all heard his voice. One of my friends could even imitate it cleverly. Laughing, we sur-

rounded him—a twelve year old in grimy shorts who spoke with the Emperor's voice. A minute later we felt afraid. We looked at one another; no one spoke. How could we believe that an august presence of such awful power had become an ordinary human voice on a designated summer day?[4]

East Asia at the End of the War

Defeat brought an end to the half century during which Japan was the dominant military and political power in East Asia. It marked the dissolution of the Japanese Empire, for Japan was made to relinguish not only Manchuria and other areas seized since 1931, but all gains since 1895. It thus opened a new phase in the history of Taiwan and Korea. The defeat of Japan also initiated a new phase in the history of South and Southeast Asia, where former colonies resisted the return of Western colonial masters. Indeed, it marked the beginning of the end of colonialism throughout the world.

For Japan itself defeat brought a sharp break with the past, for it thoroughly discredited the militarists who had brought the country to disaster, and it opened the way for new departures. For China, in contrast, the end of the war did not bring with it an immediate change, for there the shape of the future was still a subject of contention between forces locked in civil war. The end of the great war brought no peace to that long-suffering country. Nor would it permit a peaceful determination of the future of Korea and Vietnam.

On the broad international scene, the war left the United States and the Soviet Union as the two giant powers who maintained a presence in East Asia and had the capacity to influence events in that part of the world. And Hiroshima and Nagasaki had demonstrated just how dangerous a place that world could be.

NOTES

1. The term "incantatory symbol" comes from Masao Maruyama, in Ivan Morris, ed., *Thought and Behavior in Modern Japanese Politics,* Expanded edition (New York: Oxford University Press, 1969). p. 376.

2. Stuart R. Schram, *The Political Thought of Mao Tse-tung* (New York: Frederick A. Praeger, 1963), p. 209.

3. Jerome Ch'en, *Mao and the Chinese Revolution* (New York: Oxford University Press, 1965), p. 337.

4. Ōe Kenzaburō, *A Personal Matter,* trans. John Nathan (New York: Grove Press, 1968), pp. vii–viii.

PART SIX

East
Asia
since
the Second
World War

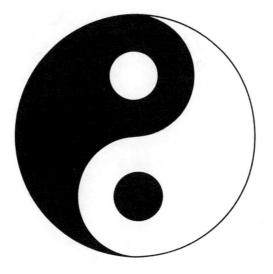

第二次世界大戰
餘燼下之東亞

23 The Aftermath of the Second World War in East Asia

Civil War and Communist Triumph
  in China (1945–1949)
The International Situation
Japan under the Occupation
Postwar Korea
The Korean War
International Relations after the Korean War
Korea after the Truce
Vietnam
The Vietnam War (1946–1975)

Throughout East Asia, the third of a century following the Second World War was a period of change unprecedented in its rapidity and scope, affecting the direction of civilization, economic systems and social structure, and the very rhythm of the lives of millions of people. Two wars fought in Korea and Vietnam present grim proof that change did not always come peacefully nor without outside interference.

In China, Korea, and Japan the basic parameters of postwar history were decided during the years immediately following the Second World War. The triumph of the Chinese Communists, the war in Korea, and the remolding of Japan under the Occupation all fell into those years. This is not the case with the history of Vietnam, but since it too developed out of problems left unsettled by the Great War, it also is treated in this chapter.

The Second World War destroyed the Japanese Empire and, in the world at large, confirmed the eclipse of the Western European powers, thereby completing a process begun by the First World War. In Asia the once great British Empire was steadily dismantled as India and Burma attained independence in 1947 and the Malay Peninsula followed suit ten years later. Hong Kong alone remained a Crown Colony. The Dutch in Indonesia and, especially, the French in Indo-China did not yield as gracefully as did the British, but everywhere old-style colonialism was on the decline. Only two world powers remained in a position to exercise major influence over events in East Asia: the United States and the Soviet Union. During the immediate postwar years they developed a bitter Cold War rivalry that remained the prime fact of international relations for a whole generation and has yet to be resolved.

Civil War and Communist Triumph in China (1945–1949)

For China the end of the Second World War brought not demobilization and peace but a rapid transition from an anti-Japanese war to civil war. The country, which had been at war for four years before Pearl Harbor, did not attain peace until four years after Japan's surrender.

When Japan surrendered in August 1945, its generals in China were ordered to submit only to Nationalist forces. To enable the KMT armies to accept the Japanese surrender, the United States undertook to transport them by water and by air to those parts of the country up to then occupied by Japan. However, they were not allowed into Manchuria until January 1946. Manchuria had been occupied by the U.S.S.R. during the last days of the war, and the Russians did not completely withdraw their troops until May 1946, by which time they had allowed the CCP to gain substantial control of the countryside there. Chiang Kai-shek, determined to retain the area where the Japanese had begun their aggression, disregarded American warnings against overextending his forces and stationed almost half a million of his best troops in Manchuria.

During the year or so immediately after the war, the Nationalists appeared to have formidable resources, at least on paper. Recognized as the legitimate government of China by all the Allies, including the Soviet Union, they had three or four times as many men under arms as their Communist rivals and enjoyed a similar superiority in armament. They were, therefore, in no mood to make concessions to the CCP. The Communists, on the other hand, had come through the war battle hardened, with well-established bases of support in the countryside, and high morale. Their leaders, too, were convinced that victory would be theirs in the coming struggle. It was against this background that the United States sought to mediate between the KMT and CCP. In December 1945, President Truman sent General George C. Marshall to China to help the parties compose their differences. Given their history of conflict, divergence of views, and confidence in their respective causes, there was little chance that American mediation could bring about a genuine meeting of minds between the bitter Chinese antagonists. The American initiative was probably doomed from the start. Marshall's efforts were also hampered by general American support of the Nanking government, even though President Truman stipulated that large-scale aid to China was contingent on a settlement. As during Mao's visit to Chungking in August–October 1945 (see Figure 23-1), there was a show of cordiality, but the Marshall mission produced only a brief breathing spell before fighting broke out in earnest in mid-1946.

Initially, until July 1947, the KMT armies enjoyed success, even capturing the wartime CCP capital at Yenan. However, these were hollow victories. Like the Japanese before them, in North China and Manchuria the KMT controlled only the cities in the midst of a hostile countryside. Moreover, the military efficacy of the armies was undermined by the rivalries between their commanders; by Chiang Kai-shek's penchant for personal decision making even when he was far removed from the scene; and by his abiding concern to prevent any possible rival from amassing too much power. Also much in evidence were the harshness and corruption that had sapped the soldiers' morale during the war against Japan and were even more demoralizing now that they were supposed to fight fellow Chinese.

In other respects too, far from stimulating reform, the defeat of Japan resulted merely in the transfer to the rest of China of the ills that had been incubating in wartime Chungking. A nation badly in need of political, economic,

Figure 23-1   Chiang Kai-shek and Mao Tse-tung exchanging toasts, Chungking, August–October 1945.

and social reconstruction was subjected to a heavy dose of autocracy and to a galloping inflation. There was talk of reform, but the assassination, in the summer of 1946, of the poet and professor Wen I-to (1899–1946) disheartened intellectuals who shared his liberal ideas and hoped for greater freedom to criticize the government. But intellectuals and students were not the only ones disenchanted with the regime, for many suffered from the arrogance of the Nationalist soldiers and the rapacity of those with political connections.

The situation was particularly bad on Taiwan, where carpetbaggers from the mainland enriched themselves at the expense of alleged Taiwanese "collaborators"—a convenient charge against any noncooperative Taiwanese who had done at all well during the preceding half century of Japanese rule. When the Taiwanese rioted in protest in 1947, the Nationalist government responded with brutal and bloody repression. The exact number of casualties is not known—Taiwanese leaders in exile claim that over 10,000 were killed.

The government, inefficient as well as autocratic, proved unable to halt rapidly accelerating inflation that threatened all those whose incomes did not keep up with rising costs. Toward the end, people in the cities had to carry enormous bundles of paper money on their daily rounds of shopping for the necessities of life.

In the CCP areas, in contrast, the political and military leadership offered models of earnest dedication to their cause based on the conviction that this cause was just and would ultimately triumph. Unlike the KMT, which promised reform only after the fighting was finished, the CCP offered immediate change, instant liberation from the exactions of local authorities, landlords and usurers. As they gained new territory, the Communists organized the poor and oppressed, convincing people, by deed as well as by word, that their military organization deserved its name: the "People's Liberation Army."

In July 1947, the Communists turned the tide of war decisively against Chiang Kai-shek and the Nationalists. Communist armies attacked along several fronts in North China. In Manchuria, General Lin Piao (1907–71) organized a campaign that put the KMT forces on the defensive and ended, in October 1948, by completely routing them. During that same month and into November, the last great battle of the war was fought at the strategic city of Hsuchow on the Huai River where the Peking-Nanking Railway line joined the Lunghai line, which runs from Shensi to the sea. Around half a million men on each side were involved in this battle, generally known as the battle of Huai-Hai after the Huai River and the Lunghai Railway. When it was all over, the Nationalists, under Chiang Kai-shek's personal command, had lost 200,000 men and no longer had any way to supply their forces to the north. In January 1949 Nationalist generals surrendered Peking and Tientsin. Throughout the campaigns the Communist army gained not only military advantages from its victories, but also captured valuable military equipment and supplies and increased its manpower as Nationalist soldiers defected or surrendered and were incorporated into the People's Liberation Army.

During 1949 the Communists continued their advance. They crossed the Yangtze in April, took Nanking the same month, and were in control of Shanghai by the end of May. On October 1 Mao Tse-tung, in a great ceremony in Peking, formally proclaimed the establishment of the People's Republic of China. (See map, Figure 23-2.) There was still some fighting in the south, but clearly the CCP had won control of the Chinese mainland. Meanwhile, Chiang Kai-shek and other Nationalists took refuge on Taiwan and vowed continued resistance.

The triumph of the Communists in 1949 began a new chapter in China's long history. It was the result of a long revolutionary process that had begun well before the founding of the CCP, but in terms of the party's own programs and goals the revolution had only just begun. The story of China's continuing revolution is told below (see Chapter 25). First, however, let us consider its immediate international ramifications and its indirect influence on Japan.

The International Situation

Although hailed with enthusiasm in Moscow and bitterly deplored in Washington, the Communist victory of 1949 was a Chinese achievement very little affected by the plans or proposals of the two great powers. Just as Mao disregarded Stalin's prognosis that the Chinese revolution had little prospect for early success, Chiang turned a deaf ear to American counsels. Neither leader was amenable to foreign direction or inclined to accept unwelcome foreign advice. Nevertheless, partly for ideological reasons and partly in response to continued although unenthusiastic American support for the Nanking government, the CCP aligned itself with the U.S.S.R. in a policy of "leaning to one side" enunciated by Mao in July 1949.

Although some American observers had taken the measure of Chiang Kai-shek's regime, large sectors of the American public continued to view him as China's savior, a view fostered by wartime propaganda and the efforts of ex-missionaries, politicians, and others who argued that China had been betrayed and that continued support for the KMT was best for the Chinese people as well as in the interest of the United States. Yet, there may well have been room for diplomatic accommodation between the People's Republic and the United States had not war broken out in Korea in June 1950.

The Korean War brought the United States into conflict with China on two fronts. First, President Truman ordered the American Seventh Fleet to patrol the Taiwan Strait, creating a buffer between the Communist government on the mainland and the Nationalist regime on Taiwan. This prevented Chiang Kai-shek from trying to invade the mainland, but it also prevented the Communists from extending their rule to the island. Indeed, the Communists viewed the move as extending American protection to the KMT in order to prevent reassertion of historic Chinese sovereignty over Taiwan under CCP

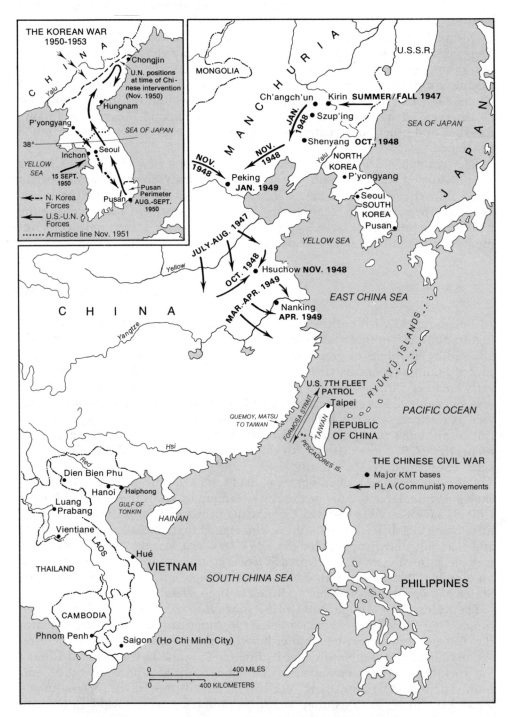

THE KOREAN WAR 1950-1953

Chongjin

U.N. positions at time of Chinese intervention (Nov. 1950)

Hungnam

P'yongyang

38°

SEA OF JAPAN

YELLOW SEA

Inchon
Seoul

15 SEPT. 1950

Pusan

Pusan Perimeter AUG.-SEPT. 1950

CHINA

Yalu

- ◄- - - N. Korea Forces
- ◄——— U.S.-U.N. Forces
- .... Armistice line Nov. 1951

MONGOLIA

MANCHURIA

U.S.S.R.

Ch'angch'un   Kirin   **SUMMER/FALL 1947**

Szup'ing

JAN. 1948

NOV. 1948

Shenyang   **OCT. 1948**

SEA OF JAPAN

JAPAN

NOV. 1948

Peking   **JAN. 1949**

Yalu

NORTH KOREA

P'yongyang

Seoul
SOUTH KOREA

Pusan

CHINA

Yellow

YELLOW SEA

JULY-AUG. 1947

OCT. 1948

Hsuchow **NOV. 1948**

EAST CHINA SEA

MAR.-APR. 1949

Nanking **APR. 1949**

Yangtze

RYUKYU ISLANDS

U.S. 7TH FLEET PATROL

Taipei

PACIFIC OCEAN

QUEMOY, MATSU TO TAIWAN

FORMOSA STRAIT

TAIWAN

REPUBLIC OF CHINA

PESCADORES IS.

THE CHINESE CIVIL WAR

- ● Major KMT bases
- ◄——— PLA (Communist) movements

Hsi

Dien Bien Phu

Red

Hanoi   Haiphong

Luang Prabang

GULF OF TONKIN

HAINAN

Vientiane

LAOS

Hué

THAILAND   **VIETNAM**

SOUTH CHINA SEA

PHILIPPINES

CAMBODIA

Phnom Penh

Saigon (Ho Chi Minh City)

0   400 MILES
0   400 KILOMETERS

Figure 23-2   **East Asia after the Second World War**

auspices. Secondly, as we shall see below, Chinese and American troops clashed head-on in Korea, after United Nations forces under General Douglas MacArthur approached the Yalu River, China's boundary with North Korea. After the Korean War, antagonism between Communist China and the United States hardened into the established foreign policy of both nations.

The United States came to the military assistance of the government of South Korea partly as a result of its worldwide policy of resisting the expansion of what American leaders then considered a monolithic Communist empire directed from Moscow. But what gave Korea its special importance, now as earlier, was its strategic location in respect to Japan. Therefore, before considering the Korean War further, it is important to consider what had been happening, in the meantime, in Japan.

Japan under the Occupation

Japan was in ruins, cities largely destroyed, the economy wrecked. The devastation extended also to the psyche of the Japanese people, for whom the known world had ended in a cataclysm of destruction. Unprepared for defeat, they could not turn to their own history for guidance, for never before in historic times had their country been occupied by a foreign victor. They had no inkling what the future held in store for them. The whole nation now found itself in a psychological position not unlike that of the rare Japanese soldier who during the war, despite his best efforts and contrary to all expectation, found himself an American prisoner. Such men, their old orientations and expectations shattered, were usually most cooperative toward their former enemies, and the Japanese people too were disposed to cooperate with the Occupation authorities. In both cases, decent treatment of the defeated also helped. Thus, when defeat came, the Japanese evacuated many women to the countryside and even the government ordered its female employees out of town. It is not difficult to imagine people's relief when such measures turned out to have been unnecessary.

In theory the Occupation was placed under the authority of the Far Eastern Commission, which sat in Washington and whose members included representatives of all the countries that had fought Japan, but actual control was in American hands. The Japanese government continued to function but did so according to the directives and suggestions of the Occupation authorities, who assumed ultimate responsibility for governing Japan. At the head of the Occupation was General MacArthur, Supreme Commander for the Allied Powers (SCAP). Despite the reference to Allies in the title and the presence of some British and Commonwealth officials, the Occupation was essentially an American undertaking. In MacArthur it had a leader who won easy credibility among the Japanese, for he was a commanding figure, confident in his sense of historical mission, a military man who commanded respect and exuded confidence.

Among the initial and pressing tasks of the Occupation was the disarming of the Japanese military and the provision of relief to prevent famine. The widespread destruction of capital goods and industrial plants, a soil starved for lack of fertilizers, the loss of the natural resources from the former empire and of the entire mercantile fleet, and the need to provide for six million Japanese expatriates and refugees from overseas threatened economic catastrophe. In this situation, suffering was unavoidable. By supplying food and medical supplies, the Occupation authorities helped to avert the worst. But it was not until around 1947 that the Occupation, in the light of the emerging Cold War, became seriously concerned with rebuilding the Japanese economy, particularly Japanese industrial strength.

The basic long-term policy of the Occupation was to demilitarize Japan and turn the country into a peaceful and democratic state; or, we might say, "a peaceful because democratic state," reflecting the optimistic American belief that the one equaled the other. The American conviction of the righteousness of their political values, as well as confidence in the problem-solving powers of American "know-how," were important ingredients in the history of the Occupation.

Demilitarization entailed the dismantling of the military establishment and a purge of militarists from positions of leadership in government and business. Individuals charged with wartime brutality were placed on trial. At the top, twenty-eight leaders were charged with responsibility for the war and were brought to trial before an international tribunal in Tokyo, which sat from May 1946 to April 1948. When the sentences were handed down in November 1948, seven leaders were condemned to die. Foremost among them was Tōjō, the rather colorless general who had headed Japan's wartime government. His role during the war had been more like a chairman of the board than a dictator, but wartime propaganda had cast him as a Japanese Hitler, and it was as such that he was tried and condemned. The lengthy judicial proceedings produced voluminous records but never attained the legal clarity nor the moral authority achieved by the trial of Nazi leaders at Nuremberg.

The emperor was not charged with war crimes, but his person was subjected to a process of demythification. He was required to substitute a more open life style (akin to that of the British monarch, for example) for the secluded and ritualized existence traditionally led by Japanese emperors. An example of the demythification process was the emperor's unprecedented visit to MacArthur at his headquarters. The resulting photograph (Figure 23-3) showing the stiffly formal emperor standing next to the open-shirted general caused considerable shock and dismay throughout Japan. In his New Year's message of 1946 the emperor publicly and explicitly denied his divinity, and under the new constitution he became a symbol of the nation.

This constitution, which went into effect in May 1947, was practically dictated by the Occupation. It stipulated that sovereignty belongs to the people, placed the highest political authority in the hands of the Diet (to which the executive was now made responsible), and established an independent judi-

Figure 23-3   General
Douglas MacArthur and
the Emperor of Japan.

ciary. Another noteworthy set of political changes were those decreasing the
power of the central government, particularly the Home Ministry, and fostering local self-government. Accompanying these structural changes were provisions for universal suffrage and human rights, including the equality of
women. A unique feature was the renunciation of war that became Article IX
of the constitution. This stipulates, "The Japanese people forever renounce
war as a sovereign right of the nation and the threat or use of force as a means
of settling international disputes" and goes on to say, "land, sea, and air forces,
as well as other war potential, will never be maintained."[1] In this way the authors of the constitution hoped to incorporate peacefulness into the very
framework of the new Japanese state.

The authorities at SCAP headquarters knew that Japan could not be turned
into a democracy simply by changing the political system. Consequently they
tried to change Japanese society itself and to do so in the relatively short time
allotted to them. Since many American officials lacked previous study or experience in Japan and high military officials could be quite narrow in their outlook, there was a tendency to rely excessively on American prototypes without
taking into sufficient account Japan's own experience and situation.

An example of limited success was the Occupation's reforms of the educational system. This was restructured to conform to the American sequence of elementary school, junior high school, high school, and college. The Japanese were forced to eliminate their old technical schools and special higher schools, which previously covered the eleventh to thirteenth years of education and prepared students for university study. Under the old system, only the student elite had access to a university education, but under the new, all students were to be given equal educational opportunities through high school. In an effort to expand opportunities for higher education, many of the old technical and higher schools were upgraded to become universities. But these new universities were not of a quality comparable to the old established schools like Tokyo University. Competition for admission to this and other prestigious universities remained brutal. Entrance examinations confronted students with an "examination hell" comparable to that which once faced the Chinese degree candidates; in both cases passing the examinations opened entry into the elite.

In order to reform the content of education, the Occupation abolished the old ethics courses and purged textbooks fostering old militaristic and authoritarian values. Its attack on these old values was rather successful, especially since they had in any case been largely discredited by defeat. It was rather less successful, however, in its attempt to create a positive sense of individual civic responsibility and citizenship.

Social change entails a transformation of values and thus naturally takes longer than institutional change, but changes in the legal system can encourage social change. Among the Occupation's notable efforts in this area were measures to enhance the status of women and limit the powers and privileges of the family's male head. The new constitution stated explicitly, "Marriage shall be based upon the mutual consent of both sexes, and it shall be maintained through mutual cooperation, with equal rights of husband and wife as a basis."[2] The presence of many thousands of Americans in their country also gave the Japanese an unusual opportunity to observe foreign mores. It may have encouraged them to become somewhat more relaxed toward authority and also stimulated a measure of cosmopolitanism.

It was generally recognized that the political and social changes desired by the Occupation demanded an economic foundation, and the authorities set about restructuring the Japanese economy. Most successful in this respect was the Occupation's program of land reform. This prohibited absentee landlordism and restricted the amount of land a resident landowner could hold to a maximum of 7½ acres to work himself and another 2½ acres to rent out (except in Hokkaidō where the average farm is twelve and one-half acres because the climate precludes intensive rice cultivation). Anything in excess had to be sold to the government, which resold it to former tenants. There was provision for compensation for the landlords, but inflation made this meaningless. The old inequity in the countryside was eliminated. In terms of productivity too, the land policy was a success, for the agrarian sector was the first to recover.

In the urban industrial sector, the Occupation tried to eliminate or at least to reduce the concentrations of economic power, which Americans viewed as a major component of Japanese authoritarianism. One policy was to foster labor unions. The constitution guaranteed "the right of workers to organize and to bargain and act collectively."[3] As intended, a vigorous union movement developed, but contrary to American wishes, the Japanese unions did not, like the American AFL and CIO, limit themselves to economic demands. Much like European unions, they were political in orientation, developing into labor arms of the Socialist and Communist parties. In February 1947, the Occupation banned a planned general strike and thereafter was less friendly toward the unions.

On the management and ownership side, the Occupation did break up the old holding companies and purged the old *zaibatsu* families from positions of economic leadership. Contrary to initial expectations, however, this did not lead to genuine decentralization. Where old systems were broken up, new and equally pervasive patterns of trade and finance developed, bearing a marked resemblance to the old. Furthermore, a plan to break up operating companies petered out: of 1200 companies initially considered, only 28 were, in the end, broken up. Economic power and decision making remained concentrated. The reasons for this are instructive for understanding the accomplishments and failures of the Occupation as a whole, for they include both a Japanese and an American component.

On the Japanese side, strong support for land reform contrasted with a marked lack of enthusiasm for American-style trust busting. Few shared the American faith in the ultimate benefits of maximum competition. Instead, the feeling was that Japanese companies needed to be large in order to compete in the international market. Radicals and conservatives disagreed about ownership and control, not about the structure of industry and commerce.

Decentralization of the economy also faltered because of a change in American policy. By 1948, developments in Russo-American relations and the turn of events in China made the rebuilding of Japanese economic strength a more important goal of American policy than economic reform. As the Cold War developed, the United States increasingly looked upon Japan (as on Germany) as a potentially valuable ally. Since an armed ally, capable at least of self-defense, would be more valuable than one unarmed, the United States now also had second thoughts about Japan's total renunciation of military force.

The United States also sought to end the Occupation—an idea MacArthur broached as early as 1947. In 1947 the United States approached the Far Eastern Commission to draft a peace treaty, but this diplomatic move failed largely because of Russian opposition.

The Occupation continued, but by July 1950, when MacArthur took command over the United Nations Forces in Korea, the work of the Occupation was practically complete. The next two years were little more than a holding operation awaiting the conclusion of peace. This was finally accomplished after the signing of a peace treaty in September 1951, an event which took place without Russian participation. (Relations with Russia were normalized in 1956.)

An assessment of the Occupation must naturally take into account the history of the post-Occupation years (see Chapter 24) when the Japanese could again make their own decisions concerning their society and its institutions. However, it is possible to draw a few preliminary conclusions. Perhaps the most significant of these is that the Occupation was most successful where Japanese precedents and Japanese support were available for its programs. Although the Occupation authorities failed to realize it, this was true of much of their political program, their plan for land reform, and their advocacy of liberal values. Representative institutions, after all, went back to the early Meiji period, and demands for land reform, for equality, and for a rejection of authoritarianism all predated the rise of Japanese militarism. Thus, despite the Occupation's misconceptions and mistakes and despite the contradiction inherent in a plan to foster democracy by command, much of what the Occupation attempted did actually take hold.

The Occupation also had unplanned side effects, including the influx of foreign culture. Intellectuals eager to catch up with the recent Western developments devoured translations of Western books, and popular culture was equally open to foreign influence. In some respects the scene resembled that after the First World War, and it is well to remember that it did not take the Occupation to introduce the Japanese to baseball and jazz. However, this time change went deeper, and there was to be no radical turning away such as took place in the thirties.

The constitution has now remained in effect for thirty years, and if Japan did not develop exactly along the lines envisioned by the Occupation authorities, neither was there a reversion to authoritarianism. Whether the Occupation merely hastened inevitable changes or served as a catalyst without which Japanese history would have developed very differently remains a subject of scholarly disagreement and dispute. What we might note here, however, is the contrast between the comparative American success in Japan and the total failure of United States policy in China. In both countries, the Korean War confirmed the direction of internal development as well as international orientation.

Postwar Korea

Korea's last decade under Japanese rule was in many ways a bitter one. The Japanese relentlessly stamped out Korean nationalism, sending its leaders into prison, exile, or underground activities. In the late thirties the Japanese expanded their suppression of political nationalism into an attack on Korean cultural identity. In line with a policy of total forced cultural assimilation, they stopped Korean language instruction in all secondary schools in 1938, and soon elementary schools followed suit. No longer could Korean children learn their own language in school; the use of Japanese was mandatory. In 1940 the Korean press was closed down. The Japanese made strong efforts to propagate the official State Shinto. To help the war effort they first launched a movement of voluntary conscription. Then, in 1943, military service became compulsory. At the same time, the Koreans had to bear the hardships and deprivations of war.

During the war, the United States and the Soviet Union agreed on the 38th parallel as a dividing line: north of this line the Japanese forces would surrender to Soviet troops; south of the parallel they would submit to the United States. Perhaps the 38th parallel was selected by Pentagon officers in order to assure the inclusion of Seoul in the American zone. In any case when the Soviet army entered the peninsula three weeks before the Americans, they abided by the agreement. What was not clear at the time was that this was to become a semipermanent dividing line.

In the north the Soviet army backed the creation of a Communist state under Kim Il-sung (1912–), a former leader of Korean guerrilla fighters in Manchuria who had spent some time in the U.S.S.R. and now entered Korea as a major in the Soviet army. Gradually Kim overcame factionalism among Korean revolutionaries and fashioned a party and government along Soviet lines. Officials and policemen who had served the Japanese were purged. Industry was nationalized with minimal opposition, since it had mostly been owned by Japanese. Land reform followed, and a start was made in economic planning. And a military force was created.

In the south the American army did not arrive until three weeks after the end of the war. The American military government then refused to recognize an existing interim government, suspecting it of pro-Communist or pro-Japanese leanings. The initial American policy was to await the outcome of negotiations for unification, and there seemed hope that these would reach an early settlement when the United States and the Soviet Union agreed on a joint commission to supervise a five-year period of transition to independence of a unified Korea. This plan, however, ran into the vociferous opposition of a group of Korean nationalists who demanded immediate unification, and when the Soviet Union wanted to bar such men from participating in scheduled elections, Soviet-American cooperation came to an end.

The United States then initiated moves to give South Korea a representative government and in the meantime allowed the economic status quo to persist. Since the Japanese had effectively suppressed organized political activity, there was at the end of the war something of a political vacuum. The victor in the battle over who was to fill that vacuum was Syngman Rhee (Yi Sung-man, 1875–1965), a longtime Christian Nationalist who had suffered seven years' imprisonment as a young man. Forced to leave Korea in 1911, he had lived in exile (mostly in Hawaii) before returning to his native land after Japan's defeat. A strong advocate of immediate unification, Rhee was an eloquent speaker and a capable organizer. He was also strongly antileftist. In August 1948, the septuagenarian Rhee became president of the Republic of Korea, and American military government came to an end. Thus Korea was divided into two mutually hostile parts.

The Korean War

Increasing international tensions between the United States and the Soviet Union as well as bitter hostility between the governments of North and South Korea reduced the chances for unification by negotiation. Both the Communist state in the north and the anti-Communist government in the south harbored the ambition to rule over the entire country. These ambitions erupted into war in June 1950, when North Korea attacked the south.

The period of intense fighting can be divided into three main phases, each with its own subdivisions. First, from June to September 1950, the North Koreans were on the offensive, pushing the South Korean and American forces back until they established a defense perimeter around Pusan from which they could not be dislodged. The second phase began with MacArthur's amphibious landing at Inchon in September, which led to the recapture of Seoul and then to an offensive intended to unify Korea by force. Then, in November, the Chinese, alarmed by the American advance to the Yalu River, and having had their warnings ignored, sent massive "volunteer" armies into Korea. These succeeded in regaining the north but were unable to win control over the south. This became clear in late May 1951, and in July of that year truce talks began. Earlier, in April, President Truman had dismissed General MacArthur, thereby making it clear that America would not extend the war beyond Korea. His dismissal of the eminent and popular general also demonstrated the American system of civil control over the military, a demonstration which had considerable impact in Japan.

Casualties in this war were heavy on both sides. They included over 800 thousand Koreans (approximately 520 thousand North Koreans and 300 thousand South Koreans) and probably as many or more Chinese soldiers. The southern forces were sanctioned by the United Nations and fought under a United Nations command, but approximately half of the ground troops in addition to most of the air and naval forces were supplied by the United States, which suffered 142 thousand casualties. South Korea supplied two-fifths of the remaining United Nations troops, and thirteen other countries combined to make up the remainder.

The truce talks dragged on for two years until an armistice was signed in July 1953. Although marred by incidents, this armistice still remains in effect today. For the long-suffering Korean people, so recently freed from very harsh Japanese rule, the cruel war accomplished nothing: their country remained divided essentially as before, only more bitterly.

International Relations after the Korean War

The Korean War did not alter the international configuration of power in East Asia, but it did considerably embitter Sino-American relations. Both sides were now more convinced than ever of the enmity of the other. In the United

States, proponents of a moderate China policy were removed from influence and subjected to slander. The American commitment to the Nationalist regime was confirmed. Taiwan was given economic and military assistance, and in 1954 the United States signed a mutual defense treaty with the government of Chiang Kai-shek. Meanwhile, American troops remained in Korea. The United States also retained bases in Japan and on Okinawa, for the conclusion of a peace treaty with Japan was accompanied by the signing of a defense agreement. The Chinese, alarmed by these developments, were convinced of their wisdom in allying themselves with the U.S.S.R. The formal basis of the relationship between the two countries was provided by a treaty of friendship and alliance they had signed in February 1950 directed at preventing a revival of Japanese aggression. While the Chinese viewed America as an imperialist aggressor, throughout the 1950s many people in the United States, even those in high places, considered the People's Republic to be little more than a Soviet satellite.

If the Korean War merely solidified alliances already in the making and froze the participants into their Cold War postures, it did enhance China's international status by demonstrating the ability of her peasant army, a bare year after the triumph of the revolution, to resist the formidable armed might of the United States. Among those impressed with the caliber of the Chinese military were the authors of the official U.S. Marine Corps history, who found much to admire in the Chinese style of semiguerrilla warfare, with its emphasis on infiltration, deception, and surprise. Within China, the Korean War helped the government to mobilize the people under the banner of national resistance, and it created its share of national heroes. Above all, it meant that the revolution had now been tested in foreign as well as domestic war.

For Japan the war brought profitable orders for equipment and supplies, which provided a substantial stimulant to what was still a faltering economy. Even after the war, orders to supply American troops and bases continued to benefit the Japanese economy. Under American encouragement, Japan also created a paramilitary force of 75,000, a first step toward limited rearmament. In the peace treaty, signed with the United States in San Francisco in September 1951 and ratified the following April, Japan was restored to full sovereignty. The basic pattern of internal economic growth and dependence on the United States for ultimate military protection was set. During the fifties and sixties Japan continued to take its foreign policy cues from the United States.

During the years after the Korean War, both China and Japan were able to concentrate on domestic development, although this always took place within the parameters of the Cold War. The two leading countries of East Asia, of course, remained keenly aware of each other, but they had little to do with each other. Kept apart by Japan's alliance with the United States, oriented toward contrasting models of social and economic development, influenced by different ideologies, they interacted only sporadically and then in a limited way.

Korea after the Truce

On both sides of the 38th parallel, the mutually hostile Korean governments maintained large military establishments. In the north, with about 55 percent of Korea's land area and a population which is now around 16 million, there are about 495 thousand men in the well-equipped military establishment (army, navy, air force), and this does not include paramilitary personnel such as the security forces and border guards. For South Korea, with a population of 34 million, the comparable figure is 670 thousand men under arms (army, navy, marines, air force). In both states the possibility of renewed hostilities also provided a rationale for the concentration of power in the hands of political strongmen.

The government of North Korea remained under the firm control of Kim Il-sung, who became the focus of a personality cult as intense as any in world history. When relations between China and the Soviet Union deteriorated, North Korea was able to pursue an independent line between them, and it remains an intensely nationalistic state. In keeping with its ideological objectives, the government in 1958 restructured agriculture, organizing cooperatives of about three hundred families and one thousand acres each. Industrialization, begun by the Japanese, continued to expand. Despite heavy military expenses, material conditions gradually improved for the people of North Korea. However, for many years, North Korea remained virtually closed to non-Communist outsiders, and even under the less strained international situation of the 1970s, it remains a country little known to the outside world.

South Korea was under the authoritarian rule of Syngman Rhee for a total of twelve years (1948–60), until he was overthrown by widespread and persistent student riots provoked by outrage at government repression and corruption, including dishonest elections. A brief ten months of multiparty liberal government came to an end in 1961 when the military carried out a coup under the leadership of General Park Chung-hee (1917–), who had been a second lieutenant in the Japanese army in Manchuria at the end of the Second World War. (Despite Rhee's bitter hostility toward Japan, in South Korea there had been no purge of Koreans who had served the Japanese.) In 1963 a constitution was enacted, elections were held, and Park became president. This initiated the present system of presidential rule backed by military force, but the government frequently resorted to the suppression of dissent and the repression of its critics, including the imprisonment of political opponents. Park's assassination in 1979 revealed divisions in the leadership itself but left the ultimate shape of Korean politics in doubt.

During the first ten years or so following the Korean War, the economic priority of the South Korean government was reconstruction and rehabilitation, which was accomplished with American assistance. In the mid-sixties this was followed by economic growth in association with Japan. In 1965, Park, despite student opposition, signed a treaty of recognition and reparations with Japan, and since then Japan has played an increasingly important role in the

South Korean economy, supplying capital and goods, and marketing Korean-made products. When wages rose in Japan, many labor-intensive plants were attracted to Korea. Economic growth did not benefit all equally. Fast growing cities suffered from poor urban planning, and centralized administration from Seoul did not help. Land reforms carried out in the late forties and fifties left many rural poor with insufficient land for self-support. The solution to these problems is slow, but indications are that South Korea is economically viable.

After more than thirty years of division, peaceful reunification appears as much out of reach as ever. Militarily, both governments rely on their powerful allies to extend military assistance in case they are attacked. In the case of South Korea, America's planned withdrawal of ground forces, repugnance at the government's authoritarianism, and shock at revelations of alleged Korean bribery of United States Congressmen have not changed the United States' appreciation of Korea's strategic importance nor the official commitment to assist in the defense of South Korea if necessary.

Vietnam

Comparison of Vietnamese history with that of Korea reveals significant similarities as well as differences and may help to put their postwar histories into perspective. In both countries the traditional rulers and elite looked to China as a model of organization and a source of high culture, but in both cases political independence from China was jealously guarded and cultural identity maintained. In modern times both Korea and Vietnam, after unsuccessful Chinese intervention, experienced a period of colonial rule (under the Japanese and the French) that strained and distorted traditional society and failed to prepare the countries for independence. Then, after the Second World War, both suffered division into two mutually hostile states, each supported by rival international power blocks. In both cases bitter warfare between northern and southern divisions ensued, and in each case massive American participation in aid of the south was a major factor.

On the other hand, Korea and Vietnam differ in climate, terrain, and internal geographic configuration; and in their wider cultural and regional settings. Korea's neighbors are China, Japan, and the Soviet Union, whereas Vietnam is a major power in Southeast Asia. Furthermore, there were differences in their experiences under colonialism. For one thing, the Japanese were much closer to the Koreans culturally, geographically, and even in physical appearance than were the French to the Vietnamese. And Japan and France were, of course, countries with very different histories and traditions. The present situation of the two lands is also different: Korea remains divided whereas Vietnam is now a unified nation.

French policy in Vietnam was not consistent over the years, and it also differed in the north and the south, but in neither area did it provide a viable fusion of either the modern and the traditional or the foreign and native. In the center (Annam) and the north (Tonkin) the French maintained "protectorates" with parallel French and Vietnamese systems of administration, although the French had superior authority. Under this arrangement the French maintained the Nguyen emperor in Hue with the result that the throne failed to become a symbol of Vietnamese nationalism. Even the examination system, modeled on that of China, was retained until 1919 by what Alexander Woodside has aptly termed, "the embalming agency of colonialism."[4] The south (Cochin China), in contrast, was governed as a full colony on French lines by French and French-oriented officials.

The difference between north and south extended also to economic organization. In the south, plantations (rice and rubber) developed, creating great economic inequities and dependence on the vagaries of the international market. The northern lowlands were an area of small fragmented holdings, but here too life became very hard as population growth created great and increasing pressures on the land.

In the beginning, resistance to the French came from members of the traditional elite, and it is noteworthy that men of mandarin (elite) background continued to figure prominently in the leadership of Vietnam's national and social revolutions. An important nationalist leader who shared this background was Phan Boi Chao (1867–1940), who studied with Liang Ch'i-ch'ao in Japan and hoped to transform Vietnam into a modern state along the lines of Meiji Japan. Japan was also admired by the founders of the Free School of Tonkin, in Hanoi, modeled on Keiō University. Here a romanized script was used in place of Chinese characters, the examination system was attacked, and modern political and social ideas were disseminated. Opened in 1907, it lasted less than a year before it was forcibly closed by the French.

The French could repress radical ideas, suppress insurrections, arrest, imprison, or execute their enemies, but they could not breathe life into moribund social and political structures. Nor could they restrict the import of Western ideas to Catholicism: Paris itself was, after all, a major center of Western radicalism. During the First World War 100,000 Vietnamese served in France as soldiers and laborers. Many returned to their native land ready to question the continued legitimacy of colonial rule. The most famous Vietnamese to be influenced by a stay in France was Ho Chi Minh (Nguyen That Thanh, 1890–1969). Ho was already a nationalist before he arrived in France, but it was in Paris that he complemented his nationalism by fusing it with Marxism.

Ho's status in the Vietnamese Revolution is comparable to that of Mao Tsetung in China, but the Vietnamese leader differed from the Chinese not only in having extensive overseas experience but also in coming from an impoverished but nonetheless distinctly scholar-official family. His father eventually became a district magistrate. In 1911 Ho left Vietnam as a seaman and after a period of travel spent a crucial six years (1917–23) in France, supporting himself as a gardener, sweeper, waiter, photograph retoucher, and oven stoker. He also became a convinced Marxist and assisted in the founding of the French Communist Party. Subsequently he went to Moscow and was then sent by the

Comintern to assist Borodin in Canton. However, Ho's interest always remained focused on his native Vietnam. In 1930 he succeeded in fusing various groups into the Communist Party of Vietnam (soon changed to Indo-China).

Strong ideological foundations, powerful international models, and especially dedication to organizing grass-roots support in the villages were some of the factors that gave the Communists an advantage in their competition for leadership of Vietnam's national revolution. However, in the south, highly organized syncretic religious movements such as the Cao Dai and Hoa Hao sects supplied many of the same social, organizational, and psychological needs. Furthermore, on the eve of the Second World War in the Pacific, the Communists were beset by factionalism.

But this changed after 1941 when Ho organized a broad anticolonial movement known as the Viet Minh (more formally, the League for the Independence of Vietnam). The purpose of this organization, established with Nationalist Chinese support, was to resist both the Japanese who occupied Vietnam in 1941 and the French (adherents to the puppet regime established by the Germans at Vichy), whom the Japanese kept in office until they removed them in March 1945.

From a base along the Chinese border, the Viet Minh expanded their military and political influence to the Red Delta and beyond. They built up an effective military force under the command of General Vo Nguyen Giap (1912–), who had studied guerrilla warfare techniques in Yenan. During the war the demands of Vietnam's new masters created increased economic hardships. In Tonkin, in 1940, between 400,000 and 2 million people starved to death, having been deprived of the rice reserves necessary to combat famine.

When Japan surrendered in August 1945, the Viet Minh were the most effective force in the land. On August 26 Ho Chi Minh proclaimed an independent Vietnam in Hanoi. The French, however, had other ideas, and Ho lacked the resources to prevent them from reestablishing their presence in Vietnam.

The Vietnam War (1946–1975)

The Vietnam War can be divided into two wars: one fought against the French (1946–54) and a second in which the United States became a principal party.

The first war began in 1946 after negotiations had revealed the gulf separating the Viet Minh, dedicated to achieving national independence, and the French, seeking to recover former glory and adamant in their refusal to relinquish their empire. As the fighting continued, the Cold War developed, and the Communist character of the Viet Minh came more to the fore while the French tried to attract non-Communist nationalist support by sponsoring a regime under the former emperor Bao Dai. This, however, won little support from the Vietnamese people. Furthermore, the French made little military headway against an enemy who knew the terrain and had the support of the civilian population. They committed 420,000 troops to Vietnam not counting another

200,000 in the Vietnamese army, but the end came in April-May 1954 when Giap, with the aid of artillery laboriously transported over the mountains, vanquished the French at the famous battle of Dien Bien Phu.

Negotiations at Geneva led to the partition of Vietnam at the 17th parallel into a Communist dominated state with its capital at Hanoi and a southern state ruled from Saigon. Nationwide elections were agreed upon for 1956.

The elections, however, were never held, for they were blocked, with American support, by the head of the Saigon government. This was Ngo Diehm Diem (1901–63), a Catholic Nationalist whose government lacked popular roots and administrative efficacy. In 1963 his government was overthrown and Diem* himself was killed in the coup. By that time the United States had 17,000 troops in Vietnam to assist in what the American government viewed as the containment of world communism.

The removal of the unpopular and aloof Diem and his corrupt family did not result in any marked improvements in government, which beginning in 1965, was in military hands. While the Saigon government remained autocratic, ineffective, and corrupt, the insurgents gained ground. Leadership of the southern revolutionaries was now exercised by the National Liberation Front (NLF), organized in December 1960.† The NLF was supported by the North Vietnamese, and there was logistic aid from the Soviet Union and China.

The Chinese continued to give moral and material support to their Vietnamese allies but, unlike the United States, did not send troops. American involvement meanwhile increased. Leading American policymakers justified this by drawing historical analogies from the appeasement of Germany and Japan in the thirties, when they might better have drawn lessons from the Japanese experience in China or the fall of Chiang Kai-shek. An elaboration of this approach was the "domino theory," which held that if Vietnam fell to communism the other countries of Southeast Asia would follow suit, toppling one by one like a row of dominoes. Furthermore, the United States government treated the war not as a civil war but as a case of combating "northern aggression." After gaining Senate support in the Tonkin Gulf Resolution (1964), President Johnson ordered the bombing of North Vietnam (February 1965). By July 1965, there were 70,000 American troops in Vietnam. The number continued to increase until early in 1968, when there were 510,000. In addition, Vietnam underwent the most massive bombing in history. As American involvement in Vietnam increased, the horrors of the war were brought home to the American people by casualty lists and by the sight of gruesome destruction of Vietnamese people and villages, which they witnessed daily on their television screens. At the same time, the American government was increasingly unable to justify

---

* Like Chinese, Japanese, and Korean names, Vietnamese names are written with the surname first. However, probably because certain surnames are extremely frequent, it is customary to refer to people by their personal names. An exception is made for Ho Chi Minh, actually a pseudonym.

† In the United States both the Front and its supporters were known as "Vietcong," an abbreviation of "Vietnamese communism" or "Vietnamese Communist."

the war to its own people. And the bombings and destruction reinforced the will of Vietnamese revolutionaries on both sides to persist in their struggle.

In February 1968 it became apparent that the American effort, despite its greater destructiveness, had destroyed neither the will nor the ability of the revolutionaries to continue to fight. That month they launched an offensive in which they attacked over one hundred cities. This show of strength prompted a reexamination of American policy, and the United States began to withdraw its troops from Vietnam. However, apparently in an attempt to bolster the Saigon regime, President Nixon in 1970 widened the war to include Cambodia and Laos. It was not easy for an American president to withdraw without "victory," but strong domestic pressures as well as the situation in Vietnam left him little choice. Finally an agreement was reached in Paris, and the last American military personnel left Vietnam in March 1973.

The war continued for another two years, but the outcome was a foregone conclusion to anyone who calculated military strength, not in terms of official statistics and armaments, but in terms of such factors as the participants' will to fight, the political credibility of the leadership, and the attitude of the people. Saigon fell in April 1975. In 1976 the establishment of the Socialist Republic of Vietnam, with its capital in Hanoi, was proclaimed. Saigon was renamed Ho Chi Minh City.

The first three years of the unified state were difficult. Faced with the prospect of transfer to the countryside, numerous city dwellers, many of them ethnic Chinese, fled the country. Sino-Vietnamese relations were also strained by hostilities between Vietnam and the Khmer Rouge regime established in 1975 in Cambodia (now called Kampuchea), which enjoyed Chinese support. These hostilities culminated in the Vietnamese invasion of Cambodia in December 1978, followed by the occupation of most of the country and the installation of a client government in Phnom Penh. At the end of 1979 this regime still placed highest priority on subduing the remnants of the Khmer Rouge forces. Meanwhile, the people of Cambodia, already decimated by the hardships and brutalities inflicted on them during the Khmer Rouge years, faced starvation on a massive scale while the world looked on in horror and international relief agencies did what they could. Thus, by a cruel twist of history, millions of Cambodians became the ultimate victims of a chain of events that had originated beyond their borders and over which they had little influence.

NOTES

1. Article IX of the Constitution. A convenient source is David John Lu, *Sources of Japanese History* (New York: McGraw-Hill, 1975), 2:193–97. Article IX is reproduced on p. 194.

2. Article XXIV of the Constitution. Lu, 2:195.

3. Article XXVIII of the Constitution. Lu, 2:195.

4. Alexander B. Woodside, *Community and Revolution in Modern Vietnam* (Boston: Houghton Mifflin, 1976), p. 3.

當今之日本

24 Contemporary Japan: 1952-1979

The Economy
Politics
Social Change and the Quality of Life
The Japanese Film
The Visual Arts
Literature
The Seventies

In the quarter century following the end of the Occupation, Japan achieved phenomenal economic growth and became one of the world's industrial giants. By the 1970s Japan possessed the most advanced technology. Unfortunately the country also possessed some of the most characteristic problems of the modern industrial state: most notably, the widespread pollution that contaminated what was once pure air and clear water.

Industrialization and urbanization on an unprecedented scale have left their mark on every aspect of Japanese life. The forces of modernity are testing old values and ideas, traditional forms of social organization, long-accepted patterns of life, and previously unquestioned beliefs. At issue over the past quarter century has been the ultimate identity of Japan. To what extent would new social, political, and economic forces ultimately reshape Japanese society in the image of other economically advanced countries? Would Japan once again display an ability to work out creative adaptations of foreign borrowings?

The answers to these questions are not yet available, but during the period under consideration Japan did not become a "typical" modern society, if such exists, for its people continued to respond in new and interesting ways to the challenge of working out a satisfactory blend of new and old; a challenge which characterizes the entire period since Japan first embarked on extensive change in Meiji times. Indeed, it is the juxtaposition and interweaving of old and new that continues to make Japan both fascinating and unique.

The Economy

The Japanese economy made tremendous gains during the Korean War, largely through producing goods and services needed to support the United Nations' war effort there. By 1953, economic production had practically returned to pre–Second World War levels, although the country's trade volume was still only half of what it had been previously. After 1954, the economic surge continued, transforming recovery into growth. The annual GNP (gross national product—the total goods and services produced by a nation) rose an average of roughly 9 percent per year from 1954 to 1961, followed by an even higher rate (over 11 percent) during the 1960s. GNP figures are admittedly very rough indices, but they are useful for measuring broad trends in national economic activity, and for comparing the performance of national economies. For example, in the United States, an advanced industrial nation with a mature economy, a more modest annual growth rate in the GNP is considered quite satisfactory; most economists would probably agree that an 11 percent growth rate would be inappropriate for the United States. But the comparison is a useful way of underscoring the truly remarkable vitality of Japan's "economic miracle."

Not only did Japan's industrial output increase in quantity, it also changed qualitatively, as old industries were transformed and new ones developed. During the fifties, with government support, great strides were made in heavy industry—despite the fact that Japan lacks raw materials and is poor in energy resources. For example, by building manufacturing plants in port cities, which provided the advantage of low-cost ocean transport, and through the sophisticated application of modern technologies, Japan was able to become the world's leading shipbuilder and the third largest producer of iron and steel (after the United States and the Soviet Union). With heavy industry well established, Japan then concentrated on such high-technology fields as electronics and developed a host of strong modern industries. Cars and television sets, computers and cameras, watches and even pianos—it is difficult to think of a major branch of consumer technology in which Japan has failed to excel.

Some of these products were built by new companies, such as Sony or Honda, founded by entrepreneurs who took advantage of the opportunities offered by postwar economic dislocation to build up new enterprises from scratch. Other ambitious men reorganized or rejuvenated older companies, often importing technology by buying rights to foreign patents. In the dominant position in the economy, however, familiar old names reappeared, including Mitsui, the world's oldest major firm, as well as Mitsubishi, Sumitomo, and others.

The names were old, but they now designated a new kind of economic grouping rather than the family centered *zaibatsu* of the prewar period. Each group included financial institutions (a bank, insurance company, and so forth), a real estate firm, and a cluster of companies engaged in every conceivable line of business, where its main competitor was most likely a member of a rival group. The activities of the various member firms of each group were coordinated in periodic meetings of their presidents in presidents' clubs. Interlocking directorships, mutual stock holdings, and internal loans further held the organizations together, although more loosely than in the old *zaibatsu*. However, the enterprise groupings continued to grow in size and strength until in the mid-seventies a study by Japan's Fair Trade Commission found that the six major groupings, composed of a total of 175 core companies, held 21.9 percent of all the capital in Japan and had a controlling interest in another 3095 corporations that held 26.1 percent of the nation's capital. To this must be added their substantial investments in other companies that they can influence without controlling.

Among the member firms of these enterprise groupings the most spectacular were trading companies (*shōsha*) that conducted their business not only at home but all over the world: exporting and importing, transporting and storing, financing and organizing a host of multifarious projects—an airport in Kenya, a large commercial farm on Sumatra, a petrochemical industry for Iran, or copper mining in Zaire. One of the greatest assets of these companies is their command of information gathered from throughout the world. Thus the Mitsui trading company has computers in Tokyo, New York, and London that exchange information automatically and are connected with 112 Mitsui offices in 75 countries plus another 44 offices in Japan. It is an information gathering network more extensive than that of any other private organization and larger than those operated by most governments. Furthermore, Mitsui, Mitsubishi, and the others have their own research organizations analyzing information, charting future trends, and drawing up plans to provide for future project recommendations. Their experts are engaged in city planning, energy research, research into the world's oceans and other major investigations that are likely to influence the future lives of people not only in Japan but in many parts of the world.

At the other end of the size scale from the trading companies and the huge economic groupings are the small concerns, which had for so long given the Japanese economy its dual, semitraditional, semimodern, structure. During the sixties and seventies, the small traditional enterprises steadily lost ground. They found it difficult to compete for labor with the larger firms, which could afford to pay higher wages and offer greater job security, paid for out of the increased productivity achieved by workers in modern well equipped plants.

Similar to the decline of the traditional small firms was a dramatic drop in the agricultural labor force without any corresponding decrease in production. Instead, technological improvements, including mechanization and the development of new seeds, made possible an increase in yield even as fewer people toiled in the fields. Much of Japan's rice was now grown by women and the elderly while a family's prime wage earner went to work in an urban factory.

The transformation of the Japanese economy would not have been possible without the dedicated efforts of the nation's blue- and white-collar workers. Labor unions, organized into two large confederations, did subscribe to radical theories. They did send their members into the streets with red headbands and Marxist slogans during the annual spring offensives for higher wages. However, most unions were also enterprise unions, that is, they were composed of all the workers employed in a single firm rather than all those in the same industry or line of work. Such unions included office as well as production workers and tended to be more cooperative with management than unions in most other industrialized countries.

Worker identification with individual firms was furthered by a pattern of lifetime employment, although companies did hire temporary workers when needed. The expectation of lifelong employment was also an important factor securing the loyalty of managerial personnel. On both the worker and the management level, loyalty to the firm was quite frequently strengthened by feelings of personal obligation, as, for instance, between an employee and a more senior man who had helped him to obtain his position. In contrast to the situation in most industrial countries, even highly trained men in Japan tended to think of themselves not as members of a particular profession (engineers, accountants, and so forth) but rather as members of a particular firm.

Japanese companies provided varied services and facilities for their employees, including company dormitories for the unmarried. There were company athletic teams and a host of recreational activities, such as organized outings to mountain retreats. These were intended to foster not only the health and well-being of the employees but also to strengthen feelings of group solidarity and identification with the sponsoring firm, which used them to convey an image of paternalistic solicitude. It was, of course, in the companies' interest to keep alive as long as possible the old values that had assured Meiji enterprises as well as Tokugawa merchant houses of the loyal devotion of their servants. Yet, it is important not to exaggerate their effectiveness nor to overemphasize the traditional aspects of Japanese labor relations, for company extras increasingly became matters not of traditionalistic paternalism but rather of contractual rights subject to collective bargaining, like fringe benefits in other countries.

Other signs indicated that, gradually, non-work-related activities and relationships were gaining in importance in the workers' lives even as industry's quest for economic efficiency was weakening the nexus of personal relationships which had long prevailed at work. At the same time, managerial personnel continued to receive intensive training and indoctrination in order to imbue them with company ways and spirit. Thus at Toyota, Japan's leading automobile manufacturer, white-collar men are given an entire year of training, including a month in a company camp. Recruitment patterns centered on certain universities, ties between men entering a company in the same year, an emphasis on longevity in promotions, the practice of extensive consultation, and a strong preference for decision by consensus all helped foster management solidarity.

For the most part, Japanese companies, especially the large modern concerns, retained the loyalty of their employees, who were made to feel that what was best for the company was also best for Japan. This business ideology gained credence from management's practice of plowing earnings back into the firm so that it could continue to grow and hopefully surpass its rivals. Since that rather than any increase in payouts to stockholders was the company's objective, management was long able to persuade workers to moderate their demands for wage increases and fringe benefits. Naturally, the threat of foreign competition was also used to good effect, and for many years Japanese companies enjoyed a lower labor bill and greater labor peace than many of their competitors in Europe and America. The threat of foreign competition helped to motivate employees to work harder at a time when the quest for increased GNP gave Japan a sense of national purpose.

Government in many ways helped to advance that purpose. Because of popular sentiment, constitutional constrictions, and the country's reliance on an American "nuclear umbrella," Japan was now freed from the burden of supporting a large and costly military establishment. Funds and energies were thus released for economic development.

More positively, the government fostered growth through its own policies. It did this not only by establishing a political climate favorable to economic expansion and by adopting appropriate fiscal and monetary policies but also by setting production targets, assigning priorities, and generally orchestrating the economy. At the center of the government's economic apparatus were the Finance Ministry and the Ministry of International Trade and Industry. The importance of the latter reflects the crucial role of foreign trade in Japan's economy and the determination of the government to oversee the country's economic as well as political relations with other countries. By deploying foreign exchange allocations, manipulating quotas, and establishing barriers protecting native capital from foreign competition, the government could channel the flow of investment funds according to its priorities. It could also extend or deny tax privileges. It thus had at its disposal a variety of weapons to bring recalcitrant firms into line if and when persuasion and/or pressures exerted by adverse publicity failed. Generally, however, it preferred to rely on discussion and to act as much as possible on the basis of a shared government-business consensus.

Such a consensus was possible because government and business shared common aims, and government support was a major asset for firms engaged in international competition. It was facilitated by business concentration and also by ties between government and the business community. Some of these ties were personal, for the men at the top in the private sector and those heading the influential and prestigious government ministries tended to share similar backgrounds (both included a high proportion of Tokyo University graduates). Some of the ties were ideological, since Japan was ruled during these years by conservatives. And some of the links were financial, for elections were costly and business constituted a major source of funds for conservative politicians.

Politics

Under the Occupation electoral politics was reintroduced, and political parties representing a broad range of ideas and a variety of interests battled for votes. The Diet again became the central arena for national politics. The general trend favored conservatives.

The leading political personality to emerge during the Occupation was Yoshida Shigeru (1878–1967), a former diplomat who had opposed the military leadership in Japan during the thirties. Yoshida dominated Japanese politics for the better part of a decade, serving as prime minister in 1946–47, and again from 1948 to 1954. A coalition of conservatives and socialists of various shades of radicalism held power briefly in 1947-48, but it was unable to create a viable government, partly because of divisions within its own ranks, and partly because of Occupation hostility toward socialism. Upon reassuming the prime ministership, Yoshida called a new election. Held in 1949, it provided his Liberal party with an absolute majority. He remained in office until he was forced to resign in 1954 in the wake of a scandal involving the shipping industry.

In foreign affairs Yoshida's policy was pro-American and anti-Communist. In 1951 he signed the San Francisco peace treaty for Japan, officially terminating the state of belligerancy between Japan and the United States. In domestic affairs Yoshida was a conservative. His policies favored business and economic development. In 1950 he received permission from the Occupation to form a National Police Reserve of 75,000 men, a paramilitary force that assumed responsibility for internal security, thus releasing American troops for duty in Korea. In 1953 this was expanded to form the Self-Defense Forces.

Ever since the resumption of party politics under the Occupation there had been rival conservative parties, and Yoshida as prime minister had his conservative critics. However, the main opposition to Yoshida's policies came from the Socialists, who in 1951 divided into left- and right-wing parties. In 1955, after Yoshida's downfall, they reunited in their quest for political power, but again split into two parties in 1959. In the elections of 1955 the conservative Democratic party won a plurality of seats in the Diet but required the cooperation of the Liberal party to govern. Negotiations between the two parties led to their merger in November 1955 to form the Liberal Democratic party (LDP), which continues to this day.

Since 1955 the LDP has been opposed by the two Socialist parties (Japan Socialist party and the Democratic Socialist party), by the "Clean Government party" (Kōmeitō, formed in 1964, first ran candidates for the lower house in 1967), by the Communist party, and by independent politicians. This opposition was too divided to constitute a serious alternative to conservative rule, but it was sufficient to prevent the LDP from gaining the two-thirds majority in the Diet needed for revising the constitution. Some conservatives, concerned about Japan's security, favored the revocation of Article IX so as to enable Japan to acquire her own military power. In the light of a dangerous world and in response to American urgings the Self-Defense Forces were expanded to include well-equipped naval and air arms and the defense budget continued to increase. However, Japan continued to forego offensive weapons or capabilities, and total defense expenditures remained limited to approximately 1 percent of GNP.

Once the LDP was entrenched in power, the party's internal politics had a decisive influence on Japanese politics and government. Dominating the internal dynamics of the LDP, and thus determining the composition of Japan's government and influencing its policies, has been the interplay of political factions. These are formal, recognized political groupings built around a leader, usually a man with prospects of becoming a prime minister. From his faction a member derives political as well as financial support in his election campaigns and backing in his attempts to gain high government or party office. In return he owes his faction leader political support, especially during the complicated political maneuvering that determines the party presidency and thus Japan's prime ministership. Since the occupant of this post is elected by a limited number of national and prefectural politicians, the men who have presided over Japan's government have generally been seasoned politicians skilled in the art of assembling votes and working out combinations rather than leaders with wide voter appeal. What has counted has been skill in political manipulation, not popular charisma.

This kind of factionalism was not a new phenomenon in Japanese politics. The LDP's origin as an association of independently based politicians also helps to account for the strength of the factions. Also helping to perpetuate it was Japan's system of multimember election districts. In these districts there were frequently more conservative candidates than could reasonably expect to win election. For example, in a five-member district, there might be four LDP candidates with only three likely to win. In such cases, the conservative politicians would be backed by rival factions within the LDP.

The power of the factions set limits on the prime minister's authority. Factionalism also weakened the party itself, which remained weak, particularly at the grass-roots level where each politician cultivated his own local support organization composed of various groups within his constituency. This local political machine was kept oiled by the politician's ability to further the interests of the community by obtaining public works and other special interest legislation, by his support for various community activities, and by his personal assistance to constituents. In seeking to fulfill these expectations, politicians naturally found political clout and a full purse to be obvious assets. Although some politicians were solidly entrenched, there were enough shifts in political fortunes on both the local and the national level to provide for political interest during two decades of single-party rule.

For the opposition parties of the left these were years of frustration. The two Socialist parties were closely associated with labor, each linked to one of the labor confederations. They depended on organized labor for votes, and labor leaders figured prominently in their leadership. Many of their Diet members also came from a labor background. Ideologically the Socialists ran the gamut from Maoist radicals calling for revolution to moderate reformists. During the fifties the Communist party was very weak, but it picked up strength in the late sixties after adopting pragmatic policies. However, even had they been able to unite, the three leftist parties lacked the strength to topple the LDP regime.

Domestically the opposition parties viewed with special alarm LDP measures that seemed to represent a retreat from Occupation reforms and a return to the past. These included measures to recentralize the police and education functions and to give Tokyo greater control over local government. Socialist fears of LDP intentions may have been exaggerated, but they were fortified by the prominence in the conservative leadership of men who had held cabinet offices in the thirties and had been purged from politics by the Occupation authorities.

The left was adamantly opposed to government moves to recreate a military establishment and did what it could to block or at least delay the expansion of the Self-Defense Forces. They also objected to the government's consistently pro-American foreign policy, protested against the continued presence of American bases, and protested against American nuclear weapons and tests.

Unrestrained by expectations of forming a government themselves, the Socialist parties did not conduct themselves like a loyal opposition but engaged in bitter struggles, including boycotts of the Diet and physical disruptions of Diet proceedings leading to police intervention. The LDP for its part did not refrain, on issues it considered important, from using its majority to ram legislation through the Diet with little regard for the niceties of parliamentary procedure let alone any attempt to conduct a genuine exchange of views.

Political animosity reached its greatest intensity in 1960 over the issue of renewing the Security Treaty with the United States, first signed in 1952 along with the peace treaty. Opponents of the renewal were not limited to advocates of revolutionary ideologies. Many felt that instead of providing for Japanese security it endangered Japan, threatening to involve the country in American wars. The specter of nuclear war was particularly terrifying to a people who had experienced the holocausts at Hiroshima and Nagasaki. The Socialists mustered impressive support for their opposition to the renegotiated treaty. Union workers, housewives, students, professors, and members of diverse organizations took to the streets in mass demonstrations in which hundreds of thousands of people participated. There was also a one-day general strike. All this activity did not block ratification or enactment of the treaty, but it did lead to the resignation of Prime Minister Kishi (in office, 1957–60), who had pushed the treaty through the Diet in what many thought was an undemocratic manner.

After the 1960 confrontation, politics simmered down to less violent exchanges as the success of Japan's economic progress became apparent and the government concentrated on providing more of the same. This was the policy under Prime Minister Ikeda (1960–64) who announced a plan to double income in ten years—it actually was exceeded in seven. Ikeda was succeeded by Satō Eisaku, who continued in office from 1964 to 1972, longer than any other prime minister since the promulgation of the Meiji Constitution. During the Satō years, the government continued to work closely with the business community and to follow the American lead on major foreign policy issues. In 1970 the Security Treaty was renewed with little trouble.

In 1964 the political scene was complicated by the appearance of the new Clean Government party formed by the Sōka Gakkai (Value Creation Society), a religious sect. As implied by its name, the party program opposed corruption, but it was vague on other issues. After obtaining 10.9 percent of the vote in the 1969 election, it declined to 8.5 percent in 1972. The LDP for its part aroused little enthusiasm and was particularly weak in the cities. Before 1967 its candidates had received over 50 percent of the vote, but in the election of that year its percentage declined to 48.8 percent, and the trend continued slowly downward after that. However, it remained by far the largest vote getter and was also helped by an electoral system that favored rural areas. The party was therefore able to continue in power despite the erosion of its voting strength.

Social Change and the Quality of Life

The growth of the economy brought with it an unpredecented degree of affluence. The very physiognomy of the Japanese people was affected as an improved diet produced a new generation taller and healthier than their parents. People now ate more fish and meat, although the proportion remained modest by American standards. Dairy products became a staple of the daily diet. Changing tastes were reflected in a steadily rising consumption of wheat at the expense of rice, which, thanks to the government's price support policy, was in overabundance. While traditional cuisines continued to flourish so did Western foods and beverages. Japan became a nation of coffee as well as tea drinkers. During the seventies, the influx of Western foods continued apace as the arch of McDonald's hamburgers spread from Tokyo's Ginza to less likely places, where it was soon joined by the figure of Colonel Sanders inviting passersby to partake of Kentucky Fried Chicken, and Mr. Donut and Dairy Queen did their part to propagate popular fast-food culture American style.

Japan became a nation of Western-style consumers. The washing machine, vacuum cleaner, and refrigerator of the fifties were soon joined by the television set (preferably and increasingly color) and the air conditioner. Meanwhile, the worsening traffic jams that clogged Japan's roads demonstrated that many a family had realized its dream of owning a private automobile. Thus a solid domestic market supported Japan's major consumer-export industries.

Figure 24-1   The bullet train passing Mt. Fuji.

Ownership of the new products was not confined to the cities, for the countryside also participated in the general prosperity. This was partly because the economic boom produced a labor shortage, so that wage scales were set and plant locations determined in such a way as to draw rural manpower into the factories. At the same time, as already noted, agricultural production nevertheless increased. Another source of rural well-being was the LDP's policies, including the support of rice that the government purchased from farmers at several times the price current in the international market. Thus the stark economic distinction between city and country, which had existed in prewar years, was eliminated. At the same time, the spread of television accelerated the process, begun by radio, of diffusing the culture of the cities to the countryside. However, despite the omnipresence of the television set, the Japanese remained the world's most avid consumers of the printed word, supporting a flourishing newspaper and magazine industry as well as more bookstores per capita than any other country in the world.

Japan also led the world in the excellence of its public transportation system, including the bullet trains which by the mid-seventies connected Tokyo and Northern Kyūshū, whisking passengers past Japan's greatest mountain at 125 miles per hour. (See Figure 24-1.) Plans are to extend this line until eventually it will run from Nagasaki, in southern Kyūshū, to the far north, and experiments are underway for a futuristic linear propulsion train, which, riding on a magnetic cushion, is envisioned as making the trip from Tokyo to Kyōto in an hour. Within the cities, public transport is frequent, punctual, and efficient, although in Tokyo's rush hour ("crush hour" would be more appropriate) "pushers" are needed to cram the people quickly into the overflowing subways.

Public transportation, communication, and security were excellent, but in other areas the state did little, preferring to leave matters to the private sector. While this worked quite well in certain respects, in others it proved highly inadequate. An example of the latter was the government's laxity in pollution control. As a result Tokyo became enshrouded in a semiperpetual screen of smog while elsewhere chemical pollution made some waters downright poisonous. Most notorious was the "Minamata Disease" caused by people eating fish contaminated by methyl mercury discharged by a fertilizer plant in Kyūshū. The full dimensions of this tragedy are still to be determined by the courts, but the company has acknowledged that the poisoning brought death and suffering to the village of Minamata. Japan's long industrial area, running along its Pacific coast, became one of the most ugly and noxious to be found anywhere. While the Japanese people continued to cherish nature in miniature, lovingly tending tiny gardens on the most unlikely bits of land, Japan's leaders, in their rush to modernize, sacrificed much of the larger beauty of the natural landscape that had once been Japan's beloved heritage.

A serious social and economic problem was the constantly escalating price of land and housing in Japan's large cities. Young married people, despite their modern wish for independence, found themselves forced to live with their in-laws because they could not afford separate establishments. Others were crowded into tiny apartments in drab and monotonous buildings made of reinforced concrete. Raising a family in such confined quarters was no easy task. Although the small apartments reduced women's household chores, releasing time for other activities, the residents of such buildings were slow to develop a sense of community, since they regarded these quarters as temporary expedients marking a stage of their lives and careers soon to be surmounted. This outlook was not unreasonable, since in Japan promotion, particularly in the early career stages, was generally by seniority.

The absence of grandparents in the new housing was but one of the factors making for discontinuity between the generations. Such discontinuity was not unique to Japan, for in other countries too, rapid changes during the postwar years created a "generation gap." Indeed, the presence of this phenomenon in Japan can itself be regarded as one more sign of Japan's modernity. However, in Japan the gap was particularly severe. Not only did the younger people grow up in a society that had suddenly become very different from that of their parents, but a whole generation of leaders had been thoroughly discredited and the old values blamed for leading the nation to catastrophe. Included were many of the old values that long had helped to provide Japanese society with its cohesiveness.

New life styles and values appeared in the factories as young workers preferred to spend their leisure time manipulating pachinko (vertical pinball) machines or listening to rock music rather than going on company outings, and their valuation of skill over length of service, although very much in tune with the new technology, set them apart from their elders. Furthermore, they tended to regard the factory not so much as a second home but merely as a place of work.

Meanwhile, those fortunate enough to survive a brutal entrance examination system found themselves admitted to universities oriented largely to research and graduate work. Ostensibly paternalistic, the universities demonstrated their supposed concern for the youngest members of the academic community by virtually guaranteeing graduation to all matriculants. Neglected after having worked so hard for university entrance, the students expressed their discontent in radical political activities. Their dissatisfaction helped fuel widespread demonstrations and disruptions in the later sixties, their protest directed against both national and university policies. In this, again, Japanese young people were, of course, not alone.

In other ways, too, the postwar generation resembled their counterparts in other industrialized countries, and there is hardly a mode of dress, a style of music, or a social or political movement from consumerism to terrorism that did not attract at least a modest following in Japan. Thus, just as Japanese designers were scoring their first major triumphs in the sophisticated world of international haute couture, stores specializing in jeans began mushrooming in Japanese cities. In the meantime, the kimono, although still worn for special occasions, was losing ground. In other respects too, particularly in the practice of the old crafts, traditional elegance was giving way to modern practicality.

The general loosening of traditional patterns and values presented contemporary Japanese with a wide range of choice but within what remained, by and large, a closely knit society. For example, young people increasingly insisted on making their own selection of a spouse, and they were now always consulted before a marriage was arranged. Nevertheless, even in love marriages, most young people still asked their employer or teacher to serve as an official matchmaker. Others continued to leave the initiative to their parents. Under the postwar legal system, wives as well as husbands could now initiate divorce proceedings; however, the divorce rate remained low.

Most wives remained content with their traditional roles, which gave them a predominant influence over their children and firmly established the home as their field of authority. Although submissive to their husbands in public, most wives controlled the family budget and ran the household. Many treated their husbands as they would an older, somewhat difficult, and rather special child. They accepted their exclusion from much of their husbands' social lives, which the husbands spent largely in the company of their fellow workers. Like their Tokugawa predecessors, wives also tolerated visits to bars and overlooked occasional frolics with female playmates as long as nothing serious developed and their husbands continued to look after their families.

However, as in all periods of social change, there were some who suffered because change was too rapid and others for whom it was too slow. Among the former were old people bewildered and distressed by the whirl about them. One of the strengths of the old society had always been the dignity and security afforded to the aged, but now cramped quarters and new ideas ate away at old values and threatened traditional comforts. These were people who found that the social rules had changed just when it came to be their turn to reap the rewards the system offered to those who played by the rules. While the erosion of respect for the aged diminished the traditional attractions of longevity, forced retirement at an early age (usually 55) and the devaluation of savings because of continual inflation, deprived the old of a sense of economic security. Most families did manage to take care of the elderly one way or another. Most old people were not shunted off into nursing homes or set up in special retirement communities, but the social arrangements made for the elderly by their children were often grudging and poisoned by resentment. Niwa Fumio's short story "The Hateful Age" (1947), a revolting portrait of senile selfishness, was an early expression of the new attitude.

At the other end of the spectrum were those who felt that change was coming too slowly, such as the young and middle-aged adults who felt constrained to maintain and live with their parents. They felt stifled rather than supported by a social system that still expected the individual to be subordinate to the group whether it be family or company. They also balked at conforming to a social hierarchy that had lost much of its theoretical support. The discontented were a disparate group. They included women who wanted to make a career of work and found themselves discriminated against and artists and intellectuals seeking to fill the vacuum left by the passing of the old values with something more solid than consumerism and the race for increased GNP. This discontent was frequently shared by students and by radicals impatient for a more egalitarian society. Meanwhile, some of the young men who had no prospects for university study vented their frustrations by joining motorcycle gangs. However, most of the disaffected worked out a *modus vivendi* for themselves, and many, especially among the young, gradually came to terms with society.

The great majority of the population, however, neither mourned the passing of the old nor were impatient for the arrival of the new. Appreciative of the increase in material wealth, they were nevertheless unsure of the future. Many turned to new religious sects, seeking to satisfy their spiritual hunger and to cure a psychological malaise brought on by the loss of community entailed by moving from traditional village to modern city. Attracting the largest membership was Sōka Gakkai, which we have already encountered as the sponsor of the Clean Government party. Doctrinally based on Nichiren Buddhism, it denounced all other faiths and insisted that its members proselytize relentlessly. One of the obligations of the faithful was a pilgrimage to the head temple at the foot of Mt. Fuji, where an average of ten thousand people a day came to pay their homage. By passing a series of examinations, the faithful could rise in an academic-like hierarchy of ranks. For the devoted members, the sect provided not only spiritual community but a sense of personal worth and of belonging to a large, integrated, purposeful group.

Others found it more difficult to find new certainties, however, for the world offered a bewildering range of choices.

The Japanese Film

If, as is often said, the film is the characteristic art form of the twentieth century, then the worldwide acclaim accorded Japanese films is but one more indication of Japan's full participation in the culture of that century. All Japanese films were by no means masterpieces: Japanese film companies were second to none in turning out ephemeral entertainments—samurai movies that were the artistic equivalents of American westerns, lachrymose melodramas with torrents of tears intended to induce a similar flow in the audience, horror and monster films, and, in the seventies, a wave of erotica with little artistic or social value but much sexual action. Such films, reflecting social stereotypes and people's daydreams, are of considerable interest to psychologists and social scientists, but it is important to remember that the stereotypes they contain—the self-sacrificing but self-centered mother, the wife finding herself, daughters in various degrees of revolt—are never simple mirror images of society. The more ambitious and truly fine films also reflected the times and the society, but, beyond that, they provided new insights into the Japanese and the human reality. And they did this while drawing an enthusiastic mass audience as had the kabuki and *bunraku* (puppet theater) in their day.

The major films were the creations of fine actors, sensitive cameramen, and above all great directors. While some fine directors were remarkably versatile, the most outstanding were able to use the medium to create their own personal styles, conveying their own personal visions. If they had anything in common, it was a superb visual sense employed to create an atmosphere. Some may be said to have used the camera to paint their vision on the screen. Many are best viewed as one would view a painting—with a contemplative eye.

Exercising classic restraint in his insistence on a strict economy of means (empty spaces, simple objects, minimal plot) and avoiding anything superficial or artificially clever was Ozu Yasujirō (1903–1963), whose traditionalism also extended to his subject matter, for he was the film maker par excellence of the Japanese family. Describing the effect and tone of Ozu's films, Donald Richie has used the old term, *mono no aware,* first encountered in our discussion of *The Tale of Genji.* Richie went on to say that Ozu's "emphasis on effect rather than cause, emotion rather than intellect" and "his ability to metamorphose Japanese aesthetics into terms and images visible on film" made Ozu "the most Japanese of all directors."[1]

Other directors did not take as positive a view of Japan's social tradition and the old values. For example, in *Harakiri* (*Seppuku,* 1962), directed by Kobayashi Masaki, the hero sets out to avenge his son who had been forced to commit an unimaginably painful *seppuku* (ritual suicide) using a sword with a bamboo blade, but in the end the whole system is revealed as founded on hypocrisy. Or there is *Night Drum* (*Yoru no Tsuzumi*, 1958), directed by Imai Tadashi, in which a samurai kills the wife he loves and thereby deprives his own life of meaning, because this is what society demanded. Such vivid and moving historical films were among the triumphs of the postwar cinema, a part of a continuing and sometimes bitter dialogue with a still living past.

Outstanding as a truly great director is Kurosawa Akira (1910–), who, while remaining Japanese in his aesthetic and historical vocabulary, displays a concern for truly universal themes. Thus his world famous *Rashomon* (1950) suggests the relativity of all truth through a demonstration of the power of human subjectivity and self-interest. In *Ikiru* (1952) the viewer is taken through a Faust-like quest for meaning in life. The main character, a petty bureaucrat dying of cancer, in the end finds fulfillment in one meaningful social act—surmounting endless red tape and bureaucratic obstructionism, he gets a small park built. A gripping, powerful film, filled with action and drama, is *Seven Samurai* (1954), the story of seven *rōnin* who agree to defend a village against its bandit enemies. It is one of those rare films in which powerful and sensitive acting, beautiful visual composition and realistic detail, story line and structure, friction and harmony, violence and stillness, blend into a major artistic statement, a masterpiece.

The Visual Arts

Not only Japanese films but also the work of Japanese painters, potters, and architects won international recognition for their contributions to the world of art. As in the prewar years, some artists found their inspiration in, and took their cues from, the latest trends, so that Japan had its practitioners of abstract expressionism, action painting, pop art and the various other international art movements that at their best reflected the search for a style appropriate to a bewildering age and at their worst degenerated into fads. The cacophony of the art scene may be suggested by the disjointed ears in Figure 24-2. What are they listening to? No doubt their metallic color is appropriate for the age of the machine. Do they symbolize modern (Japanese?) man? Are they all that is left of humankind—disembodied ears?

More in keeping with the Japanese aesthetic tradition was the work of artists who strove to create beauty without attempting to convey a symbolic message. Japanese potters, both innovators and traditionalists, continued to blend shapes, textures, and colors to create works worthy of the great tradition to which they were heirs.

Another area of excellence was architecture. Although many opportunities for architectural excellence were missed in the surge of postwar reconstruction and some of Japan's industrial centers are among the ugliest cities in the world,

Figure 24-2
Miki Tomio (1937–),
Ear 201. Bronze, 1965,
41.4 cm × 34.7 cm.

there were also new buildings of great distinction. The architect Tange Kenzō (1913–), designer of the Hall Dedicated to Peace at Hiroshima, won a deserved international reputation as one of the great masters of his art. His work can be seen not only in numerous structures in his own country (the Swimming Pool and Sports Center he designed for the 1964 Tokyo Olympics is one of the most famous) but also in Europe, North Africa, the Middle East, and in the United States, where the Arts Complex in Minneapolis (1970–74) has been completed, and he is involved in the Inner Harbor Residential Redevelopment project in Baltimore. As illustrated by the latter, not only has Tange designed superb buildings, he has also been deeply involved in urban planning. Also in the interior design of modern buildings, the Japanese aesthetic of simplicity, of clean lines and uncluttered spaces, proved most compatible with modern tastes and sensibilities.

An area of major artistic achievement was the modern woodcut. Unlike the earlier *ukiyo-e* artists, those who now worked in this medium took responsibility for the entire process of print making. They did their own cutting and printing, although they might have students assist them in the more routine aspects of the process. Among the finest was Munakata Shikō (1903–75), a gifted painter as well as print artist, whose style was influenced by traditional Japanese folk art but who also developed new techniques. One was to add color to his prints by hand, applying color on the back of the print and letting it seep through the paper to create gentle, diffused coloring. This helped Munakata create a general decorative effect. Munakata's concern with decoration is well illustrated by his rendition of the clothing in *Lady in Chinese Costume*, shown in Figure 24-3. The lines marking the folds in the cloth and suggesting its ornamentation are repeated in the remainder of the print, giving it its rhythm. Strong black areas and lines contrast pleasingly with soft blues and browns.

A similar love for the decorative is evidenced by Munakata's frequent use of written characters for ornamentation. In subject matter his work ranges from the religious to the sensuous and the whimsical (for example, a nude with the artist's eyeglasses resting on her belly). In tone his art is positive and life

Figure 24-3
Munakata Shikō,
Lady in Chinese Costume.
Woodcut, 1946,
45.5 cm × 32.6 cm.

affirming—there is no echo here of the agony of the century. There are strong hints of Persia and India, but in the vigor of his lines, his gentle eroticism, and the decorative qualities of his art, Munakata resembles Matisse while his coloring is also reminiscent of Chagall.

Literature

The literature of the postwar period continued to sound many themes pursued in a variety of styles, as older novelists published manuscripts they could not release during the war and new writers appeared to sound new themes. An outstanding example of the former is the long novel by Tanizaki translated as *The Makioka Sisters* in which the author of *Some Prefer Nettles* examined an Osaka family and the contrast between the old, traditional, and Japanese on the one hand and the new, modern, and Western on the other.

In 1947 Kawabata published the last installment of *Snow Country*. Previous segments of the novel had been published in various journals over the course of the preceding twelve years, each part appearing as though it might be the conclusion, as though each part were a stanza in a *renga* (linked verse) rather than a building block for a novel. Characteristically Kawabata's novels sacrifice structure and plot for the sake of naturalness and poetry. *A Thousand Cranes* (1948) and *The Sound of the Mountain* (1951) followed, each imbued with the author's visual sensibility and with his concern for beauty and sadness, inseparable as ever in Japanese literature, and evoking what one critic termed a "vibrant silence."[2] The essential Japaneseness of Kawabata's method and vision was clearly demonstrated in his Nobel Prize acceptance speech (1968). Translated as *Japan, the Beautiful, and Myself*, it is an evocation of the Japanese tradition, a string of poems and images held together by a shared perception of beauty and truth.

In his youth Kawabata had been influenced by Western literary theories, but his work and its themes were classically Japanese. For the younger Mishima Yukio (1925–1970), however, the classically Japanese had been lost and could be regained, if at all, only through great effort. Brilliant, prolific, versatile, and uneven, Mishima, in a series of well-constructed novels, developed his ideas on such universal themes as the relationship between art and life, warrior and poet, and the nature of beauty. One of his most compelling novels was *The Temple of the Golden Pavilion* (1956). Based on the actual burning down of the Golden Pavilion (Kinkakuji, see p. 287) in postwar Kyōto, it includes powerful psychological and philosophical explorations. A noted dramatist and critic as well as novelist, Mishima's work defies summarization. And it went beyond literature, for he tried to mold his life and his body as he did his art. Wishing to be both athlete and artist, he took up body building and succeeded in developing a strong torso (but on spindly legs). Seeking to achieve a unity of knowledge and action as in the philosophy of Wang Yang-ming whom he admired, Mishima's culminating act was a public *seppuku* committed after the completion of his final work, a tetrology entitled *The Sea of Fertility*. His ritual suicide was both a protest against what he perceived as contemporary Japanese decadence and an act fulfilling his life's work.

Among Mishima's contemporaries, a writer with a substantial national and international reputation is Abe Kōbō (1924–) perhaps best known for his novel, *Woman in the Dunes* (1962), subsequently made into a well-known film. In this work as well as later novels such as *Face of Another* (1964) and *The Boxman* (1973), and in such plays as *Friends* (1967), Abe explored some of the universal themes found in existentialist writers and thinkers of the postwar period in many countries. Although one of these themes is the search for identity (and for Abe this includes identification with place and community), he did not, like Mishima and others, draw on his specifically Japanese heritage but set out to make artistic statements valid for his time rather than only or even primarily for his place. The search for identity and for roots also infuses the work of Ōe Kenzaburō (1935–), two of whose novels, *A Personal Matter* (1964) and *The Silent Cry* (1967), have been translated into English. Insight into psychological complexities of modern people, including the sources of violence, a concern for social morality, a strong personal symbolism, and his grapplings with basic problems of existence in the second half of the twentieth century mark him as a major writer and one who speaks to the central problems of his age.

The Seventies

During the early and mid-seventies there were no sharp breaks with the preceding decades, but there were signs of longer-term change as well as a series of short-term economic and political shocks. The latter began in 1971 when the United States, Japan's largest trade partner, placed a 10 percent surcharge on imports and effectively devalued the dollar by floating it, that is by allowing the international monetary market to determine its value vis-à-vis the yen and other currencies rather than maintaining a fixed rate of exchange. Both of these American actions were aimed at reducing, if not eliminating, a mounting United States trade and payments deficit in its dealings with Japan. They demonstrate the way in which Japan's economic success created new problems.

A political blow followed these economic acts when, still in the same year, Washington announced the impending visit of President Nixon to China, an act on which Japan was not consulted and which undercut Prime Minister Satō, who, primarily to please Washington, had been following the unpopular policy of maintaining the fiction that the Nationalist regime on Taiwan was the government of China.

Other shocks followed. The Arab oil boycott in 1973 reminded Japan of her dependence on imported energy and was followed by a quadrupling of the price of this vital import. Then, early in 1976, the Lockheed scandal ("Japan's Watergate") shook the political world as it was revealed that millions of dollars of the American company's funds had been used to corrupt the highest Japanese government officials. Among those indicted was Tanaka Kakuei, prime minister 1972–74. The seventies closed with intensified uncertainties over oil as world prices rose and Japan worried over events in Iran, its major supplier.

Both the economy and the LDP survived these shocks without serious restructuring. In the 1976 election for the lower house the LDP declined to 41.8 percent of the popular vote and achieved a one-vote majority only by including eight independent conservatives. Hoping to do better, Prime Minister Ohira (1910–) called for elections in October 1979, and the party's share of the vote rose to 44 percent, but it gained only one seat and again had to depend on independents to form a majority. The LDP retained its control of the upper house, but the days when it could ram legislation through the Diet on the sheer strength of its majority were past. Also, the outcome of efforts to strengthen the party internally remained in serious doubt, since the factionalism showed no sign of abating. However, the LDP remained by far the largest party, and during the seventies continued to provide Japan with continuity and seasoned leadership. But only time will tell whether it will also be able to provide the statesmanship and vision the nation will need in coping with the future and its problems.

On the international front, Japan recognized the People's Republic of China after Prime Minister Tanaka's visit to Peking in 1972. There were also efforts to broaden Japan's trade pattern, particularly to increase trade with the countries of Southeast Asia and to diminish Japan's dependence on trade with the United States. There was, however, no major change in the general direction of foreign policy nor much enthusiasm for any shift away from reliance on American atomic protection even though the uncertainties of President Carter's Korean policy (withdrawal of ground troops) caused uneasiness in Japanese government circles.

Japan continued a cautious, "low profile" foreign policy stance, aware of the country's dependence on the international economic system. With the achievement of economic success the Japanese government was increasingly prevailed upon not only to open new home markets to foreign companies but to restrain the country's exports of cars, television sets, steel and other products to the United States and the countries of the European Common Market. Furthermore Japan's economy had reached a size which made its trade and monetary policies themselves important factors in the operation of the international economy. Thus any action undertaken by Japan affected the whole system and brought repercussions back to Japan itself.

During 1974–76 Japan suffered a severe recession, but on the whole the economy weathered the shocks of the seventies remarkably well. Now the consensus of economists is for continued long-term economic growth, although at a slower rate (5 to 8 percent) than before, but nevertheless at a very respectable rate for an advanced industrial country. A decrease in the growth rate is also in keeping with a new climate of opinion that developed in the seventies when people became disillusioned with the single-minded pursuit of economic growth as the social costs of such a policy became apparent. There was now an emphasis on the need for cleaning up air and water, for improving housing and social services, and there were those who were ready to abandon growth for these ends. Others argued that some growth was necessary in order to finance the needed improvements without increasing the tax load.

The new goals were generally supported by the public but were not capable of generating an enthusiastic sense of national purpose. In addition to those who had all along been unhappy over Japan's previous national purpose, there were now those who felt that the country lacked any such purpose at all. Many turned from company to home for personal satisfaction, but others felt that the pursuit of private goals (*maihōmushugi*, that is, "my-homeism") was an unsatisfactory solution.

Perhaps this was yet another sign of Japan's full participation in the international culture of the industrialized non-Communist world. Compared with the countries of Western Europe and with the United States, Japan continued to demonstrate comparatively greater social cohesion, although the breakdown of old patterns of behavior and old values was also apparent. Whether Japan would be able to achieve a creative synthesis between the new and old remained very much an open question, but the people's continuing quest for the answers gave the land much of its vital excitement.

NOTES

1. Donald Richie, *Japanese Cinema* (New York: Doubleday, 1971), p. 70.
2. Masao Miyoshi, *Accomplices of Silence: The Modern Japanese Novel* (Berkeley and Los Angeles: The University of California Press, 1974), p. 120.

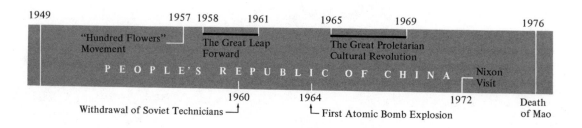

1949   1957   1958   1961   1965   1969   1976

"Hundred Flowers" Movement

The Great Leap Forward

The Great Proletarian Cultural Revolution

PEOPLE'S REPUBLIC OF CHINA

Nixon Visit

Withdrawal of Soviet Technicians ⅃   1960   1964   1972

⅃ First Atomic Bomb Explosion

Death of Mao

25 The New China

When Mao Tse-tung proclaimed the People's Republic (October 1, 1949) it marked a watershed in the history of modern China. Establishment of the new regime brought an end to over a century of increasingly severe political and social instability. It also represented a new beginning, for it brought China under the rule of leaders who were deeply committed to the revolutionary transformation of the nation. Mao and his associates were determined to create a new egalitarian society at home, and to make China respected abroad.

The new leaders faced problems as immense as China itself, but they brought to their task some powerful assets. This was a leadership tempered by long years of struggle. They could draw on the experience of having led a mass movement and of having actually governed, an experience not found in the history of any other Communist party prior to the seizure of power. They were dedicated Marxists, but as Mao had insisted all along, they recognized the need to adapt the foreign ideology to Chinese conditions. In retrospect this duality (Chinese *and* Marxist) seems so obvious that it is hard to understand how the United States and the Soviet Union failed to perceive it. For many years the United States saw only *Communist* China, while today the U.S.S.R. denies that the Chinese are genuine Marxists at all. As in the case of Taiping Christianity, what from one vantage point appears as a creative adaptation of a foreign faith is seen from a different perspective as the sheerest apostasy. However, whatever the ideological perspective within or beyond Marxism, there can be no doubt that during the quarter of a century following its establishment, the new government ushered into being a new China.

The transformation of China was not always smooth nor did it proceed at a uniform rate; Mao himself coined the formula "two steps forward; one step backwards." Nor is the transformation complete. But it is substantial.

The First Phase (1949–1958)

The first nine years of the new regime were marked by substantial progress in social, economic, and governmental affairs. This first phase may be subdivided into an earlier period of consolidation (1949–52), followed by a period of Socialist Construction, which was initiated by the publication of the first five-year plan in 1953.

Politically, the years after 1949 saw the establishment of the basic machinery for governing China. A characteristic feature of the Chinese system (as it was, also, in the Soviet Union) was the creation of parallel government and party structures, and the practice of appointing high party officials to top government posts. Thus Mao was head of the party (that is, Chairman of the CCP Central Committee) and, until 1959, also officially head of state. Party control was also exercised in other sectors by the same means. High party members held positions of leadership in various quasi-official organizations such as trade unions, and, as during the pre-1949 years, party members served as political commissars in the army. An important factor in the smooth functioning of this system was the cohesiveness of the CCP leadership. The only political conflict to erupt openly was an attack on Kao Kang, the head of the Communist party in Manchuria, who was accused of separatist ambitions. His suicide was reported in 1955.

Administratively China was divided into provinces, and these remained the primary political subdivisions after an additional governmental level between the provinces and the central government was tried but discarded. The three most highly populated metropolitan areas, Shanghai, Peking, and Tientsin, were placed under the central government, and "autonomous regions" were created in areas inhabited by a significant number of minority people. These "autonomous regions" were Kwangsi, Inner Mongolia, Ningsia (southeast of Inner Mongolia), and the vast western regions of Sinkiang and Tibet. The latter was incorporated into the People's Republic after Chinese troops entered that mountainous land in October 1950, the same month in which Chinese "volunteers" intervened in Korea, but Tibet did not receive "autonomous region" status until 1965. (See map, pp. xxii–xxiii.)

The People's Republic was clearly determined to guard China's frontiers and to reassert China's sovereignty over outlying areas. However, the Chinese recognized the independence of Outer Mongolia, where the Mongolian People's Republic had been established in 1924, under Soviet sponsorship. Indeed, the relationship with the Soviet Union was particularly important to the Chinese leadership in these years. The U.S.S.R. provided a working model for social, economic, and governmental development; it provided moral, political, and economic support for the Chinese regime; and the alliance with Russia was the mainstay of China's foreign policy. A close relationship between the two countries was maintained despite the fact that the U.S.S.R. drove a hard bargain in agreements between the two states and was slow to relinquish special Russian interests in Manchuria and Sinkiang.

After the Korean War, the People's Republic gained in international standing, and Peking's representatives played an important role in the Geneva Conference on Indo-China (1954) and at the conference of Asian-African states held at Bandung (Indonesia) in 1955. However, the People's Republic was not accorded membership in the United Nations, nor was it recognized by the United States and many of its allies. The buildup of Nationalist strength on Taiwan rankled. However, with the U.S. Seventh Fleet patrolling the Taiwan Strait, actual fighting was limited to sporadic shelling of two Nationalist held islands off the coast of Fukien Province.

Internally during 1951–52, there was a "three anti" campaign against waste, corruption, and bureaucratism aimed at disciplining the greatly enlarged CCP membership, and a "five anti" campaign against bribery, tax evasion, fraud, the stealing of state property, and the theft of economic secrets. During this campaign many wealthy men had to pay heavy fines. In accordance with Mao's "On the New Democracy" (1940), members of the national bourgeoisie were initially tolerated, and only capitalists with KMT or foreign ties were considered enemies of the revolution. Gradually, however, private companies were turned over to the state, although their former owners often remained as managers and continued to receive some dividends into the 1960s.

Not all drives were directed against human evildoers; there was also a concerted Attack on the Four Pests: a war against rats, sparrows, flies, and mosquitoes. Partly by campaigns such as this, the People's Republic achieved enormous improvements in public health. Furthermore, by involving all the people in these campaigns, the leadership not only made use of China's most precious asset (manpower) but also gave the people a sense of participation and pride in the resulting accomplishments.

Economic Policies

Economic matters were of central concern to the new government right from the start. It had inherited a land ravaged by war and floods, with both agricultural and industrial output badly down from prewar levels and the monetary system wrecked by inflation. Furthermore, the underlying economy had serious structural weaknesses. In the agrarian sector, the prevalence of small, uneconomic, scattered landholdings and uneven land ownership helped to perpetuate traditional farming techniques and discouraged capital formation and investment in agriculture. China's industrial sector, on the other hand, consisted primarily of light industry concentrated around Shanghai and heavy industry in Manchuria. It had been developed to meet the requirements of foreign capital rather than the needs of China and its people.

Any government would have had to restore and strengthen the economy to increase production, but as Marxists, China's new leaders were also committed to a complete restructuring of the entire system, including the transfer of the means of production from private to public ownership and the creation of an egalitarian system of distribution. Their aim was to create a socialist state with a strong proletarian (working class) base. The necessary precondition for this was vigorous industrialization, and since this was also required for the attainment of national strength, economic ideology and patriotism pointed to the same end.

By 1952, despite the strains of the Korean War, the economy had been restored to prewar levels. Factories had been put back into operation, railway lines had been repaired, and inflation had been brought under control. Furthermore, a program of land redistribution had been carried out. Landlords and rich peasants had been forced to relinquish land they did not require for their own support. At this time, the former landowners were frequently denounced at mass "speak bitterness" meetings, where they had to confront the long suppressed fury of the rural poor. As a result, many former landlords lost their lives. There was not, however, a centrally directed drive to kill landlords.

With economic recovery achieved, China was ready to embark on planned economic growth. A planning organization was established, as was a statistical bureau, and in 1953 China took its first modern census, which registered a total population of 582,600,000 on the mainland. Although demographers have questioned its accuracy, this figure is accepted as a general indication of the size of China's population at the time.

China's First Five-Year Plan followed the model of the Soviet Union's economic development in stressing heavy industry, with some 85 percent of total investments going into this sector. The role of the Soviet Union was important also in other ways. Russia supplied technical assistance (plans, blueprints, and so forth), assistance in training Chinese technicians (28,000 Chinese technicians and skilled workers went to the U.S.S.R. for training during the fifties), and it also helped by sending about 11,000 of its own experts to work in China. Development was also accelerated by importing entire plants from the Soviet

Union. However, the financing of this effort was predominantly Chinese, since loans advanced by the Soviet Union amounted to only 3 percent of China's total state investment.

The funds for these investments came out of the government's budget. The government, in turn, derived much of its revenue from taxes and from the income of state enterprises. Ultimately, a considerable portion of investment capital was supplied by the agricultural sector, for agriculture remained the heart of the Chinese economy. To increase output and channel agricultural surplus more effectively into capital formation, the government in 1953 began a campaign for a more radical transformation of the pattern of land management. To replace the existing system of small fields, individually owned and worked, the government planned to collectivize agriculture by pooling land, labor, and other resources. The change was not accomplished in one fell swoop. At first, "mutual-aid" teams, which shared labor, tools, and work animals, were organized. The next stage was to create village producers' cooperatives in which land also was pooled. Initially the program was voluntary, but when there was resistance, party cadres applied pressure to the peasantry. In 1957 the process was completed.

When the First Five-Year Plan came to an end, the Chinese could view the results with considerable satisfaction. The government was now firmly in control of the industrial sector, and agriculture had been reorganized. In such key areas as iron, coal, and steel, the production targets set by the plan had been exceeded, and, altogether, remarkable progress had been made on the road to industrialization. There was cause for confidence as China's leaders prepared for an even more ambitious Second Five-Year Plan.

Thought Reform

The leaders of the People's Republic were convinced not only of the scientific correctness of their doctrine but also of its moral rightness, and they believed that virtually everyone could be brought to share their vision and act accordingly. They were optimistic not only about the course of history but also about the nature of human beings, and they retained a traditional Chinese faith in the moral perfectibility of man as they set about creating an ideal socialist man to replace the traditional models. It was their belief that given the proper environment and correct guidance, people would become selflessly devoted to revolution and community.

Naturally the most promising were the young, uncontaminated by the old society, and the government saw to it that they were educated in the new values. Special attention was paid to the political awareness of Communist party members and cadres, who were relied on to set examples of personal conduct and lead ordinary people. Not only were the masses of peasants and workers to be educated, even the most unpromising human material was considered redeemable. In the Chinese view, the elimination of undesirable social classes required the reeducation, not the liquidation, of their members.

To further the thought reform and moral transformation of such people, the authorities devised techniques of group discussion, self-criticism, and public confession. By using the individual's own feeling of moral inadequacy and guilt, and by applying external pressures, the authorities induced people to renounce old values and prepared them for conversion to the new faith. Perhaps the most famous example of such a change of heart, accomplished in the controlled environment of a correctional institute, is provided by P'u-yi. As an infant he had been the last occupant of the Ch'ing throne, and more recently he had served the Japanese as puppet ruler of Manchukuo. After undergoing thought reform, he reemerged in Peking as a citizen in good standing.

Not only prominent personages but also ordinary people now spent a good deal of time in small discussion groups, analyzing their lives as well as problems or incidents at their places of work. In this way the new ideology was transmitted to the people, and they were taught to use it in analyzing everyday problems. At the same time, social pressures were applied to everyone to conform to generally accepted standards of behavior.

Policy Toward Intellectuals: The "Hundred Flowers"

The thought reform of intellectuals presented special problems. Highly trained and educated people were rare. They constituted a precious resource for a nation bent on industrialization and modernization. Yet few came from peasant or worker backgrounds. More serious than the question of class background was the persistence of traditional elitist attitudes among intellectuals, as well as their critical habits of mind. They tended to resent taking directions from party cadres less well educated than themselves. Their special knowledge and skills were needed, but could they be trusted? The integration of intellectuals into the new society remained a difficult problem.

The extent of dissatisfaction among intellectuals was revealed when Mao invited writers and thinkers to "let a hundred flowers bloom; let a hundred schools contend." When this invitation was first issued in May 1956, there was little response, for writers and intellectuals had grown wary of exposing themselves to attack. Then, in February 1957, Mao delivered a speech, "On the Correct Handling of Contradictions Among the People," in which he said that nonantagonistic contradictions should be resolved by persuasion rather than force. After some further reassurance, the floodgates of criticism were opened.

Criticism was directed not only against the behavior of individual party functionaries and at specific party policies but also at the CCP itself for seeking, as one editor declared, "to bring about the monolithic structure of a one-family empire."[1] Intellectuals and writers asked for independence from the party's ideological control. Academic problems should be left for professors to solve: "Perhaps Mao has not had time to solve these problems for us," one history professor suggested.[2]

The criticism was more than Mao had bargained for. Weeds grew where he had invited flowers. Soon criticism exceeded acceptable limits. Therefore, in

June 1957 an anti-Rightist campaign began, which in December quickened into a purge. As a result, some prominent intellectual and literary figures, most notably the writer Ting Ling, disappeared from the literary scene. Others, however, confessed their sins and were later returned to favor.

The underlying issues remained. One of these was how to insure right thinking and moral dedication to the revolution. Another was how to balance the requirements for ideological purity essential for the achievement of the aims of the revolution with the professional competence required to operate a modern state and build an industrial system. Without the former, the revolution would be jeopardized and a new elite of experts, technocrats, and managers would pursue its own aims. At issue was the emphasis to be placed on Redness over against expertise. Beyond this, since it involved everyone, was the tension between spontaneity and control: how to encourage individual initiative and foster enthusiasm without disrupting social and economic progress, how to create disciplined spontaneity and spontaneous discipline.

The Great Leap Forward

During the Great Leap Forward, initiated in January 1958 and terminated in January 1961, all emphasis was placed on Redness and revolutionary enthusiasm. Earlier the government had intended to implement a Second Five-Year Plan, but this was now displaced by an attempt to accelerate China's economic development and progress toward socialism through the mobilization of the enthusiastic efforts of all of the Chinese people. All along, of course, extensive use had been made of massive manpower in labor-intensive projects, such as the building of waterways, roads, and other giant construction works. Now all China's human energies were to be harnessed, and the spirit of the people was to be the main motor for China's continuing economic growth.

As the prime vehicle for this effort, rural communes were formed by combining the already existing cooperatives. By the end of 1958 there were 26,000 rural communes in which 98 percent of China's rural population lived. Each averaged about 25,000 people. The communes themselves were divided into production brigades, each corresponding roughly to the traditional village, and these were in turn divided into production teams. The communes were intended to function as China's basic political as well as economic and social units, integrating all aspects of the lives of their members. As economic units the communes supervised agricultural production and distribution, provided banking services, and also established small factories and machine shops operated on the commune or production brigade level, depending on the size and degree of specialization of the plant. The communes were further responsible for police functions, and they operated schools and hospitals, provided day care facilities and mess halls, took care of the aged, and staged plays and other entertainments. They represented an ambitious attempt to create new, large-scale communities. But they turned out to be too large. Their size was therefore reduced, so that by the end of the Great Leap Forward the original number of communes had almost tripled to 74,000, with a corresponding decrease in the size of their memberships. Later the communes lost many of their functions to the smaller production brigades.

There was also a movement to establish communes in the cities by combining or transforming earlier street associations, but this movement was briefer and accomplished less than its rural counterpart, perhaps because of the greater complexities of cities or because it ran into opposition. The street associations, which included the inhabitants of one street (or of several small streets, or of a portion of a large street), had originally been organized for security and welfare purposes. They were now given additional responsibilities for economic enterprises as well as for educational and medical facilities. In general, the formation of urban communes involved the transfer of authority over factories from central and provincial ministries to the local party committee that controlled the communes. Some of the communes consisted of workers in one large factory, others included the residents of one part of a city, still others, located on the outskirts of cities, included some farmland along with an urban sector. Whatever the form of urban organization, an effort was made to release women for work by establishing mess halls, nurseries, homes for the aged, and service facilities such as laundries.

To enlist the enthusiasm of the people and encourage local initiative, local authorities were granted substantial leeway in deciding how to implement government directives. The central government still set general economic policy and retained control over the largest heavy industrial plants, but 80 percent of all enterprises were decentralized. No longer was there to be reliance on experts in far-off Peking making all the decisions and operating with a centralized bureaucracy such as that of the U.S.S.R. This new policy was consistent with Mao's belief in mass participation and in the power of the human will.

High social as well as economic expectations were raised by the creation of the communes. According to Communist theory, the achievement of a truly communist society entails a change from paying people according to their productivity to paying "each according to his needs." In line with this, experiments were conducted in paying people approximately 70 percent of their wages in kind (produce to satisfy their needs) and the rest in cash according to their productivity. Meanwhile, impressive production targets were announced, including the goal of catching up with British industrial production in fifteen years. To the Chinese leaders, the social and economic goals seemed entirely compatible.

A major accomplishment of the Great Leap Forward was in furthering the emotional involvement of numerous people in the creation of a new order through the catharsis of intense participation. They were made to feel that the making of a strong China was not something to be left to the experts and technocrats; it was to be done by, as well as for, the people. People and government were to join in one vast common effort.

If the Great Leap Forward achieved some of its political and psychological goals, it was less successful economically. The initial statistics concerning production were impressive, but they turned out to have been grossly inflated.

One unanticipated consequence of the Great Leap Forward was a breakdown in China's statistical services, and serious mistakes were made because the government accepted the exaggerated figures forwarded by overenthusiastic local authorities. As a result, the government stopped publishing statistics after 1960.

Some projects originally pursued with enthusiasm later had to be abandoned as unworkable. Perhaps the best known was the campaign to build backyard furnaces for making iron and steel. The plan was vigorously implemented. All over China small furnaces were set up, but they proved incapable of turning out iron of acceptable quality let alone steel. Still, even the failures helped to spread an understanding of modern technology to the countryside, and the Great Leap Forward helped to introduce machine shops and other useful small operations into the country.

The most serious failure of the Great Leap Forward was in agriculture. Here too the government worked with misleading statistics, as local units vied with each other in reporting productivity gains. The harvest of 1958 was seriously exaggerated, leaving China poorly prepared for 1959 when bad weather harmed the crops and for the harvest of 1960, which was still worse. The gravity of China's economic situation was increased when in August of 1960 the Soviet Union withdrew all of its technicians.

The Sino-Soviet Split

From the founding of the People's Republic on, there were areas of tension and potential conflict between China and the Soviet Union. As we have seen, the CCP was not successful in achieving power until it went its own way, forging its own policies in accord with Chinese realities rather than with Moscow's theories. Furthermore, the Chinese leadership was as determinedly nationalistic as the Russians, who, ever since Stalin first came to power, had operated on the principle that what was good for the Soviet Union was also good for the cause of world communism. This was an equation with some plausibility as long as there was only one great Communist power in the world, but it was a thesis that the Chinese, sooner or later, were bound to challenge.

Initially, the forces holding the alliance together were stronger than those pulling it apart. These included not only the ties of a common ideological heritage but also a set of common Cold War enemies. However, around the mid 1950s the first cracks in the alliance began to appear.

One cause of friction and potential antagonism was territorial. The Chinese did reluctantly accept the independence of Outer Mongolia, whose historical status resembled that of Tibet, but they were very unhappy about their northern and western boundaries with the Soviet Union. These borders had been drawn in the nineteenth century and thus formed part of the history of imperialism that China's new government was pledged to undo. As early as 1954 Chinese publications indicated the country's refusal to accept vast regions of Central and Northeast Asia as permanently belonging to the U.S.S.R.

Another source of trouble was the Chinese desire for recognition as leaders within the Communist world. After the death of Stalin in 1953, they expected that Mao would be honored as the leading living contributor to Marxist ideology. Instead, Khrushchev went his own way, first shocking the Marxist world by denouncing Stalin, in a famous speech in 1956, and then by developing his theories of peaceful coexistence. Neither the rejection of Stalinism nor the U.S.S.R.'s new international stance accorded with Chinese needs, nor had the Chinese leaders been consulted before these major shifts in Soviet policy were announced.

Khrushchev's denunciation of Stalin sent shockwaves throughout the Marxist world and loosened the reins of Russian control over the Communist states of Eastern Europe. This gave the Chinese an opportunity to play a more important role within the Communist alliance. Even when they backed the U.S.S.R., as in supporting the Soviet suppression of the Hungarian uprising in the fall of 1956, they demonstrated a potential for independent action.

Despite signs of renewed friendship, including Mao's visit to Moscow in 1957, the strains in the alliance continued to mount. One reason for this was the U.S.S.R.'s unwillingness to exploit its temporary supremacy in rocketry to support a possible attack on Chinese Taiwan, an attack that would have had no hopes for success unless the United States were neutralized by Soviet threats. Khrushchev's relatively unbelligerent stance toward the United States seemed to the Chinese like a cowardly betrayal, while Mao's belittling of the dangers of nuclear warfare made him appear to the Russians as a dangerous adventurer gambling with the lives of millions. Consequently, the Russians were hesitant about sharing nuclear secrets with the Chinese, and that, in turn, furthered the strains between the two nations.

The dispute also had a strong ideological dimension. The U.S.S.R. could hardly be expected to welcome Chinese claims, made during the Great Leap Forward, that their communes represented a higher stage on the road to the ideal society than anything achieved in the Soviet Union after forty years of Communist rule.

Khrushchev's visit to President Eisenhower in the fall of 1959 confirmed Chinese suspicions that the Russians were ready to come to terms with the United States. The CCP leaders did not mince their words, and relations deteriorated. When the Russians withdrew their technicians in the summer of 1960, they even took their blueprints with them. The split was final.

Sino-Soviet Relations after 1960

Despite occasional attempts to settle their differences and despite limited cooperation on specific issues, such as supporting the North Vietnamese during the Vietnam War, efforts to reconstitute the Sino-Soviet alliance failed, and relations between the two countries tended to worsen.

One aspect of this situation was the U.S.S.R.'s support of India in its disputes with China. Relations between China and India had generally been friendly during the 1950s, but in 1959, after the Chinese suppressed a revolt in Tibet, the Indians welcomed Tibetan refugees, including the Dalai Lama, the spiritual and sometime secular leader of Tibet. Furthermore, China and India, the world's two most populous nations, were natural rivals for Asian leadership. The resulting tensions would not have led to outright hostility, however, had it not been for Indian intransigence over border disputes. The result was a short border war in 1962 in which the Chinese quickly humiliated the Indian troops. The Soviet Union continued its policy of friendship for India, and China cultivated good relations with India's arch rival, Pakistan. Meanwhile, within the Communist world, China defended and allied itself with the bitterly anti-Soviet regime of Albania.

The Chinese continued to challenge Soviet claims to ideological leadership, insisting that Mao's thought constituted the guidelines for revolution in the underdeveloped countries of the world. Going a step further, they denied the Marxist validity of the U.S.S.R.'s own development and charged both Khrushchev and his successors with deviation from the true revolutionary path. In doing so they struck a responsive chord among those revolutionaries in various parts of the world who were dismayed by the U.S.S.R.'s domestic bureaucratism and the Soviet Union's comparative lack of zeal for world revolution. Russian and East European ideologues, for their part, responded in kind, explaining Chinese aberrations as arising from their lack of a firm proletarian base and an inadequate understanding of the principles of Marxism.

Militarily the Soviet Union remained much the stronger of the two powers, but the People's Republic was also developing its armed strength. A milestone was reached in 1964 when it exploded its first atomic bomb. Numerous clashes along the border between the U.S.S.R. and China endangered the peace between them, and both sides feared that the situation might evolve into a full-fledged war. Peking invested in an extensive system of underground shelters for use in case of an attack by air. The hostility of the Soviet Union continued to be a basic reality in China's international situation. It was one of the factors that made the Chinese leadership receptive to the limited normalization of relations with the United States symbolized by President Nixon's visit to Peking in 1972.

Domestic Developments (1961–1965)

The failure of the Great Leap Forward led to retrenchment in domestic policies, a willingness to accept, for the moment, more modest interim social and economic goals. It also led to a decline in Mao's personal authority, not only because of the economic depression that had followed the Great Leap, but also because political and economic processes were becoming institutionalized and bureaucratized. The new system was settling down.

Mao was still chairman of the party, but in December 1958 he had resigned as head of the government. That post was filled by Liu Shao-chi (1898–1969), a hard-working organization man long associated with Mao. Liu had a number of supporters in high party and government positions, but the supervision of the state's administrative machinery, including the various ministries, remained under the direction of the head of the State Administrative Council, who had the title of Premier. This position had been filled since 1949 by another trusted party veteran, Chou En-lai. Chou also served as Foreign Minister until 1959, and continued even after he left that post to serve as China's main spokesman in foreign affairs. By all accounts, Chou was one of the most capable and versatile of all the CCP leaders, a superb political and military strategist, a truly gifted administrator and negotiator.

Another important government position was that of Minister of Defense. In 1959 a veteran general was ousted from this post for going too far in criticizing Mao and the Great Leap Forward, for pro-Soviet tendencies, and for overemphasizing professionalism, allegedly at the cost of failing to imbue the troops with sufficient ideological spirit. His successor as Minister of Defense was another distinguished general, Lin Piao.

Under the direction of Liu Shao-chi, the government relaxed the tempo of social change. There was now greater appreciation of expertise and less reliance on the revolutionary enthusiasm of the masses. There was an increased use of economic rather than ideological incentives: in the communes the more productive workers could earn extra work points, and in the factories there were wage increases, bonuses, and promotions to be earned—measures later castigated as "economism." Peasants were also allowed now to have small private plots and to sell on the free market whatever they could grow on them, while still under the obligation to produce a fixed amount of grain for the state.

After the great exertions and the disappointments of the Great Leap Forward, there was a natural slackening not only of the pace of change but also of revolutionary fervor. This alarmed Mao, who sought to combat this trend by initiating a socialist education movement in 1962 without, however, much effect. Furthermore, there now appeared in print thinly veiled attacks on Mao himself. Among them was the historical play, "Hai Jui Dismissed from Office," written by the Deputy Mayor of Peking. In this play the sixteenth-century Ming official (see Chapter 10) was portrayed sympathetically as an honest minister who stood up for the peasants and was dismissed by a foolish and autocratic emperor. What was implied was a critique of Mao's own dismissal, in 1959, of the then Minister of Defense. In November 1965 an article was published in the Shanghai press denouncing this play. Thus began the Cultural Revolution.

The Great Proletarian Cultural Revolution (1965–1969)

The Cultural Revolution was, from the beginning, both profoundly ideological and strongly political. In its intentions and consequences it was cultural in the broadest meaning of that term, since it sought to remodel the entire society and to change the consciousness of the Chinese people.

At the center of the Cultural Revolution was Mao himself, determined not to allow the revolution that had been his life's work to drift into Soviet-style revisionism, resolved to combat the reemergence of old patterns of bureaucratic arrogance and careerism, convinced that drastic measures were necessary to prevent the entrenchment of new vested interests in the state and party apparatus so that the people would not be robbed of their revolution. Now an old man, Mao was unwilling to rest on his laurels and enjoy the acclaim of his people as the father figure of the revolution. Instead, he actively involved himself in the Cultural Revolution and displayed great physical as well as mental energy. He demonstrated the former dramatically in July 1966 when, five months before his seventy-fourth birthday, he publically swam the Yangtze, covering some ten miles at remarkable speed.

The obstacles to the Cultural Revolution were formidable because it affected the vested interests of a majority of party functionaries both at the center and in the provinces. But among Mao's assets were not only his unequaled prestige but also the support of the People's Liberation Army, which under Lin Piao, emphasized guerrilla-style revolutionary spirit and fostered solidarity among officers and men by deemphasizing and reducing the importance of rank. In the summer of 1965, insignia of rank were abolished. Nor were there any other differences in uniform to differentiate officers and men. Mao and the other leaders of the Cultural Revolution hoped similarly to reduce or, if possible, to eliminate the distinctions and privileges of rank in society at large.

To accomplish this, required the destruction of the Establishment. A popular image of the Cultural Revolution was that of Monkey from *Journey to the West* (see Chapter 10):

> The Golden Monkey wrathfully swung his massive cudgel,
> And the jade-like firmament was cleared of dust.[3]

The author of the article in which these lines appeared in May 1966 went on to explain that the cudgel was Mao's thought. To carry on the battle, the country was innundated with copies of *Quotations from Chairman Mao*, the omnipresent Little Red Book cited on all occasions as the ultimate source of authority. Similarly, Mao himself was glorified as never before.

By all accounts the most enthusiastic wielders of the cudgel were the Red Guards, young people mostly born since the founding of the People's Republic. Mao hoped that their youthful spirit would revitalize the revolution and keep it from sinking into comfortable revisionism. In Mao's view it was not enough for these young people merely to read theoretical and historical works and to sing revolutionary songs. They must actually live and make revolution, so that they would be molded by direct personal revolutionary experience, much as Mao and his generation of leaders had been. Thus the youthful Red Guards were to form the vanguard of the Great Cultural Revolution. To some they represented the wave of the future, but others suffered as their uncontrolled spontaneity got out of hand, and they administered public humiliation to prominent men, administered beatings and took captives, ransacked houses, and destroyed art.

Opposition to the Red Guard and the Cultural Revolution was considerable. In many places the local authorities were able to draw on popular support. There was rioting, and pitched battles were fought between rival groups, each claiming to represent the thought of Mao Tse-tung. Much of the information on these struggles comes from the posters written in large characters that were the prime means of public communication during the Cultural Revolution. Mao himself, in August 1966, wrote such a poster, "Let Us Bombard the Headquarters."

Many party headquarters were indeed attacked, and the party was crippled. Leaders of the government from Liu Shao-chi down were made to confess their sins in public and then disappeared from public view. Universities were closed, scientific and scholarly journals ceased publication (although nuclear development went on apace), intellectual and cultural life were disrupted, and there was turmoil in the cities. However, Chou En-lai managed to keep the basic machinery of government working and was able to protect some from attack. Meanwhile, Mao's wife, Chiang Ch'ing (ca. 1915–), and his secretary, Ch'en Po-ta (1904–), emerged as leaders of the Cultural Revolution group.

With the party out of commission and the country badly divided, the army grew in importance as the single organized and disciplined institution capable of forceful action on a national scale. During many of the local struggles, it was ordered to remain neutral, but in September 1967 it intervened in fighting in Wuhan, suppressing local antigovernment insurgents. From then on military men gradually became more prominent in the various revolutionary committees set up to administer provinces, factories, and communes.

During the Cultural Revolution, party cadres and intellectuals were frequently "sent down" (hsia-fang) to work the land among the peasants, and now thousands of Red Guards were similarly removed from the cities for a stint of labor in the fields. This was not only a practical measure for restoring order but also had a theoretical basis in the "mass line," which embodied Mao's conviction that the people were the source of valuable ideas and that the function of leaders was to obtain these ideas from the masses, to concentrate and systematize them, and then to take them back to the masses. Mao thus envisioned "an endless spiral, with the ideas becoming more correct, more vital and richer each time."[4] The function of party members and other leaders in this process was humbly to learn from the masses and also to teach them. Whatever else the procedure may have accomplished, was there any better way for leaders to achieve identification with the masses?

China after the Cultural Revolution (1969–1976)

The Cultural Revolution continued until 1969, increasingly under army auspices. In April of that year a party congress officially confirmed the new prominence of the army's head by promoting Lin Piao to become Mao's successor, officially so designated in the constitution.

Attacks on "economism" made during the Cultural Revolution reflected a desire on the part of the leadership to return to the Great Leap Forward policy of placing primary reliance on ideological rather than economic motivation. This was also the policy of Lin Piao. Thus, payment for farmwork was now to be calculated according to political criteria rather than on the basis of an individual's productivity. There was also a move to place more authority in the communes at the expense of lower levels of organization. This policy, however, encountered resistance, including that of regional army commanders. The conduct of these generals revealed that Lin Piao did not have solid control of the army. Furthermore, Mao had come to mistrust Lin, and without Mao's support Lin proved very vulnerable. His fall came in the autumn of 1971. The official account is that he tried to save himself by staging a coup, and that when these plans did not work out, he attempted to flee in an airplane, which crashed in Outer Mongolia killing all aboard. From then on, denunciations of Lin Piao matched in vehemence those accorded Liu Shao-chi.

The fate of Liu Shao-chi and Lin Piao demonstrated the hazardous position of those who rose to high leadership and were marked for the succession, but Chou En-lai, as usual, was on the winning side. Chou continued as Premier, and with Mao aging, he played a more important role now than ever. In the political arena, there was a decrease in army influence and a rebuilding of the party. More moderate economic policies were adopted, and there was a general relaxation of emphasis on revolutionary fervor. For example, when universities were first reopened in 1970, after a four-year hiatus, admission was based on a candidate's recommendations from comrades in the candidate's work unit and the approval of the appropriate revolutionary committee. In 1972, however, academic criteria for admission were reintroduced. That year, the first scientific periodicals also reappeared, but the new emphasis was on applied rather than theoretical science. Public exaltation of Mao was toned down. There were even attacks on the Little Red Book; CCP members were now urged to pursue a thorough study of Marxist writings.

In dealing with the Chinese past, the political and intellectual leadership took great pride in the antiquity of their civilization and in some of the early accomplishments of the Chinese people. There was therefore a great interest in archaeology, and many discoveries made at construction sites greatly advanced the study of the origins of Chinese civilization and the history of its material culture. This work continued during and after the Cultural Revoltion, when some fine discoveries were made by amateurs. Other aspects of the Chinese past, however, were treated with less enthusiasm, in the continuing process of reinterpreting Chinese history according to the catagories of Marxist theories of historical development.

One of the historical figures who fared badly in the process of reappraising the past was Confucius, who, of course, had been under attack ever since the May Fourth movement. However, Confucius was denounced with special vigor and frequency during 1973–74 in a campaign linking Lin Piao with Confucius. Both men were portrayed as "political swindlers," sinister reactionaries standing in the way of historical progress. Thus Confucius was depicted as representing a declining slave-owner class, while Lin Piao was charged with wanting to restore capitalism, each man exerting himself to reinstate an outdated system.

The campaign against Confucius and Lin Piao suggests that the advocates of Cultural Revolution, including Chiang Ch'ing, still commanded some influence. Furthermore, the ancient philosopher and the modern general made a strange pair, and there is some evidence suggesting that Confucius was really a surrogate for Chou En-lai. As it was, the campaign died down without producing any living political victims.

The Arts

From the beginning the new regime had a direct and fundamental impact on the arts, insisting that they serve the masses. What was valued was not technique, or subtlety of expression, but revolutionary content and easy communication with the people. In keeping with this approach, major efforts were made both to broaden popular participation in the arts and to put artists in closer touch with the masses, so that they might draw inspiration from them.

As far as possible, literature and the visual arts were to be not only for the people but also by the people. Thus, during the Great Leap Forward teams were sent out to collect the people's literature and to encourage peasants and workers to compose poetry and otherwise participate in the creation of art. As a result, in Shanghai alone some 200,000 people participated in producing 5 million poems. Many thousands undoubtedly were exhilarated at achieving recognition in a field previously reserved for an exclusive elite.

During the sixties and seventies, workers and peasants continued to be encouraged to participate in the creation of art. There have been efforts at collective writing and painting. Another arrangement is for part-time writers to get a day off from their factory jobs in order to work on their literary projects. Professional writers are periodically "sent down" to factory or commune, so that they will not loose touch with the people. They also, as a matter of routine, invite popular criticism of their work and respond to suggestions for changes. For example, before *The Broad Road to Golden Light* (1972) was issued, 200 copies were sent to communes and factories for criticism. This novel by Hao Jan (Liang Chin-kuang, 1932–) went on to sell 4 million copies.

As earlier in the Soviet Union, the challenges and triumphs of a socialist society became the main topics of art and literature. The theme of *Broad Road*, for example, is the change from individual farming to the creation of mutual-aid teams. The same themes occur over and over: the ideals and struggles of the revolution, the wisdom of Mao, the heroism of soldiers, the triumph of socialist virtue over selfishness, and the glories of work. Although the style is usually designated "socialist realism," it is romantic rather than realistic, intended to inspire, not to mirror life, which in practice inevitably falls short of the ideal.

Figure 25-1   Mao Tse-tung.

A central reality in Chinese life is the importance of work. This is hardly surprising in a socialist state striving to feed its people, assure its national security, and otherwise catch up with the advanced industrial nations of the world. Everyone is exhorted to work hard and to contribute to the building of a new society; indeed, there is an almost puritan ethos of devotion to work. The arts both encourage and reflect this tendency. Thus Yüan K'o-chia (1921–) wrote in 1958:

> Labor is joy; how joyful is it?
> Bathed in sweat and two hands full of mud,
> Like sweet rain my sweat waters the land
> And the land issues scent, better than milk.
>
> Labor is joy; how joyful is it?
> Home from a night attack, hoe in hand,
> The hoe's handle is still warm,
> But in bed, the warrior is already snoring.[5]

Once Yüan was an admirer of T. S. Eliot, but all that is far behind him now!

Content is emphasized over form in the arts, and since that content is determined by the political authorities, the line between art and propaganda is often thin. To Western eyes, much that is now produced lacks appeal. Thus, none of the numerous paintings glorifying Mao Tse-tung matches in human appeal the sympathetic photograph shown here. (See Figure 25-1.)

Perhaps the most refreshing and enjoyable paintings come from the brushes of peasants and show scenes of people at work. Figure 25-2 shows a work of peasant art exhibited in Peking in 1973. It is filled with people at work. Most of the work is done by human muscle; children too are mobilized to help out, as in old China, although now they march in formation behind a red banner identifying them as little red soldiers. But there are other sources of power too, including a power station testifying to the electrification of irrigation, which is now general in China and has greatly helped agriculture. In accordance with the time, the painting also has an immediate political message: in front of the wall-poster stand, in the lower right, is a man making posters, "Criticize Lin, Criticize Confucius," and the theme is repeated in the painting's title. Like many peasant paintings, this one is done in bright and cheerful colors. Its tone is optimistic.

An art exhibition was held in Peking on the occasion of the twenty-fifth anniversary of the People's Republic in 1974. The works displayed suggested no

Figure 25-2　Hang Kao-she, *Criticizing Lin Piao and Confucius Promotes Production.* Peasant painting from Huhsien. Exhibited in Peking in 1973.

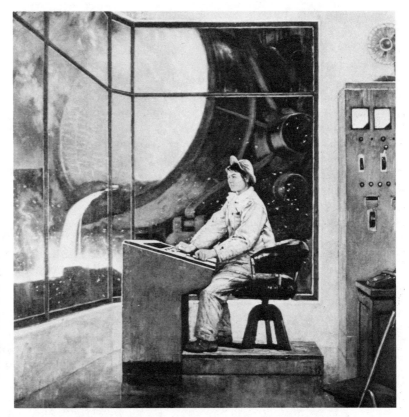

Figure 25-3
Liu Ch'ing, *Youth Red as Fire.* Oil. Exhibited at the National Exhibition Commemorating the 25th Anniversary of the Founding of the People's Republic of China.

new artistic departures but did offer further insights into Chinese life and art. Many of them show women at work, for China is determined that women become fully equal with men. In *Youth Red as Fire* (see Figure 25-3) a young woman sits at the controls of a huge steel furnace, and the red of the title is echoed by the red glow of the furnace pouring out liquid white steel.

In the performing arts, the influence of Chiang Ch'ing, herself once an actress, was particularly strong. One of her main aims was to create revolutionary operas celebrating contemporary themes in place of the old Peking opera and its traditional plots. There were also some innovations, notably in staging opera accompanied by a piano. Some of the results are far from Western tastes. Orville Schell decribes one performance as sounding "like some providentially lost Khatchaturian score," and goes on to describe an "ingeniously choreographed" harvest dance called, "We Are So Happy Because We Are Delivering Grain to the State."[6] After describing a dance featuring a father-daughter duet expressing their joy at the completion of an electric power plant, Clive Barnes, formerly the dance critic for the *New York Times,* suggested that if this seems bizarre to us, the Chinese might be just as startled by the story of a prince falling in love with a swan (Swan Lake).[7] Examples could readily be drawn from the other arts to illustrate the gulf separating contemporary Chinese and Western aesthetic perceptions.

Foreign Affairs

After the fall of Lin Piao in 1969, and with the knowledgeable Chou En-lai in charge, China was ready to adjust to the continued enmity of the U.S.S.R. by moving in the direction of wider diplomatic contacts with the United States and other Western powers. Throughout the fifties and sixties contact with the United States had largely been confined to exchanges of views between the ambassadors of the two countries in Warsaw. However, a thaw in Sino-American relations became possible when it became clear that President Nixon, elected in 1968, intended to withdraw the United States from the war in Vietnam. One of the original motivations behind American support for the anti-Communist South in Vietnam was to "contain" communism and China. Unlike the earlier war in Korea, the Vietnam War did not bring massive Chinese intervention, but the Chinese naturally supported the Communist North Vietnamese. As long as the war raged in full force and threatened to escalate still further, a change in Sino-American relations was unlikely. But a high-level Sino-American dialogue did not have to wait for the actual end of the war—a shift in direction toward peace was enough. By 1971 both sides were ready to talk. A new approach to China was deemed a logical corollary of the Kissinger-Nixon concept of international balance-of-power politics. The Chinese were receptive. The rest of the story is familiar, including the Chinese invitation to an American ping-pong team, whose members were personally greeted by Chou En-lai, and culminating in President Nixon's visit to Peking in February 1972. Sino-American relations had come a long way since John Foster Dulles, then Secretary of State, had refused to shake hands with Chou En-lai at Geneva in 1954.

The success of China's new policy was marked by the entrance of the People's Republic into the United Nations (and the expulsion of the Nationalists), the rapprochement with Japan, and recognition by almost all other countries that had not extended it earlier. One country, however, that did not establish full official relations was the United States. The United States was reluctant to terminate relations with the Nationalist government on Taiwan.

Taiwan

Both the government in Peking and that "temporarily" housed in Taipei regarded Taiwan as an integral part of China, a view also endorsed by the United States. But Taiwan is more than a piece of unfinished business left over from the Chinese civil war and the global Cold War. For one thing, the island has not, with the exception of the period 1945–49, been a part of mainland China since 1895. For three-quarters of a century its history has diverged from that of China proper. During the most recent quarter of a century it has experienced very considerable economic success along with long-term political uncertainty.

Taiwan's economic success is apparent in both agriculture and industry. In the agrarian sector there was an effective land redistribution program during the fifties, creating a peasantry that largely owned the land they worked. Here at last, with American advice, the government finally implemented a principle it had talked about for years: land to the tiller. Industrial development (stressing light industry) was advanced through the investment of great sums of money that had been brought by the Nationalists from the mainland, and was given government encouragement under a series of Four-Year Plans that began in 1953. American economic assistance also helped, until it was terminated in 1966 as no longer necessary. Another major source of capital came from Japan, as Japanese companies invested heavily in Taiwanese plants. Thus Taiwan became a participant in Japan's economic boom and attained a level of per capita income second in Asia only to that of Japan.

Among the approximately 2 million civilian refugees who came to Taiwan with the Nationalists, many brought to the island advanced training and skills that contributed to economic development. The same cannot be said of the 500 thousand or so military personnel who also made the trip. Still, on balance, the influx seems to have benefited Taiwan economically.

Although outnumbered, the mainlanders retained political control. While Taiwanese, that is people of Chinese stock who had earlier settled on the island, did win election to positions in local government, real control remained in the hands of a central government that claimed to speak for all of China. Those who grumbled were watched by the secret police and frequently ended in prison. Censors kept scrutiny for subversive ideas.

In many ways Taiwan became a modern country. For example, over 90 percent of the population is literate, an achievement comparable to that of any modern land. It became the home for institutes of higher learning, and a museum was built to house the priceless Palace Collection of Art, which the Nationalists had brought from the mainland. Many of Taiwan's intelligentsia saw their mission as one of preserving the old Chinese traditions, but there was also a small minority who sought to draw on their tradition in order to create new forms of expression suitable for their historical situation. As Liu Kuo-sung (1932–) explained: "We are no longer ancient Chinese nor modern Westerners. We do not live in the Sung or Yüan society, nor in the modern European or American environment. If it is false for us to copy old Chinese paintings, isn't it the same to copy modern Western painting?"[8] Liu is deeply conversant with both traditions. His *Metaphysics of Rocks* (see Figure 25-4) includes calligraphic brushwork and collage. The latter is described by Chu-tsing Li as follows:

> In the lower middle part are two pieces of collage, one large and the other small, both suggesting rock shapes. The paper is in color, but combined with some textures printed with wrinkled paper. Thus there seem to be several kinds of rocks, done with different techniques and brushwork. Yet none of them are realistic enough to resemble real rocks. But each gives us an idea of some quality of rocks, such as jutting up, having interesting textures, or showing watery surfaces.[9]

The political, and therefore the cultural, future of Taiwan remains in doubt. In 1972 Chiang Kai-shek died, but there was little change as the government continued under his son, Chiang Ching-kuo (1910–). Expelled from the United

Figure 25-4
Liu Kuo-sung,
The Metaphysics of Rocks.
Ink and acrylic with
collage on paper, 1968,
68.6 cm × 67.3 cm.

Nations and increasingly isolated diplomatically, Taiwan remains economically prosperous. But international politics are likely to be a major factor in settling the destiny of the more than 16 million people (well over twice the number at the end of the Second World War) who inhabit the island.

New Directions

The year 1976 was a momentous one. In January Chou En-lai died. The struggle over who should succeed him as premier grew so intense that it led to rioting in Peking before the matter was finally settled in May by Mao, who indicated his preference for Hua Kuo-feng (1920–). Hua, known as a capable administrator, was soon called on to demonstrate his talents, for in July China's worst earthquake in four centuries devastated Tangshan, an industrial and mining city a hundred miles from Peking. Casualties were high, and the quake did untold damage. But the government coped effectively in organizing relief.

On September 9 Mao Tse-tung died. Architect of the triumph of the CCP, he had been responsible for initiating most of those features of the Chinese revolution that made it unique. He had worked mightily to have the masses of the people participate fully, not only in the labor of building a strong economy, but also in the creation of a new culture and society. He had been in failing health for some time, so his death was not unexpected. Still, it came as a shock to the people he had led for so long.

Thus 1976 marked the end of an era. But it also saw the emergence of new directions. While Hua succeeded Mao as party chairman, the leadership in instituting new policies was taken by Teng Hsiao-p'ing (1904–), a party veteran who, disgraced during the Cultural Revolution, made a brilliant political comeback that culminated in his appointment as First Deputy Premier in July 1977. In contrast, Chang Ching, Mao's widow, suffered a precipitous decline. She was denounced and arrested for her purported role as leader of the "Gang of Four," which was blamed for all that had gone wrong in China over the last decade or more.

Teng's policies aimed at turning China into a modern industrial state by the end of the century. Professionalism was now encouraged, factory managers received greater authority, and measures were taken to improve workers' lives. Arrangements were made for sending specialists overseas for study and training. Pacts were signed with Japanese, American, and European firms for a massive importation of advanced technology. Negotiations with the United States led to the establishment of formal diplomatic relations in January 1979, which meant that henceforth America would have only informal ties with Taiwan. To commemorate the new Sino-American relationship, Teng* himself visited the United States. China continued to regard the Soviet Union as its main enemy.

At home, disgraced political and cultural figures were rehabilitated and, within limits, there was greater tolerance of diversity. Not only did banned Chinese works appear in print and on the stage, but Shakespeare and Beethoven could be heard again. Foreign tourism was fostered and, to accommodate international travelers, contracts were signed for the construction of American tourist hotels and the bottling of Coca-Cola. Pragmatism was the order of the day. Once again the Chinese revolution had taken a new turn.

NOTES

1. Ch'u An-p'ing, quoted in Merle Goldman, *Literary Dissent in Communist China* (Cambridge: Harvard University Press, 1967), p. 192.

2. Yang Hsiang-k'uei, quoted in *Ibid.*, p. 193.

3. Quoted in *The Great Cultural Revolution in China*, compiled and edited by the Asia Research Center (Rutland, Vt. and Tokyo: Charles E. Tuttle, 1968), p. 114.

4. Stuart R. Schram, *The Political Thought of Mao Tse-tung* (New York: Praeger, 1969), p. 317.

5. Hsu Kai-yu, *The Chinese Literary Scene—A Writer's Visit to the People's Republic* (New York: Vintage Books, Random House, 1975), p. 227.

6. Orville Schell, *In the People's Republic: An American's Firsthand View of Living and Working in China* (New York: Random House, 1977), pp. 59–60.

7. Clive Barnes, "Shanghai Ballet and Us—Two Different Worlds," *New York Times*, June 12, 1966, sec. D, pp. 5, 6, 24.

8. Quoted in Chu-tsing Li, *Liu Kuo-sung—The Growth of a Modern Chinese Artist* (Taipei: The National Gallery of Art and Museum of History, 1969), p. 32.

9. *Ibid.*, p. 53

---

* In 1979 most American newspapers and magazines switched to the *pinyin* system of romanization, so Teng Hsiao-p'ing became Deng Xiaoping. For *pinyin*, see pp. ix–xi of the introduction.

Suggestions for Further Reading

The bibliography in English on Chinese and Japanese history and civilization has increased enormously during the last twenty or thirty years, making selection all the more important as well as difficult. The intent here is to give an idea of what has been published to date so that the reader may know where to look for what. No attempt has been made to be comprehensive. Rather the effort has been made to select books that are broad enough to serve as introductions to their topics, that incorporate sound and recent scholarship, and that in their totality reflect a variety of approaches. Furthermore, the selection has been made with an eye toward readability.

Originally it was planned to list only books, but, where necessary, a few articles have also been included. In all cases in which only the author and title are given, the book has been published in a paperback edition. In the case of a few paperbacks that might otherwise be difficult to identify, the place and date of publication have been added, as has been done for all hard-cover books. Where, as is often the case, a book falls under more than one category, it has been placed under the category that reflects its primary content. Except in special cases, books are mentioned only once. General classroom collections of readings and, with two exceptions, art catalogs have not been included.

General Works

Approaches and Interpretations

A number of books composed of essays introduce the reader to various facets of East Asian history and culture. Recommended are Raymond Dawson, ed., *The Legacy of China*; John W. Hall and Richard K. Beardsley, eds., *Twelve Doors to Japan* (New York, 1965); John T. Meskill, ed., *An Introduction to Chinese Civilization*; and Arthur Tiedemann, ed., *An Introduction to Japanese Civilization*. The latter two include historical surveys as well as essays on literature, economics, geography, political institutions, and other topics. For a stimulating and influential interpretation of Japanese society, see Chie Nakane, *Japanese Society*. An older and famous work is Ruth Benedict, *The Chrysanthemum and the Sword*, which is still worth pondering. A fascinating book, with implications for comparative psychology, is Doi Takeo, *The Anatomy of Dependence*, translated by John Bester. These books do not have counterparts in Chinese studies, but three recent compendia, all published by Stanford University Press, offer good overviews of anthropological approaches to the study of China: Maurice Freedman, ed., *Family and Kinship in Chinese Society* (1972); Arthur P. Wolf, ed., *Religion and Ritual in Chinese Society* (1974); and Margery Wolf and Roxanne Witke, *Women in Chinese Society* (1975). Also see C. K. Yang, *Religion in Chinese Society—A Study of Contemporary Social Functions of Religion and Some of Their Historical Factors*.

One good approach to the study of East Asia is to read the works of some of the major scholars who have contributed to our understanding of China and Japan. Most such works are listed under the appropriate headings below, but in some cases their concerns

610

encompass a broader range. A case in point is Etienne Balazs, *Chinese Civilization and Bureaucracy: Variations on a Theme,* edited by Arthur F. Wright, and the latter's own, *The Civilization of Imperial China: Traditional Culture, Religion, and Rule,* edited by Robert Somers (New Haven, projected for 1980). Another scholar who contributed to the intellectual excitement of Chinese studies after the Second World War is the subject of a volume of essays: Maurice Meisner and Rhoads Murphy, eds., *The Mozartian Historian: Essays on the Work of Joseph R. Levenson* (Berkeley, 1976). For a more traditional approach, pursued with vast and impeccable erudition, see Lien-sheng Yang, *Excursions in Sinology.*

Some worthy books on China and Japan cannot be subsumed under any specific heading. Two which offer novel, exciting perspectives are K. C. Chang, ed., *Food in Chinese Culture: Anthropological and Historical Perspectives* (New Haven, 1977), and Ivan Morris, *The Nobility of Failure: Tragic Heroes in the History of Japan.*

The Arts and Literature

Sherman E. Lee, *A History of Far Eastern Art* (New York, 1964) includes a consideration of Indian art that is helpful for understanding the Buddhist art of East Asia. It is a well written, perceptive, but also demanding book. An excellent introduction to Chinese art is Michael Sullivan, *The Arts of China,* and a similar function is performed for Japan by Hugo Münsterberg, *The Arts of Japan.* Two valuable older books are Laurence Sickman and Alexander Soper, *The Art and Architecture of China,* and Robert Treat Paine and Alexander Soper, *The Art and Architecture of Japan.* For a sensitive and knowledgeable introduction, see Roger Goepper, *The Essence of Chinese Painting,* (Boston, 1963). *The Heibonsha Survey of Japanese Art* in thirty volumes is now available in translation (Tokyo and New York, 1972–77), as are eight volumes in the *Arts of Japan* series (Weatherhill/Shibundo, Tokyo and New York, 1973–75). These books are particularly useful because Western scholars of Japanese art participated in redacting them to meet the needs of a Western audience. Fortunately, further volumes have appeared, and the series is being continued under the title *Japanese Arts Library* (Kodansha International, Tokyo and New York, 1976–).

The best survey of Chinese literature is Liu Wu-chi, *An Introduction to Chinese Literature.* The same author is also coeditor with Irving Yucheng Lo of an outstanding anthology of Chinese poetry, *Sunflower Splendor* (also available in Chinese). Cyril Birch, ed., *Anthology of Chinese Literature,* 2 vols., includes both prose and poetry, as do two works edited by Donald Keene, *Anthology of Japanese Literature* and *Modern Japanese Literature.* Highly recommended as a literary introduction to its subject is James J. Y. Liu, *The Art of Chinese Poetry.* A similarly excellent volume is C. T. Hsia, *The Classic Chinese Novel: A Critical Introduction.* See also the same author's *A History of Modern Chinese Fiction.* For a collection of essays, mostly on literary subjects, by a master of the art of translation and a leading interpreter of Japanese literature and culture, see Donald Keene, *Landscapes and Portraits: Appreciations of Japanese Culture* (Tokyo and New York, 1971). A useful reference is Edward Putzar, *Japanese Literature—A Historical Outline,* adapted from a Japanese work. Recent work on Chinese literature is the subject of James T. C. Liu's thoroughly annotated essay"The Study of Chinese Literature in the West: Recent Developments, Current Trends, Future Prospects," *Journal of Asian Studies* 35, No. 1 (November 1975): 21–30. Unfortunately, no similar survey exists for Japan. Additional bibliography on art and literature is included in the chronological sections below.

History

A standard account is *A History of East Asian Civilization,* Vol. 1, *East Asia: The Great Tradition* (Boston, 1958 and 1960) by Edwin O. Reischauer and John K. Fairbank, Vol. 2, *East Asia: The Modern Transformation* (Boston, 1965) by Fairbank, Reischauer, and Albert M. Craig. These two volumes formed the basis for the more recent *East Asia: Tradition and Transformation* by the same three authors.

In addition to Tiedemann's *An Introduction to Japanese Civilization* mentioned earlier, recent surveys of Japanese history include John W. Hall, *Japan from Prehistory to Modern Times;* H. Paul Varley, *Japanese Culture: A Short History;* and Peter Duus, *The Rise of Modern Japan* (Boston, 1976). An extensive treatment by an older master is Sir George Sansom, *A History of Japan,* Vol. 1, *To 1334,* Vol. 2, *1334–1615,* Vol. 3, *1615–1867.* Sansom is also author of *Japan: A Short Cultural History,* which can still be read with great profit as well as pleasure. One approach to the study of history is to examine a country's own historians; see W. G. Beasley and E. G. Pulleyblank, eds., *Historians of China and Japan* (London, 1961). Also see Donald D. Leslie, Colin Mackerras, and Wang Gungwu, eds., *Essays on the Sources for Chinese History* (Columbia, S.C., 1973).

Diverse views on Chinese history are included in John Meskill, ed., *The Pattern of Chinese History: Cycles, Development, or Stagnation?,* published by D. C. Heath in the paperback series *Problems in Asian Civilization* (Boston and Lexington, Mass., 1963–70). For a recent, very stimulating interpretation, see Mark Elvin, *The Pattern of the Chinese Past.* The following are recommended as up-to-date and comprehensive: Charles O. Hucker, *China's Imperial Past: An Introduction to Chinese History and Culture* (Stanford, 1975), and Immanuel C. Y. Hsü, *The Rise of Modern China* (New York, 2nd ed., 1975). A truly comprehensive project, *The Cambridge History of China,* began publication in 1978 (see "Part V" below).

Particular aspects of Chinese history are treated in *Chinese Thought and Institutions* (Chicago, 1957), and *The Chinese World Order: Traditional China's Foreign Relations* (Cambridge, Mass., 1968), both edited by John K. Fairbank. For intellectual history, there are four volumes of essays: *Studies in Chinese Thought* and *The Confucian Persuasion,* edited by Arthur F. Wright; *Confucianism in Action,* edited by David S. Nivison and Arthur F. Wright; and *Confucian Personalities,* edited by Arthur F. Wright and Denis Twitchett. A convenient bibliography that includes listings of the individual articles in these volumes is Chun-shu Chang, *Premodern China: A Bibliographical Introduction* (Michigan Papers in Chinese Studies, No. 11).

Philosophy, Religion, and Science

A basic resource for the student of Chinese philosophy is Wing-tsit Chan, *A Source Book in Chinese Philosophy,* which covers all periods. The most extensive treatment of the history of the subject is Fung Yu-lan, *History of Chinese Philosophy,* translated by Derk Bodde (Princeton, 1952, 1953). Also see Wing-tsit Chan, *An Outline and an Annotated Bibliography of Chinese Philosophy* (New Haven, 1961). A current specialized source is the *Journal of Chinese Philosophy.* Another journal, *Philosophy East and West,* contains articles on Japanese and Indian, as well as Chinese, philosophy. For a nontechnical introduction to Chinese language, see Richard Newnham, *About Chinese.*

An excellent brief introduction to Japanese religions is H. Byron Earhart, *Japanese Religion: Unity and Diversity.* Another excellent book, which gives a fuller treatment of the subject, is Joseph M. Kitagawa, *Religion in Japanese History* (New York, 1966). Also see Carmen Blacker, *The Catalpa Bow: A Study of Shamanist Practices in Japan* (London, 1975). For China, see Laurence G. Thompson, *Chinese Religion: An Introduction* and the same author's *Studies of Chinese Religion: A Comprehensive and Classified Bibliography of Publications in English, French, and German through 1970.* Also see the volume edited by Arthur P. Wolf already noted above.

A truly monumental work of scholarship, which stands by itself, is Joseph Needham et al., *Science and Civilization in China* (Cambridge and New York). The following volumes have been published so far: Vol. 1, *Introductory Orientations* (1954), Vol. 2, *History of Scientific Thought* (1956), Vol. 3, *Mathematics and the Sciences of the Heavens and the Earth,* Vol. 4, *Physics and Physical Technology,* in three separately bound parts:

1. *Physics* (1962), 2. *Mechanical Engineering* (1965), and 3. *Civil Engineering and Nautics* (1971), Vol. 5, *Chemistry and Chemical Technology,* two parts now available: 2. *Spagyrical Discovery and Invention: Magisteries of Gold and Immortality* (1974), and 3. *Spagyrical Discovery and Invention: Historical Survey from Cinnabar Elixirs to Synthetic Insulin* (1976). Also see Needham's *Clerks and Craftsmen in China and the West: Lectures and Addresses on the History of Science* (New York, 1970). Also recommended is the highly distinguished M.I.T. East Asian Science Series. Among the books published to date is a varied collection of essays, Shigeru Nakayama and Nathan Sivin, eds., *Chinese Science: Explorations of an Ancient Tradition* (1973), and the superb, but difficult, Manfred Porkert *The Theoretical Foundations of Chinese Medicine: Systems of Correspondence* (1974).

PART I   The Classical Civilization of China (Through the Han)

Archaeology not only illuminates the beginnings of Chinese civilization but also provides invaluable information concerning its development. The leading American authority in this field is Kwang-chih Chang, who has presented a synthesis of his findings in *The Archaeology of Ancient China* (3rd ed., 1977). He has also written an important article surveying recent developments in this rapidly changing field and including much bibliographical information: "Chinese Archaeology since 1949," *Journal of Asian Studies* 36 (August, 1977): 623–60. Also recommended is William Watson, *The Genius of China: An Exhibition of Archaeological Finds of the People's Republic of China* (Westerhan, Kent, 1973). On the art of Chinese bronzes, see Max Loehr, *Ritual Vessels of Bronze Age China* (New York, 1968). On ancient Chinese writing, see Tsueh-Hsuin Tsien, *Written on Bamboo and Silk—The Beginnings of Chinese Books and Inscriptions* (Chicago, 1962).

The great historical changes that took place during the Eastern Chou are analyzed in Cho-yun Hsu, *Ancient China in Transition: An Analysis of Social Mobility, 722–222 B.C.* Also useful is Richard L. Walker, *The Multistate System of Ancient China* (Hamden, Conn., 1953).

Burton Watson, *Early Chinese Literature* is a masterly account that takes its subject through the Han. Two fine translations of early Chinese poetry are Arthur Waley, *The Book of Songs,* and David Hawkes, *Ch'u Tz'u: The Songs of the South.* Still useful is the monumental work by James Legge, *The Chinese Classics,* 5 vols. (Orig. 1893–95; reissued, 1960).

Much Western scholarship has been devoted to the classical Chinese philosophers, who are well represented in Chan's *Source Book* (see "General Works" above). In addition to the translations included in Chan's work, the following are recommended: Arthur Waley, *The Analects of Confucius;* D. C. Lao, *Mencius;* and four translations by Burton Watson: *Chuang Tzu—Basic Writings, Hsün Tzu—Basic Writings, Mo Tzu—Basic Writings,* and *Han Fei Tzu—Basic Writings.* For general accounts of early Chinese thought, see Frederick W. Mote, *Intellectual Foundations of China,* and Arthur Waley, *Three Ways of Thought in Ancient China.* A major work, whose publication is announced for 1978 (Princeton), is Kung-chuan Hsiao, *A History of Chinese Political Thought,* Vol. 1, *From the Beginnings to the Sixth Century A.D.* translated by Frederick W. Mote. Two good introductions to Taoism are Holmes Welch, *Taoism: The Parting of the Way,* and Max Kaltenmark, *Lao Tzu and Taoism* (Stanford, 1969). On Taoism and Legalism, also see Herrlee G. Creel, *What Is Taoism? And Other Studies in Chinese Cultural History* (Chicago, 1970).

Outstanding among recent interpretive works is a short but brilliant book by Herbert Fingarette, *Confucius—The Secular as Sacred.* For a sophisticated philosophical analysis of the text usually known as the *Doctrine of the Mean,* see Tu Wei-ming, *Centrality and Commonality: An Essay on Chung-yung* (Monographs of the Society for Asian and Comparative Philosophy, No. 3). An important book on a major topic is Donald J. Munro, *The Concept of Man in Early China* (Stanford, 1969).

Derk Bodde is the author of two standard studies on the Ch'in: *China's First Unifier: A Study of the Ch'in Dynasty as Seen in the Life of Li Ssu, 280?–208 B.C.* (Leiden, 1938), and *Statesman, Patriot and General in Ancient China* (New Haven, 1940). For contemporary Chinese reassessments, see Li Yu-ning, ed., *The First Emperor of China: The Politics of Historiography* (White Plains, N.Y., 1975).

A good way to learn more about the Han is by reading Burton Watson's *Ssu-ma Ch'ien: Grand Historian of China*, and the same author's translations of the great Han historian: *Records of the Historian: Chapters from the Shih Chi of Ssu-ma Ch'ien*, and *Records of the Grand Historian of China: Translated from the Shih Chi of Ssu-ma Ch'ien*, 2 vols. (New York, 1961). Watson has also published translations from the writings of the Han's other great historian: *Courtier and Commoner in Ancient China: Selections from the History of the Former Han by Pan Ku*. In addition, students of Han poetry are also indebted to him for his *Chinese Rhyme Prose: Poems in the Fu Form from the Han and Six Dynasties Periods*. Another good study of the *fu* is David R. Knechtges, *The Han Rhapsody: A Study of the Fu of Yang Hsiung (58 B.C.–A.D. 18)* (Cambridge and New York, 1976).

An important book-length study by a major student of the Han is Hans Bielenstein, "The Restoration of the Han Dynasty," *Bulletin of the Museum of Far Eastern Antiquities* (Stockholm), 26 (1954): 1–209, 31 (1959): 1–287. A general overview of a major subject is provided by Ying-shih Yü, *Trade and Expansion in Han China: A Study in the Structure of Sino-Barbarian Economic Relations* (Berkeley, 1967). A volume that contains fascinating information is Derk Bodde, *Festivals in Classical China: New Year and Other Annual Observances During the Han Dynasty, 206 B.C.–A.D. 220* (Princeton, 1975).

PART II   China and Japan in a Buddhist Age

The literature on Buddhism in English is rich and varied. A straightforward introduction, written in simple language and presuming no background in the subject, is Kenneth Chen, *Buddhism: The Light of Asia*. Another fine introduction is Edward Conze, *Buddhism: Its Essence and Development*. A useful collection of Buddhist writings is Wm. Theodore de Bary, *The Buddhist Tradition in India, China, and Japan*. For a translation of a text enormously influential in East Asia, see Leon Hurvitz, *Scripture of the Lotus Blossom of the Fine Dharma (The Lotus Sutra). Translated from the Chinese of Kumārajīva*. Another translation of a very important Mahayana text is Yoshito S. Hakeda's rendering of *The Awakening of Faith, Attributed to Asvaghosha*.

For a brief account of the history of Buddhism in China by a historian who views the interaction between China and the Indian religion as a rich and complex historical process, see Arthur F. Wright, *Buddhism in Chinese History*. A great deal of useful information is contained in Kenneth Ch'en, *Buddhism in China: A Historical Survey* (Princeton, 1964), which, however, is short on interpretation. Also worth consulting is the same author's *The Chinese Transformation of Buddhism*.

Of all the sects of East Asian Buddhism, Ch'an (Zen) has attracted the most attention in the West. The most scholarly translation of a key text is Philip B. Yampolsky, *The Platform Sutra of the Sixth Patriarch: The Text of the Tun-huang Manuscript* (New York, 1967). The standard history is Heinrich Dumoulin, *A History of Zen Buddhism*. The foremost twentieth-century Japanese spokesman for Zen is D. T. Suzuki, author of *Zen and Japanese Culture* and other books. *The Zen Life* by Koji Sato, with photographs by Sosei Kuzunishi presents a good picture of a contemporary Zen monastery. Philip

Kapleau, ed., *The Three Pillars of Zen* is well regarded for its treatment of the subject. Also see Else Hooykaas and Bert Schierbeck, *Zazen,* translated from the Dutch by Charles McGeehan.

The relationship between Zen and the arts remains as difficult to define as the religion itself, but the arts, especially painting, not only testify to the power of Zen but also offer an approach to understanding it. Enthusiastically recommended is Jan Fontain and Money L. Hickman, *Zen Painting and Calligraphy* (Museum of Fine Arts, Boston, 1970. Distributed by the New York Graphic Society), the catalog of an exhibition of both Chinese and Japanese works. Also recommended for the study of Chinese Buddhist art are J. Leroy Davidson, *The Lotus Sutra in Chinese Art* (New York, 1954); Michael Sullivan, *The Cave Temples of Maechishan,* with photographs by Dominique Carbois (Berkeley, 1969); and Terukazu Akiyama and Saburo Matsubara, eds., *Arts of China,* Vol. 2, *Buddhist Cave Temples,* translated by Alexander Soper (Tokyo and New York, 1968).

A major theme in the history of China during the period of disunion is the interaction between Chinese and non-Chinese peoples. An important work on this subject is Owen Lattimore, *Inner Asian Frontiers of China,* first published in 1940. Contributing to the historiography as well as the history of the period is Michael C. Rogers, *The Chronicle of Fu Chien: A Case of Exemplar History* (Berkeley, 1968). The study of the social history of this period has been advanced by Patricia Buckley Ebrey, *The Aristocratic Families of Early Imperial China: A Case Study of the Po-ling Ts'ui Family* (Cambridge and New York, 1978), which deals with the period from A.D. 100 to 800. Also recommended is Yen Chih-t'ui, *Family Instructions for the Yen Clan: Yen-shih Chia-hsün,* translated by Teng Ssu-yü (Leiden, 1966).

Studies of China's secular culture during the period of division include Robert Van Gulik, *Hsi K'ang and His Poetical Essay on the Lute* (Rutland, Vt., 1970, reissue of 1940 work), and James R. Hightower, *The Poetry of T'ao Ch'ien* (London, 1970). Richard B. Mather has translated the *Shih-shuo Hsin-yü* by Liu I-ch'ing under the title *A New Account of Tales of the World* (Minneapolis, 1976). This very learned and meticulous translation makes available in English a major source for the study of the period's sophisticates.

The Cambridge History of China, vol. 3, *Sui and T'ang, 589–906,* pt. 1, edited by Denis Twitchett (Cambridge, 1979), is a major resource, as are *The Sui Dynasty* by Arthur F. Wright and *Perspectives on the T'ang,* a collection of essays edited by Wright and Twitchett (New Haven, 1973). On the early T'ang, see Howard J. Wechsler, *Mirror to the Son of Heaven: Wei Cheng at the Court of T'ang T'ai-tsung* (New Haven, 1974). The best study of T'ang economic history and administration is Denis Twitchett, *Financial Administration under the T'ang* (Cambridge, 2nd. ed., 1970). For a view of the T'ang as seen through the eyes of a visiting Japanese monk, see Edwin O. Reischauer, *Ennin's Travels in T'ang China* (New York, 1955), a book of enduring fascination.

T'ang poetry is well represented in anthologies as well as in studies of individual poets. Selecting from a number of titles is, at least in part, a matter of taste, but it is generally recognized that one of the best books by a master translator is Arthur Waley, *The Life and Times of Po Chü-i* (London, 1949). Although not as fully biographical as Waley's book, the following studies of T'ang poets also provide windows on T'ang life: Arthur Cooper, *Li Po and Tu Fu;* A. R. Davis, *Tu Fu;* Stephen Owen, *The Poetry of Meng Chiao and Han Yü* (New Haven, 1975), and *The Poetry of the Early T'ang* by the same author (New Haven, 1977); A. C. Graham, *Poems of the Late T'ang;* James J. Y. Liu, *The Poetry of Li Shang-yin* (Chicago, 1969); J. D. Frodsham, *The Poems of Li Ho (791–817)* (Oxford, 1970). A leading student of T'ang culture is Edward H. Schafer. Two of his finest books are *The Golden Peaches of Samarkand: A Study of T'ang Exotics* (Berkeley, 1963), and *The Vermilion Bird: T'ang Images of the South* (Berkeley, 1967).

The standard book on early Japan is J. E. Kidder, *Japan Before Buddhism* (New York, rev. ed., 1966). He also wrote *Early Buddhist Japan* (New York, 1972). A good book on the marvelous clay figurines that decorated the outside of Japan's great tombs is Fumio

Miki, *Haniwa: The Clay Sculpture of Proto-historic Japan*, English adaptation by Roy Andrew Miller (Rutland, Vt., 1960). Miki is also the author of *Haniwa*, volume 8 in the *Arts of Japan* series. Volume 4 of the same series is Haruki Kageyama, *The Arts of Shinto*. A good source for further titles on Shinto and Japanese folk religion is Earhart's book on Japanese religion (see "General Works"). For an affectionate and knowledgeable study of Nara art by a master, see Langdon Warner, *Japanese Sculpture of the Tempyo Period: Masterpieces of the Eighth Century*, edited and arranged by James Marshall Plumer (Cambridge, Mass., ca. 1959). The *Kojiki* has been translated by Donald L. Philippi and published under that title (Princeton, 1969); for the more historically reliable *Nihongi*, see William G. Aston, trans., *Nihongi: Chronicles of Japan from the Earliest Times to A.D. 697*, 2 vols. (London, 1956). Japan's oldest anthology of poetry is also available in English: *The Man'yōshū: The Nippon Gakujutsu Shinkokai Translation of One Thousand Poems* (reissued, New York, 1969).

For Heian institutional history, see John W. Hall and Jeffrey P. Mass, eds., *Medieval Japan—Essays in Institutional History* (New Haven, 1974), about half of which is devoted to the Heian period. Also recommended are John W. Hall, *Government and Local Power in Japan, 500–1700: A Study Based on Bizen Province* (Princeton, 1966), and G. Cameron Hurst III, *Insei: Abdicated Sovereigns in the Politics of Late Heian Japan, 1086–1185* (New York, 1976). A delightful and especially well written book on the life of the Heian aristocracy is Ivan Morris, *The World of the Shining Prince*. The prince in question is Genji, and we are now fortunate in having two translations of Murasaki's great novel. Both bear the title *The Tale of Genji*. The earlier translation, by Arthur Waley (London, 1935; reissued, New York, 1960), takes liberties with the text and is less accurate than that of Edward G. Seidensticker (New York, 1976), but it continues to demand attention for its literary merits.

Recommended with enthusiasm for its all-around excellence is Earl Miner, *An Introduction to Japanese Court Poetry*, as well as the more extensive study on which it is based, Robert Brower and Earl Miner, *Japanese Court Poetry* (Stanford, 1961). Earl Miner has also translated *Japanese Poetic Diaries* (Berkeley, 1969). The following translations of Heian literature are also recommended for their literary grace as well as historical value: Ivan Morris, trans., *The Pillow Book of Sei Shonagon* (New York, 1967); *As I Crossed a Bridge of Dreams: Recollections of a Woman in Eleventh-Century Japan*, also translated by Morris; Edward G. Seidensticker, trans., *The Gossamer Years: The Diary of a Noblewoman of Heian Japan* (Rutland, Vt., 1964); and H. Jay Harris, trans., *The Tales of Ise* (Rutland, Vt., 1972).

The best book on Shingon and its founder is Yoshito S. Hakeda, *Kukai: Major Works* (New York, 1972).

PART III   China and Japan: Gentry and Samurai

China

James T. C. Liu and Peter J. Golas, *Change in Sung China: Innovation or Renovation?* (Problems in Asian Civilization series) presents a good selection of scholarly views on the Sung and its place in Chinese history. The same series also includes a collection of essays on the dynasty's most famous reformer: John Meskill, ed., *Wang An-shih: Practical Reformer?* Also recommended on Wang An-shih is *Reform in Sung China: Wang An-shih (1021–1086) and His New Policies* (Cambridge, Mass., 1959) by James T. C. Liu, who has also written a study of another important Northern Sung political and intellectual leader: *Ou-yang Hsiu: An Eleventh Century Neo-Confucianist* (Stanford, 1967). Recommended reading on the Sung economy is Shiba Yoshinobu, *Commerce and Society in Sung China*, translated by Mark Elvin, and the pioneering articles of Robert Hartwell, including "A Cycle of Economic Change in Imperial China: Coal and Iron in

Northeast China, 750–1350," *Journal of the Economic History of the Orient* 10 (July 1967): 102–59, and "Financial Expertise, Examinations, and the Formulation of Economic Policy in Northern Sung China," *Journal of Asia Studies* 30 (February 1971); 281–314. A standard work on a major topic is Edward A. Kracke, Jr., *Civil Service in Early Sung China, 960–1067* (Cambridge, Mass., 1953). Village structure is analyzed in Brian E. McKnight, *Village and Bureaucracy in Southern Sung China* (Chicago, 1971). A readable book filled with interesting detail is Jaques Gernet, *Daily Life in China on the Eve of the Mongol Invasions, 1250–1276*, translated by H. M. Wright. For a recent collection of articles on the Sung, see John Winthrop Haeger, ed., *Crisis and Prosperity in Sung China*.

For the study of Sung poetry, James J. Y. Liu, *Major Lyricists of the Northern Sung* (Princeton, 1974) has the great merit of including for each poem the Chinese text, a word for word rendition, and a polished translation. A thoughtful and highly commendable book is Jonathan Chaves, *Mei Yao-ch'en and the Development of Early Sung Poetry* (New York, 1976). Chaves is also the author of the excellent and delightful, *Heaven My Blanket, Earth My Pillow—Poems from the Sung Dynasty by Yang Wan-li*. Two of the dynasty's most beloved poets have been sensitively translated by Burton Watson: *Su Tung-p'o—Selections from a Sung Dynasty Poet* (New York, 1965), and *The Old Man Who Does As He Pleases—Poems and Prose by Lu Yu* (New York, 1973). There are a number of other worthy books on Sung poetry that cannot be listed here, but we should mention a study of China's foremost woman poet: *Li Ch'ing-chao* by P'in-ch'ing Hu (New York, 1966). For readers interested in the history of music, there is Rulan Chao Pian, *Song Dynasty Musical Sources and Their Interpretation* (Cambridge, Mass., 1967).

A prime source for the study of Sung and later Neo-Confucian thought is Wing-tsit Chan, trans., *Reflections on Things at Hand: The Neo-Confucian Anthology Compiled by Chu Hsi and Lü Tsu-ch'ien* (New York, 1967). For a penetrating analysis of Sung philosophy, read A. C. Graham, *Two Chinese Philosophers: Ch'eng Ming-tao and Ch'eng Yi-ch'uan* (London, 1958). For bibliography on Chu Hsi, see Wing-tsit Chan, "The Study of Chu Hsi in the West," *Journal of Asian Studies* 35 (August 1976): 555–77. A landmark in the study of Ming thought was achieved by the publication of Wm. Theodore de Bary and the Conference on Ming Thought, *Self and Society in Ming Thought*, which includes an important major essay by de Bary. On the dynasty's most influential thinker, there are now two complementary studies: Julia Ching, *To Acquire Wisdom: The Way of Wang Yang-ming* (New York, 1976), and Tu Wei-ming, *Neo-Confucian Thought in Action: Wang Yang-ming's Youth (1472–1509)* (Berkeley, 1976). Also see Wing-tsit Chan, trans., *Instructions for Practical Living and other Neo-Confucian Writings by Wang Yang-ming* (New York, 1963), and the same author's, "Wang Yang-ming: Western Studies and an Annotated Bibliography," *Philosophy East and West* 12 (January 1972): 75–92. On late Ming thought, see Wm. Theodore de Bary and the Conference on Seventeenth-Century Thought, *The Unfolding of Neo-Confucianism*. An excellent book on Chinese views of aesthetics during the Sung–Ming periods is Susan Bush, *The Chinese Literati on Painting: Shu Shih (1037–1101) to Tung Ch'i-ch'ang (1555–1636)* (Harvard-Yenching Institute Studies, No. 27). Christian F. Murck, ed., *Artists and Traditions: Uses of the Past in Chinese Culture* (Princeton, 1976) is a collection of distinguished papers of particular importance for the study of Chinese painting and culture, mostly (although not exclusively) Sung through early Ch'ing. For additional material on intellectual history, readers should also consult the volumes on Chinese thought listed above under "General Works."

For those who would like to explore Yüan culture, there are two recent books that are both authoritative and sensitive: Chung-wen Shih, *The Golden Age of Chinese Drama: Yüan Tsa-chü* (Princeton, 1976), and James Cahill, *Hills Beyond a River: Chinese Painting of the Yüan Dynasty 1279–1368* (New York and Tokyo, 1976). The latter is the first volume in a projected five-volume series on late Chinese painting. Both books include up-to-date bibliographies. For a general history of the Mongols, see Berthold Spuler, *The*

Mongols in History (New York, 1971). The life of the founder of the Mongol empire is presented by René Grousset, *Conqueror of the World: The Life of Chingis-khan.* John W. Dardess, *Conquerors and Confucians: Aspects of Political Change in Late Yüan China* (New York, 1973) is an important study of Yüan political history. The study of Marco Polo is a field all to itself. His account of his travels, a subject of enduring fascination, may be read in *The Travels of Marco Polo* translated by R. E. Latham. Also very highly recommended is Leonardo Olschki, *Marco Polo's Asia, An Introduction to His "Description of the World" Called "il Milione."* (Berkeley, 1960).

An excellent description and analysis of the Ming state is provided in a short book by Charles O. Hucker, *The Traditional Chinese State in Ming Times, 1368–1644* (Tucson, Ariz., 1961). Hucker is also the editor of *Chinese Government in Ming Times: Seven Studies* (New York, 1969). An authoritative study of an important subject is Ray Huang, *Taxation and Government Finance in 16th Century Ming China* (Cambridge and New York, 1974). Another good book is James B. Parsons, *The Peasant Rebellions of the Late Ming Dynasty* (Tucson, Ariz., 1970). A real treasure house of information is the monumental *Dictionary of Ming Biography 1368–1644*, edited by L. Carrington Goodrich and Chaoying Fang (New York, 1976).

A number of studies on social and economic history concern themselves with the Ming and Ch'ing periods. They include two very influential books by Ping-ti Ho: *Studies in the Population of China, 1368–1953* (Cambridge, Mass., 1959) and *The Ladder of Success in Imperial China: Aspects of Social Mobility, 1368–1911* (New York, 1962). For an introduction to the examination system as it operated in late traditional China, see Ichisada Miyazaki, *China's Examination Hell: The Civil Service Examinations of Imperial China*, translated by Conrad Schirokauer (Tokyo and New York, 1976). An important, rather technical book is Dwight H. Perkins, *Agricultural Development in China, 1368–1963* (Chicago, 1969). A-tu Zen Sun and S. C. Sun, trans., *T'ien-kung k'ai-wu, Chinese Technology in the Seventeenth Century* (University Park, Pa., 1966) is a gold mine of information.

Hilary J. Beattie, *Land and Lineage in China: A Study of T'ung-ch'eng County, Anhwei, in the Ming and Ch'ing Dynasties* (Cambridge, 1979) is a major contribution to social history. Literature provides fascinating vignettes of Ming life. See, for example, Cyril Birch, trans., *Stories from a Ming Collection—The Art of the Chinese Story-teller.* The most accessible translation of *Water Margins* is Pearl Buck, *All Men Are Brothers*, 2 vols. The first volume of Anthony C. Yu's projected complete translation of *Journey to the West* (Chicago, 1977) is now available, along with the abridgment of this marvelous novel published by Arthur Waley under the title, *Monkey.* For painting, see James Cahill, *Parting at the Shore: Chinese Painting of the Early and Middle Ming Dynasty, 1368–1580* (New York and Tokyo, 1978), the second volume of Cahill's five volume series.

Japan

For Kamakura and Ashikaga institutional history, see the previously noted collection, *Medieval Japan*, edited by John W. Hall and Jeffrey P. Mass. Mass is also the author of an important technical and specialized study, *Warrior Government in Early Medieval Japan—A Study of the Kamakura Bakufu, Shugo, and Jitō* (New Haven, 1974). Other books recommended for the political history of the period are M. Shinoda, *The Founding of the Kamakura Shogunate, 1180–1185* (New York, 1960), and two books by H. Paul Varley: *Imperial Restoration in Medieval Japan* (New York, 1971) and *The Onin War* (New York, 1967). A recent and distinguished collection of essays dealing with the political, social, economic, cultural, and religious history of the Ashikaga period is John Whitney Hall and Toyoda Takeshi, eds., *Japan in the Muromachi Age.*

Recommended for Kamakura religious history is Alfred Bloom, *Shinran's Gospel of Pure Grace* (Tucson, Ariz., 1965). The piety of the times may be appreciated in its stories: see D. E. Mills, *A Collection of Tales from Uji: A Study and Translation of Uji shui monogatari* (Cambridge and New York, 1970). The heroes of an age reveal a great deal about society's values: see Helen Craig McCullough, trans., *Yoshitsune—A Fifteenth-Century Japanese Chronicle* (Stanford, 1971). Also recommended for Kamakura literature are Karen Brazell, trans., *The Confessions of Lady Nijo,* and Robert Brower and Earl Miner, *Fujiwara Teika's Superior Poems for Our Times* (Stanford, 1967).

For fourteenth-century literature, see Donald Keene, trans., *Essays in Idleness: The Tsurezuregusa of Kenkō,* a masterful translation. The Nō theater has received much attention in the West; a good collection is Donald Keene, ed., *Twenty Plays of the Nō Theater.* For those interested in the influence of the Nō on modern English theater, see Ezra Pound and Ernest Fenollosa, *The Classic Noh Theater of Japan* (New Directions paperback, with an essay by William Butler Yeats). A good and helpful book is Takaaki Matsushita, *Arts of Japan,* Vol. 7, *Ink Painting;* also Volume 3 of the same series, Ryoichi Fujioka, *Tea Ceremony Utensils.* An older appreciation of tea by a leader in the late Meiji revival of interest in Japanese culture is K. Okakura, *The Book of Tea.*

First Encounters

An excellent introduction to the initial contacts between modern Europe and East Asia is provided by George Sansom, *The Western World and Japan.* A well-written informative account is C. R. Boxer, *The Christian Century in Japan* (Berkeley, 1951). Also see Michael Cooper, S.J., *They Came to Japan—An Anthology of European Reports on Japan, 1543–1640* (Berkeley, 1965). Recommended for China is L. J. Gallagher, trans., *China in the Sixteenth Century: The Journals of Matteo Ricci* (New York, 1953). Also recommended is Arnold H. Rowbotham, *Missionary and Mandarin: The Jesuits at the Court of China* (Berkeley, 1942). European knowledge of Asia in early modern times and European reactions to Asian cultures and peoples is the subject of an exhaustive multivolume work still in progress: Donald Lach, *Asia in the Making of Europe* (Chicago, 1965–). For the influence on each other of European and East Asian art from the sixteenth to the twentieth century, see Michael Sullivan, *The Meeting of Eastern and Western Art* (New York, 1973).

PART IV   Traditional China and Japan: The Last Phase

Many fine works concerned with the Ch'ing and the Ming periods (in addition to those noted in "Part III" above) are available. Outstanding is the collection of essays edited by G. William Skinner, *The City in Late Imperial China* (Stanford, 1977). Two highly regarded books on economic history are Evelyn Sakakida Rawski, *Agricultural Change and the Peasant Economy of South China* (Cambridge, Mass., 1972), and W. E. Willmott, *Economic Organization in Chinese Society* (Stanford, 1972). Chang Chung-li has published two important and influential books on Ch'ing social structure: *The Chinese Gentry: Studies on Their Role in Nineteenth Century Chinese Society,* and *The Income of the Chinese Gentry* (Seattle, 1962). A different approach to the analysis of social mobility is taken by Wolfram Eberhard, *Social Mobility in Traditional China* (Leiden, 1963). A good way to begin reading on Ch'ing local government is to go through T'ung-tsu Ch'ü, *Local Government in China under the Ch'ing* (Cambridge, Mass., 1962), or the more recent John Watt, *The District Magistrate in Late Imperial China* (New York, 1972). On law, see Derk Bodde and Clarence Morris, *Law in Imperial China* (Cambridge, Mass., 1967), and Sybille Van der Sprenkel, *Legal Institutions in Manchu China, A Sociological Analysis* (London, 1962). For a recent thoughtful analysis of Ch'ing government, read Thomas A. Metzger, *The Internal Organization of Ch'ing Bureaucracy: Legal, Normative, and Communication Aspects* (Cambridge, Mass., 1973). Robert B. Oxnam has devised a novel way for groups to get the feel of the Ch'ing bureaucracy; see *The Ch'ing Game Simulation and the Study of History* (obtainable from Learning Resources in International Studies, Suite 1231, 60 East 42nd St., N.Y., N.Y. 10017).

A useful monograph on the early Ch'ing is Robert B. Oxnam, *Ruling from Horseback: Manchu Politics in the Oboi Regency, 1661–1669* (Chicago, 1975). Also see Lawrence Kessler, *K'ang-hsi and the Consolidation of Ch'ing Rule, 1661–1684* (Chicago, 1976). Jonathan Spence has written two fascinating and informative books, *Ts'ao Yin and the K'ang-hsi Emperor, Bondservant and Master* (New Haven, 1966) and *Emperor of China: Self-Portrait of K'ang-hsi.* The other great emperor of the Ch'ing is the subject of Harold L. Kahn, *Monarchy in the Emperor's Eyes: Image and Reality in the Ch'ien-lung Reign* (Cambridge, Mass., 1971). For biographical information, consult Arthur W. Hummel, ed., *Eminent Chinese of the Ch'ing Period*, 2 vols., (Washington, 1943).

As usual, much can be learned about a period from its literature. *The Scholars* by Wu Ching-tzu has been translated by Yang Hsien-yi and Gladys Yang (Peking, 1957). China's most admired novel, *The Dream of the Red Chamber* by Ts'ao Hsüeh-chin, is available in partial translation by Chi-chen Wang. David Hawkes is engaged in preparing a complete translation, two volumes of which have appeared to date, published as *The Story of the Stone* by Cao Xueqin. The leading authority on the Chinese stage is A. C. Scott; see his *Introduction to the Chinese Theater* (New York, 1959). For a sensitively drawn portrait of a gentleman-poet, see Arthur Waley, *Yuan Mei: Eighteenth Century Chinese Poet.* For a man with a very different intellectual outlook, see David S. Nivison, *The Life and Thought of Chang Hsüeh-ch'eng, 1738–1801* (Stanford, 1966), a very rewarding book for advanced students.

A brilliant and well formulated interpretation of the Tokugawa political system is provided by Harold Bolitho, *Treasures Among Men: The Fudai Daimyo in Tokugawa Japan* (New Haven, 1974). Readers would also do well to consult Conrad Totman, *Politics in the Tokugawa Bakufu, 1600–1843* (Cambridge, Mass., 1967), and Herschell Webb, *The Japanese Imperial Institution in the Tokugawa Period* (New York, 1968). Excellent studies less broad in scope are John W. Hall, *Tanuma Okitsugu, 1719–1788, Forerunner of Modern Japan,* and John W. Hall and Marious Jansen, eds., *Studies in the Institutional History of Early Modern Japan* (Princeton, 1968). A splendid study of Tokugawa economic history is Thomas C. Smith, *The Agrarian Origins of Modern Japan.* A major work on Tokugawa social history as well as on the history of values is Ronald P. Dore, *Education in Tokugawa Japan* (Berkeley, 1965). On Tokugawa values, also see Robert N. Bellah, *Tokugawa Religion: The Values of Pre-industrial Japan.*

The intellectual history of the Tokugawa period is one of the important subjects underrepresented in Western scholarship. Shigeru Matsumoto, *Motoori Norinaga, 1730–1801* (Cambridge, Mass., 1970) is worthwhile. A useful book on Tokugawa Confucianism is Joseph J. Spaeth, *Itō Jinsai* (*Monumenta Serica* monograph, Peking, 1948). A very influential interpretation by a leading twentieth-century Japanese intellectual, published in 1952 but only recently translated, is Masao Maruyama, *Studies in the Intellectual History of Tokugawa Japan,* translated by Mikiso Hane (Princeton and Tokyo, 1974). It is an important but not an easy book, suitable more for advanced students than for beginners. Recommended as a delightful book on "Dutch Learning" is Donald Keene, *The Japanese Discovery of Europe, 1720–1830* (Stanford, 1969).

The lively culture of the Tokugawa townspeople is dealt with in a number of scholarly and entertaining books. A good place to begin is Howard Hibbett, *The Floating World in Japanese Fiction.* Saikaku may be read in translation in Ivan Morris, trans., *The Life of an Amorous Woman and Other Writings by Ihara Saikaku,* and Wm. Theodore de Bary, trans., *Five Women Who Loved Love.* For the theater, see two translations by Donald Keene: *Four Major Plays of Chikamatsu* and *Chūshingura—The Treasury of Loyal Retainers.* Keene's *World Within Walls: Japanese Literature of the Pre-modern Era, 1600–1867* (New York, 1976) evidences the mature scholarship of a leading student of Japanese literature, who is also a gifted stylist. It is the first volume to be published of a projected four-volume history of Japanese literature. Recommended on the art of the woodcut is Richard Lane, *Masters of the Japanese Print—Their World and Their Work* (New York, 1962). For individual artists, see the volumes in the *Masterworks of Ukiyo-e* series (Kodansha International, Tokyo and New York, 1968–). There are other worthy books on Tokugawa art, popular and aristocratic. One that stands out is Elise Grilli's superb *The Art of the Japanese Screen* (New York and Tokyo, 1970), a truly beautiful book. Finally, for an introduction to the poetry appreciated by all levels of Japanese society, see Harold G. Henderson, *An Introduction to Haiku: An Anthology of Poems and Poets from Bashō to Shiki.*

PART V   China and Japan in the Modern World

Most books concentrate on either China or Japan. An exception is Ernest R. May and James C. Thomson, Jr., *American–East Asian Relations: A Survey* (Cambridge, Mass., 1972), a collection of seventeen essays that emphasize bibliography.

China

A major work is *The Cambridge History of China*, vol. 10, *Late Ch'ing, 1800–1870* (Cambridge, 1978), edited by John K. Fairbank. A collaborative effort, it presents a synthesis of scholarship on this period and includes both a bibliographical essay and a bibliography. The publisher also plans to issue in 1980 the next volume in the series, volume 11, *The Fall of the Ch'ing, 1870–1911*, edited by Fairbank. Surveys now available include that by Immanuel Hsü, included above under "General Works," and a two volume work by Jean Chesneaux, Marianne Bastig, and Marie-Claire Bergère, translated from the French by Anne Destenay, *China from the Opium Wars to the 1911 Revolution* and *China from the 1911 Revolution to Liberation.*

John K. Fairbank, *Trade and Diplomacy on the China Coast: The Opening of the Treaty Ports 1841–1854* begins with an excellent account of the Canton System and its breakdown. A good account of the Opium War is Peter Ward Fay, *The Opium War, 1840–1842.* Three other books on the war are recommended: Hsin-pao Chang, *Commissioner Lin and the Opium War;* Arthur Waley, *The Opium War Through Chinese Eyes* (London, 1958); and Jack Beeching, *The Chinese Opium Wars.* An important book on the Opium War in terms of social history and Chinese responses to Western intrusions is Frederic Wakeman, Jr., *Strangers at the Gate: Social Disorder in South China, 1839–1861.*

For diplomatic history, see Immanuel Hsu, *China's Entrance into the Family of Nations: The Diplomatic Phase, 1858–1880* (Cambridge, Mass., 1960). A general survey helpful for those seeking to view Ch'ing foreign relations in a Chinese perspective is Morris Rossabi, *China and Inner Asia: From 1368 to the Present Day* (New York, 1975).

The best way to begin the study of China's nineteenth-century rebellions is to read Frederick Wakeman, Jr., "Rebellion and Revolution: The Study of Popular Movements in Chinese History," *Journal of Asian Studies* 36 (February 1977): 201–37. This article analyzes various approaches, discusses and lists the very substantial bibliography in this field. Although not limited to the nineteenth century, it includes many works on this period, which is more fully documented than earlier times. For the Taiping Rebellion, see Franz Michael, *The Taiping Rebellion: History and Documents*, Vol. 1. A massive and detailed study by an expert is Jen Yu-wen, *The Taiping Rebellion* (New Haven, 1973).

For the dynasty's response to the great rebellion, see Mary C. Wright, *The Last Stand of Chinese Conservatism: The T'ung-chih Restoration, 1862–1874*, a landmark of scholarship in the field. Another very influential book, although it does not make for easy reading, is Philip Kuhn, *Rebellion and Its Enemies in Late Imperial China* (Cambridge, Mass., 1970).

The following books on the attempt at Self-Strengthening are recommended: Albert Feuerwerker, *China's Early Industrialization: Sheng Hsuan-huai, 1844–1916, and Mandarin Enterprise* (Cambridge, Mass., 1958); John Rawlinson, *China's Struggle for Naval Development, 1839–95*; and Knight Biggerstaff, *The Earliest Modern Government Schools in China* (Ithaca, N.Y., 1961). Feuerwerker has also written *The Chinese Economy ca. 1870–1911* (Michigan Papers in Chinese Studies, No. 5), recommended as a starting point for the study of the period's economic history. Among Feuerwerker's additional contributions to the field is the editing of *Approaches to Modern Chinese History* (Berkeley, 1968), which includes an important article on Li Hung-chang by K. C. Liu.

Kenneth Scott Latourette, *A History of Christian Missions in China* (London, 1929) is a good historical survey of its subject. A variety of views is presented in Jessie G. Lutz, ed., *Christian Missions in China: Evangelists of What?* (Problems in Asian Civilizations series). An important, more recent publication is John K. Fairbank, ed., *The Missionary Enterprise in China and America* (Cambridge, Mass., 1974). Also recommended are Irwin T. Hyatt, Jr., *Our Ordered Lives Confess—Three Nineteenth Century Missionaries in East Shantung* (Cambridge, Mass., 1976), and K. C. Liu, *Americans and Chinese: A Historical Essay and Bibliography* (Cambridge, Mass., 1963). The anti-Christian movement is analyzed with verve and erudition in Paul Cohen, *China and Christianity: The Missionary Movement and the Growth of Chinese Antiforeignism, 1860–1870* (Cambridge, Mass., 1963).

The study of modern Chinese intellectual history has been deeply influenced by the brilliant writings of Joseph Levenson, especially his *Confucian China and Its Modern Fate*, 3 vols. He is also the author of *Liang Ch'i-ch'ao and the Mind of Modern China* (Cambridge, Mass., 1953), which should be read in tandem with the more recent Hao Chang, *Liang Ch'i-ch'ao and Intellectual Tradition in China* (Cambridge, Mass., 1971). An excellent exemplar of what can be accomplished by a master in the field of intellectual biography is Benjamin Schwartz, *In Search of Wealth and Power: Yen Fu and the West*.

The best book on the Boxers is Victor Purcell, *The Boxer Uprising: A Background Study* (Cambridge and New York, 1963). The standard study of the dynasty's last-minute reforms is Meribeth Cameron, *The Reform Movement in China, 1898–1912* (Stanford, 1931). For additional perspective on the period, emphasizing problems of regionalism, see Roger V. Des Forges, *Hsi-lang and the Chinese Revolution* (New Haven, 1973). For the revolution of 1911, an excellent collection of essays is Mary C. Wright, ed., *China in Revolution: The First Phase, 1900–1913*. Also see Ernest Young, *The Presidency of Yüan Shih-k'ai: Liberalism and Dictatorship in Early Republican China* (Ann Arbor, 1977). Recommended on the "father of the Chinese Revolution" are Harold Schiffrin, *Sun Yat-sen and the Origins of the Chinese Revolution*, and C. Martin Wilbur, *Sun Yat-sen: Frustrated Patriot* (New York, 1977). Another important and good book is Marius Jansen, *The Japanese and Sun Yat-sen* (Cambridge, Mass., 1954). For Japanese influences on an earlier Chinese leader, see Philip Huang, *Liang Ch'i-ch'ao and Modern Chinese Liberalism* (Seattle, 1972).

A good survey for the years between the Revolution of 1911 and the Communist triumph of 1949 is James E. Sheridan, *China in Disintegration: The Republican Era in Chinese History, 1912–1949*. A highly regarded study of the first decade of this period is Edward Friedman, *Backward Toward Revolution: The Chinese Revolutionary Party*. On this period, also see Andrew Nathan, *Peking Politics, 1918–23: Factionalism and the Failure of Constitutionalism* (Berkeley, 1976). On the warlords, see Donald G. Gillin, *Warlord: Yen Hsi-shan in Shansi Province, 1911–1949* (Princeton, 1967); James E. Sheridan, *Chinese Warlord: The Career of Feng Yu-hsiang* (Stanford, 1966); Robert A. Kapp, *Szechwan and the Chinese Republic: Provincial Militarism and Central Power*

1911–1938 (New Haven, 1973); and Hsi-sheng Ch'i, *Warlord Politics in China 1916–1928* (Stanford, 1976). For the twenties, also see F. Gilbert Chan and Thomas H. Etzol, eds., *China in the Nineteen-twenties: Nationalism and Revolution*. A book filled with information on intellectual history is Chow Tse-tsung, *The May Fourth Movement: Intellectual Revolution in Modern China*, which may be read in tandem with Benjamin Schwarz, ed., *Reflections on the May Fourth Movement: A Symposium* (Cambridge, Mass., 1972). For an excellent intellectual biography of a leader of the May Fourth movement, see Jerome B. Grieder, *Hu Shih and the Chinese Renaissance: Liberalism in the Chinese Revolution, 1917–1937* (Cambridge, Mass., 1970). Also recommended are Charlotte Furth, *Ting Wen-chiang: Science and China's New Culture* (Cambridge, Mass., 1970); Laurence A. Schneider, *Ku Chieh-kang and China's New History: Nationalism and the Quest for Alternative Traditions* (Berkeley, 1971); and especially Charlotte Furth, ed., *The Limits of Change: Essays on Conservative Alternatives in Republican China* (Cambridge, Mass., 1976).

For a sensitive and perceptive account of the period's literature, see Leo Ou-fan Lee, *The Romantic Generation of Modern Chinese Writers* (Cambridge, Mass., 1973). Among the novelists available in English translation are Lu Hsün, Lao Shaw, Mao Tun, and Pa Chin. On individual literary figures, see David T. Roy, *Kuo Mo-jo: The Early Years* (Cambridge, Mass., 1971), and Olga Lang, *Pa Chin and His Writings: Chinese Youth Between Two Revolutions* (Cambridge, Mass., 1967). For poetry, see Hsu Kai-yu, trans. and ed., *Twentieth Century Chinese Poetry*. For further reading consult *A Bibliography of Studies and Translations of Modern Chinese Literature (1918–1942)* by Donald A. Gibbs and Yun-cheng Li, with the assistance of Christopher C. Rand (Cambridge, Mass., 1975). Michael Sullivan, *Chinese Art in the Twentieth Century* (Berkeley, 1959) is still the best book on its subject.

The basic book on the period of KMT rule is Lloyd E. Eastman, *The Abortive Revolution: China under Nationalist Rule, 1927–1937* (Cambridge, Mass., 1974). Two other good books are James C. Thomson, *While China Faced West: American Reformers in Nationalist China, 1927–1937* (Cambridge, Mass., 1969), and John Israel, *Student Nationalism in China, 1927–1937* (Stanford, 1966). Also see Chiang Kai-shek, *China's Destiny and China's Economic Theory*, with notes and commentary by Philip Jaffe (New York, 1947). Chiang is also the author of *Soviet Russia in China: A Summing up at Seventy* (New York, 1957).

A brilliant book on the beginnings of Chinese Communism is Maurice Meisner, *Li Ta-chao and the Origins of Chinese Communism*. A long, detailed analysis of the CCP is James P. Harrison, *The Long March to Power: A History of the Chinese Communist Party 1921–72*. On the march itself, see Dick Wilson, *The Long March, 1935: The Epic of Chinese Communist Survival*. Recommended on Mao are Stuart Schram, *Mao Tse-tung*; Jerome Ch'en, *Mao and the Chinese Revolution*; and Stephen Uhally, *Mao Tse-tung, a Critical Biography*. A valuable firsthand account of the CCP in the thirties is Edgar Snow, *Red Star Over China*. On the united front, see Lyman P. Van Slyke, *Enemies and Friends: The United Front in Chinese Communist History* (Stanford, 1967).

F. F. Liu, *A Military History of Modern China, 1924–1949* (Princeton, 1956) is the best book on its subject. On Wang Ching-wei and his puppet regime, see John Hunter Boyle, *China and Japan at War 1937–1945: The Politics of Collaboration* (Stanford, 1972). For an absorbing and sensitive, sympathetic firsthand account of China in the forties, see Graham Peck, *Two Kinds of Time* (Boston, 1950). A very readable account of the American involvement is provided in Barbara W. Tuchman, *Stilwell and the American Experience in China, 1911–1945*. For analyses of the CCP triumph of 1949, see "Part VI" below.

A useful survey of the period's economic history is Albert Feuerwerker, *The Chinese Economy, 1912–1949* (Michigan Papers in Chinese Studies, No. 1, 1968). The literature on the nature of China's agrarian economy and on the economic impact of imperialism is discussed in the Wakeman article mentioned above. For the industrial sector, see John

K. Chang, *Industrial Development in Pre-Communist China* (Chicago, 1969), and Jean Chesneaux, *The Chinese Labor Movement, 1919–1927* (Stanford, 1968). For anthropological perspectives, see Maurice Freedman, ed., *Family and Kinship in Chinese Society* (Stanford, 1972). Another major collection is Mark Elvin and G. William Skinner, eds., *The Chinese City Between Two Worlds* (Stanford, 1974). A good book on a fascinating topic is Ralph Croizier, *Traditional Medicine in Modern China: Science, Nationalism, and Tensions of Cultural Change* (Cambridge, Mass., 1968).

Japan

Modernization is one of the broad themes that has stimulated scholarship on nineteenth- and twentieth-century Japanese history. This was the general theme of a series of conferences that resulted in the following collections of essays: Marius B. Jansen, ed., *Changing Japanese Attitudes Toward Modernization;* William W. Lockwood, ed., *The State and Economic Enterprise in Japan;* Ronald P. Dore, ed., *Aspects of Social Change in Modern Japan;* Robert E. Ward, ed., *Political Development in Modern Japan;* Donald H. Shively, ed., *Tradition and Modernization in Japanese Culture;* and James W. Morley, ed., *Dilemmas of Growth in Prewar Japan.* To these may be added Albert M. Craig and Donald H. Shively, eds., *Personality in Japanese History,* which also concentrates on the last two centuries. Together, these volumes provide a good review of current American scholarship and thinking about many of the key issues and developments in modern Japanese history.

Modern Japanese history begins with the Meiji Restoration, and this event, or series of events, will continue to excite scholarly curiosity and debate. A major work, built on sound scholarship and balanced judgment, written by a senior British historian, is W. G. Beasley, *The Meiji Restoration* (Stanford, 1973). A very different kind of book, which places the Restoration in the history of consciousness, is H. D. Harootunian's brilliant and demanding *Towards Restoration: The Growth of Political Consciousness in Tokugawa Japan* (Berkeley, 1970). For a fine interpretive study of a key domain, see Albert M. Craig, *Chōshū in the Meiji Restoration* (Cambridge, Mass., 1961). Another leader is the subject of a book-length study: Marius B. Jansen, *Sakamoto Ryoma and the Meiji Restoration.* A useful compilation is W. G. Beasley, trans., *Select Documents on Japanese Foreign Policy, 1853–1868* (Oxford, New York, 1955). For an influential older view of the Restoration, see E. H. Norman, *Japan's Emergence as a Modern State* (New York, 1940), which is included in a recent reissue of a collection of Norman's writings published under the title, *Origins of the Modern Japanese State.* Norman should be read in conjunction with the critical articles of John Whitney Hall and George Akita in *Journal of Japanese Studies* 3 (Summer 1977).

The most influential analysis of modern Japanese economic history is William W. Lockwood, *The Economic Development of Japan: Growth and Structural Change* (Princeton, 1954). For the economic policies and accomplishments of the crucial early years, see Thomas C. Smith, *Political Change and Industrial Development in Japan: Government Enterprise, 1868–1880.* The long-range importance of the industrial effort must not obscure the significance of agriculture, which made it possible. For background, see Smith's *Agrarian Origins,* cited in "Part IV" above. For Meiji, see James I. Nakamura, *Agricultural Production and Economic Development of Japan, 1873–1922* (Princeton, 1966). For interesting discussions of the men who built Japan's modern enterprises, and of the values and ideas that went into them, see Johannes Hirschmeier, S.V.D., *The Origins of Entrepreneurship in Meiji Japan* (Cambridge, Mass., 1964), and *The Development of Japanese Business, 1600–1973* (Cambridge, Mass., 1975) by the same author, in collaboration with Tsunehiko Yui. For a more systematic analysis of the ideas that justified and inspired the effort, see Byron K. Marshall, *Capitalism and Nationalism in Prewar Japan: The Ideology of the Business Elite, 1868–1941* (Stanford, 1967.)

For Meiji political history, see George Akita, *Foundations of Constitutional Government in Modern Japan, 1868–1900* (Cambridge, Mass., 1967). Also useful for the early years are Nobutaka Ike, *The Beginnings of Political Democracy in Japan* (Baltimore, 1950), and Joseph Pittau, *Political Thought in Early Meiji Japan, 1868–1889* (Cambridge, Mass., 1967). A study of a major Meiji statesman is provided in Roger F. Hacket, *Yamagata Aritomo in the Rise of Modern Japan, 1838–1922* (Cambridge, Mass., 1971). For Japanese and Western historians' evaluations of Meiji statesmen, see the survey conducted by Richard T. Chang, *Historians and Meiji Statesmen* (University of Florida Social Science Monograph, No. 41). An important institutional development is examined in Robert M. Spaulding, Jr., *Imperial Japan's Higher Civil Service Examinations* (Princeton, 1967).

A good way to begin studying Meiji intellectual history is by examining the life and ideas of Fukuzawa Yukichi. His *An Encouragement of Learning,* translated by David A. Dilworth and Umeyo Hirano (Tokyo, 1969), is a collection of essays written in the 1870s. Also well worth reading is his *Autobiography,* translated by Eiichi Kiyooka (New York, 1966). Important secondary studies are Carmen Blacker, *The Japanese Enlightenment: A Study of the Writings of Fukuzawa Yukichi* (Cambridge and New York, 1964), and an article by Albert Craig in the previously noted collection, *Political Development in Modern Japan,* edited by Robert E. Ward. Also see William R. Braisted, trans. and ed., *Meiroku Zasshi: Journal of the Japanese Enlightenment* (Cambridge, Mass., 1975). Two other valuable books on intellectual history are Kenneth B. Pyle, *The New Generation in Meiji Japan: Problems of Cultural Identity, 1885–1895* (Stanford, 1969), and Irwin Scheiner, *Christian Converts and Social Protest in Meiji Japan* (Berkeley, 1970).

For a variety of interpretations of Japanese expansionism, see Marlene Mayo, ed., *The Emergence of Imperial Japan: Self-Defense or Calculated Aggression?* (Problems in Asian Civilizations series). A good survey of this topic is James W. Morley, ed., *Japan's Foreign Policy, 1868–1941: A Research Guide* (New York, 1974). A detailed study is Francis Hilary Conroy, *The Japanese Seizure of Korea, 1868–1910* (Philadelphia, 1960). Indispensable for an understanding of Korea itself, and a fine starting point for anyone interested in modern Korean history, is the excellent book by James B. Palais, *Politics and Policy in Traditional Korea, 1864–1876* (Cambridge, Mass., 1975).

On the Russo-Japanese War, see Shumpei Okamoto, *The Japanese Oligarchy and the Russo-Japanese War* (New York, 1971), and John A. White, *The Diplomacy of the Russo-Japanese War* (Princeton, 1964). Also see Richard Neu, *The Uncertain Friendship: Theodore Roosevelt and Japan, 1906–1909* (Cambridge, Mass., 1967). I. H. Nish has written two books on Anglo-Japanese relations: *The Anglo-Japanese Alliance: The Diplomacy of Two Island Empires 1894–1907* (London, 1966) and *Alliance in Decline: A Study in Anglo-Japanese Relations 1908–23* (London and New York, 1972).

Late Meiji politics is analyzed by Tetsuo Najita in *Hara Kei in the Politics of Compromise, 1905–1915* (Cambridge, Mass., 1967). The best study on the political system as it evolved during the next decade is Peter Duus, *Party Rivalry and Political Change in Taishō Japan* (Cambridge, Mass., 1968). A valuable and stimulating collection of essays is Bernard S. Silberman and H. D. Harootunian, eds., *Japan in Crisis: Essays on Taishō Democracy* (Princeton, 1974). A book rich in detail is George O. Totten III, *The Social Democratic Movement in Prewar Japan* (New Haven, 1966). Recommended for foreign policy is James W. Morley, *The Japanese Thrust into Siberia, 1918* (New York, 1957), and Akira Iriye, *After Imperialism: The Search for a New Order in East Asia.*

Maruyama Masao, whose book on Tokugawa intellectual history was noted in "Part IV" above, is also the author of a number of perceptive essays on Japanese ultranationalism published as *Thought and Behavior in Japanese Politics,* edited by Ivan Morris. Morris has also compiled and edited *Japan 1931–1945: Militarism, Fascism, Japanism?* (Problems in Asian Civilization series), which can well be used in conjunction with George O. Totten, ed., *Democracy in Prewar Japan: Groundwork or Facade?* in the same series. For a distinguished recent political analysis of the thirties, see Gordon Mark Berger, *Parties Out of Power in Japan: 1931–1941* (Princeton, 1977). A major stream of opposition to urbanization and capitalism is traced and analyzed in Thomas R. Havens, *Farm and Nation in Modern Japan: Agrarian Nationalism, 1870–1940* (Princeton, 1974). On the official ideology prevailing in the thirties, see R. K. Hall, ed., *Kokutai no Hongi. Cardinal Principles of the National Entity of Japan* (Cambridge, Mass., 1949). *Dilemmas of Growth*, edited by Morley and previously noted, also deals primarily with the thirties. A key incident is studied in Ben-Ami Shillony, *Revolt in Japan: The Young Officers and the February 26, 1936 Incident* (Princeton, 1973).

Of the quite extensive literature on Japanese expansionism and the origins of the Second World War, recommended as especially stimulating and scholarly are Robert Butow, *Tojo and the Coming of the War* (Princeton, 1961), and James B. Crowley, *Japan's Quest for Autonomy: National Security and Foreign Policy, 1930–38* (Princeton, 1966). Also recommended are the following: Sadako Ogata, *Defiance in Manchuria: The Making of Japanese Foreign Policy, 1931–32* (Berkeley, 1964); James W. Morley, ed., *Deterrent Diplomacy, Japan, Germany, and the U.S.S.R., 1935–1940* (New York, 1976); Dorothy Borg, *The United States and the Far Eastern Crisis of 1933–1938* (Cambridge, Mass., 1964); and Nobutake Ike, ed., *Japan's Decision for War: Records of the 1941 Policy Conferences* (Stanford, 1967). On the Japanese military, see Ernst L. Presseisen, *Before Aggression: Europeans Prepare the Japanese Army* (Tucson, 1965); Suburo Hayashi in collaboration with Alvin D. Coox, *Kōgun: The Japanese Army in the Pacific War* (Quantico, Va., 1959); and Paul S. Dull, *A Battle History of the Japanese Navy* (Annapolis, 1978).

The Pacific War began with Pearl Harbor and ended with the atomic bomb. Both events have been written about at length and remain foci of scholarly controversies. On Pearl Harbor, see Dorothy Borg and Shumpei Okamoto, eds., *Pearl Harbor as History* (New York, 1973). For a writer, particularly an American, to deal with Hiroshima demands unusual literary sensitivity: the classic account remains *Hiroshima* by John Hersey. Also recommended is Robert Jay Lifton, *Death in Life: Survivors of Hiroshima*.

There is no general, comprehensive history of modern Japanese literature available in English, but there are two books composed of perceptive critical discussions of major novelists and their work: Masao Miyoshi, *Accomplices of Silence: The Modern Japanese Novel*, and Makoto Ueda, *Modern Japanese Writers and the Nature of Literature* (Stanford, 1976). A most enjoyable way to become acquainted with Japan's modern writers is by reading Ivan Morris's excellent collection, *Modern Japanese Stories—An Anthology* (Rutland, Vt., 1962).

For the beginning and early history of the modern Japanese novel, there are two fine books by Marleigh G. Ryan: *Japan's First Modern Novel: Ukigomo of Futabatei Shimei* (New York, 1967) and *The Development of Realism in the Fiction of Tsubouchi Shōyō* (Seattle, 1975). Studies of three novelists noted in the text are now available in the Twayne World Authors Series: *Mori Ogai* by Thomas J. Rimer (1975); *Shiga Naoya* by Francis Mathy (1974); and *Natsume Soseki* by Beongcheon Yu, author also of *Akutagawa, An Introduction* (Detroit, 1972). A study that captures atmosphere as well as insights, and is itself a literary work of art, is Edward Seidenstricker, *Kafu, The Scribbler: The Life and Writings of Nagai Kafu, 1879–1959*.

Secondary studies are no substitute for the works of the authors themselves, many of which, fortunately, are available in excellent translations. The following list is meant only to introduce the reader to this rich literature in the hope that he will then go on to explore it on his own: Mori Ogai, *The Wild Geese*, translated by Kingo Ochiai and Sanford Goldstein; the following by Natsume Sōseki: *Botchan*, translated by Umeji Sasaki, *Kokoro*, translated by Edwin McClellan, *The Wayfarer*, translated by Beongcheon Yu, *Mon*, translated by Francis Mathy; Ryunosuke Akutagawa, *Japanese Short Stories*, translated by Takashi Kojima; Kafū Nagai, *A Strange Tale from East of the River and Other Stories*, translated by Edward Seidenstricker; three novels by Tanizaki Juichirō: *Some Prefer Nettles* and *The Makioka Sisters*, translated by Edward Seidenstricker, and *Diary of a Mad Old Man*, translated by Howard Hibbett. For poetry, see Edith Marcombe Shiffert and Yūki Sawa, *Anthology of Modern Japanese Poetry*.

A useful overview of Japanese philosophy is provided by Gino K. Piovesena, *Recent Japanese Philosophical Thought: 1862–1962, A Survey* (Tokyo, revised ed., 1968); and for a statement by a major modern philosopher, see *Fundamental Problems of Philosophy* (*Nishida Kitarō's* Tetsugaku no kompon mondai), translated by David A. Dilworth (Tokyo, 1970). There is no general survey in English of the period's visual arts, but the following two books are helpful: Michiaki Kawakita, *Modern Currents in Japanese Art* (Heibonsha Survey of Japanese Art, Vol. 24, Tokyo and New York, 1974), and *Arts of Japan*, Vol. 6, *Meiji Western Painting by Minoru Harada* (New York and Tokyo, 1964). For this and other arts, including music, see also *Tradition and Modernization in Japanese Culture*, the book edited by Shively mentioned at the beginning of this subsection.

PART VI   East Asia Since the Second World War

The origins of the Cold War is one of the many issues in recent history on which interpretations have changed both as new materials have become available and as historical perspectives have changed. It is therefore good to begin by reading a recent work, a collection of essays edited by Yōnosuke Nagai and Akira Iriye, *The Origins of the Cold War in Asia* (New York, 1977). In East Asia, of course, the Cold War did not remain cold. On Vietnam seen not as a problem for American foreign policy but as a society with its own history and culture, there are two excellent books by Alexander B. Woodside: *Vietnam and the Chinese Model—A Comparative Study of Nguyen and Ch'ing Civil Government in the First Half of the Nineteenth Century* (Cambridge, Mass., 1971) and *Community and Revolution in Modern Vietnam* (Boston, 1976). The latter contains a list of suggested readings with critical comments. There is no book of similar intellectual scope for twentieth-century Korea, but the following are useful for political history: Chong-Sik Lee, *The Politics of Korean Nationalism* (Berkeley, 1963), and Sungjoo Han, *The Failure of Democracy in South Korea* (Berkeley, 1974). For Taiwan, see Douglas Mendel, *The Politics of Formosan Nationalism* (Berkeley, 1970).

There is no general history of postwar Japan, but Edwin O. Reischauer, *The Japanese* (Cambridge, Mass., 1977) provides a good general introduction. On the Occupation, see the collection of papers edited by Grant K. Goodman, *The American Occupation of Japan: A Retrospective View* (Lawrence, Kansas, 1968. Distributed by Paragon Book Gallery, N.Y.); Herbert Passim, *The Legacy of the Occupation—Japan* (New York, 1968); and Kazuo Kawai, *Japan's American Interlude* (Chicago, 1960). An important Occupation accomplishment is examined by Ronald P. Dore in *Land Reform in Japan* (London, 1958).

The Japanese economy has been quite extensively studied. Good books include Hugh Patrick, ed., with the assistance of Larry Meisner, *Japanese Industrialization and Its Social Consequences*, and Hugh Patrick and Henry Rosovsky, eds., *Asia's New Giant: How the Japanese Economy Works* (Washington, 1976), consisting of papers described by a reviewer as ranging in style "from semi-Galbraithian sparkle to semi-dissertation ponderosity" (see *Journal of Japanese Studies* 3 [Winter 1977]: 166). For rural life see Richard K. Beardsley, John W. Hall, and Robert E. Ward, *Village Japan*. Roland P. Dore is a social scientist who is also a gifted writer. His *City Life in Japan* is a classic. Dore is also the author of *British Factory, Japanese Factory: The Origins of National Diversity in Employment Relations* (Berkeley, 1973). Another very informative and revealing book is Robert E. Cole, *Japanese Blue Collar: Changing Traditions*.

Recommended for its analysis of Japanese politics is Nathanial Thayer, *How the Conservatives Rule Japan* (Princeton, 1969). Another aspect of the political system is discussed by Kurt Steiner, *Local Government in Japan* (Stanford, 1965). Another useful book is Nobutake Ike, *Japanese Politics: Patron-Client Democracy* (New York, 1972). See also Donald C. Hellman, *Japanese Domestic Politics and Foreign Policy: The Peace Agreement with the Soviet Union* (Berkeley, 1969), and Martin E. Weinstein, *Japan's Postwar Defense Policy, 1947–1968* (New York, 1971). There is a rich social science literature on contemporary Japanese culture and social trends. The reader will enjoy David

W. Plath, *Adult Episodes in Japan* (Leiden, 1975). Another collection of social science essays, with contributions by specialists interested in the future as well as in the present and the recent past, is Lewis Austin, ed., *Japan: The Paradox of Progress* (New Haven, 1977). A good source for current developments in Japan is the journal, *The Japan Interpreter.*

Donald Richie, *Japanese Cinema—Film Style and National Character* is a well informed and thoughtful historical survey of the Japanese film. A good way to begin reading in contemporary Japanese literature is by using Howard Hibbett, ed., *Contemporary Japanese Literature—An Anthology of Fiction, Film, and Other Writings Since 1945,* which was published in 1977. Major postwar novelists are analyzed in the works by Miyoshi and Ueda cited above. Many novels have been translated, including some by writers not discussed in this text. The following listing of translated works by writers who are treated in the text is not complete but is representative of their best work. For Kawabata, read the following, all translated by Edward G. Seidensticker: *Snow Country, Thousand Cranes, Japan the Beautiful and Myself,* and *The Sound of the Mountain.* For Mishima: *The Sailor Who Fell from Grace with the Sea,* translated by John Nathan, *After the Banquet,* translated by Donald Keene, and *The Temple of the Golden Pavilion,* translated by Ivan Morris. E. Dale Saunders has translated Abe Kōbō: *The Ruined Map, The Woman in the Dunes, The Box Man.* See also Abe's play "Friends," translated by Donald Keene and included in Hibbett's anthology. Two novels by Oe Kenzaburō are available in English: *A Personal Matter,* translated by John Nathan, and *The Silent Cry,* translated by John Bester (Tokyo and New York, 1974).

The literature on contemporary China is vast and very uneven. It is also growing rapidly. A new history by a leading scholar in the field, Maurice Meisner, *Mao's China: A History of the People's Republic* (New York, 1977) unfortunately appeared too late to be used in preparation of this text. The leading scholarly journal on contemporary China is the *China Quarterly.* Donald W. Klein and Anne B. Clark, *Biographic Dictionary of Chinese Communism,* 2 vols. (Cambridge, Mass., 1971) is a useful reference work.

For analyzing the CCP triumph, the following are helpful: Lucien Bianco, *Origins of the Chinese Revolution, 1915–1949,* translated by Muriel Bell; Chalmers A. Johnson, *Peasant Nationalism and Communist Power: The Emergence of Revolutionary China, 1937–45;* Donald Gillin's critique of Johnson in *Journal of Asian Studies* 23 (February 1964): 269–89; and Pinchon P. Y. Loh, *The Kuomintang Debacle of 1949: Conquest or Collapse?* (Problems in Asian Civilization series), which presents an array of views mirroring American reactions to events in China.

For an account of the revolution based on personal experience, see William Hinton, *Fanshen: A Documentary of Revolution in a Chinese Village.* A city has been studied by Ezra Vogel, *Canton under Communism: Programs and Politics in a Provincial Capital, 1949–1968,* and more recently by the contributors (including Vogel) to *The City in Communist China,* edited by John Wilson Lewis (Stanford, 1954). The most ambitious and the most impressive attempt yet made to analyze the dynamics of the new system is Franz Schurmann, *Ideology and Organization in Communist China.* Much that has been written on the Chinese economy is quite technical and detailed. A useful overview is provided by Nai-ruen Chen and Walter Galenson, *The Chinese Economy Under Communism* (Chicago, 1969).

On Chinese politics, see James D. Seymour, *China: The Politics of Revolutionary Reintegration,* and James R. Townsend, *Politics in China.* A comprehensive book that is organized chronologically and can well serve as a history of contemporary China is Jaques Guillermaz, *The Chinese Communist Party in Power, 1949–1976.*

The leading personality of contemporary China was, of course, Mao Tse-tung. In addition to the two biographies already mentioned, the following are especially useful: Stuart R. Schram, *The Political Thought of Mao Tse-tung,* which consists of a long introduction and selections from Mao; Dick Wilson, ed., *Mao Tse-tung in the Scales of History* (1977); and, for the philosophically minded, the difficult but rewarding *History and Will: Philosophical Perspectives of Mao Tse-tung's Thought*, by Frederic Wakeman, Jr. The continuing project in Peking to publish Mao's works in English translation has now reached Volume 5: *Selected Works—Mao Tse-tung 1949–1957*.

The origins of the Sino-Soviet split are examined in Donald S. Zagoria, *The Sino-Soviet Conflict, 1956–1961* (Princeton, 1962). A recent essay, Harold C. Hinton, *The Sino-Soviet Confrontation: Implications for the Future* (1976) includes a bibliography. For a collection of essays containing the reflections of a leading senior American student of China, see John K. Fairbank, *China Perceived: Images and Policies in Chinese-American Relations* (New York, 1974). On China's foreign relations, also see Jerome A. Cohen, ed., *The Dynamics of China's Foreign Relations* (Cambridge, Mass., 1970), and *Dragon and Eagle: United States-China Relations, Past and Future*, Michel Oksenberg and Robert B. Oxnam, eds. (New York, 1978). On the Chinese Army, see John Gittings, *The Role of the Chinese Army* (London and New York, 1967). Also see Edward J. M. Rhoads, *The Chinese Red Army 1927–1963: An Annotated Bibliography* (Cambridge, Mass., 1965).

A good primary source for contemporary Chinese thought are the journals of translation published by the International Arts and Science Press. They all have titles beginning with *Chinese* and survey six fields: (1) Economics, (2) Education, (3) Law and Government, (4) History, (5) Sociology and Anthropology, and (6) Philosophy. For literature, there is a journal published in Peking entitled *Chinese Literature*. For recent developments in Chinese literature based on personal interviews conducted in China in 1973, see Kai-yu Hsu, *The Chinese Literary Scene: A Writer's Visit to the People's Republic of China*. Donald Munro, *The Concept of Man in Contemporary China* (Ann Arbor, 1977) is an analysis of Chinese ideas concerning the nature of man, with illuminating discussions on how these ideas differ from those held in the Soviet Union and the West.

Travelers' accounts generally reveal at least as much about the traveler as they do about China, and it would be an interesting exercise to compare systematically the reports of recent visitors with those of foreigners who visited China in earlier times. Among the best of the contemporary books are those by professional writers (e.g., Simone de Beauvoir, Alberto Moravia), those by journalists with previous China experience (e.g., Edgar Snow, Seymour Topping), and those by specialists in Chinese studies (e.g., Ross Terrill, Orvin Schell). A particularly valuable book that combines personal experience with analysis is David and Nancy Dall Milton, *The Wind Will Not Subside: Years in Revolutionary China, 1964–1969* (Berkeley, 1976).

With China as with the Soviet Union, Western attempts to understand political events and trends are based largely on detailed analyses of publications and radio broadcasts, the tracing of the careers of government officials, and examination of the vicissitudes of official life as indicated by the relative ranking of eminent persons appearing at public functions and the like. One of the most skilled practitioners of this difficult art, sometimes termed "Kremlin astrology," is Jürgen Domes, whose *China After the Cultural Revolution: Politics between Two Party Congresses*, translated by Annette Berg and David Goodman (Berkeley, 1977) is a fascinating example of the genre, demonstrating how much it can accomplish.

A different kind of book is Michel Oksenberg, ed., *China's Developmental Experience* (New York, 1973), in which a number of scholars examine the contemporary Chinese experience for possible applicability elsewhere—including the United States. It is a promising sign of the coming of age of Chinese and Japanese studies in America that they are at last losing their aura of exoticism and that scholars are beginning to seriously examine East Asian experiences in various fields in order to illuminate our own Western problems. A recent example is David H. Bayley, *Forces of Order. Police Behavior in Japan and the United States*. The future will surely bring more comparative studies, in the humanities as well as in the social sciences, employing Chinese as well as Japanese materials.

Copyrights and Acknowledgments

For permission to use copyrighted material reprinted in this book, the author is grateful to the following publishers and copyright holders:

GEORGE ALLEN & UNWIN LTD   For three lines of poetry from *The Book of Songs*, edited and translated by Arthur Waley. Reprinted by permission of George Allen & Unwin Ltd.

BARRIE & JENKINS   For a figure from *Japan: A Short Cultural History* by G. B. Sansom. Reprinted by permission of Barrie & Jenkins (originally published by The Cresset Press).

COLUMBIA UNIVERSITY PRESS   For a table of the Five Agents system from *Sources of Chinese Tradition*, vol. I, compiled by Wm. Theodore de Bary, Wing-tsit Chan, and Burton Watson; for five lines of poetry from *Sources of Japanese Tradition*, compiled by Ryusaku Tsunoda, Wm. Theodore de Bary, and Donald Keene; for a poem by Wang Wei from *Chinese Lyricism: Shih Poetry from the Second to the Twelfth Century*, translated by Burton Watson; for an excerpt from a rhapsody by Ssu-ma Hsiang-ju from *Chinese Rhyme-Prose*, translated by Burton Watson; and for "Reading the Poetry of Meng Chiao—First of Two Poems" from *Su Tung-p'o*, translated by Burton Watson. All reprinted by permission of Columbia University Press.

DOUBLEDAY & COMPANY, INC.   For a poem by Kobayashi Issa from *An Introduction to Haiku* by Harold G. Henderson. Copyright © 1958 by Harold G. Henderson. And for a poem by Li Po and "An Old Charcoal Seller" by Po Chü-yi, both from *Sunflower Splendor*, edited by Liu-chi Liu and Irving Yucheng Lo. Copyright © 1975 by Liu-chi Liu and Irving Yucheng Lo. All reprinted by permission of Doubleday & Company, Inc.

RICHARD EDWARDS   For five lines of poetry translated by Tseng Yu-Ho, from *The Art of Wen Cheng-ming* by Richard Edwards. Published by the University of Michigan Museum of Art, 1976. Reprinted by permission of Richard Edwards.

CALVIN L. FRENCH   For a poem by Bashō from *The Poet-Painters: Buson and His Followers* by Calvin French, exhibition catalog published by the University of Michigan Museum of Art, 1974. Reprinted by permission of Calvin L. French.

GROVE PRESS, INC.   For "In Reply to a Poem from Tz'u-shan, Thanking Me for the Gift of Sung and Yüan Lyrics I Had Had Printed" by Wang P'eng-yü, from *Anthology of Chinese Literature*, vol. II, edited by Cyril Birch. Reprinted by permission of Grove Press, Inc. Copyright © 1972 by Grove Press, Inc. And for three lines of poetry from *The Book of Songs*, edited and translated by Arthur Waley (Grove Press, 1960).

HARVARD UNIVERSITY PRESS   For a poem by Ch'in Kuan from Kojiro Yoshikawa, *An Introduction to Sung Poetry*, translated by Burton Watson (Harvard-Yenching Institute Monograph Series 17). Copyright 1967 by the Harvard-Yenching Institute. And for the Hanyu Pinyin/Wade-Giles Conversion Table from Endymion Wilkinson, *The History of Imperial China: A Research Guide* (Harvard East Asian Monographs 49). Copyright 1973 by the President and Fellows of Harvard College. Both reprinted by permission of Harvard University Press.

INDIANA UNIVERSITY PRESS   For a poem by T'ao Chien and two other poetry excerpts from *An Introduction to Chinese Literature* by Liu Wu-chi (Indiana University Press, 1966). Reprinted by permission of Indiana University Press.

OXFORD UNIVERSITY PRESS   For a poem by Mao Tse-tung translated from the Chinese by Michael Bullock and Jerome Ch'en, from *Mao and the Chinese Revolution* by Jerome Ch'en, © Oxford University Press 1965. Reprinted by permission of Oxford University Press.

PENGUIN BOOKS LTD   For "To My Younger Brother" by Tu Fu, from *Poems of the Late T'ang*, translated by A. C. Graham (Penguin Classics, 1965). Copyright © A. C. Graham, 1965. Reprinted by permission of Penguin Books Ltd.

RANDOM HOUSE, INC.   For a poem by Yüan K'o-chia from *The Chinese Literary Scene*, edited by Kai-yu Hsu. Copyright © 1975 by Kai-yu Hsu. Reprinted by permission of Random House, Inc.

ERIC SACKHEIM   For two lines by Lu Chi from *The Silent Zero, in Search of Sound: An Anthology of Chinese Poems from the Beginning through the Sixth Century*, translated by Eric Sackheim (Grossman, 1968). Reprinted by permission of Eric Sackheim.

Illustration Credits

tional Commission for Protection of Cultural Properties of Japan   **177 (bottom)** Kyōto National Museum   **178** Lore Schirokauer

PART THREE   181 (left) Sir Percival David Foundation of Chinese Art, University of London   **181 (right)** Hakone Art Museum, Japan   **187** Museum of Fine Arts, Boston   **192** Palace Museum, Peking   **203** Collection of the National Palace Museum, Taipei, Taiwan, Republic of China   **205** Tokyo National Museum   **206, 207, 208, 209** Collection of the National Palace Museum, Taipei, Taiwan, Republic of China   **224** Ōsaka Municipal Museum of Fine Arts, Abe Collection   **226, 227, 228** Collection of the National Palace Museum, Taipei, Taiwan, Republic of China   **239** Private Collection   **246–47** Honolulu Academy of Arts, Gift of Mrs. Carter Galt, 1952   **251** Collection of Mr. and Mrs. Wan-go H. C. Weng   **252** Collection of Richard Lin, London   **269** Keystone Japan/Katherine Young   **271** Keystone Japan/Katherine Young   **272** National Commission for Protection of Cultural Properties of Japan   **274 (right)** Lore Schirokauer   **274 (left)** and **275** All from Robert Treat Paine and Alexander Soper, *The Art and Architecture of Japan* (Pelican History of Art, 2nd rev. ed., 1974). Reprinted by permission of Penguin Books Ltd. [**274 (left)** Paine and Soper, p. 245; **275 (top right)** Paine and Soper, p. 244; **275 (middle)** Paine and Soper, p. 242]   **288** Heibonsha Limited, Publishers   **289** Collection Tokyo National Museum (photo from The Zauho Press)   **292 (left)** Lore Schirokauer   **292 (right)** Lore Schirokauer   **295** Kyōto National Museum (photo from The Zauho Press)   **302** Lore Schirokauer   **303** Imperial Household Collection, Tokyo (photo from The Zauho Press)   **305** Tokyo National Museum   **312** From Heibonsha Gallery of Oriental Art   **316** From *A Collection of Nagasaki Colour Prints and Paintings,* published by Charles E. Tuttle Co., Inc.   **320** Palace Museum, Peking

PART FOUR   323 Bruno Barbey/Magnum   **332** Honolulu Academy of Arts, Wilhelmina Tenney Memorial Collection, 1956   **333** Cleveland Museum of Art, Purchase, John L. Severance   **334** Earl Morse Collection (photo by Gil Amiaga)   **335** Earl Morse Collection (photo by Gil Amiaga)   **339** National Trust (at Ascott House, Wing, Buckinghamshire)   **340** Collection of Mr. and Mrs. R. W. Finlayson, Toronto, Ontario   **345** Fujii Museum (photo by Lore Schirokauer)   **360** Heibonsha Limited, Publishers   **361 (top)** National Treasure, Kenninji Collection (photo from The Zauho Press)   **361 (bottom)** Nezu Museum, Tokyo (photo from The Zauho Press)   **363** Collection W. Boller   **364** The Fine Arts Museum of San Francisco, Achenbach Foundation for Graphic Arts   **368** The University of Michigan Museum of Art, Margaret Watson Parker Art Collection Fund. Acc. No. 1968/2.22   **369** Private Collection   **370** Sakamoto Photo Research Lab

PART FIVE   377 Lore Schirokauer   **382** Peabody Museum of Salem (photo by Mark Sexton)   **384** The Mansell Collection   **387** Radio Times Hulton Picture Library   **409** Library of Congress, "Yokohama-e" Prints, Chadbourne Collection   **411** Peabody Museum of Salem (photo by Mark Sexton)   **431** Tokyo National Museum (photo from The Zauho Press)   **434** Robert Muller   **435** Heibonsha Limited, Publishers   **447** Dave Glaser   **454** Popperfoto   **455** From *China and Christianity* by Paul A. Cohen (Harvard University Press, 1963)   **468** Courtesy of the Smithsonian Institution, Freer Gallery of Art, Washington, D.C.   **481 (top)** Collection of the Art Gallery, Chinese University of Hong Kong   **501** Tokyo National Museum (photo from The Zauho Press)   **502** Takakiyu Mitsui Collection   **509** The Kyōto Municipal Museum of Art   **510** Sakamoto Photo Research Lab   **511** Tokyo National Museum of Modern Art   **534** Eastfoto   **538** Wide World Photos

PART SIX   545 United Press International   **551** United Press International   **580** Minami Gallery, Tokyo   **603** Brian Brake/Photo Researchers   **608** Lee Nordness Galleries, Inc.

Index

Page numbers in *italics* refer to illustrations.

E
F
G
H
I
J